TO SERVE THE PEOPLE

The Coat of Arms of the Independent Broadcasting Authority
"To Serve the People"

THE WHITNEY MEMOIRES

My Years at the IBA

John Whitney CBE

TO SERVE THE PEOPLE

British Library Cataloguing in Publication Data

To Serve the People: My Years at the IBA

A catalogue entry for this book is available from the British Library

ISBN: 9780 86196 710 0 (Hardback)

Cover photograph: Andrew R. Darbyshire

Published by
John Libbey Publishing Ltd, 3 Leicester Road, New Barnet, Herts EN5 5EW, United Kingdom   e-mail: john.libbey@orange.fr; web site: www.johnlibbey.com

Direct orders: **Marston Book Services Ltd:** direct.orders@marston.co.uk

Distributed in Asia and North America by **Indiana University Press**, 601 North Morton St, Bloomington, IN 47404, USA. www.iupress.indiana.edu

© 2013 Copyright John Libbey Publishing Ltd. All rights reserved.
Unauthorised duplication contravenes applicable laws.

Printed and bound in China by 1010 Printing International Ltd.

Contents

Preface	vii
1982	1
1983	19
1984	43
1985	85
1986	145
1987	203
1988	277
1989	361
Index	375

TO ROMA

Preface

In 1982 I was invited to become Director General of the Independent Broadcasting Authority. Some short time after my appointment I started keeping a detailed diary which I would write up on Sunday evenings. The book that follows is drawn from my diaries at the time and covers the years in which television and radio faced more challenges than at any time in their history. As regulator, the IBA, was subject to political pressures that brought about its abolition and rebirth as the Independent Television Commission and the Radio Authority. During my time as Director General, the IBA was in conflict with the government over the programme *Death on the Rock*, oversaw the battle between the BBC and Thames Television for possession of the rights to *Dallas*, acted as "honest broker" during the financial crisis at ITN and faced the impact of the Peacock Committee Report, which marked a turning point in broadcasting policy and signalled a decisive shift toward the construction of a market framework for the delivery of broadcast services.

More than 20 years have elapsed since my time at the IBA yet I remember so well the quality and loyalty of the staff at every level and wish to pay tribute to them.

John Whitney, July 2013

I am hugely indebted to Jane Wynborne, without whose help this book would not have been possible.

1982

It was a call from George Thomson that changed the direction of my life. Lord Thomson of Monifieth had been the Chairman of the IBA since January 1981, following the retirement of Lady Plowden. He was a somewhat distant figure to me, and I had met him only infrequently. The last time was in Monte Carlo where I was attending one of those inevitable radio occasions where delegates sat in stuffy rooms looking wistfully over the sea and thinking about the high jinks they might be able to indulge in later in the day.

On this occasion, one or two of us had decided to invite Lord Thomson to dinner so that we could use the occasion to know him better. My entertaining in London was usually done in my office, using the in-house catering, but on special occasions I would invite to cook and serve the meal a most charming woman, Ariane (now Ariane Davis-Gilbert). She was much relished by all who sat at our table, for not only was she an extremely good cook but she also had a splendid manner and the looks to go with it. All in all, lunches at Capital Radio were something of an occasion to look forward to. To add to her more visible assets, she had a very attractive apartment in the Sun Tower, one of the prime properties in Monte Carlo and it was to this venue that we had invited George Thomson.

The evening was a success and we felt that the occasion had cemented a relationship that would stand us in good order as time progressed. The call to me from George Thomson came a few weeks later. In it he said that the retirement of Sir Brian Young now needed to be filled by a new Director General, and would I like to meet and discuss it.

In many ways, his call, although unexpected, was timely. I had spent eight years at Capital, during which time I had found it not only challenging but immensely enjoyable. I was, I suppose, the king of the castle in commercial radio, and was called upon to engage in all sorts of activities – Chairman of the Sony Radio Awards (which I had overseen for some years), Chairman of RAJAR (the curiously named company to provide audience statistics and ratings to the advertising industry), on the Board of the National Theatre and numerous other roles – and had begun to feel that I had reached whatever pinnacle could be attained in my role as Managing Director of Capital.

I was also beginning to feel I should be reaping greater rewards, not just in financial terms but in the wider fields of media. Before taking on the job at Capital, with John Hawkesworth (my writing partner) and John Pringle, I had formed Consolidated, a company to 'package' television services.

Some weeks before the attention of Lord Thomson, I had been asked by John

Pringle and John Hawkesworth to consider becoming Chief Executive of Consolidated. With my background in television as well as radio, I was an eligible candidate and the prospect of slipping back into television production and the creation of television was something that excited me.

I sat down with John Pringle and talked money. As I recollect, we stumbled on reaching an agreement. I wanted a better deal than the £70,000 per annum that the Johns felt appropriate. My salary at Capital was of the order of £50,000, together with a parcel of shares which I hoped one day would become a valuable asset (although at the time I could never have imagined the giddy prices investors would pay for a piece of Capital's fortunes). I suppose I felt dismayed at the time that the Johns' offer did not, I considered, fully value my abilities. It was against this backdrop that a conversation with George Thomson might serve to signify the value that others put on my abilities.

So it was that I next met Lord Thomson, in the Café Royal for a cup of tea, with the knowledge that Sir Brian Young would be leaving. There was already much speculation in Brompton Towers, as it was humorously referred to in the IBA, that the role of Director General would be hotly contested and by individuals who had already hinted to the press and others that, if they were offered the job, they would accept. Front runners at the time were a number of in-house IBA executives, the foremost being Colin Shaw, whose role as Director of Television had provided him with a very significant track record of experience, and who was generally thought to be 'a safe pair of hands'. Others had their hats in the ring and no one, but no one, dreamt that one of the possibilities to hold this crown in broadcasting was a buccaneering individual from radio who was not, in Margaret Thatcher's phrase, 'one of us'.

In any case, radio was the noisy infant overshadowed by television and, like an ugly duckling, squawking for attention.

After I had agreed with George that my name could be put forward on a confidential basis, I began to think about Capital Radio and my replacement. Another consideration was the renewal of Capital Radio's franchise, which would be considered by the Authority in the coming months. Capital was now seen as a goldmine, and others who viewed its performance began analysing how best they could unseat its pre-eminent role. It would not be so much a question of a takeover but rather a rival consortium bidding against Capital, and emphasising the qualities it could provide to the transmission area.

Whilst the Board, under Richard Attenborough's expert hand, had spoken with one voice, there had been, over a number of years, Board members who had voiced their dissatisfaction with the indulgence that I had shown from time to time in programming and other matters. They continuously drew their inspiration from Canadian broadcasting experience which in many ways was, and still is, more closely related to American commercial radio: in other words, cheap, cheerful and cost effective to audience size. I was never of that persuasion, believing that quality, retaining a bond with the audience and reflecting the social mores of the time were significant parts of the role we had undertaken from the outset.

After my tea-time conversation with Lord Thomson, I resolved to talk to Richard

Attenborough and tell him what had passed between us. He was immensely supportive and said that – if it really was my wish to take on this role – he would give me every encouragement.

During the period that followed, and the uncertainty at the IBA over the next appointment, I gained an insight into Lord Thomson's thinking. Still under a cloak of secrecy, he confided to me that what he wanted in his tenure as Chairman was to appoint a person who would help 'shake up' the stodgy regime that he had inherited both from Lady Plowden and, before that, from Sir Robert Fraser. Rightly, he judged that broadcasting – both radio and television – would be going through a considerable sea-change and that technology and competition would go hand in hand to disturb and shake the cosy status quo that had existed for decades. I am not sure whether his colleagues on the Board realised what his ambitions were and whether – had they known – they would have taken quite the same attitude.

My first encounter with the Members of the Authority passed, I thought, reasonably well. I was introduced to each, and questions asked of me – which in the main I responded to well. This was the meeting George Thomson hoped would give blessing to my appointment, and was not just any old occasion. After the meeting, he asked me to wait in an anteroom. About half a hour later he emerged from the Board Room and said, 'It has been more difficult than I expected. I thought it would be unanimous but I am afraid it wasn't. Three members were hesitant.' Lord Thomson then told me, candidly, that Sir John Riddell didn't think I had enough business experience, Paula Ridley said I didn't have enough political background and Denis Hamilton didn't know who I was or what I did!

However, the outcome had been an approval to appoint me as Director General.

All this activity had been under the cloak of confidentiality and total secrecy. George wanted to lift the cloak and announce the appointment, but Dickie rightly said that the Board of Capital should be informed first and that he would do this.

I went to Dorset that weekend and bought the Sunday papers only to find there was nothing in them about my appointment. Dickie did a ring-round to Capital Board members who sent me their best wishes and said they would give an encouraging response to the press when asked.

The following week the IBA held a press conference. Of course it came as a surprise to those who were gathered, but on the whole the response in the press was positive. Mary Whitehouse had been ramping up her attack on decency and violence on television and I was much quoted as saying I thought she was a 'beacon of sanctity'. Nobody but nobody could argue with that!

For the next two or three months, I was titled Director-General-Designate and sat in a smallish office in Brompton Road meeting people and reading the numerous papers the IBA circulated to staff. I visited Crawley Court, the headquarters of the IBA's engineering function, and met legions of staff who appeared blissfully unaware of the ever-growing world of competition circling them. Unlike Brompton Road, Crawley Court had a peaceful air, being surrounded by green fields, country lanes and a sense of insulation from the real world. My first impression was that it resembled one of those holiday camps that offer tired executives and frazzled mums a holiday from the stresses and strains of life.

Capital laid on a splendid dinner to – I was going to say 'celebrate my departure', but I hope and think it was to say thank you. Dickie, with his usual grace, said some very kind and flattering words, followed by other senior executives. Roma was presented with flowers and looked, as she always did, stunning. All in all, it was a jolly occasion.

The next farewell occasion was at Capital itself. A coach-and-four collected us from our home in Wadham Gardens and we clip-clopped through Regents Park and down the Euston Road to Capital's building. At the entrance, a red carpet had been laid down and a guard of honour blasted a salvo of trumpet fanfares to usher me in. I can't remember much of the occasion except that I was presented with a marvellous boxed crystal set, which later – when I installed it in Brompton Road – would only tune in to LBC and the BBC. I felt very genuine pangs of sorrow at moving away from the glitzy world of Capital and showbusiness to the austere interior of the IBA Headquarters.

Throughout the period when I was Director-General-Designate, Brian Young deliberately tried not to influence me and said that he knew I would form my own views and draw my own conclusions.

Looking back at the events that followed over the years, I should have been much more savvy to the political climate which coloured and set the agenda. It was only later that I discovered the real antipathy that the Conservative leadership had for the IBA and all its workings. To them it was a barrier to free marketing and a hindrance to competition. An example which should have given me insight was the request from Duke Hussey, Chairman of *The Times* newspaper and later to become Chairman of the BBC, to come and have lunch at Capital to hear my views about the advertising market and the role of the IBA.

Had I researched more thoroughly at the time, I would have appreciated the close friendship that Mrs T. had with Murdoch, the proprietor of Times Newspapers and, at that time, with Dukie, its Chairman. As far as Mrs Thatcher's advisers were concerned, the IBA was 'one of the most backward-looking organisations in television'.

Back in those seemingly tranquil days, in my period as Designate. I was filled with confidence that, as with Capital, I could set the pace of change in a manner that would provide the best opportunities for the organisation, advertisers and the audience. I should have asked Brian for his views on the climate at the time, but I never did. Instead, we attended a round of enjoyable occasions where he was saying goodbye and I was picking up the reins and whether the changes that were to come would have provided him with food for thought still remains for me a question mark.

At some time thereabouts, I was invited to have lunch with Willie Whitelaw at the Reform Club. He was held in good regard by the Tory high command and by Mrs Thatcher. It was on this occasion, towards the end of the pudding, that Whitelaw leant forward and said, in a most conspiratorial tone, 'I have only one real purpose in the Cabinet and that is to manage Mrs Thatcher's enthusiasm. Margaret hoovers up ideas that she likes and her enthusiasm for them knows no bounds.' He continued, 'I have learned that I must take her enthusiasm down from 120 per cent to 60 per cent'. And then, chuckling, he added, 'I know she will lift it back to 80 or 90 per cent, which is about right in most cases'. Whether this story was to warn me that, unless managed, Mrs Thatcher would sweep aside commonsense, I don't know. I took it at the time as a friendly aside but, thinking back, I don't believe that Whitelaw ever said anything without purpose.

I met Douglas Hurd on a number of occasions and one particular incident I remember quite vividly. It was later in my term of office, and I had been summoned to see him. He had a very large, extensive room with many tokens of affection that had been presented to him by foreign dignitaries. I thought most of them in doubtful taste.

The telephone on his desk rang. Douglas froze and very nearly stood to attention as he took the call. 'That was the Prime Minister', he said. 'I must conclude this meeting.' So saying, he made for the door. I had a vivid image of him about to enter the headmistress's study and, had he had a telephone directory handy, I am sure he would have stuffed it down his pants!

During this interim period, before I took over the role as Director General, the IBA's indomitable Controller of Information Services, Barbara Hosking, made sure that I had the opportunity of meeting a range of television executives, one even being Charles Wick, Director of the US International Communications Agency.

I invited Mr Wick to the Garrick. He arrived attended by two aides from the US Embassy, and accompanied by two bodyguards ('Security Advisors'). The female bodyguard looked as though she had walked straight out of an American Cops' series: tall, elegant and cool. Her male counterpart spent much of his time apologising that he was there.

I invited Colin Shaw to join us for dinner and it soon became clear that Mr Wick felt badly let down by not only the British but the rest of Europe as well. 'We were your buddies during the War', intoned Mr Wick. 'We fought alongside you. Now we don't know who we are fighting.'

The ICA, Mr Wick explained, funded 'The Voice of America' and various cultural institutions dedicated to planting good old US democracy where it was most, or least, needed, depending upon which side you were on.

His main grievance turned out to concern a programme which he had inspired and which was intended to be a tribute to solidarity and a fight for freedom. Although I never saw it – it was never shown in the UK – it was brimful with good old American sentimentality and corn and was considered thoroughly nauseating. Many countries took it and Mr Wick was at a loss to understand why we had not. Colin Shaw told him! Adding that it would be advisable in future if his Agency consulted with broadcasting organisations in Europe before predetermining their attitude.

Mr Wick ate Moules Marinieres with beans and potatoes! He left in a Cadillac with smoke-tinted glass windows. All that was missing were the outriders.

Another opportunity to mingle followed shortly afterwards. Roma and I went to a cocktail party at 10 Downing Street. The place was much bigger than I had expected. Rather like the Tardis. Mrs T. had the irritating habit of shaking your hand and at the same time moving it sideways. The result was that one was taken off-balance and catapulted onward and outward.

Denis T. was just like his caricature, rushing up to us (we were with Peter Murray) and bellowing, 'I've been working like a black – whoops! Slip of the tongue.' Several robed guests looked on unmoved.

Each year the good, the great and the not so great in television gather in Edinburgh for the International Television Festival and everyone takes it extremely seriously. Like all conferences, it was a wonderful opportunity for scandal, gossip, speculation, rumour, talk of hiring and firing and of course much wining, dining and carousing. All in all, a good opportunity to tell the world how marvellous television and radio are, how marvellous the people working in them are.

This was my first opportunity to see it unfold at first hand. As the Director General Designate, I didn't need to make speeches but instead listened to a great many, including the key speaker of the Festival, Ted Turner of Atlanta Cable Network. He was the man whose single-minded determination and guts had got his cable network up and running and had launched an attack on the major networks with the provision of a 24 hour continuous cable news service. Turner was a colourful character; an experienced yachtsman, he had inherited a near-bankrupt petrol filling service after his father committed suicide. The service he started was beginning to find favour throughout the States and Ted Turner fulfilled the American's idea of an adventurer. His reputation as a tough-talking, shrewd businessman was known worldwide and his picture had been on the cover of *Time*.

Unfortunately, his inaugural keynote speech at the Festival failed to live up to his reputation and he came across as a small town hick with enormous pretensions. He apparently saw himself as a warrior against the networks, a modern Napoleon. Inadequately briefed, he irritated and infuriated delegates with his ignorance, referring to Government control of the BBC.

Another executive who always caused suppressed mirth, but was fawned to in his presence, was the Director General of the BBC, Alasdair Milne. Alasdair had the reputation of being a tough talking, no nonsense believer in the Reithian philosophy. At the Festival, he was always surrounded by acolytes, taking notes and digesting his every utterance.

There were many at the Festival who considered the BBC to be arrogant and out of touch with the turbulence that technology would bring to the status quo that had been enjoyed by the BBC hitherto.

Each night at sundown Alasdair would stride the grounds overlooking the hotel where he stayed and play the bagpipes. This appeared to be a ritual considered of great consequence.

The central theme of the conference was 'Television in Transition'. There was much talk of an electronic grid covering the country, an idea first put forward by Kenneth Baker. In his speech, Kenneth Baker placed emphasis on the extended role of cable, saying it would play a positive part in the wider acceptance of direct broadcasting by satellite. This whole debate about cable and satellite was very much in the melting pot. The Hunt Committee was due to report at the end of September and I was keen, even at this early stage of my life at the IBA, for us to take a prominent role in ushering in and supervising this major development, which would undoubtedly change the existing infrastructure of the media.

George Thomson and George Howard, Chairman of the BBC, shared a platform with Kenneth Baker and it was upon Barbara Hosking's recommendation that our interest in satellite and cable, or rather cable and satellite, should be put firmly on the record during this session. The result was better than I had hoped and there were few voices raised that the IBA should not be seeking this role. Maybe it was because the Authority might be a case of 'better the devil ...'. or that the ITV companies felt that to be in the lee of the IBA would protect them from government incursions into what they believed to be their rightful territory.

After the session, I spent two hours with Michael Moriarty, talking about the introduction of DBS Broadcasting. Moriarty was one of the elegant breed of Civil Servants who appeared to be, on the surface, confused and unsure of matters going on around him, but in fact was shrewdly aware of his role and the wishes of his masters. There were drinks in the Great Northern Hotel where he raised with me his concern over the Satellite Broadcasting Company which he knew I had been interested in funding and indeed I had been, until recently, one of its Directors. At the time, the Satellite Broadcasting Company (SBC) was using the OTS, the Orbital Test fixed point satellite, and had begun successfully broadcasting English-speaking programmes down over Europe, many of them supplied to the company by Thames Television and London Weekend Television.

Some European countries had accepted the service via cable into the home, the most recent being Switzerland, but Moriarty was concerned that the entrepreneurial broadcaster Brian Hayes, who headed up Satellite Television Ltd, would be casting his eyes towards the UK and encouraging cable operators and dish manufacturers to accept his nightly two-hour transmissions.

Moriarty was also worried that some other European countries, notably Belgium and Denmark, would be angered by SBC's apparent ability to usurp the 'due processes' of regulations, and the arrangements being hammered out by the European Broadcasting Union to provide for a standard use of DBS.

I reassured Moriarty that, to the best of my belief, SBC had no intention of attempting to bring about a viewing alternative in the UK without legitimising this approach. At the same time, I pointed out that the company was serving a number of useful functions, acting, as it was, as a vanguard in space and a test bed for programme-initiation. Apparently, SBC, through their research, had already established that the European audience showed a marked preference for sport, drama and documentaries. The company, I went on to say, was also demonstrating that British ingenuity was alive and well and that the company's determination to succeed could well attract a favourable reaction from the doubters that DBS transmissions would ever survive on a viable, attractive basis as far as programming was concerned.

Finally, we talked about the IBA's own hopes for DBS now that the BBC had gained Government approval to operate the first two transponders on the Unisat satellite, which was due to begin service in 1986, presenting UK viewers with two more options: the first channel devoted to the first run of new movies, the second a compilation of the best of its own terrestrial output and from outside sources.

I referred to my discussion with Alasdair Milne, in which he had confirmed his concern over the high cost of the BBC's entry into satellite transmission and had remarked that perhaps the IBA might consider taking over one of the two transponders. Moriarty declared that this was still the position, and believed that the BBC had concluded its deal with BT. This left the IBA with several options. To encourage current television Contractors to provide a service unilaterally. Alternatively that the IBA should itself structure a fourth channel mode which would provide the service under the Authority's direct control. A third option was to wait until the end of the current TV contracts and offer a new consortium the opportunity of running the service.

If the ITV Contractors were to reach agreement to cooperate in some structure to enable a positive joint response, Michael indicated that the IBA commercially-funded transponders could be in operation by 1988. If this were not possible, the plan would need to be deferred until 1990 to allow for changes to be introduced into ITV contracts.

A Council Meeting of ITV companies was planned for 6th September when the EBU would be seeking to discover whether they would wish to be committed formally and legally to an experimental pan-European television service to be carried on L-Sat from 1986. Through the EBU, the European Space Agency had offered the use of one channel at no cost. The next Authority meeting would be considering the view of the IBA as to whether or not to give sympathetic support to the concept.

On the 8th September 1982, I had lunch at the IBA with George Thomson, Brian Young and our guests – George Howard and Alasdair Milne.

George Thomson was keen to assess in the aftermath of the International Television Festival the implications of George Howard's unexpected statement there concerning cable: 'offering the IBA the chalice of cable'. A poisoned chalice?

The BBC, said Alasdair Milne, was growing more concerned by the day that our entry into cable as a country would bring about the lowering of standards which everyone feared. I said that cable development was inevitable and it would be the skill of the Regulators that would ensure quality of output. The BBC's views on their satellite project were undergoing a change. Instead of one free service and a second subscription channel, Alasdair would be presenting to the Board of Governors the following day his belief that the two channels should be funded by one additional licence payment. The BBC, he said, were wholly opposed to pay-per-view.

After the lunch, George Thomson showed me the press statement he hoped to issue following the Authority meeting. In this was the reiteration of the Authority's desire to become the regulatory body. George T suggested to George Howard that the BBC and the IBA might stand together on the matter of their views on cable. Alasdair was quick to jump in and knock down the proposal. 'The BBC works alone', he said, 'and is already working on it'.

Returning to the satellite matter, Alasdair related how the costs of transponders stood at the time at £11.5m each. I asked if he thought the estimation of £23m in 1986 could be fully justified if cable was not to be available and viewers had to purchase dish aerials. George Howard believed that dishes would be freely available.

I must say that I found George Howard a roguish character, decked out as he was in a country suit with enormous baggy trousers and a startlingly garish shirt. Smoking incessantly, he looked more like a loss-making bookie than the Chairman of the BBC. Alasdair Milne adopted the manner and commanding tone of a strict Scottish nanny, chiding his charge. George seemed to accept this, although I could visualise a situation where the two might fall out spectacularly.

In those early days as Director General, I had a number of assignments given to me by the redoubtable Barbara Hosking, who was our Controller of Information Services. Early on, I picked up the rumour that all was not a bed of roses in the PR division under its leader John Guinery. I gathered that the department was something of a separate entity, its staff coming and going as they pleased. PR was not one of the strong points of the IBA and I was keen to try to co-operate in order to put across the message that I was a new broom, willing to make changes and that, with a knowledge of radio as well as television, I brought to the table something of value. This was not an easy balancing trick because of course I was most anxious not to in any way denigrate all the work of Sir Brian Young, who indeed had a most distinguished career with the IBA and was never the subject of criticism.

I had first met Barbara when, at Capital, I invited her to lunch, giving her the No. 1 service in my office, with food and wine to impress. Impress I must have done because she always spoke with great enthusiasm of the quality of the wine which I had selected. It was, as I recall, a very fine Lynchbague. Barbara naturally wanted to show off her new DG and one of my first invitations, that she organised, was with the Publicity Club of Great Britain. The Chairman of it was, I think, Derek Jameson, the Editor of the *News of the World*. I accepted the invitation and, with Roma, went to enjoy their hospitality. Barbara was keen for me to speak on somewhat weighty matters to do with regulation and the future, but I quickly realised that the occasion was not one for matters or subjects of consequence. Jameson, in his introduction, spoke from notes that I believe Barbara had given him about my time at Capital and what I had achieved there. I was much taken aback, however, when Jameson put down the prepared instruction and said he had 'much more interesting news than anything John did at Capital'. Producing a cutting from his newspaper, he went on: 'I have a picture here of his most delectable wife, Roma; a picture taken some years before he joined Capital Radio. John was successful before joining Capital Radio, so successful that he had a very fine Rolls Royce. When John was about to marry Roma, he had to make some savings, and one of them was the disposal of his Rolls. Being the entrepreneur that he was, he advertised in *The Times* that he had a beautiful fiancée and a beautiful Rolls, and one had to go.' For the first time, his audience was riveted. Jameson went on to read from the advertisement. 'Both', he quoted, 'were in tip-top condition, smooth runners and would embellish the life of anyone who acquired either. Of course it was', Jameson said proudly, 'my newspaper that printed this picture of Roma, still in the ballet, posing on the bonnet of the Rolls in her tutu and dancing pumps'. There was much laughter and applause and Roma, who is not normally given to holding centre-stage, laughed and joined in the merriment to my huge relief. Needless to say, I sold the Rolls and married Roma.

Whatever I was going to say about television and radio, I abandoned, and the lunch turned out to be very jolly, although not quite what Barbara had wanted.

I never looked forward to set occasions generally and I suffered a much worse experience when I was asked to address the Television Writers Guild. There were three speakers to introduce the Television Journalist Awards, and Barbara had prepared a rather lengthy piece for me to give. Of course, by the end of the lunch, most of those attending the Awards were quite merry and wanting to get on with the ceremony. I realised just how over long my intended speech was when I listened to the previous speaker, who rose, to much applause, to make a short and witty speech, balancing his notes on a wine glass in front of him. I was then invited to 'say a few words'. I should have abandoned my notes, but I didn't. Instead, I plodded on. Page after interminable page. Behind me, the toastmaster was shushing the audience, who had begun to chatter amongst themselves. I ploughed on to the end. My confidence level plummeted after this but I learnt some valuable lessons and never accepted speech notes unless I had done my own research about the nature of the proceedings and the expectations of the audience.

I was to go on to make numerous speeches in various cities where the IBA held conferences with their Regional Officers, who always looked after me extraordinarily well, and I was never let down by inadequate briefing. There were occasions, though, when all the briefing and preparation came to nought. One such was in Sheffield. I was to speak at a do, invited by the Mayor, which undoubtedly would be quite a grand occasion. Roma and I were staying somewhat out of the city centre where the dinner was to be held. I was most impressed when the Mayoral Rolls turned up and Roma and I took our seats. Happily unaware of where our route was taking us, I was studying my notes when the driver slid back the glass screen to inform us that he had lost his way, misjudged the time and asked what was to be done. The days when mobiles were at everybody's hand had not yet arrived so for the next three quarters of a hour we toured the back streets of Sheffield.

I was, and still am, very conscious of punctuality and consequently, by the time we arrived at the correct venue, my exasperation and blood pressure were at an all-time high. The incident, however, had a happy ending, for me at least, when we were met by the Lady Mayoress, choking back her own embarrassment. 'Thank goodness you're late', she said. 'You've saved the day'. I was told that a presentation that had been planned had very nearly ended in disaster when the specially-made cut glass fruit bowl was smashed on its way to the dinner. My late arrival had enabled a runner to acquire a similar bowl, which was duly presented to the accompaniment of huge cheers.

My appearance at the IBA very nearly coincided with the opening of Channel 4, in November. A degree of tension had built up between the ITV Companies, the IBA and the Channel 4 Board. The Contractors had been mollified to some extent by the IBA appointing a Director on to its Board – Peter Rogers, our Finance Director – but already Channel 4 had demonstrated its determination to carve out for itself independent status, free from the entanglements of the ITV Contractors. Since the ITV Contractors were bearing the cost of Channel 4's programming, they were expressing a degree of fury that they were not being involved in the programme scheduling of the channel, arguing that if it was not complementary, they would in fact be competing with themselves for an audience. This, of course, created the very competition that Government felt was much needed. The selection of Jeremy Isaacs as its Chief Executive was widely acknowledged as being a decision that displayed the wish of Channel 4 to be independent from the ITV 'family'. Channel 4 was going to be no pussycat and its Chairman, Edmund Dell, had already shown that he was not one to be pushed about by anyone, least of all by the Chairman of the IBA, George Thomson.

At a dinner I gave at the Garrick shortly before Channel 4 went on air three ITV Company MDs expressed their view to George and myself that they were alarmed by the independence already being shown by the Channel 4 Board, its Chairman and Chief Executive. George rounded on them, saying he had been surprised the Companies had not made a greater effort to secure a Board which represented ambitions closer to their own.

It was an unsatisfactory state of affairs that clearly showed that the need for bridge-building when it came to the subject of cable and who should be its regulator. The Companies were unanimous that it should be the IBA, clearly hoping that, unlike the way Channel 4 appeared to be going, cable could be an ancillary support to ITV and that both could live happily together.

A little later, when the announcement was made by the Home Office that cable was to be under the jurisdiction of a new Cable Authority, it was widely made known by Government spokespersons that cable should be seen to compete vigorously and that the Cable Authority would be given teeth. This was quite contrary to all that had been said by the Home Secretary, William Whitelaw to George and myself and I wondered at the time whether this new stance was to protect the cable companies, or to attack the IBA. Willie Whitelaw had assured us that the Government wished us to be the regulator of cable and either he had been rather deliberately misleading us or Mrs Thatcher had over-ridden the Home Office view.

Again, in those days I was too slow to read the runes and failed to recognise Mrs Thatcher's open criticism of the 'cosy monopoly' of the programme makers that the IBA oversaw and her determination to see the free market opened up. Looking back, I wish I had been much more politically aware or, recognising my own limitations, had brought in an advisor to help guide me through these whirlpools of political intrigue. In addition, in those early years of my Directorship, I failed to grasp that not only the ITV companies but, importantly, the advertisers wished to see a regime which would loosen or unshackle them from the strict rules governing them under the contract agreements with the IBA. Both parties were conniving with Government to bring about the demise of the IBA in its present form.

On Wednesday 13th October 1982, I woke up to read the press reports on the Hunt findings relating to cable regulation. Hunt was proposing a separate authority, the Cable Authority, which would have different sets of criteria and, whilst not being in opposition to the IBA, would nevertheless provide a market place for advertisers to compete with the existing regime of the IBA. I felt confirmed in my suspicion that we had been misled by Government in the person of the Home Secretary.

****

On Tuesday 2 November, Channel 4 opened to a mixed reception. A film about a mentally retarded youth was one of the first offerings of the new channel and caused considerable comment. I was not happy about the director of the programme using actual inmates of an institution along with professional actors.

Brookside, Channel's 4's equivalent to *Coronation Street*, started its run. I saw an episode and thought it predictable, and considerable concern was voiced about the amount of bad language in the series and indeed in a lot of the programmes being put out by Channel 4. Already, Mary Whitehouse was firing off letters to the Chairman and Attorney General. There were obviously to be squalls ahead.

During this month I lost the 'Designate' and became Director General. Brian Young and I met in his office at three minutes to noon one day and toasted each other in Perrier water: surely one of the most abstemious celebrations to have been enacted at any changeover. He presented me with a pair of scissors in a velvet box – to cut through regulations! I didn't know of the superstition which requires a coin to be given in return to the gift of a sharp or cutting object.

That same afternoon, Brian moved out of his office so that I could move in. I sat behind his desk for the very first time. The floor beneath his desk was cunningly raised a couple of inches, so that those sitting across from him had to look upwards as if seeking guidance from above. The furniture in the room was not to my taste, but I was concerned not to hurt Brian's feelings by making immediate changes. He had taken me around the office, pointing out different mementoes with considerable pride. The décor reminded me of a an airline waiting area in which Clark Gable and Lauren Bacall might have played out their farewell scene in some Banana Republic circa 1930s. I realised I would have to delay change, but do it I must.

Later in the afternoon, I returned from an outside meeting to find Anne, Sir Brian's personal secretary, in a very weepy state. She told me that Brian was looking so sad and lonely, sitting in the temporary office that I had just vacated. I asked for a photograph of Brian and me together to be taken. A photographer was

1982

summoned, took four shots and these later appeared in the house magazine. Some further pictures were taken of Brian, wearing a sweater specially knitted for him by Anne, with a motif of gambolling sheep: 15 white sheep on the front, 2 black sheep on the back. When I asked him what the black sheep represented, he pretended not to know, but I later found out from Anne they were the two new companies in the ITV fold: Channel 4 and TV-am.

On the Friday of my first week as Director General, I received a letter from Paul Channon inviting me to become a member of the Board of the National Theatre. Quite an honour, and one that I felt would reflect well on the IBA, who were so often thought of as merely a watchdog and not a creative entity.

At the weekend, I looked back on my last week as Director Designate and, there being no consensus of view on anything in ITV and ILR, I foresaw nothing but choppy seas ahead.

******

On Monday 15th November, Roma and I were guests of the Lord Mayor at his Banquet: a very jolly occasion with good speeches and lots to drink. Margaret Thatcher spoke with passion but I have quite forgotten what her then memorable words were all about.

On 18th November, the Authority held its farewell to Brian Young at Stationers' Hall. Roma sat next to Robert Fraser who afterwards fixed me with a penetrating gaze and warned me that, without prudent housekeeping and attention to costs, the independent Contractors would face a bleak future.

Brian gave a witty speech and was presented with a copy of his portrait. It was altogether a fitting occasion to see out the end of his career. Although I did not sense any real emotion, I am sure many were saddened by his leaving.

Just before Brian left the IBA, I attended with him the All-Party Committee on Party Political Broadcasts. Brian represented the IBA with Alasdair Milne representing the BBC. On the previous occasion the members of the Committee – Hugh Jenkins, David Steel et al – had been extremely aggressive with each other, fighting over the question of whether or not the SDP should be given time for PPBs separate to those given to the Alliance. Everyone, except for the broadcasters, had got extremely hot under the collar and exchanged insults about the claims of their opponents.

On my first occasion as the representative of the IBA, I made a short introductory speech in which I reminded them of the remit given by Parliament for the fourth channel to be different and to appeal to minorities. It was for this reason I believed the normal party political broadcasts should not apply. There seemed, to my surprise, to be almost total unanimity about this. Everyone appeared to take these meetings extremely seriously, no doubt endorsing the generally held view that the only way to reach the populace was to be on the telly.

I never really did warm to these meetings, where the allocation of time to the different parties appeared to be such a important issue. Nowadays, the standing of the various parties is so low, I don't believe TV audiences care one way or another about what is said in these broadcasts.

Towards the end of my first meeting with the Committee, I addressed the Lord President as 'Mr Chairman', which provoked startled looks and suppressed laughter.

In these first days of my Directorship, I bore the brunt of attacks by the press, MPs, Mrs Whitehouse and the ITV companies over the scheduling and content of programmes on Channel 4. There was one particular week which I named 'Let's bash Channel 4 week' with the aforementioned having a field day with almost anything that appeared on the channel. Mrs Whitehouse led the charge by demanding the sacking of Jeremy Isaacs as a consequence of Channel 4 showing an attempted rape scene in *Brookside*, the twice-weekly serial set in a 'respectable' suburb of Liverpool!

Then came the showing of a homosexual review – *One In Five* – on Christmas Day, adding more fuel to the fires of indignation, with a report in the newspapers that a pop group, recording for Channel 4, had indulged in 'simulated sex'. This announcement caused the final button on Mrs W's blouse to pop and she demanded a meeting with the Secretary of the IBA, Brian Rook. Willie Whitelaw, who had obviously been copied in with Mrs Whitehouse's letter, spoke to George Thomson, who decided to raise the whole question of taste, decency, political balance and violence at the next private luncheon for Members of the Authority.

Members warmed to a view expressed by Juliet Jowett, a Member of the Authority – to 'react but not be reactionary'. This phrase was echoed later when the Authority met formally. It was agreed that Edmund Dell and Jeremy Isaacs be invited to discuss the position with GT and myself. The following day the papers were still clamouring for action. This followed a statement by Willie Whitelaw in the House, in response to a question put by John Gorst attacking the IBA, and seeking reassurance that cable would not go the same way as Channel 4. I must say that, at the time, I was surprised that John, an old friend of mine, should have chosen to air his disquiet in such a public manner when a phone call to me would have been helpful to stave off the ominous signs of a revolution about to occur. Willie provided comfort for worried MPs, saying that the matter was firmly in hand, or words to that effect.

Later that day, Roma and I attended the premier of *Gandhi*, directed by Richard Attenborough. It was a splendid affair. We were sitting behind the Prince and Princess of Wales, both clearly suffering from the sniffles, and both blowing their noses surreptitiously from time to time. *Gandhi* will probably go down in the history books as Dickie's most memorable film and in the event it won, I think, five Oscars, so its place in history is assured.

At the dinner afterwards, I sat with Jeremy Isaacs. I began to wonder whether Jeremy was punch drunk, or oblivious to the storm around the fourth channel. He appeared highly confident and exuberant – not to say 'cocky'. I don't think he realised that the schedules of Channel 4 and the general outcry had done more damage to the reputation of the IBA as far as making out a case for cable supervision than almost any other factor – but then why should he have cared?

Not for the first time, I began to wonder if I had not made the most ghastly mistake in choosing the IBA as my final job. My mood of gloom was not lightened by the

1982

visit I made shortly afterwards to attend a meeting of the European Broadcasting Union in Tunis. The EBU took itself extremely seriously, believing that it held in its hand the future of broadcasting in Europe, not to say the rest of the world. In those days, these were solemn occasions, controlled by bureaucrats from the member companies who endlessly shuffled complex reports to each other, with a Secretariat which worked tirelessly to keep up with the torrent of paperwork that members were encouraged to read. Needless to say, I didn't; relying on Alasdair Milne to have done, together with his acolytes, the homework necessary for the BBC to give some view or other, which it readily did.

ITV in those days was considered an unruly adolescent, who could not be expected to have a grasp of the deeper philosophical and cultural aspects of broadcasting aimed at bringing harmony to the broadcasting environment. Indeed we were viewed with the very greatest suspicion and the only moment when my presence was felt to be useful was when a senior member of the BBC's team could not secure a lens in his thick glasses in order to read reports. I was able to provide a jeweller's screwdriver from my briefcase which did the trick and, although this usefulness was not recognised publicly, I hoped that it might have made a modest contribution to the workings of the EBU and of a BBC functionary in particular!

The EBU was founded in 1950 and in its Statement of Intent, published on the internet, it says that it 'promotes cooperation between broadcasters, and facilitates the exchange of audiovisual content. The EBU works to ensure that the crucial role of Public Service Broadcasters is recognised and taken into consideration by decision-makers.'

By far and away the best known element of the EBU output is in the organisation of the Eurovision Song Contest, amounting to a celebration of political vote-rigging and, at the time of writing, the ITV companies contribution to the EBU was the series *The Secret Diary of a Call Girl*! So it might be reasonable to suppose that the EBU, with all its grandeur and pomp, has lowered its sights to cater to popular demand.

On the occasion I write of, the EBU, in a moment of utter madness, had called on the Secretariat to find a location and they were under the impression that Tunis offered something special in the way of conference facilities. In the event, these turned out to be abysmal, with any words of importance we might have uttered being drowned out by a conference in the room adjoining, given by – of all people – a conference on conferences, and never have conference organisations uttered so loudly in discord.

Tunis is not a place I want to go back to: it is dirty, ugly, smelly and the people surly, unattractive and ill-dressed. Its general lack of style pervaded everything, whether it be transport, restaurants or formalities. The hotel bedroom had cockroaches which scurried about at night and disappeared at morning. For punishment, offenders in England could come out for a weekend in Tunisia!

The affairs of the EBU itself seemed in a certain amount of disarray. For too long the European Broadcasters had sat back in their carefully regulated citadels, secure in their respective governments' determination to control the airwaves. But of course all this was changing. The advent of satellite and cable, the growing number of video tape recorders, were all forcing a change on the output of the broadcasters. There was, for example, much concern and astonishment expressed when members learnt that Satellite Television, the company founded by Brian Hayes, was bidding for the Wimbledon Tennis Tournament at a sum of half a million pounds. The EBU had previously paid £80,000!

Whether the EBU would play a role for the broadcasters in the 80s was a question that would not go unanswered for long.

I have not mentioned hitherto a matter of a dispute between the IPA and Equity, which had remained unresolved for over two months. I had been trying to act as an honest broker. The issue was whether advertisers should pay the same fees to artists for the portrayal of their work on Channel 4, as Channel 4 at that time had no audience and was causing problems on many fronts, basically to do with audience ratings as well as good taste.

Advertisers were beginning to wonder whether they needed to reach agreement at all, as Channel 4 presented such an unwelcoming intrusion into the rather more stable environment that had existed hitherto. Equity's position was clear: they wanted the same money that would be paid for their artists' appearance on ITV.

What was becoming increasingly evident, from my position, was the fact that the fourth channel was seen as the unloved child of the television companies, and regarded as a cuckoo in the nest. It was to be some time before this vexing matter was resolved.

By the second week of December, Willie Whitelaw had sent a letter resulting from Mrs Whitehouse's intervention about good taste, to Jeremy Isaacs. Jeremy and I met, and he adopted a more conciliatory approach to the judgments that he had hitherto been resistant to change.

I seemed to spend more time mollifying MPs than I had bargained for. One such example was when I spoke to the Conservatives Back Bench Committee and, whilst giving me a round of applause for, to my mind, no good reason, one MP claimed that the weather forecast had shown bias because it had said that a cold night ahead would not be good for pensioners!

Northern Ireland was part of the IBA's parish and Ulster TV, a long-established and well-regarded television station under the benign rule of its Managing Director and Chairman, Brum Henderson. My first visit to Belfast was to appear for two and half minutes on Ulster TV to talk about Channel 4. Following this visit, I was horrified to discover that I had put on half a stone, resulting from the lavish hospitality I was enjoying. This hospitality on my first night consisted of Civic Leaders assembled in City Hall in Belfast with guests including Lady Faulkner, Lord Gowrie, the Lord Chief Justice and several others. A splendid dinner with a ten-man bodyguard positioned outside the door as we dined. During this visit, I went to see the IBA transmitter site on Black Mountain, just behind the by-then-notorious Falls Road. I noted that the people of Belfast veered between a nonchalance that nothing out of the ordinary was going on to wary concern about where and when the next bomb would go off.

*****

My first Christmas at the helm of the IBA, George had gone up the Nile and Christmas cheer had infiltrated the corridors and offices of Brompton Towers. One reason for my own jubilation was that the hysteria over Channel 4 was beginning to subside: there were no longer angry newspaper Leaders demanding resignations. The ITV companies, sensing a wind of change, were keen to see Channel 4 schedules attract a greater number of viewers and wanted closer consultation with regard to the scheduling of its programmes. Whether Jeremy would take heed of their wishes was something that only the test of time would resolve.

Whilst the IBA staff drank and feasted, I, too, was not left out, although I like to think that the entertainment I was afforded was for purposes other than simply good cheer. I found myself in the hallowed offices of NM Rothschild, one of the few places in the city where it appeared a car could be driven into a forecourt and would not be instantly taken away by yellow-coated wardens. I was very impressed by the grandeur of the place and my hosts, Evelyn and Leo Rothschild, could not have been more welcoming. Leo, who I came to know quite well subsequently, showed me with great pride his model railway before throwing open double doors to dine with Sir Evelyn. It transpired that the reason for this invitation was that Rothschilds were already becoming active in satellite and cable funding and were advising the consortium handling the BBC's launch.

It was on these occasions – and there were many more instances later – that my resolve, made before joining the IBA, that I would refrain from taking any alcohol, was most sorely tested. I should explain my reasoning: I was chary that I could maintain a sombre demeanour in the face of so much quite obvious temptation to become 'one of the boys', and subsequently be thought of as less than reliable. The expression 'he had a good lunch' was one frequently used to denigrate those who slipped from their high ideals. Looking back, the decision to avoid alcohol was a sound one, although many of my friends considered me beyond the pail.

At the end of December, the unresolved dispute between the IPA and Equity appeared to be no nearer to resolution. TV-am was seriously threatened unless a speedy solution could be found. Peter Jay was on the telephone ceaselessly urging action but, as I pointed out to him, the IBA was in a helpless position. Looking at the commercials on Channel 4 – or rather, the lack of them – I was beginning to think there was a plot on the part of the advertisers to keep commercials off the Channel. There must have been dozens of commercials which could go on, which did not use actors and were therefore able to be shown. Both sides appeared to have adopted the formula we had suggested; that is, basing artist's payments on a royalty geared to advertising expenditure. The IPA had put forward the previous week their offer for royalties for actors on TV-am, but Equity responded by upping their demands by an average of something like 500 per cent. The danger in agreeing a higher user charge for TV-am was that Equity would then argue the scale for ITV based on the settlement. I was more and more convinced that the only sensible way through this would be for both sides to agree on arbitration. The IPA would agree but at that stage I didn't know the response we would find from Equity.

One of my duties was to attend meetings of the ITN Board. At my second meeting there was continuing criticism of the general standards and style of Channel 4 News. David Nicholas was careful to point out that the method of presenting the news was entirely decided by Channel 4. I suspected then that we would be seeing some changes because in my submission, privately, it was one of the most boring items of television that it had been my misfortune to watch.

The end of 1982 was an anti-climax and a dismal conclusion to what had been, for me, a turbulent year where I had felt that I had contributed little towards some form of stability – even sanity – in the affairs of the ITV companies, TV-am and indeed Channel 4. The papers were filled with Channel 4, and rumours of impending devastation brought on the head of Jeremy Isaacs by dissident ITV Heads. He was a most unloved person within the system and, by standing out and determining for himself how the Channel should behave without bending a knee to ITV, his popularity was at an all time low. Jeremy had rung me to wish me Christmas greetings and told me that the press had got a rumour that the Companies had held a secret meeting: in his view, obviously to see how they might best unseat him and appeal to the IBA for some form of action that would rid them of his presence. Jeremy had challenged a number of the Companies about this rumoured secret meeting, but all denied that such a meeting had taken place.

During the same conversation he told me he was, in any case, 'strengthening the schedules' – whatever that meant at the time I wasn't certain – but he didn't want 'to slide into becoming ITV 2'.

1983

When Brian Young handed over the job to me, he said that the one thing I should do was forget all problems over the weekend – 'Leave it all at Brompton Road'. Since the very first weekend, I had to ignore his advice. At the beginning of 1983, television was going through a really rough period. The newspapers were filled with stories of declining audiences, the high cost of advertising and the low ratings of programmes, which – coupled with discord amongst the contractors over Channel 4 – all contributed to an unsettled climate which was felt as much by the contractors and the audiences as in Brompton Road and the IBA.

The BBC launched its Breakfast Time on 17 January 1983 with good reviews and expectations that were fulfilled. A particular star of the early morning was a fulsome lady, 'The Green Goddess': a 42 year old, ex-Butlins 'keep fit' woman, Diana Moran, who captured the hearts of males who choked over their cornflakes. ITV's breakfast television had yet still to begin its transmission but I had already become fully aware of the underlying tension within the Board and with its Chief Executive, Peter Jay, who telephoned me on numerous occasions to tell me how bad the climate was to launch the service, and had been an advocate for starting his service before that of the BBC. That battle had been lost, and the Authority had decreed a later start date.

Even at this early stage, I was predicting that the IBA would receive a letter asking the Authority to waive the first year's rental, for such had been the pressure on the company's funding to even get it across the start line.

David Frost, a member of TV-am's Board, came to visit me quite frequently. I was never certain of his objective, but he spent some time with me in engaging conversations over bottles of white wine that I was able to sneak from the Chairman's fridge.

The dispute between Equity and the IPA was still dragging on, despite Equity's decision to seek conciliation through ACAS. Newspapers were placing the total sums lost to the television companies at £30m. In the light of these losses, LWT were more and more vocal about seeking to reduce parts of their output, especially the number of plays and shortening the run of *Weekend World*.

In those days, much emphasis was placed on committees consisting of members of the public to advise on matters relating to television output. The foremost committee was the General Advisory Council of about 20 good men and women whose remit it was to cast their views over the quality of programming. Whilst the newspapers and the media in general had lambasted the output of Channel 4,

I was surprised at the overall positive reaction the Council had for its output and felt that it was performing a valuable function. I remember wishing I had felt the same!

On Sunday 12th February 1983, Breakfast Television went on the air. David Frost made a somewhat painful joke about the water workers and Norman Tebbit wanting to pour scalding water over their heads. Apart from that, it all went pretty well. I joined bleary-eyed guests over kippers at Ronnie Kirkwood's Agency.

Whilst TV-am had appeared to get off to a good start, it had taken a pounding from the press. Audience figures were well below the BBC's and there was a clamour to get David Frost replaced, a number of critics remarking on his inability to string his sentences together and his faltering style. When David came to see me some two months before, I was struck by the lack of precision in his speech and I had put it down to the white wine he had consumed in front of me. There was no doubt that the company was getting into serious trouble, not helped of course by the IPA/Equity strike which was decimating advertising revenues across the network, Channel 4 and now TV-am.

A few weeks after I was gloomily predicting the disintegration of TV-am, Peter Jay, who had been ceaseless in his efforts to retain his own control as Chief Executive and to seek the support of the backers of the station, resigned. The Board, under the Chairmanship of Richard Marsh, sought the IBA's approval to Jonathan Aitken taking over the role of Chairman and Chief Executive.

The press, who had been training their sights on TV-am's programming and financial woes, were quick to seize – through the grapevine of the imminent departure of Peter Jay – in lethal headlines to express the trauma in the most minute detail. The following day, the news was formally out and Anna Ford went down in television history when she responded to a question with a response that the downfall of Jay had been the work of a traitor in their midst; a traitor who she would not name.

Aitken's proposed role as Chief Executive was under fire from all quarters. *The Observer*, in its Leader column, attacked the IBA for ineptitude and lack of political awareness, describing Lord Thomson as new to his position and me as relatively inexperienced. It called on the Members of the Authority to act by ensuring the removal of Jonathan Aitken from this proposed role. Had we not made clear our intention to endorse Jonathan, I believe that the emergency would have escalated with the real danger of the financial institutions withdrawing and, with a lack of identifiable leadership, the company may well have foundered. We would then have been accused of a lack of business sense and an appreciation of the realities of life. The IBA in its ivory tower syndrome et al.

In the middle of this furore, the long-running dispute between Equity and the IPA continued. TV-am continued to be a whipping boy for the press to sling mud at. Max Hastings, in *The Evening Standard*, wrote a particularly virulent piece, calling for the replacement of the 'amateurs' who, as Members of the Authority, were incapable of forming sensible or even plausible judgments.

Members of the Authority were due to meet on the following Wednesday to consider what to do about TV-am. At the meeting, Members expressed their disquiet over the decision that George Thomson had taken on the previous Thursday with my support. The most outspoken critic of the action that had been taken was Denis Hamilton, who said that his own background and experience should have been called upon in reaching such a deeply sensitive decision. Other Members spoke their minds, agreeing with Hamilton that Aitken should not be granted even an acting role as Chief Executive. George was clearly upset by Denis Hamilton's outspoken comments on the way that the situation had been handled, but he was unrepentant over the actions we had taken. Jonathan asked to be given the opportunity of meeting Members during the Authority meeting. Whilst he did not win over any sympathy for the decision taken, the Members agreed – albeit reluctantly – to permit him to stay in the role of Chief Executive for a maximum of three to four weeks.

After the meeting, I was told that Aitken had indicated that, in the event of a decision barring him from this role, he was considering suing the Authority over the right to reject his nomination. Later, when I spoke to our lawyers, it was confirmed to me that the Authority did not have a right to demand the approval of a Chairman or Chief Executive, and I felt at the time that this should be remedied as soon as possible.

Throughout this period of TV-am's financial uncertainties, another cloud was looming: that of the relationship between Edmund Dell, the Chairman of Channel 4, and Jeremy Isaacs. Jeremy came to see me and said that, since Edmund had retired from other appointments, he was taking 'unhealthy interest in the running of programming for the Channel'. Reading between the lines, I surmised that Edmund wanted to take on the role of Editor, and Jeremy was finding this increasingly irksome. I told him that while he was employed as Programme Controller and MD, he should exercise his rights until such time as Edmund failed to respect this when it would be time for one or the other to go.

That same day, I had a meeting with Jonathan Aitken, who brought along his nephew Timothy. It concerned their fears about their expenditure: that it was running out of hand. During the meeting, Aitken said that the losses for the month of March had been higher than they had previously anticipated – some £800,000 – and that there were a number of unexpected creditors who were pressing their claims.

Timothy said he was prepared to move in for at least a year to replace Jonathan. I was all for making changes as soon as possible and we agreed Timothy would take over, subject to Members' views, on 11th April. This I felt would at least shut up those who kept up a wail of protest at Jonathan remaining in office.

At this same meeting, Jonathan said they had very nearly made up their minds to appoint Greg Dyke in the role of Editor. I asked him about the position of Michael Deakin and Jonathan emphasised it was not his intention to alter his responsibilities. I took this, I recall, with a pinch of salt.

On the subject of changes, Jonathan advised me it was his intention to announce a change in Anna Ford's duties, and believed she would be leaving the company. I advised him that he should make no changes until after the Authority meeting to be held the following Wednesday, because substantial changes would bring into question the framework of the whole Application, which was already somewhat perilously balanced. Jonathan agreed to hold his fire on the announcement.

After the Authority meeting, the announcement of Timothy Aitken was made, which effectively quelled the mutterings of those MPs who witter on such matters.

Throughout my time at the IBA, I was plagued by confrontations of every sort, including the Religious Broadcasting Consultation which was held that year in Grange Over Sands. It amazed me that, even some 30 years from the start of ITV, the Church was still erecting barriers around the Closed Period in the fear that the religious content of television would disappear. This particular consultation was called 'The End of the Road' and was to consider the role of religious programming in an increasingly multi-choice society. Most people who were present felt that the reviewing process, whereby programmes with a religious content were validated by the IBA, should continue. I wrote in my diary at the time that I believed that, since television was still the most powerful medium in the world, it would be up to the television producers and religious advisors to make the issues of religion as adventurous and innovative as possible. Nothing, I said, benefits from cosseting. The best work is often done when the going was toughest. The spiritual message was something we must all discover in ourselves in our daily lives. I felt that having an hour set aside for the programme divorced it from present day realities.

Towards the end of April 1983, I wrote 'The magic box still appears to hold a magnetic spell over the population, but not least over the press. TV-am holds the front page, whatever the rest of the news. Millions may perish in Biafra but the Camden Five and their ludicrous behaviour captivates the attention of the nation.

Michael Parkinson spoke out in the press for the two 'fallen ladies' – Angela Rippon and Anna Ford – and then, after a meeting with Timothy Aitken, recanted and announced that he would, after all, be staying. At the end of that week, Angela Rippon was reported to be holding a press conference and later I was informed the reason she had called the press together was to tell them she would not be talking to the press!

During the same week, George and I considered the contractual position of the company. I was worried that if Michael Deakin were to go, the original franchising group would bear little or no resemblance to the management of that day. The credibility of the IBA, already much weakened, would receive a body blow if Deakin were to pack his bags and be given the 'heave ho'. I was assured by Timothy Aitken that such a decision was far from their minds. Aitken was no fool and could clearly see the pivotal position that Deakin commanded.

Throughout this period, and the hi-jinks of TV-am, the IPA/Equity dispute ground on. I decided to meet Ted Willis and Justin Dukes to see whether Ted would act as a go-between and mediator between the two parties. His track record in both the creative output of television and his political leanings made him a good choice.

At the beginning of May 1983, I held one of my monthly meetings with Regional Officers of the IBA; something of a ritual and an occasion taken seriously by all

1983

concerned. It took place in the Board Room and people from across the country, representing the 15 regions, foregathered to be briefed by various staff members on radio, television and advertising matters. The routine was that at 10am I would walk in and, as always to my embarrassment, everyone would rise to their feet in what I assumed was a respectful silence. Waving them to sit down before I took my seat, I felt rather like minor royalty. I am sure that in Brian Young's day he made a more dignified entry and struck a more solemn note.

A glance at the Agenda for the meeting showed the issues to be discussed: the IPA/Equity dispute, the White Paper on Cable Broadcasting, satellite development and the IBA, early retirement, TV-am, and other items of concern to the Regional Officers.

The ROs took themselves rather seriously, seeing themselves as ambassadors of the IBA. In a sense, of course, they were and to a man and woman they performed their role with diligence but, as we moved further and further into multi-channel choice for our television watching – via satellite, VCR and cable – there was less requirement to regulate. Today observers will look back with amusement at the lengths the system went to in order to control and balance its output.

I seemed to be surrounded by advisory groups: this time it was a meeting of the General Advisory Council, a weighty body of men and women selected from across the country to advise the IBA on its social remit. I was impressed by their enthusiasm and obvious dedication. They were drawn from a wide spectrum of society although, now I think of it, I cannot recall meeting anyone who was not either middle class or a member of a profession; not a single 'worker' among them: an omission I was determined to correct.

One particular meeting concerned the role of the soap opera, and found it alive and well and, whilst not worthy of watching, nevertheless they considered it fulfilled a valuable function for many people by reflecting their lives and giving them a sense of continuity. A sad reflection on our society that it needs an electronic comforter.

The main subject of another meeting was the question posed by IBA staff about whether or not homosexuals should be allowed to advertise on television promoting magazines and a gay switchboard. The GAC were unanimously against allowing gays to take to the air. They felt it would cause offence to viewers and be deeply repugnant to some. I was on the point of asking whether or not the same could be said about the army putting out commercials inviting young men to learn the art of killing, but I chickened out!

On another day I had lunch with the IBA's Panel of Religious Advisors, yet another body appointed to guide and advise the IBA. A jolly bunch of widely assorted Men of God; no women and no Sikhs. Neither did I see a Jew or Hindu. The invited guest was the Bishop of Wakefield, Colin James, an ebullient man whose benign spirit warmed us all.

At that time there was a 'Closed Period' from 6.30pm to 7.15pm on Sundays: a time traditionally for religious output but threatened by pressure put on the IBA by London Weekend Television who had watched their ratings crumble, against the BBC's opposition programme called *Holiday*, which for some unaccountable reason the Central Religious Advisory Committee (CRAC) had allowed and the BBC put out their religious offering at 11pm. I told the Bishop, who was Chairman of CRAC, that I personally was not in favour of maintaining a Closed Period and thought that religious output should be encouraged to demonstrate its attraction without the need of regulation. I knew then that the subject would not go away.

Some time during May of 1983 Jeremy Isaacs showed me round the new Channel 4 building. There seemed to be a great deal crammed into a very small space, but everyone appeared happy, squashed into separate little sections with potted plants sprouting up between them. The Chief Engineer showed me the system of networking pictures to the regions and, as I listened, I became convinced that I was not capable of understanding the modern technology. Everything was possible, but it still did not meet the challenge of making good television.

During the same week I paid a breakfast call on TV-am and ate eggs and bacon with Timothy Aitken. He was a happy man, having persuaded his large financial shareholders to support his proposals for carrying on. He told me that he had made saving of £5m and that the unions had cooperated by agreeing to no overtime, and in some cases operating a different shift pattern than previously. All of this broke new ground in industrial relations. If TV-am could begin to attract an audience the IBA would have achieved a miracle of staying cool in the face of much adverse criticism.

An incident at the same time which may have heralded more complication was the announcement that a Managing Director of a radio station planned to stand for Parliament. The IBA decided that he should resign his directorship. We heard from the Home Secretary, Leon Brittan, that he had advised the Board of the radio station to continue employing its Managing Director. George Thomson wrote to Leon, pointing out that the Authority could not allow itself to be overruled.

Political broadcasting was another vexed issue of the time, particularly with an imminent election. George Thomson and I, accompanied by David Glencross, journeyed to Portland Place for a meeting with the BBC Chairman, George Howard, and the Director General, Alasdair Milne. We decided that a ratio of 5:5:4 – five broadcasts by the Conservatives, five by the Labour Party and four for the SDP-Liberal Alliance – should be agreed. We knew this would not please the SDP, who had indicated that they would be prepared to go to court unless offered parity with the two other parties. We would need to take advice from our lawyers to be sure that we were not found to be acting incorrectly but our decision was in the event accepted.

I had heard George Howard was not well and, throughout this meeting, which was held in his office, he smoked continuously, lighting a cigarette the second he had stubbed out the old. He smoked five while we sat with him. His face had become markedly drawn since I had last seen him, four months earlier; his clothes hung loosely about him; his jacket had been tossed carelessly on a hanger, one sleeve hanging inside out. Despite his wan looks, he was nonetheless an impressive figure with a clear mind and an articulate manner of speech.

Despite an air of confidence at Channel 4, there was a fly in the ointment, with

Jeremy Isaacs and his intransigent views about the need to balance programme output, particularly at that time concerning a series of programmes about nuclear defence. Once again he seemed to be making the case for the unilateralists, who objected to American bases in the UK. I realised I would need to speak to him to get him to understand our concern.

At our meeting, Jeremy listened politely and responded by saying his hope was to achieve balance over a longer period than was normal practice. I pointed out that the nuclear debate had been billed as a week's event and that I had expected the balance to have been achieved within that timescale. I could see that, as the Channel grew in popularity and respect and Jeremy's personal reputation escalated, it would become more and more difficult to convince him that he could not be the sole arbiter of the channel's output.

There was also the problem that Channel 4 would not be the most suitable channel for election coverage, following reports in the press that the ITV contractors would be seeking permission to transmit via Channel 4 on the morning after the election, thus enabling them to continue using the ITN back-up and resources. I told Paul Fox, Chairman of ITCA, that TV-am was the appointed contractor for morning broadcasting, and that the television Companies should comply with this ruling and not just use Channel 4 when it suited them. My hope was that TV-am would provide a genuinely attractive service. If they did not, I would have few friends amongst the TV Companies.

The IBA had issued a press release to the effect that whereas we would be funding the Direct Broadcasting Satellites (DBS) with private money, the BBC would be seeking £200m of public funding. This was incorrect as the Treasury would be making the loan to the BBC and I wrote to Alasdair Milne with a fulsome apology. I received a short note in return, thanking me for my letter but saying that the quote had 'done quite some damage'. It was at this time that the whole subject of direct broadcasting by satellite became more and more a subject of controversy. There was a collision of the technologies that could be employed to ensure a European standard of transmission. The large amounts of money and the vested interests involved, each fighting their own corner, made the ensuing years until Murdoch's Sky became the dominant force a time of claim and counter-claim with political undertones always beneath the surface. Had I realised how many interests were opposed to the IBA's continuing to regulate and oversee programming output, I may not have accepted the position of Director General.

At a meeting in Munich in June 1983 it became clear that the French were opposed to the unified acceptance of Multiplexed Analogue Component (MAC) in Europe which had been developed by the IBA and was obviously our preference.

I still had to come to terms with the job. The nearest I came to describing how I felt was to compare my energy with one of those 12 volt car batteries which, unless charged, simply run down. I felt as though I was just burning up energy without any opportunity to replenish it.

This feeling was not helped by a writer in *Campaign* – a weekly magazine for the advertising business – describing the attempts by the Authority to get into DBS as 'pusillanimous', which was rather disheartening and a little unfair when I thought of the efforts being made by us to thrust the ITV companies into space.

A meeting at the Home Office caused me further concern: there was obvious anxiety about allowing the ITV companies into DBS first, fearing their political masters would fail to appreciate the delicate balance that would need to be struck to ensure that the UK terrestrial services would not be seriously undermined by competition from outside. Such undermining would drastically erode their revenue which consequently would narrow the quality and range of their programme output.

The BBC, Aubrey Singer, then Deputy Director General, told me, felt badly let down by the Home Office allowing anyone who could afford £1.2m per year to lease a low power satellite (ECS) transponder, supplying material on to cable which would be to the detriment of direct broadcasting by satellite. The same week I received a telephone call from James Lee of Goldcrest film company to say that he had a deal under discussion with London Weekend Television and Yorkshire Television concerning the provision of film features using an ECS transponder. I called up Brian Tesler who confirmed that James Lee, acting for Goldcrest, had put together a consortium of American interests, including Home Box Office, 20th Century Fox, Columbia and CBS. I suggested Brian approach the five big ITV companies first, and then the regional companies, and that an investment in the consortium would be acceptable providing it had the backing of the Independent Television Contractors Association (ITCA).

Tesler saw the proposition as a stepping-stone towards a DBS film channel. He told me Bill Cotton, Managing Director of BBC, with the approval of Stuart Young, the new Chairman, was thinking of an approach to the IBA to see if it would join forces with the BBC to jointly own a DBS satellite. Three channels were envisaged – one film, one sport & news and one that might be music – reasoning that such a proposal would be the best possible opportunity of competing with ECS on cable. Such a showcase in space, it was reasoned, promoted by the BBC and the IBA, would attract viewers with a monthly subscription of £11.

At a meeting with James Lee, he warned me that the American interests would not be prepared to allow their film material on satellite until they considered the time to be right. This was a difficult one: the whole future of cable and satellite DBS, viz a viz the ITCA contractors, was clearly going to be fraught with uncertainties.

At a subsequent meeting with Bill and Brian, I raised the question of politics, saying that I thought there would be an outcry if the IBA were to join forces and form a virtual monopoly. Bill believed this would be acceptable if there were to be a distinct break point after, say, five years when both bodies would cease to work together and return to competing as before.

I thought the proposition ill-conceived and served to underline the growing unease of the BBC as they considered the problem of filling two DBS channels in 1986.

One of the few perks of the job was being wined and dined without any apparent agenda. I remember Roma and I going to the Cup Final as guests of Hugh Dundas, Chairman of Thames Television. At lunch, I chatted to Sir Ian Trethowan, the former Director General of the BBC, who confessed that the BBC's breakfast programme was too downmarket for his taste.

At this time, TV-am launched its new style of programming, under the new wunderkid Greg Dyke. This was a critical time for the company. For the last two weeks their ratings had remained at an average of 200,000 against the BBC's 1.7 million but with the advent of Roland Rat et al TV-am would prosper.

TV-am also made headline news around the same time when Anna Ford very publicly threw a glass of wine in the face of Jonathan Aitken, who she believed had been instrumental in having her fired from the company. I thought at the time what a world of crazy values we inhabited where a newsreader's action superseded world news.

I was at a dinner in the Penthouse at the Dorchester, with Norman Tebbit as Guest of Honour. I thought him a man incapable of emotion and, although I had been told he had a kind heart, I did not witness it. Richard Marsh was also present and, had I been Chairman of TV-am, I would have kept a fairly low profile while waiting not only for the ratings to increase but for the quality of output to reflect the company's original aspirations. Not at all. Marsh was in expansive mood, recounting to all who would listen the success the company was having in axing staff, chopping salaries and overtime, and generally behaving like the Borgias. I did mention to him that the Authority would be considering TV-am's performance at its next meeting. He did not appear taken aback and immediately offered to send a representative. I said I would think about it.

It was towards the end of June 1983 that I had my first encounter with CRAC. I found them an unsmiling body. An altogether chilling experience. The major topic was that the television companies wanted to move the Closed Religious Period forward on Sunday from 6.15pm to 1pm. CRAC did not show any enthusiasm for this. I countered by suggesting that change would give them the opportunity to attract a new audience to religious output but they decided to recommend retaining the status quo. I was minded to recommend to the Authority that for once we did not take the advice of CRAC. I had no doubt this would bring the heavens down about my head, but I found their arrogance insufferable.

At this same time, we decided we should look outside the Authority to find a suitable person to head up our satellite interests in the short term. Brenda Maddox wrote an article in *The Times*, clearly inspired by the BBC, that the BBC should seriously consider pulling out of the DBS since so many of their original ambitions had been altered by events.

On Wednesday 22 June, I had a useful and revealing dinner with Jeremy Isaacs and Justin Dukes. Once again, they raised storm cones over the deteriorating relationship between them and Edmund Dell. Jeremy spoke bitterly about Dell's determination to get into the day to day business of the company. I feared the outcome might not be a pleasant one. Over dinner, we touched on the subject of who should sell Channel 4's time. Reading between the lines, I sensed that both Jeremy and Justin would not be displeased if the current arrangements were changed to permit Channel 4 to appoint their own agency. I knew that this would cause mayhem amongst the ITV contractors but decided not to voice my unease at this time.

On Friday 24th, Alasdair Milne telephoned to suggest a meeting. From Colin Shaw, I knew that his proposition would almost certainly be that together we should look at a joint use of the satellite and that we should share a subscription film channel and each have control over a second and third channel – one funded by advertising, the other by licence.

On Monday 4 July, I rose early and at 0830 had the meeting with Alasdair Milne in Portland Place. His office still retained the original oak panelling which Alasdair had had sanded down to restore it to its former colour: a room of such expensive austerity that I could sense the malevolent shadow of Reith watching from behind the desk. Coffee was served by a waitress who could have walked out of a 1930s film. Alasdair didn't waste time. Colin Shaw's deep throat informant had been right in every respect and I said to Alasdair that I would think about the possibility of forming some sort of alliance.

At lunch that day, George Thomson and I met Douglas Hurd, the new Minister for Broadcasting, at the Home Office. His very grand office had the decorative style that I was sure would be relished by an African chief: lots of ivory, silver and beaten brass, all quite obviously gifts presented to Douglas in previous roles and which must have reminded him of his former glories.

George and I had prepared a brief to cover some detailed ground, including satellite, fourth channel etc. We left the meeting with the impression that Douglas Hurd had a keen interest in the subject and felt we had struck up a useful relationship. It turned out later that he was in fact preparing the ground for an assault on the IBA by Mrs Thatcher.

On Tuesday 5th July, following a successful breakfast meeting with Christopher Foster, Peter Rogers and Paul Fox, the latter representing ITCA as its chairman, I met with Peter Plouviez and Ian McGarry of Equity to endeavour to progress the question of the an agreement for an enquiry into the dispute between the IPA and the ITCA. Inside the meeting room was a scene that reminded me of a Hogarth print: the Equity Council, some 30 in number, were scattered around the room, filling every nook and cranny; papers were piled everywhere; the din was appalling. I sat down and waited for order. When silence at last reigned, I was asked to speak, which I did for about ten minutes. The letter that we had shown Peter Plouviez in draft form was tabled, and Christopher went through it, detailing the points. When he had finished, the floor was open for questions. They came thick and fast and from them I began to realise just how difficult it was going to be to find a solution that would suit both parties. The meeting finally concluded and I left more than a little worried at the applause the Council accorded me!

Later that week, I heard from Peter that Council had agreed to appoint a sub-committee to examine the terms of an enquiry. A major next step, if they agreed to the enquiry, would be finding a suitable chairman. Lord Windlesham, Ted Willis, Tom Harris and Merlin Rees had been suggested.

1983

On Wednesday 29 June 1983 I lunched with the Chairman and Sir Keith Joseph, then Secretary of State for Education and Science. Quite an oddball, who made much out of his claim not to look at television or even, it seemed, own a set. He was much concerned over the findings of a group of teachers to the effect that children aged five to 14 watch 23 hours of television per week, which is more time than they spend in the classroom. Sir Keith hoped that the IBA would consult with the Home Office on this. Since neither the Chairman nor I had at the time any knowledge of these findings and, coming as they did from a man who had no truck with television, it seemed odd that he was interrogating us. We heard nothing further from him.

The following day, there were formal farewell drinks for Tony Pragnell, who had been Deputy Director General of the IBA for many years. He was held in high regard throughout the Authority and his wise counsel had been a source of great benefit to me. I opened my remarks by quoting the dictionary definition of a 'pragnell': 'an instrument used in surveying…'. Tony was presented with a radio and TV set by staff. I thought that, after 28 years of regulating them both, he might be sick of the beastly things but apparently not, as it was his wish to receive them.

On Friday 1st July, Colin Shaw, who had been widely expected by those within the Authority and by the press to be offered the role of Director General when I was appointed, sent me a brief letter confirming his intention to resign. I circulated Members of the Authority with this information, including a press quote from the Chairman.

On Monday 4th July, a time when fat Americans all over the world celebrate with hamburgers and beer, I went to the American Embassy, which was ringed by police trying to look like US security men and US security men trying to pass as English gentlemen. Inside was a collection of High Commissioners and assorted diplomats standing in ethnic circles, stoutly eyeing each other and wondering which of them were in possession of US funding or busily trying to procure it, or which were encouraging revolution.

There should be a system of lapel badges at cocktail parties when one has eaten enough. At this particular party waitresses hovered like mother hens feeding their chicks, diving on guests with plates of morsels and destroying any hope of conversation.

Later that evening I went across to the Home Office to meet the new Home Secretary, Leon Brittan. In the foyer, Stuart Young – the soon to be Chairman of the BBC – introduced himself; a very different character from George Howard, whom I had grown to like and respect. Every inch the successful accountant, I felt Young would prove a very uneasy partner to Alasdair Milne; Young being a perfect fit for all that the Conservatives aspired to in broadcasting at the time, regarding commercial imperatives above those of culture, whereas Alasdair Milne was an embodiment of all that Lord Reith, founder of the BBC, had established, seeing the BBC as the guardian of public service broadcasting. This role became increasingly difficult to sustain due to the competition engendered by ITV, with the results that we see today!

Leon Brittan greeted me and we went into his office where, at half past five promptly, the air conditioning was turned off so that the drinks were served in a Turkish bath atmosphere. Leon had been the subject of a unexpected attack on a Channel 4 programme, insinuating he was homosexual, which greatly upset him. Jeremy Isaacs wrote later to Leon apologising, and this was the last that was heard on the subject.

Michael Moriarty, a rising star in the Home Office, telephoned during that week to say that Ministers would not be happy with the granting of a first satellite channel to the ITV companies, but that they would like to see open competition. They did, however, look to the IBA to be the Regulator of the Direct Broadcasting System. At the General C.C. meeting, I conveyed this to the ITV companies – that I thought it highly likely that the IBA's case for the ITV companies would be turned down. There was a shocked reaction but I sensed that a number of MDs were not all that unhappy. It was felt by some that the IBA was playing too passive a role and that we should be putting on a more resolute front.

Over dinner at the Garrick Club with John Freeman, Chairman of LWT, Aubrey Buxton, Anglia TV, and George Thomson, grave disquiet was expressed about the funding of Channel 4, fearing the Companies would be broke within two years without changes in funding. Advertising revenue for Channel 4 was still marginal, due to the low viewing figures – a fact that did not register with Equity, who still believed their members were entitled to the same rates when recording commercials for Channel 4 as for ITV.

On Wednesday 24th July, I invited the Channel 4 Board to a working dinner. I was told beforehand of the breakdown in the relationship between the chairman Edmund Dell and Jeremy Isaacs and his Deputy Justin Dukes. Edmund, now that Channel 4 seemed to be growing in popularity, was taking more and more of a lead – in other words, interfering, in Justin's view. Instead of being a chairman, he was conditioning the Board's views by his outspoken criticisms on the whole programme-output. Edmund, for his part, was concerned that Jeremy did not simply ride rough-shod over the Board. I hoped this would not result in resignations: if Edmund resigned, the Press would say the IBA had given in to the left; if Jeremy resigned, the Press would say he had been gagged by the IBA.

During this week, Bill Cotton again proposed that the IBA consider some form of relationship with the BBC, using a three-channel system. The unholy alliance that would be produced by the IBA and the BBC not only sharing one satellite, but also sharing channels *and* providing a programme mix, with the revenue from the three channels being divided equally through a jointly held company, seemed to me to have all the worst features of a monopoly and reeked of protectionism. Bill Cotton, however, claimed that the Government might swallow their determination to encourage competition in order to ensure that sufficient entertainment material was available to excite people sufficiently to want to purchase a dish aerial. I told Bill that if he wanted to trail the idea in front of the Minister, he could, and then we might consider it if there were signs of a fair wind behind it.

On Wednesday 3rd July, I was the guest of the political publicist Geoffrey Tucker, who had invited Lord Whitelaw as guest of honour. We met at Brooks's and were entertained well in a private room. Willie Whitelaw was in good spirits and spoke widely about the present Government and about his fears for the country, particularly the alarming unemployment figures. I said I thought we should stop ringing our hands over the job situation and set about making the country understand the need for leisure instead of concentrating on the 'work ethic' which only made young people feel rejected when they could not find employment. Whitelaw said 'Maggie' went too far, given any proposition she approved of, promoting it 100 per cent. His job, he claimed, was to 'rein her back'.

I read James Archibald's obituary in *The Times* this week. He was a good friend and we had had a productive relationship during the making of his film on the Royal College of Music, while I was a member of its Centenary Development Fund.

During the following week, Douglas Hurd chaired a meeting at the Home Office. We were confronted by huge piles of biscuits, their presence explained by Douglas as 'Trade Union members eat these by handfuls when the going's tough'.

We agreed with the Home Office that the IBA should not engage in the leasing of the satellite, but should appoint a contractor, thus placing ourselves more nearly in the same role as the Federal Communications Commission in the States. The Home Office insist we still remain the 'broadcaster' and wish us to hold on tightly to the control of the 'uplink' (the source of programme provision to the satellite beamed upwards from the studio.) All these talks and discussions are being carried out in considerable haste so that we can ensure legislation in the Cable bill.

I am not displeased with the way things are turning out. The Home Office is worried, even so, that ITCA companies will need to be kept sweet about the use of provisional funding the IBA intends deploying to maintain the system. I reassured them that the ITCA companies will take such a burden lightly. They want to be the programme supplier, so will gladly take on board that we will be utilising some funds derived from the terrestrial services. Tom Robson, our Director of Engineering, however, has considerable reservations about the IBA losing its grip on the satellite provider. It will mean less work for the Companies, but he is afraid of standards slipping.

The following week I took some leave, and arranged for my office to be redecorated in my absence. Every time I entered it, it reminded me of one of the departure lounges in early 50s films. Any moment I expected Clark Gable and Lauren Bacall to kiss a last goodbye before one of them boarded the Dakota, propellers turning over in the background. The new office will probably look like the waiting room of an advertising agency!

While away from the office, I heard that TV-am – or rather Roland Rat – was being watched by more viewers than BBC's *Good Morning Britain*. The ITV companies will have to eat their words, as they believed TV-am wouldn't last. The real problem for us being to determine how best to get TV-am's programmes to reflect the original remit which had won them the licence.

The first public rumblings resulting from the IBA's decision to move religious programming from its traditional spot appeared in a third leader in *The Times*;

quite a fair piece. I spoke to George Thomson about it and we decided to respond by a letter to the Editor as soon as the bishops had had their say. I hoped this was the right decision; there is nothing more histrionic than the Church on matters such as broadcasting policy, especially in the silly season! As recently as five years before, rescheduling religious programmes would have very nearly unseated the IBA, whereas in the current climate the general feeling is that the new vistas of choice that technology offered would sweep away much that was thought to be static and unassailable.

Radio still hadn't caught the imagination of advertisers even in this, its tenth year. I was to open Signal Radio in Stoke-on-Trent, the 43rd ILR station, at the same time as expecting to hear the news that Centre Radio in Leicester was no more. This demise may serve as a timely lesson to those stations which were still flabby in their output and staffing, and I hoped the dinner at the Mansion House to mark radio's tenth anniversary would focus positive attention on commercial radio.

I attended the TV Festival in Edinburgh, which this year was enlivened by Jeremy Isaac's sudden announcement that he wanted specially created programmes with a pronounced right wing bias, which seemed to me to signal his acceptance that his current programming had a distinct left wing slant.

Edmund Dell telephoned to seek a meeting with me and the Chairman because he was unhappy about Jeremy's editorial decisions and wanted the Board to take matters on their own shoulders. I said I thought Jeremy would not take kindly to the proposal, as it was fundamentally the job of a Chief Executive to take important decisions on the part of the Board. Without this, he would have no real value. I foresaw trouble ahead.

On Wednesday 7th September 1983 we were to interview the members of the TV-am consortium, a meeting which had been postponed following another stupid interview granted by Tim Aitken to the *Financial Times*. During the interview, he said that those who wanted to speak about public broadcasting should ring the BBC! Not a good start to winning friends and influencing people.

It was a frosty meeting. Lord Marsh was, as always, over-talkative and aggressive. Lord Thomson opened by remarking that TV-am had received support from the IBA and he felt that references in the newspapers had made us reflect on our generosity to the Company. Timothy Aitken said he had been misquoted and that he actually said that people who wanted to speak about 'public-funded broadcasting' should ring the BBC. He wasn't convincing.

Later, hard words and angry glares were exchanged across the table, separating the two sides; exacerbated when Sir John Riddell, our Deputy Chairman, suggested to Marsh that TV-am should be careful in what it said to the City in its attempt to raise further funds. Marsh took exception to this suggestion, but John stuck to his guns. Another City relationship bit the dust!

Greg Dyke, TV-am's 'wunderkid' producer, then launched into his piece about programming. It sounded awfully flat and fell on dulled and angry ears. At the end of the meeting, the consortium rose and left the room in silence. This meeting will, I think, prove a watershed in our dealings with the Company – a pity, because with a little sense of style and understanding the TV-am members could have made a good impression.

Following the meeting, I wrote a constrained letter to Timothy Aitken marking our dissatisfaction.

The following week I attended the Royal Television Society's bi-annual convention in Cambridge, where on the first day the Home Secretary announced publicly for the first time that the Government hoped to introduce Cable clauses into the new legislation which would enable the IBA to advertise and control the two DBS Channels. Reaction to the news was mixed. The existing contractors, who had wanted the first channel on an exclusive basis, were clearly divided in their views. Overall, I suppose the mood was positive, and there seemed to be a general acceptance that open competition for the two channels was right. No one spoke of the accelerated erosion that might now occur as new competitors sought to secure audiences from the existing terrestrial services! Perhaps, if we had argued more strongly for a complementary relationship between terrestrial and celestial services, the ecology of broadcasting might have been very different. On the other hand, if we had defended the monopoly we could have found ourselves ousted from the position of regulator. At least, under the arrangement we achieved, we could do our best to balance the requirements of the public service elements.

At the end of September, I returned from a short holiday in Minorca, having read that the Equity Council had turned down the settlement offered by the IPA. The battle lines were so hard-drawn, I couldn't see a solution but was determined to persevere, and set up a working party to take matters forward. Lord Lever readily accepted my invitation to take the chair. Economic advisor to Harold Wilson, Lord Lever is a man of such experience and perception that I was confident he would make a major contribution.

Mary Whitehouse was taking the IBA to court over the matter of *Scum* and I prepared my affidavit. Members of the Authority have been circulated with a tape of the film accompanied by a robust letter from the Chairman backing my judgment. When the BBC banned the original television version, there was a violent reaction against its suppression. I wondered how many would rally to the cause now the IBA had chanced its arm. Would hatred of the Authority prove an incentive to silence?

At the 50th anniversary celebration of the British Film Institute, of which Richard Attenborough was President, Prince Charles said he must be the only non-professional in the entire gathering. Orson Welles, an immense man who carried his weight well, delivered a hugely witty speech.

Ample proof that TV-am is in dire straights was provided by a visit from Sir Kenneth Cork, the insolvency accountant with a reputation for being the country's leading 'Company Mortician'. He confessed disarmingly to knowing nothing about television but explained that TV-am needed an immediate injection of £3 million, followed by a further £1 million, to survive. He then proceeded to lay down a number of points he believed the IBA would have to accept if TV-am were to secure further funding. The most contentious was that the IBA should make no demands on TV-am's programme output which might depress ratings. I told him this was not a condition we could contemplate.

The latest research findings emerging from BARB (British Audience Research Bureau) must be making the BBC grind its corporate molars in anguish. These show that ITV were capturing some 75 per cent of total viewing, placing the BBC in a position where, if this continued, they would find their licence money in jeopardy. After all the upheavals of the past months, it was pleasing to see the strength of the ITV system at a time when a boost of this sort was just what was needed.

Channel 4 continues to give me headaches. There has been long-running bitterness between Channel 4 and ITN over the provision of the former's news programme, which was presented for an hour each night. It was now being suggested that if the news contract were to be given to ITN they must achieve an audience of 750,000 or else Channel 4 would have the right to terminate the arrangement. This seemed a provocative salvo to me.

Lord Thomson asked me to have a private word with Richard Attenborough, Deputy Chairman of Channel 4, to see if the situation could be defused. It also occurred to me that, as TV-am were seeking additional finance, and we were looking for additional new programme input from them, there might be a good case for ITN taking a shareholding in TV-am and agreeing to assist in the provision of news.

Even in October 1983 people were still coming up to me and asking, in a friendly way, 'Are you enjoying the job?' Even after almost a year, I still didn't have an answer. 'Enjoy', I usually reply, 'is not a word I would use to describe the roller-coaster of events'. In more pessimistic mood I likened the role I played to that of a person responsible to a local summer resort council for clearing up debris washed up on the beach after every high tide. Just when everything looks neat and tidy, some great object or other is left stranded, needing to be refloated, burnt or even buried. October had seen many such objects.

I have grown to appreciate the finer points of Michael Moriarty, an Under-Secretary in the Broadcast Division of the Home Office. At the end of October, he came bearing news of covert planning engaged in by the BBC concerning their satellite DBS development. I was amazed at his revelations. It seemed the BBC and Thorn-EMI were proposing to enter into an agreement which would result in a jointly-held company for the purpose of marketing and programming the two BBC channels. I asked Michael whether he was aware of Thorn-EMI's 50 per cent interest in Thames Television which, under the Thames' contract with the IBA, required Thorn to seek our approval of any such move. Michael was not aware of this, and I said how incredulous I was that the Government was in secret talks with one interested party in satellite development when it was asking others to go through the elaborate ritual of a selection process. In any case, Thorn-EMI had a duty to Thames to compete against the BBC, not act for the BBC against the independent system!

Michael informed me that Thorn-EMI intended to make an announcement the following Thursday. I said, if they did, we would act to ensure the press and public knew that these actions were taking place without our approval and that the contract between Thames and the IBA would be jeopardised. Michael went away somewhat distressed and said that a Mr Sibley of Thorn-EMI would be likely to want to fix an appointment to come and see me, which he duly did.

When the Authority met to consider radio franchises, it took the opportunity to endorse the view I had expressed to Michael Moriarty, and later to Mr Sibley.

I dined with Kenneth Baker, the Conservative Minister for Information Technology, at the Garrick and, over rum and raisin ice cream – for which the Garrick is noted by connoisseurs of such things – I dropped into the conversation that the IBA would object to Thorn-EMI/Thames taking a share in the BBC's venture into space. Kenneth was obviously quite upset and said that he 'hadn't focused properly' on this particular aspect of the relationship between the two intended partners. Incidentally, his wife Mary was on the Board of Thames!

Following this dinner, he must have stumped off to the Ministry and delivered some well-aimed rockets at officials, as he would be made to look very foolish if his planning crumbled into dust.

The BBC are in a mess. Having grabbed the DBS channels, and having ignored my proposals to share the satellite with the IBA with one channel each, it has now gone off and attempted to align itself with one of our Companies! The BBC has bitten off more than it can chew but, in spitting out the bits, it is likely to make a mess on the floor!

I was happy for Thorn EMI to contribute to satellite technology with the BBC if talks were held between the three of us, and in the public domain.

The trouble between ITN and the Board of Channel 4 continues. The first round in this new clash was fired by Edmund Dell's letter to Jeremy Isaac confirming that, unless the audience figures for the one hour nightly news reached 750,000 by the end of this, the second year, Channel 4 would not feel obliged to continue the arrangement.

I listened to the arguments put by ITN at one of their Board meetings and told them I would try to ease the relationship by calling a meeting with Edmund Dell. Accordingly, Lord Thomson and I met with Jeremy and Edmund. They assured us they had no wish to terminate the ITN contract, but felt it right to put them on a year's notice. We said this was hardly the way to bring about a rapprochement.

TV-am is still searching for funds. The hope that Ladbrokes would take up 20 per cent equity has all but foundered. Kenneth Cork told me that Cyril Stein, Ladbrokes' Chairman, was blowing hot and cold. Kenneth believed that unless funding was forthcoming TV-am would have to declare itself in voluntary liquidation by the 1st of November. I subsequently had talks with Timothy Aitken who, like all good salesmen, was bouncing about the City full of confidence, sure that one of the interested parties would come up with the funding before the deadline.

Along with the Members of the Authority, I joined the BBC Governors at dinner in Portland Place. This was held in the newly refurbished Council Chamber, styled as originally in the 1930s. A fine spread was set before us but, as the meal progressed, it became clear that, despite the lavish surroundings, the air conditioning was malfunctioning, resulting in distinguished Governors and Members sweating profusely or removing their jackets in defiance of the propriety of the occasion. I sat next to William Rees-Mogg and found him most agreeable. George Thomson was not so lucky, and had a dispute over the provision of public service with Alasdair Milne who demonstrated a degree of arrogance that defied description. I would give a great deal to be a fly on the wall when he learns for the first time that the motto beneath our new crest is to be 'To Serve the People'.

On Monday 23rd October 1983 I came to my first birthday with the IBA. Channel 4 is getting a champagne breakfast for its first anniversary on 2nd November. What will I get?

I met with the Editorial Committee of TV-am: Richard Marsh, Tim Aitken, Sir Gordon Newton and Charles Wintour. They gave their views on the state of play. All spoke up robustly for the service; Charles Wintour believing it has caught 'the changing times'. If there was to be criticism, it was that news was sometimes too rigidly compressed: more flexibility should be aimed for.

TV-am took up more time this week. The company is in desperate need of at least £4m and if finance is not forthcoming by 15th November latest, the show will close. Timothy Aitken has been keeping me in the picture. Earlier that week the favourite for investing appeared to be Robert Maxwell, wanting to put in £3m for 30 per cent; then Fleet Holdings moved up into first place with a proposal to take 20 per cent for £2m. Later in the week, Rupert Murdoch's News International emerged as an interested party. I had a meeting with Brian Horton, their Head of Development. He said, bluntly, that they would only proceed if they obtained control. That they would then fire 200 staff and 'do a deal' for news from ITN, leaving the remaining 100 staff or so to provide the other elements of the morning programme. Behind their interest lay the possibility of using their Camden Lock headquarters as the base and uplink for Satellite TV in which they hold a controlling interest. They would also consider using the same news material for their satellite morning service.

Brian went on to say that, in their business judgment, it would take a great deal of expertise to put TV-am back on an even keel, and he doubted that £4m would be enough. I told him the IBA would have concern about News International: it was not an EEC company and would fall outside the provisions of the Act. I also said that, by requiring to take over control, they would effectively be changing the 'nature and characteristics' under Section 20(5) of the Act. Horton ended by saying that News International didn't like regulatory bodies and might in any case find the whole concept uninviting.

This was to be the case, for he telephoned me early on Saturday morning to say they had decided against taking discussions further.

During the first week of November, I lunched with the PM. She arrived late and I met her downstairs at Brompton Road, surrounded by men wearing raincoats and expressions of watchfulness. The lift to the 7th floor seemed to take forever. I tried some polite conversation but her mind was obviously elsewhere. Lunch discussion opened somewhat surprisingly with George Thomson telling Mrs Thatcher that the Government was 'dithering' over its decision on MAC, the IBA's proposed form of transmission. 'Dithering!', exploded the PM, sounding like Lady Bracknell on the subject of the handbag.

After this somewhat shaky start, which I later considered to be a supremely adroit move on George's part, the lunch proceeded smoothly. The PM expressed concern about the level of violence and horror on television but seemed to me not prepared to discuss any more weighty subject. Much later, it occurred to me that she had already concluded that any views the IBA might have were to be discounted in the final reckoning! We had fish for the main course, and Mrs Thatcher demonstrated considerable dexterity with the bones. I thought of her Ministers quaking in their shoes as she deftly lifted away the spine, revealing the white flesh beneath!

On Wednesday I rose early to attend the 1st year breakfast celebration at Channel 4, which was held at Brompton Road with bleary executives wishing they were still in bed. Jeremy, for once, was not called upon to speak. This was left to Edmund Dell, who performed in booming voice.

That afternoon, the Members sat in judgment on Radio Clyde, who were seeking the renewal of their franchise. The MD, James Gordon, now Lord Gordon, in the absence of their Chairman, gave a lively and convincing performance and, since there was but one applicant, the whole affair had a faintly bizarre quality with the outcome in no doubt.

A meeting on Thursday with David Steel and David Owen convinced me that politicians take television exposure too seriously. They came to plead for a fair distribution of reporting their activities on screen. The word 'fair' was theirs. The simple truth was that whereas the PM opening a flour mill was reported as 'news', the appearance of either Steel or Owen is not. Unless, of course, either fall into a funnel or get churned up in a vat.

Later that week I visited one of the out of London stations; on this occasion Ipswich, to see Radio Orwell. A rather dreary, down-at-heel atmosphere pervaded the place and this, together with the almost casual way in which I was greeted, made me wonder why I had bothered to travel the 60 or so miles. The next day I visited Anglia's studios. One only has to see the commitment of resources to understand why so many doubts are raised over the franchise process, whereby companies can lose their licence and realise nothing for their investment, through an IBA decision.

On Sunday, I appeared on *Face The Press*, a programme probably viewed by a round dozen, and don't believe I made any catastrophic clangers, but time will tell.

On Monday 7th November, Roma and I attended the *Royal Variety Show* in the presence of HM the Queen, who we duly met. I was introduced by Lord Delfont as 'Mr Whitley from the International Broadcasting Company'! The show was entertaining but, as always, totally lacking in style. We took one look at the cold buffet provided after the show, stayed just long enough to be polite, and left.

The following day saw another of those hurly-burly scrums in the House of Commons Committee Room on party political broadcasts. We had expected the fur to fly, as we knew the SDP Alliance were feeling mightily unloved and were claiming that they were being short-changed on the number of minutes allocated to them. However, peace and friendship reigned, and the Committee settled for six minutes (Conservatives), five (Labour) and four (SDP).

That evening we went to the re-opening of the Old Vic under the new ownership of 'honest' Ed Mirvish, a much-monied Canadian who had spent £2m on refurbishing the old place and had plans of a steak house alongside where hungry theatre-goers could take their fill.

The theatre looked superb. Claire Theraby, who also designed the new interior of the Duke of York, had done a superb job. The only sadness was what went on once the curtain was raised: Tim Rice's *Blondel*, into which I had put a little money, turned out to be a flashy, frothy musical lacking in any sort of fibre. Tim sat with us and at the interval suggested we might repair to the bar. I readily agreed and we never saw the second half! Sad, when you think about all the others he has written.

Wednesday 9th November was radio's big day; the tenth anniversary of Independent Local Radio (ILR). A celebration was held in the Mansion House with H.R.H. Prince Charles and the Princess of Wales, who I sat next to. She turned out to be a very engaging person and I was particularly touched by the research she had done in advance of meeting the line-up of the good and the great. During dinner, she dived into her handbag and produced a little notepad, showing me the notes she had made and the questions she would ask, all in her large handwriting. During his speech, Prince Charles went 'off piste' and asked whether we had any shares in Ronson as in his opinion our new crest bore a striking resemblance to a crest on a cigarette lighter.

John Thompson, as Head of Radio, made reference to 'radio in jeans' during his speech, a phrase that was well received, epitomising the way ILR was encouraging young audiences.

The 'royal week' continued with a call from the Palace the following day inviting me to a private lunch with the Queen and Prince Philip, but before that I had to return to matters of business.

The Authority met at Lainston House, a grand country hotel near Winchester, to present, during a full Agenda, a detailed paper on DBS development, which was accepted, taking us another step forward. Whilst in Winchester, the Chairman and I addressed 30 or so Regional Officers and staff, many of whom were clearly worried about their prospects in the face of the new technology, fearing that cable and satellite would eventually erode audiences from the terrestrial services. They were right in that in future there would be less need for their services but in my opinion it would be fully two decades before there was any substantial erosion.

I sat with Leon Brittan during a lunch with MPs from the Midlands. The Home Secretary is clearly 'miffed' by what he considers the stand-off approach by the IBA towards the BBC's proposed 'marriage' with EMI-Thorne, which had covert government blessing. I explained to Leon that the IBA wanted to hold tripartite consultations to ensure that both the BBC and ourselves were moving sensibly together on matters relating to DBS, in which we had a common interest. I believed the IBA and the BBC could share in the first instance a joint satellite, with one channel each, though I doubted this would be acceptable to Alasdair Milne.

At the end of the week I attended Howard Steele's memorial service at St Martin in the Fields. Howard had been one of the great pioneering engineers of the television age and the service was very moving, with beautiful singing and an excellent address. Howard's creative judgments, and the force of his personality, had secured for the IBA its reputation for engineering and he had also established Crawley Court, headquarters of the IBA's Engineering Division.

From this point on, I kept a detailed diary and will now draw directly from that:

Saturday 26th November

Still no decision on MAC despite the Chairman's 'dithering' taunt to the Prime Minister. On Monday 21st I attended the BREMA Dinner and listened to Sir Anthony Part, as guest speaker, berating his audiences over the matter, and particularly blaming the BBC for putting their heads in the sand. I sat next to Peter Thornycroft, a lively 73 year old, and former Chairman of the Conservative Party. I told him I was lunching later in the week with the new Chairman, John Selwyn Gummer. I don't think he had a high opinion of the new incumbent: 'Not enough tall men in the Party', he commented.

On Friday 25th, John Selwyn Gummer came to lunch at Brompton Road. None of us could remember the Ministry over which he presided – it was Employment. I fear for the nation's employment prospects as Mr Gummer did not fill me with confidence: an insignificant little man who looked more suited to be an insurance salesman.

During the week George was summoned to meet the Home Secretary who wanted him to forgo the ideology of the IBA and bless a marriage between the BBC and Thorn-EMI. George's response was that it was the proper duty of the Authority to safeguard the interests of the independent sector and that the BBC's proposals to Thorn EMI, a major shareholder in Thames TV, ran counter to this. I arranged a meeting with Peter Laister, then MD of Thorn EMI, to have a frank talk with him and explain why we could not agree to this merger.

Over the weekend, I watched a pre-transmission tape of *The Day After*, the much-publicised American fictional portrayal of the use of nuclear weapons. Although obviously violent, I considered it might make some small dent in the minds of people who see the women of Greenham Common as nothing more than a nuisance.

Sunday 4th December

On Monday 28th November, George Thomson and I lunched with Lord Harlech and Ron Wordley, Chairman and MD of HTV, when they both supported a higher licence subscription as, in their role as supplier to S4C, HTV would benefit financially. Ron W. was very upset about the decision to screen *The Day After*, and had written to Lord Harlech saying that he feared ITV was run by 'a load of pinkos'.

On Wednesday I lunched with Douglas Hurd, then Minister of State at the Home Office. We met at The Travellers Club, where Douglas has much difficulty in writing down the food I actually wanted on the order form. I thought this might not be a good omen for our future! We talked about Thorn-EMI and he felt the IBA was being unduly difficult. I tried to explain that we were simply protecting the integrity of the independent television system but he did not appear convinced. I have come to the conclusion that no one in Government ever listens. Perhaps that's the secret of being a successful politician.

On Thursday I was interviewed by a rather icy lady from *Broadcast* on the changing role of the IBA. I knew in advance this would be a 'knocking' piece of copy as she only wrote down the negative aspects of what I was saying.

I flew to Brussels for a meeting of the EBU, and spent two days with Alasdair Milne without either of us mentioning satellites or Thorn-EMI. I certainly wasn't going to raise it, and he didn't: rather like a game of chess. The EBU Council spent a good part of one session debating the future of Public Service Broadcasting. They made it sound like a rather unpleasant disease. All the delegates are caught up in this storm of the new technology but, like dinosaurs, are unable to adapt to the new climate, trumpeting and snorting in their death throes whilst around them circle and dive the entrepreneurial vultures, adapting to compete with every new form of competition that comes along.

I arrived back to find the newspapers full of dire warnings about *The Day After*, with Michael Heseltine demanding a slot immediately after transmission in order to calm the populace with soothing Tory words about the need to keep the nuclear strike force in Europe. There was much debate about the rights and wrongs of showing the film, which built it up to something akin to an epic even before transmission. I felt tired and depressed, with the next week looming, filled with meetings, lunches, dinners. I wished at that moment I had never taken on this role.

Saturday 17th December

Today a large bomb exploded at the rear of Harrods, killing five people and injuring 70.

On Tuesday I had lunched with HM the Queen and Prince Philip. There were six guests, including Terry Wogan, who made the Queen laugh. We were an odd mixture: Jean Muir, an oarsman, an Australian Civil Servant, and a black Archdeacon who remained silent throughout. Over coffee the Queen was utterly relaxed, laughing and joking and darting from topic to topic like a firefly. She became quite exercised at the prospect of her Kensington Palace rates going up and, having just returned from India, she was greatly impressed by their use of cow dung: bottling the gases and using them to light and heat their homes. Her interest was such that, in my letter of thanks, I included more information on this 'new technology'.

Prince Philip was also in good form and gave me his views on overcoming jet lag: that one should walk or run briefly before flying and after landing and on no account drink alcohol during the flight. At 14.50 they withdrew, with an ageing Royal corgi trotting behind.

On Thursday Stuart Young, the BBC Chairman and DG Alasdair Milne met their Governors and, contrary to most public opinion, decided to press on with their plans with Thorn-EMI. At a subsequent meeting with George Thomson, Stuart Young suggested the IBA should enter into an agreement with the BBC on their terms, originally put to me in June or July, to form a joint company controlling one premium channel and each then controlling the output of one other channel. Our contrary suggestion was that the satellite should contain one channel for the IBA and one for the BBC, which I still felt the most acceptable solution: we shared terrestrial transmitter sites so why not share celestial? This solution would provide proper backup, giving a spare channel if one were to fail.

I intended to put to the Authority at our next meeting that I was in favour of sticking to our original plan as only then could we keep both services properly separate, allowing us to finance by advertising or subscription. To merge with the BBC would have a profound effect on the whole ecology of broadcasting. To my mind, the BBC should get on with their own plans and we with ours. I feared, however, this would be only the first chapter in a fast-moving scenario.

Granada's planned one-hour *World in Action* special on Gerry Adams has dominated the week. Having seen it, I knew it to be an out and out attack on Adams as an active member of the IRA. My fear was that transmission might endanger not only Ulster TV but possibly our own engineers at the transmitter only three miles away from the Falls Road. Having spoken to all sides, I decided the right course would be to show the film. I hoped I was right. Ideally, we would have postponed transmission but to do so would be hailed by the IRA as a victory, and we would be accused of bowing to pressure. I thought the transmission might even be timely, at the very least showing that Gerry Adams was not the calm pipe-smoker he might appear but a ruthless killer.

Monday 26th December

Christmas week. Not one I want to repeat for another year, dominated as it has been by satellites and the BBC's mess, although they would strongly deny they were in a pickle. The Home Office was obviously in a state of anxiety, with Michael Moriarty, Assistant Under Secretary of State, on the telephone making enquiries to see which way the wind was blowing.

During the week I met with the Regional Officers, a somewhat odd collection of people from a variety of backgrounds. They play an unusual and rather old-fashioned role in the life of the Authority, each ruling a region with all that occurs on television and radio therein under their remit. Like all mortals, some are better than others and some considerably worse. They all paraded once a month in Brompton Road and I met them for an hour in the Board Room. I always walked away from these meetings feeling I had failed miserably to either put across my ideas or get any reaction from them. Either they were frightened to respond or else they didn't have anything worthwhile to say! Either way, it was 60 minutes I could well afford to miss.

During the week I had attended office parties on every floor of the building. A non-drinker, I have never understood the enjoyment of such occasions.

Perhaps it was just me at my most cynical, but I was beginning to feel George Thomson wanted a peaceful life, and not leave office having fallen out with Government. Our views on the BBC/Thorn-EMI issue were beginning to differ. He felt we should find some form of accommodation with the BBC and reach a positive conclusion, whereas I felt we should bide our time and do things in our own way. The two systems have competed for thirty years and this has provided the stimulus for a healthy duopoly. Put together, a soggy monopoly would be formed with little or no will to compete for audiences on the terrestrial service.

I should, however, note here that the more I see of the behaviour of the ITV contractors, the more I fear they may use the satellite channel to block competition. As importantly, they will have another activity to take their eye off the real ball – their own terrestrial services. I sense the IBA staff share my view but just how strong George Thomson will be in holding to his course of allowing the BBC/ITV merger remains to be seen.

Bill Cotton had been nominated to meet with me, rather than Alasdair Milne, whose views were considered unbending. In the event, Bill Cotton was equally intransigent, repeating Alasdair's June proposals that the BBC/ITV should share programme output and revenue on the first satellite. I put the other position: that we should each have one channel and compete. Bill Cotton found this unacceptable.

1984

Sunday 8th January

Here I am, writing the prophetic figures '1984' for the first time. When I was much younger, and reading Orwell, I never thought I would see 1984, and here it is, having lain in wait for many years.

The Christmas holidays seemed to go on for ever. There is still a deep urge in the corporate id of the average Britisher to want to work. Such a long period of enforced idleness makes us feel guilty. This year, I didn't feel any such emotion, however. I felt I deserved the break. If nothing else, it served to give me time to contemplate the future, and muddy it looks in my crystal ball.

This week was again dominated by considerations of DBS. Another meeting with Bill Cotton, who came armed with arrogance and the proposals put to George Thomson by Stuart Young. There is something about the BBC's posture that brings out the worst in me. On one hand, they consider themselves the only legitimate vessel for the propagation of public service broadcasting, but on the other they are quite content to grasp at any straw to help them salvage their ill-advised launch on DBS. Stuart Young referred to their need to 'sanitise' the revenues from advertising that would accrue to a partnership. The ITV system is in danger of being pitchforked into a situation that gives us no advantages and, worse, sucks out of our system the very strengths that have led us to compete so successfully with the BBC.

We spent the weekend with Jimmy and Ann Gordon. John Smith was a guest at dinner – a good friend who has known Jimmy for many years. Jimmy is the MD of Radio Clyde, probably the most successful radio station in terms of popular impact and general programming aimed at complementing community activity. I am hopeful we can obtain a CBE for Jimmy. Radio should have its Honour, and Jimmy would be an ideal candidate.

Saturday 14th January

I have come to the conclusion that more often than not the most difficult meetings are the ones that, in anticipation, appear the least hazardous. This week was spent in a succession of just such meetings.

On Monday I chaired our weekly Director General's Management Meeting and found myself striving to keep my team together on nearly every matter of substance. Satellite proves the most difficult: so many options, most of them unfavourable to us. I am still of the mind that to merge with the BBC would not be the way forward. Why throw into their lap our best talent, inventiveness and business acumen? In return for what? Providing a crutch to a patient who does not deserve to walk.

The BBC have no business in DBS and now, faced with the realization that they are deeply committed to Unisat to the tune of some £50m, they find themselves desperately looking for a way to get off a hook on which they were earlier only too happy to impale themselves. This self-imposed predicament is made the more apparent by the pressure from the Home Secretary to help them find a solution that won't leave them – and the Department of Industry – with egg on their faces.

The IBA's dilemma is finding a way of deflecting the interests of the ITCA companies from seizing on this opportunity to secure for themselves an extension of their terrestrial monopoly of DBS and, at the same time, forcing the Government to recognize they would need a longer contract period than up to 1989 so that their financial commitment would have a chance of returning a dividend otherwise prevented. All in all, an attractive proposition to the larger ITCA companies who fear that DBS will unseat them as the years roll by.

On the other hand, if the larger ITCA Companies can prevail on the Home Office to abandon its alliance with the BBC and instead offer the Companies a longer contract period than up to 1989, they would stand a good chance of establishing a secure financial basis.

This week I had dinner at Broadcasting House with Aubrey Singer – still celebrating his CBE! – and the Bishop of Wakefield, Colin James. The purpose was to examine our various positions and attitudes about the role of religious broadcasting in the competitive climate of the years that lie ahead. Alasdair Milne attended the meeting before dinner, when both he and I stood fast to our position that we would not abandon our historic role and that religious output should be maintained. I said, however, that I believed religious and spiritual conviction should become increasingly seen as part of everyday life, incorporated into the output in a way that did not leave it in some exclusive enclave, ghettoed from the events of the real world.

I came away from the evening feeling we had not taken an honest enough stand on our convictions. Those representing CRAC appeared uncertain, lacking any real point of view so that the discussion lacked cohesion. I hope we do not find ourselves with this lack of clarity at the main March meeting of CRAC.

Another meeting with Bill Cotton, Stuart Young and Alasdair Milne over DBS. The BBC's case rests on the belief that, for DBS to succeed – and that means in its earliest years – there is a vital necessity to ensure that, firstly, there are sufficient channels to attract audiences and, secondly, that competition does not fragment that audience, making it impossible for either competitor to succeed. I agree with the first proposition and reject the second. This difference was at the heart of the meeting.

Received calls this week from the Home Office and Unisat. Michael Moriarty told me he would like us to meet with Jeffrey Sterling (Norman Tebbit's advisor/hitman). I know JS slightly and looked forward with interest to the meeting, at which he confessed to no knowledge of technology. The outcome was not clear although I think I impressed him with my conviction that it would be infinitely more satisfactory to maintain competition on DBS than allow it to grow soggy in the grip of a monopoly. JS ended the meeting by saying he thought I should become Chairman of any corporate undertaking between the IBA and the BBC! We settled on a two-channel BBC/two-channel IBA launch on a four-channel Unisat, with open competition for the franchise. This will not go down well with the BBC.

I wrote to John Thompson, IBA's Head of Radio, telling him of my decision to hand over radio finance to our Finance Division. JT thought this wrong both for the industry and for IBA.

Sunday 22nd January

At the DBS meeting with ITCA on Monday, Paul Fox (Yorkshire) and Brian Tesler (LWT) represented ITV interests but not ITCA as a body. As I had expected, the two companies believed that the way forward was to join in partnership with the BBC, wait until the audience had reached a viable level and then compete separately. They hastened to add they would expect the IBA to help them achieve this goal by extending the contract period beyond 1989 to allow them sufficient time to recoup their expenditure and make a profit. I made no promises but neither did I reject their proposition. Obviously my candour did not impress them, with Paul saying, rather majestically, that if the IBA was not taken with the idea, his conscience would not allow him to remain silent.

The Authority met on Wednesday to discuss the options before us. I was rather surprised at the lack of enthusiasm for the road I had been advocating, i.e. that of competition on four channels, although it has to be said that, the more I read of the recently published Coopers & Lybrand report, the more uncertain I became that this was indeed the way forward. Sir John Riddell said he was 'underwhelmed' by my case. George Russell gave a short but spirited view that it was better to join and consolidate a position before competing. Maybe he is right.

The outcome of the discussion was that I agreed to hold a meeting with the BBC and representatives from ITCA to examine the BBC's proposals.

Had an interesting lunch with Michael Shea, the Queen's Press Secretary, who told us Princess Anne was the royal favourite this week following her television interviews. She had, he said, gained the appreciation of the public for her War on Want tours, and 'gained in both wit and confidence' as a result. Sir Alastair Burnet voiced his opinion that the Queen being seen chatting with Indira Gandhi, transmitted as part of the Christmas message, had done her a disservice. Shea said there had been more viewers writing in with congratulations than for any previous Royal 'Message'.

George (Thomson) and I tore ourselves away for a meeting at the DoI with Bill Cotton, Stuart Young, Paul Fox and Brian Tesler. We were greeted by Jeffrey Sterling, who announced that Peter Laister (Thorn EMI) and Admiral Lygo (Unisat) would be joining us. This caused a bit of a fracas.

I left the meeting having agreed to be part of the working party to examine four areas: programming, finance, engineering and constitution – the latter being the most important. Paul Fox was of the opinion that the aim of ITV companies should not be to attract advertising revenue and that the procurement of Unisat as their only satellite vehicle was not the only option. Both statements came as something of a shock to those around the table!

The following morning I received a call from Jeffrey Sterling saying that he and Stuart Young would like me to chair the working party. Where is Alasdair Milne? In India.

Lunched at The Garrick with Douglas Hurd, the Minister responsible for broadcasting at the Home Office, on Friday who said there was an immense amount of, to use Michael Moriarty's words, 'washing up' to be done if the legislation in the Cable & Satellite Bill was to include the extension of contracts for ITV companies. Although Douglas did not perceive this as a problem, I could see the Government altering course in this way would result in a number of voices raised in protest.

Sunday 29th January

TV-am is increasingly reminding me of a beggar who, having been given a coin, comes back asking for more. Tim Aitken asked to see me on Wednesday as TV-am had a serious funding problem, and required between £2m and £2.5m. He thought the Prudential and Fleet Holdings would stump up the required capital to offset the poor trading figures for October/November. Always the optimist, Tim claimed January/February were looking much better, but then followed this statement by saying the company would have to make redundancies and lose some 30-40 staff. He claimed the company didn't need these staff anyway: 'they sit around doing nothing on Saturdays'.

I asked about the rumour that they were intending to record programmes for Sunday transmission, which would not be on. He smiled ruefully, looking like a naughty boy, and said he expected me to say that. When he is in this mood, it is difficult to realise why TV-am staff have nicknamed him 'Pol Pot'. We talked about Michael Deakin, who I said was TV-am's last shred of the fig leaf as far as the IBA was concerned.

The following morning I breakfasted at The Hyde Park Hotel with David Frost, who tucked into bacon and his preferred flat mushrooms and continued to unfold the miseries of TV-am where Tim had left off. Frost thought the Board, which was to meet later that day, would 'go for the throat' and demand programme changes to reduce cost. He thought Michael Deakin's position could be maintained for a shortish time although his day-to-day supervision of programme output had already ended.

The following morning I met with TV-am's Chairman, Richard Marsh, and showed him a letter George intended to send to him, seeking to know what steps his Chief Executive intended to take to explain an outburst the previous day when he said, 'Who gives a damn what the IBA says on its grandiose application forms? You can only go with what is tenable. I could go into a court of law and defend what we are doing: the arguments made against us are a load of cock. Two fingers to everybody!' Dick Marsh ended the meeting by promising the management structure would be sorted out and financial information made more readily available. I listened.

Marsh would obviously like to see Fleet Holdings coming to the aid of the party, but the IBA has just turned down the request from Octopus to let Fleet have 3 per cent of their holding, so what next? The refunding must be in place within a fortnight. David Frost, at his most Frostian, had included the phrase 'Mission to Explain' in TV-am's application which impressed the Authority at the time, but now I believe Members will happily watch the company roll over and die.

More DBS activity this week. I chaired a further meeting of the Working Party, allocating tasks to various experts to review finance, the constitution and programming. There is a mood of optimism. The ITCA companies see this as a golden chance to break out of the bonds that chain them to the IBA yoke. They will not easily let this opportunity pass them by.

I am curious at the way the great British public, and the press, turn away from an issue that may well change the entire structure and future of public service broadcasting.

I had told the Home Office my review would take a fortnight, and I hope to give a run-down to Jeffrey Sterling next Wednesday. I never thought I would be presiding over the introduction of 'juke-box' television.

Listening to the radio today, I have become more and more angry at the way the pirates are fearlessly taking over the airwaves. One company, Skyline, has announced that from midnight it will be transmitting 24 hours a day on FM and Medium wave. I think I shall urge the Chairman to write to the Home Secretary warning that, unless speedy action is taken, the IBA will not be able to control the output of ILR to provide a wide service of programmes, if the next RAJAR survey shows a downturn of audience. Money will drain from the system, leading to cost cutting with inevitable results. Perhaps this is just another indication of the mood as we go further into the 80s. By 1990 the role of Regulator may be redundant. Reith must be turning in his grave.

Saturday 4th February

A busy week, with DBS dominating the scene. On Monday I paid a visit to the Department of Trade and Industry, where I had an hour's talk with Jeffrey Sterling. I informed him that I had learnt that Unisat had withdrawn from their relationship with the BBC. I was surprised this had been done during the very time that all the parties were striving to find a way forward and said that I would not welcome Unisat back to the table until a letter had been received confirming that no costs would be borne by the IBA relating to work done for the BBC.

Working party meetings took place between engineering and finance, with a full meeting on Wednesday, which I chaired. The outcome was a note summarizing the main findings of the group: in short, high risk might break even in the seventh year, could make money if all went well and a minimum of two million subscribers could be tempted to put up money. Preliminary figures, however, suggested that the monthly subscription would be in excess of £20 and that was considered the top figure that could reasonably be asked. All in all, DBS is looking a very dodgy affair and the more I learn about it the less I feel we should allow the television contractors to play a part: it will drain them of resources and result in a weakening of the terrestrial system.

Later in the week, while I was in Yorkshire, I had a call asking me to telephone HRH the Prince of Wales. When I got through, Prince Charles said he was sorry to track me down but he was worried about the DBS business, and what did I think. I told him I was concerned that a shotgun marriage with the BBC might have grave long-term effects on the system and was worried by the Government's panic to get some sort of deal patched together which would enable Unisat to fly.

The action brought by Mary Whitehouse against the IBA over *Scum* was heard in the High Court this week. A statement from our Chairman was read out in court, but things don't look too bright for us. It had been said in court that I overruled the advice of the Television Division. A decision I do not regret.

TV-am bumps along. The press, scenting a good story, duly wrote up the first year of the station with relish. No champagne cheer on this occasion was the general tone. I was telephoned by Aubrey Buxton, Chairman of Anglia Television, who was worried by rumours that Granada was buying into TVAM. I told him I knew nothing about this. Smoke without fire? Nothing would surprise me.

Sunday 12th February

Like a damned soul, TV-am moves through the fog with its clothes in tatters and its begging bowl clutched in its skeletal hands. Advertisers avert their gaze and cross to the other side of the street. Timothy Aitken, Chief Executive of TV-am, is a remarkable man, having already survived one crisis only three months ago. Now he needs £3m to bridge the gap between the advertising trough currently hitting the station and the eldorado of the Olympic Games which he is confidently predicting will restore the station's fortunes. I am doubtful. All our projections spell out that the station is set on a disaster course of low advertising and static audience. Advertisers like to harness their product to success: TV-am is shrouded in misfortune and gloom.

More agonizing over DBS and more to come. The ITCA companies have now gone public over their wish for an extension of their franchise if they are to accept the offer made by Government and the BBC. Seven years of loss until break-even does not take account of the three-year start-up period while the satellite is being built. Seen from any angle, the whole DBS proposition is highly speculative. I continue to feel that, if we allow the ITCA companies into DBS under this arrangement, we will be sucking the very life blood out of the terrestrial system. The ITCA companies would have to raise something of the order of £250m just to keep DBS afloat. If things go wrong, terrestrial broadcasting will suffer irreparable damage and there will be no one to pick up the pieces in time to save it.

At the meeting of the GAC, I was pressed hard to give a clear sign of my approval regarding the franchise extension. I demurred, referring instead to the Authority meeting due to take place on Wednesday. Our position is extremely tricky: if we are seen to be the torpedo in the side of ITV hopes, we will create enmity. Certainly the BBC will accuse us of ditching the new technology and we will become the scapegoat. Government – at least the DTI – will be furious. Unisat will be angry and accuse the BBC of reneging on their agreement. We have no friends, but nevertheless the time has come to say 'no'. The risks are too high and for what gain? A satellite that could be out of date before it is launched. I had hoped that the ITCA companies would not be able to come to a corporate view. I was wrong. At SCC the Companies announced they were unanimous in their wish to jointly share the DBS channel with the BBC.

Being of a cynical disposition, I suggest that the Companies are saying this to enforce an extension of contract. Later they can backtrack, but now they have nothing to lose by putting on a bold front. It will be interesting to see how the Authority Members react to the proposal, and whether they still feel underwhelmed by our case that the Companies should be prevented from going into DBS. George and I will be meeting the Home Secretary on Monday and I am not sure whether this view will find support from George.

The *Scum* case is drawing to an end and staff who have been attending Court are gloomy about the outcome.

Sunday 19th February

Another week dominated by TV-am and DBS, the twin-soul sisters.

George and I spent an hour with the Home Secretary on Monday. His stance was much less dogmatic than when we first talked. Clearly a number of conflicting views have been surfacing. The attitude of both the IPA (Institute of Practitioners in Advertising) and ISBA (Incorporated Society of British Advertisers) towards extending the duopoly on DBS is now making itself heard. In addition, the press are now questioning the wisdom of the BBC going into DBS.

Leon Brittan, Home Secretary, speaking off the top of his head, was anxious to know whether there were takers for DBS other than the ITCA companies. I said I was sure there were and suggested that, if we went ahead with the BBC, we should look at opening up the ITCA 50 per cent to others as well, and that we should not necessarily accept all the ITCA companies who put themselves forward. Leon Brittan thought this would be 'difficult'. The Government are clearly in a dither.

This was not helped when, the next day, the Working Party reassembled at the DTI under Jeffrey Sterling's chairmanship. Jeffrey did not conduct the meeting with skill, blundering at the beginning by announcing he hoped to be calling a press conference to announce our findings. This statement landed on the floor like a blancmange off a plate.

Stuart Young countered by saying it was now up to Government to show a lead. I said I didn't see any pressure as Unisat had stopped work on the project. If it came to sitting round a table with Unisat I said bargaining would have to start afresh. I have a strong feeling now that the BBC have gone off the boil on satellite: the fire has gone out of their belly and the will to go forward is not apparent. This could tie in with the much-leaked information that Aubrey Singer will be stepping down from his BBC MD position to make way for Bill Cotton. If this were to happen, the last thing Bill would want would be satellite television around his neck like an albatross. Much sooner 'bury the bird', or – better still – put off the evil hour and let private enterprise burn its fingers.

During the entire meeting, Alasdair sat silently except, before leaving, when he said that satellite was for the broadcasters and he would not let the BBC join forces with ITCA if there were others up there with them. This utterance gives me my cue to push for other interests. I have absolutely no desire to see the duopoly gain a victory.

The BBC is facing trouble on all fronts and I cannot remember a time when they seemed so ragged, so bereft of imagination, so lacking in purpose or grand design. I believe that the real problem lies with Alasdair. On the one hand, he is a highly competitive animal; on the other, a deeply introverted person with a burning determination to bring back the values of Reith. I feel this dilemma must be causing him great pain.

The saga of TV-am continues. The unions have accepted new shift patterns in return for the withdrawal of a redundancy threat, much to my surprise. Now an extra £4m is required. We need to ensure the new money comes from acceptable sources.

Timothy Aitken came to see me and we discussed a proposition that John Freeman, Chairman of LWT, become Trustee of Fleet's larger investment, Fleet having 24.9 per cent voting stock; Dick Marsh to resign and Timothy to become Chairman in his place; Bert Hardy, the distinguished newspaperman, to become MD and ITN to take a reasonable stake. More troubled water lies ahead both for TV-am and for us.

Saturday 25th February

A week of mixed happenings. TV-am is still putting together its financial package. £4m is quite a sum to secure when almost daily the newspapers report outstanding debts – a hire car firm owed £700 for driving Diana Dors to the studios. Diana Dors subsequently fired by TV-am – all rather squalid.

At the ITN Board Aubrey Buxton invited comments about a possible interest in TV-am. The Board rejected the idea as a lost cause, but I spoke up in the hope that they will reconsider. After all, they are part of the system and a strong and viable breakfast service can only be of benefit, but there is no love lost, the Companies round the table looking at TV-am simply as competition.

Douglas Hurd held a drinks party on Wednesday at the Home Office. A rich tapestry of broadcasting folk turned up for it. Aubrey Singer was there – bravely, I thought, as this was to be his swansong from the BBC. Ebullient as ever, he said he was off to India and would then return to a new life as an independent producer. At 58 that takes courage.

DBS moves forward at last. I now consider that the whole enterprise needs new money and entrepreneurial skills. ITCA and the BBC are too 'fat cat'. Some dynamic new blood is needed to get the adrenalin going, but both the BBC and ITCA will resist an interloper.

Central Television will transmit *Spitting Image* for the first time this Sunday. More trouble. Central's Board have rejected the sketch of the Supremes poking fun at the Royal Family and I have requested that one 'bugger' and one 'arsehole' be cut, as well as a sad and humiliating sequence showing Macmillan in a geriatric home slopping food over himself.

Sunday 4th March

Lunched with Neil Kinnock on Monday: an affable fellow whose stature, to my mind, diminished the longer he went on talking.

On Tuesday attended a party at the IBA to celebrate Alastair Burnet's knighthood. Not as big a turn-out as I had expected. Alastair gave a rather solemn response to George Thomson's speech about the integrity of the journalist and the need for vigilance – at least I think that was his drift. Edward Heath was there. We were introduced and he spoke at me rather than to me. I suspect he has built up so many barriers around himself he has forgotten how to communicate with the outside world!

Had meetings with various radio people this week. They no longer seem to have any fire in the belly, feeling an oppressed section of the broadcasting industry: rents too high, audiences too low, fearful of the pirates and unable to find a way of fighting back. IBA Members, at a meeting later in the week, seemed to agree: radio has lost its way, selling is poor, and it fails to catch the imagination. The Radio Marketing Bureau had the wrong man at the helm and the airtime sales agencies were looking towards the introduction of cable television to supplement income.

On Thursday George and I had another discussion with the Home Secretary on DBS. I reiterated my belief in the need for new money to take one third of the shares from both the BBC and any ITV allotments. Leon Brittan didn't see why the BBC should give up their 50 per cent, but I stressed the venture needed entrepreneurial skills and drive to be a success. The thought of the BBC retaining a 50 per cent shareholding appals me.

Sunday 11th March

George has received a letter from Leon Brittan confirming his belief that the BBC should retain 50 per cent and ITV and other interests will have to share the remaining 50 per cent. I can think of no more unsuitable body to give a dominant interest to than the BBC. I know the ITV companies are so delighted at the possibility of breaking out of their defined contract period that they would sell their grannies to get the concession, whatever the downside.

I have until now stuck to my guns in seeking a third participant in order to achieve a balance but George, with whom I have had a number of discussions, is unwilling to stand out against the Home Secretary's wishes. A pity, because the present intention will produce a highly unsatisfactory outcome, with the ITCA companies taking second place to the BBC. What is wanted is a lively third party, prepared to stand alongside and break up a costly and cosy duopoly.

Today's *Observer* hinted at a rift between George and me. It will be interesting to see how the Members feel at the Thursday meeting. Last Wednesday they seemed clearly willing to vote for a division into three but, in the light of the Home Secretary's letter, they will probably take the 'prudent' line. I greatly fear that a major battle has been lost without any real debate or consideration for the long term future of terrestrial broadcasting. The ITCA companies will now be sinking millions into DBS and moaning poverty as a consequence. It's a puzzlement that Mrs Thatcher's Government should be setting their sights on the extension of a broadcasting monopoly.

Sunday 18th March

At the beginning of the week was a meeting with ILR company representatives to discuss VFH transmissions and Independent National Radio. I was pleasantly surprised to hear that – on engineering matters at least – the Companies considered the IBA was looking after their interests and priorities. Their main concern lay in the future, and the power and radiation of their stations, when a new frequency spectrum for ILR would be agreed (1989/90). I had expected a somewhat stormy meeting, but it proved not to be.

INR worries the Companies, not so much because they are afraid of competition but more, I think, that they do not know what form the competition will take. I asked them to go away and think about it, explaining the number of options open to them. It was for them to decide which they felt offered the best way forward for the system as a whole.

On Tuesday a meeting with the SCC. The Companies, or at least some of them, seemed taken by surprise at the speed by which the DBS talks had been proceeding, and some of them seemed genuinely astonished when I told them of Leon Brittan's letter and his wish to see the enterprise split on a 50:50 basis. There followed a 30 minute discussion during which I made clear my preference for a 1/3 : 1/3 : 1/3. I have my doubts about Paul Fox's support although he said he had supported the idea when he had seen Leon Brittan. The Companies leaned towards my view although there was clearly no consensus.

I made it clear that the 1989 contract renewal would not automatically give them the right to continue. If performance was unsatisfactory, the contract would be re-advertised. I think this came as something of a shock to one or two people who had probably thought they would be safe and secure whatever their performance.

Later in the week, I heard the opinions of both Brian Tesler and James Gatward (the MD of TVS), who incidentally is now a millionaire from his holding in that company and I think deserves his success. He is also very modest, which is a delight.

Brian Tesler told me that he and others, including Lord Thomson, had had lunch with Willie Whitelaw on Friday when the latter had appeared genuinely surprised by the 50:50 proposition put to us by Leon Brittan. George Thomson had stressed the preference of my proposal. I think in retrospect George may be regretting his readiness to fall in with LB's proposal. Certainly the IBA will be in a stronger position if we can claw back the split, even if it eventually works out at 40 : 40 : 20 which I would find acceptable.

At an emergency meeting of the Authority on Thursday we were joined by a new member – a representative from APEX (the Association of Professional, Executive, Clerical and Computer Staff) – who is displaying a penchant for verbal exposure of his views on television, many of them ill-formed or ill-judged. We had a full discussion of LB's letter and our reaction to it. They approved the terms of a letter George would be sending to the Home Secretary. I think this is the only course to prevent a dangerous split within the Authority.

Norman Tebbit gave an uncharacteristically lacklustre speech at a weekend conference on Oracle in Jersey. I was presented with one of only six silver medallions given to visiting panjandrums. What does one do with a medallion?!

Saturday 24th March

A relatively quiet week. No horrors: the Home Office silent on DBS, ITCA silent on DBS, the BBC silent on DBS. All this reminds me of a computer chess game, set to 'High Skill' where the computer evaluates its next move in silence, as though dead, then quite suddenly the Voice speaks. I wonder which voice will speak on DBS.

I imagine there are some heart-searchings going on amidst the ITCA companies who are at last waking up to the realisation that they are heading for a relationship with the BBC that can do them nothing but damage. As a junior partner, they will pay the bills but have little control.

On Thursday I attended the Gala night of Andrew Lloyd Webber's *Starlight Express* attended by the Queen. An amazing musical, with marvellous songs, which hopefully will rocket round the world. I have invested £10,000 and, although capitalisation was £2m, I may see a return if it runs for a year. Andrew had married Sarah Brightman the day before. Very sad for the former Sarah and the children, but he seemed happy enough. I gave him three silk handkerchief's and a birthday card depicting a cat on roller skates. We left the celebrations at 1am because the following day Roma and I were due to attend a Variety Club event for Dickie A.

This turned out to be a jolly affair, with Dickie feted grandly at the Savoy and the occasion attended by a goodly number of stars and stage folk, with speeches by Edward Fox and John Mills. I kicked off the proceedings with a six-minute stint. It seemed to be well received.

Sunday 1st April

A ragbag of a week, with the silence on DBS still deafening as though everybody had withdrawn into their bunkers to consider the extent of the damage about to be unleashed.

Hosted a dinner on Tuesday with Alasdair Milne at which I presented the outgoing chairman of CRAC, Colin James, Bishop of Wakefield, with the works of Henry

James. He is to be replaced by the Bishop of London, an altogether tougher proposition. Our binging forward religious programmes to 2pm has resulted in a much closer examination of the whole religious scene on television. Good may yet come from it.

Saturday 7th April

Thunderclouds hang heavy over the DBS proposals, which need a good storm to clear the air. *The Economist* quoted me this week as likening DBS to 'jukebox telly' which won't gain me any friends in the BBC or Whitehall. There are rumours that Michael Grade or Paul Fox will step forward to run DBS: a thankless task, and one I would run a mile from.

On Tuesday I went to the Nuffield Foundation for a consultation on 'The Future of Broadcasting' chaired by Sir Monty Finniston (Chairman of British Steel Corporation). A very low grade affair which left me with the impression that it had more to do with Sir Monty finding out whether he was right to be investing in cable, rather than for the benefit of the assembled broadcasters.

Attended a dinner for IBA staff on a course for 'Facing Up to Retirement'. It must prove a jolt, especially for wives who have to learn to put up with their old men day in and day out!

On Thursday, Roma and I went to the Duke of York to see Glenda Jackson on stage for nearly five hours, playing in *Strange Interlude*, a performance hugely praised by critics but which I found rather tedious and curiously lacking in any real pathos. Perhaps it's just that I don't like sitting still for five hours.

Sunday 15th April

Friday 13th lived up to its reputation with their Lordships delivering their verdict on *Scum*, and J Whitney was the main target of their attack. No one representing the IBA was in court to hear the verdict. Outside the court, a jubilant Mary Whitehouse 'advised Mr Whitney to reconsider his role'.

The Court ruled that 'the Director General of the IBA made a grave error of judgment in allowing the showing of *Scum*, and that he was wrong in not referring the matter to a full meeting of the Authority'. Mr Justice Taylor said the film had 'an honest and sincere purpose'; Lord Justice Watkins said 'it is, I think, gratuitously offensive and revolting'. The Authority was criticised for not laying down guidelines for the DG to consult the Members but the Court ruled that the showing of *Scum* did not breach Section 4(1)a of the Act. As the Court held that the actual showing of the film had not been in breach of the law, it will be interesting to see whether they are right in law to seek to give guidance to the IBA as to how it should discharge its function. I am fairly certain that the bones of this case will be picked white by both sides.

I feel a little sad that the phrase 'grave error' may be remembered as linked to my showing of the film rather than, as intended, an error in not taking it to the Members.

Sunday 22nd April

On Thursday George and I decided that a letter from him to *The Times* would be preferable to a long-drawn out appeal with Mary Whitehouse cross-appealing.

Had a call from Timothy Aitken at TV-am to the effect that he wished to become Executive Chairman (and retain some responsibility for certain aspects) rather than Chief Executive. He told me Bruce Gyngell had been approved by the Board as Acting Chief Executive. I had been under the impression that his role as Chief Executive would continue for at least another year and that this change would require Authority approval. He told me the Board had also concluded that cuts in the workforce beyond the union-agreed 'natural wastage' would have to be made. Greg Dyke said he and two other senior programme people would resign if these cuts came to pass, and this pistol at the head seems to have brought a modicum of sense to the position.

I told Tim that Bruce Gyngell's appointment was not something that would go on the nod with Authority Members as he represented Kerry Packer interests and that the delicate balance within TV-am between unions and management could easily become disturbed.

******

Sunday 6th May

Have been in Nice attending the MIP Convention and during the last fortnight the Authority has decided to lodge an Appeal against the *Scum* findings. I think there were only two Members who thought it better not to risk a further hearing for fear that the Court's decision on 4(1)a would be debated again. It was clear that Members felt the key point for the Appeal was the right of the Court to dictate the internal mechanisms of the Authority and that, if not contested, anybody might be able to take the Authority to Court over any internal practice or judgment. Michael Caine, the newest Member, said it would be intolerable for the Executive to refer back all manner of decisions to Members. George had sent a letter to *The Times* announcing the decision to Appeal, whilst stressing that the Members of the IBA had total confidence in their Director General.

I suppose it's a double or quit situation. If we fail in the Appeal, my name will get another mauling. If we win, I hope the record will be expunged and 'grave error of judgment' will disappear. Only time will tell. I don't regret the Authority's decision and wrote to thank George.

TV-am took to the front pages again with news of Timothy Aitken's appointment as Chairman, Dick Marsh bowing out and two new Fleet Board members. The confirmation of Bruce Gyngell as Chief Executive took no one by surprise because, as usual, TV-am had been leaking like a sieve for several days before the announcement. Michael Deakin is continuing as Programme Director, however, and will provide a steadying influence. He seems to care for the quality of output in a way not demonstrated by others.

Sunday 20th May

Leon Brittan has decided that DBS will be opened up for competition just three years after the service comes into being, and has announced this in the Commons. If I was a Contractor, I think I would stand on one side and let others lose their money first. I don't think we will have a flurry of offers from the Companies, as they now know they will get an extension whether or not they apply to take part in DBS.

The Home Office are now pressing us to judge applicants for a third share by the middle of June. This is far too early as the sort of entrepreneurs I wish to see applying spend most of their time jetting around the world and must be given time to even be aware of the project. In fact, Ted and Eve Branson came to lunch at the weekend and I took the opportunity to scribble a note to Richard asking him to be in touch if he was interested.

On Thursday Roma and I went to a dinner party given by Rupert Murdoch, where I had the opportunity to tell Leon Brittan that I wanted more time to find a suitable DBS partner. He didn't seem unduly fussed.

At a Royal Academy dinner, where Sir Hugh Casson presided at his last dinner as President, Prince Charles and the Princess of Wales were guests of honour, and Laurie Lee responded on behalf of the guests. The speech faltered at times through a series of complicated digressions but there were some moments of crystal clarity and the audience loved him for it.

On Friday night I heard from my secretary that Greg Dyke had either resigned, or been pushed, from his position as Editor-in-Chief at TV-am.

Sunday 27th May

News of Greg Dyke's resignation has been confirmed. He left because he said he feared the new hand on the tiller (Bruce Gyngell) would insist on further cuts which would erode programme standards still further. Not a happy note to leave on.

David Glencross, the IBA's Director of Television, has written to TV-am seeking reassurance that any change in the programme service would be discussed in advance with the IBA. This prompted a headline in the *Mail on Sunday*: 'Stop this massacre at dawn. TV-am warned – close down threat from watchdogs.' How David's letter was leaked on the day it was sent worries me not a little! *The Sunday Times* lectured the IBA: 'What the IBA must now decide is whether enough is enough'.

On 22nd May we put out an invitation to ITV companies to join the BBC and ITCA in the first DBS services for the UK – my request for a later closing date than June having been rejected. George is suddenly of the opinion that the IBA should not have representation on the Board of the DBS Authority to avoid conflict of loyalties. It is too late for such second thoughts.

Norman Tebbit's depiction on *Spitting Image* as a bovver boy with chains and coshes is eerily accurate. He came to dinner at the IBA on Wednesday and as I listened to him talking I wondered whether he was flattered by this image. A likeable man, with a clear mind and articulate to boot.

Sunday 3rd June

Anxiety about DBS deepens. On Thursday I visited Television South West and had dinner with their Chairman and Kevin Goldstein-Jackson, Chief Executive – a small, insecure 33-year old with apparently a fear of falling out of cars and a shareholding that makes him a paper millionaire. TSW was Kevin's brainchild and he has a novel and effective flair for getting the best out of people. TSW are unlikely to take up a share of DBS, preferring to wait until the two other channels are available.

I had also heard that Central Television have misgivings. The BBC shareholding is seen as the reason for this lack of enthusiasm. I asked for more advertisements for DBS to be placed in the Sundays, and in Saturday's *FT*. Up to now we have received disappointingly few enquiries.

I have arranged to have breakfast with Richard Branson on Monday as he is nibbling at DBS. However, he has just launched Virgin Airways and may have too much on his plate.

Radio is going through troubled times. I visited DevonAir in Exeter, and Plymouth Sound. Both are at a standstill, with Devon Air nearly in the red, with the threat of bankruptcy looming. Root causes are hard to pinpoint. Over-enthusiasm in staffing levels? Lack of any real experience, especially in selling? There is an overriding concern that the proliferation of the pirates and the threat of community radio will lead to further audience erosion and that the Authority's regulations are too burdensome, allowing the pirate operators to compete effectively.

On Monday I will be lunching with Bruce Gyngell, now Chief Executive of TV-am. Another executive has left, after only four weeks. If Michael Deakin goes, I think the station has had it: the very last vestige of credibility will have gone.

A row is blowing up with Granada. *A World in Action* on Barratt Homes, yet to be transmitted, contains a vigorous attack on their selling methods and the high price of houses on re-sale. I want Barratt to be given a fair opportunity of replying. Granada and their lawyers disagree. In our opinion programme makers must deal fairly with their subject matter and not give a programme a 'slant' which is unjustified or unfair.

Sunday 10th June

I write this diary entry on a perfect summer's day, seated on the foreshore overlooking the sea with only a few ripples to confirm that this is not an idyllic watercolour.

On Wednesday Granada agreed to show their *World in Action* programme on starter homes to Barratts. This is planned for transmission tomorrow and I feel time is against Barratts to prepare their response. I showed the film to Authority Members at our regular meeting and they endorsed the view that within 'fair dealing' Barratts should be able to respond at the end of the programme. By 1720 on Thursday, Granada told us they had been unable to contact any 'key persons' within Barratts, and so I said the programme should be deferred for another week.

Granada are claiming the IBA intrusion is unheard of, and at one point threatened to cancel the programme and consider withholding *World in Action* completely. The principle of fair play has not been highly regarded by *World in Action*.

On Monday I lunched at the Garrick with Bruce Gyngell. 'Everything', he said, 'fills me with a growing sense of unease'. Gyngell is one of those Australians who has a no-nonsense outlook. This philosophy extends, I suspect, to the views the Authority might hold about the breakfast franchise. He was at pains to underline that the only product they had to sell was programme output, but this did not fill me with confidence as he then went on to talk about cartoon fillers and cutting back on ENS crewing. If Greg Dyke found Gyngell's ideas too depressing, what size fig leaf is left to cover the Authority's nakedness?! I wrote to Gyngell after the lunch underlining that a meeting called for 14th June, and referred by Gyngell as 'routine', should be given more importance.

On Thursday I went down to Eton to address 600 boys in the Great Hall. I told them they were tomorrow's decision makers and that they should guard against allowing broadcasting standards to fall. They appeared unimpressed.

Sunday 17th June

I am writing this entry down at Ower Quay, the cottage near Corfe Castle which was the former home of my parents. A weekend of high summer which makes this country the only place to live. Nests are busting with baby birds, hay is being cut, everything is throbbing under the sun. London and my labours at the IBA seem far off and so take on their proper perspective.

Last week started with a five-hour meeting of DGMM to consider the 84/85 budget. We are sadly in the red on radio and, looking ahead to 87/88, for television to the tune of some £14m. If we do not raise rentals by a significant amount we shall have to consider the next steps with care.

On Tuesday PPC, followed by SCC, followed by a special meeting on DBS with Stuart Young, Alasdair Milne, George Thomson and ITCA representatives. Quite a performance arranging seating so that all the parties were given equal status.

Alasdair said the BBC wanted the public service element – to inform and educate – dropped from the Broadcasting Act. He stressed that DBS had to be a commercial success first and foremost. What a long road the BBC has now travelled from Reith's beliefs, its shameless attitude now in direct contrast to the lofty aspirations I thought I heard when the BBC were given the go ahead. 'Juke Box in the sky' is becoming a bad joke coming true.

Brian Tesler questioned the rightness of going forward with three channels, suggesting that two might be the best way to start. Earlier, I recall that both the BBC and ITCA had plugged away for three channels, arguing that the greater the number of channels the more likelihood of people paying their subscription. If ITCA and the BBC are to be the only two participants, they will feel unassailable.

The IBA has now received over 70 enquiries from those wishing to play a part as the third element. The task of sorting this out will not be easy.

On Wednesday a further meeting was held at the DTI. I could not attend as I had a long-standing date to chair a meeting of ILR executives to talk about independent national radio. The Companies now accept the fact that INR will come, but its form is as yet undecided. There is a good case for thinking along the lines of a Radio 4 output, using speech as the basis. This would not conflict with the current output of ILR and would have the merit of bringing a different type of advertising to independent radio.

Lord Thomson sent another strong letter about the encroachment of pirate radio to Leon Brittan. I wanted this out and in the public eye to pre-empt the growing muttering from the Companies that the IBA was turning a blind eye to the pirates.

The Queen's Birthday Honours were announced yesterday and Jimmy Gordon of Radio Clyde received a CBE – the first Honour to go to someone from the Companies and a reward greatly deserved by Jimmy, who has worked tirelessly for independent radio.

Sunday 24th June

I never thought I would hear Channel 4 agreeing to take snooker in peak time. That is what was proposed by ITV in exchange for allowing the Channel an extension of hours. When I heard about it, I flipped and said what I thought. If ever there was a surer way of destroying the image that Channel 4 has built for itself, snooker will do that. I told the Authority, when it met on Wednesday, that what Roland Rat had done for TV-am's image, snooker would do for Channel 4's. I must have spoken with fervour because my view was accepted by Members.

Another week of DBS activity. By 20th June we had ready considered 14 applications to participate.

The Barratt affair rumbles on with a story in the *Sunday Times* in which Granada accuses the IBA of contributing towards the end of investigative journalism. A contrasting view was made in *Television Today*, who applauded the IBA for their decision to allow Barratts the opportunity to have the last word.

On Thursday I lunched at the Garrick with the film Censor James Firman and his key staff. I suspect they are ill prepared to cope with the avalanche of tapes that will descend on them when video takes off.

The BBC have been receiving hard criticism from journalists for the axing of *60 Minutes*. There really does appear to be a split leadership – with Bill Cotton, aided by Stuart Young, wanting to go more populist and, on the other side, Alasdair Milne still determined to be a reincarnation of Reith.

Saturday 7th July

As I write this, the sound of racquet and ball and the applause from the Wimbledon crowd comes from the television as Ms. Navratilova and Chrissie Evert-Lloyd battle it out in 85 degrees fahrenheit.

DBS has again taken up much of the staff's time in this previous fortnight. On

Monday 25th June, I met with Members and the Chairman to set the agenda for the DBS interviews with 'Third Force' parties. Kenneth Blyth has been at the heart of the whole operation. The Authority is fortunate to have a man of such clear vision and I, personally, am particularly fortunate to have him as my chief assistant.

The same day I attended a dinner given at the Hyde Park Hotel by Edmund Dell to pay tribute to three retiring directors of Channel 4. It was a pleasant evening, without formality. I hope the choice we have made for the new directors will prove as successful.

On Tuesday, I lunched with David Nicholas, who is pressing forward with his hopes and plans for one of the new channels to be news and information. The concept is strongly supported by David Plowright, next year's Chairman of ITCA. I am very keen that support should be given to the idea: DBS would then have value instead of adding to the juke-box fare that I have every fear will be the inevitable outcome. Every ITV company has now signified its intention of taking part in ITV's share, with the possible exception of TSW who have written to say they 'wish to limit their financial exposure to a maximum investment of £5'!

Radio has been taking an increasing amount of my time. On Tuesday 26th June, I met the radio unions and listened to their concerns about the financial stability of the system. They have genuine fears about the liquidity of Gwent and CBC and say that the station staff is now so depleted that there are only two journalists in the Gwent station, and that by no stretch of the imagination can they supply a realistic news service. The unions urged the Authority to do everything within our power to insist on a merger of the two stations.

The unions are also worried about the proliferation of pirate radio stations and the consequent threat to ILR staff. On Tuesday I attended the regular meeting with the Regional Officers, but this time, instead of talking to them about events occurring, I broke to them the substance of the report made to the Working Party to consider the future of ROs: in short, this means reducing from 12 locations to eight, and limiting their activities and staffing. This bombshell broke over their heads and I was surprised by the calm with which the announcement was met. I heard later that it was simply shock, not agreement. ROs have traditionally regarded themselves as the elite of staff, reporting, as they do, to the DG. Their operations have, up to now, been something of a law unto themselves. Like any other group, there are some good and some bad. How they will respond to this considerable change will be interesting.

This week brought out of the woodwork a sensitive issue over Channel 4's *Who Dares Wins*, a satirical programme which has caused us trouble since it first went on air. Because of this, we instituted a check system whereby a senior Channel 4 editor made sure nothing went out that shouldn't. The system failed last week when a reference to Leon Brittan was made, suggesting he was homosexual. This led to a rumpus. We wrote to Leon Brittan, apologising.

I received a letter from Charles Wintour resigning from the Editorial Board of TV-am on the grounds that the output was falling far short of the standards set by the Board when they were invited on to it. This is a fig-leaf we can ill afford to have snatched from us, and I fear it will be leaked to the press who will naturally have a field day.

To make matters worse, on Thursday 5th July it was confirmed that Clive Jones, TV-am's Editor, had resigned over the decision by TV-am to pull out of the Olympic Games, announced on the 29th June. The reason given was the unions' demand for payment for the live feeds this would need, amounting to some £100,000 in additional overtime. TV-am rejected this demand and announced their decision to pull out.

On Thursday Roma and I flew to the European Broadcasting Union General Assembly in Stockholm, staying at the Grand Hotel, which lived up to its name with an enormous baroque gold-leafed ballroom. Our conference hall looked like a gigantic stage set for *Romeo and Juliet* complete with balconies and gargoyles. The Swedes are passionate about their soused herring, but I felt I would scream or throw up if another plate of herring with cream was placed before me. We ate massive helpings of reindeer throughout our stay. Poor Rudolph, he tasted rich and livery.

Alasdair Milne delivered a homily on Public Service Broadcasting from a carefully prepared draft, which I gathered came from Stephen Hirst. I think he felt that the record should be put right after his last utterance at the EBU which made him sound a good deal more commercial than the ITV companies.

Representatives from Ireland (George Walters), Holland (Erik Jergens) and Portugal all spoke to me about the possibility of Channel 4 becoming a partner with them in the European satellite project. It would make sense for Channel 4 to get involved, not only for its own good but because it would open the ITV companies to the possibility of European co-operation. I intend to do some gentle soundings-out to see if the concept gets a good reception.

A distinctly chilly meeting with representatives of AIRC on 4th July. I left them in no doubt that I considered their recent statement about the IBA's perceived failure to deal effectively with pirate radio a breakdown in a relationship built up over a long period. The AIRC has genuine grievance with Government over pirate radio and the rumours about community radio. Instead of becoming hysterical with the IBA, they should recognise we are an ally and lobby Government.

Next week we hold our next interviews with groups hoping to join the DBS consortium: Carlton Services, Granada Rental and Thorn EMI. Scrambled eggs and bacon for Members at 8am on Monday morning!

Sunday 15th July

One of those hectic weeks when I have felt like the Sorcerer's Apprentice, with a rising tide of papers and decisions that need dealing with before they engulf me.

Both the GAC and RCC (Radio Consultative Committee) used up much-needed adrenalin. I suppose that, having sat on the other side of the table at RCC, I have a fully developed split personality during these occasions! The GAC gave me the opportunity of again underlining the IBA's resolve that terrestrial broadcasting should – must – not be eroded as a consequence of investment by contractors in DBS.

A sweeping victory by the Centre Forward group of Equity has provided the possibility of an end to the IPA/Equity dispute. Both Equity and the IPA have asked me to Chair their first meeting, which I have accepted in the spirit of honest broker.

RCC was a raggle-taggle of undercurrents. There is a deep rift between the IBA and the Companies over the cost of meeting IBA engineering standards. IBA engineers are used to building on excellence, and quality costs money. I have agreed to meet privately with the Chairman of AIRC to see if we can establish common ground. Until such a time that the pirates are trounced, the Companies feel they are fighting for audiences and profitability with their hands tied. In the words of Brian West, the IBA is being asked to 'take off the shackles' so that the Companies can compete on equal terms with the pirates.

Michael Deakin from TV-am is about to resign, following 'mayhem and skulduggery' at Camden Lock. The output is average but if the IBA calls a halt now it will be accused of pulling the plug just at the moment when the IPA/Equity dispute could end and lift revenue. If the station does nothing, it could go bust in November, or January at the latest, and we would have demonstrated our weakness with no redeeming feature to save us from the blistering criticism that will follow. Either way, we are on to a loser.

This week the Authority interviewed ten groups wishing to participate in the DBS consortium. From what I heard, there is enough enthusiasm in the private sector to finance and operate DBS without either the BBC or ITV having right of entry. As it is now, we have the worst of all possible worlds. What a mess, and from a Government pledged to competition!

Sunday 22nd July

The miners' strike cuts deeper into coal supplies and the miners' pockets. Mrs Thatcher appears on the Michael Aspel Show, dressed in fuchsia, and I thought beginning to bear an uncanny resemblance to Barbara Cartland!

On Monday, Linda Chalker, Minister of Transport, came to lunch. A bright, busy, rounded lady, she seemed anxious to call everyone by their Christian names. She kept the conversational ball rolling merrily, her main thrust being her enthusiasm for the trial experiment of roadside signs informing motorists of the frequency of local radio stations, so that they could listen to reports of traffic hold-ups and the like.

On Tuesday to Thames Television to celebrate the Queen's Award in recognition of their achievement in the export of programmes: some £84m within the last ten years.

Roma and I dined afterwards on the Thames boat moored beside their Teddington studios. Quite an honour as we were the only guests, the rest being 'Thames family'. One of the original and largely unsung pioneers of television, Howard Thomas, was present. He brought to the industry a sense of showmanship combined with a professional judgment that helped to establish Thames in its role as flagship of the television contractors.

An Authority meeting was held on Wednesday; DBS, IBA funding and Regional Officers being the main agenda items. Members approved the final recommendations for the Companies submitted to the Home Secretary for DBS consideration.

The Regional Officers' paper that Members were asked to consider was put back until September. This proposed a radical change to the number and composition of Regional Offices as well as a substantial diminution of their job responsibilities as regards radio, this year's accounts showing that radio had an excess budget over income of £300,000. A fair proportion of the over-spend was due to the allocation of time spent by regional staff in the performance of their radio duties, assessed at some 40 per cent.

The revenue of TV-am was considered together with the recommendation by staff that I should send a stern letter advising the company of its duty to perform with greater zeal in a number of areas. This I agreed to do. News of Michael Deakin's imminent departure has not leaked and I did not raise the subject with Members.

We remain poised – or is it spiked? – on the horns of a dilemma. If we close the station now, we will be accused of doing so just as the end of the IPA/Equity dispute is in sight. When it is over, the view is, money will flow in, enough to enable the station to pay its way and improve the quality of its programme output. If Deakin goes and we do nothing, the last shred of our respectability will have been taken from us.

I had a long talk on the telephone with Sir Geoffrey Cox, Chairman of ITN and also a member of the Editorial News Board on TV-am. In his judgment, the news coverage of the station had 'neither got better nor worse'. The resignation of Charles Wintour has still not become public. His views would have given further fuel to the fires stoked by the press in the hope that TV-am's funeral pyre would catch light.

Lunch at the Garrick on Friday with Marshall Stewart. Interesting insights into Mrs T's thinking about the ITV contractors and her belief that they were costly, monopolistic, fearful about the possible loss of their franchises in 1989, and consequently prepared to do anything in the meantime to fortify their position. She also had an interesting take on the role of the IBA's chairman, and was resolved not to appoint another chairman with a political background, preferring a businessman or someone from broadcasting. I am unsure whether George wants to continue in his role but, if Marshall is correct, we will have to come to terms with a new figurehead.

Friday also saw a last-minute tangle developing over *World in Action* – a programme on the death of a British businessman in an Oman jail and raising once again the question of the Prime Minister's role in securing a contract to build the University in Oman and the part that Mark Thatcher played. The Oman Government were trying to prevent the *World in Action* programme being broadcast on the grounds of impartiality, but had failed to persuade a Judge in Chambers to make that decision. On Friday, in front of the Master of Rolls and Sir Peter

Rawlinson (representing the Sultan), David Kemp QC (representing the IBA) offered that the IBA Chairman and such Authority Members as could be mustered would see the programme for themselves before transmission was approved.

I objected strongly to this action, arguing that the established system of IBA staff viewing the programme and making the decision should be followed. Kemp apologised but said the alternative would have been an Order of Court *insisting* that the Chairman and Members saw it.

Members saw the programme on Friday afternoon and formed the view that it gave 'in parts' an unbalanced point of view. The frustrating part of this whole incident was that when staff saw it just beforehand they reached the same decision. Granada will undoubtedly feel aggrieved that their programme is being banned.

On Monday I will chair a meeting between the IPA and Equity. At long last an end to the dispute may be in sight, but time will tell.

Sunday 29th July

At the first IPA/Equity 're-shaping' meeting on Monday, Equity was represented by their newly-elected President, Derek Bond – already in the eye of a storm for accepting a role in a play due to be performed in South Africa. The old brigade of the ousted Equity Council are up in arms. I only hope he survives.

The meeting went better than I hoped or expected. I sensed a genuine desire by both sides to find a way forward. We meet again on Tuesday 31st.

On Tuesday I attended a lunch given for me by the Broadcasting Press Guild at The Ivy restaurant. After I had given my 'state of the nation' round up of events, about 20 journalists fired questions at me for half an hour. The most heat was generated over TV-am, with the Authority being criticised vehemently over its indecisiveness. I was also pressed on DBS but declined to give any information on our submission to the Home Office, which had been delivered on Friday 27th July.

On Thursday I had a long meeting with Nigel Walmsley and Richard Findley to see what could be done about the parlous state of radio funding. They told me about a lunch they had had with Leon Brittan, at which he questioned the 'underlying wisdom' that ILR was a 'system'. He challenged this on the grounds that each station ought to stand on its own feet and not depend on IBA subsidies. The time has come, I think, to lay down a strategy for radio.

Sunday 5th August

The silly season is supposed to be a time when summer lulls and dulls the senses, when people take their holidays and forget about the traumas of the workaday world. Last week this was not to be.

On Monday morning, as a follow up to the recent Authority meeting, I met senior members of TV-am's management team. Michael Deakin's apologies had been sent in advance on the grounds of indisposition. Bruce Gyngell started the meeting by outlining the intentions of the programming staff as contained in a letter to IBA's Head of Television, David Glencross: 'TV-am's aim is to inform and entertain in a popular, populist and newsy fashion'. He went on to enlarge: 'There is a bias against foreign stories unless they are major, intriguing or funny'.

I reminded Gyngell that he was the spokesman for the original application, despite the changes that had since occurred, and that if he implemented a substantial change, then the franchise should be re-advertised.

I feel quite desperate about TV-am. There can be little doubt that their performance, and our handling of the situation, has gone badly. In the judgment of most professionals, the feeling is that we should have acted earlier and with more determination, yet, retracing events in my mind, I cannot determine when action could have been taken. The slide, if TV-am's progress can be thus described, has been a slow slippage, made the more unappealing by leaks and inept management utterances; the most recent being the former Chairman, Richard Marsh, demanding money owed to him and being quoted as saying that to wait for payment would be rather like an insurance salesman asked to quote for the Titanic after it had sunk!

During the course of the meeting, David Glencross highlighted the areas the IBA considered should be maintained or improved, which included children's programmes and regional inputs. Francis Essex was present as an advisor, brought in by Gyngell. His ideas have the ring of the early 70s about them – a child's 'good news' feature, chats with personalities like George Best! My heart sank still further.

On Tuesday, the Home Secretary announced the names of Companies that would be invited to participate in the BBC/ITV consortium for DBS. His statement was worded in such a way that it did not mention the IBA's recommendations but merely said: 'I have today indicated to the Companies listed below that I would be prepared to give my approval under Section 43(i) of the Cable & Broadcasting Act 1984 to their participation in the group to provide DBS programmes'. However, Leon B did write a nice letter to George: 'Overall, I believe that the IBA has recommended participants who should be able to bring a nice balance of contributions to the project, and I am most grateful to the Authority for all the work carried out and its quality'.

Now we have done our bit, we can take a back seat and watch the fun!

At a lunch recently, I heard from David Shaw that Unisat had now indicated that they were proposing to very nearly double their costs. David thought that this could be the final straw for the Companies, who were beginning in some cases to get an attack of nerves now that DBS was becoming a reality. Our work has been but the overture. Whether the curtain will come down after the First Act is anyone's guess.

On Monday I had lunch with Douglas Hurd. We discussed DBS and radio. On radio, Douglas is clearly looking for a way to introduce community radio and seemed to have already taken that decision. He questioned me closely on ILR and said that ILR was unhappy with the degree of regulation and the cost of engineering etc. I said that, if he were to introduce community radio in some form or another, the present range of programming undertaken by ILR would in all probability have to be reduced in order for them to remain competitive. I also said that we (the IBA) should consider inviting quotes from outside for the erection of aerials and transmission gear. Douglas is a nice man, but I don't think he really feels at home with the minutiae of broadcasting. I drank my Perrier and he paid the bill.

On Tuesday the second meeting of the Equity Council and IPA took place. Both sides got down to the first stage of bargaining but the gap remains wide. In order to save face, both sides will need a raft to cling to with some appearance of dignity.

Sunday 2nd September

A fortnight's holiday has been like a rest cure: a perfect week in Portugal staying with friends in a remote farmhouse without a television aerial in sight, or consequently in mind, and then to Dorset, where I caught up with my reading and went back to sculpting. A marvellously fascinating pastime which commits the mind wholly to the task in hand.

During the fortnight I was away, a dispute at Thames became a growing aggravation and over the Bank Holiday, and continuing on into last week, screens in the Thames area were blank. Much to-ing and fro-ing to ACAS has so far not resolved the row, which sprang from the determination by some 70 people working in the Central Technical Facility section, who were being asked to accept a change in duty hours with a consequent reduction in overtime. This, the striking men claim, will result in a drop of total earnings by between £3,000 and £5,000 per year. As their present incomes are some £22,000 to £26,000 per annum, their cause is not finding much sympathy. Despite this, the ACTT has backed the strike and attempted to widen and strengthen support. One action so far has been that some ACTT technicians have refused to handle the Fourth Channel signal, which is fed round the system through each regional contractor in order that local commercials can be slotted into the breaks. When the action first occurred, my response was to authorise the bypassing of those stations refusing to handle the signal. This has not pleased ACTT but has the support of the Companies and, of course, Channel 4. Twice, their shop has been asked to join with the striking technicians and on both occasions they have refused.

During the week, I have been keeping in touch with various key elements. On Friday, at the request of Thames, I had a meeting with Bryan Cowgill (MD) and Hugh Dundas (Chairman). Bryan proposed Thames returning to air, staffed by management. For the first week, they could stick to the schedule almost in its entirety; in the second by some 75 per cent; and in the third week there would be wide variations from scheduled output leaving perhaps 25 per cent of the original programming intact. I endorsed that, believing it is the duty of management to manage and protect the company's interests.

The ITCA Council met that same morning and decided unanimously to set on one side the industry negotiations which were in progress to reach agreement on pay for the next two years. We shall see what happens next. The Companies, and Thames in particular, are looking for diversification and expansion into the new opportunities of cable and DBS. The Unions want to retain their highly profitable grip on the jugular vein of the Companies' output. These factors, together with the need for each side to show strength during the period leading up to the national negotiations on pay, provide a clue to the tensions behind the dispute.

Spent some time this week examining the position of radio, which is causing concern within the industry. The pirates remain virtually unchecked by the Government. The main London pirates – Horizon, Skyline and Jackie – increasingly show their confidence by advertising their presence with distribution of stickers and discs. I lunched with Tim Brinton, who is Chairman of the Conservative back bench Media Committee. He is most concerned that Government is two-faced in their approach to pirate stations. I have come to the conclusion that it suits them to allow matters to drift and deteriorate as then the audience have greater choice, the ILR stations have to adapt or go under, and the free market philosophy of the Tories gains a victory. All this would be fine and dandy if it wasn't for the fact that much of what the pirates do they do at little cost to themselves, deliberately ignoring both copyright and royalties. Either the pirates must be stopped or the ILR stations must be allowed to compete on equal terms.

During this unsatisfactory period, the IBA has become increasingly isolated with, on the one hand, the Companies more and more dissatisfied by the standards and conditions imposed on them by the IBA and, on the other, the Government distancing itself from the Authority and allowing it to be seen as the fly in the jam, insisting on expensive technical standards and imposing heavy overheads by layers of bureaucracy.

Next week sees our first full meeting with AIRC representatives to examine the whole status of ILR and hoping to find common ground for sensible adjustments to be made. The IBA holds, whether it likes it or not, the sticky end of the lollipop.

TV-am and Michael Deakin finally parted company. Deakin went, very sensibly, on a world cruise and TV-am issued an anodyne statement. Michael has, despite all the criticism, acted as a valuable lightning conductor between TV-am and the Authority and on a number of occasions has saved the day by stabilising relations and standing back from the yo-yo game played by successive top management. His departure will be unsung, but he will be missed nonetheless.

Finally, the week has seen the usual motley gathering for the Edinburgh TV 'wordathon': a general blood-letting which does little to benefit the industry but allows excesses to be aired in a convivial atmosphere of brown ale and gin and tonics. Denis Forman, Chairman of Granada, elevated the occasion with the McTaggart lecture 'Will the Centre Hold?'

Sunday 9th September

Rumbles from the over-indulged journalists who attended the Edinburgh bash still echo. Stephen Murphy's 'a little violence before bedtime settles the stomach' received wide coverage as did Philip Whitehead's criticism of the Authority over TV-am which, he said, 'turned the Authority into a laughing stock'. Stout defence of the IBA was offered by David Glencross over our handling of the Oman affair. All in all, I suppose the BBC fared worst, with reference to Alasdair Milne 'brooding in the Gallery whilst the Corporation came under fire over its role in public service broadcasting'.

There is still, it seems to me, a mood of indignant shocked horror over the collapse, or perceived collapse, of public service standards and yet at the same time the voices that have been calling incessantly for wider freedom and more choice are faced with a dilemma. As Linda Agnew put it, 'Why should I spend my life putting together 60 hours of programming for moose droppings?'

Last Sunday I had dinner privately with Graham Greene at his table at the Connaught, the night before the private showing of 'Dr Fischer of Geneva and the Bomb Party', made by Consolidated, a company of which I had been a Director and still run by friends John Hawkesworth and John Pringle. Graham Greene was unhappy. Apart from his dislike of the air-conditioning in the restaurant, he had received a letter from an 'old girlfriend' who warned him not to expect too much from the film. A good start!

Graham was troubled over the decline of the writer and of the novel. His view of 2000 AD was bleak and he blessed the fact that he would not be here to see it.

In the event, the showing, at the National Film Theatre, was a pleasant surprise – with the Director, Michael Lindsay-Hogg, holding true to the book and preferring static set-ups rather than his usual weird set-ups which I had feared he might go for. Graham left immediately after the showing, so I don't know how he felt about it all.

Radio had dominated most of my time this week, including a longish meeting on Tuesday with AIRC representatives, who brought their concerns and grievances over radio costs and the IBA's control of the system. We made some headway, but there is still much to be done concerning the very fundamental role played by the IBA at a time when many stations face an uneasy future.

Tonight sees the first episode of *Lace*, the corn and porn titillation adapted from Shirley Conran's book. On Thursday, a full page advertisement was taken in the *Guardian* by Thames, which I thought was in exceedingly poor taste. I wrote accordingly to Bryan Cowgill, CEO of Thames, and have yet to receive a response, but I was somewhat pleased to see in the *Guardian* on Saturday a reader's letter attacking the advertisement and asking: 'Is attempted murder, sexual assault, abandoned babies the only thing that our so-called entertainers believe will make us rush to our television screens? This is not entertainment and should not be advertised in a manner that suggests it might be.'

Sunday 16th September

On Monday 10 September, I attended a BREMA (British Radio & Electronic Manufacturers Association) lunch given by their Council. BREMA, which represents the interests of set manufacturers and is not known for its leadership role in the broadcast industry, has suddenly, and without prior consultation, decided to unilaterally go along with French proposals for a D2-type MAC system.

For months now, we and the Government have been struggling to secure recognition for C-MAC, which had won the approval of the EBU (European Broadcasting Union). C-MAC will provide broadcasters with technology capable of bringing high quality picture improvements and a 3x5 aspect ratio, and could sustain these services for at least 20-30 years. D2-MAC, on the other hand, is intended to serve short-term interests, particularly cable interests, for the next 5–7 years. It has limited development scope, but provides a cheaper way to obtain a short-term advantage.

Not unnaturally, we were dismayed and angry at BREMA's action – the sort of typical response that I suppose one must expect from an industry which has time and time again shown itself incapable of looking further than the end of its nose.

This example of short-sightedness points the way to the British malady of never following up on an advantage. Here we are, world leaders in a technological breakthrough, allowing ourselves to be seduced by the wily French. No small wonder the Japanese, Germans, French and Americans leave us bobbing in their wake.

I had been worried about the meeting on Tuesday with the 15 Managing Directors, which are sometimes not the easiest. Sitting as Chairman, I sometimes felt like a General issuing orders and seeking to act as an overlord in the knowledge that I have no troops to support my words. I sometimes think the MDs know that as well and play the game.

During the meeting, I had asked the Companies to comment on recent DBS happenings. Brian Tesler articulated the dilemma facing the broadcasters with what I thought was alarming candour. 'If we are too successful in our programming', he said, 'we shall divert too many eyes from the terrestrial scene. If we fail to attract viewers, we will be shovelling buckets full of money into space without sufficient return, and that will deplete our strength on the ground.' With devastating accuracy, he was articulating precisely my fears, and the reason I had been unhappy with the degree of participation permitted to the ITV Companies by Government.

Before the meeting David Glencross and I lunched with David Plowright (Managing Director of Granada) and Mike Scott (Programme Controller). After the *World in Action* programmes on Barratts and the Oman, I had decided that we needed a quiet opportunity to chew the fat and see if there were any lessons to be learnt. I am concerned that we should not go into another series of *World in Action* and again face last-minute cliffhangers over our own intervention, or that by solicitors, Governments and the like. David Plowright spoke with spirit about the integrity and professionalism of his team and the concern Granada felt about the encroachment on their freedom as investigative journalists.

I said that, whatever the matter under investigation, the basic intention was that the subject should be dealt with fairly and that this should be seen to have been done. We concluded by agreeing that in the next series of programmes as much warning as possible would be given to David Glencross and that Granada and the IBA would work closely together – but I will be surprised if this solves the problems that will surely arise.

On Wednesday, George and I visited Leon Brittan. Leon always reminds me of a

6th Former who has just finished running round the playing field, has struggled into a suit, forced on a pair of socks and grabbed the nearest handy pair of shoes, usually in need of a good polish. He greeted us warmly.

We spent an hour talking about the extension of two Authority Members. One was Jill McIvor, a strong, well-balanced barrister from Northern Ireland, who played her role with a quiet distinction and whom we all regard highly. The other was George Russell, MD of Alcan; a shrewd businessman with an abrupt manner that occasionally appears to border on rudeness, but his judgment is sound and he makes a valuable contribution. Leon agreed readily that both should be invited to continue.

We then turned to the appointments for the Satellite Board. We proposed George Russell, Alec Cullen and Michael Caine. Leon was content with our view. The balance is a good one: Michael Caine is a businessman, Alec Cullen an eminent engineer, and George's weight ought to balance the Board more than adequately.

We turned to radio. Leon wanted an update on steps we proposed taking to ease the lot of the radio contractors. I went over our plans to prune our internal overheads. Michael Moriarty told me later that Leon had been delighted with our proposals.

At the close of the meeting, I told Leon of BREMA's position on C-MAC, inviting him to stand firm behind the Government's original intentions, but did not find his response reassuring.

The day before leaving for Minorca, I chaired a further meeting of IPA/Equity. This time the offer made by the IPA seemed attractive to Equity, who would put it to their full Council on Tuesday. There is, I think, a good chance that finally agreement will be reached: the deal is a fair one for both sides.

Just before leaving on Friday, I circulated to DGMM Members the paper I had written on radio, and how I think we should be viewing the pirates and possible introduction of community radio.

I have a feeling I have set the cat among the pigeons and that John Thompson will be less than happy, but I have come to the conclusion that the best possible course of action for JT would be to accept early retirement which would leave him enough time to reap the benefits of his experience.

Saturday 29th September

The IPA/Equity dispute is at last over. A telegram sent to Minorca, where I was on holiday, on 19th September read: 'SETTLEMENT IPA/EQUITY DISPUTE AGREED TODAY. WARMEST CONGRATS FROM ALL IBA MEMBERS FOR YOUR PATIENCE AND SUCCESS IN BRINGING THIS ABOUT. GEORGE (THOMSON)'.

Arriving back this week, I received a number of nice letters; one from Paul Fox suggesting I might go on and solve the miners' strike!

This week has been much taken up with radio. JT has drafted a detailed paper which I hope will be put to Members on 17th October, and which I hope will enable us all to see the wood for the trees, or maybe it's the trees for the wood!

At one meeting I was able to question figures for engineering expenditure which, if cut from the budget, could save £1.2m. I feel sorry for Tom Robson. He is an engineer of the very highest quality who has masterminded much of the achievements of ILR and ITV, including the Fourth Channel transmission building programme. Now he is being asked to slash major cost elements in sound broadcasting. As a perfectionist, it must be especially hard to have to come to terms with this situation.

I am worried that JT's paper might fog the major issues facing radio. He is adept at producing answers that are only half-answers. This time I am going to have to demand clear-cut replies so that decisions can be arrived at. If we fail to get clear insights, the albatross of excessive costs will dangle round our necks and bring disgrace and failure. I am afraid some tough and unpleasant decisions will have to be taken.

Sunday 7th October

I dined this week with Jeremy Isaacs and Justin Dukes at the Connaught, which still remains in a class quite of its own. JI and JD were bitterly disappointed by our preliminary assessment of their 1984/85 budget. They claimed Channel 4's success was not reflected in our allocation and that in a year when television revenues had never been higher, the Companies should be asked to dig deeper into their pockets. There will be some lively debate over this in the weeks to come.

They also made the point that, now the IPA/Equity dispute was at an end and the two minutes additional peak advertising time was being withdrawn, if the Companies had proved they could accommodate advertising, now they should be asked to use the time instead to promote Channel 4.

The opportunity came up the next evening to get a reaction, when we held for the first time a dinner for MDs of ITV Companies and Members of the Authority. Brian Tesler and David Plowright immediately sought to deny the relevance of cross-promotion. Brian T insisted that peak time ITV promotion of Channel 4 would be a waste as the ITV audience would be unmoved by an appeal to go to Channel 4 for 'minority appeal programmes'. A very flimsy argument, and one I shall be challenging as I intend raising the subject at GAC on Tuesday.

David Plowright was quick to suggest that perhaps a trade-off could be reached whereby, in exchange for retaining one minute of peak time on ITV, the second minute of peak time could be given to Channel 4! Nothing like a little horse-trading, and in fact there is, I think, a case for providing advertisers with more commercial airtime.

The evening with MDs provided a further eye-opener when the subject of DBS was raised. Brian Tesler, who was deputed to speak on the Companies' behalf, now chose the route of all-out competition, although at GAC he had said the DBS project would require a skilful balance of objectives on the part of the Companies who, on the one hand must protect their territorial base, while on the other needing to make DBS enough of a success to prevent them from losing sizable sums of money. He now said they would strive to make DBS commercially successful in the shortest time possible. I questioned him on the change of attitude and he admitted there had been a marked shift in emphasis.

The more I listen to the Companies talking about DBS, the more I am convinced that many of them are getting cold feet. There is little enthusiasm for the task that lies ahead. My guess is that, given an excuse – almost any excuse – they would turn their backs on the whole project, grateful to give someone else the heartache, but they don't want to be seen to be the first to abandon ship. They would like the BBC or the Independents to pull the bung out first.

More meetings this week with staff on the future of ILR – it is a slow and painful process, like drawing teeth. Trying to get to the bottom of engineering finances is a nightmare. No one, for ten years, has lifted the stone. Consequently, all sorts of practices have become part of the way of life without ever having been properly examined. I feel sorry for Tom Robson (Director of Engineering) approaching the end of a distinguished career to find in the last two or three years before retirement his empire is put under the microscope. Everyone wanted excellence in engineering standards, and this is what Tom has provided, but now, in a changing climate, some of his actions look like profligacy.

John Thompson moves through the debate on radio like a sapper through a minefield, picking his way through the arguments, manoeuvring with a light touch and, where possible, keeping all his options open. Whether the final paper he submits will have taken on board the progress towards sanity that I think has been achieved so far remains to be seen.

Sunday 14th October

Television has once more brought into millions of homes the reality of the destruction wrought by the IRA. The Grand Hotel bombing in Brighton was centre-stage for nearly every camera crew positioned for the Tory Party conference. Those who claim that television does not mould or influence opinion should look at the coverage of this event. The IRA, far from gaining a victory, will have hardened every heart in the UK against their aims.

We are now at the very centre of discussions on the future of ILR. The fourth and final meeting of DGMM (Director General's Management Meeting) took place on Wednesday and ran from 0800 to 1230. Slowly and painfully we are arriving at conclusions that will determine the reshaping of ILR for the next decade and more. During the past ten years, and in its setting up, radio was considered in much the same light as television: contractors, appointed by the Authority, were regulated and monitored with a degree of attention that left little to the Companies.

Bit by bit, the ecology of the broadcasting terrain has altered: more choice, more freedom – much of it resulting from the political doctrines of the Government and its ambition to promote privatisation, competition and the 'market economy'. Whether for good or ill, radio has been swept up in the gusts of enthusiasm blowing along the corridors of Westminster into Whitehall. I suppose the pirates have been the trigger, releasing a flood of protests from ILR itself.

My speech at lunch to the LRA was followed by the Director of the Association of Independent Radio Contractors (AIRC) Brian West, which threw into stark relief the frustrations of the radio industry. This weekend I have been reading the final draft of John T's paper on radio's future which will be going to the Authority. If accepted, it will produce a distinctly easier climate for the contractor to work within. Radio has to make savings of some £2m per annum if the Companies are to compete in the marketplace with any degree of success.

Friday brought welcome news that four pirate stations operating in London have been raided and the equipment confiscated.

The television companies are pressuring for a seven-minute advertising slot in the hour, instead of the six minutes which has been the rule since ITV was born. Where do I stand? I do not want to see more advertising time permitted. The ITV companies have Channel 4 to promote. They are used to their fat monopoly providing them with a full belly come what may. The thought of actually having to earn money by marketing Channel 4 is something they have little stomach for. No doubt they will deploy arguments centring on the appalling risks they are being forced to take over DBS!

Sunday 21st October

TV-am's coverage of the Brighton bombing has ignited a bitter wave of recrimination from the ITV Companies. George T. received an outspoken letter from the Chairman of Anglia Television, Aubrey Buxton, claiming on behalf of the Board of ITN that TV-am had brought the entire ITV system into disrepute; that ITV was being judged on TV-am's ineffectual coverage of the event. I have counselled GT to maintain a distance from the war of words and in the meantime we will conduct our own enquiry.

ITN's reaction was fairly predictable. ITV wanted a large hand in running breakfast television. They were not offered the contract and felt their rejection bitterly. Then TV-aim failed to reach an agreement with ITN to use their material. So a rift developed which was never bridged. The Brighton bomb has given ITV a perfect platform, not only to attack TV-am's performance but also by innuendo to attack the wisdom of the IBA in appointing TV-am in the first place and also not instructing TV-am to use the services offered by ITN.

There can be little doubt that, as so often, we stand on thin ice. TV-am has been over-extended financially and under-resourced. The Brighton bomb has thrown into sharp relief the inadequacy of TV-am to meet a major challenge of this nature. Once more, it throws also into focus the inadequacies and difficulties that result from our fragmented regional system. Unlike the BBC, who can call upon their national unity to cope with sudden emergencies. As I write this entry, I am unaware of comments that may be in the Sunday papers. Timothy Aitken has now publicly stated that he would welcome ITN involvement as a shareholder in TV-am. My guess is that ITN will now play exceedingly hard to get.

On Wednesday the Authority hosted a lunch for Dr Runcie, the Archbishop of Canterbury. Runcie is a warm, outgoing man with a beady, inquisitive mind and no overriding love for ITV, being 'horrified' by the 'paucity' of research undertaken by the television programme *Credo* which 'purported to survey bishops' attitudes to Christianity'.

Thames is locked in a dispute with its editing staff, who are demanding a 30 per cent rise to compensate them for 'learning to use new technology'! Bryan Cowgill (MD of Thames) has said that he intends for management to operate the station from Monday if the strike is unresolved. This could well have a knock-on effect on the rest of the television system.

Sunday 28th October

Autumn is here. Leaves are falling and so is the ITV's advertising revenue! The market appears to have gone flat. Still, they've enjoyed an unprecedented run of success so a little of what the rest of industry is facing may not be such a bad thing.

I spend a large proportion of my time looking at problems. Two years ago, when I took up the post, I had visions of reflecting quietly on the future of television in the unhurried calm of 'Brompton Towers'. How wrong I was. Sometimes I feel as if I am on a treadmill, or the White Rabbit: 'I'm late, I'm late'. Time races past and I feel I'm struggling to keep up, and succeeding only in keeping my head above water. Enough of these grey thoughts; they match the day outside.

The progress of TV-am after the bomb is occupying my time. I would like to see ITN and TV-am kiss and make up. I held a meeting with David Nicholas (Editor ITN) and Aubrey Buxton to test the idea of bringing both sides together. There will be much work to do if old scars are to heal. ITN still look to get 50 per cent of TV-am's shares, which is a non-starter, but there is the possibility of a three part package. Firstly a bought-in service of ITN news, live from Wells Street. Secondly, a transfer to ITN of TV-am's shares. At a later stage, a further tranche of TV-am shares could be made available.

Timothy Aitken came in to see me and stated bluntly he was looking for some form of marriage. I have now arranged for the two to meet to see if something can be worked out.

On Tuesday I attended The Thirty Club and listened to Robert Maxwell; a cross between Churchill and Napoleon with the underlying manner of the barrow-boy-made-good. Talking of cable, he used an expression which summed up his credo. He said, 'I am convinced that cable will succeed and I am going to be right there, taking money from the consumer in their own home'.

The Thames strike continues. Alan Sapper (Secretary of the ACTT) sought help from the IBA and was advised by GT that it was a matter for ACAS and industrial conciliation. If he wanted to speak to me, I would be happy to see him. No word has come back from Soho Square. Meetings are now due to take place at ACAS.

The final draft of JT's paper on the funding and future of ILR has now been completed and some tussle it took to finish. JT has a dogged streak of determination and hangs on to his point of view like a terrier. In the end I made some changes to the final text which did nothing to foster our relationship. The paper goes to the Sub-Committee of Members this week.

I have spent this weekend working on the draft of my speech to NACRO, 'Crime and Broadcasting'. Not an easy subject to pin down in 30 minutes.

Sunday 4th November

The assassination of Mrs Gandhi erupted on to our breakfast screens on Wednesday. This time, TV-am matched the BBC and managed to acquire, even at that early hour, a turn-out of Indian commentators.

On Saturday I watched the funeral of Mrs Ghandi, switching between the BBC and ITN. The pictures were the same but I thought the BBC's grasp of the moment conveyed more than ITN's commentary, which at times was prosaic in the extreme.

The extraordinary close-ups that television can obtain provide minute insights that even an eye-witness could never hope to see. Two sawn-in-half petrol cans were tipped on to the pyre. They looked oddly out of place, but perhaps for me symbolised more than anything else the essential simplicity and ordinariness that is at the root of any service for those departing this world.

The Thames Television dispute is over. The technicians have settled for a compromise. In fact, it gives Thames management what they were after – a hold on payment for the use of new technology until the new technology is actually used! The dispute marks a significant landmark in television's labour relations and for the first time the unions have found, to their consternation, that the blackmail of a blank screen has been successfully challenged.

On Monday, Giles Shaw, the Minister responsible for broadcasting at the Home office (replacing Douglas Hurd) came to lunch at the IBA. Not an impressive performer and woefully ill-briefed on his subject. I meet him again on Monday and hope to revise my first impressions.

On Tuesday, I lunched at the House of Commons where Northern MPs were invited by the Labour Party. Bob Lorimer, our articulate, hardworking Regional Officer for the area, joined with us in celebrating the 100th birthday of Manny Shinwell. Lively as ever, full of fire in his belly, Manny spoke about 'communications being the key to the advancement of civilisation'. GT presented him with a copy of *The Times* published on the date of his birth, and a bottle of whisky!

I should have mentioned the dinner the previous night, when GT and I were guests of Edmund Dell, Jeremy Isaacs and Justin Dukes at Claridges. A celebration to mark the second year of Channel 4. I am a little sad that, amongst all the tributes to the Channel, no mention is ever made of the part the IBA has played, keeping its cool and standing firm in earlier times when the press, MPs and 'opinion formers' were hellbent on bringing about the extinction of Jeremy and the programmes he was scheduling. Never mind.

The Finance Committee meeting held on Tuesday endorsed my proposals on local radio. I am determined to see a 10 per cent reduction on rentals as a first move and would like to get this announced as soon as possible. The Authority meets next week and, unless my plans go astray, a press conference could be held on Monday 12 November.

On Tuesday evening I went down to Devon to see the IBA's training establishment at Seaton. It brought home to me the need to nurture and protect these roots of our business.

Next week my speech at NACRO: 'Crime and Broadcasting'.

Sunday 11th November

Lunched again on Monday with Giles Shaw. Found him more responsive and able than I had first thought. A useful discussion, but I became worried over his very evident desire to placate the pirates if the DTI succeeded in convictions. I reminded him that there were many honest contenders to run new stations, and it would be wrong to pardon the criminals to the detriment of others. I think he took the point. The idea of a third London station, specialising in ethnic output, appears to have found favour with the Home Office.

In the afternoon I met George Ffitch (MD of LBC) and Christopher Chataway and tried them out on my thoughts on INR – getting rid of IRN and replacing it with a news output on INR, which could be fed to the ILR stations at a greatly reduced charge. The suggestion did not seem to worry either of them unduly.

I was pleased I had spoken to them because that same evening I met with 'the big five' radio companies. George Ffitch was there and I floated the idea, which received a good reaction. I also tried testing the water for an ethnic station. George F exploded, choked and very nearly expired. He resented the idea and said he would resign from LBC and from radio altogether if such a shocking course was adopted.

The Authority duly met on Wednesday and deliberated on my plans for streamlining radio. After a morning's debate they accepted my proposals. JT lost most of his support when he spoke in favour of abandoning much of the role of the Regional Officer. The press will be told on Monday.

On Thursday, lunch at TV-am to meet Lord Matthews, Tim and Jonathan Aitken and Bruce Gyngell. A good opportunity to have my say and alert TV-am to the fact that higher audiences and increased anticipation of quality should be matched with action. They should either do a deal with ITN or put up sufficient new money to resource their enterprise.

In the evening the NACRO speech I have been working hard to prepare on 'Crime and Broadcasting'. It went better than I had hoped for. About 35 minutes of questions afterwards but ones easily dealt with.

Next week Cyprus and then the 'News Conference on Radio' in New York.

Saturday 17th November

The end or the beginning of another week. I feel like a rider going over the course: two jumps clear, one to go. NACRO was first, Cyprus second and New York to come. So far, so good. The NACRO speech seems to rumble on. A letter in *The Times* today calling me 'naïve' and claiming kids do become more violent after watching television. A letter from Denis Forman commending the speech as 'a firm utterance, much wanted from the IBA'.

Last Monday was the unveiling day of our changes to radio financing. About 30 journalists crowded into the conference room to put a barrage of questions. Most interest was centred around the possibility that this was the IBA's first move towards deregulation. I was at pains to maintain that, on the contrary, all the steps we are taking lie within the provisions of the 1981 Broadcasting Act.

The AIRC welcomed the IBA moves, which give the contractors greater responsibility and were obviously delighted at the prospect of a 10 per cent reduction in rentals from April 1985.

The next stage in radio will be to sit down with the Companies and discuss community radio and INR. I suspect I will have the same problem – trying to push along JT – but I think he's now got the message that I'm not easily put off.

To Cyprus on Wednesday with Roma and to the Radio Advertising Conference. Arrived in grand style on Concorde. The first time the plane had landed on the island. It drew hundreds of onlookers and we all descended the stairs on to the tarmac feeling like superstars with flashbulbs popping.

The following morning I gave the keynote speech: 'Radio is not the dodo: it can survive and thrive'.

The bedroom we were given was located beneath the main ventilation system, which rumbled and groaned throughout the night, expelling strong odours of stale chips and fried onions! Wherever we go on IBA business, we always seem to land up in such rooms – near the laundry, kitchens or other unsavoury places.

The Cypriots are a friendly lot, mostly unshaven, and looking like refugees from a spaghetti western. The conference was well attended by advertisers and their agents and the speakers and presentations were first class.

Flew back into winter on Friday and am writing this prior to going to New York tomorrow.

Sunday 25th November

Back to the peace of Ower – sweeping up fallen leaves and clearing gutters. High tides have left long trails of flotsam. A lovely time of year, with winter colours and Beethoven on the wireless.

Television and New York seem so far off, as they are.

New York is bustle. On arrival, we dined with Richard Attenborough and his assistant Claire in a jolly restaurant called 'Something Pink'. The bill came to US $254 – that I do remember!

Dickie is in New York to shoot *Chorus Line* and two days later we saw an eight minute excerpt which had enormous energy and style, and which bodes well for the outcome. Dickie was working amidst the usual chaos and hugely enjoying himself, kissing and cuddling everyone regardless of gender. He brings to everything he does an amazing warmth and sincerity. He gets the best out of people because he makes them bring out their best.

The Emmy Awards presentation was on Tuesday night: drinks beforehand and lots of speculation. I said hello to Sidney Bernstein, who looked, I thought, rather frail, but at 84 you're entitled to look anything you like. He said he was determined to make his speech, come what may, and he did: getting applause when, at the start, he enquired of the audience, 'Can you hear me? Well, I can hear you!'

In the event, ITV and Channel 4 walked off with five awards out of 143 entries from 25 countries. No small achievement. We were all delighted, coming as it did at a time when Michael Grade had recently joined the BBC and was sounding off about the lowering of standards of ITV.

The following evening I spoke briefly at a dinner given by the Museum of Broadcasting, making the point that quality and commitment to the culture of one's own country could, and had, produced programming that appealed to international audiences. 'Be true to thyself' is a maxim that broadcasters would do well to remember.

On Wednesday to lunch with the veteran American newsman Gene Mater. We talked about the fragmentation of the medium. CBS see a part of their future in co-production abroad. The Emmys will certainly have helped the UK programme makers to be taken seriously.

Back to London and mountains of paper to plough through. Next week speaking to staff at Crawley Court and station managers to reassure them that they are not going to be out of a job by Christmas! People hate change and always consider it to be for the worse.

Sunday 2nd December

The British Telecom share issue looks like being a smash hit. Unfortunately, the staff and Members of the Authority are prohibited from purchasing shares because of our business dealings with BT regarding the lines between transmitters and studios. A pity because it looks likely that a sizable premium will be established.

Pirate radio is under the hammer again with a writ being served by Mercury Broadcasting on Radio Jackie. This has the blessing of Michael Havers, the Attorney General, and so my lunch with him a while ago may have paid a small dividend. MH asked to see the *Scum* film. I am afraid he may take an unhelpful view although the matter, when it comes before the Appeal Court, will be out of his province.

On Monday last I attended an ITN board meeting, where a main item was TV-am and a report from Aubrey Buxton about his talks with Timothy Aitken. A rather dismal story emerged. There is little or no will on the part of ITN to treat with TV-am. The ITN board displays the kind of arrogance I find distressing and shows the 'family' of ITV at its least attractive. The fact that ITN lost out in the initial contract awards has left their *amour propre* deeply scarred. They do not wish TV-am success and nothing would have given the Companies and ITN greater satisfaction than to have seen TV-am crumble. It seems unlikely that this will be the case. The company has settled down and is making a serious attempt to get its news commitment strengthened. I am minded to sympathise with TV-am if it is their decision to go it alone.

A report on TV-am comes before the Authority on 15 December, and I have called Timothy and Aubrey in to have a meeting and see if there are stones as yet unturned that could provide the basis for further discussion, but I am doubtful if much will come of it.

On Tuesday a meeting with Quentin Thomas, Head of the Home Office Broadcasting Department, to examine community broadcasting and INR. John Thompson agreed to put down on paper our thinking on community radio. I must remember to make certain that the paper gets a proper airing at the Director General's Management Meeting before it goes out.

Drove down to Crawley Court on Wednesday to attend a meeting of the station managers during their Annual Conference. In the afternoon I addressed some 60 people. It was an important opportunity for me to put over the policy of management towards the changes in the business approach of the IBA: the need for cost control. It seemed to go well. I got a round of applause when I finished (perhaps because I *had* finished!)

On Tuesday next week I meet with the staff unions and I expect this to be somewhat more bumpy.

This week I have been reading Minutes of the GAC which are disturbing. They appear to have abandoned the firm role I would have expected them to adopt to make sure the MAC system for DBS was pursued. Instead, they have agreed a 'wet' approach, hinting that it must be for Government to take the lead. Secondly, they appear to be favouring some weakening of the IBA position regarding terrestrial television rights. I believe that the IBA, just as the BBC, must have the right to decide what programmes it will allow to be shown first on DBS. Our plain duty is to protect the existing independent television stations and that can best be achieved by ensuring that ITV provides the best possible product for terrestrial viewers. I do not think I am at one with George Thomson on this point, and it will be interesting to see how matters develop.

Sunday 9th December

Another week of treadmill activity. I wish I could find moments that give me genuine pleasure or satisfaction. The task often seems like that of a caulker, consistently pressing substances between the planks to keep the ship afloat.

Last Monday I had a successful meeting with Timothy Aitken and Aubrey Buxton. The occasion was an important one because I felt that something had to be done to bring TV-am and ITN closer together so that a working arrangement could be advanced in the wake of the Brighton bombing. I was pleasantly surprised when Aubrey agreed to secret meetings with Ian Irvine, Chairman of TV-am's Executive Committee, to consider and formulate a deal both sides could put to their respective boards. While this was going on, I agreed a moratorium should be declared on TV-am's actions to build up their newsgathering resources. I subsequently wrote to Timothy suggesting a two-month period while talks took place.

In the evening, with Roma to the Radio Advertising Awards at Grosvenor House. A disappointing selection of commercials. It seemed to me that most of them had been thought up in the hope of impressing the judges and winning prizes rather than to impress audiences and win sales for advertisers. After the Awards ceremony we attempted to dance, but the band and amplification were quite deafening. Is this just me getting old?

On Tuesday to lunch at the Mansion House, hosted by the Chairman of the Police Committee of the Corporation of London. Just as well I turned up because, although not at the top table, I was prominently positioned directly under the eye of the Chairman, Edwina Coven and the Home Secretary, who made a good speech, praising the British bobby. Willie Whitelaw was a few places along, looking, I thought, rather peaky. He seems to have lost weight and with it bounce! Still, he has agreed to be our star speaker next year at the Banqueting Hall. The event will replace the IBA's lectures that have grown repetitive and boring, with the same old faces turning up each time to gossip and brag over the chicken and plonk provided by the IBA afterwards in the Broadcasting Gallery.

In the afternoon, a fairly sweaty meeting with the staff union representatives, deeply miffed at the IBA's recent decisions taken on radio and Regional Offices. The main grouse was lack of consultation. They have a point, but I rather doubt whether I would have got what I wanted from endless meetings. Still, perhaps I should have tried first. The decisions reached have not lifted staff morale, rather the reverse. They see, I think, GT and JW as the unacceptable face of commercialism. I am speaking to managers at Brompton Road tomorrow: not an easy task and one I shall be pleased to see behind me.

In the evening to dinner with the ITV chairmen in the House of Lords, hosted by GT. Surprisingly, many of the chairmen have never met one another.

The subject of the role of the Authority in determining whether ITV companies could transmit material first on DBS came up for debate at the Authority meeting on Wednesday. The Members endorsed my view that the IBA should have the power of veto, but asked that I should consult the Companies on the best way of expressing this. It will be interesting to see what the Companies say at the GAC.

On the plane home from the EBU (European Broadcasting Union) meeting, I read the report prepared by Andrew Quinn, Chief Executive of Granada TV, on DBS. A copy has obviously been leaked to the *Sunday Times* which predicts the cost of Unisat will force the consortium to look elsewhere for hardware. ITV should never have got involved in the whole bizarre enterprise.

Sunday 16th December

This has been BBC-bashing week. A week in which the BBC disclosed their ambitions for their license fee: £67 per annum, an increase of 41 per cent since 1981 as the critics were quick to point out.

Beeb-bashing is, I suppose, an acknowledged pastime when the time of review is upon us. This time round, the BBC's strategy is obviously to tell the worst and hope for the best but, for perhaps the first time in many years, there is a very distinct groundswell of discontent. This is partly because of an apparent lack of leadership and partly because the BBC flagship of respectable and admired successes has not been in such evidence as in former years. *The Thorn Birds* saga – seen as a slithering towards mediocrity and an attempt in the crudest way to compete against ITV for audiences by abandoning *Panorama* for the occasion – has stood against them on the record.

Added to this is the well-orchestrated assembly of advertisers and their agents conducted by the newspaper lobby, who relentlessly demand advertising to help balance the BBC's deficit. Mrs T. appears willing to consider a change, but it could be to put the frighteners on the politburo of Portland Place. The other threat against the vast broadcasting battlements of the BBC is to axe Breakfast Television and BBC Local Radio. Stuart Young, BBC Chairman, and Alasdair Milne may come in for yet more barracking and disillusion when the accountants – Peat, Marwick & Mitchell – provide their financial review of the Beeb's husbandry.

Christmas fever is seeping down corridors and into offices and boardrooms like an invisible effluence. If every company in the land were to put the money spent on desk diaries and cards into helping mitigate the suffering of others, Christmas might have real purpose.

Next week, the Authority considers the progress of TV-am. I wrote recently to Timothy Aitken inviting him to meet with ITN and work out a sensible way of combining the two talents. I have now had word with both Timothy and Aubrey and from their comments it is clear to me that a little banging of heads is necessary. I shall set about this by inviting David Nicholas, Chief Executive of ITN, to come and talk to me.

Boxing Day, 26th December

The carol singers have departed and Christmas lies behind us for another year. Another week when the BBC came in for every sort of brickbat. The worst, though, is probably over. Giles Shaw – Douglas Hurd's successor as Minister of State at the Home Office – said in the House of Commons on Friday 21st December that 'a limited injection of advertising was a tempting proposition (for the BBC) but the line between feast and famine in marketing and advertising was very thin'. If advertising were introduced into BBC programmes, it would have to be done gradually with the license fee revenue remaining the major part of the Corporation's income for some time.

The levy arguments are surfacing at the same time with speculation mounting in the press that the Treasury will produce some mix of revenue and profit-based levy. All in all, all the Companies must be approaching 1985 with considerable doubts and hesitation.

A paper by the DBS Consortium has now been circulated and a letter sent to Leon Brittan clearly stating that, if DBS is going to have a chance of success, there must be a re-think of Unisat costs. The Report recommends an open tender approach. They also want a contract life of 15 years instead of 10, and are contemplating the introduction of advertising from the start of DBS. They also endorse 20/10 MAC which now means the whole of Europe has accepted the MAC system.

On Wednesday 19 December we held our last Authority meeting of 1984. A Report on TV-am went through without much comment. I spoke about the meetings I have been holding with both parties. Also under review was the extremely difficult question of permitting Public Service Broadcasts on the subject of counselling for homosexuals in the light of the emergence of the AIDS virus. The Authority Members were divided on the subject. There is a strong case for permitting PSBs on this subject, but this view is not sustained by the findings of the research we privately carried out. Whatever our decision, there will be an outcry either from the pro or anti lobby; both are highly vocal; both will demand to know our reasons whatever decision we make. I offered to take back the subject and come forward again with a proposal. I would like to see PSB carrying homosexual counselling information.

At the beginning of Christmas week, on Monday 17 December, Roma and I went to see *Cosi Fan Tutti* performed by the English National Opera company at the Coliseum. We were guests of Luke Rittner, Chairman of the Arts Council of Great Britain, and it was the night of the announcement by the Arts Council of their reduced grants to the National Theatre and the Coliseum. Luke appeared very relaxed and, in fact, snoozed away quietly for part of the First Act!

Next year I have agreed to become President of the Television & Radio Industries Club – a prospect which gives me little pleasure and will, I am afraid, consume more time than it should.

I went in to the IBA on Christmas Day with a small gift for the girls who work in 'Lines', the operation within Brompton Road which links the various transmitters together for networking purposes; an important job and one which gets little notice or praise.

With the passing of the old year in a few days, some good news from Channel 4. For the first time last week it gained more audiences than the BBC, snooker being the main reason for the increase in ratings.

One further postscript to the year. When Michael Havers came to lunch he asked to view a copy of *Scum*, rather to our vexation. This week GT received a letter from Michael which is interesting for what it does not say:

14 December 1984,

Dear George,

I have now had a chance to look at the recording of the film *Scum* and read the judgment of the Divisional Court. I think you are being unnecessarily concerned about the effect of that judgment, which I think was based upon quite extraordinary facts which I think will be most unlikely to reoccur.

I think, if you accept the general evidence contained in the judgment, which, curiously enough, could not agree among themselves whether the film should be shown, you will have very little to worry about.

Yours ever,

Michael

We shall see.

On 24 December, Sean Day-Lewis, writing in the *Daily Telegraph* about the year's events, got it wrong when he said, 'The other side (ITV) also found problems. The Court agreed with the censorship lobby that ITV should not have shown the cinema version of *Scum*'.

Thursday 27th December

At least I hope Christopher Dunkley got it right when, reviewing the year in the *Financial Times*, he wrote: 'When the media sociologists of the third millennium come to write the history of television, it could be this that they see as the most significant aspect of 1984. Perhaps it was the influence of the new Director General, John Whitney .... Best of all, the Independent Broadcasting Authority seemed to be changing its ideas and lining itself up solidly with the Companies.'

I read this today and like it:

'He who kisses the day as it flies
Lives in eternity's sunrise'.
William Blake

1985

Sunday 6th January

A quiet week, with people returning to work like moles caught in the sunlight. Paul Fox got a CBE, which pleased us as this Honour had been strongly recommended by the IBA for his sterling services to television.

I have made a New Year resolution not to go out so much in the evenings, and do less!

Sunday 13th January

My promise for the New Year still appears to be holding good: another reasonably quiet week apart from demands to bring hellfire and damnation down on the heads of those who make *Spitting Image* for making a caricature of Princess Margaret when it was known she was in hospital for a check up.

I am afraid that I have a particularly nasty, not to say deadly, time bomb ticking away beneath me. If it goes off, at least I know I have done everything possible to defuse it.

A book by Barrie Gunter, a member of IBA staff, 'Dimensions of television violence' is shortly to be published. I was invited to chair a press gathering, and consequently a brief was written and circulated to those who would be attending. Unfortunately, one of the book's main findings was that home produced drama is perceived as more violent than its overseas counterparts. This is not a very satisfactory finding and ought to have been properly discussed with the Companies and the Authority before it hits the headlines. I have now sent a letter to the Companies enclosing a copy of the book, which I hope will calm them. Time will tell, but I fear the anti-violence lobby will pounce on this to make more brouhaha about violence on television.

Next week the Authority meets to consider the subscription level for Channel 4 and S4C. My own inclination is to give Channel 4 a budget which would be at the upper end of the scale – something of the order of £128m.

The Companies are bound to whinge at this because they have seen a recent downturn in revenues and they are worried about possible levy implications, but I think Channel 4 needs to be financed sufficiently so that it can extend the area of programming that fell within its remit.

More storm cones are being raised over radio finances for Companies who claim to be in peril. I have called a meeting of the Companies next week to take stock, and also called a meeting of the Unions.

No word yet from Government about their views on the DBS Report submitted to Leon Brittan just before Christmas. It is rumoured that Unisat will reconsider their quotation of approximately £80m per annum, but they will have to come down a long way to satisfy the consortium. The prospect that the IBA should advertise for other takers is being canvassed. I would favour this. I have never been happy with the current proposals.

Sunday 20th January

Television is becoming more like Fleet Street every day – the less salubrious parts.

This week it is the saga of *Dallas* that has hit the headlines. Opening my newspaper over breakfast last Thursday, I was greeted with a banner headline: 'ITV SNATCHES DALLAS FROM THE BEEB'. Thames Television had gone behind the back of the BBC and done a deal sewing up the rights for UK presentation of 30 episodes. The method adopted by Thames in securing this 'coup' was nothing short of conduct unbecoming a gentleman, there being an unwritten code that any major American series should not be bid for or bought by the opposition during a current run. This gentleman's agreement has not been observed by Thames.

I invited Bryan Cowgill of Thames to see me that same morning. He confirmed that the contract had been signed and that there was no going back. I said the situation was one that was far from satisfactory and would reflect badly on both the IBA and ITV. I reminded Bryan that the Authority approves schedules and could stop *Dallas* being broadcast if it considered that otherwise the wider interests of broadcasting policy would be harmed. A number of Companies have already indicated that they would refuse to transmit the programmes.

Quite apart from these factors, I wondered how Thames could justify their action at a time when so much attention was focused on BBC and ITV funding and resources. What was galling, and embarrassing, for the other Companies was that there had been no prior consultation and that the previous day the Companies had presented their case to the IBA for holding down increases to Channel 4's subscription. The cost of the Thames purchase was almost double that paid by the BBC. I told Cowgill that he should hand the series back to the BBC on the grounds that he had been over enthusiastic in his desire to acquire the series and that, since other ITV Companies were not prepared to transmit the programmes, we – the IBA and the Companies – would be seen as responsible for preventing viewers from watching a popular programme.

On Tuesday I cancelled a visit to a Management Meeting out of London, to attend a hurriedly-called Authority meeting on *Dallas*. At the end of about an hour and a half, Members endorsed the proposal I put to them – that Dallas be handed back to the BBC. After much to-ing and fro-ing, Thames held a Board meeting and subsequently informed me they were not prepared to hand back the series. They will come in and talk next week.

Sir Robert Fraser died today. He was 80. As one of the principal architects of ITV, and the first Director General of the IBA, he made an outstanding contribution to the esteem in which independent broadcasting is now held.

Sunday 27th January

Sad news. Yesterday George telephoned me to say that David Harlech, Chairman of HTV, had been killed in a motor accident driving home the previous night. He was a fine man and will be a loss to television. He did much behind the scenes to oil the wheels and was never pushing out in front to capture headlines.

This has been a week of sad news. Lady Fraser died two days after her husband. She had been ill for a long time, and Bob had been a tireless comrade to her. I hope they are happy together. Sir Robert's funeral is on Tuesday and the memorial service in about two weeks.

The *Dallas* saga continues. Thames have now said privately that they will return the series to the BBC. Hugh Dundas, Chairman of Thames, is flying someone out to L.A. for a meeting next week. George is having a word with Stuart Young (Chairman of the BBC) to tell him of developments. Awkward questions are already being asked about the nature of the arrangements broadcasters make between themselves over acquired American series. MPs – John Gorst in particular – believe that there are sufficient grounds to table an Early Day Motion.

I finally made *The Sun* – surely the greatest accolade! Headed 'Come off it', it read 'John Whitney is the Director General of the Independent Broadcasting Authority. He is also a twit. He solemnly tells Bryan Cowgill and Thames Television to give back the *Dallas* series to the BBC in the interest of "gentlemanly conduct". Come off it, Mr W, Thames are playing in the harsh world of big business, not on the croquet lawn. They won this series by offering more money than the opposition. Just how does that make them more wicked than J.R. himself?' (Monday 21 January)

Another drama, of a different kind, began to unspool later in the week. This time it was Television South West and a call from Sir Brian Bailey to say that his Board had taken the decision to oust Kevin Goldstein-Jackson as Managing Director. Apparently Kevin went off on holiday leaving his subordinates with the unpleasant and difficult task of making top staff redundant. This turned out to be the final straw and the Board decided to act. The announcement was due at 4pm yesterday. I scanned the Saturday papers but no mention was made of a boardroom upheaval. Kevin is not a person to take things quietly. As one of the principal founders of TSW and a large shareholder, he will not give in without a fight.

On Thursday (24 January), Leon Brittan answered a question from Mr Hayward. 'Would Mr B. make a statement about the development of community radio?' Leon gave a long response which amounted to the Government endorsing the development of both low-powered neighbourhood radio and 'community of interest' stations serving an ethnic minority for example. I read the statement out at a meeting of the Radio Consultative Committee that I was chairing. The IBA will have to act to ensure there isn't widespread chaos.

I am writing this diary entry before reading the Sunday papers. There may be much to reflect upon. On Monday, for example, Channel 4 will be broadcasting extracts from the Clive Ponting trial, with actors reading to camera material taken down by shorthand during the proceedings. Ponting has been charged with leaking an internal MoD document concerning the General Belgrano, the Argentinian cruiser which British forces sank during the 1982 Falklands War, killing 360 people. The government line had been that the Belgrano was threatening British lives when it was sunk. But the document leaked by Ponting indicated it was sailing out of the exclusion zone. Its publication was a huge embarrassment for Mrs Thatcher's government.

This programme is bound to cause consternation and already has, because I received a call from Quentin Thomas at the Home Office enquiring if Authority Members were aware of the programme. I said they were!

I nearly forgot to mention one of the week's highlights and a television breakthrough. The televising of the Lords began on Wednesday. The Commons cannot be far behind, and about time.

Sunday 3rd February

The funeral of Sir Robert Fraser was held on Tuesday: a quiet affair which purposely I did not attend as it was intended for close friends and family.

Instead, I attended a TRIC event with an after-lunch speech by Alasdair Milne. During question and answer time, Alasdair sounded off about the difference in costs between the BBC and ITV. I pointed out in response that the BBC was a unified system while ITV was federal. Thus ITV had to duplicate its unit costs as each Company had to support its own sales, accountancy, engineering, publicity and costs associated with running a separate enterprise. To my astonishment, Alasdair, instead of arguing back and defending his statement, simply said, 'I take your point'.

Dallas has gone underground this week. I bumped into Stuart, who said they appreciated the stand we were taking and hoped for news soon.

Hugh Dundas has undertaken to open talks with Worldvision Enterprises tomorrow. Much depends on the outcome. HD would like to see Bryan Cowgill as the next Chairman of Thames. He stands a slim chance of taking up the role if he fails to unscramble the mess he's got himself and the Company into.

Paul Fox, writing in *The Listener* on 24th January, summed it up with characteristic crispness: 'The danger is that the damage *The Thorn Birds* did to the BBC, *Dallas* may now inflict on ITV'.

The Channel 4 programme on the Ponting trial has been generally regarded by critics as so boring that it would only send people off to sleep. However, looking at Friday's offering, I noticed that the producer was breaking up the cross-examination by giving the questions and answers to different newsreaders. I telephone David Glencross this afternoon to point out that this was a departure from the first evening's offering, when chunks of the narrative were read by one newscaster. It would be too awful if the judge considered that the change was in contempt. I don't think David was overly concerned and he pointed out, quite rightly, that Mark Carlisle, QC for Channel 4, was in the studio vetting every camera move, so perhaps I am being over-cautious.

Kevin Goldstein-Jackson's departure caught the trade headlines and slowly the causes behind his resignation are emerging.

The DTI sent in their heavy mob and took Radio Jackie off the air on Friday, and about time. Radio Jackie have said they will be back and the DTI have said so will they!

Sunday 10th February

Radio Jackie resurfaced and so did the DTI. Radio Jackie again responded by saying they would be back on air, but must have had a change of heart as they've now said they've had enough.

Another week with the future of *Dallas* still in the melting pot. Bryan Cowgill flew to Los Angeles to see the man from Worldvision. Hugh Dundas telephoned George on Friday to arrange a meeting with the four of us on Monday. The results of the visit are not likely to be good. I had a word with David Plowright to see if he could throw any light on the sort of contract that Thames might have signed. He said that it would probably be a fairly standard one, allowing Thames the UK rights, which would mean that Thames could be in a position to negotiate with the BBC. David P. says that the Companies will pay the difference – about $10,000 per episode – as he thinks the BBC will go to about $50,000. If there is a will on the part of Thames to return *Dallas* to the BBC, I am sure a way can be found.

On Monday last, I attended a screening of the first episode of the new Granada series *History of Television* – a magnificent opening episode which should again give Granada the documentary equivalent of *Jewel in the Crown*. I had to leave early to meet Michael Shea, the Queen's Press Secretary. This was a preliminary discussion to set the agenda for a visit to the IBA by the Queen later in the year. Some good ideas emerged and those he will put to Philip Moore, personal private secretary to the Queen, so that detailed planning can be got underway.

On Tuesday I attended the annual lunch at the Savoy of *What the Papers Say*, and enjoyed the traditional fare of oysters and steak-and-kidney pudding. Guest of Honour was Norman Tebbit, who looked woefully pale but had lost none of his 'bovver boy' image and lashed into television for trivialising the news. Sitting amongst so many television people, and enjoying their hospitality, it seemed an unnecessary stance to take but it is typical of the man and people admire Tebbit not for his politics but for his style.

Problems with Central Television. The Chairman, Gordon Hobday, is retiring and a successor has to be found. Gordon Hobday very properly came to us to see how we react to the various proposals. I think he would have liked John Jackson to succeed him but JJ represents a large shareholder interest and would not, on those grounds, be acceptable. There must be somebody from the area who would fit the bill.

No news yet on the satellite front. I hear that the consortium have definitely turned down Unisat but whether the Home Secretary will now try and free Unisat's hand to reduce their costs only time will tell.

Sunday 17th February

The *Dallas* saga continues. At the beginning of the week, Hugh Dundas and Bryan Cowgill came to see George and me. Bryan's mission to America had not proved a success. We sent them away to think again. I believe that Bryan has no real will to hand over the series and is playing for time. We meet again tomorrow and I think I will say to them that they should simply tell Worldvision that Thames wishes to pass back *Dallas* to the BBC on terms already agreed.

Spent the greater part of the week wrestling with a programme C4 wants to transmit, which contains interviews with Civil Servants disclosing information clearly protected under Section 2 of the Official Secrets Act. Jeremy Isaacs was pushing for approval to transmit yesterday, but I told him that it must be a decision for the Authority. I very much doubt whether Members will agree to show it. I am against broadcasting the programme on the grounds that the people concerned in the programme should have, and could have, properly discharged their duty by submitting their evidence to an appropriate office in Whitehall rather than to a programme company for transmission on television.

The Ponting Case, I do not believe, has direct relevance to the principle. Should a publicly accountable body – in this case the IBA – be a party to an action which is clearly endorsing an act of lawbreaking? I think not.

On Tuesday I attended a dinner at Leeds Castle to consider the future of local radio, hosted by the IPA. A very grand location which seemed somewhat at odds with the subject of community broadcasting.

On Wednesday off to Liverpool and a visit to the *Brookside* set. *Brookside* is now an established twice-weekly series on Channel 4, attracting some five to six million viewers per episode. The credit for the programme must go to Phil Redmond, the enterprising Executive Producer and creator of other television series, including *Grange Hill*. Phil represents the new generation of television entrepreneur: very laid back and professional; full of exciting ideas and notions; a man who will undoubtedly wish to contest Granada's franchise in years to come.

A visit to Granada's newly purchased site in the dockland area, now being developed. This will be used as a base for Granada's news-gathering operations.

Then on to Radio City and a tour of 'Beatle City', a mecca funded by the city in memory of the Beatles. Very stylish and attractive. I hope it proves financially viable – it deserves to succeed.

On Friday to Winchester, and an exhilarating tour of departments concerned with transmitter erection and maintenance. A good team.

Next week, Monte Carlo or bust! Today spent in tidying up my keynote speech.

Sunday 24th February

A week of happenings:
- Monte Carlo and the Advertising Conference
- The Fourth Channel subscriptions
- The banning of the film on MI5 surveillance

1985

- The row with ITN over Mrs T's broadcast from Congress
- The Queen Mother on *Spitting Image*

There were many long faces in Monte Carlo when news of our apportionment of Fourth Channel subscriptions was announced. Channel 4 should be pleased because their apportionment came well up to their highest hopes. They had asked for £34m but knew that would be out of reach. The Companies rather hoped that their falling revenues in November and December, together with a disappointing January would have made us more sympathetic to their pleas for a much lower subscription. On the whole, they took their medicine well but I expect we will get some shot and shell when they've had time to consider the figures away from the brandy-impregnated air of Monte Carlo.

Dallas continues to fill the newspapers. This time the BBC decided to go on showing it in sequence instead of withdrawing it as they had intended. Thames have now sent out a letter to all Contractors (including LWT – much to their amusement) inviting each Company to tell them if they will transmit *Dallas* and, if not, what reasons they would give. Hugh Dundas claims that this evidence will make it easier for the Company to confront Worldvision when they come to negotiate the series back to the BBC. I think, however, that it is a Thames ploy to demonstrate to us the extent of support for the programme and therefore a case for showing the series on ITV.

The Authority viewed the programme made by the independent company '20/20 Vision', entitled *MI5's Official Secrets*, on Wednesday morning. George and I had breakfast before the viewing with David Glencross, Barbara Hosking, Shirley Littler and Brian Rook. We discussed how to handle the press. I think that, by this time, everyone knew that the showing to the Authority would lead to a decision not to transmit, and this was the case. The film makes allegations about the surveillance methods used by the security services against individuals and organisations who are not suspected of terrorist or subversive activities. Cathy Massiter, an MI5 officer who left the service after 12 years, made disclosures in the programme that the telephone lines of the Campaign for Nuclear Disarmament (CND) and National Council for Civil Liberties (NCCL) had been tapped. The MI5 had classified these organisations as 'subversive' which in her opinion was being overzealous. The papers exploded into headlines after Channel 4 showed the film to journalists and MPs. The real attention centred not on our decision but on the content of the programme.

Just before I left Monte Carlo I had a meeting with David Nicholas, Chief Executive of ITN, who had flown over specially to catch me before I left. He was mightily upset by the IBA's decision not to mandate transmission of Mrs T's speech from Congress. Three major Companies had refused to show it: Central, Granada and Yorkshire. David Glencross, (IBA's Director of Television) had told ITN that he would not permit some to take it and some not, as this might be interpreted as political bias. David Nicholas told me that it was the worst decision that had been taken in all his experience. Aubrey Buxton then got into an even greater tizz and wrote a singularly abrupt letter to GT referring to me simply as 'Whitney'.

The real trouble over the affair, to my mind, was the lack of time to consider the matter. Personally, I would have liked to see the programme transmitted but I was not prepared to overrule David Glencross.

The pressure on the BBC to accept advertising still continues. There was a strong move from advertisers at Monte Carlo to suggest that all the arguments put forward by the advocates of the status quo were falling on deaf ears. I have come to the conclusion that ITV and the IBA are in real danger of wrong-footing ourselves. The satellite consortium still maintains that they do not want advertising to fund the DBS project. The advertising business interprets this as another example of the ITV Contractors calling the shots and protecting their monopoly. I believe that ITV should abandon the pretence that DBS is part of public service broadcasting.

Tonight, *Spitting Image* is going to lampoon the Queen Mother and everyone is thoroughly upset – including, it is said, the producers. If the producers are unhappy, who the hell is controlling the production? More next week!

Sunday 3rd March

We are probably the least-loved statutory body in the United Kingdom or, at least, the least-loved in the last seven days, due to the decision we took to ban the showing of the Channel 4 MI5 secrets programme.

I have never seen such condemnation of one of our decisions. The *Guardian* led the chase, printing the full text of the programme. *The Observer*'s Sunday leader was headed 'IBA as Nanny!'. Earlier in the week, the Prime Minister passed the 'tapping' buck to Lord Bridges and his Committee on telephone tapping. Labour MPs insisted that this wasn't going nearly far enough. Gerald Kaufmann called our action 'pusillanimous'. Not one voice was raised in our defence. Perhaps we had got it wrong but, while the Official Secrets Act remains on the statute books, we would have been in breach of the law. Whether we should have taken our courage in our hands and 'transmit and be damned' is the question.

Those critics of our decision now argue that there is nothing left to prevent us from showing the film. After all, they argue, video cassettes and tapes are freely available and a number of public showings in cinemas are taking place, backed by the 'generosity' of Richard Branson who has stepped in to ensure a wider public showing. Both Channel 4 and the independent producers have written asking us to reconsider our ban.

The Authority holds its meeting on Wednesday and obviously the question of reviewing their earlier decision will be on the Agenda. It is likely to prove difficult. On the one hand, nothing has changed that would make showing the film acceptable within the law. On the other hand, now that so much has come out in other media, should not the IBA make the programme available to its audience and let people judge for themselves?

I gave a lecture to the Royal Society of Arts this week, which was well received, but the MI5 issue necessitated that I start with a longish statement on our reasons for banning the programme. I gained the impression that, if there had been a vote taken that evening, our action would have found endorsement, but maybe that is just me looking for a ray of hope in an otherwise doleful and disgruntling week.

Sunday 10th March

I talk much of 'shaping the future'. I seriously wonder if I can shape the present! So much seems in chaos: radio, pressure on revenue, disillusionment amongst the Contractors, the threat of added competition (possibly without fair balance), complaints and criticism from AIRC that we over-regulate, that we cost too much and even so our transmitters fail to match the BBC's. Disenchantment is rife. The unions claim that we went too fast and too far, constructing smaller and smaller radio stations that we should have known would prove unviable. Add to all this the radio companies' deep suspicion of the IBA and its intentions, and ability, and you have a situation that will only be exacerbated when the next station failures through bankruptcy make their impact.

Television is little better. The IBA decision to award Channel 4 a higher than expected subscription from the Companies has angered and surprised them. Television revenue since October/November 1984 has lost its buoyancy. The threat of the Government to introduce advertising on the BBC has not receded. DBS hangs around the necks of the Contractors like an albatross. Their only purpose in remaining in the consortium is to give themselves some protection from the IBA in 1989 when contracts come up for re-advertisement. Now ITCA has turned on the IBA and thrown out our proposals for mid-term financing of the system. This has been under review for some little while but the Companies' formal response was made just before the weekend. In it, they attack the IBA for over-spending on engineering, research and development, site maintenance and construction. Competition, or the threat of it, has sharpened their teeth. They question the need for the standards the engineering division have proposed.

Our problems lie deep in our own infrastructure. For years the IBA has dictated its own terms, its own pace and its own criteria. Successive managements have ensured security and certainty for their staff, with little or no regard for the future and, to be fair to them, few could possibly have seen the rate of change which has taken place in the last five to seven years. The IBA is over-staffed and has been for a long time. The introduction of the Fourth Channel gave a reason to pull out the stops and staff-up to a level that, once on the payroll, could not be shed. Now we are saddled with a workforce that has had to be absorbed and that has meant creating jobs. Self-justification is the ruin of good business practise!

On Wednesday the Authority met. Pressure had been building during the week for a lifting of the ban on *MI5's Official Secrets*. Not one single column inch in any newspaper took our side. We appeared more and more isolated, more and more out of step, more and more 'wet'. When Michael Havers, Attorney General, announced on Tuesday that Cathy Massiter would not be prosecuted, the last impediment was removed. Allen & Overy, our solicitors, argued that we would still be in breach of the law. Our position has become untenable. If we were to stand out and refuse to show the programme, we would look simply stubborn.

The Authority took four minutes to reconsider its position. I telephoned Jeremy Isaacs and gave him the news.

On Thursday I appeared on *Right to Reply*, answering questions and putting the IBA's view to Gus McDonald and to Roger Boulton, who had written strong words about our initial decision in *Broadcast Magazine* and *Time Out*.

MI5's Official Secrets was shown on Friday evening, along with my interview. Miss Massiter came out of it as the only really sane person.

On Friday I lunched Sidney Bernstein at the Garrick. Now somewhere between 82 and 85, he is incredibly spry. We talked about DBS, competition from European satellites, the BBC and the implications that advertising on it would have on our terrestrial system.

Sidney felt saddened that television appeared no longer to be considered a national asset; that the structure he had worked so hard to build was in danger of crashing. He spoke fervently and passionately about the need for television to retain its core of young talent; that only through encouraging talent, as Granada had done, would film and television prosper in this country. He finished his meal with figs, cream and stone ginger!

Finally, in what was a black week, we paid our respects to Sir Robert Fraser. The good and great turned out. Willie Whitelaw took a pew in the front and faces from the past were scattered among the congregation. Brian Young read from T.S. Elliot's *Four Quartets*: 'Home is where one starts from. As we grow older the world becomes stranger, the pattern more complicated of dead and living.' I read the second reading from John Stuart Mill's *On Liberty*. It was a simple service with the address given by our Deputy Director General, Tony Pragnell.

Sunday 17th March

Probably the bleakest week of my time at the IBA: the combination of events coming together in a most unholy alliance.

I suppose the backwash of *20/20 Vision* is still rocking the boat, in what seems more and more to be an oily swell. Eric Kaufman, in the Commons, 12 March: 'In recent weeks particular disquiet has been expressed following the allegations made in the television programme 'MI5's Official Secrets', the programme that was cravenly banned by the IBA'.

On Tuesday John Thompson, Director of Radio, held a meeting of senior executives to look into further cost savings in the radio branch. It turned into a depressing examination and ended ironically with an additional £10,000 added on to research and development!

The sad fact has to be faced that, while the IBA operates as regulator and provider of services, the burden on the radio Companies is out of all proportion to the actual service provided. The overheads, including staffing, were geared to an age where the hurricane wind of change was not even a draught along the corridors of Whitehall. In some respects there is a similarity with the current dispute over the funding of the Arts. The excellence of the theatre in the 60s and 70s that led to the support of the Arts has been replaced by the Thatcherite dictat of the survival of the fittest. In many ways the IBA resembles the beleaguered National Theatre with few friends and a growing number of enemies. In this new climate of competition and widening choice, the dreadnoughts of the Reithian age look vulnerable and anachronistic.

We cannot conceal this vulnerability. It lies exposed.

We have a meeting with the radio Contractors on Tuesday and I have half a mind to permit them a sight of our internal budgets! It would give them a heart attack, but might bring home the reality that we have to cut internal costs. The times of plenty have ended, and with them the atmosphere of 'spend, spend, spend'. The ITV Companies are resentful and indignant that they were not listened to with sympathy. Bill Brown, acting as spokesman, put it simply and directly: 'We feel that we have been treated less than equally'. There was a chill in the room which deepened still more when the subject of increased rentals was raised under the appropriate Agenda item. The Companies feel they have been dealt a double blow, and this at a time when the future of DBS means a high risk investment.

Looking back over the events of the past weeks, I misjudged the extent of the fall-off in revenue. Setting a high Channel 4 subscription highlights the burden that the Companies will have to bear. The infuriating thing is that if only I had had more sense, I could have minimised the aggravation of the rental uplift by bringing in a more modest subscription. I have played my cards badly and now reap the results – anger from the Contractors, fear and apprehension internally from staff looking at the cuts that might have to come. I have no one to blame but myself. That is why I conclude this diary entry as I started: 'probably the bleakest week of my time with the IBA'.

Sunday 24th March

This week, thank goodness, back on an even keel, relatively speaking.

The great debate over the BBC's funding still excites enormous interest. It is difficult to sort out which cries for change come from voices without an axe to grind. Everyone seems to be joining in with a ferocity which makes the Christians being thrown to the lions in Roman times appear child's play! Where are the voices that used once to speak up for the Corporation? Is everyone too frightened of the Wicked Witch of Westminster? Or has she cast a spell over the lot of them?

The BBC have been less than adroit at arguing their case for the status quo to continue. The hiring of Michael Grade, hailed as a sort of Second Coming, was badly mistimed if the BBC wished to rest their case on 'excellence', but those that took that particular decision must have thought that, with Mrs T snorting fire and brimstone, the introduction of MG would demonstrate that Auntie was prepared to adopt a more competitive stance.

Unfortunately, it seems to have had the effect of illustrating to the world that the BBC shake-up might as well extend to a major shake-up of all the cherished sacred cows, including the question of advertising as a source of revenue. Stuart Young's determination to see the BBC remain true to its founder has apparently confounded and angered Madam T, who believes that Young has 'gone native'.

The Peat Marwick Mitchell rebuke to the BBC for overstating its funding was a serious own goal. For Stuart Young then to publicly take to task his own *Nine O'clock News* team for inaccuracies must have been doubly perplexing and difficult to accept by the stalwarts at the Beeb. Then the *Doctor Who* furore, when Michael Grade 'rested' the series, much to the dismay of viewers.

Just when a statesmanlike stance was called for, there was another row over the switching of drama to BBC 2. The BBC's case has not been helped either by ex-employees making disparaging comparisons to the budgets employed by Channel 4's independent Companies, which are about half those of comparable programmes; the BBC's *Eastenders* being put alongside Channel 4's *Brookside*.

Peter Utley, Leader writer on the *Telegraph* was guest speaker at a Thirty Club dinner at Claridges that I attended this week. He ranted and raved against the BBC for the greater part of his speech. There was no one from the BBC present to defend itself. I spoke up but, in the atmosphere of considerable dislike for the Beeb, it had little effect. It was as if for all these years there has been a deep, slumbering resentment against the BBC which has suddenly been released, like a genie from a bottle.

On Monday I went to an ITN Board meeting. The assembled MDs were polite, but a little distant. The GAC still casts its shadow. ITN is slowly coming round to consider what it should be doing to keep live throughout 24 hours. Its capability does not include manning between 0945 and 1145. At long last there might be a sensible solution, if a relationship can be established between TV-am and ITN, but ITN have been considering going it alone. If they did, this would cost about £250k and would then only give them one self-operating studio with a talking head, highlighting again the mealy-mouthed attitude of the Companies when it comes to spending money on news facilities.

The obvious solution would be to involve TV-am and, in emergency, keep their studios open and share services with ITN. There will need to be some shelving of pride, but it must make sense to both services. I shall do what I can to get the two sides together.

Channel 4 hosted a dinner for Authority Members on Tuesday. Jeremy Isaacs, Justin Dukes, Edmund Dell and other senior executives all sat cheek by jowl round the Channel 4 Board table. The evening was far from uneventful. The subject of the separate selling of Channel 4 was raised by Justin Dukes. I said that the last thing the Channel should be doing was store up enmity between themselves and ITN, who were, after all, paying their wages and funding their programmes out of the subscription. George Thomson joined in and let fly at them in no uncertain manner: 'Just get on and do the job you're meant to be doing – don't meddle'. Jeremy was much taken aback, but it did him no harm to be reminded on which side his bread was buttered.

Next week, the *Scum* Appeal. The proceedings are scheduled in Court 3 on Tuesday 26 March and will be heard by the Master of the Rolls (Sir John Donaldson), Lord Justice Browne-Wilkinson and Lord Justice Murstill. They have indicated that they wish to see the film on Monday, so we are arranging a viewing at the IBA. My guess is that they will uphold the previous judgment.

Sunday 31st March

The Home Secretary on Wednesday announced his long-awaited decision on the BBC Licence renewal – £58 – and an Inquiry into methods of financing the Corporation, headed by Professor Alan Peacock. The press greeted the news of the increase with surprise and anger which most, if not all, the writers found too high.

Stuart Young appeared in 'the chair' on Sunday facing Brian Walden on *Weekend World*. I thought his answers sloppy and misguided. In the first moments he seemed to give away the BBC's position entirely, saying that if the Committee considered that advertising was the recommended option, 'so be it'. Then, having dug his hole, he jumped into it by confirming beyond any shadow of doubt that, if advertising was the preferred route for the BBC, he would wish to see the Corporation fighting for advertising on all fronts – a head-on confrontation with ITV and ILR. He did not consider making a measure of 'top up' advertising as practicable: 'One can't be just a little pregnant'. I wonder how his opinions went down with the BBC's Old Guard? I think he may have disclosed far too much of the BBC's strategy far too early. He seemed to have already accepted defeat. I can see the next two years taken up with speculation, rumour and skulduggery.

I hope David Shaw and others in ITCA, who spoke up for an inquiry into broadcasting, will feel content.

I had originally not intended to go to the *Scum* hearing in the Appeal Court, largely on the advice of Counsel, although I failed to understand their rationale. George Thomson, however, said he was making a point of attending and thought that, if I could spare the time, I should also. I was glad to take his advice and on Wednesday and Thursday I was to be found for an hour on each day sitting in Court No. 3 listening to *Scum* unfolding.

Mary Whitehouse appeared in Court as a spectator very near the end of the proceedings. I gained a strong feeling that their Lordships were not impressed with the earlier finding. This seemed to be the view of our Counsel, David Kemp, and our solicitors, Allen & Overy.

Radio Four's *Law in Action* on Friday evening included a piece on the hearing. The presenter considered that Mary Whitehouse might at last find a decision going against her. There is, too, a note of optimism in a paper circulated to Authority Members by Allen & Overy.

The thought that the earlier finding of a 'grave error of judgment' might be reversed and my actions vindicated is keeping me in a state of suspense that I find difficult to live with. I fear that, if it goes against me after all this, my despondency will be all the greater. One thing is clear, however: if the decision is to uphold the previous judgment, the case could not have been better presented by David Kemp or listened to more fairly by Lord Donaldson and his fellow Judges. Next week should provide us with the answer.

Two departures this week. George Ffitch from LBC and INR, and Stephen Murphy from the IBA. George took over his post as Managing Director in 1979 and brought an air of stability to LBC. Not an easy man to work with but he had a dry wit and a directness I admired. Stephen worked under David Glencross and brought to his position the long experience he had had during his time at the British Board of Film Classification. A man of extraordinary knowledge, he liked and enjoyed confrontation and debate. He will be missed from the IBA.

Giles Shaw, Minister of State at the Home Office, asked me to see him on Thursday. Bouncy as ever, he accompanied me to the door as I was leaving and invited his secretary to take me to the 'liftikins'.

Monday 8th April

I always seem to do it. Get ill over a holiday. This time Easter, and here I am, between bed and loo, suffering the effects of the dreaded Hong Kong flu. Quite an effort to summon the energy to write but a good opportunity to record the events of last week.

On Tuesday evening, Clare Mulholland told me that Allen & Overy had telephoned to drop a very broad hint that the finding of the Appeal Court would be 'all that we wanted'. Earlier in the day, I agreed with George Thomson that I would attend the 10am hearing on Wednesday and come back to the Authority meeting when it was over. I was told that the Court findings would be made available to us an hour before the hearing.

I was in the office by 0820 and a few minutes later a Clerk from A&O arrived. She handed me a large brown envelope. I tore it open and read the Judges' findings. Mrs W. had had her case overturned. The Divisional Court's rulings were quashed and my 'grave error of judgment' was withdrawn. I went to Court on a high and stopped in at the Aldwych Hotel to order a pre-court aperitif of a double fresh orange juice. Then over to No. 3 Court in order to sit one away from Mary Whitehouse, who was accompanied by a quiet, thin, rather timid looking gentleman who was, she informed me, her husband. They appeared to be in good form. We neither of us spoke about the outcome, which we both knew.

It was all over in a matter of minutes. Mrs W's Counsel asked that costs be met by the IBA. This was refused. They then asked that the Court approve their request for the case to be heard by the Lords. Mary W. left the Court and was quickly engulfed by reporters.

Heady with success, when asked by an ITN reporter how I felt, I responded by saying, 'I hope it has taught Mrs Whitehouse a lesson'. Such a response was unnecessary and I regret it to this day.

I was to learn that Mrs W. was pleading poverty, saying that she had joined in battle with the IBA as an individual, not as President of her Association. Later, I was to learn that an anonymous donor discharged her total costs, amounting to some £30,000 and was prepared to pay her costs if she appealed to the Lords.

My mood of elation has been somewhat dampened by the knowledge that all is not yet over. Mary W. has 28 days to appeal. The Lords will then either refuse her petition or agree to hear the case. On the whole, the press have reported the event accurately although I think some are utterly confused: 'Is this the man who banned *20/20 Vision* and allowed *Scum?*'

After the decision, I returned to Brompton Road and went into the Authority meeting. Everyone said nice things. After the meeting we gave lunch to the Lords' Committee on Televising the Lords. Lord Aberdare thought the experiment a success so far but Lord Winstanley doubted very much whether it would have the Lords' blessing after the trial period, concluding it hadn't done enough to justify itself. I refrained from asking him whether this might not have something to do with the material the cameras were being offered!

Sunday 14th April

A quieter week to return to after the Easter break. While unwell, I missed a meeting with Hugh Dundas to pick up on where the *Dallas* saga had got to. The short answer appears to be 'not far'. I have scheduled a meeting next week with Hugh Dundas and Bill Cotton to see what else can be done. It looks to me as though we have exhausted most of the routes open and now, unless Bill Cotton has a proposal to make, we should allow market forces to take over. I suspect that, at the end of the day, all the ITV Contractors will show *Dallas*, even Yorkshire. Passions have cooled; events must take their course.

On Wednesday I attended the Fleming Memorial Lecture to hear George Thomson give the address. A good speech, delivered with wit and style. How I envy those who appear at ease when speaking in public. GT was still working on re-writes and re-shaping during the afternoon, yet was word-perfect. Each page of his typescript ran for one minute exactly. I must remember – a useful tip.

George was introduced by Stuart Young, who spoke with sincerity about GT. Afterwards, quite a number of people commented on the excellent relationship evident between the two Chairmen – a change from earlier days. I am sure the Old Guard at the BBC are less than happy with the friendship, having always stood aloof from their commercial rivals.

Lunch on Friday with Richard Branson on his dilapidated houseboat in Little Venice. Richard's calmness belies the dynamo he must obviously possess – a £50m company does not come about by calm reflection – yet I have never seen Rick flustered. He had written the questions he proposed to ask me in a little red notebook. He has been thinking in his bath, he tells me, about seeing if the IBA would allow his 'Music Box' service to have access to the ITV transmitters after closedown. He reckons there is a sizeable youth market ready to watch pop programmes. The idea has its attractions. A correspondingly sizeable fee could be worked out to fund the service generally and help towards the cost of re-engineering the UHF service. I said I would think about it.

George Thomson has been invited to stay on as Chairman for another three years and has accepted. Good news on which to end the week. Michael Moriarty from the Home Office had approached me in confidence beforehand to ask my view. I was enthusiastic.

Sunday 21st April

Still no further news about Mrs Whitehouse. The 28 days she has to lodge her appeal are ticking by. David Kemp responded to my letter of thanks by saying that he thought it extremely unlikely that the Lords would entertain her Appeal. Like him, I cannot see what grounds there would be.

I have had a number of angry letters from viewers, who thought my utterance about Mrs W. needing to learn a lesson was arrogant. I replied to the correspondents defending my phrase and pointing out that the findings of the Appeal Court did mean that there were lessons to be learnt.

The Dallas saga continues behind the scenes. On Monday, a meeting with George Thomson, Hugh Dundas, John Read, Bill Cotton and Stuart Young. Incredible, really, to have such a top-brass meeting over such a trivial programme. It became clear that Bill wants Dallas back, just as much as ever he did. Dundas claimed that Thames had no wish to keep it, especially in view of the burdensome extension clauses which insist that, for as long as the series is being made, Thames will agree to run it. And that an additional 10 per cent must be paid by Thames for each subsequent series.

Bill Cotton didn't like the sound of this, and I don't know how an arrangement can be made to square the BBC on this account. Bill is also concerned that, under his previous agreement, he had two showings of Dallas. If the BBC lose the series, he will have lost the opportunity of replaying his series – I suppose, because he would not wish to be providing further publicity for ITV showings. Oh what a tangled web we weave!

Stuart Young has been making his presence very much felt within the BBC. First, he publicly chided his staff over not showing the Pope's Easter message, and announced it would be scheduled next year. Later in the week, there was the extraordinary pirating by the BBC of TV-am's Princess Michael interview. In an almost unprecedented announcement, the Board of Governors, who had met on the 18th, expressed their 'grave disapproval' of the breach of copyright by the BBC and made it clear that 'there must be no repetition of actions of this kind on the part of the BBC'. Strong stuff. If I had been Alasdair Milne, I think I would by now be considering whether to resign. There must be some sore heads in Portland Place.

A jolly lunch on Wednesday in Jeffrey Archer's penthouse overlooking Westminster. A 57 variety of guests: King Constantine of Greece (much younger than I expected), Andrew Neil, Michael Parkinson, Leon Brittan, Michael Edwards, a tycoon from Marks & Spencer and a strangely quiet Michael Grade. We talked of the miners' strike, Andrew Neil saying how pleased he was that Mrs T. had given them a good pasting while on her foreign junket. Another guest – Charles Saatchi – told me (without any bragging) that his company had raised, I think it was £350m in one hour in the City. He left early, without finishing his coffee – perhaps to raise, spend or make another million.

Also on Wednesday to The Thirty Club, to listen to Sir Adam Thomson, Chairman of British Caledonian. How anyone can make running an airline sound dull, I don't know, but Sir A. succeeded.

Sunday 28th April

On Tuesday breakfast with Richard Attenborough. Dickie refused to eat the mushrooms, scrambled eggs and toast that I ordered because he said he was overweight: 'Darling', he said, 'if you were my size and weight – 13 stone – you would agree'. I admitted I would. We talked about Capital and I told him I had been angry with Nigel (Walmsley) over the manner in which they had cut back on their drama. It smacked to me of high-handedness, but I had to admit that IBA staff in Radio Division had been less than nimble in alerting me to the likelihood of the cuts.

I miss seeing Dickie in the way we used to meet when I was at Capital, and we agreed to meet more regularly in future.

A long DGMM (Director General's Management Meeting) to examine Tom Robson's paper on forward engineering expenditure. He has made a good case, but I am recommending that we get Authority blessing before taking it back to ITCA for their comments. We also debated the budget for 85/86 and I managed to get agreement on a number of potentially contentious aspects without blood being spilt. I am still worried about the radio budget. Trying to find out from John Thompson (Director of Radio) what things actually cost is almost impossible. Like the Emperor's new clothes, no one seems to have actually asked the very basic questions about the budget. We are going to look very stupid with AIRC (Association of Independent Radio Contractors) when questions are put to us.

On Wednesday the news was released that George T. would have another three years in office. When I invited the senior staff for some celebratory champagne, I detected, I thought, a lack of enthusiasm. Anyway, I am pleased. I find G.T. a good Chairman. We get on well and see things mostly the same way. GT is also a good man for the complexities that lie ahead.

That evening, Roma and I had dinner with George and Grace. The other guests were John Tooley (General Director of the Royal Opera House) and his wife Patsy, Alex and Vanessa Bernstein and Leon Brittan and his wife. Leon, after dinner, spoke about the Peacock Inquiry and said that its purpose was to examine options, not to make recommendations. We shall see.

The Sunday papers this morning carried pieces about the likelihood of the Commons agreeing to have television recording their antics. About time too. It might just force them to behave like adults instead of delinquent children.

Monday 6th May

Bank Holiday Monday, and Ower full of people, dogs and noise. Not a good recipe for unwinding.

A busy week. I sometimes get the feeling that the IBA is rather like an engine spinning at full throttle in neutral. A great deal of vibration and no forward movement. Last Monday a dinner for Channel 4 with ITV Directors, Paul Fox, James Gatward, David Plowright, Brian Bailey and Mike Scott. GT consumed rather more wine than was good for him and towards the end of the evening began to repeat himself, which after a time became quite irritating. So much so that I lost my sense of humour.

The dinner had been called by G.T. to seek views on subscription appraisals and how to produce a more satisfactory way of doing things. Part of the reason for my invitation, I suppose, was due to the fact that I had already spent quite a time attempting to find a formula that would please S4C, C4, ITV and the IBA, and I had been going from one group to the next, rather like a Chinese juggler, spinning the plates on a pole before they fell to the ground. The basic difference between G.T.'s thinking and my own was that he thought the ITV Directors on the Board of Channel 4 should represent ITV and not themselves as individuals, as had been the case. The ITV Directors have always been scrupulously correct in maintaining their split loyalty in a manner that was well regarded by Channel 4. I do not want the ITV Directors becoming merely a cipher for ITCA.

Paul Fox and David Plowright wanted the Directors to speak for ITV, and Brian Bailey, Mike Scott and James Gatward wanted to keep the status quo. I maintained my own conviction that what was wanted was a formula that would operate without the need for any form of assessment, which would only lead to argument and uncertainty. I began to suspect, as the debate grew in intensity, that those who did not favour a formula preferred instead the politics and debate that went with the current manner of setting the subscription.

On Tuesday we held a one-day conference – 'Television without Frontiers'. It proved a great success. The representatives from the EEC put up a good show of solidarity with their Green Paper to produce harmony amongst countries and broadcasters. The whole ragbag of Europe is like a patchwork quilt – quite impossible to 'harmonise' beyond a 'pasty glug'. If efforts in Europe so far are anything to go by, I shudder to think what might come out of all this. One endless outpouring of Eurovision Song Contest type entertainment?

On Wednesday to Lainston House and an Authority meeting. I got the Board to agree to the mid-term funding of the UHF re-engineering of the transmitters. Now I have to go back to ITCA and convince them that this is the right way. Before leaving, I attended a demonstration of enhanced MAC – the name given to a better picture quality together with a wider screen, developed by IBA Engineering. Estimates vary, but most educated judgment is that some form of high definition will be in use by the mid 90s. Tom Robson hopes that MAC will be the interim step.

Thursday and my speech to the Nuclear Forum. Quite a hostile audience to start, but I think it went down well. One Labour MP was heard afterwards: 'What utter rubbish'. Had a conversation with Derek Ezra, ex-Chairman of the Coal Board, and talked about DBS. I said the Government had 'muffed' the whole thing: on one hand inviting entrepreneurs to chance their money on a high-risk venture; on the other preventing them from making their own deal with a satellite provider at the right price, and insisting on Unisat, who have been sitting on their hands for a year in the belief that Government would protect their favoured position. A disgraceful way of providing the right environment for commerce to operate.

Mrs Whitehouse just managed to squeeze in her application to the Lords within the 28-day notice period. Reading the Appeal, I don't see how she is going to succeed in getting the case reheard. The Appeal concludes with a summary of reasons:

    1. Because the decision of the Court of Appeal was wrong

    2. Because the issues are of general public importance and ought to be considered by your Lordships' House.

Not many bricks to build a firm case, but I am filled with gloom. Another two months or so of waiting to see whether their Lordships will hear the Appeal.

Just to add to the bizarre nature of the whole thing, I have now learnt the identify of the mystery benefactor behind Mrs W – none other than Paul Getty Jnr., who viewed Mrs W's impassioned statements about being a pensioner with no money and decided to help out.

On Thursday, attended a party at the BBC to celebrate the publishing of Asa Briggs' book, *The BBC: the first fifty years*. Many old and familiar faces trying to look eager and interested as Asa rabbited on and on under the impassive gaze of Reith, looking down from the painting in the centre position of the Board Room wall. I wonder what he would make of this bold new world of technology we find ourselves thrust into.

Sunday 12th May

A week in which the storm clouds hanging over DBS continue to swirl, but there are moments now where gaps in the cloud appear and one can glimpse the landscape.

There have been gatherings of the 'Club of 21' to assess their position, and a meeting with Unisat to listen to their latest offer. The Home Secretary has said to Unisat that, if they cannot reach agreement, all bets are off as far as the Government is concerned. That means for the ITV Companies as well as Unisat. The delays and prevarications on all sides for the past year has been disgraceful. During this stalemate the French have been racing ahead with their satellite TDF1, which has received backing from the French Government, thus enabling them to offer DBS channels at a quarter of the charge asked by Unisat. The British Government bangs the free enterprise drum but then ties the hands of the entrepreneurs by insisting that they use British technology, making no concession to reality, and then wonder why we lag behind.

During this year other developments have been occurring that put, or could put, DBS into the shadow. For some months now the ITV Companies have been looking at the possibilities of launching their own European Cable Channel called 'Super Channel'. This they intend would show recycled UK TV offerings sans commercials. Mostly a diet of game shows, quiz and comedy programmes. Super Channel would be in direct competition to Sky Channel and would be beamed down to cable heads via a low-powered satellite. This would give ITV low cost access into Europe, and it does not take a leap of the imagination to see that, if the channel proved a success, it could provide an additional service to the UK. Or, in the event that DBS became viable, the service could be switched to a DBS channel.

But now another character walks on to the stage – SMATV. The Government will shortly announce that they will allow the use of satellite dishes by hotels and private individuals through a system of licensing. The result of SMATV (Satellite Master Antenna Television) could mean that users will be able to pick up cable channels *and* DBS signals from the EEC. Just to complicate matters further, it looks possible that the French will abandon C-MAC in favour of maintaining PAL/SECA. This will result in Europe having one system and we another. Much of all this – if not all – stems from Government stupidity, crass ignorance and arrogance in pursuit of ideas without recognising practicalities.

The next two weeks or so should clarify the DBS state of play. My guess is that Unisat will offer a lower, compromised deal which the Companies will turn down. The IBA would then be back in the driving seat, offering for tender the UK DBS channels. This time we would have one valuable advantage: the BBC would no longer have any part in the venture!

Next week I appear as witness for the IBA before the Public Accounts Committee. On Friday we met with Brian Cubbon, Permanent Under Secretary of State, to discuss our position. It is thought that the PAC will seek to question the costs of Channel 4 in the light of the reduction of levy payments by the Companies to the Treasury. They may also have a go at the IBA for allowing the cost of productions to be high – thus enabling programmes to appeal to overseas markets where the returns are currently outside levy collection.

Dallas flitted back into our sights this week. Hugh Dundas telephoned me to say that their US lawyer had advised Thames that there was good cause for simply assigning the contract over to the BBC and letting Worldvision stew in their own juice. Hugh made the point to me that, if they proceed on these lines, the BBC must understand that the Contract will have to pass to the BBC, warts and all. I said that I thought the BBC would recognise that they could not expect to have Dallas returned without accepting some further negotiation on terms for its future showing.

Wednesday 22nd May

I am writing this in the unfamiliar but friendly surroundings of daughter Fiona's home in downtown Los Angeles. The house was built in 1906 and is full of delights in its design. Being largely made of wood, it's a mass of interesting angles and perspectives, full of character and, thankfully not modernised, has retained its charm, although badly in need of a coat of paint on the outside. All this a far cry from Brompton Road and the IBA. Trying to catch up on the week just past focuses the mind and sorts out the real from the trivial.

On Tuesday (14 May) I chaired the SCC. A number of major items of business still remain on the table: the mid-term financial review now nearly completed, and due to be considered by ITCA. No change in our original stance but I think sufficient justification to support the figures. The largest single item of expenditure is the rebuilding of the UHF transmitter system.

The Companies had hoped that the rebuilding programme could be delayed for as long as possible, but the risks of not starting until after 1987 are too great.

Another agenda item is to find a sensible solution to the annual fourth channel subscription wrangle. A proposal lies on the table from David Plowright. When I get back I hope we can move it forward but I have said to David that, if there is a gap in our views, I can't negotiate any further on the deal, and will either have to come up with another formula or abandon the attempt and go back to the existing formula.

The largest item of outstanding business is, of course, DBS and whether or not the Companies will do a deal with Unisat. This is a critical time for the Club of 21 and the omens are not good. The Companies are disunited in their purpose; falling revenue has made them increasingly wary of committing themselves to a run of years where their cash flow will be going in the wrong direction. DBS is, after all, only a message-carrier. No one cares where the picture comes from, just as long as it provides entertainment. The magic of technology has long since ceased to have 'magic'.

At SCC, I tackled the Companies about their reported interest in the French TDFI DBS system. The visit to Paris by a number of representatives from the Companies had been widely mentioned in the press and obviously caused some embarrassment. As stated earlier, TDFI has the financial support of the French Government and allows them to offer channels at greatly reduced rentals to anything that Unisat can offer. This makes a big difference and is obviously a tempting proposition to the Companies. But, if they chose TBFI, they would lose their rights to continue after 1989 without a franchise appraisal and they would need the IBA's approval.

Another stumbling block to the French satellite is the footprint which reaches only into the south of England – but using a larger dish overseas could possibly get a good picture through the rest of the country.

The real interest in TDFI could be as a carrier for signals intended to reach cable users in Europe. This is where the ITCA plan to launch a cable system channel would come into play. This is also where the real problems of the IBA become focused. If ITCA hire a TDFI channel from the French for relaying Super Channel to European cable users, the IBA would find it hard to object. Indeed, we have already said that we have no objection in principle. Where the whole thing becomes suddenly extremely complex is if, as a result of the signals being clearly received in the south of England, viewers invest in dishes, ITV would be fragmenting its own UK national audience. What's more, it would be operating outside IBA jurisdiction. If, as mooted, Super Channel consists of repeat material held together with news live from ITN and transmissions from TV-am, we could land up in the ludicrous position of seeing ITV becoming the supplier to a larger, more popular service. We really are at a crossroads. The Authority and staff are already split on the issue. Those that say 'you can't stop progress' and those that say 'keep the ITV Companies doing the job they are contracted to carry out'. It's a difficult knot to unravel. Either it will just happen or there will be thought, shape and order put into the course of events.

On Wednesday 15 May, I attended – with Peter Rogers and Bernard Green – the Public Accounts Committee hearing at the House of Commons, with Brian Cubbon representing the Home Office.

PAC calls every so often major public bodies to answer questions concerning the way they spend and husband the funds under their care. The IBA has not been before the Committee for several years. The main concerns of PAC appeared, from the Auditor General's report, to be about the manner of handling the levy. Disappointment had been expressed in the report about the low level of levy receipts from the Companies after the introduction of Channel 4. Another bone of contention was the monies outside the levy made by a number of the Companies (particularly Thames) resulting from the sale of programmes overseas.

The meeting lasted longer than I anticipated. The questions were tougher and more complex than I had imagined. I found the whole thing quite a strain. I was asked why we didn't control the spending on programmes intended for overseas. I replied that programmes were primarily intended for home use and that to draw a line between expenditure on programmes for home consumption and for overseas consumption would be impossible. In any case, I went on, programmes were excellent ambassadors for this country and provided a form of export which had been given an incentive by Government when they excluded overseas sales from levy compilation.

As to the low level of levy repeats after Channel 4, I said that this was due to the IPA/Equity strike and the need to wait for the growth in audience that would enable the Companies to recoup a major part of their subscriptions through the sale of Channel 4's advertising spots. It had been quite a going-over and I was relieved when the meeting concluded.

We return from Los Angeles on Sunday. I dread the pile of work that I know I will meet on my return.

Saturday 25th May

Los Angeles has, I feel sure, much to give its dwellers but to a tourist it presents an ugly, unattractive face – dirty pavements and lacking any kind of style except brash insensitivity. As you will gather, I am not in love with Tinsel Town. Driving out of town yesterday, I saw the mushrooming – or rather the inverted mushrooming – of the new satellite age: 15" diameter dishes plonked outside motels and pull-ins, pointing their antennae into space like great unblinking eyes. Dishes on American buildings won't be seen as an environmental or unsightly problem but in the rest of the world, where the remnants of cultural heritage remain, the satellite dish will be regarded as an intrusive eyesore, as solar panels are already.

Sunday 2nd June

Roma and I have just returned from celebrating 25 years of the White Elephant Club, owned by the redoubtable Stella Richman, who has made her mark in both her careers – of successful restaurateur and television tycoon/entrepreneur. I owe a very great deal to Stella, for it was her faith in my early television projects that paved my way. Latterly she has drawn in her horns and is taking things more quietly. We are the losers. Today's party at the White Elephant was like turning back the pages, as face after face from the past appeared to have a drink and something to eat from a table laden with good things: Gerald Savory, Dick Marsh, Paul Knight, Philip Mackie. A warm and friendly reunion.

On Thursday I flew to Munich for the EBU Council meeting. The poor old EBU is still trying to come to grips with the new dimensions of broadcasting: who should be allowed into membership and who should not. The old order changes but what exactly is the new? No one has the answer. Our meeting was blighted by the tragic news that 39 football spectators had lost their lives before the European Cup Final between Liverpool and Juventus at Heysel Stadium. A disgraceful and shaming episode as it appears the blame lay squarely and directly on the shoulders of the Liverpool supporters.

The match was played despite the disaster in order to prevent further violence. The BBC came in for criticism in the press today for continuing to show the match after the tragedy had occurred. Some countries ceased transmitting out of respect – and anger. On balance, I think the BBC made the right decision.

Sunday 9th June

The BBC top management this week came under the myopic and blurred vision of the press, who put it under their microscope yet again.

What a change from two years ago. Alasdair is now the hunted and hounded. Jeremy Isaacs the knight in shining armour. Will Alasdair Milne be removed and Jeremy Isaacs take his place? Two years ago, JI was heading for the tower and the chop if the newspapers were to be believed; now JI is letting it be known he has no intention of quitting Channel 4!

On Tuesday Stuart Young reaffirmed the Governors' loyalty to their Director General and moved Alan Protheroe (deputy Director General) sideways and Michael Checkland upwards (making him Deputy Director General), a move obviously intended to strengthen financial grip at the top.

Dallas lurched forward again. This time the press were obviously linking events at the Thames Board which suggested that the staff were for retaining the series and the non-executives for returning it to the BBC. Hugh Dundas asked GT for a firm letter from the Authority supporting this latter action. A great deal of drafting went into what resulted in a lacklustre response on the advice of Allen & Overy. GT decided he would ignore their advice and went for a firmer line. I am convinced this is right but it could lead to problems later. Thames have now decided not to seek financial support from the Companies to make up the difference between what they paid and what the BBC are prepared to pay to buy back the series.

HD, armed with GT's letter, has now gone to see O'Sullivan in New York. I don't rate his chances highly, but he didn't win the DSO for nothing and he will be as good an advocate as anyone else, if not better. Where this places Bryan Cowgill I do not know. His position must be precarious, coupled with the fact that Thames have not been overly successful in sales terms, nor indeed in programming.

While the BBC is still under a shadow, the IBA's 30th Anniversary was commemorated by the first Robert Fraser Lecture. We held it in the Banqueting Hall and the address was given by Willie Whitelaw. Excerpts were shown later that evening on Channel 4. Willie was in fine puff, singling out for particular attention the case, which he now backed, for a single regulatory authority to control radio broadcasting. Much praise was heaped on Channel 4, Edmund Dell and Jeremy Isaacs. The great and the good turned out in force: Sidney Bernstein, Denis Forman, Baroness Pike, Howard Thomas, Giles Shaw, Bridget Plowden, Lord Hill and Brian Young. It was a good evening. Afterwards, Roma and I had supper together at the Garrick. I heard this week that Mary W's Appeal to the Lords is likely to be heard on 20 June. That is to say, the Appeal to see whether or not the Lords will accept the hearing. She has nothing to lose by going forward and the bills are being paid by Getty. Mary was at the Willie W. lecture. We exchanged friendly commentary. For all her strange ways and hang-ups, I continue to admire her. Society needs its Mary Whitehouses.

Talking of society needing fearless fighters, George Brown died this week. He appeared regularly on Capital Radio when I was MD and I had proposed him for membership to the Garrick on his promise that he would remain sober while there. He became a Member, but sadly did not keep his promise. He will be missed.

On Tuesday a visit by the Authority to TV-am and lunch with staff and Board. The station is looking towards a successful future with an audience twice the size of the BBC's Breakfast programme and billing that could reach £28m this year. TV-am is out of the doldrums.

The following evening to dinner with David and Carina Frost. While we were having dinner, Bernard Ingham telephoned and urgently advised David to look at the *Ten O'Clock News*. We all thought the world must have fallen in but, although we watched every second, there was not the remotest piece of news we thought of direct interest. It was planned for David to interview Margaret Thatcher for 45 minutes on Sunday morning. I watched the interview on that Sunday. All went smoothly until Frost started in on Mrs T and the Falklands War and in particular her decision to sink the Belgrano whilst it was steaming away from the exclusion zone. For fifteen minutes he probed and poked into her decision and in particular her cover-up or stonewalling used to mislead Parliament. Under attack, Mrs T. began to get rattled. I was surprised by the force of David's questions. I suspect he may have gone too far and unbalanced the interview, simply by using up so much time on one subject, although it was fascinating and the sort of thing only a good television interview can do really well.

I imagine the Directors of TV-am may not have welcomed the way the interview went. I am quite sure Mrs T didn't. Poor old Bernard Ingham. I imagine madam will give him a roasting for allowing her to be put in that unfortunate position. David Frost went up in my estimation. Few other interviewers would have had the courage to conduct the interview on grounds of his choosing, not hers.

This week I visited Scotland and spoke to a dinner gathering at Gleneagles. I visited North Sound Radio in Aberdeen, Grampian Television, Radio Tay in Dundee and STV the following day. A busy time and it served to remind me just how troubled are our radio Contractors.

Roma collected me from the airport and we drove to Dorset. While eating lunch we suddenly remembered that it was our wedding anniversary. Just how many years I have conveniently forgotten!

Sunday 16th June

How the weeks race by. I never seem to get a moment to sit back and indulge in a little introspection. I am always being asked what I think. Half the time I wish I knew! Are all of us unwilling passengers on a downhill racer, hanging on for dear life and hoping that we won't be dislodged before crossing the finish line.

Mrs T was indeed upset at Frost's Falklands interrogation. After the recording she declined to join senior staff on the station for a cup of tea. On the whole, the press marked her high for her performance. I also had it whispered to me that madam had suggested a patch of rough questioning so that she could demonstrate that she had not become a softie and that her resolve over the Falklands remained undiminished. On both counts she succeeded.

On Monday I wrote to Sophie Brown expressing my sadness at George's passing. I did not attend the funeral, but sent flowers.

That day I lunched with Howard Thomas, ex-Chairman of Thames and a man of wide experience of broadcasting and all its facets. Although retired, he is no less active today, with fingers in many pies including television in Hong Kong and soon, if he has his way, China. We talked about Dallas and about Bryan Cowgill's action. I was left in no doubt as to Howard's views.

Another chapter has opened on Dallas. Dundas returned from the US without having reached an outcome. He suggested to George that he should meet O'Sullivan and put the Authority's view. While we were thinking that one over, the weekly trade magazine in the US – *Variety* – published what could only be a first hand account of what was going on behind the scene and raising the spectre of fixing and the anti-competitive stance that would attract unfavourable attention from the UK Office of Fair Trading. The article made the front page banner headline: 'Brit Government probing *Dallas* Deal. American distributors rejoice over price-fixing row'.

In the light of this, I advised GT not to hold any meetings until the smoke had cleared.

On Tuesday I became President of TRIC and was introduced by the outgoing President, Aubrey Singer, who seemed well-pleased to be rid of the role.

The DBS Club of '21' has finally concluded that it cannot back the Unisat proposition. An announcement has still to be made publicly. A wasted sixteen months. What a fiasco. Even the Government's blackmail of the Companies has failed to make them a pawn of Mrs T's hopeless aspiration. Common sense and business might now prevail.

Barbara Hosking has got a well-deserved OBE in the Queen's Birthday Honours. Pat Lambourne either an OBE or CBE, I am not sure, and, I believe, Geoffrey Littler a K., so Shirley will now be Lady Littler!

Sunday 23rd June

A celebration in the office for Barbara and congratulations to Shirley – no other Honour for ITV, ILR or the BBC. I think we are definitely not the flavour of the month with Mrs T. More so than ever after David Frost's Belgrano assault. There is a story going about that after Mrs T had done the interview, her complaint was not about Frost but about too many commercials interrupting the programme!

To Scotland and attended the Scottish Advisory Committee. All well-intentioned, middle class, mostly middle-aged and white. Our fault. We select them. Stayed the night in a hotel called 'The Hospitality Inn' in Glasgow. Bedroom like an airport waiting room: enormous, bare and uninteresting. The only hospitality was a miniature bottle of whisky with the Manager's compliments.

Super Channel continues to occupy the minds of the ITV MDs since the demise of the satellite project. Now we have a difficult decision. If we allow Super Channel it will be picked up here on the large dishes that Government are now permitting. On balance, I don't think we should object. Some of the Companies are thinking of inviting the BBC to share in Super Channel. I am against this. The BBC can row their own canoe if they want to sell-in programmes, but to allow them anywhere near the business end would be fatal.

On Tuesday and Wednesday we devoted most of the Authority's time to thinking about our approach to Peacock. Looking at our options, I am quite convinced that we should concentrate on protecting as far as possible our source of revenue and then fight for our corner of the market.

Thousands of words will be written on Peacock. I do not intend adding to them more than I must.

Sunday 30th June

Dallas continues to take up time. O'Sullivan called us on Monday. I have counselled George to be careful that this whole business doesn't become a story of the silly season – it has all the makings. O'Sullivan seemed genuinely upset that he appeared to be the villain in a situation that he claimed he had no reason to be typecast in. Thames had offered a sum of money beyond which the BBC were prepared to pay. Telexes had been exchanged between the BBC and himself, spelling out the state of the negotiations. O'Sullivan could not believe that Companies in ITV would refuse to show *Dallas* and he was planning to hold talks with them.

Later in the week we heard he had met with them and seen the strength of feeling, and concluded that if the BBC were prepared to invite him to negotiate new terms with them, he would consider a new arrangement. Now it remains to be seen if Stuart Young and Alasdair will take up the offer. If the BBC get it back, we are going to need to play our PR role extremely carefully.

In the words of Sue Summers writing her 'Langham Diary' in *The Listener* (27 June 1985): 'Those who believe that British broadcasting is a cosy cartel must feel thoroughly vindicated by the contortions of ITV overlords as they bend over backwards to accommodate their supposed rivals in Broadcasting House'.

A meeting on Monday with David Plowright to see if I can get nearer to an agreement with the Companies over funding for Channel 4. I have a suspicion that, at the end of the day, we will have to continue with the old formula.

A breakfast meeting with Aubrey Buxton at the Hyde Park. AB is currently Chairman of ITN and believes that others on the Board may be thinking it time he gives up his seat after some years. The problem is, who would be suitable to follow? Perhaps Bill Brown, or Paul Fox? I had another breakfast meeting with Alastair Burnet on Friday, who wanted to see me about the broadcasting of Parliament. He would, I think, favour Paul Fox.

On Wednesday, I invited representatives of *The Times* to lunch. Charles Douglas-Home and some others turned up at 1.20pm, having been invited at 12.45 for 1pm. Not an impressive bunch of people, and the conversation was puerile and a total waste of time. I felt flat and depressed afterwards.

The plotting behind the scenes, following the collapse of the DBS venture, is intriguing. I suspect that the Satellite Broadcasting Board would like to stay in existence. GT and Stuart Young see themselves as a powerful duo, who quite relish the prospect of taking on all comers. The ITV Companies are thinking about Super Channel and whether they should entertain the notion that the BBC be invited into the consortium. My first reaction on hearing this is one of deep despair: this could be a ploy to attempt to keep a duopoly position open, albeit on low-powered satellite, and then use it to ensure that, if successful, they would progress to DBS, thus keeping the door open against the re-advertisement process in 1989.

I have a feeling, too, that GT would agree to this. I shall do my best to nip this one in the bud. I think it better to open up competition and advertise the DBS franchise to all comers.

Two days at the end of the week interviewing a replacement for Tom Robson, our Director of Engineering. There is one obvious contender against the in-house applicant, but I doubt if we can attract him for the money.

Sunday 7th July

The Oracle people – Peter Bailey, their MD, and Peter Paine, their Chairman – want to allow subscriber use of teletext and are doing a deal with BT to act as agent. But they want to make arrangements that will continue after 1989 when the franchise renewals come up. I told them I couldn't allow that. They went away disgruntled.

My feeling about Oracle is that it has always been a soft toy of the ITV Companies, who have played with it to keep the IBA happy. I am convinced that if Oracle were put up to other private bidders, we would see the teletext field blossom and some real developments and marketing take place.

On Monday, dinner with the big five radio Companies, who put a plan to me for forming a company to actively look at ways of promoting, and owning, a radio facilities company. The group would also want to fund consortia in trouble. There is a better feeling within the ILR Companies: at last they are thinking about how to project a positive face to the world instead of adopting the whingeing tone and hysterical cries that have been their posture for the last twelve months or so. In the middle of dinner, Nigel Walmsley was handed a note to say that both London FM transmitters had been put out of action by a fire! IBA engineers installed a temporary rig and the stations went out over the air a few hours later.

The Home Secretary spoke at the first ILR Congress held at the IBA. A good speech and with plenty of detail and some praise of the IBA. No new announcement about community radio. The Authority broke their regular meeting to attend.

Went to Naples on Thursday for the European Broadcasting Union Conference. We are hosting next year's in Bournemouth. I hope we do better.

Dallas continues to rumble. The DTI have asked us if they can help! Apparently O'Sullivan paid a call on the British Ambassador in Washington and described in detail the tricks the BBC and ITV were getting up to.

Long talk with Alasdair Milne. He is quite convinced that High Definition is the road to take and that EMAC is a poor substitute.

Sunday 14th July

The *Dallas* time bomb has finally exploded, covering everyone concerned in a shower of debris which is still falling as I write. On Thursday I was telephoned by Hugh Dundas to say that the Board had decided that Bryan Cowgill should go. Terms were being discussed. At the same time, I heard that the BBC were not being particularly helpful in re-opening negotiations with the UK representative of Worldvision. I bumped into Stuart Young at a DT reception and he said that Thames would have to pay the difference if the BBC failed to reach an agreement.

On Friday BC announced that he would be resigning from Thames and laid the blame for his decision on the IBA and, in particular, George Thomson and myself. His claim that we put pressure on Thames, threatening the company with termination of their contract if they did not return *Dallas* to the BBC was widely quoted in the press. BC appeared on Friday night's *News at Ten*, portraying a man who had been unfairly treated and repeating his concern about the IBA's stance. The *Sunday Times* carried a front page story quoting BC as saying that the action of GT in particular was contemptible. GT and I spoke on the telephone and agreed to call a meeting to assess the position on Monday morning at 7.45.

I understood from GT that Hugh Dundas was issuing a press statement this afternoon repudiating the accusation made by BC that we had threatened Thames with taking away their franchise. So far, O'Sullivan hasn't let off any bolts from the USA, except to again say that the relationship between the BBC and ITV is a cosy and complacent one that works to prevent competition.

I am perplexed by the recent action of BC. In resigning, he has opted for what I am sure will prove to be a handsome sum. Either he should remain quiet, having taken compensation, or else speak freely, having rejected a payment. He shouldn't be permitted to 'tell all' and collect his severance money. His was a stupid and dangerous act of folly, which has split the Companies. What a life – *Scum*, *Spitting Image* and *Dallas*. So much for 'shaping the grand concepts of independent television'.

Turning to other matters: on Tuesday I chaired SCC and had the opportunity of closely questioning David Plowright about intentions for Super Channel and, in particular, about the rumours I had heard about his hopes to persuade the BBC to join them in its formation. DP grew quite angry when challenged, and said that he had had some private talks with the BBC but that was as far as it went.

Brian Tesler spoke against the BBC joining in, giving as the reason the political conclusions that would be drawn from such an association, and also the lack of need in the past for the ITV Companies to engage with the BBC. No good purpose would be served.

Turning directly from the BBC's relationship with Super Channel, I asked about the effect of receiving in England signals intended for Europe as a result of the Government's decision to allow dishes capable of receiving ECS transmission. DP must have thought I knew more than I was letting on, because he unexpectedly started talking about a BBC/ITV special cable service beamed to this country and consisting of specialist material. This was the first I, or anyone else around the table, had heard about it. David saw his mistake and shut up.

Next week, we review the candidates for the job of Director of Engineering. To my mind one man – Alan Rudge – stands out head and shoulders above the rest. I had breakfast with him on Wednesday to sound him out about salary.

Sunday 21st July

GT and I had an early meeting on Monday with Brian Rook, David Glencross and Barbara Hosking to decide on our PR approach to Dallas and Cowgill's onslaught in the press. GT had prepared a press statement and so had Barbara. My own feeling all along has been not to get into a tangle of accusation and counter-accusation. Hugh Dundas' rebuttal on behalf of the Thames Board had said it all. GT was naturally angry at the views about him and particularly wanted to lay the lie that all the parties, including O'Sullivan, had met together.

On Tuesday we decided, in the light of comments received by Allen & Overy, not to take any action. I think it was a wise decision. The trade magazines by and large considered that BC had burnt his boats and acted foolishly. I feel sorry for BC, and particularly for Jennie, who has stuck by him and will do so no matter what happens.

The actual *Dallas* business isn't getting any easier.

Stuart Young spoke to GT on Monday and gained the impression that the BBC were in no hurry to settle. He told Stuart Young that it was up to the BBC to make some positive moves, but I think this fell on rather stony ground.

On Monday, I attended the Channel 4 dinner in the private room at Claridges. Dickie was there, having just flown in from America. The dinner was a disaster. GT and Edmund Dell have a hearty dislike for each other. Also, GT has never liked Jeremy Isaacs and once the wine flowed attitudes became polarised. Channel

4 distrust us over our attempts to tidy up our relationship with them. Since the agreement was first drawn up, nothing has been altered and Shirley Littler has been working on an updated document. Edmund Dell took quite violent objection and said we were trying to move the goalposts. GT retorted by accusing Channel 4 of working towards the aspiration that one day they might become a separate broadcasting body and that was the reason they wouldn't countenance our efforts.

Later in the evening, Jeremy Isaacs gave a lengthy dissertation on the way we should consider judging violence, taste and decency on Channel 4, arguing that research would back up his belief that few people were upset by programmes late at night when they had been given advance notice of their content. We broke up in gloomy mood, having seemed to drift further and further apart for no good reason.

On Wednesday *Face the Press* lunch at the Hyde Park given by Tyne Tees with guest attraction Margaret Thatcher. MT extolled the virtues of the North East in a manner that reminded me of those early railway posters depicting the countryside in a glowing light. MT looks more and more like her caricature in *Spitting Image*. It was a good performance but wholly lacked substance.

The BBC, after a weekend's deliberation, announced a series of cuts which boiled down to a number of small cost-saving exercises. The speed with which they find cuts has been criticised in the press.

I will have a tricky meeting next week with GT, who has been forging ahead with a plan to launch, with the BBC and ITCA, a 'Friends of Broadcasting' lobby. The trouble is, it needs £100,000 to fund. Quite apart from the money, I cannot think of a worse time to join hands with the BBC, or indeed ITCA. The press would have a field day.

Just heard the news on television that the commentator and author of the *Wendy* series, Dorian Williams, has died. Roma and I had been to see him a week ago. He was obviously very ill but managed to walk to the front door to wave us goodbye. A very fine man, who gave so much to everything he did. A sad evening.

Sunday 28th July

The hot air currents of high summer are eddying upwards. Hot air is very much in evidence also as journalists work hard to construct stories. *Dallas* continues to bubble along. On Wednesday 24 July, *The Times* carried a major piece examining the background: 'Power play with the real JRs'.

On the following day, on the Order Paper in the Commons, a quest for Written Answer by John Gorst, MP for Hendon North: 'to ask the Secretary of State for Trade and Industry what steps Her Majesty's Government has taken to seek to ensure that the arrangements made by the British Broadcasting Corporation and the Independent Broadcasting Authority or its contracts for the acquisition of film or other programme material are consistent with the Government's policy on competition; if he will refer these arrangements with particular reference to the circumstances surrounding the purchase by Thames Television of the Dallas programme to the Director General of Fair Trading for examination; and whether he will ask the Director General of Fair Trading to satisfy himself that there are no arrangements made by the British Broadcasting Corporation or Independent Television for the purchase of programme material that are (sic) in contravention of the provisions of the Restrictive Trade Practices Act'.

With friends like this, who needs enemies? John Gorst is perfectly entitled to ask what he likes, but I did feel that he should have shown a little decency and told me that he intended putting down a question.

The actual situation of *Dallas* itself is stuck in a limbo land between the BBC and Thames. Dundas does not want to pay the difference between what the BBC are prepared to offer and the original price agreed by Cowgill. He had been hoping the ITCA Companies would help make up the difference, but Bob Phillis has told me in strict confidence that they were not aware that BC had purchased a second series from Worldvision, entitled *Highway to Heaven*. BP has told Dundas that the Film Purchase Committee will take *Highway* if Thames settles over *Dallas*. This second piece of skulduggery will have serious consequences for BC and show him to be what he is: a cowboy!

Another story surfaced this week. The IBA's attitude over the making for television by Zenith of *The Profumo Story*. *Men & Matters* in *The Times* carried a story that could have only come from someone leaking the confidential PPC papers. One guess only. BC is obviously going to do all he can to throw mud at the IBA, GT and me. The Profumo film surfaced some months ago and I spoke to RP and said that we wouldn't be happy to have it offered by Zenith for showing. Profumo is still alive and if any man has paid his debt to society, Profumo has. I said this to Bob who told me that he would not be offering it to the network. It would be made as a film and Central would not be putting up any funding. GT spoke about the project at PPC and a brief minute was recorded. The papers now claim that we had tried to stop it being made into a film, which is rubbish.

This week saw the Home Secretary making his long-awaited announcement about the two-year experiment in community broadcasting. From memory, four Community of Interest stations in London. We issued a press statement with the reminder that this experiment would mark the first time that Government had taken a direct control of the broadcast medium. There has been a total lack of interest in the announcement from Leon Brittan. Peacock and television dominate the scene.

Lunched with Michael Montague, Chair of the Consumer Council, on Monday. MM told me his Council had considered Peacock and decided that no harm would come from the BBC taking 'a little advertising'. I told him that a little, or a lot, the effect would be the same.

Good news about our Director of Engineering. Alan Rudge has been enticed back to consider terms that he might find acceptable. This is an interesting development because, if Members agree to the salary Rudge is asking, this would mean that consideration has to be given to mine!

After Margaret T's ill-considered decision on top people's pay, I have no scruples in expecting Members to give me a rise.

The IPA published its Annual Report this week; altogether a more readable document than in previous years – complete with pictures.

A meeting with David Glencross this week, and the case being brought by Norris McWhirter against the IBA with regard to *Spitting Image* wherein he claims that a subliminal image of his face was inserted on the body of a naked woman.

On Friday, Roma and I went to the funeral of Dorian Williams. A short and joyful occasion, well organised, with tea afterwards at Foscote Manor. He would have approved.

Sunday 4th August

A whirlwind of criticism hit the BBC as a result of their plan to show a documentary *Real Lives* featuring the views of the IRA's Chief of Staff, Martin McGuinness. News of the programme first hit the headlines on Sunday 28 July. I note I didn't even comment on it last Sunday! What happened in the wake of the storm will be well documented. Suffice to say that Mrs T's 'starve them (the terrorists) of the oxygen of publicity' speech in America had already set the seal on her determination to show up the BBC if it strayed from the path.

Shooting from the hip because she hadn't seen the programme, she is reported to have said in Washington: 'I would condemn it utterly'. The scene was thus set and actors took up their accustomed roles; BBC management claiming the film was balanced and fair, MPs crying foul and the Governors, in the absence of Alasdair Milne, who was on holiday, deciding to cancel transmission.

Sunday 11th August

I am on holiday in Dorset which is wet and windy. Everyone else seems to be leaving the country to avoid getting sodden. The thunder and lightning still roars round the BBC. More column inches have been given to the 'censoring' by the Governors of the BBC than to the memory of the thousands who died 40 years ago from the two atomic bombs dropped on Japan.

Alasdair Milne, who had been fishing quietly somewhere in Scandinavia, came home too late to prevent the disaster engulfing the BBC and declared 'I am in charge'. Stuart Young clearly thought otherwise and so did the journalists of both BBC and ITV, who took Wednesday off in protest. While the Governors and Milne looked wet, the villain of the piece was clearly thought to be Leon Brittan, who wrote an ill-considered letter advising the Governors of his displeasure should the film be shown.

It's always easy to stand on the sidelines and say how things ought to be done. The sad thing is that the whole affair is a monstrous cock-up on the part of all concerned: the Governors for being weak and panicking, Leon B. for going too far, the Board of Management for not maintaining a solid front and allowing reporting procedures to get muddled – the Features Department apparently unaware of the rules applying to Current Affairs and News.

The victors were the IRA, who have been given a strong whiff of oxygen paid for at the expense of the BBC's reputation throughout the world.

The relationship between Milne and Young will be hard to mend and, if I was a betting man, I would lay fairly long odds on one or the other deciding to quit, but I think perhaps I am being too hasty. Both men are vain, and filled with their own conceit, so neither will allow the other the satisfaction of being the one to stay on.

While all this has been going on, *Dallas* has been slowly fermenting. Hugh Dundas is anxious to clear up matters and I put Richard Dunn, the new MD of Thames, together with David Plowright, who has promised to do all that he can to negotiate the series back to the BBC. The OFT has now written to the IBA, the BBC and ITCA inviting comments about the 'arrangements' surrounding *Dallas*. I can almost hear the squeak of quill nibs in the poisoned ink as the critics of the BBC and the IBA get ready for a field day.

On the *Spitting Image* front, I wrote to Norris McWhirter, sending him a copy of our press statement and suggesting that we could both save our money by not going to court. If he decides to go ahead, then I'm afraid we're in for another long, legal slog with precious few prizes at the end.

Thursday 15th August

Have just heard from my office that Norris McWhirter has decided to press forward with his claim against us, using the Magistrates Court as his starting position. It will be interesting to see what headway he makes.

The day before yesterday I spoke on the telephone with Hugh Dundas, who said that Thames had come to the end of the line over *Dallas*. They did not wish to use ITCA as a negotiating instrument with the BBC, neither did they wish to negotiate themselves. Dundas said he was content to offer the BBC compensation of £300,000 to assist the BBC in purchasing the new series of *Dallas* and if some of the ITV Companies, through ITCA, were prepared to give their financial support, Thames would be clearly grateful.

Reading between the lines, I think that Dundas is now out on a limb with his Board and his staff. They see his actions as a capitulation. Undoubtedly, some Board members would wish to see Thames keep *Dallas*. I asked Hugh if he personally wanted to keep *Dallas*. He replied no. He just wanted to 'get shot of the whole ghastly mess'. I said that what it appeared to come down to was that Thames weren't prepared to do a deal with ITCA and didn't want ITCA to do a deal with Worldvision on their behalf. There was a stalemate with the BBC and a decision would have to be taken before the schedules were published in early September. I told Dundas it seemed the IBA were the only source left to determine the future of *Dallas*, and that I would speak to the BBC and see if they would settle for £300,000.

Later, I spoke to George T, who agreed with this action. I then spoke to Michael Grade, Bill Cotton being on holiday. Grade said he would speak to Bill and call me.

Friday 16th August

Grade has come back to me and agreed the deal. I telephoned Hugh with the good news. He was clearly very relieved. Now the BBC will need to agree their contract with Worldvision. When this is done, £300,000 will be paid into ITCA for onward payment to the BBC, thus avoiding Thames making a direct payment to the BBC. All of us hope that the sum paid will not become public knowledge, but I am sure it will leak.

Sunday 18th August

The 'great' Peacock debate is on today at Edinburgh. Interesting to see what the luminaries there will have to say. Thank heavens I am in Dorset, worrying about the moles tunnelling like demented Channel developers under the front lawn.

Today's *Observer* headlines another BBC 'cover up'. This time revealing facts supporting the allegations that MI5 are regularly used to vet and comment upon BBC new recruits and freelancers. Won't do much good for our image abroad: first censoring, now mole catching! The words of Alasdair Milne during the recent *Real Lives* shindig are already coming home to roost. The *UK Press Gazette* of 12 August: 'Stuart Young, Chairman of the BBC Governors, is beginning to look as if he wishes he had never taken the job in the first place. Alasdair Milne, Director General of the BBC, is telling everyone in sight, 'I'm in charge' – a phrase remarkably reminiscent of that used by General Alexander Haig after President Reagan had been shot, and carrying about as much conviction ….'.

Reading the mountains of advice to Peacock and his Committee, I came across one of the very few sensible rationales for retaining the present position, as opposed to pulling it down and applauding while the dust settles and waiting to see what destruction has resulted. Brenda Maddox in *The Listener* (15.8.85), argues that the system, and the BBC in particular, should stand firm on their achievements and demand the continuation of the licence fee. She concludes her article with these words: 'As the new possibilities crowd in, what is needed is not the boldness to take apart the present broadcasting structure but the will to preserve it as one strand in the inevitable multi-channel future'.

Sunday 1st September

No news on *Dallas*.

On Monday, writing in the *FT*, Raymond Snoddy reported on the state of play with such accuracy that he could have been bugging my telephone. Every detail correct, even down to the final views of the Thames Board. Next week, something must happen if we are going to get the damned thing shifted, otherwise it is likely to go into the Thames schedule with accompanying egg on numerous faces, including my own.

The IBA has been given leave by a High Court Judge to seek orders stopping Norris McWhirter's claim and summons against me for the *Spitting Image* case to be heard in a Magistrates Court. The Judge has said that we have 'an arguable case'!

We will then ask the High Court, at a full hearing, to quash the summons and ban the Magistrates from hearing the case on the grounds that no crime was committed.

Evidence pours in to Professor Peacock from ITCA, the Newspaper Society, the Arts Council, National Consumer Group, HTV Ltd, BAFTA, AIRC, IPPA. The Authority meets this week to discuss, and hopefully approve, our submission. It reads well and contains much of substance. Early days yet, but the pendulum of public opinion appears to be swinging slightly in favour of separate funding.

We have a knotty problem coming up: Robert Maxwell and his intended participation in the French satellite TDFI. I think we must tell him that this is a direct conflict of interest with his shareholding in Central and he must decide which to give up. Again, the Authority meets to discuss this. Some members of DGMM (Director General's Management Meeting) are undecided and a few want to take the soft option and let him ride both horses.

On Tuesday Aubrey Buxton came to see me to discuss his decision to give up the chairmanship of ITN. His nomination for his replacement would be Paul Fox, now that Bryan Cowgill is no longer in the running. Paul would be a good candidate.

Held a meeting this week over the Royal Variety Show. What a lot of fuss for 90 minutes.

Sunday 8th September

The BBC Governors got round to considering a transmission date for *Real Lives* and agreed a showing in October. Not much else they do can really. BBC Management looks painfully thin on top. If Alasdair Milne had resigned, the choice of a replacement would have been woefully meagre. People of the stature of Paul Fox or David Plowright don't seem to be waiting in the wings.

Leon Brittan out – Douglas Hurd in. Thus the ever changing scene of politics. My guess is that Douglas will give us a better run than Leon. His heart is nearer to broadcasting. He is almost certainly more sensitive and, I suspect, has a better grasp of the complexities facing broadcasters. We shall see.

No news on *Dallas*.

I spoke to Hugh Dundas again this week. The BBC are awaiting confirmation from ITCA that they will be taking a Worldvision mini-series *East of Eden*. If this is confirmed, Worldvision will transfer ownership of *Dallas* to the BBC.

The Maxwell saga was reviewed by the Authority at its meeting on Wednesday. I said I thought we could rely on Central to ensure that Maxwell didn't rock the boat with a conflict of interest that might prove damaging to Central's contract with the IBA. This view was accepted readily. I don't think anyone has much stomach for a tussle with Captain Bob!

I spoke to Brian Tesler and David Plowright. Both thought the idea of Maxwell having a foot in both camps would be a travesty of the role of Directors engaged in maintaining a terrestrial system against competition. DP believes Maxwell should resign from the Board of Central. I can smell trouble!

Our Peacock submission got the green light from the Authority on Wednesday. It reads well and should command a wide platform of sympathy and, more importantly, understanding. Much, if not all, credit should go to Kenneth Blyth, who has steered it with deftness and skill through the many rapids of dissension. I want to get it circulated before the Cambridge RTS convention in a fortnight's time and am planning to hold a fairly low key press briefing on the 16th.

On Thursday I went to Manchester and opened an exhibition to celebrate 25 years of *Coronation Street*. I still haven't dared confess that I have never actually seen an episode from start to finish.

James Gatward of TVS (Television South), one of the new breed of telly-magnates, spoke to me last week about his company's hope to bid for the film and distribution part of Thorn EMI, which is said to be up for grabs. He thinks it will be in the region of £50m. I am in favour inasmuch as it would keep these considerable assets within ITV but there are others who think TVS would be biting off more than they can chew.

Tomorrow morning to see Giles Shaw with John Thompson, Director of Radio, to speak about INR and twist his arm a little to make sure that he doesn't give away the frequencies to the BBC.

Sunday 15th September

Giles Shaw bounces like the centre of a golf ball when its outer coverings have been removed. He is worried about how to reconcile the pressures from the BBC and us over who gets first bite at the FM frequencies due for reallocation quite shortly. The BBC want the frequencies to be split between BBC 1 and 2, thus further strengthening their hold on the national audience. We want an early start for INR, arguing that to allow the BBC in first will be to increase the difficulties for INR if it were to come in afterwards, and further increase the difficulties for ILR in sustaining current audience levels. I think we will lose. Giles fears a backlash from ILR Companies, who by and large take the view that INR could deplete ILR prospects by increasing their share of advertising revenue.

GT is seeing the Home Secretary next week. It wouldn't surprise me if this was on the agenda.

I have heard more from those I think worth listening to on the subject of Maxwell and his interest in TDFI. Bob Phillis would like to see a strong line and Denis Forman called me to say that he would go further than David Plowright, considering Maxwell to already have too many fingers in too many pies, citing Australian television and radio as an example of media control in too few pairs of hands.

I am bringing this subject back to the Authority table for discussion on Wednesday but I have a feeling that GT has little stomach for the fight between us and Maxwell that will undoubtedly occur if the decision is to ask for his removal from the Board and a sale of his shareholding in Central.

Tomorrow sees my briefing of the press, called for 1115 in the Board Room. I have prepared an opening statement which I may use and which, if I do, I will include in this diary.

On Friday I attended with Roma the 30th anniversary dinner given to former and serving members of ITN staff – a very happy occasion. Informal, and much appreciated by those who had worked all their lives for ITN.

David Nicholas introduced two former ITN Editors-in-Chief. Both spoke warmly of the ITN tradition of friendship and professional pride which unquestionably has survived and been further strengthened by David Nicholas, who continually surprises me with his puckish sense of fun coupled with an unassuming manner which conceals a rock-like determination. I felt very privileged to have been invited.

Next week the RTS and Cambridge.

Two further events occurred this week. The first was the finding of the Monopolies Commission in regard to the ITV Companies and the BBC publishing advance programme schedules only in the *TV Times* and *Radio Times*. The Commission ask only that 'consideration' should be given for others to publish programme details a week ahead for a reasonable fee.

The second event was the findings of the Public Accounts Committee published on Friday about which I am not so sanguine. So far a strangely ominous silence in the press apart from a small item in the *FT*. I suspect I haven't heard the last of PAC. The findings appear less than helpful with the suggestion that the levy should be re-examined.

Sunday 22nd September

A hectic week, finishing today with my return from Cambridge and the RTS.

Last Monday we unveiled our evidence to the Peacock Committee to the press. I had hoped for a larger turnout. Perhaps it was Monday morning blues, but only a handful turned up. I had prepared some carefully chosen words, which in the event I thought pompous as I sonorously intoned them into the quarter-filled room. I drew the analogy of the high rise tower blocks of the 60s, the planners and experts, with whole communities uprooted and piled on top of one another. Out of sight, out of mind. We now know the result of those decisions – the tearing apart of tight knit communities. All the king's horses can't put back those families and those communities again now that, 20 years on, we recognise the damage wrought upon people never given any real opportunity to choose where they wanted to live.

I likened these events to the mad chase for options facing the Peacock Committee. If the wrong decisions were taken, we would see the bulldozing of a structure that had stood the test of time for 60 years. If the decision to allow advertising were to be taken, there could be no winding back of the clock. Little of my speech was quoted, except the bit about bulldozing, which I suppose was the only phrase that caught the ear.

On Tuesday we got a reasonable press. Peacock's submission keep thumping down on the desks of Fleet Street editors. We are all slowly sinking into a quagmire of cliché and rhetoric.

My fears about the PAC seem groundless. If there is a time bomb ticking, it's got a fully wound spring.

On Tuesday off to Wales on one of those 'royal progresses' beloved by the Authority.

Being nice non-stop is a terrible trial, I find. I have been 'nice' for too long. Tuesday evening was a 'be nice to everyone' occasion at Cardiff Castle. Dinner excellent hosted by GT. I sat next to Baroness White, 22 years a Labour MP and former Minister of this and that. A formidable person with so many fingers in so many Welsh pies. She must strike terror in the hearts of all lesser mortals who meet her in her different roles. I liked her.

The Minister for Welsh Affairs made a weak speech, which showed a lack of homework. GT spoke about the value of ITV and its success in selling programmes overseas. It went down well.

Rose bright and early for the Authority meeting. Starting with congratulations to John Riddell and his (surprising) appointment as Secretary to HRH Prince Charles. I think he might be quite good. A bit quirky but fast on his feet. I suspect, though, he has little idea of the pressures he will find himself under. He and Princess Diana will either hit it off, or come to blows. I suspect the latter.

Two items on the agenda were TVS's plans for acquiring Thorn-EMI cinema and distribution interests and Robert Maxwell's interest in TDFI and Central. On TVS, Members thought that the proposition was too risky for TVS to go it alone. David Glencross described their track record as less than perfect. It would mean that top executive talent would be tied up. I saw James Gatward later in the week and he was unhappy, which was to be expected.

Members took my advice that Maxwell should be invited by Central to decide which interest he wanted to pursue and that, if he chose the French satellite, he would need to resign his position on the Board of Central. This decision is going to make Mr Maxwell very cross indeed and I foresee a brisk exchange of correspondence while he claims his right to maintain his role in Central.

Media Week ran a centre page article (20.9.85) on my three years as DG. It was better than I had feared. Why am I so sensitive about what is written? I suppose I still feel I am masquerading in the job and waiting to be rumbled.

After the Authority meeting, to Culverhouse Cross – the Cardiff studio of HTV. Enormous, impressive and devoid of any activity. Still, we had our pictures taken and walked down long corridors and shown, with pride, a make-up room, a 'drying room' (for I know not what), a wardrobe room etc, etc. I would have preferred to see a room in which people were making a television programme, but that was not to be.

These royal progresses, and the visits made by Members, remind me of governesses being shown round the homes of those they governed when little, but who have now grown up and display a benign tolerance for their former guardians. Ron Wordley, HTV's Managing Director who conducted the tour, reminds me of a Sergeant Major who doesn't want to officiate but is prepared to bend a little.

A flying visit to the beleaguered and broke CBC Radio, our ILR station in Cardiff. The staff continue to put out a good service, I am told, despite the fact that bankruptcy has been staring them in the face for six months or more. They are all hoping for a miracle to happen on Friday and that Owen Oyston, their knight in shining armour, will be able to save them and Gwent. On Friday I heard from John Thompson that he had!

Dashed back on the train on Wednesday and then off on Thursday to Cambridge and the RTS's bi-annual thrash. This time addressed by Douglas Hurd, the 16-day-old Home Secretary, who gave a boring speech focused on community radio, which had little of interest to the Royal Television Society.

In the evening, a Cambridge Union debate: 'Should the BBC accept advertising?' Paul Johnson for, John Mortimer against. Pretty predictable stuff, with much emphasis on virgins and whores by Paul J. The case for advertising was lost overwhelmingly.

A good 'hypothetical' on Saturday: 'Terrorism and Television'. A stunning performance from the barrister acting as interrogator. ITV's response to the various imagined crisis situations was of a much better calibre than the BBC's.

David Frost, guest of honour at the RTS dinner on Saturday, misjudged his audience and was weakly applauded. I sat next to Lucy Faulkner, ex-BBC Governor, who was deeply distressed at the path the BBC seemed to be taking internally – the split between Managers and Governors.

Alasdair Milne told me that Stuart Young could not reconcile himself to accepting that the *Real Lives* crisis would be forgotten and it would be business as usual. I don't think this will occur until the BBC have formally decided who is 'in charge'. Both of them have refused to face up to this crucial issue.

Sunday 29th September

Another week without news of *Dallas* and its final resting place! I've done as much as I am prepared to do. If it gets lost in transit, somebody else will have to send out the search parties.

For a while now, we have been looking at our expenditure of some £200m per annum – divided between Engineering and Brompton Road. We commissioned a study from Peat Marwick McLintock, who advised that they should be under one heading. I have always felt this to be the logical rationale, but when the report was circulated there was bitter dissent. I am going to have to bite the bullet and insist on the changes. It may take a year or more but the present set-up is crazy.

On Tuesday I went and had a drink with Richard Branson – an amazing entrepreneur with fingers in nearly every entertainment pie. At 36, he looks relaxed and happy. His houseboat is moored in Little Venice and he enjoys it in much the same way as a weekend canal-user would. I was sounding him out on DBS and whether he was still interested now the Club of 21 was disbanded. He is. Although at heart a pirate, I suspect Rick will take the best opportunity that presents itself. Who wouldn't?

This week I wrote to Bob Phillis, copying him with the letter the IBA has sent to Maxwell. Maxwell is not a man to be crossed and, having lit the blue touch-paper, I have got my fingers in my ears waiting for the explosion, but I cannot see how he will be able to justify his two commitments without acknowledgement that they represent a conflict of interest.

Brian Tesler has raised with me the question of the BBC's possible participation in Super Channel. I told him I didn't see it as a problem. If the BBC and ITV want to go together on cable in Europe, good luck to them. My original objection to BBC participation was with DBS, quite another kettle of fish.

On Thursday I attended the official commencement of construction of the Museum of the Moving Image on the South Bank. Tony Smith is the leading light behind it. They are still short of £1m. So far the ITV Companies have declined to pass the hat round.

Sunday 6th October

A week of squalls and sunshine.

On Monday to the Garrick and lunch with Andrew Quinn, the co-ordinator for the ill-fated Club of 21, the consortium of satellite interests, which, together with the BBC and ITV, considered the launching of a UK Unisat DBS and concluded that it would prove too high a risk.

Andrew now believes that the future of DBS lies in a high-power transponder beaming from a pan-European satellite with other countries sharing the cost by using similar transponders to beam to their own audiences. Following the lunch, he sent me – under plain wrapper – a letter he had received from the DTI, which appears not to count out of court the notion of a European partnership along these lines. Although we are putting on a bright face over our failed 'trawl' of UK interests in the British DBS, the results so far are disappointing.

On Tuesday I had a call from Richard Dunn of Thames. Could I meet urgently, and away from the office? We met at the Inn on the Park and sat together drinking a cup of tea in a large bedroom suite, just like a couple of secret agents.

The tale he told was startling. Carlton Communications were making a bid for the total shareholding of Thames and both existing major shareholders were prepared to consider the offer. My first reaction was to say that I would be surprised if it got past first base.

He told me that, on 30 September, Hugh Dundas had agreed to consider the offer of just under £83m. Thorn-EMI had also agreed in principle, subject to the IBA. Dunn was obviously concerned about the future stability of Thames. However, he indicated that, if the Management had proper safeguards and the IBA was satisfied, the proposition ought to be considered.

On Thursday I had a meeting with Sir John Reid and Hugh Dundas. They asked for the meeting as a matter of urgency. I listened to their side of the argument. Both indicated their willingness to sell if, and only if, the IBA felt this to be right. I said that I was extremely doubtful that the IBA would agree to the terms as stated. This acquisition would be subject to the clause in the Act which gave the Authority power to decide whether or not to allow a substantial change of ownership through the phrase 'nature and characteristic'. I said that the nature and characteristic would be substantially changed and I could not see the Authority agreeing to this and would certainly wish to re-advertise the Contract. I said that I would think on. Hugh Dundas was afraid that rumours of the Carlton interest would emerge in the press at the weekend. I agreed that the IBA would not comment.

On Friday, I had breakfast with Michael Green and Michael Luckwell, both pressing for an urgent decision. The plan was for Carlton to acquire the total holding of Thames for £82m, then form a company – Thames Carlton – and then offer shares in the new company in the ratio Carlton 40 per cent, Thorn-EMI 50 per cent and other investors 10 per cent.

I asked Brian Rook, IBA's Secretary, to liaise with our lawyers. Brian spoke to me later, on Friday evening, to say that in principle Allen & Overy believed that such an acquisition would be feasible but would have to rest on the decision of the Authority.

Subsequently, I received a call this morning from Richard Dunn to say that he had held a meeting with his advisors at County Bank, and now felt that the offer by Carlton would be dangerous for Thames as it would put too much control in the hands of Michael Green. County Bank were advising a further issue in June which would attract a wide spread of investment interest but not diminish British Electric Traction's present holding of 47.5 per cent and provide 15 per cent for staff, with the remainder placed with County Bank. So back to square one!

George T comes home today and I will have to do some careful briefing but it wouldn't surprise me if there isn't a major difference of view between management and shareholders.

On Tuesday next we meet James Gatward and Lord Boston to hear further from them about their plans for TVS to acquire the Worldvision interest of Thorn-EMI.

The Board of Central have now acknowledged our decision to ask them to remove Maxwell because of his interest in TDFI. So far a deep silence from Mr Maxwell.

On Wednesday, Roma and I travelled to Nottingham. At the Royal Hotel we changed into evening dress and I donned the chain of office of President of the London branch of TRIC and duly appeared as Guest of Honour at the Silver Centenary Celebration of the Midlands branch of TRIC. I sat next to a lady with blue hair who had been President for it seemed a thousand years. The toastmaster – a man of massive girth – presided while we ate, and had a drink at a small table on the dance floor. He looked more like the Guest of Honour than I did. After he had performed his function, he pulled out a packet of fags and walked off. Altogether a splendid evening, with everyone toasting everyone else, including the serving staff.

Today's headline in the Business Section of the *Sunday Times* announced that Thames was in a 'take over' situation. It was a piece of accurate reporting, but failed in one vital respect: the name of the company bidding for Thames had not been discovered.

The telephone calls started at 10am and haven't stopped. I told our Press Office to simply state that no formal proposals had been made to the Authority and no statement was therefore forthcoming.

I spoke to GT last night and warned him to expect a leak. The next few days are going to prove interesting.

Richard Dunn believes that Hugh Dundas should stand down as Chairman of Thames. I agree with him. He put forward a tentative proposal by Mary Baker, a director of Thames, that he himself should become Acting Chairman. I am not in favour.

This morning, Bryan Cowgill has a piece in the *Sunday Times* on Peacock and takes the opportunity of having another go at the IBA and the BBC for 'colluding' on *Dallas*.

Saturday 13th October

The main focus of all eyes this week has been Carlton's proposed merger with Thames. Interesting to see how different elements in the industry reacted.

The ITV Companies rightly felt threatened: if it could happen to Thames could it happen to them? The media writers during the week balanced the arguments. None said outright that the IBA should let it take place, but at the same time none believed the idea so offensive as not to merit consideration.

On Monday Lord Thomson returned from holiday and we had three meetings. The first with Hugh Dundas and Sir John Reid. The second with Richard Dunn. And finally with Michael Green and his partner Mike Luckwell.

Michael Green is a very charming, presentable tycoon. Certainly the next generation of media boss. His enthusiasm for the merger was almost infectious but the more I looked at his proposal, the more I became concerned that it was not a 'merger' but a take-over with Carlton holding some 40 per cent of the enlarged company, with Michael Green and Mike Luckwell holding some 21 per cent of the stock.

However one looked at it, the fact could not be obscured that both BET and Thorn-EMI were proposing to sell out at a premium. What point the franchise process, if all a company had to do was wait until an attractive offer came along and then get out at a profit?

As the week progressed, I took soundings from our solicitors – John Wotton & Geoffrey Sammon. They had no doubt that we would be in error to allow the 'deal' to go through.

During the early part of the week, I encouraged Richard Dunn to push forward with his examination, together with County Bank, of an alternative proposition. Richard telephoned me several times, late in the evening, expressing his growing concern that, if the deal went through, staff would not back it.

On Wednesday, at DGMM, I expressed my own view for the first time – that the bid should not be allowed to go through – and my view was generally endorsed.

In the evening, Roma and I went to Peter Gibbings for dinner. Dick Marsh and David McCall were guests, with their wives. After dinner the conversation inevitably turned to Thames. David McCall and Peter Gibbings were of the view that Carlton should be seen off. Dick Marsh thought there could be merit in the deal.

The following day the broadcasting unions added their voice, asking for urgent meetings.

Mary Baker asked to be telephoned at the Tory conference. I spoke to her on Thursday morning. She was against the deal. I saw GT and told him that I thought we should wait no longer and that, as Thames had a Board Meeting scheduled for that evening at 5pm, we should declare our hand. I said that to wait would increase the pressures on Thames' management and we would appear indecisive. GT agreed. He spoke to Authority Members Alec Cullen and Michael Caine. I had spoken earlier to George Russell.

Hugh Dundas and I had spoken on the telephone the previous day and he had asked me if I could give him a 'steer' for his board. I had promised to speak again to him and called him to say we would not agree the deal. I said that I would call him formally with the exact words of our decision. Finding the right words was more difficult than I had expected. I was anxious to avoid detail, and yet I didn't want to create precedents by a statement that was too vague.

Brian Rook, Head of Legal affairs, and his deputy John Norrington and I agonised until Bryan and I felt we had got it about right. John disagreed. The words I telephoned to Hugh Dundas were: 'The Authority has concluded that the Carlton Communications proposal, which would lead to a major change in the nature and characteristic of a viable ITV programme company, is not acceptable, having regard to the Authority's responsibilities under the Broadcasting Act'.

I telephoned Michael Green and read him the statement. He said he was astonished and dismayed. The Thames Board duly met and the following morning Hugh Dundas put out an announcement from the Board stating that they accepted the Authority's decision.

Predictably, the Sundays have called the findings 'potty', but in the same breath as condemning the Authority for having its head in the sand they talk about the 'rich resources and programme material' that could make the company worth many millions more than Carlton's £82m bid. The papers hint today that Carlton may try and insist on acquiring the shares despite our refusal, going for a break-up value of Thames without its television contract interest. The Authority meets on Wednesday. I hope all Members endorse my action. I fail to see how they cannot, but whichever way one looks at the events of last week, Thames Television will never be the same again.

A less dramatic but nonetheless important decision was taken by Members at the meeting to give TVS permission to go ahead and make a bid for World Screen. And on their own head be it if as a result they fail to deliver a good television service.

Another surprise at the meeting was the conclusion reached by Members who had interviewed the candidates for the Portsmouth & Southampton radio franchise. Instead of Radio Victory (the incumbent) the Members have granted it to a new consortium. A final parting gift from Sir John Riddell! Poor old Victory. They performed adequately but in the interview gave a lacklustre performance and were clearly second place to the case made by Ocean Sound, who had a much more realistic assessment of costs.

Sunday 20th October

Another week dominated by the Thames furore.

The Authority met on Wednesday and I knew in my bones the natives were restless. GT had already got wind that a number of Members were seriously upset that they had not been consulted prior to the announcement of our decision to abort the move by Carlton to acquire Thames.

I sensed at the time that the notice sent to Members was pitifully inadequate, but I reasoned (incorrectly) that Members would endorse the decision and not require a lengthy explanation.

In the event, the meeting with Members proved one of the most unpleasant since I joined. They very clearly had already vent their spleen on GT before I came in, during a private session to discuss salaries and pensions. GT had taken the opportunity in the private meeting to apologise for failing to consult the Members. This did not prevent some searching questions to elicit why I had advised the action I did. I explained as best I could. Listening to the debate that followed, I was glad I had taken the decision when I did. I suspect that, had it waited for the meeting, I would not have got a clear signal and the result would have been to throw more confusion into the wind.

On the Tuesday preceding the Authority meeting, GT and I held an 8.15am meeting with Nicholas Wills of British Electric Traction (BET), Hugh Dundas and Colin Southgate of Thorn-EMI. They came to seek clarification of the IBA's decision. I formed the view that neither Wills nor Southgate really had any idea of the kind of responsibilities that their two Companies had inherited when they undertook to become partners in Thames Television. They appeared genuinely to think they had a right to trade the shares with whoever they wished and without consideration of duties laid on them by the Authority of the day. This was exemplified by an apparent restructuring agreement reached between Carlton, BET and Thorn-EMI, which had not been brought to the Thames Board. I said I would do what I could to help guide the thinking of the Thames Board when the whole matter of restructuring the company came before them.

Back to the Authority meeting. Members were alarmed to see a letter to the IBA from Carlton stating clearly that their legal advisors believed BET and Thorn to have entered into binding agreements with Carlton to sell their holdings regardless of IBA approval. It was most probably this frontal attack by Carlton that helped GT and me get the endorsement to the actions we had taken.

Subsequently Hugh Dundas wrote assuring me that Carlton had no such right. Allen & Overy are arguing that, before guidance is given to the Thames Board on next steps, the threat of Carlton to acquire the shares regardless of our wishes must be withdrawn. We now await a formal letter to confirm HD's note to me.

Carlton have not gone away though, and the Sunday papers today speculate on their next move. Richard Dunn told me that Robert Maxwell had telephoned Hugh Dundas and said that he would 'top' any offer made by Carlton.

The IBA really can't win. This week's *Broadcast* in its leader takes us to task for not having moved earlier to broaden the shareholding base of Thames!

Dallas was very nearly settled this week – or at least I thought it was. Michael Grade telephoned to ask if the IBA would act as 'honest brokers' between Thames and themselves and co-ordinate press statements so that neither side took advantage of the other. He hoped the announcement would be made on Friday or, at the latest, Monday. Yesterday, during my conversation with Richard Dunn, he said that there was a new snag: Worldvision had cabled to say that they would only agree to the assignment if Thames would agree to underwrite the terms of the original contract if the BBC, for one reason or another, failed to continue playing the series. Thames will say no, and hope to call their bluff. What with the OFT sniffing around, the last thing we need is yet another 'side' agreement to confuse the issue still further.

This week saw agreement between ITV, Channel 4, the IBA and S4C over subscription charges for the next three years. A good step forward and one that will save us the palaver of making a judgment each year.

Finally, in a crowded week, a new saga is unfolding at Eggcup House. Timothy Aitken is making a bid to become Executive Chairman. If he gets his way, Bruce Gyngell will leave and we will all be back to square one.

I lunched with Tony Vickers at the beginning of the week and he related the sorry tale. I am due to lunch with Timothy Aitken on the 28th October. On the 29th there is a Board Meeting and TA hopes to be able to say that I have approved his bid. One uncharitable reason for his sudden enthusiasm to become active at TV-am is so that he can claim a share of some 400,000 shares that are being issued to Executive Directors!

I invited David Frost to hear his views. He drank half a bottle of white wine and smoked an old stub-end of cigar that still stinks in my office. He has no love for TA and backs Bruce.

Later I met Bruce and he was outspoken in his criticism of TA.

To add complications to an already potential powder keg – Fleet Newspapers have been bought out by United Newspapers. Fleet owns 31 per cent of TV-am and the Authority will have to decide whether to allow United to continue to hold the same amount, sell off their interest or wait until a share floatation is agreed.

Thursday 24th October

Dallas lurched another step towards the brink this week. I told Richard Dunn I would seek a 'feel' from the majors and consequently spoke to Bob Phillis, Chairman of the Film Purchase Committee of ITCA, on Monday evening. Bob, quickly but politely, left me in no doubt that the 'big five' would not go back on their decision not to make up the difference. Bob said he had coerced the regions into agreeing the *Dallas* package and that a return to the previous position would be unthinkable. He concluded by saying that the stock of Richard Dunn with his colleagues would go down if he now went back on the agreements reached. If Thames decided to show *Dallas*, they would show it alone.

I spoke to RD and conveyed this reaction. RD said he would follow this up with Bob.

On Wednesday I received, by hand, a telex from Worldvision addressed to Hugh Dundas, in response to a letter he had sent the day before to Kevin O'Sullivan. The telex left Thames in no doubt: Worldvision were not prepared to move from their position.

I spoke to RD and said that the decision would have to be made by the Thames Board. The IBA was not going to prejudge or step into the situation. I did add that they might decide to bite the bullet and agree to the conditions. At least it would bring an end to the sorry story.

Flew to Paris today to speak at a seminar on sponsorship at Versailles. Received a message from Sally (my P.A.) to say that *Broadcast* magazine had published details of a meeting between GT, Shirley Littler and Sir John Reid and a meeting between GT, myself, Hugh Dundas and Stuart Young. A copy of a letter sent by the IBA to Allen & Overy is also published, dealing with our understanding regarding the Office of Fair Trading. I write this on the plane home, and have not yet read the article, but I counselled GT not to issue any statements. I fear that this is but the first of a number of mis-informed leaks that are set to cause maximum embarrassment.

From the account given to me from Sally, it would appear the leak has come from a Thames source and not from us, which is a small blessing.

Thames is taking up an inordinate amount of time. HD last week asked me to be as helpful as possible to their Board in considering restructuring.

On Monday, Brian Rook, the IBA Company Secretary, worked hard to draft a letter outlining our considerations, and also took account of RD's concerns expressed to me last Saturday.

On Tuesday, however, BR told me that he had been notified by Allen & Overy that BET's (British Electric Traction's) lawyer had agreed to the contractual understandings of both BET and Thorn-EMI to Carlton not to agree any change in conditions except with Carlton until 30th November. I spoke to HD and told him we could not offer any steer until the position with Carlton had been clarified.

Dundas was upset by this news. I told him he should have highlighted this clause when seeking earlier advice on the substance of the agreement with Carlton. He said he thought it was such a 'usual' clause he had not thought it worth bothering about! I told him a letter was going round by hand setting out our views and invited him to circulate his Board with copies.

The Thames Board held a meeting yesterday, no doubt discussing their response to Worldvision and their reaction to my letter.

I read today in the newspapers that a MORI poll had shown a 64 per cent vote by the public in favour of accepting advertising on the BBC.

The Versailles seminar was disastrous. Eighteen speakers and 30 delegates, but my speech struck a good note and might get wider airing when it has been circulated to the press here at home.

I close this part of the diary as we fly into London airport, knowing little of the problems that await my return.

Sunday 27th October

Back to Dorset and an early drive to Corfe's newspaper shop to see what stories the Sundays have to tell. Thank goodness nothing to tear hair over. A mention of *Dallas* and a piece about United Newspapers' holding in TV-am.

When I landed at London airport last week, my driver David was waiting with a copy of *Broadcast*. Not as horrendous as I had feared. The leaked memo was stated as being from the pen of Hugh Dundas. A reference to Shirley Littler as 'Deputy DG' which won't go down well on the 8th floor! A passage from HD's memorandum that the behaviour by Cowgill was such that he (GT) could not forgive and forget, was attributed to GT. Despite the fact that it could have been worse, I am not at all happy at the leak. It could give Worldvision an excuse to pull away from a final resolution. O'Sullivan might take exception to the insinuation that Worldvision had behaved improperly.

Yesterday I had an hour-long telephone conversation with Richard Dunn. I did not mention to him that, on my arrival back from Paris, I had been given a handwritten letter from HD containing the line '*The Broadcast* spread on *Dallas* is terribly distressing to me'. I had also been handed a formal letter from HD responding to my letter hand-delivered on Thursday morning. The substance of this second letter was to defend as 'reasonable' BET's and Thames' agreement to allow Carlton until 30 November to decide whether or not to proceed. This had never been stated before.

There was also another reference to 31 January which, on re-reading the letter several times, still is not clear to me, although it appears to suggest that if the IBA changed its mind they (Carlton) could make a renewed offer up to and until that date.

My conversation with RD confirmed my suspicion that the Board of Thames had no idea of these clauses.

In the *Parliamentary Bulletin* of 22nd October, Michael Howard, Junior Minister for Trade and Industry, answered John Gorst's question to the Secretary of State, which asked what steps Her Majesty's Government had taken to seek to ensure that the arrangements made by the British Broadcasting Corporation and the Independent Broadcasting Authority (or its Contractors) for the acquisition of film or other programme material are consistent with the Government's policy on competition ... with particular reference to the circumstances surrounding the purchase by Thames Television of the *Dallas* programme.

Mr Howard replied: 'The Director General of Fair Trading has statutory powers to initiate appropriate action under the competition legislation in respect of any arrangements that may exist between the British Broadcasting Corporation and the Independent Broadcasting Authority or independent television Companies concerning the acquisition of film or other programme material'.

He went on say that the Director General had written to the BBC, the IBA and the ITCA making enquiries in connection with the purchase of overseas television programmes. All three bodies 'denied the existence of arrangements concerning the purchase of film or other programme material which might require registration under the Restrictive Trade Practices Act 1976'. The Office of Fair Trading is now considering whether, in the light of these replies and other information available, further action is justified under the competition legislation.

Sunday 3rd November

On Monday, lunch with Timothy Aitken in City Road. Timothy, as always, immensely confident and forthright. Obviously wants to float TV-am as soon as possible (early 1986). I thought he would bring up the subject of becoming Executive Chairman. I may have got in first by saying I thought Bruce was doing a good job and hoped the Board would allow things to move forward at a sensible and measured pace, because not a word was mentioned. I said the IBA would lose patience if, for some reason or another, TV-am were to be thrown into confusion!

Bruce later telephoned to say the Board meeting had gone better than he had dared hope, so what I said must have struck a chord with Timothy.

To the Lords on Monday, and a dinner hosted by GT for ILR Chairmen. A good PR exercise but not without its embarrassments. The recently deposed Chairman of Radio Victory was sitting immediately below our top table and I suspect he has now made it his mission to cause the maximum fuss about the 'iniquity' of the IBA's decision, having written to GT with copies to the PM and heaven knows who else.

Spoke for nearly two and a half hours on Wednesday to the Station Managers at Crawley Court. This time I had decided to do it by myself, rather than with GT. I felt more comfortable than before and I think the session was a success. Am doing the same with Managers and some senior staff at Brompton Road on Monday.

In the evening a good dinner with an excellent speech by GT and a lively toast to Members sung by the diners with special lyrics to the tune of 'Rule Britannia':

> 'When Britain first had ITV
> Arose from out of Parliament
> An Act, a brand new Broadcasting Act for ITV.
> There was no Charter, no Board of Governors,
> But Guardian Angels, an Authority.
> Hail! Authority,
> Authority Members all.
> Lord T's merry, merry, merry band of twelve.
>
> Today Lord Thomson has the Chair,
> Sir John Riddell his Deputy.
> With them, with special care for our provinces three,
> Scotland's John Purvis, Gwilym Peregrine for Wales,
> From Ulster Jill McIvor hails.

Hail! Authority,
Authority Members all.
Lord T's merry, merry, merry band of twelve.

To represent our modern life
Are Roy Grantham and Paula Ridley,
Then Alec Cullen next and Yvonne Connolly,
Juliet Jowitt, George Russell, Michael Caine
To them, with glasses raised, our toast shall be
The Authority,
We drink our toast to thee,
Long life, health to the Authority.

Attended the Booker Prize given on Thursday at the Guildhall. Altogether a much less dazzling occasion than I had expected, with a less than dazzling decision by the judges to award Keri Hulme's *The Bone People* with the Booker. Three strange ladies chanting a mantra came forward to accept the prize. None turned out to be the author.

No more on Thames or *Dallas* this week. Is silence golden?

I nearly forgot – perhaps a good sign – that after three years all's well, very nearly. Channel 4 is three years old this week, and *Crossroads* has done 21 years hard labour but still attracts huge audiences and Roma finds it riveting.

Sunday 10th November

Armistice Sunday. The old soldiers get older, the shadows seem to grow longer as they fall across the Cenotaph. I wonder if thousands of young men would answer again to the call to arms as they did 40 years ago. Next time there won't be a declaration of war, just a big bang.

A week of mixed blessings. On Monday I talked to about 30 staff at Brompton Road. I told them things look brighter than they had a year ago when I addressed them last. I said too often praise was in short supply for the IBA and the staff. I told them our finances were better controlled and better spent. Afterwards we had drinks. Several people said they appreciated what I had to say.

My self-satisfaction was short-lived: two days later Sally told me that Bob Towler, our Head of Research, had said to her he thought it had been patronising and a waste of two hours. I felt quite upset and asked Bob to explain what he meant. He thought I had misdirected my remarks to senior people and that, if it had been those lower down the scale, it would have been acceptable. I suppose the fact I write about it shows how vain one is and how much I hate criticism. Are we all like that?

Nothing daunted, I have decided to speak to staff lower down the system. I will use the same text and see what effect it has on them.

A meeting of GAC (General Advisory Council) on Tuesday. They are a lively lot and give much thought and time to Authority business. This time they gave their views in no uncertain fashion on violence and were harsh in their criticism of *Dempsey & Makepeace*. They were also concerned about the representation of ethnic minorities on the box and behind the camera. I admire the GAC and am considering whether we really take up their views with enough seriousness. It is too easy for the Members of the Authority to feel aloof from the GAC, although I think that Yvonne Connolly shares much the same concerns. I shall read the Minutes with care this time and see if something more positive can result.

In the evening, a dinner to celebrate Channel 4's third birthday. GT promised me beforehand that he would not over-react or get rubbed up the wrong way (which he always seems to when in the company of Jeremy Isaacs and Edmund Dell). This time all went well until the speeches were past and it was time for comments. GT suddenly got astride his hobbyhorse – balance and impartiality. He chastised Jeremy for continuing to get it wrong. The celebration deteriorated into a wake.

I had arranged a birthday cake decorated with Channel's 4's musical theme. It was brought in with two sparklers sparkling. GT tried to blow them out, much to everyone's amazement and concern.

On Friday, Jeremy Isaacs telephoned me to say how upset he had been over GT's words. There is a liaison meeting next Tuesday and I have arranged to have an item on the Agenda which should allow us to discuss GT's remarks seriously and maybe at long last get some sort of rapprochement.

Reports in the newspapers say that Worldvision has now offered evidence to the OFT about *Dallas*. It will come to haunt us like Banquo's ghost.

On Thursday, Mrs Whitehouse announced to the world that her Association had compiled a tape of seven days of violence consisting of some 220 items. ITV and Channel 4 were attacked, as was the BBC, but BBC 2 fared better. It was *Dempsey & Makepeace* that made the headlines for violence. I hoped the GAC would keep quiet. Thankfully, they did. I asked Information to get out a short analysis showing how viewers were reacting to violence and I received their review on Saturday. It throws a steadying light on what is rightly a highly-charged subject.

On Thursday I lunched with friends and sat next to Peter Cadbury – a splendid buccaneer and a man whose energy and arrogance obviously upset Lady Plowden and the Authority of the day. He said that much water had flowed under the bridge and he would welcome an invitation to lunch if GT felt so inclined. I relayed the message to George, who seemed disinclined to take up the offer.

Sunday 17th November

Marcher Sound (Cheshire and North East Wales) has been taking up time this week. The station is insolvent (technically) and must either do a deal with outside backers (in this case Chiltern Radio) or go to the wall. Held a meeting with the Chairman of Marcher and the Chairman of Chiltern. Not convinced the solution offered is attractive to us, or to Marcher. Still consider it might be best to pull the plug and start again.

Victory's Chairman is still causing much aggro. On Monday (18 November) GT and I will be seeing a deputation and will be presented with a petition containing 25,000 signatures. Barbara Hosking tells me that Brian Young refused to see deputations. I restrained GT from going to the other extreme and offering coffee!

On Tuesday attended annual Cable and TV Association lunch at the Dorchester.

Why do these events go on for so long? Giles Shaw finished at 2.55 pm, just in time for me to get back to SCC at 3.25. The cable industry feels let down by Government. Mrs T's 'white-hot technological revolution' has gone stone cold and the Companies are facing a long, uphill struggle.

John Jackson, a Director of Central and also on the Board of Sky, tells me that the Companies see Super Channel as a first stepping stone to a European DBS opportunity. At SCC on Tuesday, I underlined to the Companies that, if the Authority endorsed their plans for Super Channel, it would be strictly for satellite to cable. After SCC I met Richard Dunn, who asked me whether I would be upset if Thames decided not to participate in Super Channel. I said I wouldn't be. It was up to Thames to decide where its priorities lay.

At SCC, I caused some consternation by asking to see the ITCA business plan for Super Channel. Some around the table, who I don't think have shown it to their own Boards, were obviously taken aback.

On Thursday, I went to the launch of the Howard Steele Foundation at BAFTA set up in memory of Howard who had been the IBA's Director of Engineering until his death in 1983. Nobody from the upper echelons of the BBC or ITV. We are giving it a cool reception until we have more information.

Next week Belfast.

Saturday 23rd November

This week the world of broadcasting has lurched a little further into the relative unknown. I sometimes feel like the men on the tea clippers, lashing themselves to the mast and hoping the ship will keep on course through the storms.

On Monday to ITN and the regular meeting of the Board. Last item on the agenda was Super Channel and Aubrey B. kicked off the item by expressing his concern and disappointment at the lack of consultation by the working party and the Executive of ITN, whose particular and very real worry was that Super Channel had already struck a deal with the BBC to supply the main 9pm news slot. This they felt – and rightly in my opinion – would give the BBC a prestigious role to play, which would serve to endorse and confirm the view that the BBC was the pre-eminent news provider in the UK and, since Super Channel itself was being marketed under the banner 'Best of British', the title would itself confirm the BBC's superiority. David Plowright said that no arrangements had yet been fully discussed with the BBC, but that the BBC were most anxious to supply the service and, if they couldn't, might well abandon their role altogether as programme suppliers.

Alastair Burnet commented that, if this was the case, it illustrated how much value the BBC placed on establishing this role for itself.

I felt that I should have the IBA's concern recorded for the Minutes and said that, whilst the Authority would not wish to interfere with business judgments, it would, I believed, be concerned if actions brought about by the Super Channel Board appeared to be demoting or downgrading the services provided by the independent system and that, if this were to be the case, I could imagine the Authority having something to say.

I shall follow this up next week with a letter, so that there can be no later misunderstandings. My overall feeling about Super Channel is going through a change – the Companies have rushed headlong into it and, from all accounts, the business plan reflects the hurry and also the optimism that some Companies have privately criticised.

I am sure that the same plan of the majors – or at least Yorkshire, Granada and LWT – is to get Super Channel up and running at whatever risk and, once established on cable, make a case to Government that, together with the BBC, a DBS option is within realisation if – and this is the bargain – Government will give them an extension of their terrestrial contracts and if they can use an alternative carrier than Unisat in order to bring the costs down. I am against this.

At the Authority meeting on Wednesday, I spelt out my fears and received a generally warm endorsement of the approach I had adopted at the ITN Board meeting.

On Monday evening, I got a call from Robert Maxwell to tell me that on the following day there would be an announcement about his role in the French TDFI venture. He said that he believed the IBA's resistance to him having both an interest in the French satellite service *and* a seat on the Central board was mistaken and that, if we persisted in our wish to have him removed from the Board of Central he would 'vigorously' apply to the Courts to reverse our 'quite unacceptable decision'.

If there was a sound reason, he said, he would like to hear it. I said that it was quite simply a conflict of interest.

Actually, I was somewhat premature in making that statement because, on Tuesday, the press stories carried the news that Maxwell had agreed to rent one DBS channel on TDFI for a rumoured £5.2m per annum, which he would use to transmit programmes in English to a footprint that would cover Europe and the UK. Earlier, when the matter had first come to our attention, Maxwell was considering acquiring a 20 per cent holding in the project as a whole. This current deal means that the Authority will have to take a decision afresh. I will advise them to stick to their guns and ask Central to ensure his resignation from their Board but the going will undoubtedly be rough.

The news of Maxwell's acquisition has sent tremors through the industry and may well lead ITCA to review their intention to launch Super Channel. Maxwell, in one move, has positioned himself as a real force to be reckoned with, not only as a competitor to UK terrestrial services but also to Rupert Murdoch's Sky Channel. Rupert must be extremely displeased and I imagine will now do his utmost to secure a similar means of transmission. Star Wars of a different kind.

This week I have been hearing from two groups, both wanting to get into DBS: Granada and James Lee who has founded SBC, the Satellite Broadcasting Company. We have been asked to submit the report we are preparing on satellite interest for the UK DBS to the Home Secretary by the end of December. Last week

I prepared a paper for the Authority in which I said that I considered that the role of the IBA would be best served if we indicated to the Home Secretary that we believe our best course be that of a regulator for the existing terrestrial services and not grasp for wider opportunities. I added that we would, of course, not wish to close any doors and that, if invited, would play our part.

At the Director General's Management Meeting on Tuesday, I came up against unexpectedly strong opposition to the stance I was proposing to adopt. DGMM felt that I had been too negative and that there was a positive role to be played within the development of DBS. I agreed to amend my oral report to the Authority on Wednesday, which I subsequently did. I don't think Members really understand the gravity of these decisions or else they are being simply pragmatic.

To Belfast on Wednesday and Thursday. The car taking us to the hotel rolling over 'sleeping policemen' set in the road outside the airport was a physical reminder that Ulster is not like anywhere else in the UK.

That evening to Hillsborough Castle to attend a dinner in our honour given by Tom King, newly appointed Secretary of State for Northern Ireland. Hillsborough Castle was defended like Fort Knox but we swept inside in a hire car without any kind of search or identity check. Tom King was very relaxed and we chatted over dinner about the Anglo/Irish agreement. He said he thought the path towards reconciliation was going to be rough and long.

The following day we were the guests of Ulster Television at the City Hall. This turned out to be a lively affair which caught the headlines. After we had sat down to eat, a group of Unionists rushed in and started to yell abuse at the guests and, in particular, the Lord Mayor, who they clearly considered had behaved in a traitorous manner, sitting down as he did beside the Secretary of State for Northern Ireland. Not the most popular man in Belfast. The whole event had undertones of farce, except that it was played out in deadly earnest. We tucked into our first course, whilst white-faced angry Protestants banged on our tables, mounted the platform and screamed slogans. The police duly arrived, having taken their time, and manhandled the protestors outside, where they eventually fell upon poor Tom King as he was leaving. The papers and television made a great hoo-hah about the incident but I don't think it warranted all that attention.

A week of deaths. Leslie Mitchell, aged 80 and well remembered as a commentator for British Movietone News, especially in his wartime commentaries; Tony Preston, Deputy MD of Yorkshire, died in a motor accident – a charming and likeable man who will be sadly missed.

Finally, on Friday evening, to Lainston House and a dinner hosted by Tom Robson to celebrate the award to him of the Edward Rhein Prize in recognition of his pioneering work on MAC.

While I was making my speech of praise, I was thinking what a pity it was that all the money and expertise would very likely be wasted as the French and Germans were discarding the E MAC standard for the greatly inferior D2 MAC. Ah well.

Oh – I very nearly forgot: on Wednesday night the Commons, in their mighty wisdom, decided by 12 votes to reject the experiment to televise the Chamber.

What utter wets! Viscount Hinchingbrooke once said, 'Parliament must work with the tools of the age or it will sculpt no monuments for the future'. The sad truth of this quote is that it was uttered in the early 1960s.

Sunday 1st December

The lights in Oxford and Regent Street are glittering and glowing. The message is Merchandise – peace on earth so long as the cash register rings.

On Monday evening Roma and I attended the Royal Variety Performance at the Theatre Royal, Drury Lane. This being white tie and tails, GT and I stood in a freezing draught just inside the front door waiting for the Queen, who arrived on time looking quite stunning. We bowed and shook hands, and GT said how much we were looking forward to her visit to the IBA the following day.

This year's show was infinitely better than previous ones: a line-up of famous stars not just the usual old telly puddings. Jean Simmons, Elizabeth Welch, Anna Neagle (looking very frail), Norman Wisdom (looking like he has looked for 30 years), Joan Collins (looking like a Joan Collins lookalike) and Celeste Holm.

In the interval, Roma and I went to the Royal Retiring Room and met the Queen again and Prince Philip. The Queen was in a skittish mood. She has an attractive way of suddenly dropping her royal mask and behaving like anyone else. We spoke about the show and the Queen suddenly said, 'Last Sunday, when I was upstairs, I heard great chuckles coming from below. It was Prince Edward, rocking with laughter, watching *It'll Be Alright on the Night*.' The thought of the Queen 'upstairs', I find very amusing. A sort of typical family scene in Watford, not upstairs in Buckingham Palace. I've never before thought of any room in the palace being 'upstairs'. A very jolly evening, landing up in the River Room at the Savoy where tickets to attend the buffet supper had been selling for £1,500 each.

Earlier in the day, a sobering meeting with representatives from AIRC, again searching and hoping for signs from us that we could reduce our costs still further and prevent the imposition of another cost of living increase. I don't think we can. The sad thing is that if radio were regulated separately it could be done for much less.

In the evening, dinner with the Regional Officers.

On Wednesday, a meeting with the Local Advisory Committee chairman and a further meeting with groups interested in launching a UK DBS system, with Robert Devereux from Virgin and Michael Green from Carlton.

A quick dash to the National for a preview of Peter Schaffer's new play *Yonadab*. Incredible performances from Alan Bates and David Warner. We joined Peter and Petra Hall in the interval. I felt I could truly praise the play. It's immensely powerful and I think will get good notices.

A quick dash to Leeds on Thursday to give the CAM Lecture at Trinity & All Saints College on 'The Future of Independent Radio'. I never know whether my performance is any good or not. Speaking from a text for 45 minutes is a hell of a bash. The questions afterwards were good. We dined with the Principal of the

College afterwards and I returned to London early the next morning feeling somewhat knackered.

Much ado on Channel 4's programme *Right to Reply*, with further criticism of Derek Jarman's plays *Jubilee* and *Sebastiane*. David Glencross put up a good response to the attack by Milton Shulman but I am not certain, having seen a bit of *Jubilee*, that this was something I would have shown.

The Sunday papers today all ran stories about Mrs T's determination to reduce violence and sex on television. This is timed purely for a Private Member's Bill due to have its hearing on Tuesday and which hopes to make television as accountable as the Act on Obscene Publications. There is no doubt that a strong mood is running against television violence. Mrs T will find plenty of support.

The great Peacock Debate, held on Thursday, seems to have been a damp squib. Still, it enables Peacock to claim that he allowed the people to speak, or at least a chosen few.

Monday 9th December

Most of the blessings this week were not mixed! Most indeed seemed to have been conjured out of the devil's own brew.

The swarthy shadows of Tebbit and Thatcher continue to fall across the television screen, declaring vengeance on violence and censure on sex. The Sunday 'filth' wring their hands over the decline into the depravity and vice shown on television, even summoning up enough righteous conviction to enable them to reproduce stills from the most offending scenes. (Despite the fact that they were shown after 11pm and were in the context of the drama.)

Singled out particularly for criticism are *Sebastiane* and *Jubilee*. *Eastenders* and *Dempsey and Makepeace* came in a good second.

I rather wish we hadn't shown *Jubilee* and *Sebastiane*, but I have only myself to blame. David Glencross asked my view of *Sebastiane* and I said that, despite it being extremely sexually liberal, it merited showing. Much has been said in criticism about the opening sequence, showing a dance of lust by masked characters holding enormous penises, which ended with a giant explosion of spunk over the face of a recumbent figure. (Even as I describe the scene, I can imagine the opinion of those who did not themselves witness the opening sequence.) I wonder how many of those same critics would object to the primitive dances of African tribes celebrating the rites of fertility.

Like so many things in life, I fear our greatest sin was the sin of bad timing. It would not surprise me if the Authority didn't feel the need to conduct their own witch hunt and, by declaring their innocence, purge themselves of collective guilt. No, I am being grossly unfair. They stood by me over *Scum*.

Speaking to David Glencross last week, he was genuinely prepared to say, if required, that in allowing the showing he had misjudged the public mood. I think I would agree with him but it is odd how silent are the voices of those that were raised over our banning of sequences from Channel 4's intended showing of *Brazil: Cinema, Sex and the Generals*.

Lord Young lunched with us on Monday and urged us to transmit the positive news on unemployment figures. I reminded him that the Government should start thinking about leisure not as a sin but as an inevitable result of the drive to create modern technology and labour-saving processes. This did not fall on appreciative ears.

Also on Monday, I held a meeting with the broadcasting unions. They asked a number of questions about our position viz-à-viz the BBC and engineering rationalisation. I assured them that no discussions had taken place at the highest levels. Tony Hearn said he didn't believe me. I looked hurt. If we do start discussions, I must honour my statement, like it or not.

The Authority meeting on Wednesday confirmed our view that Robert Maxwell should not remain on Central's Board in the event that he was establishing his own channel on TTFI.

An extraordinary outburst after the meeting by a member of the Authority, Jill McIvor, who was greatly angered at the display of our coat of arms hanging in the boardroom. She had not been consulted over it in the first place and found the whole thing objectionable. Very odd.

On Tuesday the Queen's visit. Much last-minute licks of paint and general scurrying around. We were due to show a 20 minute presentation illustrating the work of the IBA. All the rehearsals had fallen short of perfection. Tom Robson intones his piece in the manner of an undertaker describing coffin fitments to a conference of morticians. The demonstration of high definition television, using a wider screen – and on which the IBA engineers have spent thousands upon thousands – crackled and kept giving out muffled squeaks like a pig having its throat cut.

At precisely 3pm, the Queen arrived with Susan Hussey, Robert Fellows and two elegant officers – one from the Navy and one from the Army. For a moment I thought she'd got her engagements muddled!

Susan and I followed the Queen upstairs where she met the Members of the Authority. After lunch Jill McIvor commented that she thought the Queen was particularly boot-faced. She certainly went down the line like a dose of salts.

Much to my surprise, the presentation went off without a hitch. Tom behaved less like an undertaker, and the high-definition came in on cue, in colour, and without wobbling. Susan Hussey asked me the perfect question: whether it would be detrimental to public service broadcasting if the BBC were to take advertising, which gave the opportunity to express our opinion. The Queen listened and said, 'I rather hoped that would be your view'.

After the questions, GT presented the Queen with an album of photographs taken on visits by the Royal Family to television studios throughout the country. She seemed pleased.

On the preceding day, we entertained Sir John Riddell to a farewell dinner at the Hyde Park. Nice speeches. Lousy food.

On Thursday, Friday and Saturday in Geneva with Roma to attend meetings of the European Broadcasting Union. Then back to Harrogate for another royal occasion – this time, YTV's Youth Gala. Met the Queen again and chatted quite happily. A busy week, all in all.

Sunday 15th December

It's odd that in a week when Tebbit and Kinnock regularly attack each other with a violence rarely seen in the House of Commons and when two Euro MPs engage in fisticuffs before the television cameras of the world, that MPs should be accusing the television authorities of bringing an unacceptable degree of violence into the home.

Next Tuesday, GT and I – together with Stuart Young and Alasdair Milne – have been summoned to attend upon the Home Secretary to be told to behave or else.

This week there has been a debate instigated by Geoffrey Johnson-Smith, a former BBC TV presenter, on young people and violent crime:

> 'That this House views with great concern the problem of violent crime committed by the young: notes the important influence which parents, the schools and the media can have in their formative years: and calls upon the Government to lead a renewed and vigorous effort to develop in our young people an increased sense of responsibility and awareness of the interests of their fellow citizens and to encourage their more active participation in their communities.'

Then he went on to say:

> 'It is estimated that young people aged between nine and 14 years of age spend an average of 23 hours per week watching television, sometimes far into the night. What a waste. Just think what could happen if some of them spent 23 hours practising a musical instrument ...'.

Yes, Geoffrey, but the world isn't like that.

> Geoffrey then conjured up the respectable figure of Lord Lane. He was reported in July this year as saying that violence in films and on television, including in news reports, had contributed to an alarming increase in violent crime. He went on to say that it was 'now accepted as common form that once you have your victim on the ground you kick him, preferably in the stomach, or in the head, where the blows are likely to maximise injury'.

If Lord Lane is unaware of the pitched battles that have been fought down the years by hooligans, long before film or television and in which the protagonists used all means at their disposal, he has not been looking to the left or to the right.

At the end of the debate, the Parliamentary Under Secretary of State for the Home Office, David Mellor, closed with these words:

> 'It is important to remember that broadcasters are applying standards far stricter than those contained in the 1959 Act (Obscene Publications Act).'

At SCC this week, I received at long last a copy of the Super Channel business plan, which I have taken home to study. It's called 'Best of British' but it envisages 30 per cent imported material. I suspect that the whole output will be pretty rubbishy. There was a general feeling at the meeting that the Authority might begin to intervene in programme matters. I said that this was not the case but I did want to ensure that ITV was used in a responsible and important way.

Went on Wednesday to the BREMA Dinner. Mrs T. shook my hand with little enthusiasm and I hers. She grows daily more like her Spitting Image.

On Friday off to Rome. Met on the tarmac by a car filled with Italian police and whisked off at high speed to speak to about 200 members of a new group of communicators sponsored by RAI. I spoke about the effectiveness of regulation, and the need to stand firm against the encroachment of DBS and cable in order to protect an excellence of output through PSB. It was well received. The Italians are in a mess over their broadcasting arrangements and are trying to bring back some order into the chaos.

We have now completed our study on DBS options to place before the Home Secretary. Members will be asked to approve our conclusions and at the same meeting the proposals put by Thames for reorganising their voting structure.

The electricians are taking some action over wages. ITV could be off the air over Christmas – wot, no violence?!

Sunday 22nd December

I always succumb to a strange melancholy as the year draws to its end. Perhaps it's because I inevitably feel that much has been left undone, and much could have been done better – or perhaps even done not at all.

Perhaps it's the sense of minuteness of the things upon which we place such store. I clear up piles of papers and see empty headlines, stories long since forgotten, moments of victory and defeat. No matter now. Another empty ring in the tree of life.

I suppose that another birthday acts as another landmark or step towards the Reaper standing in the shade. What terrible introspection. How maudlin at such a time of good cheer and happy greetings.

This, I suppose, has been the week when sex and violence reared their head in the shape of Douglas Hurd, who had on Tuesday the task (no doubt at Mrs T's behest) of giving the broadcasters a wigging.

The day before, GT and I went to Broadcasting House and met Stuart Young and Alasdair Milne to decide on the line we should take. It was pretty clear they hadn't spoken to each other prior to the meeting. Alasdair said to Stuart he thought the BBC should offer viewers who wished to complain direct access to Will Wyatt (Chairman of BBC Guidelines on Violence). Stuart didn't think that was good enough and said Alasdair should be the recipient of letters on the subject. Alasdair agreed. Stuart asked GT what the IBA would do. GT responded, as we had agreed, that the IBA would not take any new action. The Guidelines had been updated in April. The task for the broadcasters was one of interpretation. Stuart informed us that Douglas Hurd, after his meeting with us the following day, was attending a broadcasting journalist luncheon and would obviously be saying something about our talks.

On Tuesday, we sped into the courtyards of the Home Office, avoiding a gathering of press and TV cameramen waiting outside the main entrance.

Douglas has picked up the infuriating habit when shaking hands of moving his arm gradually to the right, thus propelling one sideways and away. A thoroughly nasty habit, learnt at the knee of the All Powerful One – the Matron herself, who was the first person who did it to me. I noticed that he did it to all his guests, which made me feel marginally better.

The broadcasters sat on one side of a long table, Douglas and his acolytes on the other. The meeting lasted longer than I had expected, some 70 minutes.

Douglas kicked off by seeking reassurances that we were attending to our duties. Stuart Young and George Thomson described the way we set about ensuring that shock and horror were not the order of the day. Douglas referred to *Sebastiane* and *Jubilee*. I said that they had been played late at night but had nevertheless caused us to think hard about the appropriateness of showing them. On balance, I said, we had probably misjudged the reaction of our audience.

Douglas said that he wondered if we would like to consider setting up some outside body to long-stop both the BBC's and our own judgments on programme content relating to violence, sex etc.

Stuart and George gave this proposal short shrift, pointing out that both had advisory bodies in addition to the Governors of the BBC and the Members of the Authority. To add another tier to the edifice already created would be unnecessary and cumbersome.

Douglas changed tack and said that he believed that whatever we did in the way of monitoring should be seen more publicly so that viewers might be reassured about the seriousness the subject rightly merited.

He then passed on to Winston Churchill's Private Members Bill to bring broadcasting authorities within the provisions of the Obscene Publications Act, due out around the 10th January and down for debate on 26th January. The Government wasn't yet minded to support it through the House, but he thought it would be hard not to see how it might find a wide measure of support. What did we think?

We told him. We believed that to embrace us within the Obscene Publications Act would be to shackle us needlessly. It would bring discredit to the broadcasters and would limit creativity and expression.

It would censor without sensitivity. Beyond all that, it would mean that Governors and Members alike would be subject to criminal proceedings for decisions taken by programme makers.

Douglas listened to all this, and then pointed out that we had said earlier, when talking about our contracts, that we exercised greater constraints than was contemplated within the Obscene Publications Act. If this was the case, why, he wondered, should we be upset?

It is a Catch 22 situation. Douglas knew he had us cornered and asked us to go away and see what case we wished to mount against the proposals that would be made by Churchill. At a press conference after the meeting, however, Douglas spoke in softer terms than I had expected, or that the tone of our meeting would have suggested.

GT reported back to Members and it was agreed that a letter be sent to the Home Secretary setting out the views of the Authority.

On Wednesday the Authority approved a draft report on DBS proposals and gave their blessing to the Thames reorganisation of their share structure. We had a jolly Christmas lunch afterwards with everyone wearing paper hats and with much laughing and giggling.

On Thursday to Jeffrey Archer's shepherds pie and champagne party, packed with media folk all trying to recognise each other. I left before Matron arrived.

Today I picked up the *Sunday Express* and saw one of the better headlines of 1985: 'TV Sex Beast Storm', about a Thames investigation by the *TV Eye* team, who, it was alleged, had filmed a self-confessed child abuser. Nothing else in the papers about sex and violence. Most people, I suspect, are heartily sick of the whole subject.

Richard Dunn telephoned me on Friday to say that Thames' lawyers had agreed the small print with the BBC over *Dallas*. We shall see whether, at long last, the saga is over.

1986

Sunday 12th January

First entry in the New Year. Sun shining in Dorset if not on Margaret Thatcher. The Heseltine resignation provided one of the most riveting hours of television on *Weekend World* that I have ever seen. I imagine every political commentator and MP was out to telephone calls between midday and one o'clock whilst Brian Walden probed and ferreted around for truth – if not truth then facts as interpreted by Heseltine, who came out well, responding and looking more and more like a possible future Prime Minister, though that prospect fills me with deep despair.

The Christmas season came and went on television, with Channel 4 demonstrating that variety is the spice of life. The BBC claimed a substantial ratings victory. It's ironical but when the BBC does present light entertainment it does it better than ITV, who have the reputation for popular programmes. Conversely, ITV, when it puts its back into it, delivers an impressive range of serious output, not only in the Arts but in documentaries and the field of current affairs.

Before Christmas I noted that the press was making much of Thames interviewing a man who claimed to be a child molester. Thames stood their ground after the transmission, defending their decision on the grounds that if they had disclosed the identity of the man to the police it would have led to a confidentiality being breached and the likelihood that the man would have gone to ground and not seek psychiatric help, which he had promised to do in return for his identity being concealed. The story ran out of steam.

Since the New Year which, incidentally but importantly, secured a CBE for Tom Robson, I have spent much time ensuring that two matters reached a satisfactory conclusion. The first was our DBS report to the Home Secretary and the second the letter from the Chairman to Douglas Hurd following our meeting with him over the question of violence on the screen. I think it was a good letter – fairly putting down our concerns, both about violence and how we govern our business, and also our reaction to the proposal to be embraced within the Obscene Publications Act. I sent a copy to the Companies and will discuss it with them at SCC on Wednesday.

Ken Blyth did a first rate job on the DBS report. I don't imagine the ITV Companies are going to welcome the outcome and I fear I may have to point upwind when its contents become public. In short, we are in favour of going forward and believe that there is sufficient interest in the private sector to warrant our confidence.

I always did think the private sector would respond positively, and the last eighteen months have been frittered away all because the regional television companies' Club of Twenty One wanted to have a monopoly and Government believed this to be the only solution. How misguided.

On Tuesday 7 January I had a breakfast meeting with Brian Tesler, David McCall and David Plowright with Lord T. to discuss Super Channel. Facts still emerge that cause me to believe that the chances of ITV going forward are some way off. It would not break my heart if it fell away to dust. The meeting discussed an increase in foreign material. This would be a travesty of the Best of British concept that attracted me in the first place.

Thames are considering replacing their Controller with David Elstein. A bold choice but one I could endorse. It will give Thames some edge.

Dinner with Justin Dukes on Wednesday. He wants to see Channel 4 in the next franchise round set up as a separate channel in competition for advertising.

Sunday 19th January

This was the week to get away with murder. No one, least of all the media, would have cared one jot. The stage was entirely occupied by the Westland affair – who didn't say what to whom. In the wings, ITV notched up its first billion in advertising revenue.

Granada and Ladbrokes came closer to talking in the open about their plans to merge. The Home Secretary came to lunch and the Companies decided yet again to give more time to shuffling their feet over the launch of an ITV equivalent to *The Listener*.

For a man so much in the storm's eye, Heseltine seemed blissfully unaware and unconcerned that the collar of his shirt always seemed to have a life of its own, popping up at an incongruous angle and distracting attention from his words, reminding me somewhat of the choir boys who always seem to be fiddling with their hymn sheets while prayers are being said at the Cenotaph.

This week we sent out our brief on the Obscene Publications Act to those MPs we think might be sympathetic. I hear that the BBC have decided/are considering playing down their dislike of the Bill on the grounds that they will lose the battle anyway. We are holding a briefing meeting on Wednesday.

On Tuesday, SCC met and the main topic was Super Channel.

It is clear that the Companies are still not agreed on whether they should go forward. I suspect that, since Bryan Cowgill left, some of the fire in their belly has departed. Also, Thames and Central are far from content to join in the project. Granada and LWT seem the most committed.

To a Board meeting of Independent Television Publications on Wednesday. ITP have little or no taste but have done well on it, since the majority of ITV viewers appear to have little taste either. *TV Times* magazine reflects this and consequently has a huge circulation and makes huge profits. Now ITV have launched a weekly magazine *Chat*, which is as far downmarket as any magazine on any newsstand. The good news is that it is not selling as well as hoped or expected. With any luck, they might even get a bleeding nose. I suppose I am feeling prickly because once more the Companies decided to postpone a decision on the launch of an upmarket magazine similar to *The Listener*. ITV badly needs a little gravitas. Although it does much that is good, it is still seen by opinion formers (whoever they might be these days) as the channel with more quiz shows.

Some Authority Members attended the dinner party I hosted for Tom Robson, a double celebration: to applaud his award of the Edward Rhein Prize for his work and that of his team in the development of MAC, and secondly his CBE. I made an impassioned plea to Government to stand by MAC, which didn't get a line of coverage.

On Thursday the Members met and the main subject was the Obscene Publications Bill. Members were shown a video compilation of excerpts from plays, news clips, comedy shows that were close to the boundaries of taste and decency in the judgment of David Glencross. I saw for the first time the man in the hat sequence from the Brazilian film on *Censorship and the Generals*. Actually, quite a funny sequence with a man bonking away with a pretty girl; he wearing nothing but a hat, she talking ten to the dozen about nothing.

Taken out of context, the opening sequence of *Sebastiane* looked grossly indecent and a sequence from *Jubilee* showed two skinhead girls attacking a policeman. So unpleasant I couldn't watch. I can well appreciate how horrible these things can be made to look when taken out of context.

We lunched Douglas Hurd, Quentin Thomas and Wilfred Hyde. Douglas tucked into his steak and kidney pie like a schoolboy. I don't think we're going to get much backing for Independent National Radio (INR) but Douglas seems to want DBS to be up and running.

In the afternoon, a meeting with Alex Bernstein, Dennis Forman and David Plowright to hear about the merger proposals between Granada and Ladbrokes. This is going to be a headache for us. The precedent of Thames/Carlton is there and any significant change of ownership is bound to bring up similarities. We will have to tread extremely warily.

Sunday 26th January

This week Mrs T. must have been reminded of Macbeth in The Scottish Play: 'Come what may, time and the hour run through the roughest day'.

But the hours are still to run their course and she stands on her own to face the Commons on Monday and to explain to all of us, did she know and, if so, when did she know.

This afternoon she appeared on *Face the Press* and for just under an hour was questioned by Gillian Reynolds, Karen de Young of the *Washington Post* and James Naughtie of the *Guardian*. This was a call to the party faithful. Maggie was sweetness and charm, smiling at every thrust, smiling, smiling, smiling.

On Tuesday Richard Luce, Minister for the Arts, lunched with us. An agreeable man who seemed keen not to upset or cause alarm. He told us that television and radio 'made an important contribution to the arts'.

The previous night GT had dined with Winston Churchill. The following morning he painted a dispiriting picture of Churchill's attitude to the Bill he was bringing. His pessimism was to be borne out later in the week. On Wednesday David Glencross and I went in to bat with a briefing to the press. It went better than I expected and resulted in some good press on Thursday, with the exception of the *Guardian* who suggested that I showed little concern over children's viewing of unsuitable material. In fact, I was pointing to research that indicated that 58 per cent of parents interviewed considered that responsibility for children watching TV was that of the parents themselves. It was perhaps fortunate that my press briefing coincided with the release of our annual research: *Attitudes to Broadcasting in 1985*. The figures all support the fact that viewers' concerns over taste, violence and language have stayed at around the same level for the last ten years (5–8 per cent). The highest complaint – 'too many repeats' – 24 per cent in 1985.

On Wednesday a private dinner with radio MDs at the Café Royal. A good discussion on INR with a number speaking up for it. Some talk, too, about the IBA selling off its transmitters and letting the Companies operate under their own steam.

The General Advisory Council met on Thursday and were generally in good heart. Their questions about programmes are more penetrating and less guarded than Members.

An early start on Friday to Frankfurt and to a summit meeting of EBU Council Members. The hotel was depressingly expressionless. We discussed the future for a day and a half: should the Union embrace new members obviously dedicated to competition and 'naked commercial gain'. Overall, we decided that we should hold on to what we've got and be certain we were getting a quid pro quo if we invited others in. There was a general view that the Union should look at ways of moving faster when decisions had to be made. I was conscious of my own need to look in the mirror because Super Channel is not exactly a public service concept! Everyone seemed to think that we had accomplished much – I'm not sure.

One problem has gone away of its own accord, thank goodness. Granada and Ladbrokes have decided not to go further on their plans for a merger. It would have been difficult for the IBA to make a decision consistent with our attitude to Thames.

On Friday night, I telephoned Barbara Hosking to ask about the Second Reading – 137 votes in favour, 31 against Churchill's Bill. I am afraid *Sebastiane* and *Jubilee* have done much harm. I wish I had said no to *Sebastiane* but I didn't, so that's that.

Sunday 2nd February

This week the Companies finally agreed amongst themselves to form Super Channel. There were two exceptions: Thames and Yorkshire. Central, who appeared at one time to be opting out, decided to go in. I still have my doubts that it will ever get off the ground and I have a feeling that the Companies would really rather it went away. I was none too pleased to see no mention in the news release issued by ITCA that the Super Channel proposals still had to be approved by the IBA. I said as much to Ivor Stolliday, the Secretary of ITCA.

A meeting of the Radio Consultative Council (RCC) on Wednesday. Never an enjoyable occasion. The AIRC has put in an unhelpful submission to the Home Office complaining again about the cost of Regulation.

This week's issue of *Television Today* carried a bitchy piece about George Thomson and me being 'at daggers drawn' and the suggestion that ways were being looked at to get me out of the IBA, and that the IBA had never been as weak as under our control. The writer of the article went on to say that Colin Shaw was definitely not behind the rumour. Someone in the IBA is obviously still gunning for me or my job. These things still hurt. When I think of the brickbats politicians have to put up with, I take some comfort.

At least one thing did go right last week. Norris McWhirter lost his case in the courts to bring us to the Old Bailey on criminal charges for allowing a freeze-frame showing his head on the shoulders of a lady with no clothes.

Sunday 9th February

I heard this week that the Moderator of the Church of Scotland, on being asked what he thought of the film *Sebastiane*, said he was pleased ITV was showing religious programmes, even if it was at a late hour!

Met Giles Shaw on my return to London. He seemed eager to make sure we understood Government reluctance to step in on the Obscene Publications Act and was relieved to hear about our plans to introduce some sort of codification on screen. I shall be discussing this with the Companies at PPC this week.

Giles Shaw warmed to the thought that INR might become an enlargement to the output of ILR and not, therefore, subject to outside advertisement. If Government buy the proposal, it could win over the Companies and actually assist them in competing for revenue rather than threatening to take it away.

We spoke about new Authority Members, and Giles suggested we could do with more weighty representation.

At an Authority meeting on Thursday and received the welcome news that Sir Gordon Borrie, Director-General of the Office of Fair Trading, had found 'no evidence of a gentlemen's agreement between the BBC and independent television companies on the buying of overseas television programmes'. One in the eye for the former Director of Thames and a certain MP in a North London constituency!

On Friday to the Savoy and the *What The Papers Say* lunch. Always an entertaining occasion. I sat between Hugh Cudlipp and Sidney Bernstein. David Owen made a stupid and ill-informed speech attacking the BBC and the IBA over costs and 'outmoded labour practices'. Hugh Cudlipp has been advising Robert Maxwell on various media matters. I asked him how it was going. 'Downhill', he replied.

Then on to Lainston House near Winchester for the Authority five-year review. After dinner that evening, with snow falling silently across the landscape, I gave my 'sermon', as GT decided to call it. I finished with the words Kenneth Clarke used at the Guildhall dinner marking the opening night of ITV: 'The ITA is an experiment in the Art of Government. An attempt to solve one of the chief dilemmas of democracy. How to reconcile a maximum of freedom with an ultimate direction?'

The speech I made seemed to strike the right note and the sessions that followed the next day, and on Sunday morning, all showed that the Authority Members were well attuned to accept that major changes in technology would inevitably bring major changes to our broadcasting landscape. My thoughts about reducing engineering capacity were not welcomed by the Engineering Division.

I drove home in a snowstorm. I wonder whether the Authority will ever meet again in such surroundings.

Saturday 15th February

Ower Quay.

Bitterly cold weather. The birds on the lawn all fluffed up to protect themselves from the biting easterly wind which blows relentlessly across the foam-specked waves of the harbour.

Pleased to see the announcement of my election as a Fellow of the Royal Television Society. I have been asked to speak at a dinner in May, when I will receive the Fellowship.

Dallas is scheduled to start again on the BBC on Wednesday 5 March. Bryan Cowgill's only comment so far: 'I am glad the OFT has confirmed the existence of a no-poaching agreement'.

Heard this week from the Home Office that a Parliamentary Question down for next week, probably Thursday, would give the Home Secretary the opportunity to announce his decision that the Government was giving the go-ahead to DBS, and inviting the IBA to press ahead with our plans to select a suitable DBS contractor. This will mean one hell of a lot of work in a very short time. I must find a DBS supremo to oversee the developments. I have it in mind to ask Brian Morgan, who combines legal knowledge with intelligence and a quick mind.

George has been unwell this week, stricken by flu, so I stood in for him at PPC. It was a lively one. A paper by David Glencross was discussed, inviting the Companies to consider how best to promote better understanding of the IBA's control mechanisms regarding taste and decency, sex, violence etc. Particularly, we invited comments about how to promote our family viewing policies.

The paper proposed some form of on-air information on a regular basis to accompany films considered to be of an 'adult' nature. I detected little real desire on the part of the Companies to take this on. Reservations were more apparent than constructive proposals. It was agreed that a small sub-committee formulate a policy.

The committee examining Winston Churchill's Private Member's Bill begins its sittings next week. On Thursday I stood in for George at a cocktail party and had an opportunity of meeting Virginia Bottomley – an outspoken critic of ITV and BBC programme policy regarding violence. I find it extraordinarily difficult to communicate with people like Virginia Bottomley. She sees little television but, despite this, feels deeply that television is the root of all evil, at least as far as conditioning young minds (3-5 year olds). She sums up her anxiety by paralleling it with her concern, 20 years or more ago, about smoking as a health risk: 'No one could prove then that there was a causal link; we just believed there was'. She told me that parents who wrote to her cited the *A-Team* and said that immediately after viewing the programme their children would run about emulating the antics of their heroes. I said, 'What about cowboys and Indians? Children have played similar games for years.' VB represents a serious, perfectly responsible section of parliamentary thinking. Hearts and minds cannot be changed in a week. We have brought a lot of this on ourselves.

The subject came up again at my liaison meeting with Jeremy Isaacs on Thursday afternoon, when I criticised *Saturday Night Live*, which I consider plummets new depths of banality and crassness. The jokes are juvenile and littered with gratuitous obscenities. I said that, if it does not improve, it should come out of the schedule. Jeremy defends his babies, but I don't think his heart is in this one. *Saturday Night Live* is a perfect example of lowered standards and brings no credit to LWT, Channel 4 or the IBA. It damages our case and lends strength to the arguments put up by our detractors – and there are enough of them around without inviting more!

Earlier in the week at SCC I asked the Companies about the business plan for Super Channel that the Authority required to see before endorsing the Companies' role in the project. I warned them (perhaps a little over dramatically) that if they made any further plans without our approval, on their own head be it.

An early breakfast meeting with Clive Leech raised again the proposition of YTV – that of providing, through the night, a service of programming based on Music Box. Clive told me that YTV, Granada and Thames believed in the project and requested an early decision to go forward. Two days later I heard that David Plowright was alarmed at the prospect and believed it unwise to press forward. I have put the subject on the DGMM for discussion on Tuesday. I think we may be getting ourselves into some difficulty. Clive also asked my reaction to the suggestion that YTV might wish, before the franchise round in 1988, to merge with Tyne Tees Television. What would the IBA think? I said, 'Not much'. It would create a precedent and would invite every Company to start playing around with its boundaries before it was time to do so, if at all.

Douglas Hurd wrote to GT this week and indicated that he was not minded to push forward on INR while so much was in doubt. I got John Thompson to draft a response which GT sent, telling Douglas that at our Lainston weekend the Authority had warmed to our proposal that INR could be effectively financed and linked to ILR. I mentioned to Giles Shaw that I would be doing this, and he said it might help to change Home Office thinking. My guess is that the letter from Douglas was prompted by my earlier meeting with Giles Shaw, when I put to him the thought of an ILR/INR package.

On Thursday I endured a one and a half hour grilling from Martin Jackson, Editor of *Broadcast*, and gave him a 'state of the nation' overview. How I hate these interviews. While every word is recorded, a photographer wheels around one's head like a vulture, grabbing morsels of expression to subsequently plaster across the page containing the interview. I don't think I did well but time will tell. It probably comes out next Thursday. *Broadcast* doesn't like the IBA and this could give them a golden chance to put the boot in. I mustn't be so sensitive, but I am and there's little I can do about it.

A busy week in every way. On Friday our one and only meeting with the Peacock Committee at the Home Office. One member said nothing; another had a dreadful cold, blasting suddenly through his nose and startling us all. Sam Britton is obviously cast in the role of court jester. I came away thinking that they had most probably already made up their minds and our session was simply for the look of the thing. If I were in their shoes, I would ditch Radio One and hand it over to us. And possibly Local Radio too. Perhaps I would also consider making Radio Two a subscriber service and call it a day. (Not a bad day at that.)

Finally, on Friday night, the telephone rang in Dorset and Clare Mulholland told me that storm clouds were gathering over a programme due to be shown this Sunday evening on Channel 4, *My Britain*. This week's subject David Steel. Clare said Conservative Central Office had telephoned to enquire if we were serious about transmitting what they believed to be a 45 minute Party Political Broadcast, particularly as they had been alerted to the fact that the programme was the subject of an article in this week's *Liberal Weekly*, inviting readers to record the programme and show it to their friends.

Clare watched the programme with Robert Hargreaves and Neville Clarke and all three had decided the criticism by Tory Central Office was justified. Consequently Clare was inviting me to endorse their decision to withdraw the programme. Others featured in the series have been Jim Prior (no longer in the Cabinet and standing down at the next election), Jimmy Reid (an acknowledged communist) and Miles Copeland (far right private entrepreneur). Why on earth this discrepancy wasn't picked up earlier, I can't imagine.

We agreed to sleep on it. This morning Jeremy Isaacs put his side of the case. He bluntly said that if the IBA took the programme off air the Liberal balloon would go up, that there was no reason to do it and that we would be accused of bowing to Tory pressure. An echo of *Real Lives*.

I called GT and said I wanted to share the dilemma with him. GT, on balance, thought that the programme should go forward; a view I agreed with. I subsequently spoke to Clare who, having slept on it, felt that her decision of the previous night had been wrong and that damage limitation would be best achieved by showing the programme and, if accused of political imbalance, create an additional programme to redress this. I am afraid there is going to be a hullabaloo over the programme – especially as I now hear from Clare that it was made by the same team who make the Liberal Party politicals.

Sunday 23rd February

What was supposed to be a relatively quiet week turned into something of a whirlpool.

The major media news event was a sudden attack on Granada by the Rank Organisation on Monday. Rank offered £753m, which was rejected outright by Granada.

I suppose they had it coming. As soon as the City saw 'friendly' merger talks between Granada and Ladbrokes cease, it was a signal for sale notices to attract predators, and few come with sharper teeth than Michael Gifford, Rank's Chief Executive.

We face a difficult decision. Granada voting shares cannot be held by anyone with over 5 per cent of voting stock so effectively the IBA can block a takeover attempt by refusing to allow Rank to acquire voting shares. But since television business accounts for only 17 per cent of Granada's turnover, the pressure will be on us with the argument that to stand in the way would be anti-competitive. Today's *Sunday Times* makes this point and suggests that the time has come for the IBA's grip on Companies to be loosened.

There has been some speculation about how the IBA will in fact respond. So far we have remained silent but on Friday GT and I had breakfast with Denis Forman, David Plowright and Alex Bernstein. Staying true to the contracts, they would resign if the deal went through as Rank would treat the television side in a very different way from Granada.

They looked like worried men, and I felt sorry for them. Granada has been a very special Company in the system and the thought of Rank possessing it sends shivers down my spine.

GT and I called a meeting of the Authority for next Tuesday. David Plowright called me in Dorset today to say that over the weekend the three of them had been working on a letter to GT which we would receive in advance of the meeting.

At this stage, I really don't know which way the Members will vote. My vote will certainly be for Granada staying the way it is.

On Thursday, Douglas Hurd made the announcement in the Commons that the IBA would be responsible for DBS franchises so we must put on our skates.

Last weekend's panic over *My Britain* ended like a damp squib: nothing, but nothing followed in the wake of showing the programme. I thought it rather good and not at all like a Party Political. It's funny how the things you think will explode don't, and the ones you least expect do.

Another breakfast meeting on Wednesday with Bill Cotton and Michael Grade to talk about tobacco sponsorship. We all want to toughen up our rulings. Michael was off to chair the BAFTA meeting on the Obscene Publications Bill and has raised a goodly head of steam with John Mortimer and Michael Winner leading the pack. It was Michael who reminded listeners on the *Today* programme that the *Well of Loneliness* had been banned 30 years ago and now was the BBC's *Book at Bedtime*!

Sunday 2nd March

A week largely dominated by the Rank bid for Granada. The Members met on Tuesday to consider their position. Whilst it wasn't a full turnout, it gave a pretty good cross-representation: Paula Ridley, George Russell, Michael Caine and Alec Cullen. Brian Rook had done a good job putting together a very complete file so that no one could accuse staff of skimping on paperwork!

GT asked me to open the debate. I said that Granada had proved over the years to be good servants to the Authority and had provided good service to the audience. To abandon them would be a folly of the greatest magnitude. Rank had known the score and were surely trying to bulldoze their way in. On the other hand, there would be those who would say that, if proper conditions were placed on Rank, why shouldn't the normal competitive climate affect Granada as any other company? Should not shareholders expect their company to look to their best interests? Taking this into account, would not the IBA be seen to be acting in an obstructive and negative manner, especially as Granada's interests in television represented less than 20 per cent of their turnover.

There followed a considerable debate, during which I thought Michael Caine put up the most convincing argument for permitting talks with Rank before slamming the door in their face.

I reminded Members that, if we decided to tell Rank to get lost, we should recognise that we ran a real risk of having to face up to the possibility that if Granada accepted, or were forced to accept, the offer, we would either have to retract or re-advertise the contract. Members decided this was a risk they were prepared to take and, with no dissensions, decided that Rank should not be allowed to purchase voting shares over 5 per cent.

Following the meeting, we gave a brief press statement that the Rank bid for Granada was 'unacceptable'. The Chairman of Rank, Sir Patrick Meaney, issued a statement stating they were seeking an urgent meeting with the IBA. No such meeting was in fact requested but on Friday, at about 3pm, Rank issued another statement stating that, unless by 10am on Monday, the IBA agreed to a meeting, Rank would begin judicial proceedings to seek a court ruling on whether the IBA was acting within its rights!

We certainly do not intend to hold a meeting with Rank, so once more we seem launched on a sea of litigation. I am just glad that Carlton didn't take the same line when George and I virtually took the decision alone to stop their bid (and that bid was with the support of the two major shareholders!). I don't believe that on that occasion we would have carried Members so confidently as we do on this. I hope everyone keeps their nerve.

During the week I had three or four conversations with the Takeover Panel Directors, who said we might expect to go through a 'fairly sweaty period'. They could be right.

Last week, I decided that we should show our hand over *Sebastiane* and *Jubilee*. Channel 4 produced the research figures. Since the two films have arguably been at the centre of the row over violence, it seems only right that we should publish the findings of the survey. Interesting aspects are that the majority of those who had seen both films, disliked them both – disliking *Sebastiane* more than *Jubilee* and young people tuned to *Jubilee* because they wanted to hear Adam Ant's music, couldn't understand the plot and thought the punk scene of the early 80s a drag! Those who watched *Sebastiane* disliked the homosexual aggression and found the opening sequence of masturbation disturbing. Perhaps the most important finding of the research was that almost 100 per cent of those questioned thought they should have the right to decide whether to watch the programme or turn it off.

This research will be revealed on Monday, along with an announcement that the IBA will conduct two new studies – on violence and the desensitising effect (if any) of television.

Just had a call from Denis Forman, who wondered what the Authority would do if Rank bought up all the voting shares, regardless of our position. Would we agree to the takeover? Or re-advertise? I said we would re-advertise.

On Wednesday and Thursday I went to Cheltenham to attend the Consultation on Entertainment. Clive James gave a stirring and thoughtful opening address, majoring on the theme 'Words Count', and making a firm plea to evaluate the use of bad language before transmission.

The first of my two interviews in *Broadcast* was published on Thursday. I thought I came across as particularly inept and confused.

Sunday 9th March

A busy week, with more on my plate than can, or ought to be, digested.

A meeting with Aubrey Buxton. I wanted to put in his mind the real opportunity I believe ITN has to make its own way as a separate entity, still funded by the ITCA Companies but able to draw on outside finance. This would allow them to develop without being tied to the strings of the Companies. They need to expand and, by doing so, will strengthen their own resources against the competition of CNN or anyone else who chooses to come along.

Lunched with European MEPs. Actually only two bothered to turn up but, despite that, it was a useful meeting. There is a growing belief that the Commons will start behaving over broadcasting as they are behaving over butter, meat and other commodities. I said that broadcasting was a service, not a commodity.

Have wrestled this week with our evidence to the courts over Rank and Granada which a judge will hear tomorrow morning in the High Court. If we do eventually lose the case, we can say goodbye to regulation and the IBA.

Had dinner on Thursday with Peter Cadbury, founder of Westward Television. A nice man, but can see why he got up the nose of previous IBA folk.

Heard sad news that Jeremy Isaac's wife is very ill and may not have long with us. So difficult to convey feelings.

Lunched with Harry Turner on Friday at Waltons. Kevin Goldstein-Jackson still planning his book about the unfairness of the franchise system. Why he should complain I don't know – Kevin must be more than a millionaire from his exploits with TSW.

An interesting meeting with Mel Rosser of HTV about the vexing question of their alleged overcharging of S4C by some £14m to £15m pounds.

This weekend to Arundel Castle, where we stayed with the Frosts. Marvellously mixed bag of house guests: Andrew Neil, Mark Wembley, Charles and Carol Price, Ronnie Corbett and his wife, Terry Wogan and his wife, Sarah Ferguson and Prince Andrew, both jolly and relaxed. Andrew, methinks, is too young to marry but Miss F. could handle him. Bedroom dreadfully cold but huge log fires brought late night cheer. Suggested to David that he should think about launching an initiative to put down a TV-Am marker for a DBS channel. Interesting to see if he bites! All in all, a splendid weekend and something I wouldn't have missed for the world.

Thursday 12th March

Roma and I attended the funeral service of Tamara Isaacs at Golders Green. A simple, moving occasion with many of Jeremy's friends there. I do think that the Jewish form of prayer and music in many ways better than our own.

Tonight in the Garrick, over dinner, Roma told me that she wants her ashes scattered over the foreshore in Dorset. 'Not on the water, but on the green where we barbecue in the summer.' And she doesn't want the coffin sliding out of view during the service but just lying there until everyone has left.

Tomorrow, at 1030 am, we will know the outcome of the judicial review of the Granada/Rank case. My money is on us winning, but I suppose that is tempting fate.

Friday 13th March

At just after midday, I learnt by telephone that we have won the case. The judge backed the IBA's decision to prevent Rank's takeover bid.

Tonight I watched a recording of last night's BBC *Dallas* episode.

Sunday 16th March

Another sad death this week. Huw Wheldon, at the age of 69. He was a remarkable man, whose gift to television was one of undiluted enthusiasm and vitality. Huw was a kindly, warm hearted man who made time to share the concerns of others. He will be much missed, and his passing removed another pillar from the original edifice of broadcasting.

Spent part of the week wrestling with the question of diversification policy for ITN and, to a lesser extent, ILR Companies. How we respond to the questions raised by Maxwell and his purchase of DBS interests in TDFI will have major repercussions on all kinds of diversification issues.

The jagged edge of our dilemma is best illustrated by Maxwell. If we decide that his participation in Central is a conflict of interest, then what would be our stance with ITV Companies who wish an involvement in UK DBS? It could be argued that this represents just as much competition to PSB as does TDFI.

Members on Thursday are going to be asked for their views. More and more I am convinced that the decision should be a matter for the Boards of Companies themselves and not the IBA. If the Members agree, we will be accused of selling out, or bowing to Maxwell and his bully-boy tactics. If we decide otherwise, we shall be accused of interference and stifling genuine competition – can't win!

A lively SCC on Tuesday, starting at 2.30pm and continuing until 4.45pm, very nearly a record for SCC business. Main bones of contention were how the levy on overseas sales should be applied and, secondly, the relationship between terrestrial broadcasting and DBS. The Companies are fearful that PSB constraints will be eased for DBS contractors with a consequent impact on revenue.

I decided to call a special meeting of SCC to go further into these two questions. I fear it will not be an easy meeting because they will need to come to terms with the IBA's role in controlling the new DBS services. They will be very different to the accustomed regulations for the terrestrial channels.

On Thursday, the IBA Regional Officer for the Midlands, Jack Reedy, hosted a buffet lunch for MPs – about 20 turned up. Largely, I suspect, for the beer. What an unruly, crass, boring, bigoted, self-indulgent, bullying, pompous, self-satisfied lot they are. Full of wind and conceits. How we can sleep soundly in our beds at night with that crazed bunch representing us, I do not know. They hardly listened to what was said from our side, only what they wanted to hear: television was violent; the Fourth Channel is left wing; programmes are unbalanced. With friends like these, who needs enemies?

On Friday, a meeting with Authority Members and GT, who met in sub-committee to examine our draft DBS contract over which Ken Blyth has been slaving.

One major element of the discussion was to decide whether to leave the door ajar to enable applicants to put forward proposals other than C MAC in the technical specification for transmission. I am utterly opposed to making any concessions, but we have had pressure from the Home Office and DTI which leads us to think that Government has been got at by some pressure groups to enable other means of transmission standards to be considered. I agreed that we should take a leadership role and that, having instigated MAC as the standard in Europe, we would look pretty stupid if we faltered at the last fence and showed that, after all, we were less than fully convinced that MAC was the system.

GT, old political warrior that he is, was reasonably careful to position himself in the middle but he showed enough of his colours during the opening debate to demonstrate that he believes a door ajar was acceptable. I think I managed to swing the view of Members, who began by supporting GT. An important victory.

On Friday afternoon, a meeting with David Nicholas, who wanted my views on Aubrey Buxton's paper about ITN diversification and Super Channel. The paper resulted from my breakfast meeting with Aubrey. I agreed with David that at the ITN Board on Monday a proposal that a subsidiary company should be formed by ITN to exploit their position would get a favourable nod from me.

Tonight, off to the BAFTA Production Awards where I have heard that the BBC will reign supreme. The more humiliating since it is LWT's turn to televise the occasion. Oh well – grin and bear it. There's always next year!

Sunday 23rd March

On Thursday we were told that our decision to block the £750m take-over attempt by Rank Organisation of the Granada Group was upheld for a second time in the High Court.

Patrick Meaney, Rank's Chairman, said he would 'pursue every avenue in an attempt to continue with the take-over bid'.

We certainly haven't heard the end of this affair but what the next twist in the saga will be is hard to predict. I still believe that at the heart of the affair was Morgan Grenfell's inability to read small print! And now they have the matter of saving their dented reputation to think about. An injured rhino is a dangerous beast in a charge; a charge that has cost Rank to the tune of some £58m in the acquisition of 8 per cent of Granada and underwriting costs of £900,000 a week, adding up to nearly £4m since the bid was launched.

An important week in a number of other respects. On Tuesday the Authority met and confirmed the contract specification for our DBS plans. The day before, a sub-committee of the Authority met to resolve the difficult question of tactics regarding DBS technical standards relating to C MAC. The problem has arisen because Government is in a dither. There's obviously been pressure from some quarters – John Jackson and the DTI – to allow applicants to make their own assessments of the standards they want to adopt. I, and others – Tom Robson and Ken Blyth – think that to open the option by even a chink will throw a wobble across the whole enterprise and result once again in no-one knowing how to proceed, especially the set manufacturers who will not know which components to make whilst, in the general confusion, the French and Germans press on with a form of D2 MAC, an inferior option that will see much of the capability of C MAC discarded in preference to a quick, short term gain. If only Government would show some determination to carry through its pledges. It has backed C MAC and now it appears to have lost its nerve.

Giles Shaw telephoned me on Wednesday to express the Home Office view that the IBA should leave the door open for applicants to put forward their best options. I said I didn't agree but that my view might not be upheld by the Authority. A letter from Giles duly arrived by hand and I arranged for it to be tabled at the Authority meeting.

However, the sub-committee endorsed my view and this was ratified by the full Authority on Thursday. Giles will not be happy at the outcome but to have bowed to pressure would have been a nonsensical step to take. It must now be for Government to decide whether to put down a PQ which would enable them to quash our decision but I think they will not risk the outcry this would cause. We have called their bluff. Time will tell. I hope I shall be proved right. I think the Authority would have been minded to take the easier route if left to their own devices.

The next important matter discussed at the Authority meeting, and agreed, was the vexed question of how to deal with the growing complexity of diversification by companies, their directors and major shareholders in other activities, particularly activities which could be seen to be in conflict with the aims of the contractors themselves. Staff spent a great deal of time considering the question and finally resolved to recommend to the Authority that, as a principle, (i) the Companies should still be required to obtain permission from the Authority for their plans to diversify but that (ii) ultimately whether this action would represent a conflict would be up to the Board of the Company to decide. The Authority approved these recommendations.

This would mean Maxwell would now be free to sit on the Central Board and at the same time compete for revenue in the Central area through TDFI, the French Satellite channels he is now signed to.

Maxwell will undoubtedly signal this as a victory for his stand and I am sure do as much as he can to make this known. The Companies, on the other hand, will claim that we have bowed to Maxwell and that we should have stood our ground. I am sure we have come to the best decision. We must choose the right moment to release the news. There is good PR value to be gained if we take the initiative.

Dinner on Friday at Odins with Dickie Attenborough, telling me about his new film on the life of Biko. We talked about the Chairmanship of Channel Four. Marcia Falkender was one thought I had, which Dickie considered worth pursuing. I told him about GT and my idea to appoint George Russell to the Deputy Chairmanship and then possibly Chairman. Dickie wasn't impressed and said (I think rightly) that people would expect to have heard of the Chairman of Channel Four.

I subsequently spoke to GT, who believes MF is still too politically involved and therefore an unsuitable candidate.

On Monday I attended the ITN Board and listened as the Board members kicked into touch the idea of ITN forming an enterprise to give them opportunities to expand and operate on a commercial basis and not be tied to the apron strings of the Companies. I think there may be some merit in seriously considering whether or not ITN should be offered this opportunity in the next round of contracts.

The subject of new dimensions came up at our C4 liaison meeting with Edmund, Jeremy and Justin on Thursday. Justin mentioned the thoughts the channel was having about a breakfast programme offering more cerebral fare than TV-am. I responded enthusiastically. I hope we shall hear more.

On Saturday to Cardiff with Roma to attend the Radio Industries Club 48th Anniversary Ball. I offered a toast from the guests. The Welsh enjoy themselves in a thoroughly rumbustious way, pouring pints down their throats and over their clothes with equal enthusiasm.

This week we said goodbye to Juliet Jowitt, a Member of the Authority. She was a stalwart Conservative but played every issue with a good Yorkshire straight bat.

Tuesday 1st April

A devastating fire at Hampton Court last night. James Cagney died over the weekend and the papers all carry pictures of Sarah Ferguson and Prince Andrew. Channel Four has been quietly achieving its goal – that of reaching and sustaining a 10 per cent share of audience – and this is above BBC2 without any lowering of sights.

Last Monday I attended the funeral of Huw Wheldon at St Mary's Parish Church, Richmond. As the coffin was borne in, I swear that everyone in the congregation had in their mind's eye Huw, vibrant, gesticulating enthusiastically, intensely alive.

Before attending the funeral, Members met Dr John Forrest, the new Director of Engineering, for the first time. He doesn't appear to have much sense of humour but he knows a klystron from a cathode ray tube. I hope he will bring a cost-conscious view to Engineering. I am sure we have made a good choice. Tom speaks highly of him.

Mr Churchill goes in front of the Commons on April 25th. I fear the Bill will go through largely unscathed, with the broadcasters swept up in it like so much litter in the gutter. Mary Whitehouse will have the last laugh and we will be subjected to constant demands by outraged viewers through the DPP to face prosecution. Back to the Middle Ages.

I sent round a copy of the letter I had written to Giles Shaw, informing him that we wished not to compromise our standards for DBS. No PQ was issued on Thursday to widen the opportunity for a choice of standard, so it appears we have called his bluff.

The SCC meeting on Wednesday went off better than I had dared hope given that we had issued the Specifications for DBS the same day. The IBA walks a narrow parapet: on the one side upholder of Public Service Broadcaster; on the other licensee of visual jukeboxes, hellbent on eating into the traditional audience of both BBC and ITV.

ITCA prepared an agenda and contributed by nominating speakers to address different sections: David Plowright with an overview; Bob Phillis on programming; Bill Brown on regulation; David McCall on the levy. We quickly got stuck into the central theme – would the Authority expect the status quo to continue into the next franchise round, taking competitive elements into consideration? Would DBS be different in its regulation? Would we be even-handed?

Answers. Public Service Broadcasting, as known and understood today, would continue. Brian Tesler said he believed that by 1997 33 per cent of existing revenue to ITV would be taken by DBS services. I said I didn't agree. It was a debate with no clear answer.

Yes, DBS would be handled differently. In two respects. Firstly, there would be no requirement to offer a wide range of programmes. Secondly, advertising would be positioned at the beginning and end of programmes. In all other respects the same conditions would apply.

Received a nice letter from Giles Shaw, wishing us well over DBS and confirming the Government position regarding C MAC. We issued the press release on DBS on 1 April (actually, a mistake. We had intended releasing it on 2nd). Received reasonable press the following day, which usefully linked up with our advertisements in *The Times, Telegraph, Guardian* and *FT*. On Monday evening I recorded a piece for *ITV News at Ten*.

We have appointed Bernard Green, our Chief External Finance Officer, as DBS 'supremo' and I think we have made a good choice.

In the press release, my quote 'in inviting applications we will be looking for proposals which take advantage of the new technology and provide an attractive addition to the existing television services'.

In Friday's *FT*, there appeared a piece claiming that the new French right wing Government had cancelled the concessions given previously by the socialist administration to Robert Maxwell, Jerome Seydoux and Silvio Berlusconi. If true, this will be a major blow to Maxwell and Bryan Cowgill. The French Government instead intends setting up a National Broadcasting Commission to replace the High Authority. They will tender out again the satellite channel to bidders.

That same day, Friday, I was telephoned from Luxembourg by Gust Grass of CLT. Gust asked what my reaction would be to his making an approach to ITV to bid for TDFI. I said that he was at liberty to approach them, and that I couldn't say how the IBA might react, although I believed we might be concerned to ensure the competitive strength of ITV's terrestrial services. Gust concluded by saying might it not be better to have allies than enemies in TDFI? I said perhaps so. Either way, this new move by the French Government poses new questions.

Roma and I are off to Mauritius on Sunday, returning on 19th or 20th April. Should make a break from the cares of Brompton Road.

Sunday 27th April

Mauritius was paradise; a perfect place to forget everything. I never read an English paper or heard a news bulletin, though the news of the US bombing of Tripoli filtered across the oceans to us two days after that dreadful event. I cannot comprehend how the Americans, or Mrs T., believe they can achieve an end to terrorism by retaliating in a manner that must inflame Libyan passions. Madmen don't lie down under force. I fear this action by the US will stand out as an action that will only serve to alienate world opinion against Reagan and Mrs T.

Our holiday had an eventful start. We had just taken off from Heathrow in the giant Jumbo 407 packed with Halley's Society members en route to a hopeful sighting in Mauritius. About four minutes into the flight, and while the engines were at full throttle and the plane still rising steeply, there came from the forward compartment a muffled sound we all believed to be an explosion. A brief flash lit up the cabin; the plane continued to climb. We sat transfixed. I held Roma's hand and what truly unnerved me was the sight of the two stewardesses strapped into jump seats also holding hands. I honestly thought the end had come and that the explosion had been a bomb going off somewhere under the forward cabin. I felt a strange sense of emptiness and calm. It was as though time suddenly slowed down. No thoughts of loved ones, regrets or emotion went through my mind. I know I was waiting for smoke or flame. It seemed inevitable that these would engulf us. The question in my mind was 'how soon?' No word from the pilot. We went on upwards as if nothing had happened. What seemed an age later (about four minutes) the pilot came over the PA system and informed us that the plane had been struck by lightning but that, as far as could be determined, no damage had been sustained. Not an experience I ever want to go through again.

Roma and I had also gone to Mauritius to see Halley's Comet – it being supposed that a better view could be obtained in the Southern Hemisphere. The first few days were overcast, but eventually we made out a dim circle of light, looking rather like the headlamp of a car in fog. This was Halley. Later, we did see it as I had imagined: the comet of my childhood drawings, with the trajectory taking it further away from earth. Worth every penny of the trip. We returned safely.

I tried to slip gently back into work at Brompton Road but things never work out as one wishes and I was pretty soon plunged into a round of hectic meetings and decisions.

One decision I'd come to in Mauritius was to appoint Shirley Littler as my Deputy Director General. It will relieve me of some duties and will, I think, complement my efforts. The announcement hasn't been made yet and I know it will be met without joy by DGMM.

I suppose the big news this week is that Winston Churchill's obscenity bill was talked out of the Commons on Friday. Something like 75 votes for, 15 against, but insufficient to vote it through to the Lords. Mrs W. said she would press on but was 'disappointed'. I must say I thought we had lost the battle but inertia really won the day. So many MPs speeding home on a Friday. We've had a fight. We must learn some lessons. We went too far, I think, with *Jubilee* and there is undoubtedly a strong resentment against wanton violence and bad language. Now that the immediate threat is removed, it would be sensible to maintain a close watch on output.

On Monday the Queen's 60th birthday was celebrated with a Gala Concert at the Opera House. The expression 'glittering' is overworked but this really was such an event. The production was put out live by Thames, with a commentary by Alastair Burnet. Not a very good one. I don't think he'd done his homework and seemed at one remove from his audience. Nevertheless, it was one in the eye for the BBC and I took satisfaction from that. Afterwards we adjourned to the Savoy, where we ate a good buffet supper and went to bed exhausted at about 2am and dreamt of tiaras and jewels.

The Home Secretary has asked to see George and me on the 15th May – I think about radio. I am pretty sure it will be bad news. Government is planning a Green Paper on sound broadcasting and I believe that the screams of anguish from AIRC may have been heard. In which case a likely option will be to separate radio from the IBA and put into one parcel Community Radio, ILR and possibly BBC radio if Peacock recommends allowing Radio One or Two to go commercial. This is the latest rumour and may well have some weight behind it.

I forgot to mention that Lord Goodman wrote, at GT's request, a good letter to the *Times* on the Winston Churchill bill, which Tim Brinton read during the debate. It must have swayed some waverers.

Finally, I attended a private lunch given by Aubrey Buxton to say farewell to ITN, whose Chairman he had been for some five years. I sat with Bernard Ingham and

Eddie Shackleton. Aubrey was a good, forward-looking Chairman. I hope his successor, Paul Fox, will contribute as much.

Monday 4th May

Another one of our Bank Holidays, but this time with radioactive fallout mingling with the rain. The public having been reassured there was no risk of contamination, on the news just now the Water Authority National Radioactive Protection Board are advising that rain water should not be drunk if you live in certain areas – charming!

Last week passed like an express train. On Tuesday I presided over the annual TRIC Celebrity Awards lunch. David Frost was compere and the BBC again scored the highest number of awards. Altogether an extremely jolly occasion, made the more hilarious by my being joined on stage by a big and very busty lady who was there to hand me the awards to be presented. She got so over-excited, she began by presenting the award to the winners herself, much to everyone's mirth.

Dinner at the Garrick on Wednesday for radio MDs, ostensibly to welcome their new Chairman of AIRC, Ron Coles. Turned into an interesting evening with, I believe, a genuine attempt by both sides (John Thompson and Peter Baldwin on my side) to come to terms with some of our joint dilemmas and differences.

Thursday, a meeting with the executives of Mullards of Blackburn over MAC standards for DBS. I think they are beginning to weaken over their position of hitherto endorsing C-MAC. They hinted at pressure coming from their French and German partners that D2 MAC might be more advantageous to get things started. I intend re-emphasising the IBA stand for C-MAC in my speech to the RTS tomorrow.

BBC this week announced changes to their hierarchy. Brian Wenham becomes Director of Radio in place of Dick Francis, who after 28 years leaves the Corporation. Who will be the next BBC DG? I would not rule out Michael Grade as a long-odds possibility, but Jeremy Isaacs could be the chosen one.

Sunday 11th May

On Tuesday I was a guest on the Brian Hayes Show on LBC. A chat and phone-in programme. It went pretty well and I didn't get the sort of spine-rattling questions I thought might come from ill-wishers. Am listening to Capital's new split frequency output as I write this. I am only amazed that we, or the Companies, didn't push split-frequency harder and faster earlier. In a few years time, if anyone else bothers to read this, they will think that we must have been living in the dark ages of radio – only two stations, financed by advertising, for the whole of London. Well, I never!

In the evening, my Fellowship Award presentation by the RTS followed by an address after dinner – 'Looking Forward'. I started my speech with some fierce, but honest, words about a disgraceful article that had appeared in the April edition of the RTS magazine *Television* in a regular feature called 'Tavistock Diary'. It was written by a Council Member, Nicholas Mellersh, a one-time Director of Capital Radio and now employing himself as a freelance broadcasting consultant.

The piece was an attack on the IBA and was couched in the most virulent terms. I kicked off my speech by saying that I found it quite extraordinary that a serious journal, devoted to promoting debate about broadcasting, should entertain an opinion that was 'spurious, spiteful, juvenile and inaccurate'.

I also said that Public Service Broadcasting enjoyed no God-given right to exist but had to serve a recognisable public need for it to compete against the new wave of broadcasters.

After I had finished, there was a stunned silence. Both the author and the editor were present. *Broadcast* magazine and the *Sunday Times* reported it as an 'attack'. I don't regret it.

This week I am being interviewed by the *Sunday Times* and I think I shall go more on the attack than I have in the past.

On Wednesday I attended the Memorial Service in Westminster Abbey for Huw Wheldon (1916–1986). The service brought out all the old figures in broadcasting and the BBC were well represented by early DGs. Alasdair was not there. Amongst the throng were Sir Hugh Casson, George Sholti, Stuart Young, William Rees-Mogg, Kingsley Amis, Wynford Vaughan-Thomas, Peter Dimmock and about two thousand others. *The Times* the following day listed the lot with the exception of John Thompson, David Glencross and me. Did the BBC prepare the list, I wondered, as I read the papers. On Friday, the *Times* and *Telegraph* printed the error in a special box but I think we had to pay!

The service was very moving. David Attenborough read the First Lesson – Proverbs 3:1–12; Jessye Norman sang *Dido's Lament*; Paul Fox paid a moving tribute and the Choir of Westminster Abbey accompanied by the BBC Symphony Orchestra sang *Zadok The Priest*. At the end of the splendid occasion, the bells rang out. A great man, who should have been Director General of the BBC.

On Thursday an important Authority meeting. The Board approved the concept of my paper on radio and television expenditure not being separated on actual costs but rather on ability to pay. I sent a letter to Giles Shaw on Thursday afternoon. If the suggestion is well-received, it would get us out of the dilemma we are in regarding radio expenditure and at the stroke of a pen we could shift at least £3m out of radio and into television.

The ITV Companies won't like it but, with the contract coming up, I don't think they will want to make too many waves. I shall be interested to see how Giles responds. Even if the idea gets the cold shoulder we at least will be seen as trying to do something. My regret is that we didn't try three years ago, although I don't believe we would have had much change out of the Government if we had.

The other important step taken by the Authority was to agree that a three-month experiment be undertaken by Yorkshire Television to launch a through-the-night Pop video programme using the material put out on cable in Europe on 'Music Box', Richard Branson's company. Ray Snoddy of the *FT* got the story from someone and published an accurate account the following morning. Today the *Sunday Times*, for once, couldn't criticise the IBA and said the decision heralded the way for more 24 hour broadcasting. One of the papers on Saturday grumped away that it would keep children up all night and deafen neighbours.

I am pleased that we have gone down this road. Firstly, it will be one in the eye for the BBC. Secondly, it will pre-empt a similar attempt by Maxwell. Thirdly, it demonstrates the IBA isn't a killjoy, and perhaps fourthly – and importantly – now that the Companies are using the night they will find it difficult to resist the attempt by Channel 4 to extend its own broadcasting hours.

After the meeting, we lunched with ITN staff and they gave vent to their frustrations and hopes. Chief amongst their hopes was that they could be free to expand into other channels and DBS and do it by selling their services to the ITV Companies and others. I am going to pursue this further.

When George and I go to see Douglas Hurd soon, I am going to advise that we should make a strong pitch for Community Broadcasting. Nobody else will on our behalf, so nothing ventured nothing gained.

Finally, in a busy week, Roma and I went to Lake Windemere for me to speak to an after dinner audience made up of TRIC members from the North West. Frankly, I could have talked about how to grow carrots!

GT gave an interview earlier this week to Ray Snoddy of the *FT*. Snoddy is an astute journalist and the Chairman must have thawed considerably over a Glenfiddich. The result, when published, suggested that he at any rate considered that there might not be good enough reasons to go through the contract process in 1989, and that the existing contracts should be extended or rolled. This view was in direct conflict to answers I gave the RTS on the same question. I said that the 1989 contract round should be the last and thereafter the case for rolling as competition grew amongst the contractors seemed a sensible way forward. I tackled the Chairman, who said he was sorry. He had been carried away. Nevertheless, he was pleased he pressed his own views.

Sunday 18th May

Peacock appears, from the outside, to be leaking like a sieve! I suspect that they are deliberate, to draw comment, so that when the Committee comes to its final meeting before publication, it can adapt or alter its recommendations in the light of public debate.

Peacock seems to be saying that the prospect of allowing BBC Television to go commercial is unlikely but instead there would be an index increase in funding over the next ten years.

On Tuesday I'm off to New York to represent the IBA at a dinner celebrating a season of Channel 4 arts programmes. I have written my speech and hope it catches the mood of the occasion.

Oh how times change. On Friday TV-am acted as host at Eggcup House to the Members of the National Committees. Bruce Gyngell had decorated the dining room in pink – flowers, walls, menus. He remarked, when speaking after an excellent lunch, that pink was his colour and made him and everyone cheerful.

He should be cheerful with a flotation of about £40m around the corner. The Board of TV-am should be able to laugh all the way to the bank!

On Tuesday at SCC I gave the Companies my thinking on the subject of ability to pay. I prefaced my remarks by assuming such a grave air that I believe they were expecting something far worse.

Monday 19th May

John Thompson and I drove together to the Home Office and our meeting with Douglas Hurd. GT had arrived earlier but before that I had had the opportunity of setting out what I hoped would be the approach we would make over the role I saw for us regulating radio. It turned out to be a good meeting, better than I had thought possible. GT was in good form and spoke eloquently about the hardships of the radio contractors and how, if we were to offer assistance, we would need to look at the question of apportionment.

We were duly ushered and I noticed that, since our last meeting, Douglas had now gone heavily into middle eastern trappings: a side table had reposing on it, alongside an array of ornate daggers, a handsome framed picture of an Eastern mogul, resplendent in flowing garments and jewels.

In my letter setting out my hopes, I had used the phrase 'ability to pay'. On our drive to the Home Office, JT wisely suggested that this might be a hard pill to swallow for a Tory Government so 're-apportionment' seemed a more seemly phrase and in the event the one I used when I outlined my grand plan for the future role of the Authority. 'All depended', I said, on the necessity of getting our bottom line down to an acceptable level. That could only be done by re-apportionment. If this was achieved, then we could properly take charge of the oversight of not only INR but also Community Radio.

Monday 26th May

On Tuesday I flew by Concorde to New York, leaving from the new Terminal 4 at Heathrow. Difficult to find off the motorway but, once inside, very stylish.

Concorde hurtled into the sky, feeling a bit like a hot-rod. Masses of raw energy and not much else. This was Concorde's tenth year and each passenger was presented with a memento – surely the most useless present every dreamt up. For the man or woman who has everything, a silver luggage tag. The steward who handed them out advised me on no account to put it on my luggage: 'It will get nicked'.

I don't like New York, and I don't like New Yorkers: brash, rude, unstylish and intensely parochial. I stayed at the Regency on Park Avenue. I asked for a room with a view – they gave me one looking over the back of a tenement block and a playground set in deepest concrete.

In the evening, I went to a dinner party held in my honour by Shirley Lord. Her apartment has the most stunning view of Central Park. Shirley's friends at this quiet, informal dinner were the actress Beverley Gill, Barbara Walters, Ed Kosh (Mayor of New York), Abe Rosenthal, Henry and Nancy Kissinger. Everyone sparkled and glittered and made witty speeches. I rose to my feet and said something about diversity and the fact that the Albert Hall had been designed and built by Francis Fowke who had also designed a portable bath for army officers! I think I must have been horribly jet-lagged, or drunk on Perrier water.

Shirley let me have a copy of her new novel. She is an amazing person who has constructed her life rather as an engineering feat, rising to a highly successful position through sheer determination, talent and guts. Her novel is called *One Of My Very Best Friends*. I have started reading it and so far find it riveting.

Got back to the hotel at 5am London time, took two sleeping pills and parted company with my consciousness until woken by Sally with messages from London.

At 11am, attended the opening of the six-week programme at the Museum of Broadcasting to celebrate Channel 4's activities in the field of the arts. Masses of people came to hang on Jeremy's words. I was pitch-forked on to the stage to say a few words. I did two and a half minutes and raised a laugh by concluding that I considered C4 was failing in its duty to innovate and experiment if I heard nothing in the course of a week that gave me cause to panic!

In the evening, a cocktail party at the Museum, before I hosted a dinner in honour of the Museum and Channel 4 at the St Regis Hotel. I closed the evening with a speech quoting C.P. Scott: 'Television. The word is half Latin, half Greek. No good can come of it', and, just for good measure, James Agate in 1937: 'I wonder what it is in the New York air that enables me to sit up all night in an atmosphere which in London would make a horse dizzy but here merely clears the brain'.

Back to London by Concorde – three hours and nine minutes. Another eight minutes standing in the aisle waiting for the gangplank to be positioned.

Thankful to be home, and to Dorset for the weekend. Saw our badger trotting across the back garden at 5am. Sensible fellow, he will never know New York.

Sunday 1st June

Roma and I have just returned from Zagreb, where we have spent the last four days at an EBU Council Meeting. The Council is still deliberating over its role in the world of expanding media competition. Biggest problem of EBU functions is how to prevent food being pressed on you by your hosts. They are always so very hospitable. Food equals friendship. I wish there could be another form of fraternal ceremony.

Sunday 8th June

In two weeks' time it is the longest day. I have been working in the garden in Dorset in my winter sweater and still feeling chilly. I put it all down to the sophisticated meteorological reports we get nowadays: too many busybodies tracking the work of the Almighty.

Plans continue to put up Shirley Littler as Deputy DG. She is obviously voracious for the position and actually wanted her appointment brought forward so that the announcement would come the day before she was due to address the girls at her old school. Whether the enhancement of her current role will actually help me remains to be seen. Shirley is a hard and skilled diplomat, who had trodden on many toes within the IBA and there are some who would like her to trip up. The next stage in the appointment is for a letter to go to Authority members, accompanied by a brief on her proposed role and duties. If this is accepted, I will have the unenviable job of telling my colleagues and the even more unenviable job of reading the press comments. Still, the timing is right – there has to be someone to deputise in my absence and Shirley has the right qualifications.

Dinner on Tuesday with Christopher Chataway at his home. William Rees-Mogg was also a guest. I found him much less frigid and rigid than I had witnessed before. Perhaps it is because he is coming to the end of his time as Deputy Chairman of the BBC, which – from his comments – does not seem to have given him much pleasure. He launched into a strongly-worded attack on the BBC's lack of humility, common courtesy and inability to apologise with any sense of grace. So much antagonism by MPs – Ministers and others – simply rested on the correct belief that the BBC saw themselves above outside criticism. They were an elite who did not need to behave like ordinary mortals. I should say that William was expressing those views to me before dinner, not to the assembly at large, but I think he would have done if he'd been asked.

GT has gone to Montreux for the Festival. Before he went, we decided on the steps to be taken in presenting his 'Better Way' paper. It is being circulated to DGMM members and to Authority Members. I will discuss it on Monday at DGMM. The more I consider his proposals, the more I believe them to be misguided. It is going to be an important debate when it comes before the Authority and I will need to marshal my arguments if I am going to win friends.

Another meeting with David Young and GT at the Ministry of Employment. This meeting was to point up the role of the IBA as the body to appoint the body of the College of the Air Limited. 'The IBA will live forever', said the Minister jovially. 'Better to have you overseeing it than Channel 4 or someone else who might disappear. As for the BBC', he went on, 'the only person I will have to square is my mother. She doesn't like us brothers falling out.' General laughter all round.

On Wednesday went with Roma to the Derby and held a Channel 4 liaison meeting with Jeremy Isaacs and Justin in a restaurant filled to overflowing with punters. My real purpose in having the meeting, at almost any cost, was to ensure that Jeremy and Channel 4 were told that the IBA was to act as anchor for the College of the Air. Justin seemed relieved when I told them it would not be the BBC, but I am expecting a whole series of problems to surround the launch of the College. In my experience, there are no more savage fighters than educationalists and with this project every educationalist in television will be after some morsel from the carcass.

The Authority meeting was held in Winchester. The meeting approved my proposals for Super Channel. Jill McIvor, who sometimes seems to be acting even more strangely than usual, became quite agitated about my decision to bypass public consultations about DBS. This was for Members to decide, not the DG!

She was right. Members could decide if they wanted to. No one voiced any particular inclination one way or the other.

Sunday 15th June

More leaks on Peacock. This time, confirmation privately that the concept of selling a franchise to the highest bidder subject to the IBA's quality control is in the report – with four voting in favour and three against. My inclination is to do absolutely nothing until the report comes out and let everyone else comment. The whole thing is a monumental farce. No one has any intention of doing anything about it. When it does get published, the Government certainly won't want to push forward with any of its recommendations, at least until the next election and even then it will be doubtful the recommendations will be worth the paper they are written on.

What is so extraordinary is that the Committee started off looking at the funding of the BBC and have finished up throwing rotten eggs at independent broadcasting. We really are the unloved child.

This week saw the first reaction from the DGMM to GT's paper on the next franchise round: 'There must be a better way'. I expressed my views to DGMM and then sat back and listened. I was taken aback by the reaction. The only person backing my view was Kenneth Blyth. The rest, in varying degrees, believed that a major change was preferable to the chaos and uncertainty that occurred just prior to the earlier franchise decisions. We return to the subject next Tuesday. It looks as though the battle is already lost. Perhaps I am wrong? Am I really the only one out of step?

The Queen's Honours List came out on Saturday and I was delighted that two of our recommendations were accepted – Brian Tesler a CBE, and David Pinnell an OBE. I had hoped that Harry Theobalds, Controller of Advertising, would have got an OBE but it was not to be.

The new French government has decided to grant Robert Maxwell his satellite on TDFI, so we are spared Bryan Cowgill flapping his arms above our heads!

On Tuesday I attended my last function as President of TRIC. I had to leave the ceremony early to get back to SCC but not before I had passed on the Badge of Office to Robert Maxwell, who taught me one thing I never knew before – that is to say 'whisky' when being photographed. It apparently makes one pull the right facial muscles. I always look so dreadful, anything to improve the result would be a blessing.

Returning to SCC, I was able to confirm the Authority's agreement to Super Channel going forward. I think it was a foregone conclusion.

Earlier in the week, I sent off the Authority's response to Lord Young, providing him with the assurances he required that Independent Television and Radio were, subject to the right deals being worked out, willing to set about forming a College of the Air. Much water is going to flow under this bridge.

On Monday night, Roma and I celebrated our 30th wedding anniversary. A jolly evening amongst friends. I used the dining room at the IBA. The cook served up as a main course chunks of fish which would have looked more appropriate on the plates in an army barracks.

Sunday 22nd June

World Cup fever has struck the country. England appears to be in with a chance. The BBC and ITV are at daggers drawn over showing the Quarter Final match. ITV claims that a gentleman's agreement has been breached. The BBC say there was no such agreement and, in an article today in the *Sunday Times*, Alasdair defends the BBC's actions, claiming that ITV only 'cherry-picks' the best sports offerings, leaving the BBC to carry the less popular sports. But in addition, Alasdair sounds the most arrogant note, claiming the BBC has an inherent right to cover events of national interest. From a look at the background papers, it does appear that the ITV case is a strong one. There was an agreement signed by both ITV and the BBC in 1979 that accepted the case for alternating important matches.

At the Authority meeting on Thursday, Members endorsed George's concern that it ran contrary to public interest to allow the ludicrous situation of two channels both showing identical pictures. He left the meeting to speak to Stuart, reappearing to say that his appeal for common sense had been rejected; that the BBC would have nothing to do with 'tossing a coin'. One day the BBC will realise that this holier than thou attitude wins few friends, and I am disappointed that the Sundays I have read so far, with the exception of *The Observer*, do not take issue one way or the other.

The Authority on Thursday confirmed Shirley Littler's new role as Deputy Director General. Plans for the College of the Air proceed but I have now learnt that the radio companies appear far from happy at the prospect. They are a miserable lot, teetering on the margins of bankruptcy and complaining about everything as long as it has nothing to do with their own ability to perform, which they have singularly failed to do.

Tomorrow I hold a press conference to announce and confirm a contract with Marconi for 14 transmitters, costing £11.5m. It will provide services for ITV into the 21st century.

At DGMM on Tuesday we had another go at discussing GT's 'Better Way'. This time, things went more my way with most Members coming round to the argument I have been making: that it would be ethically wrong to close off options from outsiders wishing to compete in the next contract round as well as, importantly, proving an opportunity for real change in contract specifications to be realised, e.g. removing Oracle from the ITV contract. It certainly needs new life breathed into it.

Sunday 29th June

The Peacock Paper whirlwind is gusting back and forth as leak after leak blows opinion in one direction or another. Last week's talking point was 'selling off ITV to the highest bidder'. This Sunday's *Mail on Sunday* headlines the leak that the future of television will be in pay-as-you-view and that, by the end of the century, we will choose entertainment by paying for our choice. Out of the window seems to have gone the belief in Public Service Broadcasting.

Another broadcasting story in the Sundays is the news that the Government has decided to stay its hand on Community Broadcasting until late autumn when it intends publishing a Green Paper. Yet another example of Government folly. At least the notion of considering sound broadcasting in the round will be marginally better than piecemeal as had been its intention. With any luck the Home Office will conclude that the IBA might as well run the whole caboosh rather than breaking it up for others to get their hands on.

On Wednesday I chair the Radio Consultative Committee and am bracing myself to sit through another two hours of moaning and whinging. If radio companies sold themselves positively and stopped complaining, they might have a future. As it is, their revenue shows no sign of rising. Advertisers see ILR as fourth division stuff and the operators do precious little to alter the image.

On Tuesday, Douglas Hurd addresses the AIRC at their Congress, this year at the Café Royal. He may take the opportunity to announce the postponement of Community Broadcasting, unless of course it's just another rumour!

Next week is a busy week all round. DGMM on Monday will consider a paper prepared by Shirley Littler which attempts to offer the pros and cons of options to find a Better Way. GT has a copy to study this weekend. He has already said that he wishes to reserve his position. I think he wants to leave his mark. If he has his way, it may turn out to leave a scar!

On Thursday, Roma and I go to Bournemouth for the EBU General Assembly. It will open on Friday morning, the day after Douglas Hurd makes his statement on Peacock in the Commons, so a jolly time will be had by all!

Last Thursday, attended with Roma a cocktail party at Winfield House, the residence of the American Ambassador in Regent's Park, and bumped into Alasdair Milne, who looked sheepish and uttered the nearest thing to apology that he's ever likely to make. The event that brought this about was none other than the World Cup duplication which had caused so much spilt blood last weekend. I suspect that the Governors had been alarmed at the overkill deployed by AM and Bill Cotton to justify their stand. This Sunday's *Sunday Times* throws further light on the nature of the 'gentleman's agreement' and shows there was substance behind the understandings.

Saturday 12th July

A fortnight has elapsed since I last entered my thoughts in this diary. A great amount has happened. The AIRC held their Congress on 1 July at the Café Royal. The rumours about Community Radio had been confirmed by Douglas Hurd in Parliament. The Government had decided to abandon the two-year experiment because, as DH said, 'the exact form was still causing difficulty'. The reason uppermost in the minds of his Cabinet colleagues, as Raymond Snoddy put it in the *Financial Times*, was 'unregulated stations would broadcast political propaganda in the run up to the next election'.

Whatever the reason, DH spoke out about the decision at the AIRC Congress. In the event, this turned out to be a more civilised affair than I had imagined. Ron Coles gave a good opening speech, welcoming the Home Secretary and applauding the decision over Community Radio. George and I sat in the first row as DH spoke about the resolution of the IBA to find effective ways of reducing costs. The delegates listened politely and then, after we'd left, carried a motion unanimously that we should halve our regulation costs.

That said, it became clear to me during the Congress and subsequently at the meeting of the RCC the following day, that two things were beginning to work in our favour. Firstly, revenue from advertising was creeping forward and secondly the latest figures showed that audiences of ILR had increased and now placed ILR in first position over the BBC so some of the gloom was giving way to very cautious optimism.

On Thursday, Roma and I drove down to Bournemouth, the Peacock Committee's findings finally seeing the light of day. They were universally dubbed a failure. The leaks had proved accurate, and the BBC to get off scott free. Poor old ITV has borne the brunt of the criticism. The auctioning of contracts being the high spot. There has been a predictable range of comment. The IBA kept quiet. I did a small piece for ITN News warning that Peacock was treating broadcasting like selling baked beans, as a commodity not a service.

Generally, Peacock has been deemed to have laid a rotten egg but the smell and disposing of the yolk is going to be quite a problem. The most damaging element of the day's events was the statement in the House by DH that he was looking, with the IBA, at the possibility of lengthening or extending the present contract period in order to allow more time for Government to decide on how best to deal with television franchises. This came as something of a surprise to us since no words had been exchanged between anyone on the subject. Hurd's worry is that we will lock in our contractors until 1998, effectively putting paid to any thought of auctioning off. And a good thing too! The one thing television doesn't need is instability. How can television production come to fruition if every moment the contractors are looking over their shoulders to see who is going to snatch them up. Certainly, if we delay in announcing the contract opportunity in 1989, we would be responsible for bringing great uncertainty to the broadcast environment.

The EBU Bournemouth Conference went like clockwork and reflected great credit on all those who made and carried out the arrangements.

On Thursday of last week the Authority met to discuss the contract process and whether we should agree to DH's suggestion that we hold over our contract process using the 1984 Cable & Broadcasting Act to extend the period. There was a lively discussion and, much to my relief, the Members agreed that the contract process be conducted as planned. GT will write next week and tell Douglas Hurd, who will not like it.

On Friday, we had a Chairman's Liaison Meeting with Channel 4. Edmund Dell dropped a bombshell to the effect that he proposed considering seriously the pros and cons of one of the Peacock recommendation – that Channel 4 should have the option to sell their own airtime. Dell is proposing to speak at the RTS Seminar on 12 July at the Barbican. I said that I thought he was most unwise to start this horse running. Dell seems adamant. I think he feels like making a splash before he retires from the chairmanship next year. If Dell makes a statement on the subject it will appear to everyone that he supports change.

Sunday 18th July

I have mislaid my diary for last week, so will have to make do with my memory!

On Monday, spent a lengthy session at a National Theatre board meeting following the attack by the *Sunday Times* that Peter Hall was engaged in commercial theatrical ventures at the same time as running the National Theatre. The mood of the Board is quite hard to define. I think everyone wants to remain loyal to Peter but at the same time there is an undercurrent of unease. To run the National should be quite enough for any one man, but Peter has an insatiable appetite for work which takes him further afield, to the highways of Glyndebourne and the byways of commercially-funded stage productions. You can't have a man of unquestioned genius and then expect him to only perform an ordinary role and not stretch himself creatively. The National itself would be the loser. It was revealing that at the Board John Mortimer alone spoke out about the unsatisfactory relationship between the National and commercial theatre. The cross-funding of productions is anathema to John, who believes that, to do good work, the National must stand alone without any commercial interests. The Board has decided to spend an evening discussing this issue.

But back to broadcasting. Post-Peacock blues have set in, at least as far as I am concerned. Now it's out, some people continue to urge a debate – some that it should be put away in a drawer to gather dust. GT sent off his letter to the Home Secretary giving the view of the Authority about the extension of the present ITV contracts. It is a good letter and I hope will give Douglas pause for considered thought.

At SCC on Wednesday, I gained the impression that the mood was more in favour of rolling contracts than fixed terms, but as far as I could judge the main concern was for keeping to the 1989 contract round. There is now little doubt that the ITV Companies – or many of them – see value in discussion with the Authority over regional boundaries. I had dinner with Bob Phillis of Central, who wants to make a case for having fewer companies. I suspect that, as we get nearer to the day, every company will make a similar representation.

George and I had words separately with David Shaw and David Plowright about the need for caution that should be exercised by Companies before putting up their rates by a 27.5 per cent increase year on year, which could land us all in a deal of trouble. If ever there was a case for auctioning off ITV Companies this would fan the flames. David Plowright took the point and, after SCC, he held a closed session with the Companies and the outcome, I think, will be that they will agree to hold their rates for six months.

This week, TV-am had a successful public offer which was twelve times oversubscribed. It will make a few of the original shareholders a great deal of money.

On Friday, the Minister of State launched the College of the Air, a rather muted affair held at BAFTA. I think it is somewhat to our credit to have held ITV, Channel 4 and ILR together in order that the IBA could speak for the totality of independent broadcasting. It will be interesting to see if the College ever takes to the air. I think it will.

Next week, the Great Wedding, which Roma and I are attending. I bought them a Dartington Glass salad bowl and have already had a thank you. What manners!

Also next week, I address staff at Brompton Road. Difficult to give them a rousing call to support Public Service Broadcasting when everyone seems bent on giving it the push.

Sunday 27th July

Quite a week, one way and another. The wedding of Andrew and Sarah must, I suppose, take precedence over everything else. Television was very much at the centre of the occasion and over 300 million worldwide, it was claimed, saw every stitch and hem of the royal dress.

Roma and I got to Westminster just after ten in the morning, having driven in regal splendour along the route that would be taken by Prince Andrew and his bride-to-be a little later on. I got quite carried away by all the waving and cheering and made my own royal progress down the route, waving back to the crowds.

At the entrance to the Abbey, we bumped into the US Ambassador, Charles Price and his wife Ann and were about to enter with them when we discovered that our entrance was a more lowly one around the side. We duly took our places and for the next 40 or so minutes watched the comings of the congregation. Lord Snowden, looking creased and old, took his place quite near to us – below the salt, as it were. When you are out, you are out, in royal circles. It must have prompted many memories of another occasion, when he was at the very centre of a royal event.

Striking a somewhat incongruous note was Elton John with his wife and there, for all the world to see, was his celebrated bald patch which he is supposed to have spent thousands on trying to re-fertilise.

Finally the wedding itself. A service of great beauty, Sarah F. looking absolutely stunning, as calm as anything and obviously enjoying every moment. The Queen looked more relaxed than usual and the couple spoke up for the whole world to hear. A jolly good time was had by all.

Back to broadcasting. And on Monday a Board Meeting of ITN. A lively affair which became quite heated when the discussion turned to the role that ITN should perform for Super Channel. Apart from David Plowright, most other ITN Board Members appeared hellbent on securing, if at all possible, the cheapest service they could decently get away with. David Nicholas very nearly lost his temper, claiming that this was the blackest day in ITN's long history, etc. etc. Afterwards, I took David aside and told him that we were as mindful as he was to ensure that ITN got proper exposure on Super Channel.

I can foresee choppy waters ahead. When it comes to spending their own money, the contractors are the meanest lot imaginable.

Dinner that night with the Chairman of AIRC, Ron Coles. We dined in a room that was a cross between a launderette and a cabin on a banana boat. Very loud air conditioning and foul food. Try as I might, I cannot work up enthusiasm for AIRC these days. A miserable lot of people. I told them that we hoped to get our re-apportionment of television and radio budgets approved by the Home Office. On Friday I heard that this had indeed been cleared.

Two meetings with staff this week – one at Brompton Road, the other at Crawley Court.

I have now decided with George that I will speak on Peacock at the RTS Conference on Tuesday, so I have spent very nearly all day working on my opening statement. The whole event seems vastly miss-timed and inappropriate, but I shall say my piece.

Dinner on Friday night at the Garrick with Roma, Shirley Lord, Abe Rosenthal, Ludovic Kennedy, Moira Shearer and Chris Chataway with his wife (a dreadful woman who looks as though she is permanently bored, and probably is). Apart from her, an amusing evening, with Ludo in good form with many funny stories.

On Friday, sat at lunch next to Sue Stoessel of Channel 4, who confirmed that Edmund Dell would be having his say about Channel 4's option to sell advertising. I told her I thought it was ill-timed and inappropriate. She said she would pass my comments on to Justin Dukes.

I am looking forward to my holiday in Portugal.

Sunday 3rd August

Rain coming down from a leaden sky, falling on wet grass and the moles busy exploring beneath, all add up to another glorious summer in Dorset.

I am now officially on holiday but next week I am going into the office a couple of times before leaving for Portugal on Thursday.

This was the week of the RTS Symposium on Peacock, but before that, on Monday, GT and I paid a visit to the Home Secretary at his request.

Douglas wanted to hear more from us about extending the current contract period. He argued that we were failing to take account of the many likely changes in the broadcast firmament, and that to lock away the contractors for another eight or ten year period would cut down our options. We responded by saying that stability was what was required, not uncertainty.

On Monday evening, Roma and I went to the Bolshoi and saw a very disappointing *Ivan The Terrible*. A great deal of prancing about and little else. The audience attending the Royal Opera House is largely a scruffy lot. We ate a hurried meal in the interval in John Tooley's private dining room. I think somebody had it in for us: I swear the pepper mill contained ground glass.

The RTS Symposium was a dampish affair. Rather like trying to make yourself sick by sticking two fingers down your throat – not much came up.

Sam Britton heckled Alasdair, who gave an abrupt denunciation of the RPI indexation element of Peacock. Peacock himself sat, eyeing mournfully each speaker, occasionally muttering, shaking his head or – like Sam – heckling. They both behaved like barrow boys and did little to elevate the occasion. Simon Hoggart gave the best analogy of Channel 4 – that of a lady of virtue kept by ITV. Edmund Dell delivered his magisterial acceptance of Peacock's invitation to consider the selling by Channel 4 of its own airtime: 'Our funding system has been one of the key factors in the success of Channel 4, but someone may notice that it is almost too good to be true. Someone, or some government, may say that this funding system could be justified in the first five or even ten years of Channel 4. But how can such a system be justified indefinitely? Is not Channel 4 just too insulated from the pressures with which everyone else has to live.'

To all of which I would say 'yes, that is why it has been able to flourish'. Ratings are not important. In fact, ratings which demonstrate popularity are a sign that the Channel is turning from its remit. The important statistic is reach – how many people in the course of the week at some time or another turn to Channel 4. I believe it is over a quarter of the entire television audience.

I said my bit, not included in the pot pourri of Radio 3 the following evening. In it, I made a stout defence of the present ITV system, opposing the notion of auctioning. Despite the BBC's lack of interest, it received a line or two from most of the heavier journals the following day.

In the evening, I attended a dismal TRIC Dinner. The Guest of Honour was Frank Chappell and my guest was Quentin Thomas. We dined in dim, fading light, lowered to diminish the awfulness of the surroundings. Indeed, there was good cause to avert the gaze. This was to be the last night of the Grosvenor House Dining Rooms. A final meal, after which the place was to be turned into something completely different. They should have, at least, toasted the old girl. I did have, however, a useful talk on the pavement with Quentin, who pressed the matter of contract extension. He said that Douglas had not made sufficiently clear a view not brought out in Peacock – that Government might wish to see ITV going towards subscription rather than advertising. I said I couldn't see much sense in that. Quentin said he'd get Douglas to write and enlarge on the idea.

Douglas Hurd did write. The letter came by hand and was delivered during the Authority meeting on Thursday. This was an important meeting of Members. The matter of the 'Better Way' was up for discussion. The outcome was, I think, a good one: a ten-year contract with the option to allow continuation by the IBA – a review with a clear indication two years before the end of the ten year period of the performance of the contractor. If the review was not positive, the IBA would consider it right to offer the contract up for re-advertisement. Finally, that during the period, the Company would no longer have the absolute certainty of protection from take-over and that the Authority would be the judge of whether or not 'the nature and characteristics' of the Company would be damaged by any take-over.

A few minutes ago I spoke to GT and we talked about Edmund's statement at the

RTS. GT, rightly, is concerned that we take a firm decision about how we play our next card (if we have one). We meet on Wednesday for breakfast.

Sunday 17th August

It's astonishing the effect a holiday has on one's perspective. One week in Portugal has spring-cleaned the mind of much rubbish, leaving only seemingly immoveable objects to worry about. With one week more to go, in Dorset, even some of these might get shifted.

On our return from Faro, I spent the drive back home from Gatwick catching up on the week's mail, which had been collected by our driver from Brompton Road. Incidentally, Gatwick – which suffered a similar reputation to Scunthorpe; a sort of picture postcard ribaldry – is today, in many respects, superior to Heathrow: cleaner, smarter and the inhabitants generally more polite. Reading week-old notes and correspondence, Minutes and reminders is normally a sobering task but the lot I had on my knees as we drove into London proved far less daunting than I had feared.

One message that stood out informed me that Michael Green had been approached by Lord Young to become Chairman of the company that would be responsible for running the College of the Air. It's a surprising piece of casting. Michael is clearly an astute businessman, and has made his mark in communications. Despite the brush we had with him when Carlton made their bid for Thames, he behaved impeccably. His is a typical Tory choice – young, go-getting, successful – but whether the appointment will bring satisfaction to the academic world is another matter. I shall meet Michael next week.

According to GT, who lunched with him recently, Michael does not rate an offer by Channel 4 of two hours programming a day highly. He has his eye, George thinks, on getting the College a space on ITV and not in off-peak. He also wants more freedom to tempt industry into sponsorship opportunities. I have a very open mind on all this. If the College is going to succeed, it requires someone with drive and determination, but he may not sit well with the ITV Companies. Then again, it may be no bad thing for ITV to meet its match. Up until now they have held all the cards. According again to GT, Michael believes that the IBA can wield the big stick if necessary to get them into line. The answer could be to appoint ITV MDs and radio MDs on to the College Board as, without their goodwill, George believes the College will fail.

Catching up on the press cuttings, I was amused to see a piece by Ray Snoddy in the *FT* about UK DBS. Far from being the last across the line, he was suggesting that we could be in lead position, the French having come unstuck. We will know in a fortnight's time whether we have succeeded in attracting bids.

In this Sunday's *Observer*, there is a useful piece about SCC and our advertisements to Companies wishing to bid for the contract. No praise for the IBA. A pity, because it is a venturesome step with new technology.

Sunday 31st August

Back from a week in Dorset. English summer no longer contains sun. Fires were lit, sweaters donned and telly watched. Was it always like this?

On Friday, I was telephoned by the office to say that Stuart Young was dead and that Howard Thomas was in hospital with cancer.

Stuart's death was not a surprise. We knew he had been ill for some two years. Cancer is a cheat. Some people who suffer from it tend to look well. Stuart did and was working until very nearly the end. He wore the mantle of Chairman well. His obvious enthusiasm and respect for the BBC were self-evident. The cock up over *Real Lives* was the result more of inexperience than weakness. He was an honourable man who faced a difficult period in the BBC's relationship with Government and Peacock with energy and a growing confidence in his own beliefs.

Speculation is already building over his replacement. Lord King of BA is a hot favourite. Other possibilities: Willie Whitelaw! Too old and I doubt would want it; William Rees-Mogg – not a favourite at the BBC and a confessed (at least to me) anti-BBC person. No doubt there will be many more.

Seven groups have come forward to operate DBS for us. Likely front runners are Carlton and Granada. I know it's water under the bridge but I remain convinced that we could have got the show on the road two years ago with UK technology if we'd offered it to open competition. The difference would have been that the contestants would have hammered the UK suppliers into offering them services at a competitive rate instead of allowing them to lounge in their corners waiting to get their snouts in the trough.

My hope for this round is that ITN be awarded one of the channels. At least some real good would have resulted from DBS.

Two major papers go to the Authority Meeting on 4th September: the IBA's response to Peacock and the IBA's views on the 'Better Way'. I am happy with the views contained in both.

Fundamentally, we believe that a two-year extension to current contracts would be wrong. We could live with four years but, if the Authority believed it sensible, we would consider an eight-year new contract advertised as before.

Yorkshire Television came to the market last week, heavily oversubscribed. Paul Fox should be smiling all the way to the bank.

Sunday 7th September

Another debate is going on in York this weekend about the future of broadcasting. I am here in Dorset, utterly sick of the future of broadcasting. No one can predict the future, but we in the broadcast profession have what almost amounts to a mania for self-analysis. No other industry, I suspect, picks over its garbage in quite the same way that we do. To make matters even more incestuous, the same people keep doing it. It reminds me of those rather sad elderly folk who I have seen rummaging continuously in their handbags, looking for something they think they have lost or seeking reassurance from seeing a familiar object.

1986

An important week for us. The Authority met on Thursday and debated the next contract position. GT criticised the plan I had put forward, and he was right to do so. It was too complicated. Instead, we reached a good position: to recommend strongly that there should be an extension of four years, not less. That, as from 1994, the Authority of the day should select suitable contractors to hold a contract for 12 years, with a review two or three years before expiry, providing an opportunity to advertise publicly should a particular contractor's area be put up to offer. Those who the Authority judged to be performing satisfactorily would be given extensions by means of a rolling contract.

I am meeting the SCC on Tuesday and will hear their views before GT writes to the Home Secretary.

The Authority also discussed the IBA's response to Peacock and broadly endorsed the paper that had been offered. There was a dicey moment when Michael Caine said that he profoundly disagreed with much of the philosophy behind our views, and there was talk of expressing a minority view. I said that this would lead to endless outside criticism – better to word our findings in a way acceptable to all parties. We are now attempting this.

GT has spoken to George Russell and indicated to him that he would like him to be the next Chairman of Channel 4.

I am very much in two minds about this. George is a good businessman with a flair for organisation, but he is no arts 'heavy' and I suspect does not, apart from opera, have a great deal of interest in the arts. This could make him seem a relative lightweight compared with other names that might be thought acceptable. It might well also appear that the IBA is putting in its own man. George Russell asked me whether I thought he should accept GT's offer. I questioned the arts aspect of his knowledge but he did not feel that would be a hindrance.

On Wednesday night, GT gave his annual Chairman's Dinner at the Hyde Park. I sat next to Hugh Dundas, who told me that on his retirement he would be recommending to the Authority that Ian Trethowan take on the role. I said I thought that would be splendid.

The new Chairman of the BBC guessing game continues. This Sunday's runners include hot tips from the *Sunday Times* that Douglas Hurd is against the appointment of Lord King and that he considers Lord Windlesham to be of the right calibre. I think it's the *Sunday Telegraph* that plumps for Lord Quinton. At another 'do' of GT's on Thursday evening, I met Lord Barnett, the new Deputy Chairman of the BBC. He seems a quiet, sensible man, but hardly capable, I would have thought, of carrying out the task.

Next week, Channel 4 shows *The Naked Civil Servant*. I wonder whether the press will get to hear that the IBA has reinstituted the line 'Masturbation is more fun than sex'. At least I think that was the line, rather than 'Wasn't it fun in the bath tonight', which was the line approved by the IBA Members in 1976 or thereabouts.

Henry Moore died this week. Pat Phoenix of *Coronation Street* is dying of cancer.

Saturday 13th September

Wind, rain, falling leaves and swallows circling high under the heavy clouds all point a cold finger towards the approach of winter. We haven't really had a summer. Was it always the same or is it that I'm getting old and the summers of one's youth seem to hold the warmth and promise of that period in one's life. Here in Dorset, the duck shooters are already out in the early mornings, slaughtering as many wildfowl as they can. It seems a massive shame to end the lives of these creatures when they've taken so much trouble, and suffered so much anguish, to bring up their offspring.

The Japanese have been in town this week. I attended a 'summit' of broadcasters from Japan. Together with Alasdair Milne, I opened the conference with a speech of welcome. In it I pointed out that co-operation and competition went hand in hand. Since they had come here to pinch our ideas, I viewed the whole occasion with some cynicism. On Tuesday evening, George hosted a dinner for them at Westminster. The Japanese made speeches praising the 700 year old historic building, the traditions, the role of Government in ensuring true democracy. I couldn't help but think while all this was going on what would have been the state of our democracy if the Japanese had succeeded in what they attempted some 40 years ago.

As the wine continued to flow, so our guests became more animated. My neighbour to the left leant towards me in a conspiratorial manner and whispered, 'Hoso'. 'Yes', I nodded. 'Hoso', he said, 'Pussycats! Hoso'. He made a sign with his fingers that failed to match with any knowledge I had of cats, but which said volumes about where his thoughts were straying. 'You mean Soho!' I said. My neighbour nodded his head vigorously. 'Hoso, very good!'. I suggested he should go back to his £170 a night hotel (The Portman) rather than spend his money elsewhere.

SCC this week was an important occasion to tell the Companies about the Authority's deliberations over the contract process. I told them our views about the four-year interim when the contracts would be re-advertised. They didn't like that. Many would prefer to go for re-advertisement in 1989 and have done with it.

The following morning, Ray Snoddy reported in the *FT* what the IBA had in mind. Pity. I wanted a clean run in making an announcement.

SCC also gave me the opportunity to mention my concern about ITN and the role it should be playing in Super Channel. There is skulduggery at the crossroads. The night before SCC – at the end of the dinner for the Japanese delegates – David Nicholas came up to me and confided he had heard the BBC had come to an arrangement to provide two new services for Super Channel: one at 7a.m. and the other at 2 pm, and – as if that wasn't enough – the Companies in Super Channel were opposing the ITN role to supply a programme at 11pm each weeknight on the ground of expense. To be exact, £400,000 per annum per programme, making a grand total of £2.4m. I said to SCC that I believed the Authority would be extremely concerned if ITN were not to play a role.

The Board of Super Channel met after SCC to consider their position. Subsequently, on Friday, I telephoned Paul Fox and, as Chairman of ITN, told him if the deal fell through as a result of cheeseparing, I would give notice that the IBA would withdraw its permission to the Companies to diversify. Paul said that he was pleased to hear the IBA's stance. We shall see what transpires on Monday at the ITN Board.

The announcement about Michael Green as Chairman of the College of the Air was finally made. I sent him a telex to wish him success.

Had a meeting with the Permanent Secretary at the Department of Education & Science, Geoffrey Holland, on Thursday and told him that we were less than happy with the way events were proceeding. No consultation over MG's appointment and rumours that MG had already selected a Chief Executive. Geoffrey agreed that things could have been handled better and assured me that there would be no appointments until careful evaluation had taken place. Geoffrey Holland is a master in the art of making soothing noises. How far I believe him is another matter.

Howard Thomas seems to be making a recovery from his illness. He wrote a warm letter of thanks. In it, he said, 'I admire the way in which the Authority is so boldly tackling its new challenges and facing its competitors', but then went on: 'The IBA has a good story to tell about itself. I do wish you could find a really first class public relations man in the role of entrepreneur.' If this is a dig at me, it certainly hit the mark. I just don't think it was intended in that spirit. Howard is much too nice a man.

The first film going out with the Channel 4's special red triangle warning symbol is transmitted this week. The French film *Themroc*. We are again in a no-win position. If the programme is too near the knuckle we will be accused of using the symbol to get on the air material that we would otherwise not have shown. If the film is considered uncontroversial, we will be accused of trying to whip up irresponsible publicity in order to attract viewers.

Next Tuesday I have agreed to meet Owen Edwards of S4C. He told me on the telephone that the dispute over their contract with HTV had reached the point where it was likely that S4C would be formally indicating to the IBA that matters were irreconcilable between them. Owen said Leading Counsel had advised S4C to make certain facts known to the Authority. How this ghastly business has remained secret for so long is amazing.

On Friday to Crawley Court to present the Harman Memorial Prize. John Forrest seems to be settling in. Tom Robson has moved out of his office to make way for John. Tom looks years younger already. Retirement must be like waking up in a different place – I think I rather look forward to it.

Sunday 21st September

An Indian summer in Dorset, like a dream from childhood. Out every evening last week.

Monday evening, a dinner at the Garrick as a tribute to Aubrey Buxton and his time as Chairman of ITN. A good occasion with many MDs paying their respects. Aubrey was genuinely moved by Paul Fox's speech and clutched the silver jug presented to him close to his chest like a small child with a favourite toy while he responded.

Earlier in the day there had been the ITN Board meeting. I raised the question of arrangements that Super Channel might be thinking of making with the BBC over the provision of news. There was an awkward silence and Brian Tesler replied that no decision had been taken. David Plowright said he was, anyway, opposed to the BBC playing a daily news role. I listened uneasily.

After the Board, the Super Channel Board convened and I made my points about the understanding I considered the Authority had reached with Super Channel – that is to say, ITN would supply a nightly bulletin and the BBC would provide a weekend news roundup. I argued that to permit the BBC more frequent bulletins would unbalance the contribution of ITN and would, in any case, prevent ITN coming in earlier in the day at a later date. After the meeting, I wrote to Brian 'bottom lining' our conversation.

This whole incident more than underlines the peculiar relationship that exists between the ITN Board and the ITV Companies. They are one and the same. ITN is merely an appendage, without a life of its own. Bad for ITN, bad for ITV.

I lunched with Justin Dukes on Tuesday and he is putting on paper his thoughts on ITN floating free. It is something that must be done if ITN is to compete on equal terms with other news agencies in the 1990s.

The S4C/HTV business is far from over. My Tuesday meeting with Owen Edwards more than reinforced my concerns. Poor Owen. I noticed for the first time that his hands shake. He had to clutch them together to control them. Owen believes that the time has very nearly been reached when the Board of S4C will decide to formally provide the Authority with information relating to the case. I pointed out that, if this were done, it would force the IBA to investigate and this in turn would lead to the Authority calling for HTV's side of the affair. What still amazes me is the fact that nowhere has there been a mention in the press.

On Friday I learnt that George McWatters and Idwyl Simmons of HTV had asked to see GT. I said that I thought the meeting should not take place without me.

George Russell chaired the Authority meeting on Thursday and did the job well. It was agreed to give Robert Maxwell a further six months to sell his shares in Central.

I held a press briefing on Thursday to give background and a statement on our views on the next contract round for ITV. Given a fairly tough time, but the results on Friday were much as I wanted.

The radio submission to the Home Office went off to Douglas Hurd under GT's signature. There seems a growing belief that the Cable Authority will be asked to handle radio matters. I doubt they will.

John Mortimer's *Paradise Postponed* went out this week and got a hammering. I didn't watch.

The Wales is on tonight. I won't watch. If I see another picture of Princess Diana, I think I shall turn Communist!

Sunday 28th September

Driving in to Corfe Castle this morning, I heard on the radio the announcement of the death of the dancer Robert Helpmann in Australia. He was 72.

Timothy Aitken came in for drinks with me on Wednesday. We talked about ITN. I had mentioned to him previously I thought it high time that ITN should be floated as a separate entity. Tim had obviously given this some thought. He explained his plan: TV-am would seek to buy into ITN in such a way that TV-am would be able to use ITN's resources to cover their news output, and this would also grant TV-am a slice of the action when ITN went public. Tim said he would have a private talk with Paul Fox and see whether there was any encouragement. It will be interesting to see how Paul reacts. ITN, in its present form, is lacking business acumen. The Companies treat it like a tiresome child always demanding pocket money. If they all shared in its success, ITN would blossom and expand. If nothing is done, it will wither in the face of new competition.

A dinner with Geoffrey Chandler, Director of 'Industry Year', on Monday to see whether there was anything the IBA could do to further Industry Year on radio and television. We dined in the elegant surrounding of the Royal Society of Arts.

The trouble with Geoffrey is that he seems incapable of giving encouragement. The result is that, instead of creating an atmosphere in which initiatives can flourish, he has seemed to pour cold water over every effort made so far. Not a successful occasion. I think Geoffrey is basically anti-media.

A meeting on Wednesday with James Gatward and Greg Dyke to listen to their case for TVS becoming a sixth networking company. They made their case well. I can see no good reason for putting a stop to their ambition.

Heard this week that we can expect a response from the Home Office to GT's letter about a four-year postponement of television contracts. I was informed that, in all likelihood, the answer will be not to give an answer! This would be most unsatisfactory. I am convinced that, if we can't get a decent response or if the answer is that Government's intention is a two-year extension, we should press for a re-advertisement in 1989. I rather think GT would prefer to settle for Government's position, but I might be misjudging him.

Two goodbyes to Tom Robson. One from Staff at Brompton Road on Tuesday, a second at Crawley Court on Thursday. I tell the same stories, and everyone claps. One more goodbye with the Authority Members at Brompton Road and that will be that. Tom has had a good career. He is a man of total conviction, who was the right man for the job during the formative years of ITV. I think that John Forrest will be the right man for the 90s.

I watched the tape of *Themroc* this week. Much was made in the press before the showing of a scene in which a French policeman gets killed and eaten. Mrs Whitehouse has been creating again – I think she must be desperate if she considers this film went too far.

Sunday 5th October

Went with Roma to see *The Magistrate* at the National. Max and Jane Rayne were our hosts and the other guests were the Chinese Ambassador and his wife.

Over dinner, I talked to the Ambassador about the dramatic advance of television in China that has occurred in recent years, pushed by the Americans and the BBC. It had set me thinking that ITV should make a concerted effort to establish a bridgehead there, rather than let the BBC have all the running.

On Tuesday I attended the Memorial Service at St Columbus Church, Pont Street, for James Coltart, who had been the first Managing Director of Scottish Television. A moving ceremony rounded off by two bagpipes playing a lament. Most of us shed a tear. He died aged 82 and was working up to the end. A good way to go.

Wednesday proved something of a red letter day for the BBC. News of the appointment of Duke Hussey as Chairman came in the middle of a Conference on film and television I was attending at the National Film Theatre. Halfway through a dissertation given by Jeremy Isaacs, a note was handed to Alasdair, who was chairing the session. Shortly after, another note was passed up to him. Jeremy stopped in mid-sentence and asked if Alasdair would like to put us all out of our misery and tell us who the next Chairman was going to be. 'No', said Alasdair. 'Well, are you pleased?' asked Jeremy. A pause. 'Yes'. Another pause. 'Quite', said Alasdair.

The session ended and immediately someone came up to me and told me that Dukie was to be Chairman. My first reaction was one of total disbelief. Someone from the press asked for my view, off the record. I confess that now, several days later, I am less than pleased at my response. It was stupid and foolhardy. I said the appointment was an obvious victory for Mrs T. and that it was tantamount to an insult to the BBC. Talk about being two-faced. That afternoon I wrote to Dukie with my congratulations and saying his appointment was at a pivotal point in the history of the Corporation. I feel extremely ashamed of my initial reaction and it would have served me right if my off the record comment to the press had been printed.

Actually, the press this weekend was ambivalent over the appointment. All talk of his war record, his bravery, his forcefulness, but there is widespread comment that the dispute at *The Times* when he was Managing Director was less than adroitly handled. Some say his bark is worse than his bite. Simon Jenkins, writing in the *Sunday Times* on the other hand, says that Tory Central Office were jubilant over the announcement and that Hussey had been selected to 'sort out the BBC'. My own guess at this juncture is that he will disappoint those who hope for this kind of action.

In the evening, the ITV MDs met Members and, after a formal meeting, dined at the Hyde Park. David Plowright and I had a brief exchange over the vexing question of exploiting ITV programmes. David said that he believed that contractors should feel able to place their programmes anywhere, including the BBC. I said that I thought a contractor attempting to do that should be asked to 'pitch his tent' somewhere else and that there would be others only too pleased to step into those shoes and take over what would still amount to be a near-monopoly franchise for at least another dozen years.

The Authority met on Thursday. Before the 0930 meeting, I had breakfast with GT at Brompton Road. Top of my agenda was the question of Edmund Dell's replacement at Channel 4. Over the fruit juice, I got unimportant matters out of the way and then, with the eggs, got round to the subject and my reservations about the appointment of George Russell. GT listened carefully and then, rather to my surprise, said as I had clearly strong feelings against George's appointment, 'we should think again'. I was much relieved. Peter Parker and Ian Gilmour are possibilities and this weekend I looked at the list of retiring MPs. I only hope that George R. isn't terribly disappointed or that he discovers I am the principal objector to his nomination.

On Thursday, shortly after noon, GT received a response to his letter to Douglas Hurd concerning the extension of ITV contracts. It brushed aside our case for a four-year extension and instead confirmed the Home Office intention to permit a two-year period.

'When Parliament reassembles, I shall want to announce my intention to bring forward legislative proposals on this matter. Until then, I should be grateful if you and your colleagues would regard as confidential this indication of my response to your views.'

The whole thing is thoroughly unsatisfactory.

Sunday 12th October

Monday saw the 100th meeting of the AAC. I hosted a lunch and we had some bubbly to celebrate. I learnt with pleasure that at their meeting beforehand the Committee had endorsed the concern that I and a number of others feel about the growing rush of commercials pandering to the fantasies of children, deliberately creating the impression that by possessing the particular toy they will enter a magical world. Some priced at astronomical figures – £75 is quite common – the time has come to put a brake on this. As a result of the AAC's deliberations, Advertising Control will be holding a series of meetings with the larger agencies to spell out the disquiet we feel.

One or two newspapers have picked up a remark made by Jack Reedy, RO for the Midland Region, who said on a Central TV programme that the IBA might be prepared to permit the advertising of condoms to help stop the spread of AIDS. I think it's a good notion. We should do as much as we can to prevent a scourge that will, in a few years time, be a major cause of death.

I spoke to GT this week about a new Channel 4 Chairman. I suggested that we should go after Sir Ian Gilmour. George agreed and we'll see what comes of the approach.

GT sent a stinging letter to Douglas Hurd following a conversation I had with an official at the Home Office. The man, whose name I have forgotten, told me calmly that the person we had been counting on to replace John Riddell as Deputy

Chairman of the IBA had been turned down by, presumably, the Prime Minister. No one had thought to tell him, or GT. Also outstanding for selection are another four Members. If no replacements are found by the end of the year, we could be down to six Members.

On Tuesday, David drove me down to Bournemouth – 110mph he told me later! – for dinner with Denis Forman. The guest of honour was Douglas Hurd. The Royal Bath gave us a welcome like returning royalty, resulting from our EBU high jinks in July. In the bar, I came across Hugh Jenkins, who confirmed my thoughts about Ian Gilmour. Then in to dinner, surrounded by police patrolling the corridors. Guests included the MP Paul Bryan and his wife, and Judy Hurd (who wanted the IBA to take an advertisement in the Conservative Ball brochure!)

After dinner, the conversation inevitably turned to broadcasting. Douglas said he thought the triangle on Channel 4's risqué films absurd.

On Thursday, went to the first night of *Phantom of the Opera*. Enjoyed it immensely and think my £10,000 'angel' money is probably safe.

Spoke to Michael Green and asked him whether his Board had been selected. He tells me he is thinking of asking Michael Grade.

On Friday Roma and I attended the TRIC Charity Ball at Grosvenor House. Robert Maxwell presided and made an inept speech. Then left without saying goodbye.

Sunday 19th October

Roma and I went to *Jacobsky and the Colonel* at the Olivier. I found it dreadfully tedious. My legs were aching and I kept fidgeting, so we decided to give up the unequal battle and eat in the restaurant instead. Sometimes I get the feeling that the National goes out of its way to stun rather than stimulate.

SCC on Tuesday. I tell the Companies that they must accept that the IBA budget requirement will re-apportion £1.6m from radio across to television. The ITV Companies are making such vast sums that to quibble over the odd million would be churlish, and time-wasting.

That morning, GT received the letter from Douglas Hurd agreeing that I should inform the Companies of Government's decision to limit the extension of contracts to two years, rather than four. Armed with this letter, I told the MDs the news, stressing its confidentiality. Within an hour of the conclusion of the meeting, David Shaw, Secretary of ITCA, called me with the news that Ray Snoddy was publishing the story in the *FT* the following morning!

Later, after an evening at the Whitefriars Club, I went over to the *FT* and picked on the Wednesday's first issue. The story was accurate in every respect.

I went to bed deeply troubled – certain that one of those who attended my SCC meeting had blown the story despite my stressing its confidentiality.

The next day I spoke to Chris Scoble at the Home Office and apologised. I rang GT and told him. Then, breathing fire and brimstone, dictated a letter to the Chairman of ITCA. I had just finished when Elliot Grant from the Home Office asked to speak to me on the telephone. It was a curious conversation. For the first time, I had insight into the expression 'coded response'. 'Don't be too concerned', he said. 'Ray Snoddy is an expert journalist. He has many high-level contacts both inside and outside ITCA. We're not unduly perturbed.' I told Elliot that GT was planning to drop a note to Douglas Hurd but he thought that 'unnecessary'. The leak quite obviously hadn't come from ITCA. I tore up the draft of my letter and got on with the day's work, wishing I hadn't spent a night agonising over the incident. I am still very naïve when it comes to the workings of Whitehall.

The year rotates smoothly at a seemingly ever increasing speed. On Thursday the BBC Governors came to lunch after an Authority meeting. It turned out to be something of an unique occasion. Duke Hussey made his first public appearance. The irony of this being on IBA ground was not lost on anyone. Dukie made a good response to GT's speech of welcome. I sat next to the immaculately suited Joel Barnett. He is still Acting Chairman as Dukie has not yet been sworn in, or whatever the BBC does on these occasions. He starts on 5th November. According to Dukie, 'Either there is a plot to blow me up, or else people think I might have chosen the date so that I can blow them up', explained Hussey amidst laughter. Michael Grade, Bill Cotton and Michael Checkland laughed the loudest.

During the pudding, Joel leaned towards me conspiratorially and confided that he is going to 'wrap up' the *Panorama* legal case started this week between the BBC and Neil Hamilton MP and Gerald Howarth MP for the alleged libel by the *Panorama* team accusing them of being extremist right wingers. Joel said that the BBC had shot themselves in the foot again after the *Monocled Mutineer*. He considered this case to be lost already and a long journey through the Courts, with the publicity attached, would do nothing to enhance the reputation of the BBC. A mistake had been made and it should be admitted as quickly as possible.

Today the news of that decision has broken in a big way in the Sundays. BBC staff are quoted as being 'furious'. The scene now seems set for another blazing round of recriminations. The new dimension will of course be the suggestion that the decision to capitulate has been made by Dukie and that this marks the opening round in a determination by the Governors to stamp their authority on the Corporation. Those who saw Hussey's appointment as Mrs T's inspiration will have a field day. I have a feeling that, compared to *Real Lives*, this will be as an atom bomb to a grenade. Joel and Dukie are right to stop the case and settle. There will be bruised and bloody feelings, but at the heart of the affair is the reputation of the BBC. If the case was to be lost, better now than later, and out of Court. It is rumoured that staff were not consulted. If so, that was foolish. But the staff concerned are an arrogant bunch and have brought much of the separation between Governors and staff on their own heads through their own actions.

On Thursday, a meeting with David Mellor and GT. This had obviously arisen as a direct result of the torpedo fired by GT at Douglas Hurd over the Home Office tardiness in selecting new IBA Members and a Deputy Chairman. David M. seems nice enough, cast in the white-hot metal mould into which Mrs T pours her ambitions.

Strangely, on the occasional table in front of us in David Mellor's office, was a fossilised sea creature. Not in keeping with the get-up-and-go image so desperately worked on by so many in the thrall of the Prime Minister.

David Mellor told us who Douglas Hurd and the PM hope will agree to serve: Detta O'Cathain, Ranjit Sondhi, Sir Donald Maitland and Lady Popplewell. GT expressed himself well pleased with the nomination of Donald Maitland as Deputy Chairman – an old friend and part of the 'Scottish Mafia'.

On Friday I ate dried up sandwiches with Michael Green. Very upset at our disinclination to join him on the Board of the College of the Air. He threatened to go to Mrs T!

A very jolly fancy dress party on Saturday to celebrate Edward Montague's 60th birthday. We, and a thousand others, joined in the revelry at Beaulieu Motor Museum. Roma went as a parking fine, and looked elegant and funny at the same time. I went with a plate hanging round my neck. On it I had stencilled numbers. 'What am I?' I asked fellow guests. Only one young man got it. A number plate.

Sunday 26th October

On Monday 20th, I attended an ITN Board. My concern over the future of ITN continues to mount. The Companies treat it as a rather unnecessary and expensive burden they have to carry.

Publicly, they speak of ITN's great contribution to the system. Privately, they consider it badly run and self-indulgent. Perhaps I am being over-critical of the ITV view, but perhaps not too far off the mark. The ITN Board considered the role of ITN and Super Channel and came to the conclusion that ITN should invest £400,000 in the channel, representing the shortfall between the sum Super Channel were prepared to pay from their budget and the sum asked by ITN.

I asked whether, by putting up this sum, the Board of ITN would seek to reduce next year's ITN budget by the same amount. I was assured by Paul Fox that no such thing would happen. I intend writing to ITN, and Paul, setting out my continuing unease. At this meeting, I said for the first time that I thought there was a case for considering the possibility of ITN floating free from ITV and going public.

On Tuesday, went with Roma to the preview of *The Mission* and afterwards a dinner hosted by Anglia. Peter Gibbings made his first public appearance as Deputy Chairman. David Putnam rushed up to me afterwards and said he was desperately concerned over the terrible battering the BBC was taking. Was there anything that could be done? David and Patsy were off to L.A., and I told him to look up my daughter Fiona. *The Mission* is a stunning film but I doubt it will do big business in the States: not really enough to satisfy the hoards of Rambo lovers who look to the cinema to engulf them in mayhem and slaughter.

Big day on Wednesday. I was the speaker responding on behalf of the guests at the Mansion House lunch to celebrate 75 years of the RNID. About 250 people were there, Lord Chalfont as President, and the Lord Mayor. I had worked hard on my speech and I think it was effective.

In the evening, at the Booker Prize ceremony at the Guildhall, I lost a tenner on

Paul Bailey's *Gabriel's Lament*. (It went instead to *The Old Devils* by Kingsley Amis.)

Was given lunch on Thursday by John Thompson at the Garrick to celebrate his membership. It's taken over four years to get him elected. I think he knows more members than I do!

Off to Walsall on Friday, with Roma, to be Guest of Honour at a Civic Dinner given by the Mayor, Councillor Brian John, a member of our Regional Engineering Staff. A good and dependable man, who warmly entertained us and presenting a superb cut-glass rose bowl, cut and engraved by a group of young disabled people who Brian John is trying to get established. We stayed the night in an amazing hotel called 'Baron's Court', the most devastatingly bad taste hotel I've ever had the misfortune to stay in. Everything mini baronial fake: a tiny four poster bed and chandelier; the room so small it was impossible for us to move about at the same time. Reading the bumph on the proud owner revealed he had started his life as a jobbing builder and lived in a two up, two down. He'd obviously got hooked on small places.

Brian John generously put his mayoral car at our disposal to take us to Birmingham North Street. To our surprise, the driver got hopelessly lost on the way to the station. We arrived with some seven minutes to spare and were just approaching the ticket barrier when Roma turned white and said her handbag had gone. It turned up two hours later. She had forgotten to take it from the car. The truly amazing thing was we didn't have a row.

Back to London and to wake up today with the headlines blazing details of Jeffrey Archer and a prostitute who, it was alleged, had been given money by a go-between to silence her. The whole story stinks of gutter press muck. The *News of the World* masterminded the revelation, which culminated later in the day in the announcement on the *Five O'Clock News* of his resignation as Deputy Chairman of the Conservative Party.

I tried calling him at home, and spoke to Mary. It could happen to anybody, any time – poor Jeffrey. I feel desperately sorry for him and the family.

The Sundays are full, too, of the abandonment of the Panorama trial. Alasdair seems short of defenders. There are calls for his resignation. I doubt very much whether it will ever cross his mind. His position is untenable and so is that of the Governors. All this is perfect grist to Mrs T. What better example could be found to finally show up the BBC and what she considers it to be – a Commie-infested tower of power in Portland Place. Goodbye the case for public service broadcasting. How, I wonder, are those working within the BBC taking this shame-making debacle and all just as their 50th celebration begins. Duke Hussey must be sorry he ever picked up the telephone and accepted Douglas Hurd's invitation to become Chairman.

Finally, as if all this wasn't enough, the death of Alan Stewart, a Thames Television producer, killed by a landmine in southern Sudan. His last words: 'I don't want to go there. I must survive', leave nothing to the imagination.

Sunday 2nd November

What a way to celebrate 50 years of British Broadcasting! On Thursday Norman Tebbit launched his long-heralded attack on the BBC over their editorial handling of the US air strike against Tripoli in April. Tebbit's 20-page dossier took apart the BBC's newscast coverage, pointing up bias against the actions of the Government and the part it played in allowing US aircraft to refuel in the UK. Since then, it has become increasingly obvious that Tebbit has overplayed his hand. His attack has been called 'over the top, out of control'. Most broadcasters, including the reporters at ITN, have pledged their support to their beleaguered BBC colleagues. They are in for a surprise.

Last night, Roma and I attended the Golden Ball, celebrating the first 50 years, organised by the RTS. Alasdair told me that his people were preparing their defence, which included some disparaging analysis of the role ITN had itself played. I advised him to speak to David Nicholas before including this. Talk about dog eat dog. I saw Geoffrey Cox and tipped him off about the BBC's intention. Geoffrey immediately said that he would defend ITV, having studied the output of both the BBC and ITN. If the BBC do go in for character assassination of ITN, it will serve only to divide the BBC's support from other quarters. It will certainly create another public outcry.

Such has been the attention given to this latest piece of Beeb-bashing, the spotlight has quite faded from the continuing debate over the *Panorama* debacle, although in today's *Sunday Times*, the Editor of *Panorama* has opened up a few wounds, both in and outside the BBC, by defending his corner. It will raise again the central issue of why the BBC decided to cave in and apologise before the case was brought to Court. It will also reawaken the criticism of Alasdair in his actions to endorse the Governors' decision to settle out of court.

Sunday 9th November

I attended a luncheon at the Cable Authority this week. The Chairman, Richard Burton, is an agreeable man in his early 60s. The cable business is still very much in its infancy, with some 180,000 homes 'passed' by cable. Since its inception, the Authority has received no complaints regarding programme standards, possibly because those paying hope for something spicy. One day cable may deliver its promise of the 'wired society' passionately envisaged by Kenneth Baker, Peacock, Sam Britton and Peter Jay. I suspect that day is at least a decade and a half away.

The Open College moved a step closer this week with the Selection Committee to appoint a Chief Executive meeting on Tuesday. David Young (Lord), Geoffrey Holland of the Manpower Services Commission, and Michael Green presiding as Chairman. We saw three candidates: Michael Deakin (late of TV-am), Naomi Sargent of Channel 4's Education Department and Sheila Innes of BBC Education. We chose Sheila Innes and I am sure she will prove an able leader of the College. The announcement will be made on Monday or Tuesday along with that of the appointment of myself and Jeremy Isaacs as Directors.

That evening, I held a cocktail party at the IBA for some 40 friends to celebrate my mid-term point as Director General. Afterwards Roma and I had dinner with Richard and Sheila Attenborough; he in good form, having just completed filming Biko in Zimbabwe.

The BBC have turned down Dennis Potter's *Brimstone and Treacle* on the grounds of 'taste and decency'. David Glencross and I decided we should see what the Members felt about it as Jeremy had indicated that he wanted to put it in the schedule for Channel 4. It is a moving and disturbing work, excellently performed, which argues the nature of love and anger on many different and subtle levels.

On Wednesday, we held a special viewing. On Thursday, Members met for an Authority meeting and the film was discussed. Michael Caine believed it should be shown. Paula Ridley, the previous day, had said she thought it right to be shown. The other Members rejected it, with GT endorsing their decision. David and I said we would have shown it. Jill McIvor, who had been sent a tape, lent her support to rejection despite the fact that she had not viewed it!

On Wednesday we also held a preliminary discussion with Members about DBS. David Glencross made a spirited contribution on programming, stating in no uncertain terms that Members should guard against making programme judgments when selecting the eventual contractor: 'Time', he said, 'would alter the best laid plans. We should not be seduced by grandiose plans, or turn our backs on strong commercial objectives.'

I raised the issue of AIDS at the Authority meeting the following day. The IBA must not be slow in coming forward. The matter of 'free' or 'paid' advertising was discussed. GT is clearly in favour of free advertising. I am not so sure. Another important decision that will have to be taken is whether to allow brand advertising for condoms. The problem here is that the major manufacturer, the London Rubber Company, has 95 per cent of the total market and they appear reluctant to want an association between AIDS and their product.

After the meeting, I issued a press release saying I considered it the duty of the IBA to educate and inform, and that the IBA was ready to play its part.

On Thursday night Roma and I attended the Gala Opening of the new opera extension at the Royal College of Music. This really represents the culmination of our efforts to raise money for the College. (I am Chairman of the Media & Events Committee). The Queen Mum was the 'Royal', and Roma very nearly fell over when she bowed low to greet her. The Queen Mum looked in splendid health, radiating a warmth that filled the room when she entered. The Opera Hall is charming and stylish. I wish the same could be said for the selection of works that were presented for our delight. Benjamin Britten is not everyone's cup of tea.

I heard from David Shaw that Elliot Grant from the Home Office had approached ITCA to find out how they would feel about a three-year extension to their contract, rather than two or four. He asked my opinion. I was against it, but subsequently – on Friday – he telephoned me again and said Douglas Hurd's advisor had said four years was out of the window. I spoke to GT and said that, on reflection, I thought we should agree to three years. GT agreed and I told David Shaw.

On Thursday, the sad announcement that Howard Thomas had died. He was a larger than life figure in the early days of ITV and the BBC. I don't think he received full credit for his achievements and dedication to television.

Sunday 16th November

The row over the BBC's coverage of the Beirut bombing has escalated with an exchange of letters between Norman Tebbit and Duke Hussey. Dukie has suggested that if Norman Tebbit is unhappy he should take his complaint to the Home Secretary.

On Monday I and Members went to ITN in the evening for a tour and to watch *News at Ten*. There is no doubt that my statement at the last ITN board about going public has sunk in. David Nicholas took me on one side and said that afterwards there had been much debate.

SCC on Tuesday. I told MDs that I had been appointed as Director of the Open College. Before that, I asked that the Board stand in silence for a minute to remember Howard Thomas. I received a nice letter afterwards from Richard Dunn, thanking me. The subject of AIDS and ITV's approach to it was on the agenda. The television Companies all believed that the maximum effort should be put into freeing television so that it could run AIDS 'commercials' across the evening viewing and not only after 9pm. I also confirmed with the SCC that the IBA would accept a three year extension of contract but so far we haven't any indication that this deal has been agreed by the Home Office.

Richard Dunn came to see me after SCC. He told me that Thames would like to agree a 5 per cent holding in the Luxembourg TDFI medium power satellite. TDFI expects to beam 16 channels across Europe, including the UK, in 1988. Richard said that Thames did not wish to become a channel provider, but wanted instead to invest in the satellite itself. This poses problems for us. If Thames are given the go-ahead, this will be in direct competition with UK DBS. I think the answer will have to be 'no'.

I am Chairman of the charity Soundaround and on Wednesday Roma and I went to their Gold Ball. I had gone intending to relax, but on arrival at 7.15pm discovered that we were not sitting down to dinner until 9pm so we had to stand around making small talk for an hour and three quarters. Our Guest of Honour was Richard Branson who, although a millionaire several times over, chose to come without a penny piece. I spent the entire evening paying for his delights. Odd how the very rich fail to recognise that to others money doesn't come easily.

On Thursday, Norman Fowler came to the IBA to find out our reaction to proposals he wanted to make over an AIDS campaign on radio and television, to support a 23 million leaflet drop in January. Subsequently, he hoped for a continuing campaign on the air through public service announcements. GT and I gave him our personal support.

Have just had a call from Shirley Littler regarding the outcome of a ballot organised by the union BETA who are resisting Management's determination to alter regulations governing house purchase and mileage costs. Our tactics throughout the negotiations have, I fear, been less than adroit and on Friday I realised (much too late) that the IBA was in danger of bringing the whole of ITV to a state of darkness over our insistence on savings which amount to only £200,000 in the first year. Not a firm enough wicket to be sure of the support of the ITV Companies.

I end this week on a more hopeful note regarding Channel 4 Chairmanship and a Deputy Chairman for the IBA. Peter Parker has indicated to GT that he might be prepared to become the next Channel 4 Chairman – a decision that would be widely welcomed.

Sir Donald Maitland has now also accepted the Home Secretary's invitation to become Deputy Chairman of the IBA. We might even see him in place in December.

Sunday 23rd November

Ripples of Tebbit appear to be spreading but losing their potency in the process. What is now apparent is that Tebbit scored a resounding own goal by his intemperate attack on the BBC. Ranks have closed round the Beeb and, rather than weaken, he has strengthened their resolve. How frustrating for Mrs T. Rather like Sir Robert Armstrong dropping his composure and hitting out at a photographer at London Airport, now Tebbit has lost credibility. He has become a 'crank' and in the process done the BBC a power of good.

Lunch on Monday at Marlborough House, hosted by Nicholas Barrington, to welcome Charles Wick of the US Information Agency, which I suppose is the 'acceptable' face of the CIA. I had lunch with him once before, three years ago at the Garrick, when he brought along two plainclothes sharp-shooters; one a very attractive sharp-shootess. This time he was less well accompanied: two boot-faced fellows wearing the traditional gabardine raincoat. We sat round a small table in an enormous room and made jokes about the Russians. I wasn't sure why I had been invited.

In the evening, dinner at the Dorchester given by BREMA, the first appearance of their new President. Frank Chappell gave a funny introduction to Gordon Borrie, who I sat next to and who gave an exceedingly dull speech in response, which I have wholly forgotten.

On Tuesday a liaison meeting between Channel 4 and ourselves. Lord T's time to chair the meeting. The only item on the agenda was Channel 4 selling its own air time. Lord T. and Edmund Dell confronted each other like old bulls. GT expressed our wish that Channel 4 would refrain from publishing Professor Alan Budd's findings until after the Authority had considered them. Edmund (I think) finally agreed with our reading of the report: that if conditions were all satisfactory, Channel 4 would stand a better than even chance of success in selling its own commercials. Certainly Budd has not presented a cut and dried case. GT pointed out that if Channel 4 did go its own way then the IBA would certainly need, and wish, to advertise the contract. Long silence from Dell.

We intend taking the view of the Authority on 11th December and we will advise them to note the Paper but restate their previously held view that Channel 4 would be best served by maintaining its relationship with the IBA. My guess is that well before 11th December the Report will have been leaked!

On Wednesday to Norwich and to a grand dinner in the evening in the Blackfriars Hall. I sat next to the Mayor, who referred to us in her welcoming speech as the Independent Broadcasting Association. It rather put us in our place. GT used the platform to speak about Peacock et al in advance of the Peacock Debate the following day. It got good press coverage the following day. We all sat down after breakfast and had our Authority meeting. AIDS was on the agenda and Members approved a decision to allow explicit wording in commercials. Harry Theobalds read out the script for a radio commercial which contained the words 'vaginal fluid'. Not a Member flinched. They also agreed to permit commercials across all programmes, disregarding the watershed time of 9pm.

During the coffee break, I organised a press release which I hoped would pre-empt the press conference that Norman Fowler was to give the next day. In the event, we got good coverage and to some extent showed our positive response, but most coverage was devoted to the BBC.

Rumour abounds that Michael Grade will take Bob Phillis' job at Central. Next week I meet Colette Bowe, who our headhunters have identified as a possible Controller of Information.

I also met Sir Donald Maitland with GT. I thought him a likeable man with an obviously good mind.

Sunday 30th November

A week in which I suppose one can say with some justice that the face of television changed more dramatically than it had since the introduction of colour.

The Authority held interviews with the consortia bidding for the DBS contract. ITN was first on Monday morning, led by Paul Fox in his usual bluff manner. The team appeared confident and enthusiastic. ITN had, before the meeting, informed us that they were identifying with BSB in their 'Now Channel'. I thought they put their case well and I am certain in my own mind that ITN should find a place in DBS.

Next was NBS at 11am. Just two representatives: James Lee, late of Goldcrest, and their money man. James did all the talking, speaking past his allotted 30 minutes for a further quarter of an hour. He subsequently wrote to GT questioning our lack of questions and probing of his programme plans, ending with 'I feel a real sense of mission to give the DBS project the leadership it needs if it is to survive the inevitable traumas of its birth. I hope you and the Authority will decide to give me that role.'

I doubt very much whether the Authority will come to that decision but the Authority has reached unlikely decisions in the past.

In the afternoon, Starsteam and BSB. Most pundits place BSB at the top of the league for the contract although Granada, Virgin, Amstrad, Anglia, ITN all have a lot to offer. A feature that attracts me is their combination of subscription and advertising, together with three strong channels.

On Thursday, the remaining contenders.

Sat UK was the entry by Bond Corporation and Alan gave a good, confident, bouncy interview, with a typically Australian flavour. DBL (Carlton, LWT et al) did not come up to my expectations, despite a confident introduction by Michael Green. The team came in wearing a rose in their buttonholes 'so you can remember which ones we are', joked Michael. The interview was messy and I didn't think they had got all their facts together – a pity. I felt their singleminded determination to opt solely for advertising-funded channels a weakness, as was their view that a film channel was not a viable proposition, considering there would not be enough films to attract the audience required.

Finally John Jackson's Group, DBS UK. JJ gave a lengthy but interesting introduction, leading to their financial objectives, supported by a mixture of advertising and subscription.

During the afternoon interviews I noted Jill McIvor nodding off. I whispered in GT's ear that she was dormousing but there was nothing we could do. I only hope it wasn't too obvious. We meet next week to see if we can come to a decision.

This week was also Chinese week. The Minister for Broadcasting and a team from Chinese Broadcasting came to visit Crawley Court and Brompton Road. The Minister presented me with two jade balls to play with!

This was followed by a dinner at the Chinese Embassy on Friday evening. A small group: Duke Hussey, Bill Cotton, Paul Fox, David Glencross and Brian Cubbon.

The week also embraced interviews for a replacement for Barbara Hosking. A good shortlist was headhunted. One candidate is Colette Bowe, ex DTI. She has been offered another position and if we are going to secure her it will have to be a rapid decision. I read the Sunday papers with interest, slightly fearful of a leak but there was no sign of our discussion.

On Wednesday the annual Tyne Tees lunch with their guest, President Giscard d'Estaing, who spoke well, wittily and to some effect about his hopes for a unified European monetary policy and leadership. Clearly he was making his own pitch for the role.

The Channel 4 saga of the Budd Report continues and the plot thickens. After the Chinese dinner on Friday evening, I drove Justin Dukes home and we stopped in Regents Park for a few words. They did not please me. Justin is convinced that the Board hostility to Edmund's proposal was 'over the top' due to the inept manner of Edmund's presentation and that his staff would react against the status quo and declare UDI. I told him that I found that extraordinary and if they did, tough titty. My own reading is that Justin himself is angry that Edmund overplayed his hand and instead of shelving the report for the time being brought about a Board rejection. Something Justin hadn't bargained for. Now Justin has to think up some reason for taking the matter back to the Board and he's chosen the threat that staff may react against the present decision. I must read the Minutes with great care and check them urgently against the recollections of those present.

I must also speak to RA and alert him to the plot I am sure Justin is hatching. That is to say, the plot to get the Board to make a 'hold' recommendation instead of a 'no' recommendation.

On Wednesday evening Roma and I went to the Guildhall and heard Alistair Cooke, a remarkable performance. He held the audience in the palm of his hand for more than 45 minutes, weaving together strand upon strand of opinion, experience and humour. The evening was a celebration. The Fulbright Commemorative Address 40th anniversary. Aged, I suppose, about 80, Senator J. William Fulbright was as spry as Cooke. The evening was introduced by Charles Price, the American Ambassador.

The following morning at 8am, I was at the Hyde Park Hotel for breakfast with Peter Parker. I have now done my best in getting him interested in being the next Channel 4 Chairman. I think there is a fighting chance.

The last thing I record this week is a paper I have written to Authority Members setting out my views on pay for Senior Directors. Quite simply, I think we are underpaid. I await developments.

Sunday 7th December

David picked me up from Ower Quay on Monday morning at 9.15am to go to the official opening by Prince Charles of Ocean Sound. It was a strange experience, leaving the Quay in a chauffeur-driven car, gliding over the potholes and cowpats. Did I ever imagine I would drive in this way when I was a small boy peddling over the heath?

Ocean Sound is the new Portsmouth/Southampton station and is sited mid-way between the two centres in a new factory lot. Much police activity was in evidence. The small crowd of onlookers was already there when we arrived. (I think it must be the same small crowd that turns up to all royal engagements).

Prince Charles duly turned up, accompanied by Norton Romsey and the Lord Lieutenant, who introduced me to Prince Charles as Lord Thomson!

A good time was had by all. After Prince Charles had departed, I went round and did my own royal tour. The station sounds confident on the air and they are already making a profit.

In the evening to the Great Room at Grosvenor House, and yet another Awards ceremony. I sometimes imagine purgatory will be something like this – much scurrying and jollity, all to no avail. This night was the ILR Advertising Awards Dinner. The presentation was smoothly executed but marred, I thought, by the recipients of the awards. The so-called creative media people, some of whom had forgotten to wear a dinner suit, let alone a black tie. Something to do with fighting convention. It was a pity that more creativity was not put into their commercials. Perhaps it really is my advanced age that causes me to find these offerings so repellent. Maybe it's just a passing fad, but they all sound as if they've been put through a food mincer and then squashed. What connection they have been product and customer totally eludes me.

I saw Kenny Everett beaming away, wholly unconscious of the stares from around him, caused I suppose by a recent article linking his name with an unfortunate Aids victim. Roma and I managed to say our goodbyes before 11.30 and returned home to watch the end of *Newsnight*.

On Tuesday, lunch at the Mansion House given by the City of London Police Committee of the Corporation of London, presided over by Edwina Coven. Guest of Honour was Douglas Hurd, who had to leave before the pudding and made a lack-lustre speech. Sitting on Ms Coven's left hand was Charles Price. With a toast to the guests, Charles stood up and was promptly kissed by Edwina, who appears to enjoy kissing. She kissed me!

I sat alongside Lord Edmund Davies and took the opportunity of bending his ear about the notion that C4 should go it alone. I think he got my point that this was not a good idea. A nice, cautious and obviously very able man.

Leaving the Mansion House, I bumped into Lord Goodman. I took the moment to thank him for the letter he had sent to *The Times* on the subject of violence on television. He thanked me warmly and then said, 'You will be needing more letters before long'.

On Wednesday, the Finance Committee of the IBA met. This was the first occasion that Donald Maitland had been present. He is clearly not intending to be a silent Deputy Chairman. The sub-committee was there to discuss senior salaries and staffing at top level. I had previously circulated a paper arguing that the Directors' salaries were not equivalent to salaries outside in television. GT did not appear to want to make any additional increase over that suggested (8 per cent over the previous year). I said we would lose people if we did not recognise the reality of the market place. George Russell said my conclusion was right but my arguments wrong. He pointed to the salary we were proposing to pay to our new Controller and the salary we were already paying to our Director of Engineering, both considerably higher than the salaries paid to the previous incumbents. It was finally agreed to make an interim pay increase, and invite an outside consultant to assess the salary scale which is, I suppose, the best I could have expected.

On staff future movements, discussion ranged over what we should do about John Thompson's and Peter Baldwin's retirements, and who could lead Radio Division. Also who should take over from Brian Rook and who should take over from Harry Theobalds. There was enthusiasm expressed for recruiting someone young and ambitious, and someone to act as a think-tank input, preferably with a Harvard business background.

After the sub-committee the Authority meeting, where the main subject was DBS and listening to the Committee's recommendations. The Members had earlier met for breakfast and I had taken them over the ground, pointing out the strengths and weaknesses of the major contenders. I did the same performance at the Authority meeting. A good and full discussion took place. The Members were all in favour of BSB, but split amongst themselves about who would have come in second. Some disquiet was expressed over BSB's funding proposals. GT concluded the discussion by proposing that the four main contenders come back to answer further points. Rightly, too, it would suggest to the press that we had yet to come to a final conclusion. On that same basis, we have agreed to hold the decision back until after the Authority meeting on 11 December, making the announcement at 3pm and inviting in the winner and losers at 2.45. With any luck we can keep them all guessing until then. I have even had the Dining Room and Board Room checked over this weekend for bugging devices. Ray Snoddy of the *FT* is without doubt a first rate journalist but I wonder sometimes whether he uses modern technology to aid his knowledge. Tomorrow, Monday, we sit down again with the remaining four candidates – DBS UK, DBL, BSB and NBS.

For the last week or so, I had been undecided about going to Geneva on Thursday and missing a Friday meeting with Douglas Hurd at his office. In the event, I decided to fly out for my visit to the EBU after my 9.15am meeting with Douglas.

The BBC was strongly represented by Duke Hussey, Joel Barnett, Alasdair Milne and Michael Checkland. I was with GT and David Glencross. The subject was the Independents and DH's concern and belief that they should be accommodated into ITV and BBC schedules as soon as possible, but in any event he wanted to see 25 per cent of air time within four years taken up by independent production.

The previous evening, I had paid a visit to Alasdair and Michael Checkland to consider what common ground might exist between us. The BBC sees sponsorship as a possible hook to catch the Home Secretary's attention and pleasure, although Michael readily admitted that the Independents were less than happy with the notion. I told them that our position was somewhat different, our structure different and our use of Independents on Channel 4 standing in our credit. Alasdair was clearly working for some sort of joint statement and he put forward the thought that we might state that together we could double the existing use of Independents, i.e. 2,000 hours over the next four years. I rang back the following day, having spoken to David Glencross and said 'no, we would prefer to go our separate way'.

The meeting at 9.15am took place without Douglas, who had been summoned to No. 10. David Mellor instead occupied his chair, apologising for the place change. He conducted the meeting well and GT and Duke Hussey opened for both broadcasters. Our position was clearly stated: that no major changes could be contemplated for the year up until 89, but that the three years following could begin to shape a way forward for the contracts in 1992.

Not wholly what David Mellor wanted to hear but he couldn't fault the logic. BBC hackles were raised by the suggestion that independent production could also be seen to cover sport and outside events generally. We left as Douglas returned. The BBC stayed behind to talk over their sponsorship proposals, which I don't think they have a hope in hell of getting on to the statutes. I left and went back to the office before going to the airport. I had the chance of another word with Peter Parker and to put to him the salary arrangement of £15,000. Peter seemed content. He asked about Jeremy and Justin – would they be pleased? I said they would. He has promised to give me an answer on Tuesday. I spoke to GT and told him I thought we should engineer an announcement before Edmund held his final meeting before Christmas on the 16th to consider Channel 4 funding.

Off to Geneva and there to do my best to get Super Channel afforded the service of news items through Eurovision and to sort out a problem over links – both accomplished to some extent.

Sunday 14th December

A crowded week of goodbyes, parties, DBS and Edmund Dell!

Monday morning saw the DBS Committee of the Authority calling back DBS UK, DBL, BSB and NBS for further talks.

Michael Green of DBL gave a much better account of himself than at the previous meeting. The group still stuck to its plan that there would be no subscription and no dedicated film channel. Their conviction was impressive. Lesser people might have bowed to our obvious disbelief.

James Lee, of NBS, telephoned me after the meeting to ask whether any Members wanted reassurance after a question (I think I now rather unadvisedly asked) concerning an article in *The Tatler* that spoke of James in very much less than glowing terms following his period as Chief Executive of Goldcrest. I assured him that it had not put off Members.

John Jackson, of DBS UK, answered questions put to him with conviction, but again I got the strong impression that his whole thrust had been a technology-led venture which allowed programming to be placed in a poor second to his first enthusiasm.

The BSB contingent spoke well and confidently again.

At the end of Monday, our minds were made up. BSB should be given the contract.

PPC and SCC the following day. Lord T. took the Chair at PPC and used the opportunity to tell the Companies about our meeting at the Home Office with David Mellor. At SCC I urged the Companies to respond positively to what I said was a clear Government intention (if they won the Election) to push forward with plans to bring in a greater degree of independent production to both BBC and ITV. The first step would be to announce their plans for a £5.6m film fund for independent production.

Wednesday. I put on a black tie (incorrectly as it transpired) to attend the Memorial Service for Stuart Young. In fact it was titled 'A Celebration' and a moving celebration it turned out to be. The Guildhall was jam-packed. I was seated rather more than 'below the salt'. As I was going in, I saw Duke Hussey waiting outside. He confessed that he really felt it a bit inappropriate to be leading events since he had never met Stuart. The great and the good were out in force. Margaret Thatcher read from Ecclesiastes; Alasdair turned up in a rather too light blue tie and gave a lacklustre address, reminding his audience that, despite their rumoured tiffs, he and Stuart actually got on famously and Stuart did like travel and did have a hard time over *Real Lives*, but he did enjoy himself. Best, and most moving, tribute came from Stuart's brother David, who spoke of their childhood and how they had gone their different ways. He finished quietly by saying, 'How much I would like to be back in those sunny days of our childhood'. I saw several hardened warriors take out their handkerchiefs, and I, too, shed an uncontrolled tear.

Dinner that evening with Members of the Authority. Roma and several other wives were invited to say goodbye to the three retiring Members. GT hosted the occasion in the Cholmondely Room in the House of Lords. Jill McIvor, Yvonne Connolly and George Russell all spoke briefly. George, replying at greater length, went I thought a bit close to the bone in his storytelling. Three good Members.

I slept badly that night, my thoughts concentrated on the DBS announcement the following day.

The Members confirmed the recommendation by the Committee that BSB be appointed.

The Agenda of the session contained the provision to see Edmund Dell, Jeremy Isaacs and Justin Dukes. Edmund was in a bull-like mood, opening with a short account of the Board meeting of Channel 4 and the views of his Directors. He then devoted his remaining time to putting forward his own view. The previous day he had written under his title as Chairman a spirited letter in the *Guardian* attacking the complacency of ITV (and by implication the IBA). Members listened to him in stony silence. I think he had hoped for some confirmation that some Members might not be in agreement with the party line. GT alone responded. Nothing really was said that changed the views of either side. My hunch is that on Tuesday next, when the Channel 4 Board meets, Edmund will either resign or say he cannot go on representing the Board on the subject of the Channel selling its own airtime.

I had hoped to get Peter Parker's assent to being the next Chairman of Channel 4, but in the call GT made it became obvious that Peter wants to continue with his SDP activities. The two interests would not go well together so we will have to look for someone else. Jeremy suggests Sir Nicholas Henderson.

We adjourned for lunch with our guest from the Alliance Party – David Steel. Then downstairs for the DBS press announcement. All the contestants were to be taken to separate offices, where they were to be handed a letter from the Chairman. The winner, BSB, would be met by Kenneth Blyth and taken to the Chairman's office. This was timed for 3.15pm. The press conference was for 3.30pm. The whole event went like clockwork. BSB representatives – Andrew Quinn and Robert Devereux – came in at precisely 3.15pm.

GT and I went down to the Conference Room first and took to the platform. GT gave a brief opening statement and then we took questions. The room was packed. GT made the running and proved just how capable he is of handling situations, fielding questions with obvious relish. Andrew Quinn and his team then came to the rostrum and gave their press conference. They did well. No one knew the outcome in advance. The result was as most experts had predicted. The Third Age of broadcasting had arrived!

Sunday 21st December

A biting wind off the sea with grey, scudding clouds threatening snow. At any time of the year, Ower has its own magic. This is the shortest day and it still casts its spell.

The pre-Christmas escalation of parties and general whoopee has arrived. Roma and I are deciding to spend Christmas and Boxing Day quietly in London and then here for the New Year.

On Monday a meeting with Ken Miles and Leslie Simmons of ISBA to listen to their case for having more advertising minutage. Harry Theobalds is considering recommending a maximum of seven minutes, but increasing the average from six to six and a half minutes, which would allow for an additional seven or seven and half minutes or so to be inserted daily in the daytime programmes replacing schools programming at the end of June. Alternatively, to abolish the average figure and allow a normal maximum of seven minutes in any one clock hour, which would provide for an additional 14 minutes of advertising daily that could be inserted during daytime.

Before coming to a decision, we will need to consult with ITCA and AIRC. We cannot please everyone. If we increase minutage, ITV profits will continue to rise even further. If we do nothing, the advertisers will scream all the louder that the ITV monopoly is causing the price of airtime to go through the roof. The radio companies will complain that money that might have gone to them will be siphoned off instead into television.

Lunch with Bob Phillis at the Groucho Club, tucked away in Dean Street. It is one of the new breed of clubs catering to the high-spending 'ad-world'. Princess Diana was discreetly tucking into an enormous salad with a couple of chums. She looked more relaxed and happy than I have seen her when she is on parade.

Bob gave me some news about Carlton's plans – or rather, I should say, no news. Carlton are not planning to bid for an SES Astra Channel but it would not surprise me if they joined forces with BSB. Certainly the BSB consortium would be strengthened by Carlton.

The rumour that Michael Grade has been propositioned by Central was true. The Chairman had met him at an RTS Dinner and asked him to consider a proposal. The proposal never came. ITV will be the loser when Bob goes and so will Central if they can't find someone with real calibre.

On Tuesday to address the Tory Back Bench Media Committee of the Commons. Not a good time of year to talk serious business with MPs but some eight or nine turned up. I told them that the IBA was much more than merely a regulatory body. We were 'enablers' and I pointed out the developments in broadcasting presided over by the IBA. The meeting went well and I think I managed to convince them that the IBA was a suitable body to oversee the expansion of radio.

Afterwards, went with Roma to Covent Garden as guests of Alan and Judy Britten to see the most static performance of *Samson*, composed by Handel as an oratorio. I dozed off several times but the action didn't seem to have moved forward during my slumbers.

Afterwards to the Garrick and Robert Tear joined us with his wife for a hilarious dinner, Robert telling very wicked and amusing stories about George Solte, mimicking him to perfection.

On Thursday the crack of dawn found me perched on a stool in Wimpole Street being photographed by Gemma Levine for a book of portraits *Famous Faces of the 80s*. I am in very good company but will probably come out looking like a second-hand car dealer. I always do.

Then a meeting with JT. Not one I had been looking forward to. I told him I hoped he would consider early retirement. I said I would like the whole matter settled by the end of January. JT took it very calmly.

Later in the day a meeting with Naomi Sargent. She is still very distressed over losing the key appointment at the Open College. There was not much I could say. The more I hear educationalists talk, the more I find them mixed up and crazy. Perhaps we made a mistake in choosing Sheila Innes – I don't know.

Friday was Barbara Hosking's last day at the IBA. Before the staff drinks, Shirley Littler had invited Colette Bowe in for a drink to meet some journalists. CB had them eating out of the palm of her hand. I made a 'goodbye and thank you' speech in front of staff. Brian Young was there, and Tony Pragnell. Several journalists had said nice things about Barbara that I was able to incorporate in my goodbyes. Everyone seemed to like it.

In the evening, the staff Christmas dinner. Much frolics but left reasonably early.

Earlier in the week I had words with Donald Maitland who I fear is going to be something of a handful. He had decided to interview my senior staff and had asked George's secretary, Asifa, to arrange 45 minute sessions with him. I telephoned him and said it wasn't the way I liked doing things. The upshot is that a lunch is being arranged with staff.

Christmas next week. A rest, I hope.

1987

Sunday 4th January

A monstrously long break. Only in this country do we feel obliged to waste so much time. Television cavorted its way through the sea of sloth like some elephantine, uninvited guest. ITV did little to commend itself: no original drama worth its name; an output dominated by repeats and old films. ITN was twice transmitted 45 minutes later than its usual 2200.

Today the BBC is locked in a strike situation with its electricians, with live output looking the first to suffer.

The *Observer* today carried a report that the Green Paper on radio will recommend ILR being handed over to the Cable Authority and the stations owning their own transmitters.

ITCA has sent to us a note of their meeting with Douglas Hurd on the subject of the Independents. From the account, it was not a good meeting, with Douglas taking a sideswipe at the IBA over our plans for a 'better way'. The trouble with this Government is that it does not consider broadcasting to be a 'service', merely a commodity.

Sunday 11th January

The new year is getting into its stride. Icy winds are blowing across Poole Harbour from their cradle in Siberia. The only good thing I have decided about moles and their very existence, is the by-product of their ceaseless labours: newly-formed mounds of dark brown soil spurting to the surface beneath the iron layer of grass prove excellent excavation sites for the birds, who would otherwise be deprived of their morning meal of worms and little grubs. So all things have purpose.

Can the same be said of television, I wonder? More particularly, Christmas and New Year television. At a time when so many are gathered around their sets, I am dismayed by the seemingly worthless output.

The Authority met on Thursday and I said I thought the offering, regardless of ratings, was a pretty poor effort. ITV has a reputation of catering to the more plebeian tastes of audiences. Christmas viewing would confirm that opinion, seemingly only catering to the knees-up spirit of Christmas. The range and diversity of genuine choice in so called 'light entertainment' was sadly missing. Everyone ('everyone' being the media pundits) have been predicting a walk over for the BBC in the ratings war. Preliminary figures that I saw on Friday show in fact that ITV and BBC very nearly split the audience down the middle. This does not alter my view that ITV could do better. At the SCC next Tuesday, I intend giving notice that a detailed paper will go to PPC to consider what plans should be laid for Christmas 1987. The ITV Companies hate criticism, so I won't be popular.

On Tuesday, a lunch with the Editor of the *Independent*, Andreas Whittam-Smith, and his editorial team. I was taken on a Cooks type tour of the building. Gone are the huge presses, the hot plate lettertype settings, the roar and thunder of activity. Whirring computer discs and display units are the new tools of the 'printer'. I suppose it's the same kind of difference you get between a steam train and a diesel. I can appreciate now just how deep the divide must be between Rupert Murdoch and his old print unions. I have a suspicion that we will be seeing the same forward thrust in transmitter technology. The day will surely come when the terrestrial transmitter will be a relic of earlier times, with satellite beams aimed at regions rather than just a land mass.

In the evening to the National and a preview of *Coming In To Land* at the Lyttleton with Anthony Andrews and Maggie Smith. The critics subsequently gave it a mixed reception. I thought it needed some cuts but the play was amusing and in parts touching. Talked to Arnold Goodman in the interval. A fortnight before, he had been celebrated in a Sunday night tribute at the English National Opera. The event had raised over £200,000. Arnold said he felt mightily embarrassed by all the fuss, but – from the twinkle in his eyes – he had obviously found the evening much to his liking. Arnold is a splendid example of a genuine art lover who, through his influence, has done so much to maintain the arts against the pillaging of funds that this Government seems convinced is the way to behave.

The thorny problem of advertising minutage on television is again hitting the trade press headlines. The advertisers and the ITV Companies both argue that more time will help reduce costs of airtime. Those that oppose the increase believe that more airtime will serve only to enlarge the revenue potential for the ITV Companies and do nothing to keep costs down.

On Wednesday I met a deputation from the five major Companies and they made their case. Battle lines are drawn. Next Tuesday I will be able to hear the views of the MDs of all the 15 Companies.

Later that same evening, I attended a dinner at Lancaster House given in honour of IBA Members. The reason behind the occasion was not so much to convey thanks to the IBA for past services rendered but more, I suspect, to sound out the Authority on its views for the future. I gain the strong impression each time I meet Douglas Hurd that he's only interested in securing short-term objectives to destabilise broadcasting in order to weaken the power of the BBC, in particular with the unions as far as both the BBC and ITV are concerned. The long term good of the services currently provided by both organisations is something that he pays scant attention to sustaining. Douglas appears determined to bring about a radical shake-up; the introduction of independent production to ITV and BBC being but a part.

Radio is also on the evening's agenda. I get a strong impression that present

Government thinking is to take control of ILR away from the IBA and hand it over instead to the Cable Authority, as the *Observer* suspected.

George Thomson, John Thompson and I are due to meet the broadcasting press on Wednesday next week to set out the way forward we see for radio. Better to lay out our stall now, rather than wait for the Green Paper to pre-empt our position.

The major item on the Authority Agenda last week was Thames' desire to participate financially in the Astra Consortium. A complex and unhappy moment for our major ITV Company, to stand apart from the others and go it alone – or appear at this stage to have that intention. The IBA would have found it very difficult to find an objection to the diversification other than on the basis that Astra would be competing with the ITV Companies and in 1990 with BSB. Thames is the only Company to have unilaterally decided not to participate in Super Channel so, from almost every angle, the Thames' decision is unfortunate. I advised Members to permit the diversification on the proviso that Thames would take a 5 per cent share in the Astra holding company and not as a channel owner. That, I told Richard Dunn, would need separate consideration.

In the letter I subsequently sent to Thames, I concluded by reminding them that at the end of the current contract the Authority would be entitled to review their performance as a contractor, taking into account any effects on their performance resulting from any other activities they might have been engaged in during the period of their contract.

The first AIDS (or rather, anti-AIDS) commercials were transmitted this week. Until the last moment we did not know which of two versions would be used. The reason for the indecision was, I think, due to Norman Fowler waiting until Mrs T. had seen them both.

This week Thames announced the appointment of a new Chairman – Sir Ian Trethowan replacing Hugh Dundas.

Lunched with Colette Bowe on Friday, which confirmed my belief that she will do the IBA very nicely. Met Donald Maitland again, which confirmed my view that he is trouble.

Sunday 18th January

Winter had the country firmly in an icy embrace: the coldest since records began, I believe, in 1940. Mostly it has taken everyone by surprise: Local Councils, Government, transport, Utilities.

George has been holed up in Kent since the week began so, as a consequence, we cancelled Wednesday's press conference on the IBA's proposals for radio.

On Monday, sat round the National Theatre's Board table to agree the appointment of Richard Eyre as the next Director. Caused some merriment by proposing that Richard should undergo a medical. I think he will be an able and visionary successor to Peter. Perhaps it's just me, but I have always found it hard to have a rapport with him. Always pleasant and courteous, he still somehow stands apart. I don't feel I share the thoughts that lie behind the remarks he sometimes makes.

I have been reading his published diary and realised what a tangled, insecure person he is, driven forward relentlessly by his creative fervour, passion and drive but at the same time a prey to his insecurity and introspection. It must drive him mad.

On Monday night, I was due to have dinner with George and Professor Brian Griffiths, the head of the Prime Minister's Policy Unit. As GT was baling out his house in Kent (the result of a leaking roof), Brian Griffiths decided that he would prefer to come when the Chairman was there. It has now been fixed for next Friday. In the interim, I sent him the two volumes of Bernard Sendall's history of the IBA for light reading!

Despite the appalling weather, Regis de Kalbermatten and Werner Rumphorst flew over from Switzerland to have a meeting with Super Channel and then go on to dinner with Kenneth and me.

We find ourselves increasingly in odd situations. We now have the EBU wanting to link the activities of Super Channel to the IBA in order that the relationship enables the EBU to prevent non-aligned Companies gaining access to EBU services. So here we are, actively endorsing an arrangement that will bring competition closer to home when Super Channel begins to compete in the home market.

On Tuesday, I met the MDs at SCC and paid tribute to Bob Phillis as this was his last meeting. Sad for ITV. He produced clarity of thought and was respected by his fellow MDs. We talked about the role of the Independents in ITV. Paul Fox was, and is, resistant to making any speedy concessions, but the flow of opinion amongst the other MDs is for action of some sort. I believe that they are right. If insufficient indication is given to Government, they will take the law into their own hands. Especially as they have pegged the BBC licence for the next three years to the RPI. The disparity between ITV and BBC costs and revenues will grow even wider. I am sure that this is intentional and Government will be the very first to draw conclusions on how best to bring about parity.

During the week, I had several calls from Michael Winner, creating a stir about the imminent likelihood of the Obscene Publications Bill coming forward to Friday's timetable in Parliament. In the event, it failed to materialise. Instead, the Bill proposing free TV licences for pensioners raised MPs' blood pressure.

Michael Winner wants to create a Committee to fight the Obscene Publications Bill, which will most certainly surface again. He has been looking for a title which sounds respectable and which will enable him to invite leaders in the arts on to a small inner council of war. I suggested 'The Milton Committee' – Milton having been the architect of freedom of printing etc., etc. We will see. Winner is sometimes a pain in the neck but he gets things done and I would rather have it that way than the other. GT has already written to a number of influential MPs advising them of the IBA's concerns over the Bill, so the battle lines are drawn.

On Thursday, I attended the memorial service for Howard Thomas in St Martin in the Fields. A good and well-attended service with a splendid eulogy given by Joe Loss, who must be in his 80s but bright as a button and very engaging.

Afterwards, clutching each other for support, we all slithered down the Strand to the Savoy and a really splendid buffet luncheon. A lovely way to celebrate Howard's passing. Bridget Plowden was in great form. I asked her whether she had ideas for the next Chairman of C4 and she said she would think hard.

Sir Donald Maitland was due to lunch with us on Friday, but again the weather forced us to cancel our plans. Instead, I met a group of Danes who had come to England to see how we arrange our Public Service system and especially how we organised C4. It's amazing how many nations think we have something in which to take pride whereas we (or rather Government) appear to be doing everything possible to bring about a reduction in the service we give to the public.

Sunday 25th January

Colette Bowe joined the IBA on Monday. I sent her flowers and we had a drink together at the end of the day. She has a ready appreciation of nuance and will bring much of value to our public persona.

On Monday, a jolly evening spent with the Hawkesworths. We went to the Siam restaurant in St Albans' Grove, which was a favourite haunt of ours when we worked together. I must say, listening to John talking about his current work, I am filled with a deep longing to work again on something creative, but then I have to pull myself together and argue (with myself) that what I am doing *is* creative.

A meeting of the ITN Board on Monday afternoon. Listening to the arguments about pricing the service for Super Channel makes me more and more convinced that sooner rather than later we must set up ITN as a separate entity. It has too many masters at present.

Met Sir Raymond Lygo on Tuesday. Came to the office to make his mark about British Aerospace interests in DBS and co-operating with BSB. Much will depend on launch dates. I hope arrangements can be made with Aerospace. It would be a sad day for the UK if Britain's first DBS service were to have American hardware.

Sat at lunch with Geoffrey Rippon, a guest at one of Bob Lorimer's occasional gatherings for MPs from the Regions. I have come to the sad conclusion that most MPs are really interested about television's impact and effects when it touches their own lives. They have what nearly amounts to an obsession over whether or not they have been left out of a local television programme, whilst their opponent succeeds in taking the stage. I spoke for a few moments on major issues. No interest whatsoever. Geoffrey Rippon has formed a television sales company called China Television Ltd. Not bad, as both the Russians and Chinese are in the commercial launch business.

George Thomson and I met Jeremy Isaacs and Justin Dukes on Wednesday morning. Jeremy wanted to tell us that he has very nearly made up his mind to leave C4 at the end of 1988 when his present contract expires. I believe he may have been offered the directorship of the Royal Opera House, but he didn't mention it on this occasion. Justin said that, in the event that Jeremy did decide to go, he would wish to be in the running for Chief Executive.

A meeting with Donald Maitland, still rabbiting on about founding a Policy

Committee. A good thought but he sees himself very much as its future leader. I hear through Shirley Littler that this is not contemplated by the Home Office.

A drink with Aubrey Buxton at his flat in Hyde Park Crescent overlooking Hyde Park. I realised for the first time how good a painter he is – pictures of far off places. The reason for the drink was Aubrey's passionate belief that Anglia should be considered as a Network Company before TVS. I suggested that David McCall should write and put the case.

Thursday's Authority meeting discussed TV-am's shareholding arrangements in the light of shareholder Alan Bond's acquisition of Kerry Packer's disposal of his shares of Channel 4 in Australia. Members decided to postpone a decision pending further consideration.

At last, the lunch with Professor Brian Griffiths on Friday, reporting directly to the PM on, amongst other things, broadcasting policy. A lively, engaging, highly articulate man, he insisted on shaking hands with the wine waiter in the general introductions. If the Tories get in at the next Election, the IBA is going to have to work hard to prevent the auctioning of Channel 4 to the highest bidder, and much else. We got on well together. I spoke of coherence in broadcasting, the need to employ a structure that would uplift and maintain the values of Public Service Broadcasting whilst allowing more competition.

Sunday 1st February

Is there any medium so hypnotising to the media and the public as television? Its hold on public attention dominating the fireside, vacuuming conversation and polarising debate through the eyes of a few commentators. Television and royalty vie for first place.

This week, television won hands down. At 1130 am on Thursday 29 January, Alasdair Milne decided to hand in his resignation 'for personal reasons'. This was far from what actually happened, no doubt to be documented and 'frame frozen' for posterity.

Sad for the BBC, sad for Alasdair. Roma sent Sheila flowers and a note: 'Shall miss you at the EBU. Love, Roma.' Alasdair's aloofness distanced him from almost everyone. When he joined in conversation it was as if he was battling within himself to sound like a mere mortal. His disdain for the commercial world of television was all pervasive.

Alasdair's attendance at EBU was where I saw him most frequently. On several occasions he insisted on moving out of the hotel room selected for his stay by ever-attentive acolytes. But he had an aura, a kind of Reithian aura that he wore like a cloak, shrouding what I suspect may have been a deep sense of his own insecurity. Easy now to analyse and deprecate his achievement. This was, I suppose, to hold up to inspection the BBC's belief that it, and it alone, was the instrument of broadcasting public service.

Who now? Paul Fox – no, earns too much, too old, but undoubtedly would have been a great DG ten years ago. All the right assets: attitude, ability. A great pity his years in the wilderness, despite his success with Yorkshire, cannot measure up to the seat he could and should have occupied.

Brian Wenham? No – if he is selected, which is quite possible, he will be a stand-still DG.

Jeremy, the current favourite? Four years ago his head was being demanded on a stake. Today a hero. Jeremy will not be selected. His radical form of leadership will not chime readily with the task the Government believes lies ahead. 'Not safe in taxis' used to be applied to certain debs' delights in years gone by. The same can be applied to Jeremy in a different context.

John Tusa? No. Michael Grade? No. Alastair Burnet? No. Christopher Bland? No. Michael Checkland? No.

Despite the suddenness of Alasdair's departure, Dukie must have an heir apparent in his sights. The rest of the week, by comparison, seems to pale into insignificance.

By dint of nudging, praising, cajoling, JT has now agreed to have his early retirement announced next Tuesday. He writes his own obit, then re-writes it, providing the Chairman with a lustrous quote.

The Advisory Liaison Committee (ALC) met on Monday and debated the possible increase in television minutage. I think I am now settled on advising a seven-minute limit in every one clock hour. It will fail to please the larger contractors, or the larger advertisers, but tough titty. Television has lived with its present advertising time for 30 years. The increase to seven minutes will put an extra 14 minutes into the system, allowing extra minutage for daytime programmes but holding peak time to its current level.

On Wednesday, RCC. The Radio Companies are more tranquil of late. I am not sure that they now believe that the Cable Authority is the answer to their prayers. Since the rental reduction, the IBA's role has not been attacked as fiercely as before. If we play our card right, the day can still be saved.

On Thursday, the postponed press briefing on the IBA's stance on radio. Well attended, quite good follow-up in the press, but seemingly not high on the news agenda. We must do more private lobbying of Douglas Hurd and David Mellor. There is still time.

Later in the day, chaired a meeting at the National to decide whether or not to hold a celebration to mark the 80th birthday of Lord Olivier. He doesn't want royalty, and doesn't want a play, but would come to a party. Decided to go ahead although time short.

Later still in the evening, attended the launch party of Super Channel at Limehouse Studios. Margaret T. spoke well about the excellence of UK products and wished the venture success. Behind the scenes, problems abound. Equity are insisting that all artists must agree the terms of their repeat fees. Why this wasn't cleared up ages ago, I cannot imagine.

On Saturday, I was telephoned by David Nicholas, vastly distraught, telling me that the EBU had telexed to say that approval for all members to go ahead on news participation had not been given and that separate deals must be struck by those who do participate. After much telephoning, the problem does not seem so formidable. A shame if the news cannot go out on Monday. Everyone trying so hard to make it work here.

Sunday 8th February

Another week of speculation and rumours over the choice of DG for the BBC. On Thursday, Jeremy Isaacs rang and told me he was applying for the job. I don't think he'll get it. David Dimbleby is now the hottest bet.

Talking of Jeremy, I have just seen a letter from him to David Glencross expressing his consternation that the IBA have turned down a showing of *Brimstone and Treacle* by Dennis Potter. Oh dear, poor old IBA simply can't win. David and I personally thought it should be shown. About half the Members agreed. GT was opposed. We haven't heard the end of *Brimstone* by a long chalk.

On Monday to the Institute of Mechanical Engineers and to a party hosted by ITN to launch their new service on Super Channel. Norman Tebbit made a brief appearance. Everyone seemed pleased by the presentation made by ITN. However, the BBC 'pulled' over 50 programmes at the last moment because they couldn't get the permission from actors required by Equity. This means that Super Channel's schedules will be awry until such time as the necessary agreements are signed. A great introduction to British television to those in Europe!

On Tuesday Paul Fox asked me to add my name to those of other Vice Presidents of the RTS on a letter to *The Times* about police access to journalist transcripts. I thought the wording over the top and suggested some amendments, which were duly made. The letter appeared the following day and since then I have heard nothing more.

John Thompson's retirement was announced this week. I am afraid that all his early work in launching ILR has been forgotten, and he now appears in the garb of an inhibitor rather than an innovator but the contribution he made to the planning and launch of commercial radio cannot be underestimated. A small drama is being played out between John and Peter Baldwin over the matter of offices. Curious how grown men can get mightily upset over a carpet, desk and drinks cupboard!

RA telephoned me on Friday to speak about his concerns over C4. He is right to be worried. With Edmund leaving in June, Jeremy wishing to become the BBC's next DG, Paul Bonner going to ITCA, Channel 4 is in for an unprecedented upheaval. Edmund (according to RA) never wanted JI as boss of Channel 4, and RA rightly is worried that while Edmund is still in the driving seat he might make decisions at odds with Channel 4's best interests without consultation with RA. Who the hell do we get to replace Jeremy? There are so few people up to it. Possibly David Elstein, or John Birt. I don't know.

What to do about the Independents? This is our next major problem. On Monday we dine with David Mellor, and he and Douglas Hurd want blood. I think we must prick both our fingers and those of ITCA's and draw, if not a gush, then one or two drops. Otherwise, when the Conservatives get in again, Hurd will have fixed quotas. Perhaps the thought put forward by Peter Rogers would be the best way – that is, to form a holding company owned by the ITV Companies to commission network programmes from both the Independents and ITV Companies. I don't know how we solve this one: there are so many diverse interests. One first step would be to put a freeze on all capital expenditure by ITV Companies. Not really very practical.

The Authority on Thursday considered TV-am's shareholding exchange between Packer and Bond. They accepted our recommendations to tell Bond to sell his new acquisition from 27.5 per cent down to 10 per cent, and for the Board of TV-am to make up its own mind whether or not to invite Bond on to the Board. I can see more ructions ahead!

The Authority saw the AIDS Public Service Announcement. This time an iceberg with 'AIDS' carved on its base; really just pussy-footing with the problem. My P.A., Sally Munton, said that she had seen the same film in a cinema and the predominantly young audience had hooted with mirth.

On Friday a lunch for Donald Maitland to meet and talk with key staff. Quite a good display of wisdom by those around the table. In the middle of the meal there was a loud crack and the empty dessert glass in front of Sir Donald split asunder!

I feel weary with the whole broadcasting world. We seem to be slipping slowly into a quagmire of mediocrity. Is it the cost that matters most, or the quality? I fear that in today's world it is the former.

Sunday 15th February

Something about this time of year adds to any feelings of depression that one might have – for me, anyway.

Speculation over the next BBC DG continues. Some names are still backed. More speculation this week on Michael Grade, David Dimbleby, Richard Dunn. Frontrunners are Brian Wenham and Jeremy Isaacs. I suppose, if I were to be honest, I would like somebody to have suggested I put my name forward, but no one has! I offer, as explanation to myself, the fact that I have little real programming experience, but am pulled up short by the realisation that neither has Richard Dunn. It's depressing, but I rather think that my talents, if I have any, are obscured by the image of the IBA, which, to say the least, is hardly glittering. I suppose the second thing that is making me feel low is the imminent Public Issue by Capital. The station was my baby and I feel dreadfully isolated from all the razzamatazz. The third thing, and much more pedestrian, is that Alasdair Milne's salary was £75,000 – mine £60,000. I should be paid more. I am growing into an embittered person.

On Monday met Prince Edward with Emma Nicholson. Poor boy – he is obviously still suffering from his decision to pull out of the Marines, doing his best to make up for it by being decisive and purposeful. Our meeting was to think up ideas to promote the Duke of Edinburgh's Award Scheme. Prince Edward arrived an hour late which didn't strike me as a good start.

In the evening, dinner at the IBA for David Mellor. A likeable, enthusiastic person who is still pushing the Government's hope to see ITV taking in the Independents, if not under a quota at least in a manner that demonstrates their commitment to change.

Much will depend on a tripartite meeting that I am due to chair on 19 March, between ITCA, the Independents and ourselves, but benchmarks must be established; vague promises will not do.

At the dinner, I pitched in again about Local Radio, but David Mellor said he couldn't comment as the Green Paper had been completed. Most people (not me) think it a foregone conclusion that radio will be taken from the IBA and given to the Cable Authority. This may be in the Green Paper, but I remain convinced that we can persuade the Home Office and Ministers to think again.

On Tuesday PPC and SCC. At PPC I spoke about my concern over Christmas and New Year programming. I was surprised to find that my doubts were in the main endorsed: that the Christmas output could have been better.

Poor old Harold Wilson is getting more doddery and pathetic. I attended on Thursday a presentation at BAFTA of 'Images of Britain' sponsored by the British Council. We certainly don't do enough to promote our culture overseas through television and film. 'A foot of film is worth a dollar of trade, say the Americans, who, enjoying special advantages, have turned every cinema in the world into the equivalent of an American consulate'. So wrote Sir Stephen Tallents in 1932. Wilson, as President of the British Screen Advisory Council, opened the proceedings, reading painstakingly from his text. I saw him afterwards standing outside the building, trying to catch the attention of a passing cab without success. Crowds hurried past him without a backward glance.

At various times through the week I have been having telephone conversations with Richard A. Both GT and I think that Dickie would be the best chairman of C4, if he can be persuaded to give up some of his other work to have enough time to devote to the Channel. I think he will. The combination of Dickie and George Russell would make a good mix of talents. Just who would be right to take over Jeremy's job, if he went to the BBC, I don't know.

A good meeting on Thursday with ITN, to talk over the possibility of ITN going public. We make headway.

On Monday, or Tuesday, Mrs Whitehouse is due to have another go at us/Channel 4 over material shown with the warning triangle. Research we have conducted supports the notion that a warning of some sort is needed, but I am worried about the clips Mary Whitehouse has selected. Like taking a close up of a small portion of Picasso's 'Guernica' and then castigating the whole work for depravity! But there is no doubt she'll win popular support from Tory bloodmongers.

Sunday 22nd February

The great 'who's to be DG of the BBC' continues. We are now told that the announcement will come next Thursday. If this is really the way the Governors and Duke H. go about their business, it seems extraordinary to me. Why not hire headhunters and quietly set about the task? At present, it's turning into a sort of gladiatorial contest. Front runners still Jeremy, David Dimbleby, Brian Wenham. Second field John Tusa, Michael Grade, Anthony Smith, Nigel Ryan.

It is said that insiders within the BBC dislike intensely the thought that David D. could order their lives. This makes me put David D. at the top of the list.

Lunched with Jeffrey Archer on Monday in the Savoy Grill. Full of bounce, of confidence, of energy. Jeffrey appears to have come through this 'strange experience' totally unscathed but determined to bring the *News of the World* to account.

On Tuesday to see Jonathan Miller's production of the *Mikado*. Very stylish set and costumes but I confess to a dislike of the whole piece.

Wednesday and the redoubtable Mr Alan Bond, who came to the office to present his credentials and make his case for hanging on to his 27.5 per cent of TV-am. In the event, the Authority took my recommendation to allow him to retain 20 per cent of his holding; 10 per cent voting, 10 per cent non-voting. Bond is another variation of Archer. Confidence has to be the most seductive of all assets in the armoury of a successful person. Confidence when things go wrong – that's the key. Bond will go on the Board and Timothy Aitken will welcome the addition. It would not surprise me in the least to find out that Tim and Bond are busy plotting something. Time will tell.

Going back a day, to Tuesday evening, Mary Whitehouse invited in ten MPs to show them excerpts from 'triangle' films on Channel 4. In the event, she appears to have scored an own goal. The newspaper reports indicate that the majority of those watching either found the whole thing boring or just plain funny. It could not have helped Mary to have to explain what she thought was going on.

Much speculation was ended after the Authority meeting on Thursday when the Members came to their decision about the amount of advertising time per hour, endorsing my recommendation that it should remain at a maximum of seven minutes but the six-minute average formula could be scratched, resulting in around a further 14 minutes a day as a result of schools programming going from ITV to Channel 4. It was the right decision and whilst it won't have pleased the advertisers, or the majority of ITV Companies, it will be appreciated by audiences.

George and I went on Friday morning to see Douglas Hurd and to hear the worst about the Green Paper on Radio. The Green Paper sounds as if it will please nobody. Instead of a coherent plan, it opts for almost total deregulation, merging ILR and Community Radio, introducing INR on up to three national channels by auction.

If we play our cards adroitly, we will win. The most important element, as far as we are concerned, is that the Paper offers three alternative regulators: ourselves, a new broadcasting authority or the Cable Authority. Transmitters will be the responsibility of the licensee. A recipe for mayhem.

To lunch later at the Savoy and to witness the presentation of awards at the *What The Papers Say* annual beanfeast. Oysters and Lancashire hotpot the order of the day. Had a long chat with Sidney Bernstein, still in good nick. This was the last occasion that Denis Forman was presiding. When he leaves the television arena it really will be the end of an era.

Talking of eras, the passing on Friday of Hugh Carlton-Green. A splendid and triumphant DG of the BBC. It must be hurtful for Alasdair this week to read the tribute to him.

Finally, down on Friday to Lainston House near Winchester and to our Authority weekend. Much useful debate and most of what I want, including assent from Members to continue talks with ITN to produce a new structure of funding. The IBA is there to serve listeners/viewers, not the other way round.

Off now to put my feet up in front of the telly and have an Indian take-away.

Sunday 1st March

White smoke finally belched out of the BBC's chimney on Thursday evening. News of the appointment of a new DG was held back until after *News At Ten*. It fell to *Newsnight* to announce that Michael Checkland was the Governors' unanimous choice. So the quiet man in the background was the man to make it. Since then, the newspapers have had a field day. 'Mr Nobody', 'Mr Checkbook', 'Mr Who?' The Press Association somehow got my home telephone number and asked me for a quote. I said he was 'his own man', which they didn't use. Whether he is in fact 'his own man' or the Chairman's remains to be seen. It is reported that there were over 300 applications. One name that they didn't get was mine. Do I hear myself sounding peeved? A case of sour grapes? Yes, in a way. It would have been nice to have had even a little speculation about whether I could be shifted across, but I don't think it occurred to anyone except me. Ah well, I wish him luck.

This week saw the publication of the Government's long overdue Green Paper on Radio: 'Radio Choices and Opportunities'. There was a press conference at 11am held by Douglas Hurd. Much on the line that Douglas had already spelt out to George and me. The press and broadcasters latched on to the prospect of another three new national sound channels. I did a series of interviews for ILR and BBC Local and National Radio, and ITN and BBC TV for the *Nine O'clock News*. I stressed that radio should not be left simply to market forces, the big elbowing out the small. The press on the whole welcomed the notion of deregulation. It was welcomed by the AIRC. ITN referred to me as 'Chairman' of the IBA. This is the second time. The BBC got it right! It's going to be a long, slow heave but I think we can hold on to radio if we demonstrate a practical understanding of need. We have much of the current mood to blame on ourselves. I should have spotted the signs much earlier. I am filled with regret.

On Thursday evening I had a call from Douglas Hurd's Private Secretary saying that the Home Secretary hoped we had not felt too badly about it all. I said, 'No, we didn't'.

The day before the Green Paper we had another meeting with Brian Griffiths. From it, I deduced:

- TV violence was on the mind of the PM
- Auctioning is still flavour of the month

- Different regulatory authority for different regimes is good for competition
- The profitability of ITV will need to be curbed

The real issue is whether or not ITV should be considered to have a Public Service Broadcasting role at all. Radio was a good test-bench. If it succeeds, do the same for television. The writing is all too plainly on the wall.

In the evening, to an appalling production of *High Society*, the night before First Night. Singing was third-rate, and the production looked under-rehearsed. Richard Eyre wrote the 'book' and directed.

AIDS is so much in the forefront of everyone's mind, that in Andrew Hislop's critique this Sunday he referred to 'the prophylactic of pre-recording'. I think it rather apt.

Unfortunately, even the 'prophylactic of pre-recording' could not save one of ITV's more ghastly newborns being foisted on to the screen, entitled *Hardwicke House*. A comedy set in a secondary school. It hit rock bottom in taste, humour and acting. Thankfully, my view appeared to have been shared by a goodly proportion of its audience who telephoned in their hundreds to ask for the series to be removed. David Glencross passed on to Andy Allan of Central our view and the series was taken off. The Company has threatened to put it back on later in the evening: 'at some future date'. Over my dead body. How it got on to the network in the first place fills me with anger. So much for the big fives' 'commitment to quality'. Andy is said to have declared that he himself did not actually see the two episodes before they went out.

On Wednesday to Gerald Savory's party to celebrate his play *George and Margaret*. Poor Gerald, he is now showing his years.

On Thursday dinner to say goodbye to Ron Wordley of HTV, retiring after serving ITV since 1958. Colourful, difficult but undoubtedly a torchbearer for ITV, he will be missed.

Now that Michael Checkland has been appointed, the question will be raised about who should become the next Controller of Channel 4. Today's Sundays gave the news that Jeremy had accepted the position of Director at Covent Garden, replacing John Tooley. Now begins the next guessing game. Richard A will, I know, pitch for Anthony Smith, and he wants the new man to have total control of Channel 4. I want Justin to stay and become MD with the new man appointed as Programme Controller. GT agrees (I think) with Dickie. So it looks as though we have a genuine difference of opinion.

Our first major AIDS programme went out on Friday: 'First Aids'. It started at 7.30.pm and featured, probably for the very first time, a French Letter demonstration – over two fingers, that is. I wonder what Mary Whitehouse will make of that?

Monday 2nd March

The news last week that Michael Checkland has got the DG role has unleashed a torrent of speculation about Jeremy's role as Chief Executive of Channel 4. Jeremy came round to see me this afternoon, greatly distressed that Edmund Dell is plotting to call a meeting of some Channel 4 Board members to consider making an early change of Jeremy's role and appointing a new Chief. This was all sparked off by Jeremy's announcement that he would be going to run the Opera House when John Tooley retires in 1989. Dell is now saying that Jeremy will only be a contender if he remains at Channel 4. Jeremy said to me this afternoon that he intended seeing out his contract with Channel 4 – that is until the end of 1988. Both GT and I will resist any attempt by Edmund to oust Jeremy.

I bumped into Claus Moser tonight at Sonia Melchit's party and he confirmed to me that, whilst they would like Jeremy to start at the Opera House earlier than at the end of 1988, they nevertheless respected his loyalty to C4.

I can see that, whatever we do to try and dampen rumours, the next media story is going to be who is going to take on Jeremy's job at C4.

Dell obviously wants to leave on a high and sees the appointment of Jeremy's successor as key to achieving this.

Sunday 8th March

The bleakest news of the year. On Friday evening, at about 6.45pm, the Cross-Channel boat between Dover and Zebrugge sank in less than a minute. Radio and television problems take on a proper perspective against this tragedy.

A lively meeting with Conservative MPs on Monday at a lunch given by Jack Reedy for Midland MPs. Amongst them Gerald Howarth. I said my bit and invited questions and comments. Violence and sex on television did not weigh unduly on their minds, or so it seemed. Afterwards, I spoke to Howarth and we have arranged to meet. He alluded to the scene in *Themroc* which was part of C4's Red Triangle series last year, described by Mary Whitehouse as horrific, and in which a policeman was roasted and eaten. I pointed out that this incident was never actually established in the film.

Held a meeting with Radio staff on Tuesday to give them a pep talk and show them that we thought we had a good chance of winning the Green Paper debate. It's always difficult to judge the mood of Radio staff, possibly because John Thompson is so unforthcoming and his staff appear terrified of upsetting him.

On Wednesday an AIDS seminar, which I chaired. Straight talking by the two Department of Health doctors, together with photographs – one in particular set someone off in a faint. AIDS is the most appalling affliction. There are no signs of a cure and every sign that we are still scarcely aware of the devastation that will be wrought on mankind. The Black Death, by comparison, was small beer.

I attended the first Board Meeting of the Open College on Thursday. A great deal of work to do by staff. I don't envy their task. Afterwards, spoke to Michael Green who wants to pursue his interest in taking over Ladbroke's share in Central. He hopes to let me have a letter from Central's Chairman towards the end of this week and asked that we take it to the Authority. I think Members will welcome the transfer. There is a problem with John Jackson. Michael does not expect him to stay on Central's Board if Ladbroke's role disappears. I said that would be a decision for Central's Board to make. Our only concern is that news of this change should not break before an announcement is made.

Much to-ing and fro-ing over C4 Board matters. I heard earlier in the week that Edmund was preparing to mount an offensive on Monday evening to dislodge Jeremy and invite him to leave earlier than his proposed retirement date in 1988. Jeremy is alarmed and, to counteract the rumours that have started to circulate, issued a statement from C4 reiterating that he intended staying until the due date. As a result of all this, I have been pushing for an agreement with Dickie that he would confirm his willingness to take over the role of Chairman. George and I breakfasted with Dickie on Friday and were much relieved when he agreed. Now it's a matter of timing. When to tell Edmund (who will be less than pleased). Dickie will speak to Edmund on Monday evening, or Tuesday morning. There may be tears before bedtime. I spoke to Jeremy on Friday, who called me from a train between London and Cardiff, I think to find out the state of play. He sounded much relieved.

The Government seems determined to get inside the broadcasters' guard. This week a piece appeared in *The Observer* suggesting that Douglas Hurd and David Mellor proposed looking at the networking arrangements. I said to GT that we should consider writing a stiff letter to Douglas telling him to keep out of our affairs. Our fears that the period between the end of the current contract and the next contract would be used to destabilise the system are proving all too true. If the Green Paper is only intended for radio, I will have misjudged our friends in Westminster. It is a precursor for television and we must be on our guard.

Next week there is a Council meeting with the Independent Producers and ITCA to see if a way forward can be found for the introduction of Independents in ITV. I am chairing the meeting and I am not looking forward to it.

Returning to the subject of Edmund Dell, I heard this week that he was making a bid to become the next Chairman of the IBA. What a ghastly thought. This would explain why he wants to move fast on the appointment of a Chief Executive of C4 and why he argued so fiercely for the channel to control its own advertising in competition with ITV. Away dark thoughts!

Sunday 15th March

'Remember you are not immortal'. So Edmund Dell reminded us at the Authority meeting on Thursday. He was referring, he said, to the practice adopted in Ancient Rome when returning heroes made their customary parade through the streets. Running behind the hero's chariot was always a slave who shouted these words repeatedly above the din and adulation of the crowds. Sitting on his right as he spoke was Jeremy Isaacs – feted as the uncrowned king of television and C4 and responsible for every deed of courage and innovation in the whole calendar of television enterprise.

The occasion was the Annual Budget meeting between C4 and the Authority. It was also an occasion for the Chairman to say a few words as retiring Chairman before handing over in June to Dickie. Behind the scenes much activity. Dick spoke to Edmund for the first time about our decision late on Monday night after the meeting to consider Jeremy's future. Edmund got squashed. The decision to retire Jeremy failed and he endorsed his own wish to stay on until his due date for ending his contract.

Edmund said nice things about Jeremy and Justin. George said nice things about Edmund. Edmund didn't say nice things about George or the Authority.

I wonder how the future will turn out. Will Jeremy decide, having gained his victory to stay on, to take his leave early? Will Edmund have his wish to become the next Chairman of the IBA? Will Justin become next Chief Executive of the Channel? It sounds like a trailer for a soap opera!

Early in the week, on Monday, lunched with David Frost in The Rib Room, Carlton Tower. More New York than New York. David as bouncy as ever. He talked about TV-am and how to get it a better position within ITV. Waiters brought our coffee and two chocolates containing billowing clouds of dry ice. It reminded me of *Macbeth* and the witches. Would our spells succeed, I wondered.

Later on Monday to Buckingham Palace and to a reception given by Prince Edward for the Duke of Edinburgh Awards Scheme. Prince Edward is a nice, gentle fellow and I can see why he had little taste for the Marines. A case of being pushed to the front. He has asked me to see what can be done to get coverage for a do at Henley to launch the 1987 Awards. I suggested he should rub sticks together and produce flames. Very symbolic for youth. It would make a good picture and that's what it's all about. Poor boy. He will soon be quite bald.

Tuesday was something of a red letter day for ITV. I chaired the meeting between representatives from ITCA, the Independents and the IBA to begin to hammer out an understanding leading to the phased introduction of Independents on ITV. Douglas H has said that he is looking for access amounting to some 25 per cent over the next three to four years. He is not going to get that from us, but he might see something nearer to 17 per cent up to the end of 1992 on ITV alone.

The meeting went rather better than I had expected. The crunch came towards the end when I indicated the kind of hours we envisaged: a range between 200 to 400 hours for locally originated programmes and between 175 to 225 hours for network programming. Despite a request at the end of the meeting that we should keep these figures confidential, Ray Snoddy had the full facts in the *FT* the following morning.

First impressions are that these figures have pleased the Independents and angered and alarmed the ITV Companies. They have asked for a meeting on Monday to express their fears. I am not persuaded they have cause for hysteria. Regional hours of 6,000 per year can surely accommodate 300! And network of 2,023 per year could stand an injection by the Independents of 200 hours. I will stick to my guns. If ITV were producing programmes of the very highest quality, it might be different but there has been an increasing load of rubbish on ITV. *Newly-Weds, Hardwick House, Highway to Heaven*. No *Brideshead* or *Jewels* for a long, long time. New blood might be the answer.

Yorkshire TV reception in the evening and met Willie Whitelaw, who rambles on like some ageing Second World War tank on manoeuvres. He doesn't listen. The greatest sin of politicians! Perhaps if they listened more they would be faced with the truth. The party was to celebrate going public. The shareholders' bank managers must be celebrating too.

Wednesday 11 March, a meeting with British Aerospace unhappy about BSB and the possibility of the consortium going for a Consat spacecraft. Second-hand, they say, and with certain deficiencies.

BSB is worrying on several counts. I begin to feel that they are running out of steam. The threat of Astra is casting shadows over their actions.

Late that evening, a private dinner with GT, Terry Smith and Jimmy Gordon to plot our radio futures.

Thursday 12th March. The Authority Meeting, Donald Maitland taking an increasingly active role. Is he the next Chairman? I hope not. Much damage can be done by men retained with little to do.

We agreed to the transfer of shares by Ladbrokes to Central.

Problems arise over a live broadcast at Piccadilly Radio by two National Front spokesmen. I ban it!

Dinner that night hosted by AIRC to meet Authority Members. I detect the awakening of real fears by the Companies as they realise that the free market, deregulated, airwaves they have been campaigning for may well leave them fighting for survival. Especially galling at the moment because radio companies generally are enjoying a prosperous new year.

Sunday 22nd March

I wonder if this will ever be read? All this effort – dust to dust. There will be many more such records near to the heart of great matters but perhaps this window on television will serve some purpose. I hope so.

Winter blasts come and go – like some old man stomping in and out of the house when the owners have already said goodbye three times. Writing this at Ower, I can see the rooks busily collecting leaves and twigs together with their mates, then flying to the top of the oaks at the end of the garden. I hope they will be happy bringing up their new families.

Last Sunday, from Euston to Manchester, met by David Lee and then, after stopping at the Portland Hotel (tiny bedrooms with hundreds of cards propped up everywhere with messages from Management, free offers, invitations to try exotic menus, warnings about leaving valuables. More money spent on the room and less on cards would have been welcome.) Driven over to Granada Television and Stage One where the Craft Awards presentation was to be held. Lots of familiar faces without names. Not included in the line-up which slightly miffed me, but then why should I be included? Guest of Honour, the Patron of BAFTA, Princess Anne made a good speech and for the next three hours or so watched BBC win every award. Shirley Bassey sang 'Diamonds Are For Ever'. She looked marvellous. Roma and I sat next to Andrew Quinn and we talked about BSB. He is worried, obviously, about Astra.

On Tuesday 17 March, a good DGMM, mostly getting our teeth into our approach to the Green Paper on Sound Broadcasting. We are coming round to accepting a role of licensor, of leaser of equipment, and giving up our role as Public Service guardian.

'It is all too often true that those who do not seek to change with the times find that the times leave them changed for the worse.' (Rab Butler). Thus I start my paper which will go to the Authority for the next meeting. It is a radical change in outlook but it could, I think, be for the best. Anyway, needs must – and if we don't grasp the opportunity we will be left high and dry on the shoreline like a beached whale. It will be interesting to see how Members react and, perhaps more interestingly, how ILR regards our stance: Granny putting on her 'sneakers'.

In the evening to Claridges, to the Thirty Club, with my guest Andrew Quinn again. Main speaker a South African – very, very boring. Andrew and I talked about how ITN could fit into BSB's plans and where they would be operating. Andrew sees the whole operation as supplying know-how as opposed to a service. He wants the news output to emanate from BSB's Upcentre, not to originate from ITN. I can see a major disagreement erupting.

I should have mentioned that on Monday I agreed to see a delegation of ITV MDs to review the IBA position on the Independents. They say they are worried. LWT announced double profits this week and their shares went up by 79p, I think. I am more and more coming round to the realisation that some form of auctioning is inevitable. The pickings are too rich.

On Monday, GT, David Glencross and I go to see David Mellor to give him a progress report on the use of the Independents. I think we have got the equation about right. The BBC have said they will be spending £20m and 600 hours by 1990 on two channels. We aim for 500 hours on one channel by the end of 1989.

Friday 20 March. Watched Channel 4 news at 7pm this evening and heard the news that John Birt was likely to accept the job of Deputy Director General of the BBC.

Saturday – confirmed today that John has accepted. What a flutter in the dovecote. John could have taken Jeremy's place at Channel 4. Many noses about to be put out of joint: Michael Grade, Alan Protheroe et al. The old brigade within the Corporation will have multiple coronaries. Who will LWT appoint to replace John Birt? My guess: Greg Dyke. Where is the quality and integrity of yesteryear?! Anyone who can transmit *The Newly-Weds* is someone the BBC is welcome to.

Sunday 5th April

A fortnight has sped by since I last made an entry. Time quickly blurs memory's image: things that seemed important get swallowed up in the crevices that time etches into the brain.

On Monday 23 March, George, David Glencross and I had a meeting with David Mellor and his advisors. Checkland went by himself to see Mellor on the same subject, and I feel slighted that I did not go alone. In the event, it was a pity because George, at the end of meeting, answering a question from Mellor said he would attain the 25 per cent introduction of Independents into the system but he didn't make clear that this figure would only be reached by adding the total time of the two channels. Home Office officials – or David Mellor himself – must have immediately upon our leaving spoken to Ray Snoddy because next morning in the *FT* was an account of the visit including the 25 per cent promise made by GT. *Broadcast* later picked up the same information and said that George had 'caved in'.

On Wednesday 25 March a breakfast meeting with Gerald Howarth and Bill Cash to discuss GH's intended Obscenity Bill. Much conviction, and ignorance, expressed. They have all the missionary zeal of earlier times and, if they get their way, anyone will be able to complain about anything they find offensive. We talked about mayhem while tucking in to bacon and eggs. I now know the debate in the Commons appeared as a resounding victory for GH with Mrs T. going into the Chamber at the head of her acolytes and waving towards Mary Whitehouse, seated in the Gallery. It may all be a one-day wonder, and so quietly disappear, but I rather doubt it.

Later went to have lunch at Lockets, hosted by Sarah Thane. Among the guests – mainly Conservative MPs from the Anglia Region – was a good example to disciplinarians: Harvey Proctor, accused by the *People* newspaper in June last year of spanking male prostitutes. He seemed to me a gentle person. Taller than I had expected, but with clear blue eyes that I suspect could turn icy.

That evening, Roma and I went to Crosby Hall, off Cheyne Walk, to a wedding reception to celebrate the marriage of Jo Sandilands and David Briggs. Hardly anyone from the past. A strangely odd affair, with apparently a number of events lined up for the guests. We left after half an hour. Roma home, me to a dinner at the IBA for Board Members of Channel 4.

Thursday 26 March. A lunch in honour of, and to say goodbye to, Denis Forman, retiring Chairman of Granada. A great pioneer and a truly significant figure in the creation and development of ITN. His sense of mission will be missed.

In the afternoon, an Authority Meeting followed by drinks in the Conference Room to wish John Thompson farewell. I made quite a funny speech, but tried to speak seriously from the heart as well. JT, after all, brought ILR into existence. A pity that the timing of his going will not enhance his reputation.

Friday 27 March. Off to Turkey, together with Roma, as guests of TRT. On arrival in Istanbul, met with flowers and whisky. Through Customs into the VIP lounge. Shown great courtesy and friendliness by everyone. Turkish broadcasting struggling into the 80s but woefully behind in technical skills and production values. Spent the weekend sightseeing, with the Assistant Director General of TRT, Halid Ertugrul acting as our guide, and then on Monday to TRT to meet Professor Tunca Toskay.

Called on Timothy Daunt, the British Ambassador, in Ankora. Very pleasant, cool in the best tradition of a servant of the Queen. Drank tea and learnt that relations with Turkey could not be better.

On Tuesday we travelled back to Istanbul and more sightseeing. On Thursday, we were given a private concert arranged by Ayhan Songar, a distinguished member of Turkish cultural society. He had brought a group of students and teachers from the University to play Turkish classical music. I mentioned I had once played the trumpet. To my consternation, a trumpet was produced and I managed to play a scale, much to my surprise! The concert was a delight – the music wistful and melodious, albeit with the deep melancholy which seems to pervade their music.

Sunday 12th April

Back from Turkey, where the pace of broadcasting is like a stately minuet as opposed to the frantic jive of British broadcasting.

A further (the fourth) meeting on Tuesday between the Independents and ITCA representatives to dig deeper into the question of access by Independents. I chaired the meeting, which lasted about two hours. The Companies see the advancing hordes and are uncertain how to respond. They are in a difficult and complex situation. If they appear to be over-welcoming, they will lose the confidence of their staff; too unaccommodating and they will be confronted by a wholly hostile Government and public opinion as well as the IBA. The Companies have few allies. This is dangerous in itself, for who do they turn to for help and support? Other opportunities beckon them from across the English Channel: unregulated expansion alluring both in wider market terms and greater freedom. Who would turn their backs on that?!

The Government is accomplishing its aim of bringing about the fragmentation of independent and BBC Public Service broadcasting without even firing a shot.

The Green Paper on Sound Broadcasting is a precursor of the road Government will travel towards the deregulation of ITV. The scramble for the lifeboats has already begun with Thames, and recently LWT, turning towards that tempting, glittering star – Astra. The exodus from Public Service constraints will gather momentum as the grip on audiences by ITV weakens through competition. Thus it is that these meetings between the Independents and the ITV Companies mark a seminal moment in the history of British broadcasting. I believe that a sense of history and chance did not escape those around the table on Tuesday.

David Glencross and I will be meeting David Mellor to report progress in about five weeks time.

On Wednesday, Brian Tesler rang to say that LWT had decided to appoint Greg Dyke as Programme Controller to replace John Birt. It did not come as a surprise. I said I thought he would do the job well.

In the evening, to the RTS Annual Fleming Lecture, given on this occasion by Albert Scharf. Poor man – a blister on one heel had gone sceptic and he appeared on stage hobbling with the aid of a walking stick. Not the President of the EBU I was used to seeing, he was obviously in considerable anguish and his performance was well below his norm. His theme was much as expected: the duty and obligation of society to maintain a healthy Public Service commitment to broadcasting while accepting strengthening competition.

This event was, I believe, the first occasion when the former DG of the BBC and his replacement had appeared in public together. I found myself having pre-session drinks with them and Sheila Milne. Alasdair was there to make the summing-up comments and to record the RTS's appreciation to Albert.

Either Alasdair is extremely courageous or extremely thick-skinned. Whichever, he walked into the Chamber, head held high, behind Michael Checkland, who was surrounded by his peers, his admirers, his critics, and in one instance, by one Governor who had helped in his downfall and with whom Alasdair refused to shake hands. I found myself in the uncomfortable position of sitting between the two during the lecture.

Afterwards, we repaired to the Athenaeum and a private dinner party hosted by Paul Fox. Alasdair and Sheila left shortly after Scharf, immediately after coffee. It had been a long evening.

I surmise (without any evidence) that the honeymoon of Checkland and the public is drawing swiftly to a close. The BBC is in a state of shock. When it comes round, there will be resistance to some of the lightning changes Michael is contemplating. At the Athenaeum dinner, I sat next to Alan Protheroe, Deputy Director General, who seems to have so far prevented his head from being removed from his neck. Alan and I talked about Channel 4, its leadership and structure. Alan turned out to be a firm and enthusiastic advocate of Brian Wenham, and an equally firm believer that the lead position should go to the programme maker and not an administrator: 'Channel 4 is about programmes, not business'. He has a good point.

At the lunch following the Authority Meeting on Thursday, I sat next to Gerald Kaufman, who during the general discussion over coffee evinced himself deeply troubled by the Conservative policy advocating deregulation. A firm believer in the IBA and in PSB. Since Labour has little chance of winning the next election, his words fell on somewhat hard, if not stony, ground.

Earlier, at the Authority meeting, Members had heard about Capital's willingness to purchase control of DevonAir. I have many reservations about this, and managed to get the Authority to postpone a decision until after we have a chance to meet the parties.

A meeting with BSB on Thursday, ostensibly to deal with further contract points but the conversation turned to the overall position of BSB, now that the spectre of Astra looms with its consequent effects on the City. Why should investors commit £600m into regulated broadcasting for a limited tenure and broadcasting only to the UK, when for millions less the same group could reach a much wider European audience, without regulation and with unlimited tenure of channel? I can see their point.

In this connection, we received a response from Douglas Hurd to George's letter about the actions of BT and Astra. Douglas said that there was no action likely by

Ministers to curtail BT's activities. Thus, the stage is set for the withdrawal of BSB from UK DBS, going instead into Astra with Thames and LWT, and then – almost certainly – Central and Michael Green's Carlton. Why bother with the IBA if you don't have to? All this would suit the Government's ambitions to destabilise UK broadcasting. With most of the ITV Companies beginning to compete with themselves, what a good case for Government to argue for the auctioning of contracts to the highest bidder and for the extension of the Radio Green Paper's argument that ITV should be allowed to float free of Public Service obligations and do its own thing in the new age of broadcasting and technology. All good, free market Tory stuff.

Mark my words, this will come to pass.

I think our best position in the face of these BSB doubts is to go to Douglas Hurd and align ourselves to BSB's position. What we don't want is to be seen as 'wrecker', oblivious to the realities of the market place, head in the sand, seemingly unable to comprehend the changes in broadcast environment. Better by far to stand alongside BSB and agree with them that the playing field isn't level and a fair, competitive stance by BSB under the aegis of the IBA is impossible. On Friday I asked GT to mull this over.

Read this Sunday that Lord Olivier's birthday party at the National would be the hottest ticket in town. So I am glad that we on the National's Board pressed forward with this.

Monday 20th April

An IBA dinner on the 13th to say goodbye to John Thompson after 14 years. I took the Milne Room at the Garrick and JT invited some 25 friends from various parts of his life – including Mary Warnock, John Riddell, Jill McIvor and Chris Chataway. GT made an excellent speech, hitting just the right note. JT stood up and made everyone laugh for about ten minutes. Looking back on his achievements, I think he will be best judged after a decent lapse of time. To launch commercial radio and make it successful, at least in its earlier years, was no small feat. His light has been dimmed by radio's traumas in recent years but those traumas were mainly to do with lack of quality management and sales.

This week's SCC on Tuesday was important because we used the occasion to inform the Companies about IBA thinking for the extension contracts for the three years commencing 1989. We will be issuing a press release on Wednesday. The major points are: no boundary changes, new plans for networking arrangements, a possible night time contractor and consideration to be given to funding ITN.

On Wednesday, dinner with the 'big five' radio Companies. A private affair, when hair is let down. The radio companies are, I think, coming round to the recognition that the IBA would be as good a regulator as anyone else and, with experience, probably better.

Channel 4 liaison meeting with Edmond on Thursday. His last before retiring. GT could hardly find the words to express the usual courtesies. He had apparently been told that a vitriolic article by Woodrow Wyatt on privatising C4 had been engineered by Edmond. Not a happy meeting. Jeremy has his mind on the Royal Opera House. A new broom will be no bad thing.

GT received a letter this week from Douglas Hurd, asking him and Duke Hussey to go and talk to him about violence. GT is angry at this further intervention, and said he is considering telling Douglas to get off his back: 'If he doesn't like what we do, he can ask us to resign'.

Sunday 26th April

A heavenly day, with temperatures in the 20s. Everyone out and about in shorts and birds nesting everywhere.

The week was a short one, starting on Tuesday after the Bank Holiday. Owen Edwards, CEO of S4C, came to see me. The saga of HTV and S4C still has some time to run. HTV propose an extension of their contract with S4C, but charging £4m more for two and a half hours less a week! This is the final straw for S4C. Times have changed since their original contract with HTV: Independents have sprung up, and their reliance on HTV has consequently lessened. The result? A letter from S4C to HTV telling them to think again or face the consequences. The next move, I suspect, will be a hurt letter from HTV to me accusing S4C of breaking their agreements. But – and it is a big but – the contract states clearly that the terms must be 'commercial'.

Lunch on Tuesday with David Barlow, Secretary to the BBC, at Gaylords. Always amusing, David is one of those rare creatures who combine intelligence with wit. His career has spanned both ITV and BBC, but I sense his star is on the wane somewhat since the new regime and that he may be looking around for something new. Alasdair, he told me, is about to embark on his autobiography but is starting by getting his diary up to date. David thinks it will be pretty vitriolic stuff when it emerges.

Over the poppadoms, David blithely remarked that much of the pressure would come off everyone if BBC2 were to take commercials.

Afterwards, walked over to ITN to attend a Board Meeting. Much heart-searching over plans to move from Wells Street to News International's old building in Holborn.

I enquired about the ITN contract with BSB and was told that an arranged meeting had collapsed when representatives from BSB failed to show up. I worry about BSB's intentions now they are within an ace of signing. I fear they will set on one side their promises and commitment to ITN and attempt to screw them down to a low-cost operation.

Dinner in the evening with Peter Morrison, Deputy Conservative Party leader. A whimsical exterior concealing a shrewd interior. Referred a little too much to his silver spoon upbringing with Eton traditions, which makes him somewhat suspect. Referred to Maggie as his 'mega star' and believes that by and large ITV and ILR were safe in our hands, whatever that quite means.

We tried him out on our decision to allot the three parties five minutes each for their political party broadcasts, and he said that he didn't think the Conservatives would object. I noted he left himself room to reverse his judgment should a different view emerge at a result of talking with his 'mega star'!

On Wednesday 23 April quizzed the respective representatives from GWR Radio, DevonAir and Capital (in the shape of Dickie Attenborough and Nigel Walmsley). Arguments on both sides for seeing a Capital takeover of DevonAir by either GWR (local and concerned) or Capital (metropolitan and profit-motivated). Dickie, as always, performed stylishly and convincingly. We gave it to Capital.

Later to ITN for dinner with Roma, to watch Super Channel News uplinked to the ECS satellite beaming down to 19 countries cabled to the Channel. The 30-minute news comes from two portacabins bolted on to the roof of ITN's building. An amazing example of shoestring endeavour and a great tribute to the tenacity, conviction and courage of David Nicholas. A great sense of purpose and challenge. We left elevated in every sense.

Thursday 23 April. A 'pitch' by Members during coffee before the Authority Meeting nearly put paid to our preparations and recommendations for the IBA's response to the Radio Green Paper. Naughty Donald Maitland used the opportunity to lobby his colleagues against our presentation of the case for the IBA. George was angry and rather thrown by the incident but, in the event, when the Paper came to be discussed sensible conclusions were drawn.

Members ratified guidelines on advertising of contraceptives, and talked about sex and violence. The Authority gave its blessing to the appointment of Sir Trevor Holdsworth, Chairman of GKN, as Chairman of BSB.

The papers on Thursday reported the IBA's decisions over the three-year extension with the *Guardian* headline: 'IBA Plans Network Shake-up'; *FT*: 'IBA Considers Changes to Companies' Contracts'; and the *Daily Telegraph*: 'ITV shake-up will give major break to small producers'.

The day before the papers had headlined the jump in profits at TV-am. 20 per cent ahead of prospective forecasts with a profit of £8.7m. Not bad for a company that was written off by City pundits three years ago.

Finally, I urged George to write a letter to David Mellor setting the record straight about our meeting with him. Will be interested to see how DM replies.

Monday 4th May

Another Bank Holiday. We British like striking, getting drunk and watching television – the last two we do in excess on Bank Holidays. Me? I lie on my sickbed, struck down with flu and feeling especially sorry for myself.

On Monday 27 April I travelled to Wakefield with various telly luminaries – Duke Hussey, Humphrey Burton et al – and then by coach to Bradford to attend the inaugural Huw Wheldon Memorial Lecture, given by David Attenborough. This was being held in the National Museum of Photography, Film and Television. A splendid place, imaginatively created to illustrate the face of television. A great tribute too, to Paul Fox, whose patronage of the Museum by Yorkshire Television made the enterprise possible.

The lecture – 'Unnatural History' – was a tour de force by David, who was in cracking form, but if one may be allowed the merest whisper of an uncharitable nature, I grew concerned as the lecture went on that David had been picking up Dickie's gestures and mannerisms. To carp in the face of such brilliance is unworthy and I excuse myself on account of my temperature and lack of food!

Huw would have relished the occasion. After a jolly fork luncheon, we departed for London.

Tuesday 28 April. A 9am meeting with Brian Tesler, John Birt and Barry Cox to see what's to be done over the splitting of weekend news provision. London Weekend were asked by the Authority to strengthen their weekend news commitment and they propose doing this by employing an independent news gathering team. So far, so good. The problem is that, in order to offer a company enough to get their teeth into, they wish to end their arrangement with Thames whereby Thames provide them with a six to six-fifteen London News programme on Fridays. Thames are naturally loath to see an end to their contract. On balance, I think it better that LWT are allowed to do their own thing but David Glencross thinks otherwise. Both arguments are equally persuasive.

Lunch at the Garrick with Laurence Cotterell, Donald Sinden and Sandra Chalmers (Editor of *Woman's Hour*). The purpose of the lunch to meet each other and prepare for Members Night of the Whitefriars, Sandra proposing the toast to *Mere Men*, Donald to *Sovereign Women* and me attempting a vote of thanks on behalf of the assembled friars and their partners.

Later in the day, hosted with David McCall a welcoming reception to delegates attending a three-day session of the Legal Committee of the EBU with dinner afterwards. Feeling pretty pooped by the end and must have shown it because I was politely admonished by the butler for requesting the removal of plates whilst some were still eating.

On Wednesday 29 April I welcome the Committee at the beginning of their first session and conveyed an actually bogus apology from David Mellor, who had agreed to open it.

Spoke to Regional Officers at 11am. So many things to say, the session went on for an hour and a quarter.

Lunch with James Lee at the Ritz; still, for my money, the prettiest place to eat but service oh so slow. James, having failed with his application to be the DBS contractor, is looking for something else to occupy him. Still, poor man, very sensible over the collapse of Goldcrest and his part in its downfall. Talk turned to who should run Channel 4 after Jeremy's departure: 'What about Michael Grade?' 'Never thought of that', I said. 'A good notion.'

A meeting in the afternoon with Nigel Dyckoff and Michael Holford to assess senior salary levels. I said that if they had to find a replacement for me, the IBA would be paying between £80 – £85k and not the £60,000 I get now. Interesting to see what they finally recommend.

Joined GT for drinks at one of his regular cocktail parties. Always a good cross section. This time no exception.

Thursday 30 April. Driven down to Crawley Court and met the entire staff for a one-hour talk-in. Quite daunting. I started with a quote from Rab and a piece of information: 'It is all too often true that those who do not seek to change with the times find that the times leave them changed for the worse' and the information that in 1921 Arnold Bennett drank a glass of Parisian tap water to show that it was uncontaminated. His splendid gesture was somewhat overshadowed by his death from typhoid some days later.

Back to London and dinner with John Wakeham and Murdo Maclean. John Wakeham, obviously gearing himself up for the election, said he could 'fix' the SNP, who were being difficult about parity in Scotland. Television is obviously going to be the battleground of the parties, this time more than ever before.

Sunday 10th May

The last seven days have mostly been spent in bed. I went down with some sort of virus, which has left me feeling low and somewhat out of sorts. This is the first time I have taken to my bed since joining the IBA. Engagement after engagement had to be put off or postponed but the world continued without me. I turned to Peter Hall's diaries for light relief. What a tortured soul he appears to be. His diaries give me no better insight into what makes him tick. He still seems an essentially cold and remote figure.

The media this week have been winding themselves up into a lather over the impending announcement of the date for the election. All bets are on 11 June. Mrs T. and the cronies of her inner circle are reviewing their options today.

GT has received a note from Douglas Hurd confirming the appointment of new Members of the Authority: Lady Popplewell, Sir Anthony Jolliffe (former Lord Mayor of London), Professor Fulton and Mr Ranjit Sondhi (a senior lecturer in Social Sciences). The appointments are for five years, which will see me out.

More news about BSB. A group representing their backers paid a visit to Douglas Hurd and set out their worries, mostly centred around their concern that they were to be regulated whilst their competitors would not be. We have bent over backwards to be helpful and recognise their risks. I suppose, if I were them, I would see how far I could get Government to go before signing the contract with the IBA.

Reports in the press about Alasdair writing his account of his departure. I wonder how history will assess his role. So far Checkland has played a straight bat and won admirers in every quarter.

This week saw the final struggle of the dying Obscene Bill, with over 200 amendments tabled. It was a raft that could not float. Sunk, but not forgotten, the Milton Committee will have to rise to fight another day.

Sunday 17th May

The Election has been called – 11th June. It looks like being a tidal wave victory for Mrs T. So piano-legs will be covered and television, theatre and film muzzled, lest someone should find something offensive. Nothing but a miracle will save the country from the worst excesses of a right wing government. There is no one to stand up to Mrs T., her own ministers and Opposition alike.

On Thursday the Authority met at Crawley Court. The matter of ITN's missing minute was discussed and Members endorsed the recommendation I made, together with David Glencross, that the minute should stay with ITN and not be lost from *News At Ten* or released to the Companies for regional opt-out news. David Nicholas will be relieved.

ITN and ITV were generally wrong-footed by the BBC when they announced their election coverage. The BBC's announcement was upbeat and impressively confident and majored on their decision to extend the *Nine O'Clock News*.

ITV, on the other hand, appeared in disarray, with ITN grumbling that they had been given only five minutes. The problem in ITV is that there is no press co-ordination worth speaking of. Each Company tries to steal a march on the others. What ITCA needs is a Press Officer. I intend seeing how this could be followed up.

The Authority also considered BSB and development. On Tuesday I had a two-hour meeting with BSB representatives. BSB still believe they should have control of the uplink. They want the teletext contract and the two additional channels proposed by Government to be brought into play three years after the first service will come into operation. On top of all these demands, BSB want the freedom to use whichever technical standard is endorsed by the majority of users in Europe. I said, during this meeting, that I thought we might arrange for a side letter to be sent to BSB signifying that the IBA would agree to a change in the British Standard in the event of a *de facto* use of a standard other than DMAC.

The Authority considered these matters and agreed to award BSB the teletext contract for the full 15 year period. The uplink would be retained by the IBA but the Authority remained adamant that the standard should be DMAC. On the question of the two additional channels, Members showed surprising equanimity. Anything, in fact, that would ensure the launch of DBS by BSB. Providing a consortium with a contract that would effectively make them the most powerful television group in the UK did not seem to cause them a moment's anxiety.

Since the meeting of the Authority, I have received a letter from Quentin Thomas inviting our reaction to BSB's proposals to have the two other channels. I think they are pushing their luck, hoping that they can panic Government and the IBA into giving in to their demands as the price for going ahead or aborting. My present mood is to say no. I think the outcry if we were to agree would be vociferous, and with some justification. It would change the nature of the contract to an enormous extent. Many other companies might well have bid for five channels. Indeed, we might have gone for a different contractor ourselves!

Incidentally, BSB announced in their press release on the award of the teletext contract that Amstrad had decided to drop out. A pity. *The Times* on Friday said that the IBA would be acutely embarrassed by Amstrad's departure. Not embarrassed, but certainly irritated.

Thankfully, the parties have agreed to the overall sharing of time for their election programmes. The SNP contested our decision but a court in Scotland turned down their application for parity.

GT and Duke H. paid a visit on the Home Secretary and he has told them, privately, that in the Manifesto will be reference to widening the powers of the Broadcasting Complaints Council to embrace the complaints about programmes generally. Talk about belt and braces. What with a Bill and now this, their seems little point in having IBA Members if nobody trusts them to act in a responsible manner.

Monday 25th May

Another Bank Holiday. The Election process is now in full swing. An apt phrase, as each party would gladly string up its rivals. The dirty tricks brigade has been out in force. First slinging mud and potentially-damaging allegations at David Steel, who responded swiftly and successfully by suing *The Sun* for libel and winning. This weekend it was the turn of Roy Hattersley, a Sunday newspaper alleging that he was running two homes, one for himself and his wife and a second 'with a friend'. With any luck, he too will reap handsomely the rich pickings resulting from the excrement dropped by some of the tabloid vultures.

Last Monday an ITN Board Meeting with much agonising whether or not to agree the purchase of the old News International Building in Gray's Inn Road and the handout to Camden Council that formed an integral part of the purchase. The Board found it extremely hard to reach a decision but in the end came to what I think was the right conclusion: they would offer to buy without making any offer to provide the additional £750,000 for Camden Council. Having bought it, they will then apply for permission to use it as an ITN operation and, if Camden refuse, take them to Court where they have been advised they would win! I am much happier that they do it this way. If the gamble fails, then they will have to re-sell the building.

Early breakfast at the IBA on Tuesday with Dickie, GT, Peter Rogers, Shirley Littler, David Glencross and George Russell to see if we could all agree a common policy on the appointment of a replacement for Jeremy Isaacs. I have done a full U-turn and now believe that we need a creative leader to head up the Channel, rather than, as I had first thought, an administrator to keep the Channel shipshape whilst a Programme Controller did his or her thing. My change of heart has come as a result of the continuing uncertainty as to whether or not C4 would be 'floated off' in the event of another Tory win. If the IBA were to insist on a business person leading the Channel, it would give a false signal to Channel 4 watchers that the IBA endorsed the notion of selling off the Channel and was preparing for this eventuality by doing so. It was agreed that we should set about the search in the autumn and that it would be 'creative led'. So far, Michael Grade, Brian Wenham and Alasdair Milne have indicated their interest. Not a bad catch before we've even advertised.

On Wednesday, in the afternoon, the LACs. GT had made his apologies for vacating the chair and departed for Dundee to watch the local football team play some foreign side. They – Dundee – lost. LAC Chairmen were all interested in how the results of the Green Paper on Radio would affect ILR. I promised to send our submission to them in advance of going public. I don't think they will like what they read.

An article in *Campaign* headlined 'IBA goes on the defensive against a barrage of hate'. All good slanging stuff with ever more non-attributable quotes giving their reasons for wishing to see the IBA dead and buried. The days when a regulatory authority was seen as something for the public good have long since gone. Now the flavour of the month is deregulation at any cost. What people fail to recognise is that the IBA is simply the invention of Parliament. We didn't create ourselves – an Act of Parliament, or Acts of Parliament, brought us into being. Never mind. My skin is hardening. I should have realised when I joined the IBA that no friends would be made.

We start the second week of the Election. It is a TV election. Everything is done for the cameras: babies patted, Cornish pasties stuffed, lambs hugged, wheelchairs pushed, promises made, broken pledges forced down opponents' throats. I shall be glad when it's finally over.

Sunday 31st May

About to enter the third week of the Election. I still believe that it is a one-horse race, although Neil Kinnock is gaining points in the polls. But not, I think, in the minds of the voters. The deluge of claim and counter-claim is deafening if one unlocks one's ears. Very few do. Reminds me of a thunderstorm without any lightning.

Roma and I have just returned from Berne, having attended the EBU Council Meeting. No Alasdair there or Sheila. No Michael Checkland either – fishing in Finland! Switzerland, and especially Berne, is still a place where life appears to be clean, decent and honest. Everything looks in place by design. Even the cows in the fields seem as if they are playing their part in a great 'Come to Switzerland' campaign.

Unfortunately, I was not able to attend the meeting of the Director Generals held on Wednesday – a special meeting called to consider how best the Union would face up to the changes in broadcasting which threaten to unseat the EBU after thirty years. Public Service Broadcasting rings like an echo from the past. Today the bottom line is competition. Competition within a country and competition aimed at those outside. With profit as the sole objective. The ideals of the founders of the EBU were realistic in a static broadcasting environment but today everywhere one looks change is all about.

Earlier in the week, on Monday, I attended two interviews. The first with Michael Mallet of the Viking Group, and then Owen Oyston of Red Rose. Both had come to represent their groups and to say why they considered it in the interests of their companies that they should form a merger. I obtained the distinct impression that MM in reality was less than enthusiastic at the prospect, whilst OO was like a two year old with a new toy just outside his reach. I had gone into the meeting believing that a merger would be sensible. I came out with my mind changed.

At the Authority meeting on Thursday I asked for further time to consider the matter. I have come to the conclusion that if permission for the merger were to be agreed it would have the effect of signalling to the industry that Companies, even if they were not in trouble, could be bought. It would trigger approaches by the big Companies to almost all the small ones. Capital/DevonAir being a classic example, although in this case DevonAir was in financial difficulty.

On Wednesday had an interesting dinner with two of our four new Members: Lady Popplewell and Professor Fulton. Both very lively and engaging. I have a feeling that when Lady P. gets into her stride she will be quite formidable. After dinner I went home to watch *The Media Show*, a Channel 4 programme dealing with the mechanisms involved in the structure of networking production, costs and participants. The thrust was critical of a system that, it was argued, was completely out of date. David Mellor appeared as an outspoken critic and a barrister specialising in restrictive practises said, 'This is a price-fixing cartel – a carve up. They should be competing and they are not. The interest of viewers and advertisers requires that the cartel be bust up.' Shares in the television Companies, that had been falling, fell still further.

It is not going to be easy to unlock the system. Although I suspect it might be done for us in 1990. You can't simply turn on the tap and hope that a *Brideshead* or *Jewel* will come bubbling out. The attack on networking arrangements coincides with the fiercest attack I have seen yet by advertising folk on the Companies and their lacklustre ratings. This, coupled with soaring rates (up 40 per cent over the last year, or so it was claimed by Ken Miles in a letter I've just read) has led to anger and resentment at the status quo of the ITV Companies and the IBA in what must seem grossly unfair market conditions. A perfect gift to Mrs T. if she does take up her bullwhip after the election. I could even make a pretty good case for auctioning ITV Companies. I have arranged a dinner with David McCall, David Shaw, Shirley Littler and David Glencross to see what can be done to get ITV back on an even keel. There is much worry at present. Internal bickering, a sense of discord that I've not felt before. Are we going to see the collapse of ITV as we are seeing the routing of ILR as we know it today? ITV is growing expert at shooting itself in the foot. Both feet. In its present mood, it could even begin to aim at the heart.

Sadly, but not unexpected, Cecil Madden died on Friday at the age of 84. A pioneer producer of great merit for the BBC.

And so, tonight, off to the National to celebrate Lawrence Olivier's 80th birthday. He may not turn up, I am told.

Sunday 7th June

90 hours or so to go to the Election. Everyone must heartily wish it over. It has been Kinnock's time to star. By contrast, Mrs T. has looked ill at ease, over-defensive and, if she says 'yes, we want this' and 'yes, we've done that' one more time, I'll scream. The two Davids plot their outside track like marathon runners without a chance of winning.

Last week I finished my entry in this diary with a look forward to the National

1987

Theatre party for Lord Olivier. It was a good event, packed to the rafters with well-wishers. The celebration itself was a rather curious affair. Just before it began, Sir Larry with Joan Plowright entered the Olivier theatre to ecstatic applause. The show itself was based on Lord Olivier's own thoughts on acting, as expressed in his book *On Acting*: Burbage, Garrick, Kean, Irving: four names that handed on the Shakespearean mantle to our generation. That's why, today performing Shakespeare, we can feel close to him, that his ink is still wet on the paper. The old actors smiling, grinning, laughing and saying 'Follow that'. 'It's not important to be top of the bill, it's important to be best ... . I will continue to learn until all ceases to function.' And so it was a kind of pageant conjuring up the past in sketches, delivered in the most part with exuberant style and humour. Peggy Ashcroft, Graham Crowden, John Hurt, Jeremy Irons, Albert Finney, Anna Carteret, Ben Kingsley, Jane Lapotaire, Maureen Lipman, Alec McCowen, Geraldine McEwan, Anthony Sher and many, many more.

At the end, a great birthday cake popped open and out leapt one of Larry's daughters: 'Happy Birthday Dad', she cried. And it was. Lawrence Olivier took a four-minute standing ovation, waving and bowing amid streamers, balloons and falling glitter. Afterwards, fireworks lit up the Thames. A great finale.

On Monday afternoon a meeting with Martin Noar of the Economic League, who had come to complain about the way the League had been treated by a *World in Action* programme. I had obtained from Granada (much against their will) a transcript of a secretly-recorded telephone conversation between Noar and the producer of *World in Action*. From this, I have little doubt – none at all – that Granada are in the wrong, in that they misused the conversation, basing the League's response on Noar's answers to questions on different issues.

Granada are not going to like being caught out and reprimanded but that is what is going to happen. We have not heard the end of this saga.

On Tuesday, another celebration for Sir Larry. This one given by LWT at the Inn on the Park. A distinguished collection of friends: Anthony Hopkins, Frank Findlay, Albert Finney and Alec Guinness. Roma and I were lucky to have been invited.

Larry got more and more frail as the evening progressed, and a little drunk. Joan Plowright watches his every move and movement. He has to be supported on both arms to walk. He is either playing a very old man or else he *is* a very old man. The actor is still, I suspect, uppermost, but the grin possibly masking a sad and somewhat lonely figure.

Towards the end of dinner, Larry rose to thank Melvyn Bragg, who had proposed his health. He thanked us for coming, knocked over his wine glass and said the evening had made him very happy. Then he was taken home. I think it will be the last time I shall see him in the flesh.

> 'No mask like open truth to cover lies,
> As to go naked is the best disguise'.
> So read the invitation menu.

Met the Radio Liaison Group on Wednesday. Not a happy meeting. The AIRC would like to see the IBA giving way now on major issues that stand between us

– selling our transmitters, ending cross-subsidisation between radio and television – but, too, they are clearly anxious to get information on our response to the Green Paper. It should surprise them! I gave them few clues but told them our timetable for publishing our views and holding our press conference. This will take place the day before the AIRC Congress and we will release a copy of our evidence to AIRC on the Friday before the Monday press conference.

Sunday 14th June

On Thursday, the Tories swept to power with a 102 majority. Public Service Broadcasting, as we know it today, has a bleak future for television. The writing has been on the wall since the Radio Green Paper was published.

At lunchtime on Monday I took John Calvert, Industrial Relations Director at ITCA, to lunch at the Garrick. Who should come into the bar but Paul Fox with Alasdair Milne! What plot are they hatching, I wonder, or is it just old buddies having lunch? The Garrick, always a good place for gossip and intrigue, lived up to its reputation. Seeking my table, I went to the Grill Room and stumbled across William Rees-Mogg lunching Brian Wenham. What deeds abroad? Old buddies?

John Calvert is a civilised person who came from industry three years or so ago to help ITV get some sense into their union negotiations. (This Sunday's piece in the *Sunday Times* won't have pleased him, although it will delight the bash-ITV-brigade, Mrs T's advisers amongst them. Apparently, a technician working for TV-am is claiming the Company owes him £92,000 odd for his 'Golden Hours' payments, whilst working on the Zeebrugge Ferry disaster.) Calvert believes that the message is very slowly getting across to the ITV Companies that unless they put their house in order somebody else will. He thinks ITV is broadly divided into two camps. The old guard – Fox, Tesler, Brown, Plowright – coming to the end of their reigns and finding it difficult to accept change, and the other camp – Gatward, Hill, Dunn et al – determined to break out of the old mould.

SCC on Tuesday proved somewhat nail-biting. It's a meeting I never look forward to. Advanced notice had been given that the Companies felt 'bounced' over the apportionment of rentals. In one sense they're right. No opportunity was given them to respond to our decision to reallocate rental costs across the Companies more in line with their NAR share. I came the nearest I could to decently apologising but countered by saying that, if a consultation had been the course taken, it would have meant that every Company, human nature being what it is, would have been demanding some change to their rental apportionment and this in turn would have meant a knock-on effect to another Company's assessment.

Post mortems on the *Roxy* – ITV's pop show and a much needed attack on the BBC's stronghold – failed to impress the critics. I thought it rather good, but my judgment may be coloured by memories of *Ready, Steady, Go*.

After SCC, a meeting with Richard Dunn and more news regarding his tentative plans for Thames' involvement in the Astra project. Thames are commissioning a review of the likelihood of a channel, or channels, succeeding to capture a market share of advertising revenue from the UK. If the business plan's findings look encouraging he will wish to seek IBA approval to go forward and lease a channel.

Dunn realises, and was at pains to underline, that the IBA's views on an involvement would bear decisively on their decision. Dunn then went on to tell me that LWT and Carlton had banded together with Dixons and Saatchi & Saatchi to consider applying for Astra's channels. (Dunn said that each channel would probably cost in the region of £3m per annum.) It would seem more than likely that if LWT went in so would Central, being currently non-aligned. If the IBA gives permission to one, it must give permission to anyone else in ITV. Now that we have committed ITV to compete with itself via BSB, it will take some quirk of logic to preclude Companies from finding their own role in DBS. The arguments for Companies to get into Astra, or stay outside, are pretty evenly balanced. Stay outside and vigorously compete with all comers or go into diversification and provide a service that will take money out of one system and put it into another.....

In the evening, dinner with David McCall, David Shaw, Shirley Littler and David Glencross in our dining room. The purpose was to see if some of our interests, which we share in common with the Companies, could be strengthened by mutual understanding. Promotion for the systems and maintaining a unified public image were two subjects discussed. The BBC appears to be suddenly the favoured child and ITV sent to bed early without supper. Some useful chords were struck.

On Wednesday, the papers were full of Ann Diamond's set-to with Denis Healey. Ann accused Healey of permitting his wife to use private health care for an operation instead of going on the NHS. I watched a recording and thought she did well.

Thursday was grey and the clouds began dropping rain early in the day. It improved later on. I went and put my cross against the name I consider to be the least objectionable, and went off to address the problems of the day.

Attended the British Council Film & Video Committee. Back to hear Paul Bonner is taking over Colin Shaw's job at ITCA. I hope he can put some spine into ITV's scheduling plans. ITV has lost its way and, unless we can do something to get it back on course, it's heading for Mrs T's knackers yard.

A meeting with David Coulson to prepare me for next week's luncheon with ISBA, always a stormy affair. Then a meeting with Graham Grist at the Oxford & Cambridge Club. A typical Pall Mall club, but graced by an extremely attractive Tina Turner lookalike barmaid.

Graham told me that BSB had had talks with Quentin Thomas regarding the possibility that they would like to see the two additional channels advertised earlier than anticipated, in the belief that a 'full shop window' would prove an attraction to consumers. What did I think? I agreed. In fact, I think it would be a damn good idea. If the price of each channel was attractive, we could see a genuine complementary service of programming.

And so to the election results. George T. gave a party. The BBC started off badly, giving an exit poll result of a 26 margin against ITV's 67.

It was obvious from the first minutes that the Tories would be back.

I went with Roma to ITN and then on to Capital, getting at last to bed at 2 am.

ITN did well, better I think than the BBC. Most of the press voted in favour of the BBC. So we now look forward to another four or five years of Tory rule.

Sunday 21st June

The longest day – 9.55pm and still quite light. In Dorset for a week, but I may have to go back to London on Wednesday for a night.

A week in which, again, the axes of the anti-commercial television lobby hacked away at the trunk. It's funny how quickly the pendulum swings away from the BBC. Now it's our turn. ITV can do no right. The Golden Hours claim of the TV-am engineer continues to dog us despite protestations from Gyngel that it's all a pack of untruths and, although ITV audiences have gone back to 52 per cent of total viewing, poor audience ratings are still dominating the media press. All grist for Mrs T's mill.

On Monday, I attended the second Board Meeting of the Open College. They seem to be getting into a sorry mess. The whole concept appears to have gone through a U-turn. From wanting to appeal to mass audiences, teaching basic skills, they now appear to be aiming for specialist skill users. This is because they are finding the task of raising money harder than they envisaged and are consequently going for sponsors who want to attract particular skills. At least I think that's what they are doing.

The meeting was appallingly handled. The Agenda was a farce – undated, showing little or no preparation. I don't know how Michael Green conducts his own business but his handling of this leaves much to be desired. Both Jeremy and I are going to write to Michael expressing our concerns. It would be a terrible misfortune if the College crashed because no one had got a real grip on it.

From the Open College, over to the Garrick to lunch with Russell Twisk, probably the best time to lunch him because he is leaving the editorship post of *The Listener* and taking on the editor role for the *Readers Digest* UK edition. I had never met Russell before, and found him most engaging. We gossiped about the BBC. Russell said that between them Duke and Joel were probably the most interventionist of Governors and Chairmen the BBC had ever had. The two of them run the show, the rest of the Governors not counting for much.

We talked about the future of *The Listener*. I suggested that ITV might offer to acquire some of the equity and become a part-owner. Paul Fox had been a leading light about a year or so ago and he was promoting the idea of a serious journal to rival *The Listener*. I have written to Paul to sound him out. Russell thought it worth a try.

On Tuesday, DGMM and a final opportunity to tidy up our response to the Green Paper on Radio before Thursday's meeting of the Authority.

In the afternoon, I had arranged a special meeting of senior staff to consider proposals for floating ITN. Peter Rogers has agreed to write a draft paper. I want to get in first.

Then to Channel 4 liaison meeting. Edmund has made a few changes to his annual report. I think it better to let the thing go than cause waves in an attempt to get

Edmund to change his mind. He's determined to go out with a bang and nothing is going to stop him. We talked about the red triangle experiment. Jeremy clearly didn't favour it continuing in its present form. Shirley Littler came up with a proposal that the symbol should be taken off for the next six months and we should gauge public reaction. We all rather thankfully took this easy road out.

The day ended with drinks at the Banqueting House to launch TV-am's Breakfast Television conference, the first of its kind anywhere in the world. About 200 delegates turned up and stuffed canapés down their throats.

On Wednesday, I lunched with ISBA. I don't know whether it achieved anything. I went over the ground with their Committee. Why no additional minutage?, the disappointing ratings, Channel 4 selling its own time and so on. We discussed ISBA's dissatisfaction over share and parity deals, with talk of the OFT. I reminded them that the ALC was the appropriate place to air their grievances.

Thursday's Authority meeting approved our Green Paper response and the signing of the BSB contract when it is ready. BSB have asked for a fortnight or so extra time because they have a scheme which they want to put in place which could save them up to £10m. I don't think they're stalling.

On Thursday, during the meeting, I had a message that the OFT have written to all ITV Companies asking about their selling methods.

The following day we also received a letter inviting answers to a range of questions on selling arrangements.

I forgot earlier to mention the session we arranged with Members after the Thursday meeting. We showed ITN and TV-am coverage of the Zeebrugge Disaster. I wanted them to see it following their critical comments at a previous meeting. I felt that they were being unfair to ITN in their criticisms. The coverage ran for some twenty minutes. It made harrowing watching. Members commented that filmed accounts by witnesses or relatives intruded wrongly into personal grief and permission had only been given because the subjects were in a state of shock. They also considered that the camera dwelt too long on scenes of suffering.

Watching the extracts again, I think that some of their worries were justified. David Glencross has agreed to write draft guidelines that Members can approve and which might help remove the anxiety that many felt about the coverage that appeared.

Sunday 28th June

Fred Astaire died last week, at the age of 88. A splendidly full life, passing on his exuberance, style and art to generations to come.

Rain has been falling almost continually to celebrate my week of holiday in Dorset. I suppose it foreshadows a glorious week of sunshine and soaring temperatures when I return to the grindstone tomorrow.

Election Night ratings were proudly trumpeted by the BBC who, after taking a hammering from *Spitting Image* placed against Jasper Carrott, picked up audiences and, as results began to come in, achieved audiences of 9m after 11pm against 4.5m watching ITV.

Roma and I drove up to London and I went into the office on Thursday, mainly to sign letters to staff to be sent out with our Green Paper response, which we are due to expose at a press conference on Monday. I telephoned Jimmy Gordon on Friday and got a warm response to the submission. I had telephoned him principally to hear from him about the notion being canvassed by a number of ILR stations and LBC that they would like to take a majority holding in IRN (£1m for 60 per cent equity). Strikes me as a good step forward and will commit ILR to a secure news output for the future.

Reports in the newspapers this week claimed that ITN has sold its Super Channel news service to Japan for showing on NHK. One in the eye for the BBC, who are hoping for funds from the Foreign & Commonwealth Office to launch a television version of the World Service. ITN is quoted: 'The BBC is talking about it, we are actually doing it'.

The trade press picked up this week on GT's letter to ISBA pointing out in no uncertain terms that the first function of ITV was to serve the audience, not the advertiser. Time it was said.

Next week, Timothy Renton, our new Minister in charge of Broadcasting at the Home Office, addresses the ILR Congress. We sent him an advance copy of our response to the Green Paper. It will be interesting to hear his reaction.

The 'Summit' meeting between ITCA/IPPA (Independent Programme Producers Association) and the IBA to agree the terms of access by the Independents has been arranged for 8 July. The main, and seemingly still outstanding, issue concerns the IPPA position on ITV shareholding. IPPA appear adamant that, if ITV Companies hold shares in Independent Companies, the output should not be counted against the indicative hours that have been assessed for Independent input to ITV. I wrote a letter to Mike Darlow, who is co-ordinator for IPPA, stating the IBA's convictions. I expect a pretty frosty response. It will be interesting to see if Home Office officials stick their noses in.

Rain continues to fall as I complete this week's entry. Next weekend Roma and I go to Copenhagen for the EBU annual thrash. It seems only a few weeks ago that we were entertaining delegates in Bournemouth.

A footnote. TV-am's boss, Bruce Gyngell, has been making headlines over his commitment to pink. Apparently, he was greatly upset that a presenter wore dark clothes and he issued his ten commandments on brighter colours to be worn.

Sunday 5th July

Arrived back from Copenhagen a few hours ago and found London sweating under a brilliant blue sky. Caught the end of the Men's Finals – Cash beating Lendel; the winner causing a stir by leaping over the ringside spectators to reach his parents in the VIP Box.

A busy week starting off on Monday with the radio press conference to launch our response to the Green Paper. About 15 or so journalists turned up and listened as GT gave an account of the Authority's position. I think we've steered, more by luck and good fortune than by intention, a pretty good line between outright competition on the one hand and the status quo position upholding PSB on the other. On reflection, I think we intended this should be so but I believe that GT has always seen our position as more PSB than I. The response, in fact, speaks about a PSB role but says little or nothing about how we achieve it. Several questioners appeared puzzled but any puzzlement there may have been did not surface at the meeting.

That evening, Roma and I went to David Frost's summer party at his home. These annual occasions become more and more glitzy. There is not one person there who isn't someone! Dougie Hayward came up and said, about himself, 'The only person I don't know here is me'. If someone had tossed a bomb over the garden wall, the entire Cabinet would have gone up with it. Andrew Lloyd Webber looked hung-over and flushed. Tim Rice was with his lady friend, whose name I forget. The Duke of York was skipping about among the guests.

On Tuesday, to the Radio Congress at the Café Royal, there to hear Timothy Renton, the new David Mellor. GT invited Renton to breakfast and got a turn-down, which I think rather rude. Instead, he has invited us over for a meeting. Renton gave a speech, obviously written for him. I was miffed that not once did he take account of the IBA's role in developing the changes that lie ahead.

By and large, the AIRC are, I think, keen to endorse the IBA as the regulatory body, although, in their submission, they are mealy-mouthed, preferring to sit on the fence. They do, however, flatly turn their backs on the Cable Authority.

In the afternoon, a meeting with Michael Dealey and Chris Rowley. Michael Dealey had flown in from L.A. especially to add his views, and those of the Independents, on the two subjects of rights and participation in Independent Companies by ITV. He put his case on both issues extremely forcefully and on both I was left with the uneasy feeling that we had got it wrong. We are in fact in a dilemma. Time is pressing and we are still some way from having a Heads of Agreement document that both ITCA and the Independents will accept. I have circulated the correspondence I have been having with Mike Darlow to ITCA. We are due to meet both groups on Wednesday. I fear the tensions that have been bubbling under the surface will erupt. The ITV Companies are mightily displeased with the IBA for pushing forward with the resolution we are showing. The Independents are standing firm against any ITV holdings in Companies. Pragmatically, I think we are right to take our present position but we may not get agreement however we play it.

In the evening, to see the National Ballet of Canada performing *Alice* at the Coliseum. Talked to Arnold Goodman, who said he hadn't enjoyed ballet since 1926. Just why this particular year was the watershed of his view on ballet I didn't ask. Afterwards, Ian Hunter, Roma and I went to the Garrick and walked out after one hour and 40 minutes, having only had our first course. They really are hopeless at getting their act together – in the Garrick of all places!

On Wednesday, the RCC meeting, which I chair. It went rather well. I think both they and we are somewhat relieved that we aren't in head-on conflict with our Green Paper evidence.

In the evening, to the AGM of the London Marriage Guidance. As President, I get a decent meal afterwards – this time at L'Escargot.

Breakfast with David Frost on Thursday in the Carlton Tower Rib Room. Nothing is cheap these days. The bill came to £19. My reason for inviting him was to test out how far TV-am were committed to trying to work out some relationship with ITN, if ITN were to go public. The answer I got was unsatisfactory. David still feels that David Nicholas would rather see them in hell than supping at his Board. I also get the impression now that TV-am are beginning to take their role seriously and actually believe they have something going for them which puts them in an equal pecking order with ITN.

Just before leaving for Denmark for the EBU, I received a note from Harry Theobalds suggesting that further and new consideration should be given by us for increasing air time in peak time by transferring two minutes into peak time. This would not be adding new minutage so it would not be a major change of position. I am meeting GT tomorrow and I have a pretty good feeling that he will agree. Personally, I don't think we've got much to lose, although I was against it before.

The rest of the weekend was spent at the EBU General Assembly in Copenhagen. The heat really is on in Europe, as it is here. Whether to allow in new members who may be seeking to compete or whether to keep them out and risk them starting their own 'club'. The French tried getting the okay to allow Channel 5 and 6 into the EBU, but were told to go away until the EBU had made up its mind about several principles.

Spent the time in the car from the airport to home reading correspondence and papers for next week. It seems sometimes as though I am on a treadmill: the faster I work, the more it seems to pile up.

Sunday 12th July

The BBC issues its response to the Green Paper – a thin read. Jeremy Isaacs claims that Channel 4 made a £20m profit for the ITV Companies selling air time, and the Government agrees to our guidelines to advertise condoms!

On Monday, I lunched with the AAC and paid tribute to Harry Theobalds, who has served the Committee and the industry for well over 25 years.

On Tuesday, an early breakfast with GT, then PPC, followed by SCC. We talked about ITCA's submission to the Home Affairs Committee in relation to our own submission. The two have shown a major difference of viewpoint. ITCA believes that all regulation will require a lighter touch in future, promoting equal competition. They do not put a timescale against it. We maintain that the present system will see us through the next major contract round in 1992. A significant difference of views. ITCA say they will come back with their response.

On Wednesday, breakfast with Dickie and Nigel Walmsley, ostensibly to talk about Capital providing their own news service (using IRN excerpts). We have up to now said no to them doing this, because it was felt that not to have IRN on the country's biggest station would be to discredit IRN's service. At breakfast I struck a deal that if the ILR Companies purchased 60 per cent of IRN's equity, we would allow Capital a six-month period to try out their news provision. The IRN buy-out is not a new proposition. LBC have been discussing this with the Companies for some time in conjunction with an additional two minutes of national advertising time built round the news.

After this had been discussed, I told Dickie that I thought Capital's output had gone more downmarket and more smutty. The innuendo and double-entendre were much in evidence and this was, I said, alienating the older sector of the station's audience. With the removal of Michael Aspel and Graham Dean the morning was taken over by loud, coarse-mannered DJs. Dickie didn't make a strong response and said that they (Nigel) were thinking about Jo Sandilands and 'moving her on'.

After breakfast, I chaired the very important tripartite meeting of the Independents, ITCA and the IBA on the question of independent access. The main sticking point was, and still is, the participation by ITV in Independent Companies. Unlike America, where the networks put up only a proportion of production costs in return for a license to play, here the ITV Companies will in all probability put up 100 per cent and will expect, with some justification, to receive part of overseas sales.

The meeting lasted for two hours and actually did make progress. I concluded by saying that the IBA would produce a policy document which would be circulated.

In the evening, spoke after dinner at a consultation on Social Action Broadcasting. At least nobody fell asleep.

On Thursday, the Authority met ITV Programme Controllers of the majors for their annual meeting. Much more spontaneous and open than in previous years. Andy Allan made a passionate speech about the Companies' need to cater to the young audience. I pointed out that John Birt had given the same speech on behalf of the Controllers about two years previously. Collapse of stout party.

Prior to lunch, the Authority had approved our proposals for IRN/LBC sell-out to ILR and had congratulated Colette Bowe on the press conference for the radio response.

Later in the day, a meeting with David McCall and Dick Emery with the news that the ISBA had reported ITV's sales practices to the OFT. The heat will be on ITV to show itself more sensitive to advertisers' needs. I said that I thought the IBA would permit a further two minutes of peak time, shifted from other hours, but we would expect share and parity schemes to be discontinued. There is a meeting of the ALC next week and I shall get GT to suggest a working party of ISBA/ITCA to work out ways for better cooperation. It might stave off action by the OFT.

Rushed down to a IBA General Advisory Council Dinner in Kent and slept in a ludicrous bedroom at the Chilston Park Hotel, owned by the proprietor of the *Antiques Guide*, a Mr Miller, who has filled the place with antiques, making it look as though it was still inhabited by an eccentric aristocrat.

Members of the GAC at their meeting thought that an interview with Edwina

Currie and Clive James was sexist because Clive kept asking her about her Janet Reger underwear. Afterwards, I revealed to a number of startled members that I was wearing underpants with hedgehogs bonking!

Back in London now, and shortly leaving for the Dimbleby Lecture, given by Denis Foreman.

Next week my after-lunch address to a *Readers Digest* gathering and later in the week to Bristol and the Radio Academy. Roll on retirement.

Sunday 19th July

The field mouse that usually busily crosses between the garage and the woodshed has, so far, kept to him/herself. It must have another life but all I see of it is the 'crossing'. I feel unrewarded. Perhaps all of us see each other just at the 'crossing'.

Main issues this week: access by the Independents.

Main success this week: the signing of our contract with BSB.

Main worry this week: do we allow Thames and LWT to attack the terrestrial base of our audience through access to Astra to compete against BSB.

On Monday I decided to telephone David McCall and put to him the other side of the coin regarding involvement by the Companies in independent production companies. So far I haven't really argued that the case for any involvement would be seen by some as the IBA endorsing the status quo, attempting to retain control of the Independents by the back door, or an involvement that would encourage 'sweetheart deals' and why, it could be argued, does ITV need an interest at all? Why shouldn't the Independents be independent? If some go to the wall, so be it. If the Companies want to support independence, especially in the Regions, let them do it by means of development funding and not by way of shareholding. I went on to say to David that it could be argued that there were other, bigger battles to fight and that Government would not look happily on the monopoly trying to hold on.

David told me later (after the Companies' meeting on Tuesday) that they, ITCA, had discussed the subject but still felt there was a strong argument for some involvement.

I put the same case to DGM on Tuesday. I gained the pretty conclusive view that my arguments were not reaching their target. Some involvement was thought to be right. Later, in Bristol at the Radio Academy Festival, I had opportunity to speak to Quentin Thomas from the Home Office. He believed that Ministers would probably accept a limit of about 10 per cent holding by ITV, so maybe my fears are overstated. In today's *Sunday Times* the Independents are quoted as saying that they will pull out of any arrangement with the IBA if it fails to deliver their objectives.

The outline policy document goes to Members on Thursday.

On Tuesday, spoke at *Readers Digest* luncheon at Claridges and attended supper with the Unions at the IBA, which ended at 8pm as a result of a bomb scare across the road.

1987

A red letter day on Wednesday. Attended the press conference given by BSB announcing their signing of the Hughes Spacecraft contract.

Talked to IBA staff and spoke at the farewell lunch to Bill Westwood, leaving our Religious Advisory panel. As a keepsake, gave him a tape of an Easter message he gave in 1982 on Capital. I think he was quite touched.

Thursday started with a champagne breakfast – another farewell to Harry Theobalds on behalf of ALC. Later, at the Meeting, GT and I were able to persuade ISBA to go back to their Council Members and see if they would withdraw their complaint to the OFT, while we set up an ad hoc working party to see what answers could be found to the problem of minutage, share and parity, etc.

Lunch with Donald Maitland at Simpsons in the Strand. A hyper-active man whose questioning and probing never stops.

Back at 3.30pm to witness the official signing of the BSB contract with the Authority. Felt quite emotional.

Off to speak at the Radio Congress in Bristol. Travelled in the train with Dick Francis, newly-appointed DG to the British Council. A jolly dinner followed by a funny speech by Ned Sherrin. Quentin Thomas afterwards asked whether I knew that C4 had gone to the Treasury suggesting a C4 buy-out. I said no. There's some dirty work at the crossroads. Edmund's Chairman Report comes out next week with the publishing of an Annual Report. QT asked what thoughts I might have about the next Chairman of the IBA. I said I would think!

The following morning listened to the Home Secretary saying nothing and did my piece 'Facing Up To The Challenge'. Returned to Ower, exhausted.

P.S. Denis Foreman's Dimbleby Lecture has ruffled feathers over his remarks about Government packing the IBA and BBC Governors and Members. (Or rather, I should say, the damage of Government trying to pack etc..)

P.P.S. On Monday evening supposed to be having dinner at the Garrick with Mary and Jeffrey Archer.

Back from Dorset to London in torrential rain.

The IBA seems to be getting a good press. *Broadcast* magazine actually paid tribute to the quality of the response to the Green Paper.

Listening to the Home Secretary, I got the impression that he was beginning to back pedal over the IBA's role. He went out of his way to say that the IBA had performed its role well and that it had striven to do it as effectively and sensitively as it could within the 1981 Act etc, etc.

I think that Douglas must be beginning to realise just what sort of task has been entered upon by Government. My guess is that he doesn't want the IBA to give up radio and is starting to shift his ground. I think that our ploy now will be to get closer to the Community Lobby so they will back us.

Re DBS, one day I will look back over my diary at the start of all the talk. Chris Irwin at least had the courtesy to say that I was right about getting the private sector to launch DBS.

Sunday 26th July

Giving blood nowadays takes on a significance that I am certain did not accompany the giver, or the given, in earlier times. AIDS stalks the pre-giving conversations of those awaiting the prick of the needle.

On Monday, I attended this ceremony at the National Farmers Union Headquarters in Knightsbridge. After giving blood, sweet coffee and a sense of achievement made up for any collywobbles beforehand.

Lunch at the Mirabelle (a place where you can almost hear the laughter and chat of the ghosts of the 30s and 40s). Leslie Jackson, Chairman of 2CR, and David Porter, his MD, wanted to sound me out on the possibility of a merger with Radio 210, caused – they said – by the fear of being swamped by Ocean Sound. (I didn't intend the pun). Both companies appear to want to combine.

Afterwards, to ITN and a Board Meeting. I have a nasty feeling that the intended move of ITN to the old Sunday Times building is going to be a slow, expensive and painful undertaking. One newspaper report this week mentioned the £600,000 sweetener that Camden Council had asked for, adding that it was most unusual. I am sure ITN did the right thing in refusing, despite advice to the contrary of Sir Patrick Layfield that a payment of that nature was in order. There will be 'I told you sos' on both sides.

Later in the afternoon, a meeting with Sarah Lawson and David Glencross and Chris Rowley re Independents. Sarah was making the point strongly, and well, that Independents should be allowed to sink or swim according to their talents, and should not be given the crutch of an ITV shareholding. Later in the week, the wording 'not normally' was to be tried out on the ITV Companies and with the Authority at its meeting. Both now appear to believe the words acceptable. The more I think about our original position, 25 per cent access by ITV, the less I think it stands up. Michael Darlow still believes we are sticking on access but this wording should show very clearly where the IBA stands over shareholding.

Dinner that night at the Garrick with Mary and Jeffrey Archer, both very cool and confident over the outcome of their action against *The Star*. Jeffrey has the capacity for bouncing back whatever the situation. I think he is actually enjoying the role. If Mary is, she isn't showing it. What she does show is a great deal of poise and self control. During the evening, we talked of many things, and poetry came into it. Mary recited 'Lies' by Kit Wright:

> 'When we are bored
> My friend and I tell lies.
> The prize is won by the one
> Whose lies are the bigger size.
> We really do – that's true
> But there isn't a prize – that's lies'

I wonder why it sprang into her mind!

Later in the week we heard that Jeffrey had won the case although, in the long run, the Judge's disgraceful summing up may come back to haunt him.

On Tuesday, an early morning meeting with GT, Derek Palmer and Paul Fox. I knew the reason beforehand – to see if the Authority would reverse its earlier decision to allow the 21 per cent Bass holding in Yorkshire to be taken up by Paramount. We listened to Paul making perfectly proper points about the virtue of having a strong US partner capable of funding and marketing Yorkshire's output. I have some misgivings. To open up the UK ITV scene and allow in US entertainment interests would bring about a tidal wave of US investment and, whilst Paramount is a distinguished company, many are not. Once the precedent had been created, it would be well nigh impossible to determine who should and who should not be permitted a holding.

On Thursday the Authority agreed this line. GT told Paul Fox and on Friday I read in the papers that Bass had placed and marketed their shareholding amongst some 40 investors, making – if the papers are to be believed – a cool £23m profit. A great pity that Bass should have done this without any prior warning and without looking to see what other groups might have come forward which could have made a contribution to the company and its expertise. I have a feeling that approval should have first been sought from the Authority. What we can do about it now I am not sure, although Derek Palmer remains the Chairman and I suppose we could invite him to stand down.

On Thursday evening went to the First Night of *Follies* – I think it will run.

On Wednesday, met for the first time properly Timothy Renton with GT. Most of the conversation turned on the Government's priority of gaining access into ITV by the Independents. I got the impression that TR would settle for 'not normally'. It transpires that he has seen delegations from practically everyone in ITV so this route through the maze may be something of a relief to him. He asked whether any other unions might come in to make life difficult for ACTT and thus weaken their stronghold. I said no, adding that if they give too much support to the Independents they could easily become infected by union bad practices. They needed to fight this course, I said. We talked about radio and I said I thought some coming-together could result from IBA assistance in bringing together community radio aspirants and ILR before a new Broadcasting Act. Thus, I agreed, taking some pressure off Government in the meantime. Renton, I think, took the point.

On Thursday, dinner with the ITV principals, preceded by a meeting with the Authority. A good occasion with the opportunity to examine serious issues, amongst them networking, night programming, Channel 4 and the Independents, ITN and the proposed Broadcasting Bill in autumn 1988.

Real movement now does seem possible over networking conditions. The Companies seem resigned to the IBA disallowing access into Independent production companies.

On Friday, I sent round to Quentin Thomas at the Home Office the draft Policy Statement approved by the Authority the day before. It will be very interesting to see what comments QT might make. Next week I intend sending the draft to both ITCA and IPPA. It is then that the balloon will go up!

An early breakfast at the Savoy with Jeremy Isaacs, at his invitation. Who will take over from him? I asked. Jeremy was non-committal. How should C4 be funded?

Non-committal. Who should be the next Chairman of the IBA? Peter Carrington? The Savoy breakfast was a great disappointment – no flat black mushrooms.

Sunday 2nd August

The Bass sale has gone un-remarked. I thought there would be a furore, but not a murmur.

Last night the first ever condom advertisement was transmitted. I suppose something of an historic moment. Durex had first bite of the cherry – a fairly innocuous 'boy lusts after girl' routine with a symbolic wire mesh between them.

Another advertisement, not yet shown, is for *Mates*. This one goes nearer to the heart of the matter. I showed it to GT because the storyline was quite clearly accepting that premarital sex was part of the lifestyle of young people. We will get a huge mailbag, I think, after showing it.

On Monday evening went with David Glencross and had dinner with the new Head of MI5 at the Carlton. Obviously much worried about bad publicity following Wright's publication of his memoir *Spycatcher*. I said it would soon be water under the bridge. I hadn't bargained for the clamp-down on press and broadcast comment imposed by the Law Lords on Friday that made us seem not unlike South Africa!

A dinner on Tuesday with Jimmy Gordon and the 'big four' to talk about the next phase of radio during the transitional period.

Appeared on *The Brian Hayes Show* on LBC on Wednesday, talking about the Green Paper and after. Sounded very prissy when I heard it played back, and thought I did pretty badly. Afterwards I lunched with the Board.

A week of retirement parties. Charlie Mayo, who gave dedicated service to the cause of education and particularly helped to introduce sub-titling for the deaf. Ted Wilson, and then on Friday Harry Theobalds. In my words of farewell I said he joined the IBA in a sea of soap suds and ended on a float of condoms! Joyce, his wife, wisely stayed away.

On Thursday to Glyndebourne for a Ravel double bill as guests of the Gatwards. James told me in the interval that the Companies would have to invest in a rights issue to keep Super Channel going. They had already cut 40 people from the workforce of 114. James said that the other ITV MDs had no concept of real competition. All I could think of was Richard Dunn chuckling to himself.

On Friday I became uneasy about the silence from Quentin Thomas on our Independent Policy Statement draft. I eventually spoke to him and heard from him that Douglas Hurd had a number of comments, some of which we can take on board and some of which we can't. On Monday I will send drafts to ITCA and IPPA. I am seeing Douglas on Thursday. GT is on holiday so I shall take Shirley Littler for company. Next week promises to be quiet – I hope.

Sunday 9th August

Saw a fox walking along the shoreline opposite the cottage today. They move with such purposefulness. Nature is very thoughtful. Foxes can't get down rabbit holes, so at least the rabbits can have a good night's rest.

At last our Policy Statement regarding use of Independents on ITV has reached a final stage. We heard back from both IPPA and ITCA that, though neither were completely satisfied, the draft met with their approval. Just as well, because I wasn't minded to make any changes.

I discussed publication with Colette Bowe and decided that we couldn't risk waiting any longer than was necessary. We decided to hold our press briefing on Thursday, after I'd seen the Home Secretary.

On Thursday, I spent about 45 minutes with Douglas and Tim Renton. I took Shirley and Kenneth Blyth with me. Douglas Hurd was obviously making an end-of-term report to Mrs T. and wanted to avoid getting his bottom smacked by not delivering the goods – the goods being the Independents. He was worried about the unions and the possibility of a closed shop operating. I told him that it was not our business and that Companies and Independents would have to make their own arrangements. In conversation with Douglas and Tim Renton, I am continually struck by the lack of consideration they appear to give to programme values: it's all to do with numbers; programming is a commodity, not a service. At least that's the impression they give.

Afterwards, went back and had lunch prior to a FBU meeting with Alan Sapper and other union representatives. I showed them the Statement we would be making.

Later in the afternoon we held a briefing with a number of papers and issued a press release. Most got the facts wrong the following morning, but ITCA issued quite a helpful comment and there was grudging approval by Sophie Balhetchet on behalf of IPPA. Much credit should go to Christopher Rowley for his perseverance with the intricacies of the undertaking.

On Friday, I was greeted by headlines in the *Mail* about a report they had been given in which research carried out by the IBA revealed that over two million people in the country experienced feelings of violence after watching certain television programmes. The Leader in the *Mail* castigated the IBA for self-satisfaction and Mrs Whitehouse promptly sent off letters to Duke Hussey and GT. What had been a risky judgment on the part of Colette had backfired: of all the papers to have chosen, the *Daily Mail* is furthest to the right in its attitudes to sex, violence and all things beloved by the anti-porn lobby. Apart from upsetting other papers, who resented this *Mail* exclusive, I was worried that it would cause rumbles within the Companies, but so far I haven't heard from any of them. What it has succeeded in doing is showing Colette just what a tinderbox television is, and anything to do with violence. A fuse to set off all manner of Chinese crackers.

Yesterday I was telephoned by Clare Mulholland to tell me that C4 were proposing to read extracts from *Spycatcher* in an LWT production at lunchtime today entitled *Network Seven*. I was assured by Clare that the extracts fall outside the ban on the book and that Counsel's opinion had been sought and approval given for the readings. I started watching the programme but decided I had better things to do. I am keeping my fingers crossed that I am not sent to the Tower.

News of Super Channel's difficulties has finally become public. The *Sunday Times* carried a piece. The high hopes that accompanied the launch are frail after only six months. It may act as a brake on ITV's decisions relating to Astra. One man who will be chuckling again is Richard Dunn of Thames, the only MD who has kept away from Super Channel.

On Friday I had a meeting with Justin Dukes, who asked me what I thought of the proposition that C4 should sell its own advertising at the start of the extension of contracts and, if that proved successful, be floated in 1992. I said it was worth pursuing!

Sunday 17th August

Writing by the side of Ann Cameron-Webb's pool overlooking the low hills that surround her villa a few miles inland from Faro in Portugal. We are here for a week. The weather, which started off looking as though it might replicate our weather at home, has now pulled itself together and the sun is now burning down from a cloudless sky.

In the week before leaving, I went on Monday 10 August to Liverpool to celebrate the 5th Anniversary of *Brookside*. I travelled with Jeremy Isaacs in the specially chartered train from Euston. On arrival, we witnessed the official naming of a British Rail locomotive: 'Brookside'. There was quite a crowd, mostly gathered I suspect to see any well-known Brookside faces. Since I have never watched a complete episode of *Brookside*, I was unable to gauge whether the crowd had found any satisfaction!

Phil Redmond pulled aside the curtain covering the nameplate, looking more like a minor communist party leader in China than a highly successful entrepreneur and businessman. I suspect his image reflects his attitude, and it is his attitude which is the source of his prodigious talent. True to himself. The B.R. officials, and local Liverpool dignitaries, looked wildly overdressed but in earlier times the occasion would have called for frock coats and top hats.

We then coached along to the Liverpool Maritime Museum at the Albert Dock for lunch. Liverpudlians are immensely proud of their new dock development and the city is gaining in self respect.

During lunch, several people stood on chairs and made both short and long speeches. Afterwards we climbed back into the coaches and were taken to the *Brookside* set. Unfortunately, the organisers of the outing had not thought to allow the party to be taken on an attractive route. Instead, we thundered along roads lined by high brick walls or half-demolished slums – a pity because until then we had been presented with a very different view of the city.

Reaching the *Brookside* set, we decamped from the coaches and were directed into a hot marquee with small tables and chairs and a raised platform with a microphone.

Once marshalled inside, we were treated to another speech from Phil Redmond – this time about his beliefs, his art and his hopes for the future. We clapped when it was over, and trooped out into Brookside Close where we were told we could mingle with the actors and visit the five or six small houses that make up the

1987

community. Visiting each house produced the feeling that one was an interloper in another's home. Personal objects lay scattered through the tiny rooms as though the occupants had just slipped out for a few moments.

The coaches left promptly at five, and we were driven back to the station and from thence by train to London.

On Tuesday, an early morning meeting with Chris Chataway and David Hayes, who wanted to sound me out over their plans to combine a number of ILR stations into one public company. I warned Chris that the Authority would not automatically approve the proposal since none of the Companies was in dire straits. I think they were somewhat taken aback.

In the afternoon I was interviewed by two journalists from *Broadcast*, who subsequently wrote a story with the headline 'IBA takes back seat in negotiations between Independents and ITCA'. Not bad, for all that.

In the evening, went with Roma, Bob Towler and Hugh Bishop (aged 80) to see *Les Liaisons Dangereuses* at The Ambassador Theatre. It was dreadfully hot but the production was superb, so one forgot the hardship and enjoyed the play. Christopher Hampton has woven together a masterpiece of intrigue, gullibility, lust and desire. A marvellous evening's entertainment. Hugh Bishop, a C of E vicar, went out muttering that it was, in his view, a highly moral tale! Afterwards, we went to the Neal Street Restaurant, where Roma and I were misguidedly tempted into trying, as a starter, some revolting-looking Italian mushrooms, that exuded a ghastly odour. They actually didn't kill us both, as I had imagined they would.

The day before leaving for our holiday, I spent about an hour and a half with Shirley Littler going over policy issues. She told me she might decide to retire somewhat earlier than planned because Geoffrey was tired of the Treasury and thought of taking early retirement. He would immediately be offered lucrative City directorships and earn double the money he makes currently. If Shirley were to up-stumps and depart it would leave quite a gap in our executive leadership. She is a stalwart trooper and works at incredible speed, covering a vast range of subjects with expert and painstaking attention. All in all, a remarkable person. She also indicated to me that if Donald Maitland were appointed Chairman she would not work under him. And so say all of us!

Thinking about chairmen, I have been looking at *Who's Who* for inspiration. Jim Prior was suggested by John Harriott, and I wouldn't dismiss the thought of Patrick Jenkin. Time to decide is not overlong with GT going at the end of next year.

On Thursday, Roma and I were driven to the Garrick by David, having received a visit from Sally with the last scraps of mail to complete. The desk is cleared and I tell Sally to do her very best to move the piles of incoming business on to the desks of others.

Holidays are marvellous things. I haven't done a thing. Ann's parrot, Sky, flew off the day we arrived. She keeps saying we should all go and look for it, but so far no one has made a move. Poor Sky.

Monday 24th August

Returned home on Thursday night from Portugal. Good news before leaving. We were woken the day before by squeals of joy from the children and our hostess: Sky had returned to his cage and was preening himself.

On the plans home we read about the horrific shooting by Michael Ryan in Hungerford, when he went berserk and killed 15 people with an automatic rifle before killing himself. The press immediately dubbed it a '*Rambo* type' killing and described Ryan as wearing a Rambo-style headband. Instantly, this gave the press and politicians a field day against the portrayal of violence on TV. Later it transpired that Ryan was wearing an ordinary sort of hat but by that time the damage had been done. He was *Rambo* as seen on the films and on video, and such stereotyping by the press is impossible to counteract. *Rambo* is the cause of the killing and, by implication, television is the root cause – not unemployment, sexual inadequacy or any other malady. No. Television. So everyone gets on the bandwagon, including the Government and the very Minister who failed earlier to tighten the gun laws.

The BBC has acted throughout the hysteria in an exemplary fashion. They have scored heavily over ITV in the way that they handled their PR, withdrawing a number of programmes with much banging of the drums. ITV withdrew two, but failed to make a telling comment on their reasons. Now today the *Daily Mail* has the headline: 'ITV back to violence as usual', with a damaging Leader item suggesting that all ITV care about is getting on with the business of peddling violence. Colette Bowe is away and the press are dealing with John Guinery. I have spoken to David Glencross and asked for his assurance that a programme – *The Bill* – going out tomorrow, and which was cited by *The Mail* as showing no respect for the killings, is in fact acceptable for transmission. David will look at it later today, although he assured me earlier that Robin Duval and Thames had seen it. I am extremely nervous about it being shown if there are any genuine grounds for concern. David today attended the unveiling of the Autumn Schedules at the Savoy. Most of the questions by the press were on the subject of violence, so we must see what sort of coverage we get tomorrow.

Tuesday 25th August

Went out early to Corfe and bought the papers. A great amount of comment from Grade about programmes he had decided should be 'postponed'. (Comment from the press was 'why postpone, why not cancel?') Much, too, about Grade wanting a meeting with ITV chief to talk about guidelines on violence. Attributed to David Glencross in the press was the observation that it had been the BBC three years ago that had declined to continue with joint guidelines, not the IBA.

On balance, I think that Grade had begun to sound off too loudly and too passionately.

Yesterday evening, and as a result of conversations I had with John Guinery, the IBA issued a press statement drawing attention to our guidelines already in existence. This was quoted on *News At Ten* and went some way to demonstrate that the IBA was awake and mindful of its duties. Late last light I had a call from David Glencross. He told me that Richard Dunn, having seen the episode of *The Bill* due out tonight, and mindful of yesterday's storming headline in *The Daily Mail*, had decided that the episode was unsuitable for screening at the present time and would be replaced by another, earlier episode. The decision-taking process at Thames, in view of public concern being expressed over the Hungerford killings, were clearly not appropriate. I had, on Friday, received assurances that both IBA and Thames staff were satisfied the episode would cause no offence. This decision was taken at a relatively junior level at Thames and by Robin Duval within the IBA who, I was told, was relying on his memory of the episode when it had been shown previously. No one in a senior position at Thames had viewed it.

This morning I spoke to Richard Dunn and told him I thought Thames had handled this very badly. He apologised. Now we are left with the press crowing over the results of their campaign and the inference more strongly embedded that ITV is lax in its control.

I ran over events with GT on the telephone and suggested to him that he should consider issuing a statement under his name after endorsement by Authority members on 2 September. This would give the right level of emphasis to Authority concerns.

Much comment also by the press on tonight's showing of *Brimstone & Treacle*. This is the original TV version, which Alasdair Milne is supposed to have described as 'nauseating'. The *Independent* described Controller of BBC1, Michael Grade's, actions in terms which should please him: 'Michael Grade is to be commended for ending a nauseating episode of television censorship'. It will be interesting to see whether Mrs Whitehouse shares this view, or indeed viewers, having watched the episode. Alasdair Milne has withdrawn from the live discussion due to take place after the showing.

Monday 31st August

Brimstone & Treacle has been and gone. Most papers took the line that, if it was Dennis Potter, it must be art. Mrs Whitehouse held her peace but I don't think it should have been shown. The rape of a brain-damaged girl by the devil would, I should have thought, have caused offence, but apparently not.

Next on the media menu will be *V* by Tony Harrison. We can't win. If it's stopped, the whole cultural universe will rise and condemn us for being cowardly. If we allow it, the whole beat 'em and bang 'em brigade will rise up and slate us. I might try counting the number of 'fucks' and 'cunts'. It will certainly beat all previous records.

The end of the holiday. Tonight back to London. I don't look forward to it with any pleasure. Over the weekend, the faithful gathered in Edinburgh to hear themselves talk to each other. As ever the press had a field day. Melvyn Bragg is not going to apply for the post as boss of Channel 4. Douglas Hurd, at the RTS Cambridge bash in three weeks time, is going to tell the world what the Government intends doing with Channel 4. The Prime Minister is going to approve a fifth channel. Channel 4 will be privatised – and so the rumours go on and on.

Richard Attenborough telephoned today to seek information about the 'summit' meeting on the 21st that the Prime Minister is chairing. I said I had no idea but would find out. A weirdly assorted group have been invited. The more I think about it, the less I like the smell of it.

I have been doing some thinking about the meeting I am due to have with the BBC on Friday. The subject is the Obscene Publications Bill. Michael Grade has already gained valuable publicity for himself and the BBC by telling the media that he called the meeting. If we don't handle it carefully we will find ourselves upstaged again with Grade making a magisterial statement on the outcome. I think after our Authority Meeting on Thursday we will issue a statement saying we will not defend the status quo and will instead cooperate in the drafting of a sensible Bill.

If I can get this accepted, we might just steal most of Grade's thunder! So back to the slog. My, how I wish the next four years would flash by: it really is the most thankless task but I have no one to blame but myself.

Sunday 6th September

Returned after the Bank Holiday with Brian Wenham at the Neal Street Restaurant. I don't really know Brian and have always considered him something of a cold fish. Like so many thumbnail guesses, this one turned out to be wrong. I found him witty and friendly. We talked about the C4 job. Brian said he'd set his heart on getting it. He is a professional through and through and, whilst not having the charisma that Jeremy brought to the position, he has a determination that I respect. I shall be surprised, though, if RA puts him at the head of the list. Brian told me that Melvyn had definitely decided not to apply. He admitted Grade might have his eye on C4, but thought he probably had his eye on anything that might be to his advantage! The next Chief Executive of C4 is going to be speculated upon more and more until the announcement.

I talked at DGMM in the afternoon about my thoughts on promoting the IBA's stance regarding the Obscene Publications Act and using the opportunity of an Authority Statement to go public before the BBC meeting. This was agreed at DGMM.

On Thursday I held a briefing meeting in advance of the Friday meeting with the BBC. Present were David Glencross, Robin Duval, David Shaw, Jane Vizard, Jeremy Isaacs and our legal advisor, John Rink. I had not got very far into the meeting before it became obvious that Jeremy and David Shaw were both opposed to us giving way immediately on the Obscene Publications Act, arguing with some force that we should wait to see what new clauses Government considers should be included. Consequently, I agreed to hold our present position – which is basically to claim that, as the IBA is governed by an Act (unlike the BBC), Government should first consider changes in the 1981 Act rather than place us in double jeopardy.

After the meeting, I lunched at the Tate with David Norris, an old friend and legal advisor to IPPA. He said that he thought our indicative figures for the introduction of Independents would be easily reached. He was worried, however, by the threat from multi-national Independents becoming involved, and hoped we would come up with a solution that would lessen fears that the Independents entertained. I said I would think about it.

In the afternoon had a useful briefing meeting with Donald Maitland before he was due to chair the Authority meeting the next day. We resolved a number of issues and took a hard look at the proposed statement on violence. Donald felt that it wasn't strong enough and didn't reach conclusions. We worked until late with Colette Bowe, re-working the statement and including a new piece about commissioning research to monitor whether we had achieved a diminution in the amount of violent activity on the screen.

The following day the Authority accepted, in the main, the statement that was to be put out that afternoon, achieving our purpose in upstaging the BBC on Friday.

At their meeting, the Authority also took the decision (on my recommendation, supported by staff) to permit ITV Companies to play a programming role, if they wished, on the Astra Satellite. So far, we have not received a direct request for this, but I wanted to get it out of the way of the Authority so we would not have an over-long gap before giving our permission. It will surprise, and I daresay shock, some people.

The Authority Members also saw Tony Harrison's film *V* and by a majority of 6:3 decided it should be shown. Whether GT will now agree will be interesting to see. I remain of the opinion that, whatever the case for showing a work of genuine merit, the language employed would cause considerable offence.

On Friday to Broadcasting House to discuss our agreement with the BBC, in the face of the Government's determination to bury broadcasters within the Obscene Publications Act. I explained our position. We wanted to wait. We wanted to be able to put up a considered defence. Michael Checkland seemed to accept our position. In any case, the eventual wording we agreed upon made no reference to the OPA.

Sunday 13th September

The big new feature in the ITV autumn schedule was *Sins* starring Joan Collins. I opened my newspaper on Monday morning to see 'ITV's *Sins*' occupying many column inches in the tabloids. They all loudly denounced the opening sequence of the two-hour epic which started at 8pm. In the morning, I caught up with the offending part. It was obvious that a considerable mistake had been made in allowing transmission. The sequence showed two children in occupied France hiding from the Gestapo and listening from a cupboard as their pregnant mother was beaten to death to obtain some admission of guilt. For good measure, there was a scene of rape and further interrogation – all quite unsuitable for pre-9pm viewing. The avalanche was predictable, Mary Whitehouse et al demanding retribution.

On Tuesday I met the MDs at our regular SCC and left them in no doubt as to my views. A mistake had been made during pre-vetting. What angers me is that none of the MDs had bothered to check the content, despite the fact it was their first big bang of the season and despite the fact that after Hungerford we had impressed on the Companies the need for proper care. Later I was interviewed on C4. *Broadcast* said on Thursday, in the headline, that I had 'panicked'! In today's *Sunday Times* a review of the incident opines that the IBA were also to blame.

We have now received the Prime Minister's outline of the discussion the broadcasters are holding with her at No. 10 on the 21st September. I am to be the last speaker, on the subject of Regulation. Here is what the outline says:

> 'The 1984 Act sought to provide a light regulatory touch for new services. Is this adequate to ensure maintenance of standards (e.g. on sex, violence and fair reporting?) If so, do the same regulations need to apply to all new services? Does this require a single new agency incorporating functions of the Cable Authority and for the IBA in relation to any new satellite services and to independent radio? Are new arrangements needed to ensure the maintenance of standards on existing services?'

Answers on a postcard not later than 21st September and addressed c/o the Prime Minister.

An interesting comment on the state of the art was made to me this week by Don Tafner, who said that in all his experience (which is considerable) he had never known a time when the instincts of the key figures in ITV were less tuned to programming and more tuned to business!

Monday 21st September

Red Letter Day, I suppose, for broadcasters and broadcasting. The so-called 'Summit' at Downing Street and a consultation chaired by Mrs T. The first such to be held.

I was due to speak just before lunch as Mrs T decided to have me as an aperitif! Before I spoke, a whole range of issues were considered. The PM appeared at three minutes before ten and bustled into the consultation room, admonishing Nigel Lawson for being late when, as she said, 'He only has to cross the street'.

Mrs T was flanked at her top table by Douglas Hurd, David Young and Nigel Lawson. In the 'audience' was Timothy Renton (very much the Junior Minister). Mrs T. opened by saying that she wanted a sensible framework for broadcasting to cope with change over the next 15 years. A regulatory structure able to offer flexibility yet able to maintain standards. There followed a number of speakers who confirmed the range of choice soon coming to the screen. Heard from a very sotto voce Michael Grade, who in fact said very little except that ITV paid too much to its employees, and we heard Jeremy's views, well-articulated as always though somewhat bizarre. He wanted to hear the Libyan point of view and Russian voices in an unregulated world where freedom of expression was valuable to enrich understanding through television. It didn't go down particularly well.

I got to my feet and said that the dilemma she faced was widening choice.

De-regulation on one hand and maintenance of the standards and values that she and we would wish to see coming into our homes on the other. I criticised the formation of a separate Broadcasting Council if its duty was the same duty as the IBA Members and BBC Governors. Second-guessing could lead to muddle and double-standards. She should widen our remit and allow us to consider wider and deeper issues of concern to society so that television would be part, but not the whole, of our attention and this would put television into proper perspective.

She wrote down in her little red exercise book what I had said, and listened with some irritation to my rationale about the Obscene Publications Act. She began to fidget as I started to talk about the conduct of our regulatory role, the fact that since 1970 there had been no appreciative increase in viewers' concerns over violence on TV. Nevertheless, since Hungerford, there was a greater public concern that television by its very strength contributed in some way to the climate of violence. We took these concerns seriously, I said, and reiterated our vigilance to ensure as best we were able to maintain a consistent high standard.

We trooped into lunch in the large dining room. I sat next to David Young, who was generally pretty convivial except when he broached the subject of transmitters and the number to be installed each year to reach a low number of new viewers. Mrs T. saw us off the premises where a battery of cameramen were doorstepping. I went straight to ITN and gave an interview and then to C4, and then back for the *BBC News* on Radio Four.

Last night Roma and I went to the First Night of *Beyond Reasonable Doubt*, Jeffrey Archer's first play, at the Queen's Theatre, packed with 'celebs': Michael Caine, of course; Carol Thatcher, who asked me how I got on with her mother!; David Owen, Tim Bell, Ann Diamond, David Mellor. It doesn't matter what we all thought of the play (not much) it has already taken £700,000 at the box office, so my little £1,000 investment may come back with interest! Afterwards we repaired to the Inner Temple, where we enjoyed some good food with the accompaniment of flashing bulbs from the press hawks.

This morning I read there had been a 'standing ovation. (There wasn't). 'Cheers for the lead'. (None). Nine curtain calls. (Five curtain calls). Ah well, that's showbusiness, but I am sure a good time will be had by countless hundreds of Archer fans for years to come.

I want to retrace my steps to 16 September onwards. There has been so much happening, I haven't caught up yet.

On Wednesday 16th, I and others from Brompton Road travelled by train up to Wakefield, took a coach to Bradford, where we were entertained by YTV at the Alhambra Theatre, splendidly refurbished. Then on to the Bradford Museum of Photography, Film and Television. The Museum gratefully accepted items from the IBA gallery, soon to be disbanded. Afterwards to the Queen's Hotel for the night.

The following morning we held our Authority Meeting. The Members confirmed their approval for the showing of *V*. I again made an objection, but to no avail.

After the meeting to Cambridge for the RTS Convention. Douglas Hurd gave the keynote speech. In the closing session, I pretended to be the new Home Secretary considering the future, which allowed me to speculate a little and get a few laughs.

On the first evening Michael Checkland made a good, solid job at a speech intended to point the BBC towards efficiency, profitability and success … .

Sunday 27th September

The impact of 'the box' is staggering. The number of people commenting on my brief appearance on the step of No. 10 is remarkable. Nobody seems to know (or care about) the reason but the fact I was there has registered in people's minds. A one day wonder.

On Tuesday, GT and I lunched John Howard Davies and S4C's Managing Director, Owen Edwards. This was an altogether better occasion than when we last met. I seem to recall that much smoke and not a little fire has been generated by S4C by their attack on HTV and the cost they felt they had been unfairly burdened with since the original agreement. Now, since they gave notice that they would take in Independents as part of their remit and would no longer continue with the previous arrangement with HTV, the relationship has improved. Both parties have agreed to bury the hatchet and the Peats Report! If this can be accomplished satisfactorily, it will be a good note on which to conclude a whole series of unhappy events between the two companies. What to me is even more satisfactory, and amazing, is the fact that over this long period of time no word of it ever got into the broadcast press.

On the same day met Richard Dunn and Ian Trethowan with GT. The visit was to spell out their wish to prepare for their Board a proposal that Thames should seek to provide a channel of programmes for transmission by Astra. The cost would be in the region of £10m. They indicated that LWT would wish to join them, although they (LWT) would be making a separate approach to the IBA. (Christopher Bland of LWT telephoned the following day. I said I would come back to them, which I duly did on Thursday to say they had been given the amber light).

On Wednesday Sir Anthony Jolliffe dropped in to have a chat. He said that he had been asked by a number of his mates in the City why on earth he had agreed to become a Member of the Authority. He said that the IBA had a ghastly reputation and he hoped something could be done to improve it. This was not said in bad humour but I think he's going to contribute some good common sense to our deliberations.

More thoughts on V. On Monday I have arranged for our lawyer John Wotton to view the cassette. I am sure that it will cause offence to many people despite the qualities of the programme. If it becomes a cause celebre and my position becomes known, I shall be labelled a philistine, but there it is. I counted – 54 'cunts' in 45 minutes, which takes some beating. I think it was in 1964 that Kenneth Tynan first used 'fuck' on television.

David Frost rang from Washington to ask about developments on TV-am's use of ITN material. I suspect there is going to be another shoot-out at Eggcup House, this time between the Board and Bruce Gyngell who has been allowing his thoughts on masturbation to be recorded for posterity by a journalist from one of the Sunday garbages.

I think I am at last winning internally to get ITN floated way from the Companies. The paper goes to the Authority on 8th October.

On Wednesday afternoon I visit the Oracle subtitling office to see what is a unique service for deaf people. The 5.45 and C4 News is subtitled 'live', which is at least a step in the right direction for assisting the deaf to enjoy television.

Broadcast on Thursday met me to do a piece on what I said to the PM, and then a meeting with Carol Haslam to hear about the sad events leading up to her parting with Super Channel. She feels, I think, that she has been made a scapegoat for the ITV MDs who got their sums wrong and lost their courage. There are probably two sides to this story but from her perspective I felt sorry for her.

Drove to Crawley Court on Friday to present the prize for the best student in Engineering Maintenance – the Bob Harman Memorial Prize. Also another opportunity to wish Alfred Witham a happy retirement with his wife and his newfound pleasure in bee keeping.

Then down to Dorset, but not before a number of telephone conversations with Bob Phillis and Central's MD over the sale of Zenith to Carlton. I told Bob that I would confirm the Authority's view of whether Carlton was an Independent and therefore qualifying as part of the 25 per cent Independent quota when the Authority meets on 8th October but reading the Sunday papers confirms that the deal has gone through. If the Authority believes it falls outside the quota, the balloon will go up and Michael Green will have his worst fears confirmed.

Sunday 4th October

One of those magical days that make this country worth inhabiting. Torrential rain last night; worries about the dangers of flooding. This morning, balmy summer back again. Driving to get the morning newspapers in short sleeves with the sunroof open. Now writing this overlooking the sea; boats moored on a mirror surface. High overhead a jet leaving its white finger marks across the sky. Soon I will hear the deep echo of its engines but it will be out of sight.

Last Monday performed a button-pressing ceremony at IRN, inaugurating their 'electronic newsroom'. An end to shuffling papers across endless desks. Now each journalist sits in front of a VDU and puts his story down which is then copy-tasted by the Deputy Editor. The Editor then builds the bulletin on his machine, indexing and adding to the bulletin until the very last moment.

Car to London Airport and shuttle to Edinburgh. Met by Bill Jamieson, our IBA man there and driven to Gleneagles to speak at the TRIC Scottish Convention. Stayed in a suite big enough to house a family. My speech was followed by Geoffrey Pattie, ex-this and ex-that, on the platform. I talked about new horizons in broadcasting for the manufacturer and retailer, then sped to the airport and was sitting in front of the Home Secretary's desk by 4.15pm at a meeting with GT and Duke Hussey, Chairman of the BBC. GT had a good brief to work from and spoke well. The IBA scored well with the announcement that we, with the Companies, were reducing foreign (American) material in peak time from five and a half hours to four hours a week. I could see Douglas taking all this in, ready to spew it out again at this week's Tory Conference.

Duke Hussey produced out of his briefcase two video 'half-nasties' as a graphic illustration that, with over half the country owning video machines, the control of the screens was no longer in the hands of the broadcasters.

Afterwards, GT and Dukie faced the journalists and on the Nine O'clock and Ten O'clock News there were pictures of us entering the Home Office. Several people remarked how relaxed I looked. The truth of the matter is that I have learned just to smile. No matter what the occasion, smile.

On Monday, GT and I are to see Douglas again – on this occasion over the amount of time we are giving to Independents.

After the Home Office, back to Brompton Road for a drink with Gordon Reece, Margaret Thatcher's 'Advisor for Television'. It had been some years since I'd seen him, but he hasn't changed. Neither had the size of his cigars – my office still reeks from that brief half hour meeting. I am not sure why he came. Possibly he brought tidings from Mrs T but if there was a message it was so well-coded that I failed to decipher it. What he did say was that, in his judgment, ITV needed a Lew Grade. Someone to bring back the smile. Someone big, brash and important who could bang about a bit and duff up the politicians. I asked him who he thought should be the next Chairman of the IBA. He blew cigar smoke reflectively into my curtains and then said 'King, Lord King'. He's bored running British Airways, and he watches television!'

Sunday 11th October

On Monday 5 October to the Home Office with GT to see Douglas Hurd again to give an update on the progress of talks between ITV and the Independents regarding the 25 per cent target set by Government. GT said the IBA believed the figure was attainable and would be reached by the end of 1992. He then went on to say that the IBA would be excluding regional news and news-related items from inclusion in the total hours counted. I was watching Douglas quite closely and either he didn't take it fully in, or else he agreed.

Possibly pressed by No. 10, DH then asked questions about the strength of union domination of the Independents and I said the Independents had a better arrangement than ITV with the ACTT. I begin to think that DH and his advisors are hoping that in some mystical way there will be another Wapping scenario to bring about the withering of union power. Murdoch's innovations in the newspaper publishing industry have reduced the power of the unions over Fleet Street but television does not have an alternative source of talent or expertise to trade with or trade off. My guess is that the union will gain greater strength and power by holding to ransom not only the ITV Companies but the Independents in the fullness of time.

On Wednesday attended the *Sunday Times* Breakfast Forum and took the platform in front of a gathering of the good and the great: Duke Hussey amongst them. I attacked the tabloid press and showed a number of their front pages, with lurid headlines, my point being that the press get off much too lightly as they exploit every opportunity to heighten passions by sexy and violent commentary. As a consequence of my outburst, the Murdoch empire gave me a very bad press, which I am sure lowered Mrs T's estimation of me still further.

Authority meeting on Thursday, one of the best since I joined, its success due to a large extent to the carefully-prepared papers forming the main part of the business. Important decisions relating to C4, ITN and the next contract round, as well as the introduction of Channel Five.

On Friday, I told Thames and LWT that the Authority would permit them an interest in Astra. I also spoke to Carlton and Central and told both of them that we would accept Zenith as an Independent.

The fact that the Authority was deeply divided over allowing *V* to be shown is emerging into the open. Tonight, I was telephoned by Colette Bowe and told that *The Mail* had obtained a copy of the script and was seeking a quote from me! The story has legs and I think will get bigger and bigger as the days go by. They have not taken public mood into account and I think we are going to find ourselves under fire. I still believe the Authority made the wrong decision but I must stay a loyal IBA man and take whatever comes.

Monday 19th October

I was right in one respect over the programme *V*. On Monday last I sat down to breakfast, picked up *The Mail* and was confronted by a banner headline: 'TV Four Letter Poem Fury', with a predictable avalanche of angry quotes from rent-a-quote MPs.

GT and I met during the week and took stock. I think we were both minded to go public with our personal opinions, to distance ourselves from the Members but we took advice from David Glencross and decided to stick to the party line that it was an Authority decision. As the week wore on, more voices protested. *The Telegraph*, Friday 16 October: Martyn Harris in *Odd Man Out*; Coleman: 'The best way of consigning it to deserved oblivion would be to put it out at 11.30pm on Channel Four', which of course is exactly what we propose. Bernard Levin's 'An Adult's Garden of Verse': Do we not show ourselves as a nation of laughing stocks when one of our most outstanding literary artists proposes to read one of his finest creations in public and is greeted by screams of hysterical outrage from people who have almost certainly never heard of him and have probably not read any poem written later than Wordsworth's *Daffodils*'.

So the stage is set for what I think will be a confrontation, with everybody enjoying themselves hugely! I retain my original position: the poem is moving and compelling but it will cause offence. However great the quality of a work, we must balance that against our duty regarding offence. The two are quite separate but I doubt whether this argument will get an airing in all the other eddies of hot air.

The BETA overtime ban continues. Last week I had a meeting with John Forrest and Stuart Bevan to go over emergency plans in the case of transmitter breakdown. If we give in, it will erode our negotiating position for years to come. 'Sod's Law' operated with a vengeance on Thursday, the night of the great wind. It hit London at about 4 a.m., tearing up trees, stripping tiles from roofs. Roma and I lay in bed with our cat while the leaves were torn from the branches and the chimney stacks rattled and rumbled.

In the morning, we woke up to chaos: no power and people walking to work. My main preoccupation has been the BETA IBA dispute, with staff still refusing to work overtime or do special duties. Both ourselves and BETA have set our faces against compromise. It is the oh-so-normal scenario. The storm of course has put a number of transmitters out of action, due mostly to power failure rather than breakdown.

Tuesday 20th October

Last night dined at the Garrick and entertained Trevor Holdsworth, Anthony Simonds-Gooding and GT. Anthony took up his post as Chief Executive of BSB that same day. He is a bluff, confident man in his mid forties. I confess to being worried about his attitude, but can't put my finger on the reason. I suspect he has been listening too much to his previous employer – Charles Saatchi – and to Saatchi's friend, Michael Green. With their interest in the Astra project, they are all for pressuring BSB into taking short-term decisions that could have a dramatic and unfortunate effect on the long-term future of BSB. Programming does not seem to be uppermost in their mind but these are early days still. I have a meeting tomorrow with them and will begin a review of their plans.

This has been a week of trauma. The storm last Friday and this week 'Black Monday' with the crash of the world money markets. Anybody with any shares has seen their holding shrink by more than a third and there's more to come. I have decided to grit my teeth and hold on.

Sunday 25th October

An Indian Summer in October! I write this at Ower, on a beautiful, still, clear day with no sign of the troubles engulfing the country. Others are still suffering from dislocated power and flooding. In Dorset we have been very, very fortunate.

The stock market is still spinning in crisis, dipping and rising like a crazed kite in a high wind.

On Wednesday morning rose early and breakfasted at the IBA with George Russell, Richard Attenborough and GT. Our main discussion centred on the replacement of Jeremy Isaacs. When Dickie spoke to us, he received only one serious bid – from Brian Wenham. Both he and George Russell had taken a dim view of Brian's determination to 'lobby' Channel 4's board members, taking each separately out to lunch. The flood of applications that was expected had not occurred. Maybe there are two reasons: firstly a desire not to stand in Jeremy's shoes, a difficult act to follow. Secondly, and more likely I suspect, the uncertainties surrounding the future of the Channel are enough to put anybody off who already has a secure and profitable job. There are three people who I think could do it, all with different assets. Michael Grade (flair, courage, native perception, but an appointment that would almost certainly lead to speculation that the Channel would be privatised). Melvyn Bragg (a natural successor to Jeremy, with all his values but possibly lacking in width of experience). My current favourite would be David Elstein (highly intelligent, articulate, a wide experience of production and someone who would command respect from the C4 team). If no one comes forward, I suggested to Dickie that he invite David Elstein out to lunch under cover of picking his brains as someone of wide experience. This would provide an opportunity to assess David at the same time.

I said I would make a discreet sounding of Melvyn. We talked of little else, except to ask RA to put to one side – for the time being – the showing of *The Life of Brian*. I think it will offend a large number of people, me included! The Authority, in their present mood, would show it I suspect. I would rather not put this to the test right now.

The V controversy continues unabated. On Saturday, the *Independent* published the poem in full. It would be no surprise to me if Mary Whitehouse or Winston Churchill make an attempt to stop the transmission.

After breakfast I chaired our first meeting with BSB. I think I may have misjudged Anthony Simonds-Gooding. He is taking in a good deal and not saying much in return. No bad thing for a Chief Executive only three days into his new role.

On Thursday the Authority meeting. An important one that has set the seal on an increase in minutage in peak time from seven minutes to seven and a half. The decision went through without noticeable dissent – as also did the discontinuation of share deals.

I took the Authority over the current industrial dispute and raised with them the vexed question of bringing in outside labour if it were found to be vital. I was pleased to get their support, although I very much hope I won't have to take this action. I will have to prepare some ground for discussion with the unions, but not while they are in their present mood. It is a delicate position. My guess is that the unions are not anxious to escalate the dispute because this would not win public support, and if screens go blank the IBA will be under great pressure to resolve matters.

At lunchtime, Members and staff piled into cars and went over to Portland Place for the annual meal with BBC Governors. I sat next to Dukie, who was in splendid form. I apologise in this diary about my earlier comments on Dukie, his qualities and his courage. I come to conclusions far too quickly and often foolishly. Dukie has shown himself quite capable of taking tough and important decisions and also in standing up and rebuffing attacks on the BBC. I find myself admiring his single-minded approach. The BBC this week came out with their five-year plan, which takes major decisions on cost-cutting and reorganisation in their services. Both Dukie and George Russell gave witty speeches at the conclusion of lunch. One sad by-line was the appearance of Bill Cotton halfway through the main course, who looked for his place at the table, could not find it and squatted down beside another guest and held an animated conversation. What a whirlwind of change has gone through the BBC since we last all met together. Dukie reminded his guests that on that occasion he had found GT introducing him to his own Senior Executives.

After lunch I took a few minutes with Michael Checkland in order to fill him in over the details of our dispute with BETA. This could, if the worst were to happen, spark a go-slow within the BBC's transmitter staff, since we share a considerable number of locations and aerials. Again, I was pleased to get a positive response to the question of standing firm.

In the afternoon, a meeting with Brian Griffiths and my staff to go over aspects of the White Paper. Brian Griffiths, when questioned, said he thought it likely that there would be a separate, and earlier, paper on sound broadcasting, followed by one on television. The following morning we held a similar meeting with Quentin Thomas and Edward Bickham. From both meetings I gained a strong impression that Ministers were determined to bring in some form of tendering. A possible way would be for the IBA to set out the criteria and invite applications. We would then select a short list from those who met the qualities we expected. They would then be invited to tender for the contract. This seems sensible although it would rock the foundations of the broadcasting establishment. Perhaps that would be no bad thing. I got the impression also that giving C4 its own selling would also find favour with Ministers.

On Thursday evening Denis Forman, Ian Hunter, Tony Smith, Christopher Lucas and I met to discuss my video biography concept, whereby the great and good would be invited to express their beliefs and opinions, to be filmed and kept until after their deaths. At last we have moved the discussion forward, with Denis offering and us accepting that Janet Morgan should put together a business plan so that we can get the project underway.

Sunday 1st November

On Tuesday, lunch at the Garrick with David McLean MP, who said that if he wasn't representing his constituency he would be quite content to have a soft porn channel on television, but he won't be leading on this from the front when Mrs T. is calling for vigorous restraints.

In the evening to the Lords and to a presentation by Robin Duval on 'Taste and Decency'. The Lords' response didn't give me much steer on their views.

On Monday a letter in *The Times* from Mary Whitehouse attacking GT and the Members for *V*. GT's response appeared on Friday. Battle lines are drawn for the showing of *V* on Wednesday next.

Very little appeared in the press following our decision to increase minutage. After all the agonising, it seems no one is the slightest bit interested.

The notion of Public Service is being lost in the general hubbub of new developments. Perhaps it was always just an ideal cherished by the broadcasters. I don't know.

Applications closed last Monday for Jeremy's post as CEO of Channel 4. A disappointing application list. Melvyn Bragg is on record as saying he is not interested. I am having a drink with him this week to find out what he really has to say. I have told Dickie that I would go for David Elstein if he could be winkled out from his share options in Thames. He is probably the best around at present and would bring very considerable flair to the role. There is seemingly a scarcity of talent around.

Spitting Image starts again tonight. I am a little worried it will go well over the top about Princess Di and her quite public rows with Prince Charles. If they behave so childishly, they shouldn't expect kid glove treatment.

Sunday 8th November

On Monday, lunched with Barbara Hosking. She is in good form but thinks she is under-used by Paul Fox, who has her on a three-year retainer at Yorkshire Television. She worries, I think rightly, about Paul's image – that of a fine broadcaster but somehow stuck in the past, giving the impression he is reluctant to face the future. Barbara reminded me of the occasion last year when Paul, as President of the RTS, spoke to mark the 50th year of the BBC. Alasdair had made a very 'wet' speech about trainees in the BBC and Paul followed with a solid defence of the BBC which won applause from his audience.

The Prime Minister, a few days later, called for the text of his speech and apparently threw up her hands in horror, claiming that it confirmed her suspicions that a cosy duopoly between ITV and the BBC was all too alive and well!

In the evening, entertained new Authority Members to dinner at the St George's Hotel before taking them over to see *News At Ten* going out. Donald Maitland was in high spirits and asked a great many questions.

On Tuesday the Annual Luncheon given by Tyne Tees. Guest speaker James Callaghan in good voice, speaking on the responsibility of the media in society.

In the evening, gave a cocktail party at the IBA. Nice mix of guests: Tim Brinton, Harold Fielding, Mary Marr, Sheila Innes, Shaw Taylor, Brian and Elspeth Rix and Heather Brigstock.

I failed to mention in my diary last week that we had an NOP Telephone Survey done on *V*. Two 'dips' into public opinion. One just before transmission, one just after. I am inclined to go for publishing the results, come what may. Letters in *The Times* and *Independent* have continued to appear but generally there was a silence. I sent a batch of letters and replies on *V* from MPs to Quentin Thomas so that he could see the tone of both the MPs and GT's response.

On Wednesday the RTS celebrated its 60th year with a Diamond Jubilee reception at the Banqueting Hall attended by the Queen. Unusually for her, she was several minutes late, due to a hold-up in Pall Mall. This, I was told afterwards, put her in an ill temper. When she was first greeted, by Paul Fox, she said she wanted to get on with the hand-shaking, but then she changed her mind and asked for a whisky and water, which put everyone in a lather because they didn't have water handy! I introduced a number of RTS members to her, and thought she looked tired and rather bored. She brightened up when I introduced her to John Suchet, mentioning that he was the News announcer on Super Channel. 'Why don't I see it?' the

Queen demanded. 'Well, unless you have a dish on the top of Buckingham Palace, you won't get it', replied John Suchet. 'They never tell me about these things', the Queen retorted.

Went home with Roma at around 11pm in time to hear the sad news of Eamonn Andrews' death at the age of 64. A great television performer and much loved by everyone. Quite a shock.

Received the top line research figures on *V*. They showed that 34 per cent of those polled believed that four-letter words were never acceptable. 51 per cent found four-letter words only acceptable when used for a serious purpose, and then only when shown late at night. 8 per cent felt it was permissible where it served a genuine purpose at any time, on any channel. Respondents were asked if *V* should be shown. 69 per cent said yes, 27 per cent said no, 4 per cent didn't know. The 'after' research will be available on Tuesday.

I read the press cuttings carefully to see the comments on *V*, which was shown the night before. There were very few.

After lunch at the IBA, I went over to the Hilton and addressed delegates at the TRIC seminar. The whole thing was a bit of a shambles and didn't inspire much confidence. Michael Checkland spoke, Anthony Simonds-Gooding of BSB went on far too long, Michael Grade was in the Chair. I spoke before the Home Secretary, who once again referred to the ITV Companies 'camping out' in the night hours. Last time, at Cambridge, he referred to them 'taking squatters' rights'. Quite apart from them having an entitlement to use these hours, it is far too early to judge the results. During my speech I again plugged away at the notion of a Standards Council and got the only round of applause for my pains!

On Friday Roma and I went to Birmingham as guests of the RTS, there to celebrate their Diamond Jubilee with a ball. Danced until midnight and went to bed exhausted.

Today have read all the papers and nothing really about *V*. Such reviews as there were, were good. I think GT and I got it wrong.

Forgot to record my meeting with Melvyn Bragg, who I sounded out over the Channel 4 post. He was pretty reluctant to give a view of his interest, but later telephoned me to say that, if asked, he would consider it.

Television shares have been tumbling this week. Several rich TV executives are now only half as rich as they were a month ago.

Sunday 15th November

On Monday, 9 November, I lunched with John Thompson at his home. John, wearing a dishcloth round his waist, greeted me. Some time later I engaged in hand-to-hand combat with deep-frozen prawns. I swear my fingertips went blue in the process. Next a side of cow as steak. We both attacked our slices with the bluntest of knives. At one point, John opened the refrigerator door and released an avalanche of frozen food, cream and other supermarket delights across the floor. 'Forget it happened', John said cheerfully. We talked of this and that. John said he wanted to do something of public service. I suggested the Broadcasting Complaints Commission, a notion that appeared to attract him.

In the evening, attended with Roma 'Faces of the 80s' at the Barbican and met some old 'faces' of the 60s. Caught Lord Montague hovering round his portrait. The idea of the exhibition was Marcia Falkender's, who gave me a big kiss. Jeffrey Archer and David Frost auctioned off 20 portraits, beginning with Denis Thatcher (£400) and ending with Margaret Thatcher (£7,500). Poor old Neil Kinnock (£150), Joan Collins (£200). The PM opened proceedings with a forceful and brilliantly delivered speech, without a note. It's easy to see why she towers over the rest of Westminster. Afterwards, we repaired to Sheekays off St Martin's Lane with Tony Vickers and Pippa. Jeffrey Archer, obviously at a loose end, asked if he could join us. Over dinner he confessed to finding Jacqueline Bisset his ideal woman (a wholly proper confession).

With the stock market still driving downwards, I decided to buy from Waddingtons a sculpture by William Turnbull at a cost of £5,100. I can't afford it, but simply had to have it. Told Roma who, as always, was very understanding.

Wednesday 11th November. A truly motley collection of European broadcasters met at the IBA under the banner 'European Institute of the Media'. The purpose was to examine broadcasting futures. So, all the old ground was turned over again. They suddenly asked me to say something, so I said the first thing that came into my head, that the EBU should look after the 'mechanics' of European broadcasting and that another body, perhaps the Institute, should seek to instil a sense of purpose, standards and quality into the developing scene. I was amused to see that, in their press announcement, this idea seems to have gained substance. The thought turning into a major statement.

In the evening, to the Lords and the Annual Chairman's Dinner in the Cholmondeley Room. A good turnout, the occasion being the last one for Aubrey Buxton to whom GT paid tribute. Earlier in the evening, the question of Channel 4's Chief Executive came up with Dickie, who rang me to report the progress he had made with the sub-committee of the Board. There had been six runners: Brian Wenham, Tony Smith, Alan Yentob, Justin Dukes and two others whose fame is such that I can't, for the life of me, remember their names.

At the same time, RA said there was one other name that had emerged. In strict confidence he said 'Michael Grade' but that was known only to himself and me. I remarked to Dickie that Michael, if he were to get the job, would have to mend his ways and stop preaching a case for creating an independent Channel 4 with separate financing. I also said that the ITV Companies had a right to reject Michael if his name was put forward. At the same time, however, the acquisition of Grade would be an exciting development that would rock the broadcasting world and put the BBC into a flat spin. I repeated, though, my main concern: his appointment would look like a victory for those who espoused change. Dickie and I agreed to say nothing until there had been an opportunity for the sub-committee to meet Grade. This they intended to do on Saturday morning. Dickie said he would telephone me after the meeting. I decided to share this information with GT, who raised similar concerns over Michael's stance. We decided to sleep on it.

At the Authority Meeting on Thursday 12 November we held a closed session and I revealed the six names that were being considered by the Channel 4 sub-committee. No one got excited but agreed to allow the names to go forward.

Dickie telephoned me yesterday (Saturday 14 November) at around 2pm to tell me that the sub-committee had met Michael Grade and unanimously considered him to be head and shoulders above any other claimants to the role. He went on to say that the sub-committee would be meeting the full Board on Monday evening and he wanted to give them the position so that the announcement could be made after the Board Meeting when it met the following day. I said all this was placing a heavy time constraint on us. I wasn't sure I could deliver GT and the Members. I asked RA about Michael's attitude towards the Channel, in relation to IBA and Channel 4's Boards' determination to keep its relationship with ITV, at least until 1992. Dickie assured me that Michael wholly accepted the status quo and that he would do nothing to upset the balance. He explained that his previous stance had been a BBC position, and that his view was different now, especially because the financial climate was changing, for the worse, and the Channel needed the protection and support of ITV. I must say I find his 'conversion' very rapid and not like the Grade I know ... However.

Grade also spoke to the sub-committee with convincing passion about the need to provide truly complementary programmes and schedules to ITV if the Channel was going to succeed. Grade believed he could increase its reach to 10 per cent, or else he wouldn't be worth employing. The meeting lasted two hours. I asked RA whether Paul Fox was as enthusiastic as the others. RA confirmed that he was. On money, RA said 'there was no problem', and that 'he could start tomorrow'. I said I would tell GT and called him in Scotland. He took the news with evident displeasure, clearly worried about Grade's stance and whether Grade had demonstrated sufficient conviction about serious programming. (Dickie had told me earlier that Grade had reminded the sub-committee that his track record while at LWT had shown him to be both courageous and innovative.) I told GT about Paul Fox's reaction and we agreed that GT should get his views at first hand, whilst at the same time concealing the fact that I knew he would be doing this, in case it embarrassed me later with RA.

GT called me back an hour later. He had spoken to Paul, who confirmed everything I had said. He believed, furthermore, that ITV would welcome the appointment. GT was much relieved by all this. We agreed that we would do what was possible to push the decision quickly. RA had said to me that he could meet with us on Monday at 6pm. GT suggested that Michael Grade should come at 6.30pm and that he would alert the sub-committee of the IBA so that they could meet him if at all possible.

I only hope the news doesn't leak out before the Channel 4 Board meeting. Channel 4 will never be quite the same again. I wonder what Jeremy will make of all this.

RA's worry is that the appointment will look as though he is presiding over a down-market Channel 4. I said that the egg on our face would be the press claiming that we had lost the political battle for the sovereignty of Channel 4 and were giving it up to commercial pressures from Government. I fear the IBA will be accused of being philistine. RA also worries that Jeremy will take the news badly as Michael will steal all the headlines and diminish Jeremy's stature, whereas almost any other appointment would have retained Jeremy's standing.

Next week should be quite interesting.

Monday 16th November

I heard this morning from GT that his call round the Members had been satisfactory. All had endorsed the proposal that Michael Grade be the next Chief Executive of Channel 4.

After lunch I went to an ITN Board Meeting where Paul Fox, chairing, winked at me and said I must be having a busy day. Confidentiality was still preserved.

In the car to the office after the Board Meeting, I spoke to Sally on the telephone. She told me RA would be calling me on my private line at 4.30 and there was a problem. Dickie rang to say that he had informed Jeremy of the sub-committee's decision. Jeremy had thrown a fit and said that if Michael was appointed he would resign immediately in protest. Michael Grade, Jeremy said, was a vulgarian, a ratings man with no sense of the Channel's needs or virtues.

This conversation had thrown Dickie into something of a spin. If Jeremy were to resign in protest, others might follow his lead and the Channel face a crisis of confidence. Dickie believed the situation called for a change of plan. Rather like a bad movie, the Members of the Authority attending the meeting went to the sixth floor of the Hyde Park Hotel. All the doors to the suite were locked. No sign of Dickie. Then along came Michael Grade with a hotel receptionist bearing keys and we all trooped into Room 622 like some secret cult about to perform forbidden rights. At this point the Members and Michael were unaware of the latest twist in the drama. Dickie and GT arrived. I took them aside, leaving the Members with Michael. Dickie told GT about Jeremy. We invited the Members in and told them. Dickie went to see Michael and told him a Channel 4 Board Member disapproved, but did not say it was Jeremy.

Dickie returned and we discussed what was best to do. GT advised as a compromise that Dickie first take his sub-committee to one side and gain their support for pressing on with Michael Grade, despite opposition from Jeremy, and then take it to the Board. This was agreed. Michael joined us, and had guessed the opposing Board Member was Jeremy. It did not surprise him, neither did it unduly worry him.

We broke up at 6.30. I cancelled the BREMA dinner I was due to attend, and Dickie said he would call me the moment the Board meeting was over.

I went home. Dickie called at 9.40pm. The Board was unanimous that Michael Grade be appointed. Jeremy had had his say. Despite his eloquence, no Board Member supported his point of view. We hope to persuade Jeremy to stay on and speak well of the appointment, although Dickie wasn't too hopeful.

Dickie confirmed to me that the press conference and announcement would go ahead as planned at 11am tomorrow.

Sunday 22nd November

Sat down to breakfast with the morning newspapers on Tuesday to read all about the appointment. *Financial Times* – BBC's Grade 'expected to head Channel 4'. *Times* – 'Grade chosen to head Channel 4'. *Guardian* – 'Channel 4 moves fast to snap up Grade'. *Daily Mail* – 'Angry Grade moves to Channel 4'. *Today* – 'Grade quits BBC to join Channel 4'. I imagine either Michael went ahead after leaving us at the Hyde Park Hotel and told the press or after Michael had spoken to Michael Checkland, the BBC publicity machine rolled into action to administer a slap to Michael's ego.

The press conference took place at 11am. Grade did a good job. He made clear that he would not be changing or attempting to change the role or remit of Channel 4. The press took it with cynical admiration. He sounded convincing. Time will tell. I think, having given his word to us, he will stand by it.

At lunch on Tuesday, I attended the House of Lords where the Cholmondeley Room had been booked by Bob Lorimer to entertain Labour MPs and Peers. Arthur Bottomley was amongst the guests, looking full of beans at 80. I find it quite moving to meet figures of the 40s, 50s and 60s. They still – most of them – retain the liveliness and spark that ignited them when they started out on their careers.

Interesting to note that throughout the week past no journalist or observer has mentioned the IBA, or the relationship of the IBA to Channel 4. If I were to be twisted or bitter, I would suggest this might be because journalists didn't feel like giving any credit to the old IBA.

On Wednesday attended a Conservative lunch at Lockets, hosted by Sarah Thane. The subject of televising Parliament came up. Opinions were divided, the strongest dislike coming from a long-serving MP who told me quite simply that he would be unable to speak his mind if television came to the Commons. 'It would have to be the views my constituents want to hear, not what I might wish to say!'

Fears that 'loonies' will fill the screen and give Parliament a bad name are argued with such intensity that those who believe it can't have realised what utter idiots they already make of themselves without the help of television!

On Thursday 19 November the *Financial Times* had an accurate account by Ray Snoddy of the Channel 4 Board meeting on Monday afternoon. Despite Jeremy's confirmation to RA that he would keep his views on Michael Grade to himself, Jeremy showed a waspish, self-centred, prima donna attitude to the appointment. MG's record as a television populist ran, he said, counter to the values of C4. 'I also opposed it because of the possibility that he might lead the Channel in the wrong direction.' The article contained this gem: 'I will bloody hold him to his undertakings'. Jeremy never did recognise that C4, whilst being his baby, was also the life of many others, who had supported him through thick and thin. Now he was making out that everyone else was wrong and that only he knew the right direction for the Channel.

In the evening, Roma and I went to the RTS Diamond Jubilee Ball at Grosvenor House, an occasion brimming with gossip and some wry humour. Terry Wogan produced a pair of red braces and asked whether they belonged to anyone. He had found them, he said, at the BBC!

The Beverley Sisters (yes, they are still around) performed the cabaret. The Duke and Duchess of Kent appeared to enjoy themselves. Lord Thomson presided. Paul Fox had something wrong with his eyes.

On Friday, George and I met briefly in the morning. Both he and I feel that Jeremy's outburst to the FT was inexcusable and that he must go now rather than see his contract out to April. George spoke to George Russell, in Dickie's absence. George Russell said he would speak to RA, who was in Zimbabwe.

After lunch I spoke to Senior Staff at Crawley Court re our dispute with BETA. It was very sad but I didn't see any solution in the near term. The climate was wrong for lifting salary rates. Ours was a fair deal. There was no other course we could, or should, have taken.

Tomorrow, TV-am could be in dispute with the ACTT over manning levels on a 'Caring Christmas' theme they will be running. Timothy came to see me and told me that the Board would fight the union to the bitter end. Tyne Tees has a dispute with the electricians over who should recharge batteries belonging to ENG crews and Thames have said they will put *The Bill* out to Independents if they cannot reach an agreement with their unions over manning. So, all in all, it looks like being the lead-up to a very happy Christmas!

I must end this entry with a quote from a speech given by John Jackson to the Marketing Club on Wednesday 18 November. (John was an unsuccessful bidder for the DBS franchise.) He is a close friend of Maxwell and speaks with the voice of authority about the Authority! 'I am suggesting we say farewell to the IBA. Whilst spectrum scarcity justifies its role as broadcaster, the IBA did a good job for the public, who have, of course, paid for it and it deserves to be thanked warmly. Personally, I believe it was at its best and most necessary while it was the ITA. However, the need for the IBA is fading and I fear the IBA's image is fading with it. This is not the IBA's fault. It is simply a question of a once useful institution being overtaken by old age in a changing world. It is time the IBA was given to its own cordon bleu cooks for embalming and restoration to former glories by being stuffed, painted and put in a glass case for all of us to look on from time to time with fond and affectionate memory.'

So there!

A final footnote: Dickie telephoned this evening, having just returned from his travels, very upset at Jeremy's outburst. Will tell him that he should leave the Board on 21 December, and not attend the weekend that has been planned. Dickie says that if Jeremy continues to act like a fool in America, he will fire him.

Friday 27th November

This morning (Friday) I stayed in bed, having caught the heaviest cold I can ever remember – nose streaming, eyes watering, a real wreck! Am reading Kathleen Tynan's biography of Ken, who I vividly remember when I was 18 or so and frequented 'Jerry's Club' off the Haymarket. Ken would sit silently for hours at the far end of the little bar, smoking endless cigarettes and looking remote and incredibly bored. He may have just been lonely, but that never crossed my mind.

Last night, sadly had to give up going to *Cry Freedom*, Dickie's film on the short life of Steve Biko, which has received rave notices. What a clever man he is, able to turn his mind and give rapt attention to the subjects demanded of him. I read in the papers tonight that not one single Tory Minister turned out to the premiere. The film is certain in its message of hostility towards apartheid and the intolerance of the South African government.

Quentin Thomas telephoned from the Home Office (we had arranged to meet but my cold intervened). He conveyed the news politely and candidly as is his style that Ministers had decided radio should become the responsibility of a new Radio Authority. He asked that I keep it confidential to GT and me. He said that the Home Secretary had greatly respected the way that the IBA had regulated radio etc., etc., etc. The Home Secretary, he said, was sure that we would carry on our work with the same enthusiasm and assist with a smooth handover. I said that we would do our best. Quentin wouldn't commit himself to a date when the announcement would be made, but he said we would get the normal courtesy warning. Sad, really. I had, I must confess, secretly thought that we would hold on to radio, but there is hostility to the IBA within the Cabinet. Douglas doesn't share the same convictions as his predecessor, or Willie Whitelaw. The cruel fact is that the Act made us perform as we did. Another Act and we would have performed differently. Must keep a stiff upper lip in public and wish the venture well. Defeat takes courage, unlike victory, which is merely coasting downhill.

A rider to Dickie's *Cry Freedom*. The South African government has given permission for the film to be shown to mixed cinema audiences in its uncut version. The SA government are learning fast that banning things leads to much greater publicity than permitting them, *Spycatcher* being the classic example.

This last week has been increasingly dominated by growing disputes in ITV. TV-am's ACTT members have been locked out for the whole week, Bruce buying in new security staff to make sure. Tyne Tees has sacked 35 of their workforce for refusing to work under Management directions. Thames TV are proposing to use Independents to make *The Bill*. STV are 're-shaping' their crewing. Alongside all these is the IBA dispute, now in its fourth or fifth week. Staff members of BETA are considering stepping up their action with selected stoppages. If this action is declared, we must decide whether to meet the threat head on and sack staff who refuse instructions. One of the most stupid errors in IBA staffing policy has been in allowing Station Managers to be members of a union, thus having split loyalties to Management and the Union. An extraordinary practice which must be stopped.

On Monday 23 November Roma and I sat through three and a half hours of the *Royal Variety Performance* at the London Palladium. George Thomson, Brian Tesler and I did our handshaking routine as the Queen came in. The Queen, these days, strikes me more and more as either being very tired or very bored. In the interval, she was squashed against a wall in a tiny retiring room filled with people she had no wish to meet, and thick with cigarette smoke. Waiters bearing trays had to hold them above their heads, such was the crush. Since the food was on the trays, and unreachable, there was nothing to keep the tummy from rumbling. The show itself was like a saloon bar frolic – where are the real stars? Has television shrunk them into obscurity? Most of the performers appeared to be mimicking other performers. The only real star was Shirley Bassey, who shimmered in a dazzling dress and had the audience spellbound. Tom Jones, on the other hand, rolled his eyes, sweated profusely and died a lingering death under the bright lights. The show ran an hour longer than scheduled. The Queen's face very clearly registered her disapproval. I don't blame her.

Tuesday 24 November – meeting with Anthony Simonds-Gooding to go over BSB problems. There is clearly going to be difficulties over the 'Now' Channel. ITN's quote for the service is still higher than BSB want to pay. ITN first quoted £20m. Came down to £15m per annum. BSB want the news input to cost not more than £10m. But behind this lies their concern with ITN. Anthony is worried about the relationship ITN has with its paymasters, ITV. How, he enquires, will they like ITN being asked to compete with them on news services? Will ITN be able to present a competing news service at the same time as *News At Ten*. Have they got the adrenalin to seek out new ways of developing news stories? Are they stuck in the past? Anthony wants the Channel to be put out to tender so that other news services can compete. I can see the doubts he has. ITN seems always to act in a magisterial manner. They somehow reflect more the 70s in style than the 80s. Certainly they do not appear to be looking forward to the 90s. My guess is that the contract will be taken elsewhere.

On Wednesday 25 November, I developed a humdinger of a cold and sat through the GAC Meeting feeling like death. The GAC briefly discussed V and applauded its showing. They seemed unhappy with their role. I think they resent Douglas Hurd's proposals to establish a Broadcasting Standards Council'.

Thursday 26th November – Authority day, still with howling, snorting cold. Donald Maitland is really too much. Argumentative, aggressive and ill-informed. I despair that he might one day sit in GT's seat. (Which reminds me – I spoke to Quentin Thomas at the Royal Variety show and suggested that, if they were determined to have a Broadcasting Standards Council, a good candidate for Chairman would be Bryan Forbes.)

I would leave if Donald became Chairman at the IBA.

Sunday 6th December

On Monday 30 November, had a jolly dinner with the Frosts. Roma and I thought we were just to be four. I was still feeling very full of cold and sniffles and earlier in the day had thought to call off the evening. We would have missed quite an evening!

The other guests arrived after us – King Constantine of Greece and his wife, Prince Andrew and Sarah, Elton John and his wife, David and Deborah Owen. Fergie spent some little while on a discussion about bottoms, likening hers to Anika Rice's, but Anika had a 'pert' bottom. Fergie gave David Frost a card game –

'Who's Had Who?'. He played it, trying to guess who had said what to whom. Renata John was a pretty girl, wearing what looked like several hundred thousand pounds worth of baubles. I found the whole evening somewhat disconcerting. Perhaps I wasn't on form, but the conversations were so superficial I simply couldn't connect. Anyway, it ended quite late. Prince Andrew had to drive down to Dorset, leaving his wife to do I know not what.

The TV-am dispute still continues with the company gaining many plaudits from the 'beat em, bash em' brigade in the press, and the audience growing by another 200,000 during the week as a result of Batman and his adventures. So much for the 'mission to explain' which went some way to winning them the contract.

Tomorrow, TV-am are going to run a live service, using management labour. It will be very interesting to see how they cope.

Our dispute with BETA staff appears to have been settled with a joint announcement in which the Unions called off their overtime ban and we agreed to renew our discussions on future relationships. All very bland, but I think quite sensible. We have gained a modest victory, not big enough to cause BETA loss of face but big enough to demonstrate we mean business.

On Tuesday 1st December I handed out prizes on behalf of the RTS at their Education Awards Presentation, held at the IBA. Very impressed by the standard of production. The awards are in memory of Enid Love, who was the first Head of Schools when she joined Redifusion. It was a good 'do' and I enjoyed myself.

On Thursday 3rd December to Geneva and the EBU's Council meeting at which Members decided to move the Technical Division from Brussels to Geneva.

Returned home to read the press criticising the Government for trying, and succeeding, to gag the BBC from broadcasting on Radio 3 *My Country Right or Wrong*. This will run and run. Michael Checkland told me that it couldn't have come at a better time. The BBC were looking for something to demonstrate to Government and the media that they had teeth, and this story falls right into their lap. A winner because emotionally the story must bring the media on to the side of the BBC.

This week the IBA issued a press release stating that it had decided that it would not permit the showing of a programme on the Salvation Army on the grounds that it was propaganda. I hardly understand the press, who wrote almost nothing about the decision. I thought it would bring about howls of protest.

Christmas is advancing with an avalanche of trivia but so far no drunken driving reported. The outside of Harrods takes on the appearance of a football scrum with very nearly more money being pinched from handbags than spent inside.

Sunday 13th December

On Monday 7th December, I lunched at the Garrick with Dick Francis who was very unhappy about the way Government is looking at funding the British Council. We talked about trying to get more notice taken of television as part of the excellence of this country's talent that should be seen abroad. He agreed to try to get ITV involved in nominating a programme a month for showing in Athens at the British Council offices. The British Council would pay for two people from each production to go to Greece and present the programme. I will put it to SCC.

Later, with Roma, to the Radio Advertising Awards dinner at Grosvenor House. Much more upbeat than in previous years, largely due to radio enjoying a minor boom. If only it had come two years or so earlier, the cry to 'unshackle' radio from the IBA would have been less strident.

Still no announcement about the new Radio Authority, although this week's *Campaign* ran the headline: 'IBA could lose administration of ILR'. I imagine Douglas might announce the change next week, tucked in just before Christmas.

On Tuesday 8th December, PCC and SCC. Spent some time trying to assure the Companies that the IBA wasn't hell-bent on offering a night time contract to someone else. Discussed the new deal set up by Murdoch and the BBC and some EBU members to operate a sports channel. ITV has missed the boat, and knows it. I am for them joining, and at the same time combining with Sky to merge Super Channel.

A pleasant dinner with Lady Harlech at her home. John Sainsbury was another guest. He seems well pleased with Jeremy but I foresee clashes. John Sainsbury is as dogmatic as Jeremy. Pamela Harlech believes that Jeremy's girlfriend will call the shots.

Breakfasted at the Savoy on Wednesday 9th December for the *Sunday Times* Breakfast Forum – 'Materialistic Britain. Does everything now have its price?' John Mortimer was the opener and delivered a searing attack against the Thatcher Britain of the 80s. The Bishop of Durham was in sparkling form and full of condemnation of present values. On the other side, James Gulliver and Brian Griffiths were both predictable. Jamie Gulliver looked and sounded as if he had only woken up that morning to the realisation that he would be called upon to speak.

Thursday 10th December – Headlines in the press about the Independents deciding to call off their meeting with ITVA on the 22nd, having concluded that they could not conduct negotiations any further and that the ITV Companies simply didn't want to do business.

I got the office to call a meeting between David Shaw and Michael Darlow to see if things could be got back on the rails. They agreed to come to breakfast on Friday.

This week's Authority Meeting debated at some length the situation between BSB and ITN. (I should have mentioned that the day before David Nicholas came to see me to express his unease over the way BSB were planning to announce their proposed tender for the news input to the Now Channel.)

The Members took a stronger line than I had anticipated. They wished firstly to be satisfied that there was a real difference of money between BSB and ITN – the gap is only some £4m per annum – and secondly to be satisfied that the tender document is describing an output they would endorse. A third point – and possibly the most vexing – is the question of editorial control. BSB want this, but Members seem determined to stick to the draft Head of Agreement between BSB and ITN drawn up and presented to the IBA when the contract was applied for. This could be a tricky one.

The Members' views were not appreciated by Anthony Simonds-Gooding when I relayed them to him after the meeting. Another breakfast meeting with David Shaw and Michael Darlow has been arranged for next week.

I foresee explosions and rumpus ahead with BSB. They are a different kind of animal to their brothers in ITV.

The Authority meeting over, a jolly Christmas lunch. Sally Munton, my PA, is leaving to work for Paul Getty. At the lunch she was toasted and responded with kind words about her time with the IBA. I shall miss her.

On Friday 11th December breakfasted at the IBA. Eggs, bacon, sausages, tomatoes and mushrooms – the only way I can be tempted to attend a meeting at the hour of 7.30am. A difficult meeting with David Shaw and Michael Darlow; neither of them willing to build any bridges. I said that the IBA would set the Agenda for the 22nd. If they liked it, would the Independents attend? Darlow said yes.

After he had gone, David Shaw remained and we talked about what might remove the deadlock. Out of the conversation came a resolution that I said I would support: that the Companies should each publish the minimum production fees they would agree to, as well as publishing details on their overseas rights. I think that, if this is done, the Independents should agree to do business. They have been hoping for a national agreement. I don't think this is reasonable. If they refuse to do business on an individual company basis, I think we should declare our hand and say that we consider the Independents are acting in a way calculated to cause a breakdown in talks. Now I hope that David Shaw can get the Companies to agree. We shall see.

TV-am continues with programmes put on by Management. Bruce is becoming a public hero with Batman. Mrs T, it is said, has sent him a Christmas card with the words 'keep up the good work'. Nothing like nailing your colours to the mast!

Sunday 20th December

My birthday! Now I am 57. I still feel as though I am 27, but one look in the mirror tells me I am wrong.

Meeting on Monday 14th December with Ian Trethowan and Richard Dunn with Lord Thomson and me. Trethowan and Dunn want to set about restructuring Thames before the next contract round. Their plan would be to get the two major shareholders – BET and Rank – to sell down to 10 per cent each and then offer the 27.5 per cent to the public by way of a market issue. Or invite four new participants to join in. GT and I said that we believed this was sensible and I will write next week confirming our view.

In the evening, to the carol service of the Publicity Club of London at St Bride's where I delivered the address. Without fear of being considered bigheaded, I can justifiably declare it was a good address and was extremely well received. It was written by John Harriott, our Television Chief Assistant on Policy, and spoke directly to the gathering about the need for the media to show and practice humility and understanding.

On Wednesday 16th December, I breakfasted with BSB and ITN at Brompton Road. There is a very obvious gulf between them. I identified the gulf with three 'Cs' – control, content and cost. Try as they might, I believe that ITN is not a favoured partner and that, no matter what can be patched up on the surface to meet the identified differences, there is an underlying belief on BSB's part that ITN has one foot in the past and is tied in such a way to its ITV owners that it cannot operate in a really competitive manner on behalf of BSB. BSB want to put the contract out to tender and, unless ITN show more fire in their belly, we will be hard pressed not to say no.

There is an ITN Board meeting tomorrow (Monday) when ITN will consider its next move. My guess is that ITN may well withdraw their offer to cooperate and take a chance on BSB finding no other suitable partner and thus being obliged to return to ITN.

On the other hand, ITN might come across with a deal that satisfies the budgetary considerations. If this happens, the IBA will be forced to act to force the marriage. This could be the worst of all possible worlds.

Thursday 17th December, Jeffrey Archer's party – shepherds pie and champagne.

Throughout the week I have been working to see how best to resolve the impasse that exists between the Independents and the ITV Companies. The block is over two issues: production fees and royalties on sales. The BBC this week closed their deal with the Independents and fudged the two issues by agreeing to a wide range of payments. The ITV Companies have dug their heels in and are refusing to talk about a national agreement, but at the same time they won't agree to publish their scale of payments on a regional basis. I have said to them that I think this is the solution. Part of the trouble is the anger the Companies feel over the way that the Independents have behaved. The Independents are equally angry at the way the ITV Companies have appeared to drag their feet over reaching a settlement. Both sides have agreed to come to the IBA on Tuesday and put their case separately. These are going to be difficult meetings unless the ITV Companies are prepared to publish details of their terms of trade. I believe that the Government will force them into arrangements much less desirable than they could negotiate. If they were sensible and got off their high horse, they could come to a reasonable deal that would settle matters. I feel inclined to read the riot act on Tuesday.

Part of the problem is that the Companies are fooling themselves by believing that doing deals with the Independents, as they are now doing, will somehow get Government and the Independents off their backs. I simply don't believe this to be the case. The ITV Companies still operate in a monopoly position and so the deals they strike are ones that give them the whip hand. They will either do business with Independents they know, or the ones that are weak and cannot negotiate with strength. Either way, Government will say (rightly, in my view) that real access has not been acknowledged.

Next Tuesday will be critical for them, and for the IBA who will be seen as ineffective if no solution can been found.

The fifth and sixth Channels have come back into the limelight this week. The report, when it is published, will back the emergence of further competition. The more new developments press in on the existing contractors the more I can visualise a next contract round in 1992 in which Government would be saying what we have done in radio we will now do in television and asking why have two services of Public Service Broadcasting when one – the BBC – will suffice. Difficult to argue.

1988

Sunday 3rd January

Christmas and the New Year have passed in the usual euphoria, hype, speculation and criticism. I feel totally submerged in other people's opinions, the state of television being one of the most discussed.

No New Year Honours for ITV or the BBC, with the honourable exception of a CBE to David McCall – well deserved for his role as Chairman of ITCA and his stewardship of Anglia TV. I had hoped that Jeremy Isaacs would get a CBE or a 'K', but this was not forthcoming.

No television crises over the holiday. The tabloids could find nothing to wring their hands over.

What are my disappointments of 1987?

- Giving a frightful performance at the Prime Minister's Seminar
- Losing radio to another Authority
- Failing to bring to a conclusion a sensible deal between ITV and the Independents
- Funking V (not only totally misreading the IBA Members but also the great British public)
- The Government's determination to set up a Broadcasting Standards Council, which I see as a calculated slap in the face for both Governors of the BBC and Members of the IBA
- Uncertainty about the expertise and judgment of Colette Bowe, although it is probably too early to tell

What to hope for in 1988?

- A sensible agreement between the Independents and ITV
- A White Paper on television that maintains the values of television and doesn't sell ITV to the commercial bovver boys
- A new Chairman who believes in ITV and can stand up and be counted in the ever-toughening environment

I start the New Year with a new P.A., Caroline, and say goodbye to Sally, who has steadied my hand since my first days with the IBA.

Tonight the BBC demonstrates its new approach to 'accountability' with Duke Hussey and Michael Checkland answering viewers' questions live. Should be interesting. My predictions for the BBC are that it is going to go through another tough period, with John Birt becoming seen increasingly as a despot and Michael Checkland as a shallow broadcaster and with staff growing more restless and bitter.

I enter 1988 with fairly black thoughts, and doubts about Government's intentions for ITV. I think they believe the Public Service ideal can be upheld by the BBC alone and will set about freeing up ITV to bring greatest opportunity for competition with other operators.

A Happy New Year!

Sunday 10th January

Last Monday's papers reported extensively on a story that Michael Checkland had apologised to Bill Cotton for announcing the BBC's adoption of John Birt's recommendations for a 10.30 fixed start to *Newsnight* without prior reference to him. Michael Checkland issued the BBC's apology: 'I deeply regret that Bill Cotton, who has been my colleague and friend for many years, was upset by the manner of the announcement regarding the fixed time scheduling of *Newsnight*'.

The BBC looks as though its time in the sun is going to be short lived. 'The Duke and Mike Show', as it has been dubbed, has found few supporters in the press this weekend. It's odd, but telling, how reputations can be lost over one foolish sentence. Duke Hussey did himself no good by asking one of his callers on the telephone how things were 'down in Bristol. Haven't been able to get to my house down there to look at the lawn', or words to that effect. Your average Joe Soap doesn't like people with two homes, let alone a lawn to look at!

John Birt continues to draw the fire of media journalists. 'They have found a sitting target in John – remote, resolute, odd'. Just how long the BBC Governors, or Duke Hussey, will watch as the savaging goes on will be interesting to see. If John were to quit, or be pushed, a mighty yawning gap would open up within the Corporation. Michael Checkland would be faced with internal convulsions of major proportions. This is the problem that will not go away: a non-creative broadcaster at the head is in a fragile position to control the troops.

On Thursday night I entertained Jeremy Isaacs to a 'valedictory' dinner at the Garrick with David Glencross, Shirley, Peter Rogers and Clare Mulholland. During the dinner we touched upon the BBC's troubles. Jeremy believes that the set-up will fall to pieces under Birt's leadership: 'He doesn't inspire confidence. He loves graphs and charts but can't handle people'.

The BBC will need all the talents of Howell James if it's going to re-balance itself in the public arena to show the qualities one looks to the BBC to provide.

During dinner, Jeremy said he would have to do something about the way his new boss at the Opera House, John Sainsbury, got in the middle of every decision. Having met John recently I can see Jeremy has met his match. Here is an able tycoon with vast business experience and time on his hands. Jeremy will not dominate John Sainsbury and Jeremy does not like being dominated. It would not surprise me if Jeremy never reaches his desk at Covent Garden but seeks new pastures.

Jeremy said, with raised glass, how much he owed the IBA for its support. I wish he would just say it in public.

The TV-am dispute continues with Bruce Gyngell – Batman – the victor of both situation and ratings. There are stories in the press almost daily of the valiant freedom-fighter bouncing on his trampoline in his office and encouraging his 17 staff on to greater acts of heroism.

I have a feeling that Bruce may fall from grace with the media as rapidly as he has risen. His demands are such that the ACTT would be destroyed in ITV if they complied. The demands are so tightly drawn that Bruce has left himself no room for manoeuvre or for the Unions to save face. It is an unsatisfactory state of affairs and will, I fear, get worse.

This week Michael Grade started work at C4 by doing the right thing: meeting everyone and listening. A sure-fire recipe for good first day public relations.

On Thursday the Members endorsed my recommendation to allow me to get tough with the ITV Companies over the Independents and, if they refuse to agree a scale of production fees and residual payments, to write these in to the next extension contracts and secondly to permit me to decide when the time is ripe to allow BSB to put out a tender for the 'Now' news service. (I was pleased, incidentally, to read in the press that ITN were themselves getting tough with their own staff in order to bring down the cost of supplying the service. Amazing what the threat of real competition does to change attitudes.)

I saw David McCall on Friday, who told me he would put a proposal to ITCA on Monday that the Companies should agree to an IBA-set scale if this was also agreed by the Independents. It is an elegant solution and one I hope will be endorsed at next week's Council meeting.

BSB and ITN met on Thursday to see if they can forge a deal. My belief is that they will fail, and the IBA will move to allow BSB to go to public tender. Time will tell.

On Tuesday GT and I have been asked to go and see the Home Secretary about radio. I will endeavour to put on a brave face but will be weeping behind the mask.

Sunday 16th January

Returning home from a traumatic and tiring visit to Belfast. I had originally been lured over by IBA Officer for Northern Ireland, Tony Fleck, to mark the 250th meeting of the Northern Ireland Advisory Committee. It was only on the plane out I discovered it was the 260th meeting. I feel slightly cheated.

I have sadly come to the conclusion that all Regional Officers have one thing in common: they are extremely bad drivers. Whether it is because they have other things on their minds or that they feel all traffic should give way to them, I do not know, but finding oneself changing lanes while other drivers hoot with indignation or slowing to a funereal pace to be shown local landmarks whilst traffic piles up behind us is not conducive to peace of mind.

Through a considerable determination to make my stay enjoyable, ROs tend to look at what they consider to be accommodation appropriate for a DG. I like staying in a modern hotel. ROs have different views and I find myself too often booked into hotels of 'character'. I have learnt to my cost that character and comfort do not go hand in hand.

On Friday morning I visited our engineering base at Black Mountain, where I met the Area Engineer, Gordon Verity, a taciturn Yorkshireman, and his staff. Every time I visit a transmitter site I wonder at the number of staff employed to maintain transmitters. Technology has moved on, less maintenance is required, replacement of faulty equipment is easier. I am afraid that an efficiency expert, looking at staffing levels in this section of engineering, would find much to criticise.

After tea and a chat, on to Downtown Radio. A lovely, well run station making a tidy profit and attracting a healthy audience. I wonder how they will prosper in the new age of licensed radio.

While showing me Ulster Folk Park Centre, Tony Fleck received a call alerting him to the fact that the BBC Northern Ireland Governor, Dr Kirkand, had been in touch with our IBA Northern Ireland Member, Sean Fulton, to say the BBC were not going to show the Northern Ireland Office's commercial for a confidential telephone facility which would enable citizens to call the Security forces directly alerting them to terrorist activities.

We watched the commercial that night. Sean did not believe it to be even-handed. Tony Fleck stoutly defended his position that each picture and each sentence of dialogue applies equally to Loyalist and IRA. The Committee where shown it and, had there been a vote, it would have backed Sean's view. Adding to the problem was the Ulster Office's intention to call a press briefing on Monday at 11.15am when the commercial was to be unveiled. To pull at this juncture would be a grave embarrassment to the Office and to the IBA.

At dinner following the Advisory meeting, I sat next to Sir John Hermon, the Chief Constable of the RUC, a bluff, forthright man who has survived for nine years at the centre of so much hatred, bitterness and violence. A brave man, whose temperament seems right for the job he does.

After dinner, I spoke to Andy Wood, the Director of Government Information Services. He was appalled that I had worries over the commercial. I talked to Sean privately, who said that changes should be made but if these were not possible in the time available, then we should bite the bullet. There is no time, so the commercial is going ahead, but changes will be insisted upon if viewers perceive a partiality. At Andy's suggestion, I will inform Defence Minister Tom King.

Events earlier in the week. A dinner on Monday at the Savoy to celebrate ten years of the *South Bank Show*. A splendid gathering to heap praise on Melvyn Bragg. Praise well deserved. I sat next to Edna O'Brien and spent much of the dinner trying to think of a title for her next novel. Opposite me was the Habitat man, Sir Terence Conran, greatly upset by Government's sudden announcement that evening that all highly inflammable upholstery is to be banned. Apparently most furniture is stuffed with the stuff.

Tuesday, an early morning meeting with John Wakeham in the Privy Council office, 68 Whitehall. The subject the Masham Report on alcohol misuse. I gained the impression that Government does not wish major changes in current legislation. The drink lobby is powerful!

In the afternoon, SCC and the major test to see if I could persuade the ITV Companies to accept scales for both production fees and residual fees. We argued for some 40 minutes. In the end, I said we would set out indicative figures on both issues.

In the evening, I met Sophie Balhetchet. She said the initiative was helpful and she hoped the Independents' committee, due to meet on the 25th, would accept the role the IBA was prepared to take on.

On Wednesday I received a copy of a letter ITN had sent to BSB. They have reduced their quote to £10.9m. A meeting between both parties was to be held on Thursday. I will hear the outcome tomorrow at the ITN Board meeting.

Saturday 23rd January

A week in which important decisions on radio were taken. On Tuesday GT, Peter Baldwin and I went as arranged to the Home Office at 10 a.m. to see Douglas Hurd. We bumped into the Chairman of the Cable Authority on his way out – grinning broadly.

We sat down facing Douglas and, like a schoolmaster at the end of term, he informed us in a detached, impersonal manner of the announcement he would be making later. He confirmed what we knew already. The task of looking after the expansion of radio would go to a new Authority.

The IBA had done a good job, but on balance, after careful consideration etc. etc. Not much to show for a 15 year slog to bring about the creation of 50 or so stations. Twenty minutes later I found myself catapulted from the room by the slingshot handshake of the Home Secretary, who has Mrs T's infuriating habit of shaking hands and pushing your hand away to the left at the same time, as if he is too busy and important to waste time. The Queen doesn't do this.

I took Peter to Mr Chow's for lunch, partly to cheer him up and partly to remain out of sight until I spoke to his staff at 3pm. I would have chosen to speak to them immediately but was afraid of a leak before the lifting of the press embargo at 3.30pm. The staff in Radio Division listened sadly, and I became rather too emotional, which I hadn't expected. I felt very sorry for them, for me and for the IBA.

Afterwards I did several interviews – for ITV, the BBC, Capital and LBC, as well as the *PM* programme. I put on as good a face as possible but felt sick as a parrot inside.

On Wednesday afternoon, I received an urgent call from BSB for a meeting. We arranged it for 5.30pm. Bob Hunter, BSB's new Channel Editor and Anthony Simonds-Gooding came over. They said whilst some progress had been made on resolving their differences with ITN, they believed the time had come to put the offer to tender. I disagreed. Talks were going in the right direction and I saw insufficient reason to take matters outside. Bob Hunter, I believe, is determined to break the understanding. He quite obviously sees himself in a strong enough position to call the shots if he appoints someone other than ITN. Anthony, on the other hand, I suspect wants to see an honourable and effective consummation of the arrangements.

The following day Anthony wrote to say he would not be putting it to tender but would 'hothouse' the negotiations – his phrase, not mine – until they were either concluded or terminated. Unfortunately, BSB appear to do their negotiating by press release or leak because the following day saw a lot of press reports that BSB had given ITN until 1st February to conclude the deal. ITN have signalled their disapproval by issuing their own press statement.

During the day I had more time to think about radio. I was pleased to see the *Daily Mail* picked up a reference I had made to 'junk radio'. There was, too, considerable criticism of the concept of three national channels, each offering a mixture of programme output. Everyone, with the exception of the Home Secretary, had believed that the sensible outcome would be for each national channel to specialise in a streamed output. To have three channels competing with each other for a similar audience would be both wasteful and misguided. In addition, a cap of 18 months (at least) before the appointment of an Authority is likely to result in chaos. I have written an article for *The Listener* that underlines the point.

In the main, the media appear to have accepted the change of control as being a fait accompli. Our position currently is to argue the case, pointing out our skills and resources and the fact that if we had the job, we could get on with it.

On Thursday, the Authority meeting. I was able to tell Members that the ITV Companies had accepted our role as middle men in the matter of setting indicative figures for Independents' production fees and distribution. During the meeting I received a note that the Independents had agreed to this.

The Members endorsed our intention of making a case for radio to remain with the IBA. It is most unlikely to happen, but there could be a miracle.

During the meeting Sean Fulton repeated his concern that the commercial in Northern Ireland was unbalanced against the Catholic minority. I had spoken to Tom King's assistant on Monday and said that if there was considerable public disquiet the IBA would look again at the commercial. In fact Ulster Television received only two complaints, as did the IBA's office in Belfast. However, on Tuesday Sean telephoned to say *The Observer* was likely to print an article about the BBC's refusal to accept the commercial on the grounds it was unbalanced. I hope they don't.

Sunday 24th January

The Sundays generally were scathing about Douglas Hurd's decision to take radio away from the IBA. Most believed more work needed to be done on framework before any real judgment could be taken, although one 'heavy' seems inclined to argue that by the time the new Authority had put on the mantle ordered by the

Home Secretary it would very nearly have the same trappings as the IBA role hitherto.

The Observer today published their piece about the BBC's decision not to transmit the Northern Ireland commercial. Fortunately, the writer emphasised that the decision was because the BBC did not want to be involved in playing 'commercials' and less on the matter of imbalance. I telephoned Sean Fulton and he agreed that the piece was actually quite positive. I think he was fairly relieved.

Sunday 31st January

A week where for the first time for a very long time I spent every evening at home with Roma. A welcome change from my usual nightlife!

On Monday, the *Guardian* published an open letter by George Thomson to Douglas Hurd: a very good piece summing up absolutely the feelings, frustrations and hopes of the IBA. It might just sound some alarm bells in some quarters.

Lunch on Monday at Scotland Yard with John Stubbs (Deputy Director of Public Affairs), Robin Goodfellow (Director of Public Affairs) and Malcolm Johns (Head of News). They are still worried about the 'yob element' in the Force. Reading between the lines, they seem happy with their new Commissioner although they think he sometimes shoots from the hip.

In the afternoon a meeting with Timothy Aitken. A complicated share structuring in Beaverbrook Investments has, or is about to, cause embarrassment and complications and must be defused. He spoke about the strike at TV-am, still continuing. Revenue in January fell, as did audiences. Timothy thinks Bruce is trying too hard to make ACTT change its ways. He has issued an ultimatum that if the union doesn't give way by tomorrow, they – some 270 staff – risk the sack.

I don't think he's going to win this dispute on his terms. The ACTT has too much to lose throughout the system as a whole. Another worry for TV-am, and the rest of ITV, is the position of the NUJ, currently moderate and still working. Whether they would show solidarity in the event of a mass sacking of ACTT staff and move to action is an open question. The dilemma for the IBA is what stance to adopt if the dispute continues with no end in sight. TV-am are not able to produce their contractual output of national news. It's an example of heads you lose, tails you lose. If we step in, we will be accused of taking the side of the union. If we do nothing, we will stand accused of failing to exercise our proper responsibilities.

The papers this week have been full of speculation about the televising of Parliament. I have absolutely no doubt whatsoever that the vote this week will be against. The reason? The rejection of television in the Commons by Mrs T. The Tory sheep will go bleating through the 'No' lobby. It is absurd that, when greater transparency is demanded of the broadcasters, the same should not be expected of Parliamentarians.

The talks between BSB and ITN grow daily more public. BSB continue to appear to conduct their business through press handouts. ITN has decided to follow suit. There is clearly a willingness on the part of ITN to clinch a deal. Bob Hunter, representing BSB, seems hell bent on putting up obstacles. BSB have issued an ultimatum that unless an agreement is signed by Monday they will go to tender. I think it's bluff. ITN have responded by saying that they cannot complete by Monday but will agree to a Heads of Agreement, subject to final Board Agreement and legal advice. BSB have been tough in negotiations but, if a deal is struck, they will have in the final result helped ITN to shift gear into the competitive world that will in any case face them over the next decade. It could be a blessing in disguise. It has certainly helped management to face up to internal problems over union practices. The sticking point, and a dangerous one for the IBA, would be if ITN turned down the proposition on the grounds of editorial control.

On Wednesday a session with ROs and, after lunch, a meeting with the Radio MDs in the forum of the RCC.

I had not been looking forward to the meeting, the first since the Government's announcement on radio. I wanted to strike the right note. If sour, it would seem we were sulking. If too glib, it would seem to minimise the effect on staff working in the radio division.

I kicked off by saying we were putting the disappointment to one side. We had all looked forward to making a success of local radio. I said I had been involved in striving for change since the middle 60s when I had been shown the door by the then Postmaster General, Ted Short. I was used to battling for radio. This was another chapter.

I finished by saying that the relationship between the IBA and the radio contractors reminded me of the love/hate relationship that existed between Tom & Jerry, the Walt Disney cartoon cat and mouse. Tom was always trying to catch Jerry, and Jerry fought back with the most terrible things being done to poor Tom – sometimes blast from a cannon, sometimes squashed under a steamroller – but always, and this was the point, miraculously regaining his strength, vigour and determination, just like the IBA. There was a round of what I think was warm applause. The meeting had worked better than I had dared hope.

On Thursday, the Press Briefing concerning violence on TV: 'What the viewers think'. I had done a foreword to the research by Barrie Gunter and Mallory Wober. A time bomb had been ticking since the *Daily Mail* published the shock/horror story several months ago that 2 per cent of their sample had confessed to feelings of aggression after watching television. If correct, this means that a million viewers experience aggressive feelings. The press latched on to this and demanded more information. As a result, two studies were commissioned to look further into the question. The press also wrote up the IBA decision to question school pupils on TV violence – *Daily Telegraph* 21.9.88.

Sunday 7th February

Lunched at the Garrick with Michael Grade. His overriding concern is slapdash production standards in many programmes. Michael wants commissioning editors to take more responsibility for the work under their control. He has strong views about the need for better scheduling with ITV and believes that much can be done to brighten up Saturday evening viewing. We talked about *Life of Brian*. Michael wants Members to see it. I said I had no objection to this, but personally had found the film offensive. Michael countered by saying that the Monty Python team were known for their anarchic humour and with special 'signposting' beforehand there should not be a problem. I shall consult GT and let Members decide for themselves.

Michael told me that he didn't think that Justin would stay longer than a further year. We talked about a breakfast service. I confirmed that, if a decision was taken to go ahead, TV-am would sell the time, keep the revenue, but pay Channel 4's costs during the breakfast period. Michael is thinking of an up-market breakfast show, pulling in AB advertisers.

The TV-am dispute still continues. Bruce Gyngell backed away from his threat to sack ACTT members. He may soon find he has to face the reality of coming to terms with the Union.

I received a letter from BSB agreeing to hold off any decision to put out the news contract to tender until after our progress meeting on 4 February. I spoke to Paul Matthews at ITN and heard they were close to an agreement.

An early start on Tuesday with a meeting at 8.15 am with Colette, John Forrest, Michael Redley and Shirley to decide on our responses to the Home Affairs Committee at the meeting scheduled for Wednesday. Later, a dry run in front of closed-circuit cameras with Tim Brinton acting as Chairman of the Home Affairs Committee. Very useful practice and gave us all confidence to face the grilling to come.

Dined with Roma and Anthony Touche in his role as Prime Warden of Goldsmiths. Very grand. I sat next to Mrs Asprey, who confided she thought Aspreys 'beyond the pale. No taste. Catering to Arabs.'

On Wednesday I woke up to read in the newspapers that BSB have signed their deal with ITN; a three-year contract for £30m. The arrangement could prove a real step forward for ITN in marketing its services in the growing competitive world. I am personally delighted (and relieved). It would have been a messy business for us to unscramble and approve.

At 3.45pm drove off to the Commons and sat down in Committee Room 15 at 4.15pm. Politely led by the Chairman into an interesting dialogue with the Committee. Difficult to come to terms with the proximity of press and onlookers seated immediately behind our chairs. Talked at length about the future of broadcasting with particular attention paid by the Committee to signals coming in from satellites in Europe and further afield. John Forrest made a good, coherent witness on technical matters. Roger Gale attacked the IBA over standards. I refuted his allegations. (This got picked up in the 'gossip' piece of *The Observer* today.) At the end I felt tired and deflated. I thought I could have done better. I had not felt the adrenalin really pumping, but others seem to think our presentation went well.

On Thursday at 9.30am a progress meeting with BSB. Congratulated Anthony Simonds-Gooding over the deal struck with ITN. Plenty of problems in almost every area of their workload but I have a feeling Anthony will get there in the end.

Not so sure about Graham Grist, who was definitely shaky, both in speech and hand. A man I thought close to breakdown, but time will tell.

At midday, a meeting with Arnold Goodman. Splendidly articulate and enjoyable. Such a twinkle in his eye. A rogue elephant but equally dangerous, I suspect, if facing him over a matter in dispute. He had come to plead for an extension in Bond's undertaking to sell off 4.9 per cent non-voting shares in TV-am by late February. Made an eloquent speech, which worked well on me.

Saw a different, rather sad, insight into Goodman on Saturday. Visited Hayward exhibition by Lucien Freud. There, three portraits of Lord Goodman. Big, overflowing, intensely sorrowful.

Press interest in next Chairman of IBA slowly increasing. Rumour that Jeffrey Sterling could be on the shortlist along with my choice, Patrick Jenkin. Personally I wouldn't fancy Jeffrey Sterling because his interests are solely mechanistic and commercial.

Can see a real bust-up with Government ahead as our plans for night time become known, probably after the Authority meeting next week.

Sunday 14th February

A momentous week for television. On Tuesday the Commons, despite Mrs T's opposition, voted by a majority of 54 to permit the experiment of televising the Chambers. A week, too, when I appeared for the second time in front of a Commons Committee.

On Monday 8 February, a meeting with Brian Cubbon at the Home Office to prepare for the PAC on Wednesday. Brian is an old warrior on these occasions and exemplifies the best traditions of a Civil Servant: sturdy under fire.

Lunch with Chris Patten, hosted by GT and a gathering of television editors and current affairs people. Patten strikes me as being almost the acceptable face of the politician: genuinely caring, listening and responding with honesty. George wanted to hold the lunch because he felt that Chris Patten, as Minister of Foreign & Commonwealth Affairs and Minister for Overseas Development, might get better insight into ITV's commitment to covering events abroad, other than reporting simply the bad news.

In the evening to Winchester and to host a dinner to mark the retirement of some eight station transmitter managers. A good opportunity to say a heartfelt 'thank you' for, in many cases, 30 years of service. Altogether a unique occasion and one that I enjoyed.

Real problems beginning to surface over shareholdings in TV-am. A complicated series of undertakings between Timothy Aitken and his cousin Jonathan Aitken led to panics over ownership of voting rights in the company, Beaverbrook Investments being re-assessed in the light of conflicts between the two aforementioned. The revelation, for such it is, that Beaverbrook is in reality owned by Saudi, non-EC voters, has put Beaverbrook's original pledges to the IBA in doubt. Undertakings made at the time of the contract award confirmed the status of

Beaverbrook Investments as being 'EC controlled'. The whole affair can, I think, blow up into a major fracas. There is no love lost between Timothy and Jonathan and blood will flow, I fear.

The TV-am dispute makes matters worse because a Board upheaval would upset City confidence. Not that this would worry us.

On Tuesday 9 February SCC in the afternoon. I told the Companies that plans for night-time scheduling must be complete by 1st June in order to be confirmed by the Authority at the end of that month. I am disappointed by their seeming lack of drive or enthusiasm. Given their lacklustre approach, I feel mightily tempted to tear up the agreement and suggest to the Authority that we put it out to tender after all – but that would be stupid, and I know it.

In the evening, to *Cat On A Hot Tin Roof* at the National, hosting a dinner for Richard and Rose Luce and Max and Jane Rayne afterwards. A superb production, wonderfully steamy and guilt-ridden.

Richard Luce left during the Second Act to vote on televising Parliament and came back much elated to claim success. We all drank a toast, me with Perrier. At last, at last.

Wednesday 10th February – The PAC hearing. Not so gruelling as I had anticipated. (The Minute will reflect the business). I watched the Cable Authority trooping into their meeting with the Home Affairs Committee. I learnt afterwards that they appeared not to have fared well.

In the evening, the First Night at the Apollo Theatre of *Best of Friends* with John Gielgud at 84. A finely polished performance. As an 'angel' in the production, I think I might just get my money back!

Thursday 11th February – Authority meeting. A full agenda. Able to report the welcome news that BSB had committed themselves to ITN and that a deal between ITV and the Independents looked to be soon agreed.

Sad news about Brian Rook. He has cancer in the lungs and is in hospital. His wife is naturally very protective but I have asked whether I might visit him.

In the early evening, drinks with Anthony Simonds-Gooding and the Chairman. Anthony worried over City confidence breaking down with all the talk about fifth and sixth channels.

The Authority approved a delay in Bond's sale of 4.9 per cent non-voting stock. I rang Lord Goodman to tell him. 'At least a dukedom', he boomed jovially.

Michael Grade attended the Authority meeting and gave a good account of his future plans. He is clearly going to make substantial changes, including a breakfast news programme.

Sunday 21st February

It seems that the pressure on the IBA never slackens. We have never been popular but the endless 'knocking' the IBA receives is beginning to get me down. I am usually more resilient to the arrows of outrageous fortune. Perhaps it is simply my need to be creative instead of being a bureaucrat. I don't enjoy being a sitting target for every vested interest. The sea looks cold, and friends to rally the spirit are few.

On Friday night I was told that Brian Rook died peacefully in hospital. He had been ill since before Christmas. Bryan was a good servant of the IBA and will be greatly missed.

On Tuesday, I lunched with Timothy Renton, an amicable, urbane man with whom I find much in common, except on the subject of radio. I told him that the IBA should at least be given the task of setting up the new body with our existing radio staff who could process the change for the next 18 months or so. Eventually the body would have a new Chairman and appoint a DG. He liked the idea. I spoke to Quentin Thomas in the Home Office and asked him to follow it up if he liked the idea as well.

On Wednesday, TV-am sacked 229 ACTT technicians. So far the NUJ and BETA have stood to one side fearing, I think, a similar fate. I still remain unconvinced that Bruce and his tactics will triumph. The ACTT is facing a humiliating defeat and cannot, I suspect, simply allow itself to lie down and die.

On Friday to lunch at the Lords to meet Gennady Gerasinov (Head of Foreign Affairs/Information at the Kremlin). The night before ITN entertained him at *Phantom of the Opera* and afterwards Annabels – all good Communist entertainment!

This morning woken by Colette with news that *The Observer* had blown open the TV-am/Saudi story, implicating Jonathan and Tim Aitken in a web of intrigue. It is all vastly complicated and could bring Aitken down for being seen as tarnishing TV-am.

Sunday 28th February

The wretched business of TV-am and its shareholders in Beaverbrook Investments continues to dominate the news. On Monday I discussed it with Shirley, John Norrington and Colette. There was little doubt that Jonathan had failed to come clean with his Board and will, rightly, be mightily embarrassed. As the week went on Jonathan admitted as much. Throughout, there has been complete silence from Timothy.

On Tuesday Alan Sapper, ACTT's General Secretary, came to see me. The poor man is quite shell-shocked from the results of the TV-am sackings. He, who in the 70s had a name that conjured up fear is now an uncertain ghost of his former self, desperately seeking some toehold in a world that has changed and is passing him and his Union by.

Also on Tuesday, lunch with David Roycroft of ITN and to listen to his misgivings about the company's future. The Board has other preoccupations but the Executive sees a future clouded with uncertainty. It is difficult to see what the IBA can do to help, other than give support.

David Frost rang in the evening to ask me what my 'dream' scenario would be to see a conclusion to the Aitken affair. I said the departure of both Aitkens.

On Wednesday, lunch with Bill Elliot, Chairman of Metro Radio and, I think, well-disposed towards the IBA. I wanted to give him our thoughts on radio and hope he will follow up some of the unsatisfactory elements of Government thinking with Timothy Renton.

In the evening, the RTS Television Journalism Awards at the Dorchester. Donald Trelford, the guest speaker, delivered on behalf of BBC journalists a vituperative attack directed at the luckless John Birt. It was a blunt instrument verbally, and I thought surprisingly lacking in normal courtesy.

On Thursday, lunch at the Commons for Midlands Conservative MPs. The lunch, hosted by Anthony Beaumont-Darke, well-known 'rent a quoter'. I delivered what I hope was a stinging attack on the Broadcasting Standards Council and the Government's muddled thinking. They were, in the main, a jolly lot, who ate heartily and listened occasionally.

In the afternoon, an interview for the *Observer* with Richard Brooks; yet another piece on 'Is there a need for the IBA?' I knew it would be rotten and today it came out and proved me right. It carried an unflattering picture of me with the headline: 'Whitney – a lack of political cunning'. The article didn't expand on the headline. I am still far too sensitive after five years!

Meeting with Michael Darlow and Sophie Balhetchet. Listened to their views on our proposals for finalising the agreement between the Independents and ITV – still problems, but I think sortable.

Later, a meeting with Bruce Gyngell and Ian Irvine to tell me the results of the TV-am Board Meeting, which had started at 11.15am and went on to 4.15pm. The Board had accepted Jonathan's resignation. They wanted Timothy out as well but he declined to be rushed. It was finally agreed that Timothy would stand down as Chairman but this would not be announced until the AGM on 27 May. So far, this information has not leaked.

Went to see *South Pacific* in the evening with Tony and Pippa Vickers, so got a blow by blow account of events in the Board Room.

On Friday, attended Brian Rook's funeral at Sussex Crematorium. George gave a moving address, saying that the IBA had always been safe in Brian's hands. A simple service, attended by many familiar faces from television and radio.

Then on to Lainston House for our weekend conference. Jeremy attended the dinner and we had his valedictory speech. A good weekend of discussion. The Members contributed well but I fear the tide of events may engulf us and broadcasting as we know it today.

Watched *Weekend World* at lunchtime with the Members. Another searching enquiry into ITV and the future! David McCall said that if competition hotted up, ITV would need to have different regulations so that they could compete on equal terms.

Shades of Brian West and radio's cries of anguish.

Saturday 5th March

Writing this entry at 11am just before taking off from Heathrow to Beijing with Roma. China seems a trillion light years away – rather like another life.

Leaving behind a really hectic week, taken up in the main by the continuing TV-am/Saudi saga.

On Monday, we held a press conference to announce our '1987 Attitudes to Broadcasting' and 'Why we broadcast *V*'. It went quite well until a woman journalist behind dark glasses from the *Mirror* said, 'Why are you allowing buggery to be shown in Episode 4 of *The Fear*'? This took David Glencross somewhat aback. Later enquiries showed no bugger of any sort in any episode and the question typified the gutter press attitude to anything and everything going on currently. Interesting, too, that no paper has yet picked up and reflected the V research. I am afraid television has been cast in the role of bad boy and any evidence to the contrary does not sell newspapers.

Later in the day, talked with Ian Coulter, a backstage guru for many organisations including ITN. He counselled me to make moves towards freeing up ITN and considering new structures. Timely advice which I acted upon with a meeting on Wednesday with Alastair Burnet and David Nicholas.

On Tuesday evening I dined with radio MDs Jimmy Gordon, Ian Rufus, Terry Smith and also Bill Coppen-Gardner at L'Ecu de France in Jermyn Street. (If I had not been a guest, I would have asked them to take the Dover Sole away. It was disgraceful: deep frozen, hard and tasteless. In addition to the atrocious fish, the oysters were hard and fly button sized.) The evening's discussion was useful and I took away with me some genuine food for thought.

If the IBA acts positively and takes a real hand in shaping radio, I believe we will stand a much better chance of playing a major role in engineering and other services.

On Tuesday, a meeting with TV-am's solicitor, Penelope Hughes. TV-am are in considerable disarray over the Aitken holding and on Tuesday were hoping that a sale of the 15 per cent of the company would be put together before the IBA Members met on Thursday. I said I believed Members would call for positive action from TV-am in the event that no sale was forthcoming. (On Wednesday, I was told that the sale had fallen through.)

In the evening, George asked me to have dinner with him. He was in sombre and introspective mood, worried about how he could resolve his own deep concerns about the nature of Public Service Broadcasting with the onslaught against it from Government. We talked about who might take over and about timing. Standards and equality must be preserved if at all possible. Fleet Street (Wapping) is a bitter reminder of what awaits if Murdoch, Maxwell et al all have their snouts in the trough.

The Authority meeting on Thursday proved the bumpiest I have ever experienced. The TV-am statement took up most of the meeting, the lawyers trying to soften the wording, GT and me wanting to toughen it. Most Members were, I think, confused. It did not help that the picture was changing so rapidly. I felt in some peril as the day went on. It started badly when GT was tackled over his handling of the last meeting, when he had decided not to give Members knowledge of the Saudi interest. They felt they had been excluded, were angry and showed it. In the end, at 4.30pm, I was able to telephone Bruce Gyngell and read him the IBA statement.

GT still found our statement too weak in emphasis. I said I felt it would get a good press. As we walked away from the meeting towards our offices, I said I thought it was the best outcome and GT turned before going into his office with the words 'Don't push me'. He looked tired and angry.

Friday's press was better than I had hoped, with opinion favouring the tough line taken by the IBA.

Well, now I depart for China, leaving behind many uncertainties and hazards. How it will look when I return, I know not.

Sunday 3rd April

Returned from China to find things moving ahead, mostly as planned. Biggest news to greet me was defection by Paul Fox to become Managing Director of BBC Television. An unusual change of job and one that has caused much speculation.

Bruce Gyngell has suffered a heart attack and must take three months' leave.

On Monday said farewell to Brian Cubbon and was introduced to Sir Clive Whitemore.

On Tuesday attended TRIC lunch and gave vote of thanks to the principal speaker, Timothy Renton. In the evening, attended dinner in honour of GT, given by Arab States.

On Thursday attended Help A London Child opening, where the guest of honour was the Princess of Wales.

Sunday 10th April

A busy week catching up with a seemingly massive amount of paperwork and reading still remaining after last weekend. Now just about up to date.

Rumours still surround the future of Bruce Gyngell. Whether or not he will return to continue his role with TV-am appears an open question. Certainly the station will suffer if he were not to return, because the station is Bruce Gyngell.

Last week, too, Michael Aspel was confirmed as the next presenter of *This Is Your Life*, putting him in the position of television's highest earner with a reputed £1m per annum for all his television activities.

On Tuesday evening I attended a jolly dinner at the BBC as the guest of David Barlow, with the BBC's two regional controllers – Pat Chalmers and the Controller of Wales, Geraint Talfan Davies. Morale inside the BBC really does appear to be at a low ebb. Duke Hussey is not the favoured child, whilst the appointment of Paul Fox appears to raise more doubts than answers, but the Controllers generally consider that Michael Checkland's move was a smart way of covering his own back and securing a heavyweight to out-gun Birt if occasion were to demand tough action.

On Wednesday, held an important meeting with the ITV Strategy Group: David McCall, Richard Dunn, Bill Brown, Jim Graham, Leslie Hill and David Shaw. The purpose was to examine major issues to ascertain which were and which were not matters in which the Companies or the IBA did not see eye to eye.

Channel 4's sales, auctioning/tendering, fifth channel and ITN's future structure and funding were on the agenda. It turned out to be a useful meeting; for the first time I can remember a much freer and honest attempt to talk frankly about our views. I came to the conclusion that the Companies would accept a form of tendering for new contracts, rather than straight auctioning, if it came to that. In broad outline, this is the proposal we included in our policy document and could be effectively introduced if our first preference – a decision based on quality – was rejected.

Shirley and Colette have been racing this week to complete the Policy Document promised at the Lainston House conference. The first draft I saw on Monday was a disappointment: too woolly, too pretentious, too long. The second draft is an enormous improvement. I think it will be well received and do the IBA a power of good by setting out our agenda for action before the Government's White Paper.

On Wednesday evening attended the Fleming Memorial Lecture given by John Birt, entitled 'Decent Media'. Birt presented his case ably but reminded me of a Born-Again Christian, revealing truths about media conduct as though discovering them for the first time. He announced what I imagine will become an albatross to hang round his neck – the creation of a post within the BBC of 'Fact Checker'. BBC journalists were quick to point out that they checked facts anyway but it was a worthy attempt to lay out the Good Man's Guide to honourable journalistic endeavour. A good time was had afterwards when the chosen few repaired to the Reform Club for dinner and gossip. David McCall and Sophie Balhetchet at last decided to forgive each other for their public differences over the disagreement between ITV and the Independents. With any luck, I might see a final agreement shortly.

Thursday 7 April. Main business of the day a hurriedly called meeting, which I chaired, between BSB and ITN to see if a last-minute problem over rights could be resolved before a split appeared inevitable. Bob Hunter and Peter Clark for BSB, Paul Matthews for ITN. It soon became evident that neither side wanted a solution; BSB because they've always really wanted to go it alone and compete head-on with ITN with no holds barred, and ITN because they have become increasingly aware of the low profit margin which would result from a collaboration. After about half an hour the argument showed no sign of drawing any conclusions other than that the deal should be considered void. Both parties withdrew, trying to conceal their obvious pleasure.

ITN, on *News at Ten* laid the blame for the breakdown in talks at the feet of BSB. A sharp response came from BSB in the press the following morning. Whether or not BSB can put together a new service for around £10m remains to be seen.

Attended wedding reception to celebrate marriage of Jeremy Isaacs and Gillian Widdecombe. Denis Forman made everyone laugh with his remarks to Jeremy when proposing the toast: 'Never has so much been paid for so few'. Champagne flowed and guests puzzled their way round the Saatchi Gallery where the do was held looking at pictures and sculpture that could have been created by five year olds. Extraordinary how one man's taste can lead the art world by the nose.

On afterwards to Odins restaurant – still my favourite choice – to have dinner with Leslie Hill. A good opportunity for a real chinwag. Leslie is the new brand of MD; a good businessman, steady and utterly professional.

On Friday 8 April, congratulated Colette on her Policy Paper and went over some aspects prior to it being sent out to Members.

To the Mansion House for Guardian's 'Young Businessman of the Year' Award. Then to meet Clive Leech in his capacity as MD of Yorkshire. Then to Covent Garden to see *Salome* with Maria Ewing in Peter Hall's production. Ms Ewing flinging her final veil to the winds, and with it her modesty. A good time was had by all.

Sunday 17th April

Work went on all week to get the Policy Statement ready for Members.

On Monday 11 April lunch at the National and then the National Theatre Board meeting. Max Rayne, in his funny, diffident manner, poked a cigarette into its holder, lit up and said that he would be stepping down from the Chair, to be replaced by Mary Soames. No reaction from the Board. I said I found it a shock. Silence. The heroes depart the National seemingly without a single trumpet blast. Bridget Plowden, John Mortimer. We must do something. Hold a wake, a party, something. The National steadily and consistently is haemorrhaging financially. The range of productions, the span of touring. I ask isn't this a national scandal in more senses than one. Peter Parker agrees. We must talk. Max could sound the alarm. Does the National really want to stand by while the heart of the theatre grows weaker? I think it is all part of the general indifference to the arts by Government.

Meeting in the afternoon with Donald Maitland and Shirley Littler. Donald considers the Policy Document is in good shape. I seek to tone down the emphasis on publishers/contractors. Colette tries to resist and is obviously attracted to the notion that it would be wrong to off-balance the stance of the IBA. Any bias towards a radical alternative would send the contractors into a state of disarray, apart from the fact it would be grossly unfair. The last time round, the IBA insisted on building up studio presence in the regions. HTV, TVS, Central – all put large sums into bricks and mortar to please the IBA's then members.

Dinner with the Home Affairs Select Committee. The event, I think, was a success with Members and the Committee engaged in lively conversation. On balance, I shall be surprised if the Committee's findings don't lean heavily towards maintaining the status quo for regulations. One piece of information came at the beginning of dinner: John Wheeler, the Committee's Chairman, spoke up plainly to say that the Government White Paper would not come out until the Cabinet Committee had considered the report from the Home Affairs Committee.

Important meeting of SCC on Tuesday 12 April. Beforehand, I telephoned Michael Checkland to find out just what the BBC was thinking it was doing in becoming the first runner in the Murdoch Eurosport Channel. The most extraordinary venture yet by the Beeb to prove its new commercial machismo under Dukie and Mike! Perhaps the single greatest surprise is that the BBC is actually prepared to sign away its birthright on sports' rights and schedules to Murdoch who, if the contract goes through, would have the right to transmit material owned by the Corporation at any time of their choosing. The BBC would be handing over their competitiveness to Murdoch. Definitely not in the public interest. I don't believe Checkland has read the small print or, if he has, then he is prepared to sell the family silver.

I spoke afterwards to Brian Tesler who said that the ITVA Council – the independent television trade body – had declined to take up Murdoch's offer on precisely the grounds of my concern.

A good meeting of SCC. I outlined my thinking on ITN. It came up against some opposition, most fiercely from Andrew Quinn, but there was a strong sense of support for the IBA's arguments that ITN must be given the opportunity to grow up and face the chill winds of competition in a way that would enable it to defend itself by being properly competitive and alive to new possibilities for expansion. The more I think about ITN's lack of business sense, the more I am convinced that Justin Dukes would be the man for the job. I met him on Thursday and confirmed that, if the position were to be offered, he would take it.

On the question of auctioning/tendering for the next contract, Brian Tesler put forward a good, logical argument for holding back on the third stage of tendering being considered by the IBA – that in the event of a tie between two contractors, they would each be invited to offer either more money or more ambitious programme plans. Which would take the process back to each vying to spend more than his competitor.

Afterwards, I discussed this view with Shirley and David and both agreed that we should argue with the Members to leave it out of our proposals.

A rift has become evident between the Companies that could lead to a crumbling of the agreement with the ACTT. Tyne Tees have decided to pull out of national agreements and instead have gone for local agreements with the unions.

Today I read that the ACTT and BETA have agreed to merge. This would have profound impact on the nature of future negotiations. BETA members man our transmitters. I am sure that ACTT have their sights on getting their hands on this jugular vein of the entire system.

On 13 April, *The Times* reported that William Rees-Mogg is destined to become the first Chairman of the Broadcasting Standards Council.

On Thursday 14 April, David McCall told GT that his meeting with the Home Secretary went well and that he thinks Hurd took on board the ITV contention that tendering for the contract would be a better way than auctioning but Hurd is so much in the pocket of the P.M. that anything he suggests could be overturned by a raised finger at No. 10.

Off to Zurich for the weekend with Roma to see our daughter.

Saturday 23rd April

The papers on Sunday 17 April carried more comment about ITN. I think it has caught everyone by surprise. The *Independent* in an article headed 'Television News Service Faces Huge Shake-up', quotes one Board member of ITN as saying 'The IBA have moved the goalposts, and the stadium too'.

Broadcast followed this up on Thursday with a critical Leader: 'Selling The News. The dangers are obvious and ITN, floated in the market, would be under intense commercial pressure. It may not necessarily go down-market. We may not find the TV version of tabloid news but would the breadth and depth of the present news service survive in such a competitive environment? John Whitney has some explaining to do.'

On Monday at 10am met Alastair Burnet with David Glencross. Alastair has put a proposition to Downing Street and to Tim Renton, who said to me that he thought it 'interesting'. In a nutshell, the proposal is to give ITN all the hours from the start of *News At Ten* until the breakfast service begins the following morning. I pointed out to Alastair that I thought the concept of an 'as of right' entry into programming inconsistent with present Government thinking on creating a competitive environment. Alastair shifted his position somewhat and said that he had never anticipated an 'as of right' but expected to fight for the franchise against other contenders. I think the idea, in its present form, is a non-starter. No, that's too emphatic. It has the merit of giving a night-time contractor a financial head-start if ITN's advertising revenue from *News at Ten* is included in the night package. But that would be counterbalanced by the loss of funds and profit to the daytime contractor.

I saw Alastair again at the ITN meeting and, unlike any other I had experienced since joining the IBA, this one positively crackled with static tension. Firstly, ITN were preparing to announce their internal reorganisation package to a largely unsuspecting staff, the bottom line being a reduction of some 142 staff as a result of new technology. This would bring the total staff down to about 980. The changes would coincide with ITN's move to a new building, the old *Sunday Times* building in Gray's Inn Road. Secondly, the IBA position, spelt out by me at the last meeting of the SCC was causing an additional shockwave. It was also the first meeting that had been called since BSB had parted company from ITN over provision of news for the 'Now' Channel. Little was said about this.

The meeting was overshadowed by the explanation by Management of their plans to reorganise ITN. Board meetings at ITN have sometimes looked and sounded like the Reform Club after lunch. Change, particularly sudden change, concentrates the mind. I left them to it and returned to the IBA to meet Mike Luckwell, who has acquired 5 per cent of TV-am from Beaverbrook Investments. Mike looked dapper and relaxed – as well he might as a man with £25m in his bank, the result of selling his holdings in Carlton. Luckwell paid 142p per share, with a total value of £4.6m. Beaverbrook minority shareholders were miffed that they weren't getting more for their shares.

On Thursday we were approached by Lord Lewisham, wanting our reaction to a purchase of TV-am shares by French Cable Vision, 45 per cent of which is owned, surprise, surprise by Al Bilad, the very gentleman of Saudi birth we took such pains to remove. But on Monday I knew only of Mike's interest which was perhaps just as well.

In the evening, a horrid Indian offering at the much-hyped Bombay Brasserie. Roma, me, Irene and George Cooper. George told me word for word the same story about selecting the new Editor of *TV Times* that he had told me when we last lunched together. He started the story by asking if he'd already told me but unfortunately did not wait for an answer. Once launched, there was no abort button to stop the story's flight.

On Tuesday 19 April up early to breakfast with George Russell, Richard Attenborough and Shirley Littler at the IBA. Dickie in usual good form but obviously sad that *Cry Freedom* had had no Oscar citation. After *Gandhi*, the Americans turned to China for their plaudits.

We talked about Justin's future and I touched on the possibility of Justin for ITN. George Russell spoke about the possibility of becoming ITN's new Chairman and said that he wanted to play a part in both C4 and ITN but this would be subject to approval by his Board at Marley. If we could pull off both George Russell as Chairman and Justin Dukes as MD of ITN I would feel much happier about ITN's future than I do at present. David Nicholas is a superb Editor-in-Chief but his management skills are undeniably weak. Justin would put a shaft of cold steel into their structure and kick-start ITN into the 1990s with a real chance of success. I don't know how David Nicholas would react but, if George Russell were to go in as Chairman and make a firm stand for Justin, this would be a strong starter. On Friday I spoke to Richard Dunn and he supported the idea.

Richard Attenborough said that he and C4 were greatly concerned about reports that Willie Rees-Mogg was asking for some regulatory control over both the BBC and IBA. This would fly in the face of assurances given in the Conservative Party Manifesto when the pledge was given that 'the responsibility for enforcing Broadcasting Standards must rest with the Broadcasting Authorities'. On 21 April GT sent round by hand to Douglas a letter asking for reassurance on the point.

Lunch with the Panel of Religious Advisors and then met Albert Scharf, President of the European Broadcasting Union, who was obviously concerned about Eurosport and the failure of the recent meeting in Brussels to resolve the worries of Channel 4, ITV and the IBA. I showed him the letter I was planning to send to Michael Checkland, which included the phrase 'selling the family silver'. To my surprise Albert agreed with my concern that Eurosport should be allowed to schedule as they see fit. An extraordinary state of affairs for the BBC to stand to one side and allow a competitor to UK audiences. I have all along thought that Albert was very much in favour of the concept. He was off to see Michael Checkland and said that the question of giving rights to Eurosport, allowing them access to sporting events when they chose to schedule was a major step and one for concern. About 11 countries wanted to participate but that left many who would not take part. I arranged to have my letter to Checkland sent round by hand so that it would arrive that same evening. I showed the letter to GT, who was attending a farewell dinner to mark the retirement of Bill Cotton along with Scharf and a number of others.

On Friday I received a response from Michael Checkland to the effect that the BBC was content and that it did *not* give first rights to Eurosport. Michael is wrong on this point and I wrote back on Friday seeking to find out why he interpreted the agreement to that effect.

In the evening, to the Globe Theatre to see Maggie Smith in Peter Shaffer's comedy *Lettuce and Lovage*. Wholly refreshing, beautifully played and superbly well-constructed. Some people are blessed with that elusive quality – a real sense of style. Maggie Smith and Peter Shaffer both have this in abundance and the audience, packed to the gunnels, loved it. Afterwards to the Garrick with our guests Kenneth Bradshaw and Stella Richman. Stella's life in television and the restaurant business has been extensively reported. Inside she still burns with the old convictions and passion about television but she admits to feeling tired. She is one of the true school of television: programmes first, business second. Today's MDs march to a different drum. Shareholders and City analysts are king.

On 20 April an early morning meeting with Owen Edwards and John Howard-Davies of S4C to shake hands on the final outcome of the Peat Marwick McLintock review of production costs and the contractual position between HTV and S4C – the outcome to draw stumps and declare the matter closed. There have been neither victors nor losers.

Dinner with AIRC Committee at Brompton Road. A good-natured occasion spoilt marginally by Brian West's remark, 'We're here to bury the body'. Far from disposing of the IBA's corpse, I think they will find considerable value in the offer by the IBA as transplant donor to provide essential 'spare parts' to give ILR a measure of health before new radio is given the midwife's slap of life by Parliament.

21 April, an exhausting Authority meeting, starting at 9.30 and concluding at 4pm. The main business of the day the Policy Statement and its eventual approval. The next evening Colette called round with the completed Policy document and a 15 page 'popular' summary. James Conway called early on Saturday to warn of the likelihood of the *Sunday Times* running a damaging story as a result of the short version of the Policy Statement being leaked to them. I spent the day worried and wondering who could have leaked it. That evening James rang to confirm the story is in print. Wholly mischievous and negative. A typical hatchet job, following Murdoch's aim to throw doubt and discredit on the IBA. Telephoned GT with news.

Today (Sunday 24) I examined the story. Having slept on it, I don't feel as savaged as I thought, but who would have leaked it and why? Anger, fuelled somewhat by a damaging and silly quote by Leslie Hill amounting to criticism of the IBA as being 'negative'.

Damage limitation of leaked story discussed with Colette. Will now await Monday's press! On Tuesday I will visit the Home Secretary and hold a press conference to unveil the full Policy Statement – 50 pages as opposed to the plain man's guide of 15. We may still retrieve our position.

Saturday 30th April

On Monday Thames Television gave notice that it is to seek staff cuts of 200. The fallout from the disgraceful leak to the *Sunday Times* failed to materialise. During the day I learnt that Jonathan Miller tried to interest the *Financial Times* in doing a follow-up but Ray Snoddy wisely declined to give the story status and credibility. I asked Colette Bowe to instigate an investigation into the leak.

The Sony Radio Awards take place at Grosvenor House. GT and I attended but could not stay for the event itself, which ended at 3.15pm. The BBC won 20 awards, ILR seven. The lunch had the atmosphere of celebration, welcoming in the new radio age.

Back to the office for a meeting with Donald Maitland, GT and colleagues to plan for our meeting with Douglas Hurd the following day. Half way through we switched to examining our presentation on the Policy Document which takes place immediately after our Home Office meeting.

I ducked out from a dinner with GT to celebrate the role change by Paul Fox to Managing Director of BBC Television and went home to study the Policy Document.

On Thursday Donald drove with me to the Home Office. GT had been there for an hour, having his private meeting. I realised I was elevated by the presence of Donald when we were offered coffee in the waiting room! Then in to Douglas Hurd and Timothy Renton. A good meeting, with Douglas listening more than on previous occasions.

We talked about ITN, the Independents, ITV and the BSC. GT delivered a firm statement to Douglas: the IBA cannot tolerate a confusion of responsibility over taste, decency etc. If rumours of Willie Whitelaw's demands are accurate, GT told Douglas, the Authority Members will have to consider their position. Douglas looked taken aback. Tim hastily explained that his text delivered on Saturday to Mary Whitehouse's acolytes had been misquoted, and important paragraphs deleted. It reads 'Your President suggested that the Council should have power to preview programmes. That is not a function which we have previously felt to be essential to the work of the Council, but we shall review the arguments for and against such a power.'

On this somewhat sombre note, but with good wishes for a successful Policy launch, we all shook hands and made for the car park.

At Brompton Road the press were gathering in the Conference Room, which had been arranged with a platform and a backdrop: 'The IBA – television in the 90s'. A good turn out. GT in splendid form, Donald perky and incisive. It was a good session. Questions were directed particularly to the yellow, red card penalties proposed by the IBA. GT delivered a carefully-worded rebuke to Jonathan Miller to the pleasure, I thought, of his fellow journalists.

On Wednesday the press gave the Policy Document a fair review:

Financial Times: 'The IBA yesterday unveiled far-reaching proposals for commercial television in the UK' and 'TV Regulators think the unthinkable'.
Daily Mirror: 'TV sex to get the red card'.
The Times: 'IBA rejects Cabinet idea'.
The Independent: 'Red Card penalty plan for breaches of TV standards'.
Daily Mail: 'New Crackdown on TV nasties'.

Breakfast with David Frost at the Carlton Tower. He looked younger and ate black, flat mushrooms and fried eggs with me. We talked about the Policy Document and TV-am's performance. I told him the Members are still not happy with the weekend output. Who will become next Chairman after the AGM? David wonders whether he should offer himself? I am reluctant to give a view but I think it would give continuity and strength as David was an original founder member.

A meeting later with Ken Blyth over Eurosport. The Companies are minded still to keep out of the proposed consortia. I await a reply to my letter to Michael Checkland. The GAC meets at 10am. I am asked to give an account of the Policy Document findings. The GAC is alarmed at the threat by Government to give BSC the right to preview programmes.

At some point in the morning, I learnt that David Glencross was previewing *This Week*, Thames' programme on Gibraltar. GT received a call from Geoffrey Howe on the same subject. I saw David and Robert Hargreaves after they had met Allen & Overy's Kemp and Wotton, who advised that the programme was not in contempt in UK law. Question – will it be prejudicial to the inquest? David thought not. Co-operation had been given to the Gibraltar authorities etc. Inquest is some way off. New evidence, etc. Legitimate public interest.

At 7.15 I viewed the programme and decided it should be shown. I wrote a note for George and left the cassette for him to view on his return from the Opera.

Joined Roma to see *The Last Emperor*, arriving 25 minutes late. I tried to put the *This Week* programme out of my mind.

On Thursday I read the morning papers over breakfast. *The Times* headlines foreshadow the growing voice of dissent from the IBA over the BSC: 'The IBA Chief threatens to quit'.

Sunday 1st May

On Monday, I talked to GT who was on his way to an ICI Board. He had seen the programme and concurs with my view of it. He had left a note for me at the office, which I saw when I arrived. With Gibraltar very much at the forefront of my mind, I chaired the regular liaison meeting between the IBA and BSB. The meeting lasted for an hour. I told Graham Grist that any reduction in the DBS signal to allow the other two channels to be used for information purposes would be strongly resisted by the IBA. It would mean an increase in receiver dish size and would be contrary to the agreed technical specification on signal power. This may become an issue later. A firm marker has been placed. I also urged that programme plans and advertising considerations should be discussed and agreed with the IBA as soon as possible. Otherwise I could visualise a crisis blowing up with deadlines forcing unsatisfactory conclusions.

The meeting over, I was told that Geoffrey Howe had called, wanting to speak to GT. As this was not possible, GH was told that he could either speak to me or David Glencross. He chose David. David took the call in his office and, returning, told me it had been to tell GT that Geoffrey wished to draw the attention of the IBA to the Salmon Tribunal findings on Aberfan in 1969:

> 'It should be a contempt if any person after a Tribunal is appointed says or does anything, or causes to be said or done, in relation to any evidence relevant to the subject matter of the enquiry which is intended or obviously likely to alter, distort, destroy or withhold such evidence from the Tribunal.'

Colette Bowe, David Glencross and I met and discussed a press statement for GT to read on his return. The *News at One* on ITN carried a headline that Sir Geoffrey Howe had asked for the programme to be postponed.

That evening I went to see a performance of *The Dream of Gerontius* at Greenwich, hosted by Alan Britten for Mobil. A splendid occasion with Janet Baker in superb voice and a flame-haired timpanist banging away on the drums like a dervish and proving once again that a woman's place is anywhere but in the home!

Roma and I travelled to the concert by boat with other guests and already there were jokes as we passed the Tower of London and Traitors Gate.

I looked at my watch at nine o'clock during the concert. *This Week* has begun and for the next 45 minutes images of the programme flashed before my eyes as Janet Baker reached down from heaven to guide the soul of Gerontius towards purgatory. I wonder if that, too, is to be my destination.

Home at about 11.45pm and I called the office and spoke to Margaret on the switchboard. My heart sank as she told me that Colette Bowe, Sarah Thane, James Conway and herself had been 'flooded' by angry callers, without exception condemning the programme. I spoke to Colette, who confirmed this response.

In bed, I experienced a feeling of a void in my stomach, a real sense of foreboding and uncertainty about the reaction tomorrow. Roma confesses that she thinks the decision we reached to be wrong but she accepts that it was a judgment taken after weighing all the evidence. In the early hours I lay awake.

The one o'clock news headlined the cold wrath of the Prime Minister when interviewed by a diminutive Japanese interviewer for a programme to Japan. Without having seen the programme, she condemned it as 'trial by television'.

Her hooded eyes glittering, her voice hushed in emphasis, she is fighting the Falklands all over again. The same voice she used when describing the sinking of the Belgrano and her 'Just be thankful'. The cat is amongst the pigeons.

GT appeared on *World At One* and made a stirling defence of IBA actions. Throughout this whole business GT has acted in a spirit and robustness that has raised his profile and rating. Members have stood solidly behind him, without exception.

On *Channel 4 News* later, at 7pm, GT repeated his performance, attacking the

Prime Minister for over-reacting. It was one of the best interviews he has given. The 'heavy' press are divided. Strong defence of the IBA by some, attack by others.

In Dorset on Sunday I collected the papers from Corfe and read them over breakfast. No more attacks from No. 10. *The Observer* defended the IBA, the *Sunday Telegraph* attacked. I spoke to Colette and GT and decided that the lines are drawn. On balance, the defence of our actions has been sufficient to prevent an onslaught.

Richard Dunn telephoned to say that Ian Trethowan is issuing a statement, which he read to me. A good one, establishing clearly that he, as Chairman, stands by the action of Thames and the IBA. I pointed out the hypocrisy of some of the press, who have accused the programme of being a 'trial by television' when they are themselves now smearing the witnesses who will be coming forward.

Earlier, when I had spoken to GT, he had concluded our conversation with the words; 'I think we can enjoy the rest of our holiday, all being well'. Let's hope so.

Very good reviews in *The Observer* and the *Sunday Times*' both giving credit to Thames (and the IBA) for a balanced and thoughtful programme.

Monday. Yesterday an announcement on the radio that three airmen had been gunned down in Holland whilst off duty, acknowledged by the IRA as their work. These killings will strengthen the voices of those who want a shoot to kill policy adopted by the SAS regardless of the circumstances. This latest atrocity by IRA will certainly muddle the issue of the *This Week* programme.

Monday 2nd May

Back in London, I read the day's newspapers. The *Daily Mail* confirms my fears with their front page heading 'TV faces new attack'. The grandmother of one of the three shot, Elizabeth Shiner, is quoted:

> 'My grandson loved his life. It is dreadful that these terrorists should shoot down young men on their night off. When I think about that television programme saying we should not have shot the IRA people in Gibraltar, I just don't know how people can think like that'.

The *Daily Mail* Leader went to the limit – 'What a propaganda bonus for the terrorists'.

The Times, on the other hand, took a hard look at the evidence of Mrs Carmen Proetta under the heading 'Witness defends version of IRA bomber deaths'. A half-page reviewing the statement made by this, the one witness to speak openly about what she claims she saw:

> 'I heard a single shot. The couple turned, looked back, putting their hands up. Then there was more shooting and I saw the girl fall.' The article describes in detail allegations made against Mrs Proetta, which she repudiates in detail. 'The Sun' ran a headline labelling her 'The tart of Gib'. Its front-page story accused her of being a former prostitute and of running an escort agency. Her husband was described as 'a sleazy drug peddler', and both were accused of being 'anti-British'.

The Guardian runs a Leader: 'The true nature of the IRA threat!' Two letters in the paper backed up the IRA stance. One from Granville Williams of the

'Campaign for Press and Broadcasting Freedom' in which he draws conclusions from the Government's active attempt to muzzle television with its determination to bring in a Broadcasting Standards Council.

For the first time since the programme went out a serious journalist has examined the stance of the popular press, under a heading: 'Fleet Street sychophants who are too blind to see the damage they do to their own trade'.

Over the holiday there has been silence from Ministers. Even the MP for Hendon North, John Gorst, after announcing that he considered the IBA had failed in its duties and should be abolished, appears to have shot his bolt – at least until another opportunity to grab a headline comes his way!

Sir Ian's defence of the programme and of Thames has received little coverage. Significantly the *Daily Mail* quotes it alongside stories of the deaths in Holland.

Trying to stand back now, even though we are so close to the event, I think the IBA's stance has been successful. The battle lines are still drawn, however.

Sunday 8th May

On Tuesday, Margaret Thatcher continued her attack on the IBA and Thames about the Gibraltar programme during Question Time. Invited to condemn the film by a backbencher, Mrs T quoted Lord Salmon's report on the law of contempt from his findings after the Aberfan Enquiry, stressing the need for care and responsibility to avoid 'the horror of trial by press, tv and radio'. 'Neither Thames TV nor the IBA demonstrated that high sense of responsibility.'

Geoffrey Howe's use of the Salmon Report, enthusiastically echoed and endorsed by Mrs T, means we may be in for a rough ride. On Saturday 7 May, Michael Zander (who incidentally I was at Prep School with) wrote an appraisal of the Salmon findings that overturned much of the thrust attributed to it by both Margaret Thatcher and Geoffrey Howe.

This will come in handy for the response we are drafting to Geoffrey Howe's letter to GT. I hope to have a draft for circulation on Monday.

On Tuesday evening came the first whispers of a story that was to move into first position: this time a programme scheduled for transmission in Northern Ireland on Thursday, the work of the *Spotlight* Northern Ireland documentary team. First reports on the programme suggest that it will be dealing with much the same ground as covered by Thames.

On Wednesday, the *Times* printed a piece suggesting that a successor to GT could be Christopher Tugendhat, the 51 year old former EEC Commissioner. Referring to the possibility of Donald Maitland, the *Times* commented, 'too Whitehall for the chairmanship in today's climate'!

I had the opportunity of speaking to Justin Dukes about his possible role in ITN. He is keen to hear whether there is serious interest in him because he has another offer that he will accept if he is not invited in for discussion before 14 May. The problem is that he wants the Chief Executive title and this will be wrong while David Nicholas is in the driving seat.

On Wednesday, I held the first Channel 4 liaison meeting since Michael Grade has taken over from Jeremy Isaacs. Michael appeared his usual confident self. The changes that he has made so far are to remove programmes rather than put in new ones. The ending of Mary Nicholson's series has been much regretted. She is perhaps one of the very few interviewers who brings to the task really mature consideration and empathy with her subjects.

Just as the meeting was concluding, I asked Michael how he thought the case for maintaining the status quo for funding the Channel was going. His response shattered me: 'We will probably have to find a fallback to satisfy our critics. I think we could work it by selling our own space using an agency. Then we could put the results into the ITV pot and draw out of the total revenue our share.' 'But that could result in competitive selling', I said. 'Not really', replied Michael, 'there would be an incentive for the agency to sell the airtime but the net result would still be the same as now'.

On Thursday I telephoned Richard Attenborough and recounted the conversation to him. Dickie professed horror and amazement and said that the subject had never been discussed. I only hope that Michael hasn't floated his idea to the 'wolf pack'. All the 'wise' sages who said Michael would sell the Channel down the river would have a field day.

On Wednesday I suggested to GT that Lord Scarman might be persuaded to write a letter to the *Times* on Gibraltar as a response to a scurrilous letter from Nicholas Fairbairn (*The Times*, 4 May). GT has spoken to Arnold Goodman, who was 'thinking'. Later he spoke to Denis Forman, who said he would speak to Scarman.

Thursday 5th May – The headline in the *Independent*: 'The BBC heads for confrontation with Thatcher'. Most of the press carried the BBC quandary over the *Spotlight* programme. Geoffrey Howe got out his pen again and wrote to Duke Hussey. The BBC told him they were considering the merits of the programme.

The programme was due to go out in Northern Ireland that evening. I watched the *One O'clock News* and no decision had been reached. There appears to be considerable agonising going on behind the scenes.

In the morning, I received one of my occasional visits from Charles Wick, Director of the U.S. Information Center, a beady 50 year old. Charlie has been an old time friend of Reagan since they worked together in films. Whether or not he is afraid of meeting his end prematurely, I know not, but each time I have met him Charles has been literally surrounded by bodyguards. This time there were only two, who 'cased' the place before the great man entered.

In the afternoon I addressed staff in the packed Conference Hall. The main items were the Policy Document, the Broadcasting Standards Council, radio, the leak to the *Sunday Times* and the Gibraltar *This Week* programme.

A meeting afterwards with Trevor Holdsworth and Anthony Simonds-Gooding. BSB is beginning to get up speed. We have agreed that they can use, as temporary accommodation, the second and third floors of Brompton Road before they move into their new offices.

BSB are causing a commotion as they are bidding for sports rights over the head of ITV. I can see sparks flying as BSB get further into their stride.

On the *Five O'Clock News*, the BBC announced that they would be going ahead with their *Spotlight* programme.

In the evening, Roma and I went to the Garrick as guests of Channel 4 to say goodbye to Jeremy Isaacs. It must have been his umpteenth farewell but he was still able to find words of wisdom, which he scattered plentifully.

Willie Whitelaw got up and congratulated the Channel, saying he hoped Governments would continue to recognise the contribution that Public Service Broadcasting was capable of making; a value that should be preserved.

Dickie spoke well and congratulated George and me, and the IBA, for standing firm over Gibraltar.

Jeremy characteristically remained silent over giving any thanks or praise to the IBA for standing by and defending Channel 4 from its earliest days. He did, however, pay tribute to Bridget Plowden and Brian Young, who were both present. Not a word about Edmond and only a passing mention of Justin, but, all in all, a good occasion.

Michael Grade was told by Jeremy at the conclusion of his speech that he would never have so much fun or satisfaction as he had done in starting the Channel. He might have turned it over and said that he wished Michael as much fun and satisfaction as he had enjoyed.

Afterwards, we drove George and Dorothy Russell home. George has still to say yes or no to taking on the Chairmanship of ITN. I should know next week.

Friday's press was filled with vituperation from Geoffrey Howe over the screening of the *Spotlight* programme.

Off to the country and a peaceful weekend with the weather sublime. So another week where Gibraltar dominated. Next week I think we may all hear that Willie Rees-Mogg has been appointed Chairman of the Broadcasting Standards Council – that or the next Chairman of the IBA. We shall see.

Sunday 15th May

Now that the froth and fury of Mrs Thatcher's anger seems to have subsided, the aftermath of Gibraltar *Death On The Rock* can begin to take on a correct perspective.

Mrs T's pivotal argument was the one she expressed in a loud whisper of blazing rage through clenched teeth to the poor little Japanese interviewer from NHK who clearly didn't comprehend what had hit him. 'The freedom of the people depends fundamentally on the rule of law, a fair legal system …. The common law has come right up from Magna Carta which has come right up through the British Courts …. A court of law is the place where you deal with these matters. If you ever get trial by television or guilt by accusation, that day freedom dies.'

Bernard Ingham's intemperate outburst on 'institutionalised hysteria' merely added to the Government's extraordinary behaviour and handling of the whole affair. A great many voices, hitherto silent, have now begun to make themselves heard. Indeed, far from stilling the voice of the discontents, the Gibraltar killings have stayed firmly in the headlines. The press, now late in the day, realising I think that television was not only the medium which confronted the smugness of the first reports (by finding witnesses prepared to stand up to the outrageous hostility of the fawning gutter-press who accepted the Government line without question) but was also the medium which smoked the 'lady not for turning' from her lair.

On Monday, I hosted a farewell party for Bob Lorimer, Senior Regional Officer and Regional Officer for the North East. A much-loved and respected IBA person. His monthly reports to me always contained both humour and penetrating observation. His final gesture was to write 'Notes to future ROs'. The concluding paragraph is typical.

That same evening, I and DGMM colleagues held a dinner for Bob at the Bombay Brasserie where after the meal we presented him with a box of Windsor & Newton watercolours. He was most grateful and I hope he gets many hours of pleasure from it.

Tuesday 19 May, some of the papers this morning contained reports that Roy Hattersley had written to Douglas Hurd seeking assurance that Jeffrey Sterling was not being thought of as the next IBA Chairman: 'the candidate whom senior IBA officials now take for granted as the Prime Minister's nominee would be wholly inappropriate'.

Hattersley also attacked the likelihood of William Rees-Mogg as Chairman of the Broadcasting Standards Council: 'Not because of his close connections with the Conservative Party but because of his well-known and constantly repeated views on the obligations that broadcasters owe to the State'.

Hattersley had obviously taken IBA officials' views as being mine as demonstrated to me in a telephone call the day before, but I had been at pains to maintain a studiously non-partisan attitude to the questions he put.

Donald Maitland hosted a lunch for David Young. It proved lively and I think David Young found it stimulating. He obviously sees the emergence of competition as a gift to enable the dismantling of regulation and opening up the airwaves across Europe. I had apologised earlier to David that GT would not be there to host the occasion. I did not explain that the reason was that George had business elsewhere. In fact, he was meeting Douglas Hurd at his home with Duke Hussey with the purpose of establishing some sort of peace over Douglas Hurd's decision to appoint William Rees-Mogg and to make the announcement on Monday in the Commons.

There he would announce that there would be a delay in establishing the statutory basis of the Council until the Television Bill likely to be introduced in the 1989/90 session. This would allow time for the Terms of Reference to be decided in consultation with the broadcasting authorities and to determine the limits within which it should operate.

The lunch was followed by SCC. The Companies gave a thumbs-up to the main conclusion reached in our Policy Document. I asked about Super Channel, having the previous night met Richard Hooper and heard from the horse's mouth the sad saga of Super Channel's problems, notably money. As a first exposure by ITV to the hard world of commerce and competition, the lesson must be a painful one.

David McCall explained that there was to be an EGM on Thursday when a life-saver package would be put to the investors. This life-saver would be primarily inflated by Virgin who, if the deal went through, would retain a 45 per cent or so holding in the Channel.

Wednesday 11 May. Car at 8 a.m. to a breakfast at P&O with Jeffrey Sterling, Brian Griffiths and Robert Maxwell. Maxwell, in sturdy form, started ordering Brian around like an office boy, demanding that a Minute be taken of the words of wisdom that would be falling from his lips. What did fall from his lips, apart from a quantity of crumbs as he demolished several pieces of buttered toast, included expletives that would be more usually heard in a barrack room mess than in the austerely elegant surroundings in which we sat to have our breakfast.

It was clear from the very outset that Jeffrey Sterling's views and those of David Young were similar. Broadcasting *is* a commodity, a vehicle from which advertisers can launch products. A channel for market-driven commerce. Service to viewers was brought into the conversation by me after the selling-off of Channel 4 had been cited by Jeffrey Sterling as a real opportunity for national advertisers to have a truly national channel. Maxwell was all for auctioning. I explained the IBA's apprehensions. 'The IBA is worse than the worst excesses of Stalinism', boomed Maxwell, eyeing Brian to make sure a proper note was being recorded. 'MDs', he went on, 'are only interested in obeying the dictat of the IBA, not in serving their Boards or shareholders'.

I remarked that perhaps the MDs were mindful of keeping the contracts that enabled them, their Boards and shareholders to enjoy the fruits of a broadcasting monopoly.

Maxwell then extolled the virtues of the IBA! 'A fair and honest bunch.' Despite their fairness and honesty, he nevertheless believed that the days of the IBA should be numbered. More channels would bring greater choice.

I asked him about the output on TFI in which Maxwell had a 10 per cent holding. 'Rather too much pornography', he said. 'But no one objects. They just have different standards.' I suggested that, to use the by now time-honoured phrase, 'more could mean less'. There was no response.

Brian doubted whether the IBA's evolutionary approach could be sustained in the face of the technological onslaught.

Maxwell said that it would be the worse for UK Limited (he made use of the title quite a lot) if the IBA were to be left on its own, broadcasting gold knobs and all. I should have said, 'but that's exactly what we should try to achieve', but sadly I didn't.

Jeffrey Sterling made an amiable host. He and David Young came from the same world: bright, confident, successful and totally single-minded. A tough adversary. If the IBA were ever to fall into his hands, I shudder for the future of Public Service Broadcasting as far as ITV is concerned. Given a clear page, Jeffrey Sterling would allow ITV to go to the highest bidder, sell off Channel 4 and permit the BBC to be the sole bastion of PSB. A scenario that has come true in radio and one which I have commented on in earlier months. It has to be still on the cards.

Authority meeting on Thursday 12 May at 9 a.m. Main item on the agenda: Gibraltar. GT tabled the letter that he intended sending to Geoffrey Howe. This was approved. All the Members endorsed the decision but the item ended on a slightly sour note with Michael Caine admonishing the Chairman for not trying to assemble more Members on the Wednesday night before *Death on the Rock*'.

So another week ends. Dorset on Friday was humming with every form of wildlife, busy home-making, hatching and canoodling.

Before leaving for the weekend, I became engaged in a series of telephone conversations with Duke Hussey's personal secretary over the announcement on Monday of Rees-Mogg's appointment. GT, who had told his Members, was in a different position to Duke Hussey, who hadn't. There may be some red faces in the BBC as a result.

Legionnaires' Disease in the BBC has spread to ITN. One poor man at the BBC has committed suicide, and another has died.

On Friday, Michael Grade launched a bitter attack on Rees-Mogg and the whole concept of the BSC.

Sunday 22nd May

Moggfinder General is just one of the nicknames now attached to William Rees-Mogg as the press gathers around to cackle and hoot at William's first attempts to identify his pet hates. It appears to be *The A-Team*. The comedy programme he likes to watch, on the other hand, is *Allo, Allo*. *The A-Team* has been scrutinised by the IBA over a long period and considered good, clean mayhem. Both the GAC and the Members considered its virtues outweighed its vices. This was further supported by research findings that showed the overwhelming majority of parent viewers considered *The A-Team* to be harmless for their tender offspring to watch. Actually, I and William share, at least in this respect, a common dislike. I have always thought *The A-Team* vulgar, macho and thoroughly lacking in any saving features. It glorifies violence and, worse, it seems to me the violence it extols provides endless excuses for even more bizarre forms of antisocial behaviour. On the other hand, I strongly object to *Allo, Allo*. I have never seen the funny side of a so-called comedy set in occupied France under the Gestapo. To raise guffaws from a period of history in which hundreds of people were tortured and killed strikes me as being infinitely more suspect in his contemplation of moral values than even *The A-Team*.

As well as slagging off William Rees-Mogg, Michael Grade announced on Monday (16 May) that Channel 4 would cease showing snooker, a decision that gives me considerable personal pleasure as I have always considered snooker a tedious and overrated spectacle and totally inappropriate for Channel 4.

On Tuesday I attended the ITN Board Meeting, most of it taken up with agonising over Super Channel's refusal to continue with the news input of ITN. Super Channel want the cost reduced to £1.5m. The conflicts within the Board are highly visible. One camp, Granada and Yorkshire, would like ITN slimmed down. They have an interest, more than the others, in ensuring Super Channel's continuation as a profit centre since they jointly own Music Box, the company that handles the supply of programmes for Super Channel. Richard Dunn, as acting Chairman, behaved well and refused to allow the Board to be bludgeoned into making any rash decisions. He pointed out that ITN had a contract and that no hasty response should be forced out of the Board. He advised waiting until the new Chairman was installed.

Another hot point occurred over the decision not to transmit 'live' the Reagan speech in the Guildhall in June after his return from Moscow. David Nicholas expressed his hope that reconsideration be given to the decision. I agreed. Small wonder if ITV loses its position as a PSB provider. Lacklustre programmes and turning its back on legitimate news stories of major importance is a sure recipe for assisting the Government to treat television as they have radio.

In the evening, I attended the Aitchison Memorial Fund's 16th Goodman Lecture, given by Duke Hussey and entitled 'Channels of Culture'. A distinctly oddball affair, held in the elegant setting of 6 Carlton Terrace. Neither Sidney Bernstein nor I had been invited to private drinks beforehand so, clutching Roma and Sidney, we took our drinks uninvited into the private reception. Arnold Goodman waddled in looking lost and later took his seat to preside over what I took to be a reading of extracts from the BBC's annual report. Very thin on intellectual nourishment and high on praise and self-justification for the wonders bestowed by a munificent corporation on the grateful licence payers. The theme appeared to be that the BBC should survive to act as the nation's cultural conscience whilst Hussey would have his audience believe that the 'other chaps', the commercial ones, would vanish without trace in the whirlpool of commercial vulgarities. No matter, said Hussey, how hard the IBA with its pseudo-Reithian beliefs attempt otherwise. I thought the 'pseudo' bit rather harsh and said so afterwards to Dukie.

The strategy of the BBC is thus becoming plain. They still stand for culture and high-mindedness whilst ITV goes down-market and ceases because it cannot afford not to compete with all the other commercial offerings, leaving good old dependable Auntie to carry the flag. All very neat and tidy and very satisfactory to a Government doing its utmost to fragment and break up the existing 'cosy duopoly'. Why, Government might well argue, should they do anything if the BBC does it for them? A perfectly consistent thesis with a quiet logic that chills.

On Wednesday, 18 May, I talked to staff at Crawley Court, which seemed to be appreciated. In the evening, attended dinner with the three National Advisory Committees. *The Times* quotes Duke Hussey's lecture and his reference to Rees-Mogg. I look forward to my conversations with him, armed no doubt with the Lord Chamberlain's white staff to admonish me!

On Thursday I talked to the three Advisory Committees and went to a dinner in their honour hosted by George, who gave the first (of many) 'last speeches as Chairman' to this body. I thought it a pity that he didn't express some confidence in the staff to carry on the good fight after he leaves the field. Perhaps he doesn't think that we will!

On Friday *The Times* led with a story suggesting that the Radio Bill will be put back and submerged into one 'massive' broadcasting bill to be brought before Parliament in late 89. It would then reach the statute book in the summer of 1990. Peter Baldwin, who sat next to Timothy Renton for lunch, thinks that Renton would like to see some sort of deal struck with the IBA so that it can 'manage' the radio business in the space between. I am going to see Renton on Tuesday next week and will see what he has to say.

George Russell on Friday was announced as the new Chairman of ITN. George telephoned me to suggest we met at the earliest opportunity. It could be an interesting conversation.

Lunch with Alan Coren, new Editor of the restyled *Listener*. An engaging, intelligent and witty man. I only fear that the ITV MDs will begin to stick their noses into editorial matters. Mr Coren would then, I think, rise from his desk, put down his pen and depart.

This weekend the heavy Sundays again inspect Rees-Mogg. He probably thrives on it. As a Garrick member, I am afraid he'll give the old place a bad name.

Big articles in the *Sunday Times* about the multiplicity of channels soon to engulf viewers. All the signs are there for a deregulated ITV and an all-powerful Broadcasting Standards Council.

Monday 30th May

Returned on Sunday from Malmo in Sweden. Today is a Bank Holiday, so caught up with the Sunday newspapers. The *Sunday Times* is serialising DG Alasdair Milne's account of his time at the BBC. The first instalment I guess was chosen to highlight the manner of his leaving. He seems to have written his letter of resignation without putting up any kind of fight.

The BBC are once again in the spotlight. Legionnaires Disease has been followed by an asbestos alert that has closed six or seven studios. Last week a group of lesbians invaded the *News at Six* studios protesting about something or other. This weekend, the press have been busy stirring up a controversy over the showing of the Falklands play *Tumbledown*. Richard Eyre has said the work is meant to be political. The BBC believes it is balanced. Anyway, they say, it is not a documentary or a docudrama! I shall miss the actual transmission because I am dining at the Garrick with Dickie. Michael Checkland, like all sensible DGs, is in Iceland. I seem to remember that Alasdair was on a boat when the *Real Lives* took centre stage.

This last week has been frustrating. I have been trying to get ITV or Channel 4 to take Reagan's speech at the Guildhall live, but they are not interested, arguing that the *News at One* will cover it. (He speaks at midday). Channel 4, Michael Grade, doesn't want it. He reasons ITV should do it. I spoke to Dickie, who was shocked that Channel 4 weren't taking it and said he would speak to Michael. David Nicholas rang me today to find out whether there had been any movement. Grade had not spoken to him. David Glencross agrees with the ITV Companies, which is a pity, but there is still time.

Another storm cloud, still a blob, could break next week before the showing of the Kurt Waldheim programme: *Waldheim: A Commission of Enquiry*. The film is an inquiry into the question of whether Kurt Waldheim committed war crimes during World War II. He served for two terms as Secretary General of the United Nations from 1972 to 1981. He then became president of Austria, holding that office from 1986–1992. During his tenure as president, information was revealed that suggested Waldheim had served as a German staff officer during the war and had participated in actions to deport Jewish people to concentration camps. In the programme two teams of lawyers present the evidence to a panel of international justices. There is testimony from Waldheim's fellow officers and eyewitness accounts. Historians express their views. At the end of the film, the judges render their decision.

I believe Thames should cut the intended ending. If we include the verdict, I believe we are in danger of breaking, at least in spirit, our guidelines and sailing dangerously close to permitting 'trial by television'. A cut at the end would allow the Great British Public to make up its own mind.

On Wednesday, I met Timothy Renton at the Home Office to discuss radio. I still feel bitter about their decision and consequently taking a shallow view over the question of whether or not to continue advertising new radio contracts. We probably ought to continue.

TV-am is bubbling up again. This time over who should be its next Chairman. I have heard that Bruce Gyngell is making a bid and that Mike Luckwell, late of Carlton, would take over as MD. I don't think the IBA will be happy with the prospect of Bruce heading up TV-am.

There will shortly be a *World In Action* film investigating TV-am. This promises to be a pretty dubious affair and I imagine has been dreamt up by ACTT members within Granada. Anyway, there is no love lost between TV-am and the rest of the network. (Not that there's much love between the ITV Companies anyway.) Once again, the IBA will be dragged through the mud. We are in a quandary since the ACTT have now succeeded in having their case – that the IBA has failed in its duty to maintain standards – upheld in court. Allen & Overy have advised us that to appear in the programme would be unwise and we would prejudice our position, which sounds like sensible advice.

This weekend has been the occasion of ITV's 27-hour Telethon, which finished tonight at 10pm. So far – at 7.50pm – they have raised over £12m. They aim at £20m and will probably succeed.

Sunday 5th June

Feelings of despair and uncertainty occupy my thoughts too much lately. Television and broadcasting is coming out of the ice-age. Am I the right person to guide the IBA across these waters? I am tired of being the accused. Have I wasted nearly eight years to leave no mark on the sand for the next tide. That was the most I had hoped for. Radio all but gone; television stumbling.

Breakfasted on Wednesday 1 June at the Hyde Park with George Russell. His plans for ITN. He goes to see Mrs T on Tuesday for tea and cakes.

Delighted to know that Channel 4 has now agreed to televise Reagan at the Guildhall. (I dined with Richard Attenborough at the Garrick the night before. He had spoken to Michael Grade on Friday and asked him to think again.) Alastair was more than convinced that ITN should go forward into the next franchise round as its own man.

Saw Jeremy Isaacs at Covent Garden in the evening, all set to become Britain's greatest opera revivalist!

Lunch on Friday with A.J. Butler, possible replacement for Shirley Littler when she retires at the end of 1989.

The Telethon achieved an incredible £22m. A huge effort by many. Television can be a friend to those in need despite the shouts for its blood by most politicians. The £1m gift by Government caused a few eyebrows to be raised.

Saturday 11th June

Last Sunday's *Waldheim: Commission of Enquiry*, a four-hour marathon, duly played itself out to an audience square-eyed in the UK and Austria, determined to be there at the end. The verdict, predictably as the case unwound and no new evidence was forthcoming, 'no case to answer'. It was deeply impressive and deeply boring.

Rumbles continue over *Tumbledown*. I think genuine misgivings over the confusion regarding its intention – was it a drama documentary or was it drama based on actuality? Or was it simply being economical with some of the truth? Ten million people had the chance to make up their own minds.

On Monday, an early meeting of the Board of the Open College, with new Board Member Anita Roddick of Body Shop fame. Very bright, as one would expect. The OC is in quite serious financial trouble. The estimates of student involvement are hopelessly out and unless we get new Government backing, which is by no means certain, the College will be insolvent by August. There is a great deal of good intention about the whole thing, but I am not at all sure that there is a business mind running it. We finally chose a mid-way option, seeking some £20m, which will take us forward another three years. Will the Government wear it? I am not sure, although one of Mrs T's Golden Boys, Michael Green, is our chairman.

In the evening, William Rees-Mogg to dinner with us. William is a curious oddity. He looks a bit like a barrister, or even a doctor of sorts. An underlying arrogance keeps showing through a thin, very thin, veneer when listening to anyone else's views. William is a High Tory in the classical tradition: aloof, distant, articulate. He appeared, his suit covered in what looked like cat hairs. Or perhaps, though this strains credulity, the long black hairs of some femme fatale left languishing on a chaise longue somewhere in darkest St John's Wood!

The dinner talk predictably circled around violence, with a little sex thrown in. The more I listened to William holding forth, the more convinced I became that he genuinely believes that he alone is the saviour of the people's virtue. I felt discouraged and sad that so little of the effort and agonising that so many people had put into striving for standards we could believe in was so clearly of little account. Perhaps some of his arrogance was due to the knowledge, we only became aware of today, that Mrs T had furthered his ascendancy by creating him a peer.

Sunday 12th June

My long-term (mid-term?!) analysis of Government strategy is to have the BSC overlord of all broadcasting standards, including the parts of the BBC that will be put out to commercial use. The IBA would become a broadcasting agency or cease to be.

On Tuesday *The Times* prints the proposals by Alastair Burnet for an all-night contractor based around *News At Ten*. A good stir of the ITN pot, which will do no harm.

Rupert Murdoch plans to launch his Astra plans on Wednesday. SCC proves to be a difficult meeting. We scraped by on our proposals to bid for an SSS satellite for use by the ITV Companies. Bruce Gyngell returned from sick-leave after his heart attack. His return does not leave his colleagues around the table celebrating. I had an opportunity of talking to Ian Irvine, the Acting Chairman of TV-am, on Tuesday evening at The Thirty Club. Ian assured me that the plot hatched in New York by Bruce to become Chairman and appoint ex-Carlton Mike Luckwell as MD had been squashed on his return.

SCC's main concerns surrounded the arrogance in the Policy Document of publisher-contractors. They are just waking up to the implications. (Although later in the week Andrew Quinn telephoned to say that he would be sending me a letter seeking advice on hiving off parts of Granada's current in-house facilities.) Publisher-contractors will, I predict, become the big talking point as time goes on.

Night broadcasting was also high on SCC's consideration. I said I was expecting the equivalent of an application for the night hours. The Companies, I think, thought that the autumn schedule would suffice. After SCC, Richard Dunn talked with me privately about Thames and Michael Green. I think I have now got to the real bottom line of Thames's real wishes: Richard would like Carlton in at 20 per cent. This would mean that Carlton would have to sell their 20 per cent stake in Central. Richard is definitely against Carlton holding more than 20 per cent.

On Wednesday 8 June, Mrs T spoke at the Press Association lunch at the Savoy and delivered another slap on the wrist to broadcasters and newspapers about standards of regulation. She also gave her verdict on more channels: 'There are some people who say that it will drive television down-market. Now I have always believed that there is a market for the best and I do not like the argument and I do not believe it is necessarily true that television goes down-market. I think British people can be a lot more discerning than that, and I think that the opportunity of more channels, or subscriber channels, will enable us also to have some very upmarket television which I am certain many people will welcome.' I think she is wrong.

1988

In the evening, a session on research given by Barrie Gunter. Very lacklustre and more than ever providing evidence that £1m a year is being spent largely on researchers speaking to researchers. Dismantling research should be tabled for serious consideration.

BSB came to the Authority Meeting on Thursday and met Members for the first time since winning the contract. Anthony Simonds-Gooding puts up a sterling performance. Trevor Holdsworth is quietly impressive and immensely likeable. Graham Grist gives a good, calm impression of someone who understands how the wheels go round. Members, I think, were impressed. Anthony at one point described BSB as the 'David to ITV's Goliath'. As Anthony must weigh in at at least 18 stone, and is built like a bull, the lack of precision in identifying an analogy was pointed out by GT to much merriment.

We lunched BSB and Aubrey Diamond, who was retiring after distinguished service on the ALC. During lunch, I learnt that BSB were to pay a visit to Douglas Hurd and David Young at the Lords that same afternoon. The reason unclear. This chimed in with an invitation GT and I received the same day to meet Douglas Hurd on Friday.

GT and I went to the Lords on Friday. Nobody seemed to know where we were meant to go. Earlier, I had received a call from Michael Grade to tell me that he thought a plan was afoot to move Channel 4 and BBC2 to channels four and five on BSB. This proved true. Douglas greeted us in David Young's office looking more than embarrassed to be with the Lords and not in his own office. David Young was answering questions on Scottish affairs in the Lords, so it fell to Douglas to unfold the latest plot. David Young's visit to Crawley Court had apparently opened his eyes to two options of moving with speed – hence the meeting to get thinking in motion. We said we would think about it. On first blush, the proposal has attractions. For the Government it has *great* attractions – freeing up two national channels.

The Nelson Mandela BBC Marathon pop concert duly took place yesterday. I thought it a great pity, indeed a tragedy, that with a potential audience of more than 400 million in 60 odd countries, the UK linking material by Lenny Henry should be so yobbishly crude. How on earth we expect others to think of us as anything else than yobs I cannot imagine. As an advertisement for UK Limited, it was disgraceful. A sadness because the cause is profoundly good and there were moments when the real spirit of the occasion was really moving.

Just as we were leaving the cottage, the telephone rang. It was Richard Dunn calling to say that the *Sunday Telegraph* was carrying an account in its City Page relating to the possible sale of Rank's shares to Carlton. I asked him whether the Board had discussed their preferences and he told me that they would prefer to adopt the method outlined in my pre-Christmas letter, that no holding should be more than 10 per cent. I asked him if Carlton acquired 20 per cent, how would he feel? He replied, 'Okay'. Richard said that he had spoken that morning with Ian Trethowan, who was weekending with Geoffrey Howe. He said the atmosphere was very cordial. I wonder how cordial it would have been if Mrs T had been included in the party!

Friday 17th June

Last Sunday's newspapers were filled with comment about David Young's proposals to transfer BBC 2 and C4 to BSB 4 and 5. The arguments and counter-arguments have continued through this week.

I held a council of war at DGMM on Tuesday and an action plan was drawn up to enable a coherent expression of IBA thinking to be provided for IBA Members before forwarding to the Home Office.

When all the talking is done, the single question that needs to be addressed is: At what point does Government wish to cease terrestrial output of C4 and BBC2. If the decision is to wait until universality is achieved, or nearly achieved, by BSB satellite coverage, that is one scenario (and most broadcasters would find little to fault in the transfer). If Government decided to switch off earlier that would have a profound effect on both financing and the concept of a public service as we know it today. This would raise issues about the licence money attributed to BBC 2 services and the money through advertising receivable by C4 (through subscription). Obviously, with less homes reached via BSB dishes, advertisers would not use the channel as they do today, but Government could, if they wanted, lower the licence fee for BBC services since BBC 2 would only be available to very few. And in the case of C4, the terrestrial companies could be made to continue a subscription which initially would be more, considerably more, than the receipts through advertising they currently enjoy.

In the year to 31 March 1988, C4's subscription of £163.4m amounted to 12 per cent of the actual total advertising revenues on ITV, and C4 (£213.3m) amounted to 15.6 per cent of the total ITV and C4 revenue. C4's programmes delivered 17.4 per cent of the commercial television audience so C4 more than pays its way under the present arrangement.

It would require determination on the part of Government to take the step of withdrawing universality as a condition of transfer, but they in turn could offer two new channels terrestrially to audiences to make up for it! If I was David Young, I would certainly look at that option.

British yobos have been out in force in Germany, kicking and brawling before and after football matches. Television brings home the realities and horrors of this appalling behaviour. A bad advertisement for UK Limited. Television, so far, has not been blamed!

On Tuesday, off to an Arts consultation in Manchester, jointly sponsored by the IBA and the Arts Council. A good turn out. Melvyn Bragg gave the after dinner keynote speech. Not much hope for the arts on television in the New World. I opened the consultation and said that Art was transferable and had a place in television's new world. Art did not only reflect, it shaped social attitudes. Its role should not be marginalised.

Andrew Quinn wrote to me, inviting the IBA to consider whether they would permit Granada to separate the production facility from the programme-making entity within Granada. In due course, they would wish to see the transmission element separated also. Granada have clearly, and rightly in my view, got the message about publisher/contractor and are planning to adapt their role before the 1992 contract review.

Returned home to a jolly dinner party with Carina and David Frost and Shirley and Abe Rosenthal at the Gay Hussar. We all decided to make it an annual occasion.

Still no news of George's successor. We have begun planning the diary for next year without any knowledge of the new Chairman.

The timetable now for the new ITV contracts means that, unless I stay on for another two years, there will be a new Chairman in 1989 and a new DG at the beginning of 1990. I could, of course, go earlier – or indeed I might be pushed!

Saturday 25th June

Wimbledon. Strawberries. Eye-shades. And the plip-plopping of balls bouncing off racquets. Touts tout, players plead to or prate at umpires, noses peel and reputations are made or lost. For me, Wimbledon *is* summer.

Last Sunday to Harrogate to attend a CIRCOM conference and speak at their dinner. CIRCOM Regional is an ad-hoc grouping of broadcasters throughout Europe who meet from time to time to discuss matters related to regional broadcasting. In my speech, I likened advances in satellite television to fast food 'hamburger' television. There was a place for it but so too was there a place for distinctive food, the specialities of different countries and regions.

Back to London on Monday and straight to Wells Street to attend an ITV Board Meeting. The first chaired by George Russell and a good chairman he will make.

Sunday 26th June

The ITN Board is now composed of accountants and sales persons. Only Brian Tesler and James Gatward remain. The ITN Board has never faced in so many directions at the same time. I really can't blame them. BSB/Astra, Super Channel and ITV all with different interests.

George Russell asked Alastair Burnet to comment on his proposals to hive off ITN into a separate night time contractor. This he did, amid a strong silence from the rest of his boardroom colleagues.

On Tuesday to see Norman Fowler about the perilous state of the Open College. Fowler ill so had to content ourselves with a subordinate. Then off to Bristol and to the EBU's Educational Working Party. I spoke after a dinner given at Longleat.

On Wednesday, Douglas Hurd gave an extraordinary speech to the Coningsby Club of Young Conservatives. In it he tilted at both the BBC and the IBA. The BBC could not, should not, depend for ever on the licence fee. The IBA might no longer be useful as the regulator. One of those speeches that rattle the tin with pebbles and cause junior secretaries to wonder if they will get paid after next week.

Having failed dismally to address themselves to the question of the future of broadcasting, they, the Government, are thrashing around trying to show off their options, not caring – or perhaps taking pleasure in – the anger and bewilderment of the broadcasters.

Dickie put it extremely well in a speech he gave on Thursday and quoted in today's *Observer* Leader: 'The Government is simply putting forward various ideas, ill-judged, ill-considered, without consultation. The finest broadcasting operation in the world is being treated as a shuttlecock and is being bashed around the court. It is entitled to better treatment.' The Leader – 'Broadcasting deserves better treatment' – is possibly a turning point in public opinion.

Dickie rang me on Friday to say that he had spoken to Duke Hussey and thought that he, Duke and George should write a letter to *The Times* spelling out their disquiet at the Government's attitude.

Really the whole thing is a sick joke. I am feeling more and more as though I am in the wrong job. Pulled in so many ways by so many different interests. George leaving at the end of the year makes the future direction of the IBA impossible to predict.

Perhaps J.B. Priestley's view will be truly tested: 'The more we elaborate our means of communication, the less we communicate'.

Tuesday 5th July

It has been longer than usual since I have written my diary because I have been in Greece over the weekend attending the Annual General Assembly of the EBU – and a rotten time in stinking heat we had out there.

On Monday 27 June an early meeting with Anthony Simonds-Gooding, Graham Grist and Peter Bell in their office.

BSB are having a radical reappraisal of their launch and marketing plans and are planning, if their shareholders agree, to bring forward their promotional expenditure to compete head-on with the Astra launch in order to spoil Astra's launch plans. The object is to get a greater penetration of dishes in the first year than anticipated in their original plan. They are not in favour of endorsing the proposal of David Young that C4 and BBC 2 should move on to the satellites. I left the meeting carrying a thick folder of plans for their launch.

Attended a performance of *Aida* at Earls Court on Tuesday. To opera aficionados the whole event was bizarre – too gaudy, too noisy, too everything – but to the audience of some 14,000 it was splendid and the applause afterwards confirmed its undoubted success.

On Tuesday ITV bid £10m to secure soccer rights away from both the BBC and BSB. A major sign of the competition for sporting events that will soon be part of everyday life.

Wednesday 29 June. Over the past week there has been mounting concern about drink-related vandalism and rowdy behaviour. I knew it was only a matter of time before Douglas Hurd, or someone else in Government, turned to the box as scapegoat. Sure enough, Douglas Hurd paraded his prejudice in a speech: 'It is probably true to say that these expectations of excitement have risen higher than ever before. Probably television helps to arouse without satisfying such expectations. Certainly that is true of stupid drinking.'

Lunched with Programme Controllers on Thursday. This year much more open and controversial than in previous years. The message was put over plainly by Greg Dyke: if you don't allow us to compete we will be wiped out. Members listened attentively.

Perhaps the message was the more stark because there were already leaks appearing in the press from the Home Office Select Committee on Broadcasting. Sufficient to provoke the *FT* to headline: 'MPs to suggest abolishing IBA'. Before I left for Greece, Members at the Authority Meeting supported the proposals put to them by ITVA for night programmes and I left Brompton Road and went to Greece and to the EBU.

Sunday 10th July

Arrived back from Thessalonica without my suitcase that thoughtful Greeks placed on a Frankfurt flight to London rather than my flight, via Munich. Pleased to get home.

Early meeting on Tuesday 5 July with David Plowright and Andrew Quinn to hear about their fears for the break-up of ITVA and the strains placed on Granada for having a role in BSB. Anglia and Granada both being treated as outsiders on matters relating to film acquisitions and, in particular, sports acquisitions. These are obvious signs of tension that will only increase as competition grows.

Tuesday's newspapers are filled with reports on the findings of the Home Affairs Select Committee on Broadcasting. Very sensible findings except for their comments on the role of the IBA. I think, however, we can live with their view that there should be one commercial television authority. If we play it long, I think we stand a good chance of becoming that authority. If they had named us as the body, we would be facing a continuous barrage of criticism. As it is, there is a silence. I am convinced that we can adapt to fit the role.

Timothy Renton spoke today on the outlook for radio at the Radio Festival, which I did not attend. Government are in a mess with the prospect of a long delay before legislation. Lunched with Timothy on Wednesday at the Garrick. He was pleased to hear that we did not fancy the C4 idea put up by David Young. We spoke about the Home Affairs Committee findings. I told him we were not displeased with the results. No news yet of a successor to GT. I suggested Joel Barnett. Renton thought that Dukie would be upset at not being invited. I mentioned Jim Prior and Patrick Jenkin. They are looking for someone with business and arts flair. Someone like George Russell. He asked me to telephone him if I had any more ideas but who, I wonder, wants to commit themselves to an Authority surrounded by so much uncertainty?

In the evening, problems over a programme made by Tyne Tees about the Cleveland child abuse report out today. Spent some time agonising over whether to allow ITN to show some clips from actual interviews between social workers and children and decided not to permit this as our view (Allen & Overy's) was that it could be found in contempt of court. Showed the film to GT, who allowed it to go forward for transmission. Think I probably made a mistake.

On Thursday, a meeting at the Home Office with Douglas Hurd, Tom King,

Timothy Renton, George, Duke Hussey and John Birt. The subject: television in Northern Ireland.

To Glyndebourne in the evening for *Die Fledermaus* as guests of Isobel and James Gatward. Marvellous cold supper of lobster and able to congratulate James on his successful acquisition of MTM in America.

Long meeting on Friday afternoon with GT, Donald Maitland and Shirley Littler to look at plans for the next five years. Plenty of scope for change!

Sunday 17th July

Ripples from the findings of the Home Affairs Committee still lap around the foundations of Brompton Towers. Most casual readers of the press will have already written-off the IBA as a spent force. To many who worked in the belief that they were public servants, the slurs and mud-slinging at the regulators must seem unfair and more than rather demoralising.

Duke Hussey has come in for some flak this week for saying, in his six-monthly review of BBC happenings, that he wants further consideration to be given to plays based on documentary truths – 'faction'. We are having the same thoughts.

On Monday 11 July the press announced that the think-tank Committee on Broadcasting were due to meet in leafy Berkshire. More rumours and speculation.

A meeting with Donald Maitland, Lord T and Shirley Littler to look at how to plan the IBA's future, at least for the next five years.

A conversation that could have far-reaching effects. GT has had second thoughts about tendering for contracts and is now prepared to accept that the force of feeling is towards some form of competitive tendering. Added to this, is the recognition that the whole manner in which we regulate through the 90s will have to alter radically if the IBA is to have any role in future developments. Consequently we agreed to start Members and staff thinking what had previously been unthinkable. Stripping out many of the duties of Television Division will not be welcomed but it will have to be.

The *FT* on Tuesday 12 July headlines Monday's meeting of the think-tank as 'Consensus reached on commercial TV'. One of those who attended the seminar said: 'It was a consolidation of the debate that has been going on for the last two years'.

Richard Dunn has agreed to serve as the next Chairman of ITVA. I paid tribute to David McCall for his two years as ITVA Chairman. Most of the meeting was taken up with a discussion on the levy changes proposed by Douglas Hurd.

The big five contractors are extremely worried over a change to NAR (net advertising revenue) which will strip out their profit and reduce their budgets for programme making.

Attended a State Banquet at Buckingham Palace with Roma to honour the President of Turkey, Kenan Evrien. Very grand. Great fun. Talked to Prince Charles and Edward. One guest so overcome that he devoured his ice-cream with a knife and fork. Overheard Mrs T. ordering Denis to take her home and make her a hot toddy. The entire Royal Family, with the exception of Princess Margaret and Fergie. Talked to Sir Denis Rook who looked pleased with himself – now know why. He has just had his salary raised from £120,000 to £200,000 odd! Left at about 1130pm with the place still buzzing. Must do it again sometime! Even though we did sit below the salt or, in our case, so far down the table that the bread rolls ran out before they reached us!

On Wednesday 13 July a meeting with the Steering Committee of the Independents. Not at all happy with the process of monitoring and say that they cannot make any sense of the figures and facts given to them. We will have to change this. It is just plain stupid to fudge and muddle the issue. I wrote to David Glencross saying just this after the meeting.

A meeting with Ian Irvine, Chairman of TV-am. He wants a total restructuring of the company with Peter de Savary, TV-am and a third group forming a holding company in which TV-am would become a wholly owned subsidiary.

In the evening I missed out on a drinks party given by Timothy Renton. GT went and told me that Douglas Hurd had been extremely stand-offish. Wonder if this is anything to do with the think tank findings?

Saturday 23rd July

A week in which the patterns of ITV could well have shifted as a result of the Authority Meeting on Thursday.

On Monday the battle for football rights was still being fought, by the BBC and BSB on one hand and ITV on the other with no end to the bids and counter-bids in sight.

Lunch at the Ritz with Sir Bernard Audley. I have always counted myself lucky to eat in the splendour of that dining room but this time it was somewhat marred by an extremely large wine waiter leaning over the table, sporting – if that is the word – one of the dirtiest waistcoats I have ever seen on anyone, let alone the Head Wine Waiter at the Ritz. If I had not been the guest of Bernard, a swift letter to the management would have followed the lunch. Bernard's company, AGB, is under a bit of a cloud because his American venture has run into trouble. The Americans still like doing business with Neilson, despite the fact that Neilson's service is out of date compared with AGB's.

Meeting in the afternoon of Tuesday with Ken Miles of ISBA over regional television in the next contract round. Kenneth is anxious to ensure that ITV does not get carved up into only six regions (plus Northern Ireland).

The IPA would like to see this happen. I said it seemed odd to me that ISBA, representing the advertisers, was at odds with the IPA who, as advertising agents, were their servants. I don't see why the advertisers can't simply tell the agencies to do as they are told, but I suppose life isn't like that.

On Wednesday a meeting with Andrew Quinn regarding Granada's intention to create a facilities subsidiary out of its studio complex, thus paving the way for more efficient cost control and the possibility of hiving it off completely if Granada decides to go in for the next contract period as a 'publisher contractor'.

I told Andrew that we would not wish to stand in their way. I think he was somewhat surprised.

On Tuesday Ian Irvine had telephoned me to say that he thought it likely that news of TV-am's restructuring proposals would get into the press. I told him that, if it did, he must recognise that the IBA had not given any green light.

In the evening, dinner with the Chairman and BBC Governors. Our turn this year to do the honours. We had a jolly evening, starting off with drinks in the anteroom and later, over coffee, GT and Duke spoke, Duke warmly praising George for his nine years in office. George, I think, was quite touched. We all rose and toasted George and Grace. I was told during the evening that the atmosphere between BBC Governors and staff had improved in great measure since Alasdair's departure. The new team, apparently, was working well and Michael Grade and Paul Fox had brought back a sense of 'gravitas' into the BBC. John Birt, who had not been able to settle in due to his manner, was spoken less highly of.

Poor Ranjit Sondhi was there, smiling after his three and a half hour incarceration in the lift of the Emley Moor transmitter tower.

IBA Authority day on Thursday and much important business. I reported on TV-am and their hopes of restructuring. Main business was certainly approval that the IBA should separate engineering resources into a subsidiary company. It went through in less than five minutes. Major policy was then discussed, relating to the IBA and its own future. Approval was given to GT to send a letter to the Home Secretary. This probably marks the single greatest shift in IBA positioning since I have been there. I think it exceedingly sensible and timely. The Cabinet Committee meets next week and this will be the last real opportunity of giving Mrs T and her colleagues an insight into IBA thinking. If the White Paper does eventually come down in favour of a new regulatory body, it will not be for want of the IBA setting out its stall. I am a little fearful of a leak but it is a risk we have to take.

In the latter half of the afternoon, our annual meeting with ITV MDs. I should have mentioned earlier that the press today gave considerable space to the news that C4 would be supplying a breakfast service next year.

The meeting with the MDs proved lively and important. Subjects discussed: the future of regulation, maintaining the strength of the ITV system, the shape of the regions in the next contract round. Afterwards we repaired to the Hyde Park Hotel for dinner. Bruce Gyngell has aged since his three heart attacks. I told him that the IBA wanted to call Ian and himself in to meet Authority Members to hear from them about TV-am's plans to get the quality of their output improved. I think he recognises that time is running out.

Just before I left the Hyde Park, GT said that he was upset by the draft of the letter to the Home Secretary, with copies to the Prime Minister and David Young. (drafted by Donald and Shirley). It was too pushy.

Ian telephoned me on Friday to say that the TV-am restructuring was off for the time being. GT re-wrote the letter to Douglas (including my name as one of those wishing to call upon him).

On Sunday, C4 finally transmitted the 'Harrods Sale', the programme that reported on the machinations behind the purchase of Harrods by the Al Fayed brothers. Stand by for writs!

Tomorrow I give blood, as a donor.

Sunday 31st July

Tomorrow off to Portugal for 14 days. It will be nice to leave behind the turmoil and turbulence of television. Maybe distance will lead to perspective. Much needed by all of us engaged in this, the most public of all media, that turns the globe into a goldfish bowl. The seemingly indefatigable Prime Minister, having chaired the Cabinet meeting on the future of television, has now taken off, in the Parliamentary long recess, to tour the world, or most of it. She leaves behind her a paper chase of rumour and speculation over broadcasting.

On the subject of blood letting, with some trepidation I attended the National Farmers Union headquarters on Monday 25 July for the annual blood donor session. I filled in a long form, which appeared to encompass all known diseases (except the one they are most worried over – AIDS) and waited in a musical chairs type queue for a doctor to give the go-ahead to the nurses who were hovering over empty beds like vultures.

The doctor looked up from the form and repeated in a whisper the word I had written against countries in the last six months – 'China?' I nodded. The doctor shook his head. 'We need 26 weeks clear from China', he said mournfully.

Hanging my head, I tried to avoid the stares from the waiting queue, who were suspicious at my rejection and were bound to leap to the very worst conclusion. 'China!' I said loudly. My voice echoed round the dome in the ornate roof of the Farmers Union. No one reacted although if over each head there had been a thought bubble it would have read 'Try pulling the other one'. 'China', I said again, brightly, and left with as much dignity as I could muster.

Lunch with Colette Bowe, whose message was simple: the IBA must huddle in smoke-filled rooms and position itself to take on the job of the new commercial television authority. Time must not be lost. Colette asked that, whilst lying beside the swimming pool, I turn this matter over in my mind.

In the evening, GT and I dined with Messrs. Checkland, Young, Burton, Newlet and Hussey and Shirley Anglesey. I asked that the napkins bearing Shirley's crest should be laid out to grace the occasion. The purpose of the dinner was to consider what actions should/could be taken to counter the dreaded Moggery and his BSC ambitions. Shirley is prepared to resist all boarders and calls upon the IBA, BBC and the Cable Authority for support. Support she gets. The Chairman decided to write separately to Douglas Hurd

Over the meal, we chomped on the unpleasant prospect that Le Mogg appears determined to exercise his will even before the ink has dried on his appointment. Dukie showed us a letter from William Rees-Mogg on the subject of a recent episode of *Eastenders*. In it, Rees-Mogg outlined Mrs Whitehouse's concern about a rape scene and remarked that, as the Members of the Council have still to be appointed, 'I should nevertheless find it helpful in the meantime to have your views on whether these episodes complied in all respects with the BBC's family viewing policy, together with any more general comments you may wish to make about the application of that policy. Perhaps you would also be good enough to let me have, for information, a copy of your reply to Mrs Whitehouse.'

Dukie, I think, felt inclined to tell William to get his own copy from Mrs Whitehouse.

We also discussed whether William still considered that different forms of entry into the home, and on to the screen, should be judged on different degrees of acceptability. At our first meeting with William, I formed the definite view that different tolerance levels would be acceptable, but Michael Checkland thought that we had either heard wrong or William had changed his mind.

As a result of our conversation over dinner, I agreed to circulate to those present a matrix illustrating the different rulings and 'objectivity' we separately applied to standards of good taste and decency.

We broke up at about 11pm. Michael went off to stay overnight at the Savoy Hotel, where we were all meeting the following morning as breakfast guests of the *Sunday Times*.

On 26 July, the press headlines announced the demise of the BBC 2/C4 satellite plans proposed by David Young and Douglas Hurd. The Government try to cover their embarrassment by hinting broadly that they will give the green light to a fifth channel funded by advertising in 1992. They are being optimistic but it helps to cover up the bungle.

Bleary eyed, I made my way into breakfast and sat down with Dukie, David Frost, the German and French ambassadors and Charles Price. Andrew Neil set the proceedings going by saying that none of his selected speakers needed any introduction. That was true.

Michael Grade gave, I think, a rather strangely unexceptionable tour d'horizon of C4, admitting good-humouredly that since leaving the BBC he believed that C4 should rely on its complementary status to ITV and not compete. Michael listed ten points for keeping the BBC as *the* major source of PSB. It sounded a little like a litany.

Richard Dunn began to lose his voice but otherwise gave a good defence of ITV.

Rees-Mogg said that he had been considered an 'old owl' for 40 years. Now he was considered a despot! During his say-so, he made it clear that he considered that there should be one standard applied to all services into the home, including video.

Rupert Murdoch took this point up and said it would be a nightmare to police. Murdoch did his turn last. He believed the British public could only benefit from competition and anyway, he said, 'Responsible people in the media do have a code of ethics'. During questions, I asked him if he felt proud of the ethics displayed by his two Sunday tabloids. Murdoch replied, 'I am proud of them both, not to say that they don't make mistakes from time to time'.

Michael Winner, writing in the *Sunday Times* (31 July 1988) concluded his article on the event: 'As the assorted guests left the Savoy Dining Room, leaving Murdoch surrounded by a cluster of press, it was how a man of Rupert Murdoch's extraordinary talent could point with public pride to his *News of the World* that left me saddened'.

Later in the morning we issued our Annual Report, which got good coverage the following day (27 July), particularly for GT's valedictory and for the doubts we again this year raised over the standards of TV-am and its output.

The *Sun* newspaper ran, as a Leader, a very funny attack against me, headed: 'Sun and Wind' finishing with, 'Windbag Whitney may enjoy looking at sunrises. Hopefully he will soon be looking at the sunset of the Independent Broadcasting Authority.' By a strange coincidence *Sun* is owned by Rupert Murdoch!

A news release is issued by the Home Office naming William's Broadcasting Council, or some of them, including Miss Jocelyn Barrow, a soon-to-be ex-Governor of the BBC. Also included in the list is Bill Westwood, Bishop of Peterborough – a good friend and, I think, a sensible person. The salary of these Members is quoted at £9,000 per annum. Our Members get £4,500, a fact that has rightly infuriated George, who will write to the Home Secretary.

On 28 July a meeting with BSB, one of our regular sessions. All appears to be going as planned: no major crises. These are still to come.

Much press comment on 29 July about the Home Secretary's plans for changing the levy to NAR-based revenues. GT's letter to the Home Secretary may make him think again.

So there we are. The end of the week and more speculation about the end of the IBA. I fear we have few friends and still fewer admirers. Being unloved for so many years should have made me testy but I think, on the contrary, I have continued to bounce. Whether in the bouncing I will go over the wall along with the rest of the IBA only time will tell.

Sunday 21st August

A holiday with Roma in Portugal made a splendid break. I wrote an outline for an outrageous mini-series to keep my hand in, and thought about an equally outrageous game show called *Swap*. I may need to draw upon these frail talents sooner than expected.

Returning to London late on Monday night, or rather Tuesday morning, we got to bed at 6am, having been delayed for over eight hours. On 16 August we were met by a doleful David Barber, my driver, who related the headlines in the *Sunday Times* of 7 August: 'Thatcher to close down the IBA in big TV shake-up'. It turns out that this was another GT stitch-up. The two reporters, who GT said had no knowledge about broadcasting or its issues, interviewed him for an hour and a half, then went away and wrote a piece that contained speculation, innuendo and inaccuracy. Colette than spent the Sunday of speculation putting out the IBA's point of view and rebalancing the story. What a homecoming! Staff morale is at a low ebb. I can understand it. Staff must find it mystifying and discouraging to be publicly vilified and held in contempt for doing the job they are given to do. If the writing really is on the wall, it will be grossly unfair on all those who have worked over many years with total dedication. Just as well I didn't read any reports whilst I was in Portugal.

On Wednesday we held a planned meeting with TV-am in the shape of Bruce Gyngell and Brian Moore. GT took the Chair, and delivered in solemn tones the IBA's growing anxiety over the standard of TV-am's output. Afterwards, we put out a statement which predictably got a mixed reception. My prediction is that TV-am will not get an extension of contract. Or, if it does, it will not get a renewal of contract in 1992. I think the Board will take the decision soon to release Bruce Gyngell from his position and give him a massive leaving present – £750,000. Peter de Savary is not an idiot and he will balance where the relative strengths lie.

I am wrestling with an article for, I hope, *The Observer*. I desperately feel that the case for middle ground opinion is not being represented. The IBA is that middle ground and our voice should be heard. A short 'Diary' entry was the result.

Monday 29th August

This weekend marks the Edinburgh Television Festival. Little appears to have come from it, except a ringing statement from one Jim Styles of Sky Channel that it will have nothing to do with the ACTT when it launches its Astra Channels. An equally ringing statement came from Greg Dyke, always to be relied on to place his mouth where his foot might more properly be. Greg believes that the time devoted to those 'boring old children's programmes', religious programmes and adult education will have to go in the 90s so that ITV will be able to compete with the new channels.

'And so say all of us.' I can hear the mass ranks of ITV Companies: 'Get rid of the IBA. Unlock the shackles and let's all get our snouts in the trough'. Actually they, the Companies, won't say that out loud for fear of damaging their relations with the IBA. Frankly, I couldn't care a brass farthing what they say, privately or publicly. I feel at present disenchanted by television. I have been attempting to write an article pointing out that the IBA is not to blame, but it sounds so defensive. I shall plod on and see what it looks like.

This week's pickle: BSB are trying to choose a News Producer. They have shortlisted three. Now two of those not shortlisted are objecting that the IBA has said those with 'significant newspaper interest' may not be acceptable. This is nonsense and I have said so to BSB.

Sunday 4th September

An important meeting on Wednesday 31 August with Anthony Simonds-Gooding and Edward Bickham. BSB would now like to see Channels 4 and 5 released as early as possible to promote greater interest in BSB's satellite than in Astra's. I am recommending to the Authority that we agree a slightly lower power and thus a slightly larger dish to enable all five channels to be on one satellite. I think that the Members will agree the proposal.

On Friday a Board meeting with the Open College. The Management is still, I am afraid, far from on top of the job. Expectations were too high at the start. David Young went at it without really thinking it through, apart from it being an initiative he wanted to father. Peat Marwick are undertaking a study. The results must be in front of the Minister by 8 October. He will then decide whether or not a grant should be given. I am surprised that Michael Green hasn't kept a firmer grip on its management structure and performance, but I think Government will wish to see it go down the pan.

This week has been quiet. Little or no activity. GT has received a letter from the Home Secretary trying to pour oil over the troubled waters about Members' salaries in relation to the Broadcasting Standards Council.

Re the BSC, Colin Shaw has been mooted as a possible D.G. Now the wheel turns full circle. Shirley Littler believes him to be a chaotic organiser, but he would be good in the job. Very much his own man with strong, well-balanced convictions. Not always, I would imagine, inclined towards the view of the Mogg.

Next Tuesday a meeting with the Home Secretary. Do not believe we will hear anything to our benefit.

Tuesday 8th September

Arrived at the Home Office with Shirley Littler to meet GT and Donald Maitland. Shown into Douglas' office with habitual moving-on handshake from Douglas. He surrounded by the squad, including Timothy Renton.

What is not in the Minutes is the detail of one aspect of the talks. Douglas asked for confidentiality. Then he delivered the death knell for the IBA: the White Paper will recommend abolishing the Authority. It still hasn't sunk in yet.

When I first became D.G. I think I said, or wrote somewhere, when asked my ambition for the time of my DG-ship, that it was 'to preside over the demise of the IBA!' Little did I really suspect it would come so soon. The comment was not actually so frivolous. I believed, when I first joined, that time and new channels would diminish the need for the IBA and that it would be good for broadcasting, and viewers, as more choice would supersede the scarcity of frequencies which necessitated the need for regulation provided by the IBA.

From this part of the meeting I took away the impression that the Home Office doesn't want us to disappear without trace; rather they want to change the name and the faces. In fact, Douglas Hurd went, I thought, out of his way to say how much work there would be in holding together the IBA during what would be an extremely testing time.

I suppose this will turn out to be the most important development since the ITA was founded over 30 years ago. We drank our coffee, shook hands and left.

Peter Rogers has heard through a junior Home Office official that the H.O. is looking for a Chairman-designate who will become shadow-Chairman of the new CTA, which will replace the IBA. If this is correct, it will be a valuable morale booster if it turns out to be George Russell. A very satisfactory position, enabling the transition from the IBA to the CTA to be accomplished without severe loss of face. This could be in the mind of the Home Office.

Sunday 11th September

On Thursday a busy, and I think profitable, Authority Meeting. I put forward the proposition that BSB should get the release of a further two channels, although not to service them themselves. I said that I thought they should determine whether or not to stand by the original specification of dish size. (I have changed my position on this as now Astra are going all out to compete. BSB will have to put on the best possible show to encourage their dish sales).

The Members, I fear, were less than enthusiastic. But later, on Friday, when talking to Quentin Thomas, he endorsed very nearly the exact proposition that I had put to the Authority. The sticking point with the IBA, and with the Home Office, would I think be if BSB insisted that a veto should be put on another competing film channel.

On radio, the Members gave approval to a further 20 community stations. We will make an announcement on Tuesday and wait for the Home Office to respond.

TV-am was dealt with satisfactorily. We said we would judge its performance again in November and I wrote to Bruce confirming the various steps he is taking to get the station back to the standard we expected.

On Thursday, C4 told us that they were planning to have Gerry Adams on a late night chat show. The telephone grew hot with calls to the IBA and we said C4 would not put out the programme. C4 climbed down, looking a little bit silly in the process.

Next week I'll meet BSB and see what can be done to get the other two channels up and away.

Sunday 18th September

A week when the curtains were pulled further apart, or so it seemed, on the content of the White Paper. It is now taken for granted that the IBA will be abolished. No tears being shed but I sensed in the *Sunday Times* the first stirrings of recognition that the future of television in this country will undergo a fundamental change. 'A mixed blessing' is the view coming forward. A further leak this week established that serious consideration is being given to allowing TV contractors to select their own news service. In effect, this will bring about the end of ITN. Without a national platform, and income, the resources to maintain ITN would not be there.

Alastair Burnet briefed Bernard Ingham to make these misgivings clear to the PM. It went in the Diplomatic Bag to Chequers last weekend with the scribbled comment: 'We could lose the baby with the bath water'.

Some flack developing around our proposals for community radio. The AIRC are mightily miffed they were not consulted over our proposals. I told Dickie when I had dinner with him on Wednesday night that the AIRC could only blame itself for not sharing in IBA thinking. I told him how bitter I still felt about the way the AIRC had behaved over radio. If they wanted competition and deregulation, they would get it! Still, I fear we have not been as adroit as we might have been over consulting. I have sent a copy of our proposals to the Home Secretary and to AIRC. I fear another angry outburst.

On Thursday I attended the opening of the Museum of the Moving Image. The Prince of Wales made the opening speech. All went well until the end of his remarks when he departed from his text and launched into a quite outrageous criticism of television, films and video, lambasting the makers as irresponsible for permitting endless gratuitous violence on the screen. The press grabbed the chance and ran banner headlines: 'Prince attacks TV violence'. I thought it mistimed and misdirected, but it made copy and that was what he was aiming for, according to John Riddell whom I spoke to afterwards. We all quite forgot the Museum and its aims in the rumpus that followed.

Over the weekend I stayed with Peter and Jane Cadbury. Jeffrey Sterling was at my table for dinner. He said he was off to read the draft of the White Paper.

Douglas spoke at a luncheon given by Yorkshire Television on Thursday and gave a strong hint that the White Paper would have 'green' edges. More an enabling document than an order!

More revelations no doubt next week.

Sunday 25th September

And the heavens fell in! I try to keep track of fuses leading to kegs of media dynamite, but the fuse that spluttered towards Friday's shock-horror took everyone by surprise.

The week started quietly enough. Rumblings from Prince Charles' speech and Douglas Hurd's leaking over the arrangements for C4. The beginnings of comment over the continuance of religious programming on ITV and the 'God Slot'.

At an early morning meeting with Christopher Foster I decided to commission Coopers & Lybrand to help us come to grips with the prospect of the IBA becoming a licensing body.

ITN Board meeting at Wells Street. Really more an emergency meeting to decide how to square up to the 'leak' that ITV stations might be able to select their own service for news provision. George Russell presented four options that had been worked out over the weekend.

I thought them all off the real point and said so. What really needed saying was that ITV should have one service of news but that service should be the decision of the Companies or, failing that, the Authority. I think this is what they will agree to do.

I bumped into Brian Griffiths at the Garrick in the evening and told him my concern. I am not sure whether he took the point.

Tuesday's press was full of Douglas Hurd's latest literary achievement: 'Designer Violence'. It sounded good, and caught the headlines. Much to my surprise, 'Act of Betrayal', the ending of which I considered much too violent and offensive has passed without so much as a murmur. One telephoned complaint, that's all. Perhaps the audience enjoyed the IRA meeting their come-uppance with one of the gang crunched up under a huge cogwheel!

Meeting on Tuesday afternoon with Chris Scoble and Quentin Thomas to look further at BSB's proposition to withdraw the moratorium not to allow a further two channels within three years. Apart from clarification and agreement between the IBA and BSB over editorial access, the road is now clear.

At 9am on Wednesday a meeting with Brian Tesler and Christopher Bland. A private talk to see whether the IBA would permit them to change LWT holdings from a publicly quoted company to a private plc. The purpose behind the change would be to offer key staff the incentive of shares in the company and to control ownership. Chris estimated a premium of a third over the price of shares in the market. I said I thought that they would be lucky! This meeting brought home again the need for the IBA to square up to the massive changes taking place and the testing time for the Companies.

The *FT* on Thursday got hold of the news that BSB has given the 'Now' news contract to IRN. This created some consternation since we had not been told of the final outcome of BSB's deliberations. Actually, it seems a very good Application, which I read over the weekend.

The Times, ever contrary, ran a Leader on Wednesday: 'A Christian Hour', arguing the case for the status quo on the God Slot.

I attended the CRAC summing-up on Thursday when they considered their advice to the IBA. Essentially, they want to see the maintenance of the back-to-back programmes of the BBC and ITV. Not what the Companies wanted.

On Friday, the *Sun* carried the splendid headline: 'God Slot Storm as TV axes Harry's Highway'. Only by reading the small print were readers to learn that actually the programme had not been axed, but was being assessed in the light of CRAC advice.

Attended a meeting with John Wotton and Kenneth Blyth to consider how rapidly the IBA could/should reconsider its attitude towards takeovers and mergers and came to the conclusion that it could and should. I will raise the issue with Members next week.

The time bomb I mentioned earlier blew up some time during the morning and a report appeared on the *One O'clock News*. A witness had appeared at the inquest in Gibraltar and categorically denied the statements that he had made under the cloak of anonymity to Thames' *Death On The Rock*. He claimed that he had been pressurised by Thames and had been offered money.

Since then, and over the weekend, the Press has had a field day. On Saturday I issued a statement from the IBA: 'The IBA accepted *Death on the Rock* for transmission as a legitimate and responsible investigative programme. The IBA will consider the report that is being prepared for the Board of Thames Television and, in the light of the report, will issue a statement of its conclusions.'

Today's press have all taken the story as their headline: calls for GT to resign, Thames to lose their contract, rent-a-quote Tories having their say.

I spoke to GT in Capri and kept him in the picture. I think he was really more worried that the press would lambaste him for being out of the country. I am afraid that this affair will have major side effects on the IBA itself. We are just entering a dark tunnel and I cannot see light at the end.

Thursday 29th September

Just back from Edinburgh and a meeting with Authority Members. Last night, we were guests of the Scottish Office at a reception in Edinburgh Castle and afterwards dinner with haggis, bagpipes and toasts. GT has had to start making the first of his goodbye speeches with no heir apparent in sight. It looks more and more as though Government is seeking to abandon the IBA.

Today and yesterday I spent much time on the telephone to Richard Dunn attempting to get a statement agreed between us about the Thames enquiry into the professional conduct of the programme makers of *Death On The Rock*. I arrived at a phrase: 'Thames Board has asked the MD of Thames to appoint an eminent QC to advise and assist in the preparation of the report'.

Today the Members took a much more determined line, despite GT and me speaking for the agreed text. They want: 'This report will include an independent assessment from a senior lawyer'. Dunn was not at all happy when I broke the news to him. He was also upset with another part of the statement that we intend issuing tomorrow. This sets out the penalties that the IBA can impose if Thames are found wanting.

Ian Trethowan called GT and requested that he delete the section on the IBA powers. This GT resisted. Then Ian made the extraordinary claim that, since GT had not told him personally about the telephone call back in May from Geoffrey Howe, he had no knowledge of the intervention by the Foreign Minister and he went on to say that, had he known, he might have wanted to postpone the programme. GT, rightly, told Ian that he found the suggestion quite surprising. The whole world had known of the intervention. All Ian had to do was pick up a telephone to him. How was George to know that Ian, the Chairman of Thames, was blissfully unaware!

Tomorrow promises to be eventful: Thames will issue a statement and so will the IBA! More to come, I fear, but hope it will not develop into another Dallas.

Friday 30th September

As I drove into the office today, I heard on the radio that the summing up and verdict on the IRA deaths would take place this afternoon.

I saw GT at 9.10am and said to him that I thought that to issue our press release today, just as the enquiry was ending, would be singularly miss-timed and inappropriate. GT agreed.

The next move came at about 9.20 when Richard Dunn telephoned. He told me that the Board had thought carefully about the matter of the independent enquiry and decided that they would, after all, welcome one. It would be conducted by two independent assessors. Their report would go to the Board and to the IBA.

I said to Richard that I was pleased to hear about their change of heart. Richard read the release to me and I said that it didn't appear to embrace the IBA's role.

We talked about timing. Richard said he wanted to issue, in the morning before the verdict expected this afternoon, so – whatever the outcome – Thames would be seen to act before the verdict.

I talked to GT and agreed with him that we should issue, instead of a detailed statement, a much shorter statement endorsing the Thames' text. I read our statement to Dunn.

The first draft read to me by Dunn did not link the IBA to the eventual decision Thames was taking with respect to an independent enquiry.

The statement that subsequently was made summed up their decision in an able and accurate manner. The two statements were issued and I await tomorrow's papers with interest.

This evening, at about 7.20pm, the jury returned their verdict on Gibraltar. A 9:2 verdict of 'justifiable homicide'. The jury was out for some eight hours. I do not think the story will end here. On Sunday, Channel 4 will be broadcasting the full text of the trial, unless it is banned before then!

Sunday 2nd October

The Olympics are over. A very moving Closing Ceremony.

Tonight C4 are presenting the case from the transcripts in *Court Report*. One day I suspect the truth will emerge and I am minded to think that the Thames' witness, Kenneth Asquez, was probably telling the truth when he first gave his account.

Looking back over the week, events have a somewhat unreal flavour. The talk is still that the IBA will be abolished. Now the press are rubbing their hands in glee and pointing to *Death On The Rock* as another good reason to have the IBA sent down. Considering again GT's conversation with Trethowan I wonder what would have happened if George had telephoned Ian. Would things have been different? News of Thames' decision to hold an independent examination has not made any of the Sundays. On Saturday *The Times* reported Thames as saying: 'There was no pressure to set up an independent enquiry put on us by the IBA'.

Lunched with Chris Scoble and Quentin Thomas at The Garrick. Quentin is leaving to take up Northern Ireland, poor fellow.

I didn't gain much intelligence. The White Paper now looks delayed until early November. Cabinet cannot decide on the future of C4.

Sunday 9th October

The state of the broadcasters as we near the White Paper is becoming positively demented. We are entering a stage now with overkill in leaks which have little or no basis. The shares of most of the Companies continue to rise.

Over the weekend, Donald Maitland must have had quite a few words with Ray Snoddy because Monday's (3 October) *FT* speculated on the ending of the networking arrangements that have laboriously been negotiated and put in place. Actually, Donald used the paper I have circulated to MDs as part of the SCC Agenda this week.

The whole question of networking arrangements is a can of worms. I should have taken a firm hand in the whole subject over a year ago. Instead of that, I rubber-stamped David Glencross's plans almost without question – very foolish.

Attended the inaugural lunch of the National AIDS Trust. The host and founder,

Robert-Maxwell, with typical sledgehammer tactics, got to his feet after the lunch and presented the Princess of Wales with an almost inescapable invitation to become the Patron. I sat next to Audrey Callaghan, who told me James C. had had a mild heart attack three months previously. He looked well but somewhat thinner than I remembered him. The problem with the public's awareness over AIDS is that it is on the back burner of people's conscience. The most terrible disease is gripping mankind in a relentless embrace and few people seem to care or are even aware. Most people seem surprised to learn that it is still in our midst.

A lot of fuss on Monday that John Birt had taken off the programme due to be broadcast by *Panorama* this week on the role of the SAS in Northern Ireland. Both he and Michael Checkland stepped in over the heads of Senior Executives to pull the programme. Whether this was to delay it until after the Tory Conference or not is an open question.

In the evening went to the National to see David Hare's new play *Secret Rapture*. Enjoyed it immensely but felt the second half ran away with itself, as did the characters.

A piece in *The Times* on Tuesday (4 October) 'Beating Broadcast Bias' by Woodrow Wyatt has got GT in a fighting mood. His letter appeared on Friday.

Went to TV-am for breakfast on Wednesday with Bruce Gyngell and Tony Vickers. The occasion was supposed to be a bridge-building, fence-mending exercise put together by Tony. Bruce duly whisked me round the operation. The man is simply power-mad. Everyone appeared terrified of him. His most irritating habit is that he doesn't listen to a word anyone else says.

Over the breakfast he told me that he had managed to secure the repeats of *Doctor Who* to replace *Happy Days*. I looked surprised and suggested that to buy *Doctor Who* from the BBC was not actually a very good idea. A company that had just declared a half-year profit of £7m and which could not find a programme except by going to its competitor didn't make sense. I thought poor Bruce was going to have another heart attack. I suspect he's already paid for the repeats.

In the evening, to Earls Court to contribute to a live programme on Radio 3 with Gillian Reynolds on the future of the arts and radio in the new age called *Third Ear*. I wasn't too happy with the result. My mind seemed to get blocked and I felt that I failed to make the points I should have. Maybe I'm just tired, or depressed, or both.

Afterwards, I entertained the BBC Regional Controllers David Barlow, Colin Morris, Patrick Chalmers and Gareth Pryce. A good dinner regaled with stories – not happy ones – about the present Governors.

Meeting with BSB on Thursday morning. BSB are either heading for the most colossal fall with the loss of all hands and many millions, or they are going to make a fortune and become one of the biggest players in broadcasting. Anthony Simonds-Gooding hopes to convince the Stock Exchange that they are good for a public placing. It will put them, in size, second to the Channel Tunnel.

Lunched with Tim Renton at The Garrick. No new Chairman in sight but I got the impression that the IBA will become a shadow CTA. Whether I shall be in it is an open question.

Timothy didn't give much of a chance to the success of the EC Directive. Personally I don't think it matters. In many ways it will leave broadcasting to each country. If viewers want to watch porn from another country, they can. The trouble with Mrs T. is that she believes that she, and she alone, has the moral values and standards to judge and control. The Italians like their sleazy shows. Why should they give them up to please Mrs T.?

In the evening, to the Festival Hall and to a concert given by the Berlin Philharmonic conducted by Herbert Von Karajan, I suspect the last concert that Von K will conduct in this country but what a way to end. A brilliant conductor.

Dickie A and Michael are pitching now that the fourth channel should be affiliated with the fifth channel. That would put ITV out in the cold and leave it on its own.

Saturday 15th October

The week of Tory triumph in Brighton. Mrs T rampant and, like the White Paper on the Future of Broadcasting, going greener at the edges.

A hurried meeting last Monday with Clare Mulholland over a paper due to go to PPC detailing the results of the first year of monitoring on incidents of violence. This was far from satisfactory and ineptly written. The content, if falling into the wrong hands (the Press), would be dynamite: 'Around 3 per cent of ITV and C4 programmes contained one or more scenes of "strong" violence. Over one quarter of all programmes with "strong" violence occurred in peak time. Around 8 per cent of programmes monitored between 7.30pm and 10.30pm on ITV contained one or more elements of "strong" violence. Another 20 per cent contained "weak" elements of violence. Levels were substantially lower on C4.'

The paper was withdrawn from PPC but will now be looked at by the Authority in November. So far, the one-page summary of the research has not leaked, although it was sent to Programme Controllers.

Went to lunch at the National and met Mary Soames, who I hope is going to prove her worth.

This week has been a dicey one for Super Channel. Rumours have abounded that it is on the point of collapse. ITN say that they have been offered it for £1. David Norris telephoned me to say that ITN was considering running a 24-hour news service. Maxwell is also reputed to be bidding. A sad ending to ITV's dreams of conquering Europe. Little or no advertising is the reason.

The newspapers on Monday contained a story that the MOD had prepared a document listing 39 inaccuracies in *Death on the Rock* and describing it as 'badly flawed'. While the newspapers all appeared to be well-briefed on the MOD's anger and that of the Government, we have still not received a copy of the report, or any indication that we will receive one. I suggested to GT that he should write to George Younger asking for sight of the report. This he did, but no sign yet. This is beginning to look like another dirty tricks episode.

Talking of dirty tricks, Oscar Beuselinck told me this week that three out of the five newspapers that he has been bringing an action against on behalf of Carmen Proetta have been unable to file a defence for stories they ran against her. 'The Tart of Gibraltar', being such a one.

A meeting on Tuesday, called hurriedly at the request of Owen Oyston, who duly turned up flanked by Ian Coulter and his solicitor Michael Connelly. Oyston is a remarkable character both in dress and looks, a throwback from the 60s – flamboyant, long hair, flower-power attitudes – helped by being a millionaire several times over. I had already guessed the reason for his visit, having acquired *Miss World*, he wants now to acquire Capital Radio, placing a value on it of £100m and prepared to offer shareholders a third more on the value of their shares! I listened to all this high finance concealing, I hope, my own feelings. Here I am, DG of a busted flush with very few allies and many enemies. Perhaps I should have stayed as MD of Capital. I would certainly be much richer. I keep telling myself that to regret is only to corrode one's own soul. Remorse, regret and jealousy are deadly viruses. Nobody else cares, really cares how you feel deep down, so I work on the theory that there is precious little point in allowing myself to fall victim to those three sirens who have wrecked many a strong vessel.

I said to Owen that I will invite the Authority to consider the matter next week. I must say I am in very much two minds: one half says let the market rip and devil take the hindmost. They, the radio contractors, brought this on their own heads and now they must face the consequences. The other voice in me calls for calm and points out that, if we allow a free-for-all, the whole industry will be, or could be, thrown into chaos. Owen's argument to me is that sooner or later, when restrictions of ownership are lifted, Capital will be the subject of a massive takeover bid and he would like to see the station go to someone who cared! I pointed out that Capital's management cared. He argued that they did not have the resources and that he was in a good position to take Capital into the 90s.

Since the meeting, I have thought it over and decided to recommend to the Authority that we declare a moratorium for the time being. Certainly until after the White Paper when the position of the ITV Companies will be known. After 15 years of maintaining consistency as far as possible, it would, I think, be foolish to kick the whole structure down, particularly as Capital is in good shape.

On Tuesday evening, Alec Cullen gave a reception and buffet to welcome delegates to the Consultation on Science jointly sponsored by the IBA and COPUS, the Committee on the Public Understanding of Science.

On Wednesday morning, bright and early, attended the opening of the Consultation on Science at the Royal Society. I gave the welcome introduction, followed by Sir George Porter. It will be sad when initiatives like this Consultation are a thing of the past. So much that the IBA does and has done is submerged and only known to the Companies. We should have made much more of these occasions; they illustrate the positive role of the IBA.

Leaving the Consultation, I drove round to the Department of Employment and met Anita Roddick, Jeremy Isaacs and Ken Graham for an appointment with Graham Reid of the DofE. We had been invited as Non Executive Directors to give our views on the future of the Open College which is still awaiting the outcome of the Peat Marwick review and subsequent decision by the Government to either continue to finance the College or close it down.

Looking back, the biggest mistake was to allow the Government to push forward on a start date without sufficient assessment of costs and likely revenue. I am afraid another root cause is a lack of real business experience. The Open College should have had a high-powered businessman at its helm. I suppose Michael Green was seen to fit this requirement.

Lunched with Richard Attenborough at The Ark restaurant off Kensington High Street, a restaurant I used to frequent years ago and still exactly the same. I said that I had been unhappy to read the letter that had been sent by RA to Douglas Hurd outlining the six options in order of preference for retaining C4's remit in the changed circumstances of the 90s.

The option that filled me with concern was a new one, not discussed with us or ITV, that C4 should link up with Channel Five.

After lunch, RA telephoned me to say that Michael Grade had told him that Quentin Thomas had made it clear to him that the Cabinet Committee had gone back to the original status quo position on funding. I view such claims with a pinch of salt. Nothing in the world would suit Michael Grade more than a link with Channel Five for who would be the Chief Executive of both channels? Michael Grade, of course.

GT held his last Advertising Liaison Committee on Thursday and was presented with a silver plate as a memento.

Sadly, I had to miss the leaving party of my P.A. Caroline, who has to give up such an active position to protect her health. In a relatively short time with me, she established herself firmly but warmly with everyone. I shall miss her. Jane Lloyd becomes my P.A. I think she will be equally effective.

I should have commented on a meeting with David Windlesham and Richard Rampton QC and GT and me on Thursday. This was the first time that we had all met since their appointment by Thames to the Independent Inquiry on *Death on the Rock*.

Both GT and I were concerned before meeting them that Thames and in particular Ian Trethowan were doing all that could be done to deflect attention from Thames and onto the IBA and the part played by the Authority in permitting the programme to be shown. We find ourselves in something of a cleft stick. If we agree to co-operate, the Authority would find itself on trial. If we refuse, the accusation would be that we are ducking our responsibilities. David Windlesham kept referring to 'those in other places' who would expect to have a full report. We will answer the seven or eight questions in writing. There is more to the Gibraltar shootings than has yet come out and I shall be surprised if the Inquiry does not lift the lid off some quite unsavoury matters.

Finally, on Thursday, a piece on the *Times* front page indicating Government's attempts to fill GT's position and failing. Little wonder when they are about to give us the chop. GT is well out of the whole sorry mess.

As a footnote to my own suspicions about young Michael Grade, the *Sunday*

Telegraph, 16 October 1988 page 13, in an article by Mandrake in Brighton suggests that 'they want a third force, another ITV but separate from and in competition with it. It would need to include the existing C4 to give it a proven base, plus a new Channel Five. Mr Grade was understood to be advocating the scheme in Brighton.'

Monday 17th October

Attended in the afternoon the ITN Board Meeting. Main item under review was ITN's consideration of the Super Channel offer to ITN for the supply of its news services. Maxwell, who had previously shown interest, has pulled out saying that it conflicted with his other interests. This left only Richard Branson who, at 2.20pm, issued an ultimatum: if ITN would continue to provide the news service at no cost and set on one side the outstanding amounts owed to ITN (some £200,000) on an interest-free repayment basis, Branson would agree to continue the Super Channel service. ITN's Board did not favour this proposal and staff were told to say a firm no. At the same time, the Board endorsed the proposal to fund the night time ITV service, making up the shortfall that had been paid by Super Channel for a further three months. As of tonight, I think Richard Branson is bluffing and will make ITN another offer.

Later in the day, GT telephoned me from Eastbourne to say that the Home Secretary was seeking a meeting tomorrow between GT, Duke Hussey and himself. He did not reveal the subject and neither did he wish Michael or me to be present. I spoke to Checkland. He and I believe it to be about Northern Ireland and the possibility that the Government are seeking to place a ban on television either reporting events or interviewing Sinn Fein. GT is meeting at the Home Office on Wednesday morning.

Sunday 23rd October

GT's meeting with the Home Secretary took place early on Wednesday morning and George telephoned me at 8.15 am to tell me that Duke Hussey (who had gone to see Douglas the previous evening) had been told that Douglas would be making a statement in the House that afternoon. I saw GT when he returned from seeing Douglas and he handed me a copy of the 'Direction' prohibiting radio and television from broadcasting interviews with members and supporters of terrorist organisations in Northern Ireland. The pending announcement meant that, as soon as the Home Secretary rose and spoke, the Directive would have to be implemented by the broadcasters. I held a hurried number of meetings and Ken Blyth, David Glencross and Peter Baldwin set up the mechanism to give the radio and television contractors the terms of the Directive at the same time as Douglas Hurd rose in the Commons.

Colette Bowe came to see me, seething with anger. She felt I had not been fair to her by not telling her in advance of GT's visit to the Home Secretary. She had learnt of the visit only after speaking to the Home Office. I told her that I had given my word to keep this confidential. Colette remained deeply unhappy, feeling that it was because I didn't trust her. I said that I remained unrepentant.

Of course I trusted her but others had placed their trust in me and I would not let them down. Earlier in the week, Colette had told me that she was resigning as she had been offered a good job with a Securities Office in the City so her feelings may have been more colourfully expressed as it was near to her departure.

At 3.25pm on Wednesday, the Home Office declared the Directive under Section 29(3) of the Broadcasting Act 1981 and at 3.30 we began telexing, telephoning and faxing the Directive. I think this action is the first time Government has directly intervened using the Act.

During the remainder of the week there was close scrutiny of the wording. Both the BBC and ourselves have found ambiguities in the framing of the Order which leave too much latitude for mishandling.

One area that is bound to cause controversy is that not only will the restrictions not apply to the broadcast of proceedings in Parliament but that during the time of Elections the 'Notices' will have a more 'limited' effect according to Douglas Hurd's statement to the Commons. I can see chaos and confusion ahead. Far from taking away the platform of publicity for terrorists, I think it will give them an unparalleled weapon to use in Australia, Canada and – most importantly – in America. What, too, I wonder will be the moment (if indeed it ever materialises) of withdrawing the ban should the spirit of perestroika eventually prevail. I can visualise a debate over many months to decide whether or not the right political climate has been reached for Directive to be withdrawn.

The day before, on Tuesday, I chaired a meeting of the RCC, the first for several months. I had rather expected a greater surge of ill-feeling from the Companies on our proposals to open another 20 small stations under our 'incremental' plan, put forward to Timothy Renton, but there was little detailed comment. I gave them an assurance that consultation would take place and I think this acted as a buffer to their anxiety.

In the evening, Roma and I attended the dinner given by Max and Jane Rayne to say goodbye to Peter Hall. The Beaufort Room in the Savoy is not a cheerful room, more a waiting room. A bad shape, bad décor and, as it turned out, bad service. We waited twenty minutes after sitting down for the serving of the first course. The salt cellar in front of me was empty and during Peter's speech two waiters crashed in, noisily marched up the entire length of the room to each take a fistful of glasses from a cupboard and march out again, the glasses jangling merrily as they thundered past the speaker on his feet and the listening guests. Peter brought his new lady, Nicky, and Richard Eyre turned up during the middle course, but he made a good speech in praise of Peter which made up for his late arrival.

The season for saying farewell to GT is also upon us. The first occasion proper took place on Wednesday when GT hosted his last Annual Dinner for ILR Chairmen in the Cholmondeley Room in the House of Lords.

On Thursday a meeting of the Authority, the main business to agree the general line to take for the IBA's immediate response to the White Paper. Entertained Evelyn de Rothschild to lunch with his team after their presentation to us of their findings on their report on Contract Tendering.

In the evening, the GAC Members had a buffet dinner and GT gave a farewell speech at the beginning. He rather enjoyed the occasion, or seemed to be enjoying it, as he spoke for about 15 minutes while the GAC Members toyed with their glasses and one or two cast envious glances towards the food, but it was a good speech and struck the right note.

I should have said something about the radio takeover situation. The Members at the meeting agreed to take our advice and put a hold on Contractors attempting takeovers or agreed takeovers. As a consequence, Crown Communications share price took a knock. Owen Oyston was told the decision. Whether this will forestall him making a bid for Capital remains to be seen.

All this week, negotiations – sometimes feverish – have been taking place over the future of Super Channel. Richard Branson's bid on Friday looked like failing. At the last moment, an Italian company made an offer. I don't yet know the details. At a time when all the talk is of new channels, it is somewhat ironic that no one seems able to make any money out of Super Channel or indeed Sky Channel. Is, I wonder, the European dream of pan-European advertising a mirage?

More and more speculation on the content of the White Paper. Richard Dunn sent me, under plain cover, the fourth draft of their paper on the handling of ITV's position on day one. It starts with these wise words:

> '*Tone*
> The tone should be measured, thoughtful, confident. We should take heed of George Thomson's advice to be calm, to be proud of our record without being arrogant and to play it long. We should not rush to embrace of reject. We should keep something in reserve for the twelve months' of debate stimulated by an "enabling" green-edged White Paper.'

Sound advice and extremely timely, for the latest word we now have on the date of the White Paper is the 7th November!

Sometimes I think that all I have slogged for and sometimes succeeded in doing is but a fragment of my imagination so it was reassuring to read the comment made by GT in this quarter's *Airwaves* (Autumn 1988). Speaking of our DBS initiatives when the BBC and IBA were unable to realise Government hopes, principally because of the high costs sought by British Aerospace, I had always argued it would be better if Government had kept out of it and left the market to find its own way through the various cost barriers. The article had this to say:

> 'The eventual decision by Government that the IBA should offer a DBS contract is seen by Lord Thomson as a great victory for the Authority and a very considerable personal victory for John Whitney, the Director General, who had spent much time on the project.'

Saturday 29th October

Still waiting for a Chairman and the White Paper, but no sign of either! A very busy week with the media speculating on almost every conceivable aspect of the White Paper.

Lunch with Michael Winner on Monday at the Capital Hotel which provided good service and good value. We talked about the BSC. Winner lamented the lack of support he is getting as spokesman on Censorship for the Guild of Directors. Michael has spoken out fearlessly and with spirit against the BSC and recently against the attack on video, film and television made by Prince Charles. John Mortimer appears to have shot his bolt and retired from view. We tried to think of suitable candidates – Lord Goodman? Winner left in his enormous Rolls Royce looking every bit like the successful film director. He said rather wistfully during lunch that he would like to make a good film, not to make money but for his own pleasure. I think he meant it.

Dinner at the IBA to say thanks to Justin Dukes who has left C4 to head up a new computerised airline booking system. During the meal it became increasingly clear that Justin had become very embittered, so embittered that I said, 'Justin, you're beginning to sound like Edward Heath'. Justin's real grouse appears to be his frustration and disappointment that the Board failed to seize the opportunity of positioning C4 as a sole entity attracting specialist advertising and standing on its own feet.

Much anger in the press over *Piece of Cake*, LWTs very expensive series about the Battle of Britain. I could have told the critics of this series that they would find it not to their liking. Written by Derek Robinson, who holds very definite opinions about the middle classes!

Talked to the ROs on Tuesday and warned them that they should expect some confusion in the interpretation by Companies of the Home Office guidelines on the Directive made by Douglas Hurd, banning terrorist organisations from the airwaves. The Home Office has now produced a further set of guidelines relaxing their first condition, but in relaxing it further anomalies are appearing. The NUJ are threatening to go on a 24 hour strike in protest at the banning. If they go on strike, they will be playing directly into the hands of the Tory Party and its leader, who will say 'There you are. You see, they are a Left Wing lot who have delighted in giving Sinn Feinn the oxygen of publicity.'

In the evening to the Garrick for the ROs dinner and to use the occasion to say goodbye to the Chairman. The ROs presented George with a cut glass flower vase with a message engraved on it along with emblems of England, Scotland, Northern Ireland and Wales. George was very touched.

On Wednesday 26 October, Snoddy in the *FT* speculates that the Government is going to auction off the remaining two channels. Super Channel still occupies the headlines with its future still in the balance and ITN looks more and more lost in the middle of the whole sorry affair.

GT wrote today to Douglas Hurd at the insistence of the Members, seeking to alert Douglas to the growing concern felt by Members over the lack of a new Chairman and the loss of two Members (Paula Ridley and Roy Grantham).

The letter ends: 'Although we realise there will be major changes in the new regime, it will in everyone's interest to ensure that the new arrangements are technically and professionally competent and that they can be produced in an orderly way, without the effects of planning blight or discontinuity becoming visible on the screen or on the air in the meantime. In these processes I believe that the skills and experience of the IBA Members and staff will provide an essential foundation for the work of a new commercial television authority and I hope that you will be recognising this as and when the White Paper is published.'

At 11am on Wednesday I addressed Brompton Road staff. I spoke for about 40 minutes and questions followed. Afterwards people said it went well. (I thought it did). The purpose was to set the scene ahead of the White Paper to make staff realise that big changes were imminent and to prepare them for the inevitability of leaked information that the IBA would cease to be the regulatory authority.

In the evening to Winchester and the Station Managers' dinner with GT saying his farewell and receiving some bottles of his favourite dram. Donald Maitland proposed the toast of the Engineers with an extraordinary speech obviously first written for some other gathering either in the past or in the future, but with only a tenuous nod at the occasion for the address.

Thursday. The day when the trade press swamps the cuttings circulated daily throughout the IBA. *Broadcast* carried a full-page article on me which does nothing to flatter my ego or bolster my confidence but I think, at long last, I am learning to wear a thicker skin than hitherto. I shall need it in the next few weeks.

I have become increasingly aware of the very real animosity felt towards the IBA from almost all quarters. Nice to keep in with when in power, but even nicer to watch as the victim instead of the persecutor. 'Oh, how sorry!' everyone says, but 'Oh, how jolly good', everyone thinks. 'Serves them jolly right.'

I lunched with the Italian Ambassador on Thursday. His guest of honour was Signor Oscar Manni, the Italian Minister of Post & Telecommunications, who is in the country to look at the way we handle television advertising control – or 'publicity' as the Italian call commercials.

Before lunch, a meeting with Anthony Simonds-Gooding, not sporting the usual brightly coloured tie and, I judged, in more sombre mood than I had previously encountered. We discussed the fourth and fifth DBS channels. I had previously sent him a letter arguing that BSB was the equivalent of a common carrier in telecommunication terms and thus could be regulated if necessary by an OFTEL arrangement with the IBA or the new CTA to enable fair prices to be struck for the satellite services made available by BSB to other users.

This contention was denied by Anthony as was the argument that, as they were in a monopoly position, this called for special powers. I said that the IBA concerns over the fourth and fifth channels were to ensure as far as possible that there would be fair competition but, if this was not possible, the Home Office must be made aware in advance of the IBA undertakings to put up the two channels for applicants to apply for.

This issue may, in fact, have already been taken out of our hands by the White Paper. We shall see.

During the meeting, I asked about BSB's funding and general financial state. BSB have received £225M as a first tranche from their investors. Originally, the total investment was of the order of £600m-£650m but now they are seeking to raise from a public flotation £1bn, (the second largest public flotation since the Channel

Tunnel). The chances of the Stock Exchange Council approving BSB's issue are, in the words of Anthony, '49 or 51 in favour'. There are obvious doubts. The whole broadcasting scene has been changing rapidly since even BSB won its contract, with Channel 5, possibly a sixth channel, and now even more recently the likelihood that subscription as method of funding C5 will be included in the White Paper. This could have a serious impact on BSB's marketing strategy as could subscription on the BBC in the night hours. Or indeed greater freedom to create subscription opportunities on Channel 3. All these potential changes have surfaced since BSB created their business strategy. BSB investors cannot be sleeping easily in their beds. 'What happens', I ask, 'if the Stock Exchange refuse your application?' 'We will be in some difficulty', replied Anthony. 'Luxembourg might be the next place to try for a flotation', he opines. 'The London Stock Exchange Council is looking for reasons to say yes.' In the interim period, that is until October 1989 when the full financing is required, BSB are going back to their shareholders to seek to raise between a further £20m to £60m as a new tranche. I suspect they will find it difficult unless, or until, the Stock Exchange gives them an answer. All in all, I am growing increasingly worried over the situation. Money is flowing out of BSB, who are on the horns of a dilemma. If they do not invest in popular films and programmes, all of which mean high cost, they will not attract audiences. If they do not attract sufficient numbers of viewers they will go bust. If they invest upfront, they must gamble on their investors not getting cold feet. I can envisage a scenario as follows:

- BSB over-extends itself and fails to get support from its existing investors;
- BSB fails to get permission from the Stock Exchange for a possible flotation. Then either;
- A TV-am situation develops with new investors coming in to save the day (and make a nonsense of the application process) or;
- BSB declare themselves unable to continue to act in the capacity of programmers and hand back their contract, retaining the satellite options to sell or leave to an incoming contractor.

Alternatively, and catastrophically, the whole project is aborted with only losers at the end of the day.

To put it in perspective: BSB will be investing £1bn for three channels; Murdoch has invested £80m for four Astra channels. One or other is going to be proven to have made the right judgment.

On Thursday evening to the National Theatre. The 'Royal' National Theatre, and to celebrate with fireworks and champagne the 25th anniversary. The Queen sat through *The Tempest*, an uninspired production with plenty of Peter Hallisms in it – masks and bared chests.

Lord Rothermere and 'Bubbles' very much in attendance. The *Evening Standard* sponsored the event. No John Mortimer but Judy Dench gave a marvellous welcome to the Royals from the stage. We ate oysters and jacket potatoes and were given a 'goodbye' containing a medallion celebrating the event when we left.

On Friday to Crawley Court and gave an address to the staff. It went well. I didn't mince my words about the future but hope that I gave enough encouragement to prevent mass suicide! (Note: I have written this diary entry without reading the Sundays. For all I know, the sky could have fallen in over me, the IBA and broadcasting).

Saturday 5th November

'It used to be said of Casanova and other habitual lechers that they had their way with women through the tedium of unremitting persistence: in short, they bored the pants off them!' So wrote Richard Last in the *Daily Telegraph* on 3 November when reviewing *Signals* on C4: 'which stretched to an unconscionable 90 minutes on sex and television'. 'Lord Rees-Mogg', has many talents wrote Andrew Hislop in *The Times* of the same day. 'One of them is to invite ridicule.' No doubt William will, in the fullness of time, rise above such petty criticisms of the task set for him by the Prime Minister.

This week has been a preparation for the White Paper. Its shadow is cast over all that we say, do or think. Knowing, as I do, that the IBA's role is definitely ruled out in its present form does not make for peaceful slumbers. My talk to staff was, I am told, helpful but, if I was middle-aged and had given my career to the IBA, I would be having even more troubled sleep and with every good cause.

The Home Secretary's ban on interviews with terrorist organisations hit more trouble on Sunday night (30 October). Channel 4's interview with a Sinn Fein councillor was stopped by the IBA because, in our judgment, it contravened the Directive.

Throughout the week, there has been continuing criticism of the Directive, culminating in a debate in the Commons on Wednesday. The motion supporting the Government's ban was carried by 243 votes to 179. Nothing to stem the disquiet that is being voiced, and will be voiced in future, over this Act which will create nothing but confusion, quite apart from the principles underlying the decision.

On Monday sat two rows back at Covent Garden to see the new production of *Madam Butterfly* by the Spanish producer Nuria Espert. A splendid production spoilt, I thought, by a gauze separating the stage from the audience throughout the performance. Jeffrey Sterling was there. I still think he could pop up as the next Chairman but difficult for No. 10 to overlook his obvious and publicised dalliance with a woman other than his wife. Still, being 'squeaky clean' doesn't seem to be essential for high office these days!

Earlier, had drinks with Peter Fiddick, who is stepping down as television critic of *The Guardian* to paddle in new waters. He has served the television industry well and will be missed.

I noted last week that I could visualise a number of scenarios for BSB as it draws closer to lift-off. Michael Flint called in to see me on Tuesday 1 November, at his urgent request. It seems that Alan Bond, who he represents, is anxious to pick up the shares in BSB currently held by Vision. This would give him (from memory) something like a 29 per cent holding and would be unacceptable to the IBA. Here we go then, with the beginning of a buying and selling merry-go-round. Michael went away to think about it.

Tuesday was 'one day in the life of television'. Future generations will be able to assess whether there are differences pre or post White Paper conclusions.

Met with Richard Evans at *The Times* to speculate on the White Paper. I wish I had been doing more informal meetings with journalists. More can be accomplished by knowing someone.

Dinner with Peter and Louise Gibbings at their home. Denis Forman another guest. Television was for the benefit of the viewer, not the advertiser, he told the assembled guests. Sir Alex Alexander, Chairman of Allied Lyons, listened and smiled. Perhaps he has read the White Paper!

The Home Secretary rose in the House at 2.45pm on Wednesday 2 November and gave details of the Government's backing to the proposals for 'incremental radio contractors'. I heard it with a slightly sinking heart. Whilst it will keep Radio Division busy, it will place an added burden on other staff and particularly on Members. The floodgates will surely open and the flood of entries will pour in.

I can see turbans and saris flying round Brompton Towers. Wait till the Triads move in. After the announcement, I had the nearest thing to a full-blown row with Peter Baldwin, who I thought – and still think – tried to bounce me with an announcement welcoming the decision that included a deadline for Companies to express their interest in the area and category of station of their choice. All ridiculously compressed and without consultation. I reverted to old habits and slammed the door!

An important meeting on Wednesday with John Wotton and our team to assess what changes we could recommend the IBA taking on the subject of television company takeovers, both contested and friendly, or changes in ownership. I had in mind Central, Yorkshire and LWT in particular. I think I got a green light for putting a paper to the Authority but still have to see what the White Paper has to say.

Lunch with Jeffrey Archer and Mary at the Capital Hotel. An hour between the starter and main course has, I am afraid, finished my brief romance with that establishment. Jeffrey was in bouncy mood, despite tooth problems, busy writing a new play about a newspaper, entitled *Exclusive* – each main scene another day in the weekly cycle. He asked me what I would do if I left the IBA. I said I did not know.

Dinner to celebrate Justin Dukes given by Dickie at the Garrick. Jeremy gave an odd speech, starting off by remarking that whilst C4 would be there for a bit, the IBA might not. Justin said solemn words about the freedom of the broadcaster and not being tied to the coat tails of Government.

Thursday. I think, I think, I think Super Channel has now finally been sold by the ITV Companies to an Italian major shareholder, Video Music, with a 55 per cent holding and liabilities of £8m. Richard Branson retains 45 per cent. ITN will receive £1.9m per year to provide news and summaries. Oh, how are the mighty fallen and all this while a new, red-hot dawn of television is being anticipated. Nobody, I suspect, has seen the full irony.

Up early on Friday to breakfast at the IBA with Andreas Whittam-Smith, Matthew Symonds, Peter Jenkins and John Torode, all of the *Independent*. Another opportunity for an 'off the record' briefing. They make a good showing, asking difficult questions but listening as well, which makes a change. The rest of the day on the White Paper, together with the Chairman, preparing the line to take and approving the draft statement that we plan to issue under my name. Next week is going to be tough.

In the early evening a drink with Andrew Lloyd Webber who asks me if I would like to become MD of the Really Useful Company.

Saturday 12th November

Last Sunday, 6 November, I hosted a 'London Screenings' reception at Lancaster House. About 200 overseas delegates attended, including buyers from the Soviet Union and China. This was the second year of the Screenings and we met for the reception the day before the Government published the White Paper on Broadcasting, so amongst the IBA people present there was a great deal of speculation and apprehension, despite the fact that so much in the White Paper seems to have already been leaked.

I left the merriment quite early, determined to get a good night's sleep.

Monday 7th November – This date could, and possibly should, become engraved or etched by acid into the hearts of broadcasters. I read the morning newspapers in the car going to the IBA where I was due to meet GT before going on to the Home Office. Most of the press again repeated the catalogue of changes anticipated in the White Paper.

At 10am George, Shirley and I presented ourselves at the Home Office. We were kept waiting until 10.10 by Douglas, who apologised and greeted us in his usual breezy manner. Quentin Thomas was wearing a tie of garish hue, quite the most unpleasant article to tie around anyone's neck, least of all his own I thought. He described it afterwards as his 'media' tie. Quite why this was so, I haven't quite discovered. Perhaps it was an omen of television as it will become in the age of unlimited choice!

We sat down facing Douglas, who – after seeking the approval of Wilfred Hyde – handed George a copy of the White Paper: 'Broadcasting in the 90s: Competition, Choice and Quality'. The order in which the three objectives are placed becomes more obvious after reading it. Douglas then proceeded to run through the main features. Nothing new until Engineering, when he explained that it was Government's intention to separate the operation of the transmitter network and offer it on a regional basis to competition from outside contractors. They would also, he said, be offering the two DBS Channels for use as soon as the IBA could advertise them, early in 1989. Although it did not concern us as such, the BBC would be encouraged to use one of their channels during the night hours for programmes funded by subscription, while the other channel during the night hours would be handed over to the ITC for commercial use. (Shirley told me after the meeting that the name ITC was not the first choice but selected only after the first choice, that of the ITA, Independent Television Authority, was discovered to have been the precursor of the IBA! That, if nothing else, was quite enough for Mrs T. to reject any further consideration).

As we left, we bumped into Jon Davey and his Chairman. Greetings and false smiles as we passed at the entrance to the lift.

In the car, returning to Brompton Road, GT asked me whether he should disclose the fact that we had been given a copy of the White Paper. I advised against it.

As soon as we got back, we gathered in George's room with Colette, Kenneth, Peter Rogers, John Forrest and Don Horn. Shirley read from her notes the gist of Douglas' remarks. Colette left to re-write part of the statement that we were to issue later under my name. There was a good deal of shock registered when the Engineering proposals became known (although my guess is that John Forrest had some inkling beforehand). I and other senior executives lunched together upstairs.

After lunch, some of us met again to go over the press statement, which we approved.

At about 3.40pm I went down the corridor to Colette's office where I could listen, along with others, to the direct feed from the Commons.

Douglas Hurd rose (according to Hansard) at 3.58pm with the words: 'With permission, Mr Speaker, I wish to make a statement about the Government's plans for broadcasting legislation. I have laid a White Paper before the House today. Our broadcasting system has a rich heritage which is a tribute to the efforts and enterprise of the broadcasting authorities and to all those engaged in the broadcasting enterprise. Our proposals seek to build on these achievements in developing services of quality, range and popularity.'

Hurd spoke for about ten minutes and then Roy Hattersley rose and, after welcoming some parts of the Home Secretary's statement went into the attack, concluding: 'This White Paper reflects commercial values rather than broadcasting values as is to be expected from a policy that owes more to the Department of Trade & Industry than it does to the Home Office. It pretends to offer choice. In fact, many of the new channels will do no more than offer vast profits to the tycoons of international television. It is a giant retreat from the concept of public service broadcasting. Its result will be less diversity and lower standards.'

Others spoke, including John Wheeler, Robert Maclennan, Geoffrey Johnson-Smith, David Owen and Tony Banks. Then it was over.

What followed is, even after so little time, beginning to blur in my mind. *The Independent* Leader sounded a note of disquiet: 'Neither convincing nor coherent'. *The Times* Leader wags an admonishing finger in my direction: 'The IBA is already showing itself reluctant to give up its hold on the levers of regulation. Its Director General, John Whitney, spoke yesterday of the new Independent Broadcasting Commission as though he were already in charge of it. He should be disabused of this view.' I suppose this was only to be expected from a paper owned by an arch opponent of the IBA and no friend of mine – Rupert Murdoch.

Depending on the political hue, the popular press echoed the will of their paymasters.

At 2.30pm a meeting of the SCC. A room filled with grey faces trying as best they might to take the last 48 hours in their stride. I opened the meeting with the rather banal remark that probably not since the founding of the ITA has there been a White Paper outlining Government policy which will so radically alter the structure of broadcasting.

I told the MDs that the IBA will shortly be considering what changes may be necessary in the period of the contract extensions to allow ITV Companies to make changes in their shareholdings to ready themselves for the competition ahead. Some look pleased; some still more worried, if that is possible. There were not many laughs.

In the evening, went to a performance of 'Mrs Klein' by Nicholas Wright in the Cotesloe Theatre, packed to the ceiling and much enjoyed a play about Melanie Klein who practised psychiatry in England in the late 30s and 40s. I am an 'angel' in the production, which moves to the Apollo on 7th December. So fingers crossed, lest I get them burnt.

George and I met early on Wednesday 9th November. We are both depressed. GT has opened his heart to Richard Evans of *The Times*. The headline in the paper reads 'Too much, too quickly: 'Lord Thomson makes no attempt to veil his distaste for the Government's plans – "I think the time for a really radical broadcasting bill was not 1988 but 1998. The Prime Minister and her colleagues regarded broadcasting as simply an economic activity and did not realise it was much more than that."'

I sat with George and we brooded together over the future. I tell him about Andrew Lloyd Webber's proposal to me. If there is nothing positive for me to do in the IBA, why waste time, I speculate. Obviously, and central to whatever decision I might take over my own future, is the question of the IBA staff. To abandon ship as it approaches the iceberg is not something I have the heart for. Yet the prospect of swinging the ball at the end of the chain and deliberately setting about to smash up the IBA, its staff, its history and its spirit, is an act of vandalism I find hard to countenance. GT says that, whilst all that I say is true, I must think of myself. He feels greatly that it was he who got me to come to the IBA. He believes that I have honoured my task with a commitment and integrity that in today's world is rare. He says there is little praise for me in this new world and considers that the duty to myself must come first. Shirley Littler, he believes, could wield the ball on the chain and probably enjoy it!

'See if you can get Lloyd Webber to give you time to consider your position', he advises. 'I think many people would understand if you were to accept the offer.'

It is food for thought. I am much troubled and, as I think more and more about the contents of the White Paper, I begin to realise how much at its very heart it sets about destroying the strengths that have sustained the IBA system, networking, real public service obligations, and the IBA as the enabler to help shape and encourage the values that can be exploited to the real benefit of the viewer and not simply a fruit machine with the levers pulled by advertisers. I have come such a long way, only now to be facing a scrapheap of good intentions and be part of a system held without respect by a Government hell-bent on razing to the ground not only the IBA but all that it stood for. Is this the price we pay for *Death on the Rock*? I think it could be.

An old name from the IBA's and my past appeared in the headlines. Colin Shaw has been appointed Director of the BSC: 'It's tremendously exciting. I love being in at the birth of things', he is quoted as saying in *The Standard*.

The BSC has certainly been born, but will it prove to be healthy, wealthy and, above all, wise?

In the evening, a presentation by Robin Moss and his team from the Education Department. Of all the Divisions within the IBA, Education has won the day. It is referred to positively in the White Paper. They gave a good presentation to the Members of the Authority gathered to listen. This was the first chance for the Members to talk together since Monday's White Paper. They, too, seem shell-shocked angry. Afterwards we had dinner in the Members' Dining Room. I looked at the two framed portraits: at one end, Robert Fraser, architect of ITV and, at the other, Brian Young smiling, confident and assured. If Robert were alive, what would he be saying?

A 'storm' broke over the Home Office on Thursday 10th November when the all-powerful Public Accounts Committee charged the Home Office with making a 'serious error of judgment' that they claim lost the Treasury £38m in ITV levy. This was the Committee in front of which I appeared and, I thought, made a hash of things.

The day before, I had been unable to attend the Tyne Tees Television Annual Lunch. The speaker was Willie Whitelaw, who said that he would 'sniff critically' at the implementation of the White Paper.

Reports in the *Daily Telegraph* describe Andrew Lloyd Webber's determination to bid for a London-based classical music station. When Peter Baldwin gave me this news in the Authority Meeting, I left and asked my P.A. Jane to sell my shares in The Really Useful Group. Another nest egg gone but I don't think there is any way that I could hold shares in a company and at the same time decide who should win contracts.

Writing this on a clear, bright Sunday morning, I have no idea yet what the papers have said about the White Paper. So, in blissful ignorance of the slings and arrows, I shall write on.

A programme in the series *Dispatches* on C4 has been causing me great concern. This programme, made with the use of secret filming, claimed the Chinese invasion of Tibet had led to genocide, starvation, cultural destruction, impoverishment and torture.

The part of the programme which required a decision on our part was the testaments of three nuns who described the horrifying ordeal they suffered. The nuns wanted their identities revealed so that there could be no doubt as to their authenticity. Tibetans living in London and elsewhere expressed alarm that further punishment, including possibly death, could result from revealing their identities. Listening to the arguments on both side, particularly from Clare Mulholland and David Glencross, I came to the same conclusion as they did: that the identity of the nuns should be allowed to be revealed. If their courage was to be marred by our fear for their safety we would be preventing the full horror to be realised.

The meeting of the Authority was a sombre affair, each Member expressing their personal view of the White Paper, Michael Caine and John Purvis predictably applauding much of its contents, a feeling that the ship had already sunk. I felt miserable and couldn't lift myself out of a black pit of despair which the next few days did nothing to eradicate.

After the meeting, a conference with David Kemp and John Rink prior to our meeting with David Windlesham and Richard Rampton, a meeting called by the former to question us further on Geoffrey Howe's accusation that *Death on the Rock* had 'contaminated' the evidence of witnesses. David and John put their questions and sought permission for GT's letter replying to the Foreign Secretary to be put into the Appendix of the report which they now hoped to complete in order that we could have sight of it before the last meeting that George will chair before leaving the IBA. During the following meeting, and as a consequence mainly of the questions being put by Richard on 'contamination', John Rink became increasingly uneasy about the position the IBA has got itself into, that of the tail wagging the dog, i.e. the report, commissioned by Thames, examining the function and responsibilities of the Authority. I think we probably have made a ghastly mistake in not, from the outset, putting our foot down over the terms of reference that we agreed with Thames: 'To investigate the making and screening'. By allowing 'and screening' we, instead of Thames, are in the dock, or very easily could be. John Rink expressed himself clearly at the meeting but GT said that he had agreed the terms during a meeting that he and I held with David and Richard. What a way to end the year and GT's role as Chairman. We have been out-manoeuvred and are powerless and have no one to blame but ourselves.

In the evening a dinner party given by one of the 'great and good', Peregrine Worsthorne. He left me in little doubt that the *Sunday Telegraph* was greatly in favour of Douglas Hurd and the White Paper.

On Friday, *The Times* apologised briefly to the IBA by previously stating that we had 14,000 employees instead of 1,400. This error first appeared in an article by Nicholas Mellersh in the *Royal Television Society Journal* condemning the IBA.

The Times published a letter signed by Professor Huw Morris-Jones, Lady Plowden, Mary Whitehouse and many others which ended 'we believe the abolition of the IBA would be an irretrievable loss'.

On Friday afternoon, I called a meeting of DGMM and the next four hours was spent examining the White Paper to see what consensus we could reach. Engineering plans must come top of the agenda. For the rest, the hole in the hull is too big.

Earlier in these notes, I remember I had not read the Sunday papers. Now I am home, I have read the lot. The *Sunday Telegraph* in an article by Bruce Anderson headlined 'Why the BBC has nothing to fear' has this to say about ITV: 'ITV has also suffered from the weakness of the IBA, whose Director General, John Whitney, a hapless and hand-wringing figure, makes Alasdair Milne seem effectual.' How to end after that? Well, I suppose I square my shoulders and go on. But I wonder to where?

One final piece in this week's ghastly jigsaw came on Friday afternoon and is just another time bomb ticking away with a very short fuse: C4 has sought advice from their Counsel on the Home Secretary's Directive challenging the terms and effect of the notice. On 1st November the Executive Directors of C4 met and decided to recommend to the Board that, subject to the BBC and IBA proposing to take action, they would make an application to the Divisional Court and, if necessary, to the European Commission on Human Rights.

I spoke to GT a few minutes ago. We will be meeting our Counsel at 11am tomorrow. My view, expressed to George, is that the IBA should not stand alongside C4 without first taking our own legal judgment. If our advisers consider there to be a case, then our Members should be asked their opinion. At the moment, whatever the legal advice, I think we would be wrong to fight the issue. Government took a decision, the Act permits Government to make a Directive. Is it naïve to think that Government has a right to decide, however mistakenly? I think it has.

Sunday 20th November

I have made it a practice not to look back at any diary entry I have made since I have started writing up each week's happenings. I fear this either means that I may I have repeated myself too often or, conversely, left out matters that in retrospect will seem important. But its virtue, if any, is that I am not guilty of re-writing my view of events.

I whispered the other day to a journalist that I had heard the name of David Steel mooted as the next Chairman of the IBA. *The Observer* swallowed the bait and added a new name – Sir David English, Editor in Chief of the *Daily Mail*. I lunched with Barbara Hosking this week and she had dined Chris Scoble the night before. Scoble told her that the name of the next Chairman would be announced within the next fortnight.

Peter Fiddick, writing in *The Guardian* on Monday: 'One word, or at any rate, one polite word, sums up the broadcasting policy that Mrs Thatcher's senior ministers and advisors have struggled so long to devise – reckless'.

Sat down with Bernard Green for the first time since the White Paper and talked about the timetable and problems for launching our advertising to see who would come forward to provide programmes on the fourth and fifth DBS channels. It's going to be a race to meet a timetable that includes advertising in January 1989 and appointing a contractor in November 1989.

In the evening, attended a dinner given in GT's honour by the Board of C4. Very nice atmosphere. George made an eloquent speech and then took me by surprise by launching into an attack on press comments attacking me. I didn't know whether to look solemn, or laugh it off, but it was nice of him and I thanked him afterwards.

Attended the opening of the One World Broadcasting Trust conference on Tuesday and introduced the first speaker – Jack Hamilton – who spoke on global interdependence: The Challenge of the Local Reporter.

A meeting with Anthony Simonds-Gooding and Graham Grist. My fears, expressed a few weeks ago, look like becoming a reality. Anglia and Virgin do not, or cannot, raise the additional monies BSB now require for the next tranche of investment funding. But who should be waiting in the wings? Our old friend Aussie entrepreneur Alan Bond. He who presently is about to come before the courts in Australia on charges of being an unfit person to own a broadcasting chain of stations. Shades of TV-am. Once the shareholding starts to rollercoaster, who knows where, or with whom, it will end. They, of course, want an answer immediately. I am taking the problem to the Authority on Thursday.

Lunch with John Pringle and his advisor from Jacob Rothschild. John wants me to head up a new company. Very flattering. I said I would think about it.

The BBC 'miffed' at White Paper comments. (*The Times*, Wednesday). 'The BBC are just beginning to realise that the White Paper hasn't passed them by.' The *Daily Telegraph* goes in for Chairman-picking – Lord Windlesham, Alastair Burnet, Robin Day, Jeffrey Sterling (again!).

Channel 4 liaison meeting in the afternoon. Michael Grade asked that the Authority consider C 4's request that they join with us in challenging the Government's Directive on banning terrorist interviews. So far, this extraordinary stand by C4 hasn't leaked but, when it does, it will certainly make headlines. My view, which I stated at the Meeting, is that it would be a senseless act of folly to fight the Government over this, but Channel 4 clearly think otherwise.

Thursday. A BBC survey claims television viewers are more concerned about boredom than sex!

Visited John Pringle again and we talked about the company he wants to form. I would be Executive Chairman. We would invite a really good MD to run the company. We talked about Bob Phillis, who I have long admired and who John believes is looking around for something to get him back into broadcasting again. I told John that I would like to take on the job but I will need an open brief. I will not, in nearly my 60th year, be somebody's runabout.

Breakfasted with David Frost on Friday. Met with Clive Leach. Clive wants to take over Tyne Tees, if necessary by making a hostile bid.

Working lunch with colleagues to consider implications on manpower and staffing to ensure success of advertising incremental radio contract. Decided we're okay.

Capital Radio results announced. A pre-tax profit of £9.26m.

The Observer today (Sunday) opens up questions over the Gibraltar shootings.

Saturday 26th November

Still no news of a new Chairman, but GT told me on Thursday that a new

Chairman would come in to the IBA from 1st January and that his role would additionally be to act as Shadow-Chairman of the ITC.

I have been thinking a good deal about taking the new job in the New Year. John Pringle is coming to see me tomorrow. On Monday I am due to meet Jacob Rothschild with John, and I think he wants to hear about my ideas in advance of making me an offer.

ITN Board Meeting on Monday 21 November. David Nicholas described the dying gasps of Super Channel – very sad. George Russell talked about ITN in the period of contract extension. He does not believe that ITN should, or could, change its structure, or invite in new shareholders, before the new contract period in 1992. I think GR is wrong. I think that, if he doesn't shift ITN out of its 30 year old straitjacket and demonstrate that new blood can be brought it, ITN will be seen as a has-been and its dynamic will simply not stand up to the competition that will have emerged by the beginning of the 90s. I passed a note to Alastair Burnet, who sent back a very cryptic response: 'There will be many changes after Christmas!'. I wonder what he has in mind?

Nothing revolutionary in the Sunday newspapers except *The Observer* still pursuing its somewhat lonely course in re-examining the findings of the inquest in Gibraltar. One particular article claims Kenneth Asquez gave false evidence during the hearing. David Windlesham and Richard Rampton are still sifting mountains of evidence. I received a copy of the Thames journalists' submission. I found it rather heavy on paper and a little light on definite facts. Although, in fairness, their case over the Asquez findings (or rather lack of findings) appeared to me to have been carefully gathered. None of the whole ghastly business would have backfired as it has if Thames had got a signed statement. (A case of crying over spilt milk). Windlesham wrote to the Chairman on 16 November. He confirmed that we will have sight of the section dealing with the IBA's role 'in good time before the meeting of the Authority on 15 December'.

GT took a fairly pessimistic view of the tone of the letter, believing it to be reflective on a decision that could damage the IBA. This view was not endorsed by John Rink, who wrote to GT on 22 November, 'I think the response is helpful …. provided that he does, indeed, only refer to the IBA factually in describing the production process and that any comments upon the likelihood of contaminating the evidence are not attributed to the IBA. Then I suspect there will be nothing to fear from the report.' We shall see. I do not take such a sanguine view. Thames have much to lose if the report goes against them. The IBA is on the way out. No harm would be done by discrediting us still further! A cynical view, perhaps. I hope with all my heart that things don't turn out in this way.

On Monday evening, attended a dinner given by BREMA. Norman Tebbit was the guest speaker. He spoke clearly and concisely from notes with a dry sense of humour and an underlying cutting edge to his subject. 'The White Paper', he told his audience, 'was a bad Paper. It did not go far enough.'

Tuesday's papers were full of reports that Rupert Murdoch had done a deal for the Disney Channel on Astra. This gives him a definite plus in terms of credibility and attractiveness. BSB badly wanted Disney. This bears out something Brian

Tesler was saying to me after the ITN Board Meeting. In Los Angeles, Murdoch is taken very seriously. A big player. Whilst BSB (according to Tesler) is considered a likely casualty in the big stakes of satellite television – a bit player. I hope he's wrong but, compared with Murdoch's £250m, BSB billion pounds is one hell of a gamble. Alan Bond is increasing his stake in BSB and, as a consequence, we have had to alter, again, our rulings over non-EEC participation. Virgin and Anglia can't keep up and their shareholdings, as a consequence, will be watered down.

Wednesday. I am growing increasingly worried about my pension arrangements. If the IBA ceases and I go, I have only a promise, albeit Minuted from the Members, that I will receive two thirds of my salary, rather than one third of my salary which is what I would have received if I had not come to this agreement before I joined.

Lunched with John Riddell at the Garrick. John thinks that Margaret Thatcher is 'going slowly mad'. Over coffee he produced an enormous cigar and, in the car back to St James's Palace, very nearly put my car to the torch. He then gaily sauntered through the main doors of the palace, waving the offending cigar and obviously delighted that his employer wasn't waiting to scold him.

Talking of his employer, he told me that he, Prince Charles, had finally separated him, John Riddell, from the filing cabinets. 'I am now seen as a person, not a piece of office furniture.'

In the evening, another goodbye to George. This time given by the ITV Chairmen. A good natured affair with a silver inkstand and an album from Aspreys containing messages from each Chairman. It was a nice gesture. Gesture! I learnt afterwards that the inkstand cost over £2,000.

Trouble with the Iraqi Ambassador over *News At Ten* and *Dispatches*: programmes accusing the Iraqis of using poison gas on the Kurds. Alastair Burnet behaved quite disgracefully, turning away from the Ambassador before cutting him off in mid-sentence. I wrote to ITN enclosing the letter I sent to the Ambassador apologising for the incident.

Authority Meeting on Thursday. The Members endorsed our view that TV-am had improved. David Frost wants to acquire the Saudi holding (still in TV-am). The ACTT withdrew their claim that the IBA has not been safeguarding standards on TV-am.

The Members came to a rapid view on C4's wish to take to judicial review the Government's ban on broadcasting interviews with known terrorists. GT indicated that the BBC would not join with C4 if they were asked and neither will the IBA. Interesting to see what C4 does next.

In the evening, the Robert Fraser Lecture. GT and I got stuck in a student demonstration and had to hoof it from Victoria Station to the Banqueting House in Whitehall, I having refused to use the Underground for fear of being mugged or sat upon by 'steamers', much to GT's amusement. The walk did us good.

The Lecture was a tour-de-force. GT was in good voice and afterwards many people congratulated him. He spoke forcefully of the 'zealots of Whitehall'. I think that George will prove an able advocate of Public Service Broadcasting in the Lords. Afterwards, we gave a buffet for our guests. GT, Brian Young and I were photographed grouped around the portrait of Robert Fraser.

On Friday the papers carried a good account of the lecture. The *Times* headline: 'Changes to ITV are wanton destruction, says Lord Thomson'.

A quick meeting at home on Sunday with John Pringle. We talked about the meeting tomorrow with Jacob Rothschild. I said I planned to be bombastic and aggressive and say that the broadcasting world is my oyster.

Next week we should learn who the next Chairman is going to be.

Monday 28th November

Every month I read Celeste in *Queen* magazine. This month's predictions for Sagittarius is very much to the point and I would do well to take her advice. 'Face situations head on and exercise free will and you must be able to come to terms with anything the planets now demand of you. But be prepared to alter your outlook, methods, routine or projects which are no longer productive or viable. Saturn, new in Capricorn, is without doubt a great builder of character and if you are prepared to analyse this period of casting-out then it must be apparent that all you are losing is a stockpile of insecurities collected over a period of many years. With this thought in mind, approach December with courage and determination and, above all, don't lose your sense of humour. You are being tested only to become a more complete individual. Much will depend on whether you are now willing to settle for less than you deserve to purchase your freedom.'

Monday 5th December

Last Thursday, GT asked me for a private word. He told me that George Russell had been appointed Chairman of the IBA and that the announcement would be made on Friday at 3.30pm.

So we were all wrong. Some weeks earlier I had said to Timothy Renton that the ideal Chairman would be George. It's a good choice. GR will not be a hands-on man. The industry will be delighted.

The Times quoted me: 'Mr John Whitney, Director General of the IBA, said that the appointment was good news for television. "We can now plan forward to assure the successful development of the next phase of UK broadcasting".'

He will be the Shadow Chairman of the ITC and that should put heart into our staff. The next challenge will be to find a good Chairman for ITN and a Deputy Chairman for C4.

This week has been pretty hectic. I am writing this entry having just returned from the EBU Council meeting in Cairo, arriving there late Thursday night.

Last Monday (28 November) I had a meeting with Jacob Rothschild and John Pringle. Jacob is one of those apparently unassuming, quiet people who look as though they wouldn't say boo to a goose. This manner obviously conceals a hurricane-force drive. The meeting went well, or so John told me afterwards. They seem keen to get a company started.

The appointment of George Russell will obviously need some thinking about as far as my own plans are concerned. I am seeing GT tomorrow and see how he views my continuation.

Proposed vote of thanks at a TRIC lunch on Tuesday 29 November for Andrew Ehrenberg of the London Business School. He was adamant that the new advances in choice would be slow in coming. Very much the GT line. In my thank-you, I said I thought it would be faster, citing VCRs and breakfast television developments.

In the evening my dinner for GT and Grace at the Garrick. A very jolly occasion with a good collection of close-ish friends including Merlyn Rees, Tim Renton, Brian Cubbon, Ian Trethowan, Richard Dunn, Chris Scoble, Michael Moriarty, Tony Butler, Wilfred Hyde, Quentin Thomas, Richard Attenborough. Received warm letters afterwards and I think GT enjoyed it.

I realise this entry hasn't been overly colourful but am feeling rather exhausted from Cairo.

Must think about the future now ....

Friday 9th December

At about 4.30pm today I received the draft of the Enquiry Findings on *Death on the Rock*. Earlier in the week I had had lengthy conversations with David Windlesham over the question of who should be permitted to see the draft and when. Finally it was agreed that we – that is, GT and I – should have sight of the draft where it referred to us (the IBA) and that, after reading it over this weekend, we would meet David Windlesham and either approve it or ask for further time for consideration.

I didn't get a chance to read it until I got home tonight and even now I haven't read it through word for word but, on first reading, I am delighted to be able to say that the report endorses the decision that we took in showing the programme. It rejects the case put by Geoffrey Howe that the programme led to contamination of evidence or that the programme was unbalanced. The Findings make the best Christmas present I could possibly ask for.

Unfortunately, the Findings will not be made public for some little time so we will have to stay silent until they are published.

I had my first meeting with George Russell on Tuesday. We talked about my future plans. George said he greatly appreciated my wish to get back to positive and creative work but hoped that, if I did decide to leave, I would announce the job I would be taking up so that it would not look as though we had had a row. I can understand his feeling. This would suit me too.

George Russell's style will obviously be mightily different to that of GT's. Fewer meetings, less red tape, more responsibility on staff, less bureaucracy. I think that his leadership will tune into the times and, if I had the interest, I would have no hesitation in staying, but I want change. I must make some money and be a free agent again.

On Wednesday I had lunch with Bob Phillis. We talked about him joining me. I think we would make a good team.

Also on Wednesday, a meeting with Anthony Simonds-Gooding. Virgin are pulling right out of BSB. The other founder-shareholders – Pearson, Granada and Anglia – do not want to acquire Virgin's shareholding but Alan Bond has come forward. The company will soon be owned by Bond if things go on like this. BSB is spending ludicrous sums of money. I predict that we will see a collapse of titanic proportions.

How long they will keep going is anyone's guess. At all events, no one outside believes they have problems but the omens are there. If I was a shareholder I would not be sleeping easily at night.

Sunday 11th December

The Astra Satellite has been launched successfully from somewhere in Guyana. So, unless there is a slip-up in the next four days or so, Rupert Murdoch will have his six channels ready for the receiver dishes in the UK.

Nothing today in the press about the *Death on the Rock* programme. Last night, Colette telephoned me in Dorset to say that Donald Trelford wanted to speak to GT and get his reaction to a report that the Enquiry had exonerated the broadcaster. I told Colette to tell *The Observer* that George could not be contacted. He is spending the weekend in London packing his things and tearing up masses of paper before his departure. He must feel somewhat like a despatched Prime Minister, going out of the back door.

I have been giving a great deal of thought to my own future. On the one hand, I don't want to leave the IBA and its staff rudderless. On the other hand, if I stay until 1990 I won't be able to take on a job in television as it would then be too close to the next round of contracts.

I had a long talk with GT on Friday. He has a radical shape for the future he believes he can sell to Government:

> Firstly, Tendering. George Russell believes that the incumbent contractors should be allowed to continue their contracts if they can match the highest bid. I asked him what would be the point of others bidding if, at the end of the day, the winner was the original contractor with sitting rights? I find it hard to believe that Ministers will accept the proposition. GR argues that it is equally unfair for existing contractors to lose their rights simply because someone else comes along with more money. GT acknowledges that this could cause dissatisfaction and proposes that, after three years, a company could be subject to takeover.
>
> Secondly, GR believes that C4 should be permitted to make its own selling arrangements. That if there is a shortfall, money to support the programmes remit would be made available by the ITC.
>
> Thirdly, disposing of IBA Engineering in its entirety, staff and all, to an outside company. The result of the sale would go to the ITC as opposed to the Treasury. This could then be dipped into if necessary.

GR considered that these proposals all meet the basic White Paper imperative and can be argued through with Ministers. Each needs careful thought. The idea is right but can it be sold, I wonder?

Sunday 18th December

The Christmas season comes rattling round again, with cash jingling in the tills and shoppers with fixed expressions and haunted eyes seeking presents with a sense of desperation sometimes bordering on the manic.

The terrible events of the last two weeks – the devastation in Armenia with now some 55,000 dead followed on our doorstep by the rush hour rail crash near Clapham leaving 33 dead and 113 injured – brings home the suffering that many hundreds of thousands of people over the world will be enduring this Christmas. These two events have sunk into the national conscience.

On Monday, a meeting with David Windlesham and Richard Rampton to go over our points relating to the Enquiry. They accepted the majority of our amendments and said they proposed sending a copy to Geoffrey Howe. I was nervous that today *The Observer* would publish a copy of the report, but nothing has appeared.

To Jeffrey Archer's in the evening for champagne and shepherds pie. Got stuck with Freddie Forsyth and couldn't, for the life of me, see how he could write so brilliantly and successfully. Avoided Geoffrey Howe and had a giggle with David Frost avoiding Jonathan Aitken.

On Sunday 11 December, the Astra Satellite was successfully launched and is now in orbit. This week has seen the start of what will be a heavy promotional campaign to give Astra the edge on BSB.

The Lords sat down, or rather stood up, to debate broadcasting. Lord Ferrers rose to move 'that this House takes note of the White Paper Broadcasting in the 90s: Competition, Choice and Quality'. He kicked off the debate with an eulogy on the IBA and in particular on GT. From the general tone of the speeches and the remarks made on the Granada programme the previous Sunday, it is becoming increasingly clear that the Government is facing considerable difficulty in getting through the main elements of the White Paper, in particular the auctioning off of the ITV contracts.

Advertisers, and agencies, are beginning to look harder at the small print in the White Paper. The *FT* ran a feature on Tuesday. In it, a strong note of caution and disenchantment is struck: 'The Government White Paper, which at first glance seemed to meet so many demands of advertisers, long frustrated by the increasing cost of the ITV monopoly, does not, on closer perusal, offer quite the relaxing scenario that had been expected'.

'UK clients', says Mr Winston Delaney, Chairman of Delaney Fletcher Delaney, 'will look back on this era as a golden age when mass audiences could be reached without the expense of buying time on hundreds of different media'.

So all is not perfect from anyone's point of view.

SCC in the afternoon. We took the paper on changes in ownership. The Companies were mostly silent on the subject. Their thoughts were busily engaged on survival of the fittest.

Christmas drinks with Colette and assorted hacks. I go to the Thirty Club and take Bruce Gyngell as my guest. It is kiss and make up time, in my judgment. We eat mince pies and sing carols. Frank Muir is very funny.

Wednesday 14 December. The press comment widely on the Lords' debate.

The last Authority meeting on Thursday 15 December at which GT will preside. A full turnout of Members and one of the speediest meetings I can remember. I report that Virgin has withdrawn from BSB. As a founder member, this is an important change. Taking Virgin's place is the ubiquitous Alan Bond. The company is heading for a very sticky end. I sound very pessimistic but nothing I see of their progress gives me confidence, and confidence is what they're going to need. So far, the news that Virgin has withdrawn has not leaked. (The reason for the withdrawal is Virgin's decision to go back to being a private company).

Like many moments in history, the meeting came and went without a feeling of the moment being of importance. Donald Maitland said some words and that was it.

Earlier, at the beginning of the meeting, in a private session, GT gave Members the more than welcome news that the Enquiry would be satisfactory as far as the IBA was concerned. He was unable to say more.

In the evening, black tie again for GT's farewell dinner at the Hyde Park Hotel. A curious speech by Donald Maitland with an unfortunate joke about tarts and fingers, or rather fingers in tarts. I don't recall the joke itself. GT spoke well, and so did Paula Ridley who retired at the same time. Bridget Plowden came late from presenting prizes. Brian Young looked ten years younger than when he was DG. GT sped off at 1030 to attend an ICI Ball!

The Sun made an unreserved apology on Friday to Carmen Proetta: 'The Tart of Gibraltar'. The news got good coverage and is the first action of several against other newspapers who printed similar stories. I am delighted.

The final, final, final farewell party for GT took place in the Conference Hall where he received a television set and an album of pictures and I paid tribute to his eight years in office. And so George Thomson leaves the IBA and I must make up my mind what I do.

Saturday 24th December

Christmas week. A terrible plane crash. Pan-Am 103 with 270 souls on board. The Christmas season has been a sorrowful time. For some reason I have failed to put out my Christmas cards in the office and for the first time since it was given to me by John Pringle, my lovely indoor plant is dying. The leaves, which have always been so green and shiny, are turning brown and brittle. Omens for the future perhaps!

Monday 19 December. Crowds jostle around the entrance to Harrods. The pickpockets do a brisk trade, then dart down the stairs to become lost in the crowds going into the Underground.

Attended the ITN Board meeting, the last chaired by George Russell. Drinks afterwards.

Had coffee with Andrew Lloyd Webber on Tuesday in his flat. I suggested that the Really Useful Company be used as the receptacle for the bankers' money being put together by John Pringle. Andrew is interested but, in talking later to John,

1988

he does not believe that we should go in to the Really Useful, but instead the Really Useful group should invest in CCQ. So I think I've started off making a bog. My real task over Christmas is to sort out what I want to do and I mustn't make a bog of that decision.

As I write these notes, I am listening to *Phantom* on CD. Andrew was going off to Vienna and he later told me the show received a 20 minute standing ovation. He must be very pleased with the way things are going. *Aspects of Love* has already taken £2m at the box office.

Roma and I went to the Great Room in Grosvenor House to attend a Christmas Lunch put on by TRIC. After the meal I was presented with a plaque commemorating me as a Companion of TRIC. The Chairman read out bits about my life. It sounded dreadfully like an obituary. I forgot to record that this was also my birthday, and everyone sang 'Happy Birthday'. A jolly event.

A meeting later in the afternoon with Anthony Simonds-Gooding. Virgin have taken the decision to sell their shareholding to Bond. This makes Bond the biggest shareholder. BSB were counting on Bond underwriting £13m by Thursday. This would permit the company to draw down £31m as a bank loan so that the first payment could be made to MGM for the eventual purchase of their film library for use on BSB. I learnt on Thursday, or was it Friday, that Bond has not given the expected undertaking. Quite what this means to BSB and MGM and the bank and the other shareholders I don't know, but BSB is treading a tightrope without a safety net and there are plenty of people itching to give a gentle shove, push or nudge. Some, indeed, would not hesitate to sever the rope if they were given the chance.

BSB are now pushing hard to put all five channels on the first satellite.

An article in the *Independent* highlights Government's determination that the smaller Companies should not receive subsidies from the larger ITV Companies.

Mark Fisher, Labour Front Bench spokesman on media, is quoted: 'These plans mean the advent of tabloid television'.

Peter Baldwin's Radio Division made a press announcement giving details of the locations of the 20 'incremental' community radio stations.

Broadcasting journalist have lodged applications in the High Court seeking a judicial review of the order issued by Douglas Hurd banning television and radio interviews with terrorist organisations and their supporters. This will be a long and expensive struggle. George Russell told me on Friday that the Channel Four Board had 'agonised' over whether or not to join with the journalists but had decided against it.

David McCall and George Cooper came to see me urgently. They told me that the ITV Companies and ITP had come to the conclusion that they wished to dispose of *TV Times* with the ending of the monopoly on copyright. They consider the value will be badly hit. I hazarded a guess that its value would be of the order of £150m. 'Not far out', said McCall. I said I was surprised that, just as the White Paper was calling for the fragmentation of ITV, the ITV Companies would themselves want to get rid of the publishing business that had contributed to welding together the regional stations. They said that rather than watch the value go down and down the Companies would rather clear a profit and, since other publications including *TV Times* under new ownership would still be covering ITV output, the information would still be provided. I said that if it was a unanimous decision on the part of the Companies, the IBA would acknowledge their right to sell. This incident is an example, I think, of the real uncertainties confronting the Companies.

Today I spoke to David Windlesham as a result of a conversation GT had had with him the day before. There had been what appeared at any rate to be an exchange of words over two elements of the report. Firstly, timing. GT agreed that DW appeared critical that *Death on the Rock* had only been seen by GT only on the Wednesday preceding transmission. I explained that this was incorrect. On that Wednesday it had first been seen by Robert Hargreaves, then by David Glencross, then by me and finally by GT. DW did not comment when I explained the sequence. The second point was to do with Thames offering the programme in rough form to Television Division before completion on the Monday before transmission. The implied criticism being that the IBA should have previewed earlier. I said that it was not the practice of the IBA to look at incomplete programmes which would take us into the role of editor, which we were not. We fulfilled the role of publisher and, if we didn't like what we were being asked to put out, we had the power to reject a programme or ask for alterations. Windlesham asked me to send him a note. On Friday the note was sent by hand to DW by David Glencross.

A BSB meeting on Thursday morning. Staff Christmas lunch. Many old faces around: Brian Young, John Harriott, John Guinery. A jolly occasion.

At 4.30pm farewell drinks with GT in his room, now bereft of his personal bits and pieces. Grace and he in jovial mood. Champagne for the girls in the office, Vic (his driver) and Shirley. A moment, like other moments, that will grow in the memory but which at the time seemed almost commonplace. We raised our glasses and toasted George and Grace and their future happiness. I have to leave to go to Artsline. We shake hands and I kiss Grace.

The newspapers on Friday 23 December report the sale of Virgin's interest in BSB to Bond. It has taken them all, including Ray Snoddy, by surprise. The *Daily Telegraph* commented: 'Both the IBA and BSB seem remarkably calm about letting such a large stake in BSB go to a man facing charges that he used his television influence to hound Australia's largest mutual society AMP and has every chance of losing his local licences'. It concludes: 'Mr Bond has also been revealed as the secret purchaser of Van Gogh's 'Irises' for $49m. He has a large spread of assets and has shown himself quite happy to liquidate them at short notice. He may give the IBA a few anxious moments before long.'

If the truth be told, 'he' of course is already giving the IBA and BSB more than a few anxious moments. This is a classic no-win situation, exactly the same situation as occurred at the beginning of TV-am. To pull the plug on BSB would be an act of sheer folly. That they have no-one else at the moment to turn to, to raise money to prevent Bond from stepping in, is quite outrageous. But when, and if, things do go wrong, you can be sure that the IBA will stand accused of allowing Bond to hold such a dominant stake!

At 10am I went down to the maintenance department to meet the staff and present them with a crate of beer. This ceremony has become something of a tradition. We talk about the year that has passed and the year to come. The boys who work on maintenance have, in many ways, a better grasp of the situation and are in closer touch with events after the White Paper than many others who work in the IBA.

In the afternoon, the office closes at 3.30pm. I expect GR. He comes at 4pm and we are able to talk without disturbance. I ask him for his views about the assimilation of the IBA into the ITC, or whether he sees the setting up of an operation parallel but quite separate. George is specific. It is the former, with the IBA being absorbed into the ITC. 'Obviously', George says, 'there will be some staff who will be made redundant but there will be many senior staff who, if they want, can stay'. We talked about 'networking'. GR has very clear thoughts. He sees the network supply of programmes coming from a separate agency, paid for by the Companies with a Chief Executive appointed jointly by the Companies and the ITC. The network company will provide programmes of quality to the station, playing directly into programme schedules. GR does not expect the network company to do other than supply drama and perhaps arts programmes and a national current affairs programme. I questioned him closely, pointing out that each Company's programme schedules vary according to the tastes of their audience. I suggest that to block off air time for national networking would, in all likelihood, be resisted by Companies who felt that, by being 'closer' to their audiences and their taste, would know better what programmes to schedule. George disagreed. He believed advertisers would prefer a 'solid' network output. I pointed out that the White Paper envisaged the ITV Companies being more regional than before, thus making way for a more national service on Channel Five. I also pointed out that directing Companies to take network programmes would entail more control rather than lighter regulation. It seemed inconsistent with the intention of the White Paper. GR grunted. He does not like opposing opinions. I think he is being naïve on a number of issues.

I can foresee a time in the quite near future when some of his views are going to run into some heavy criticism. He rightly is trying to find an overall shape for the system, but the frame he envisages is not in any judgment going to stand up to close scrutiny. It leans too heavily on status quo for current Government thinking. I, for one, do not agree with his wish that the current ITV Companies be given the right, if the money is forthcoming, to go into the next contract period unchallenged.

During the discussion, which lasted about an hour and a half, not once did George enquire about my plans. I can see a cat-and-mouse situation developing. For my part, I must lock-in my new job so firmly that when I negotiate myself out of the IBA I will be certain of my future.

Tuesday 27th December

The newspapers are published today. *The Times* Spectrum feature assesses people who will matter in 1989. Under media:

'Russell could turn out to be the unlikely media hero of 1989. A first class business man with a well-deserved reputation for one shaping ailing industrial concerns. He knows the problems and difficulties facing ITV, having been Chairman of ITN and Deputy Chairman of C4. Could persuade the Government to drop some of the more illogical proposals in the Broadcast White Paper.' (Richard Evans, Media Correspondent).

1989

Monday 2nd January

Not many bows in the Honours list towards television. Peter Gibbings is knighted and John Gau made a CBE. I have continued to think about my future. I am much tempted to leave the IBA and join the Really Useful Company. It would make an exciting career change. Winding down the IBA and watching the ITC take over does not thrill me with anticipation.

I was thinking over the weekend that, somewhere at the beginning of my diaries, I wrote that what I hoped I might accomplish in the IBA was to 'preside over its winding up'. This has turned out not to be a ball far off the mark. What has changed, without my fully realising it, was – or has been – my attitude to broadcasting whilst I have been with the IBA. Had I maintained my first convictions, I would surely have done more to speed events along. As it is, I have allowed things to drift. I could have done much more to speed the deregulation of radio. Instead I sat on my hands. Our press relations have been, and are still, quite appalling. If there is time left, I intend to remedy this.

Sunday 8th January

The press claim BBC victory over ITV in the ratings.

BSB showing their irritation and anger over Rupert Murdoch's advertising attack on them with claims and counter-claims. BSB have taken their grievance to the OFT but Gordon Borrie has told them to go to the ASA. BSB have told him that this would mean an unacceptable delay.

George Russell came in early on Wednesday 4 January to meet DGMM colleagues and we lunched him in the Members' Dining Room.

GR made it clear that he wanted to see the IBA absorbed into the ITC. This view doesn't equate with a note I read of a meeting between Shirley Littler and Chris Scoble in which Chris was at pains to draw a distinction between the two bodies, believing that it would be cleaner to start the ITC on a blank sheet of paper.

Meanwhile, the Labour Shadow Broadcasting Minister is preparing a response to the White Paper which backs the continuation of the IBA and its duties. A forlorn hope.

I asked GR about the appointment of a Chief Executive of the ITC. He said he would like to advertise the post towards the end of October 1989. This response strengthens my feeling that I should be making my departure clear before this date. I don't want to take a side seat while all the usual hubbub goes on over this appointment. Anyway, I should have better fish to fry by then.

I met with BSB at our regular liaison meeting on Thursday. Anthony assures me that the payment to MGM has been made possible by interim arrangements with Bond. I tell him that the IBA hopes to advertise the fourth and fifth channels at the end of February and that the channels will be complementary to the three BSB channels.

GR brings in his personal effects to his office: a stark contrast to GT's house style. GR's pictures include two made out of Marley bricks and a picture of GR as a gargoyle!

GR appears to have already shifted his ground on competitive tenders. Before Christmas he was saying that existing companies should have the right to continue if they paid the going bid price. Now he says that he is considering quality judged within different 'bid bands'. In other words, if, say, three companies make high bids within a given band, a quality judgment would be made between the three bids. I said that seemed much more sensible.

Talked with Richard Dunn about timing on *Death on the Rock*. Thames are now dithering over whether or not to do a *This Week* programme on the findings. I said that, if we did not get the inquiry papers on the 20th January, we would not be able to give a comment by 26th. He has gone away to think about it. They have a Board Meeting on the 11th and will come back to me afterwards.

GR telephoned me on Friday about 11am to tell me he had just been told by the Home Office that Alun Chalfont was to become Deputy Chairman of the IBA and subsequently Deputy Chairman of the ITC. GR appeared pleased and said he welcomed the appointment.

The Leader in the *Guardian* was less commendatory: '… a man whose ferociously right wing views, especially on defence … '.

It looks as though Mrs T has now armed herself with two stout defenders of Tory ideology: William Rees-Mogg and now Lord Chalfont. I am rather relieved he won't be at the IBA on 26th January.

On Wednesday GT came into the office. We sat and talked for some time. He seemed sad and, I thought, rather uncertain.

Sunday 15th January

John Pringle, my old mate and partner in Consolidated, has struck a deal with Jacob Rothschild to start a new media company. Rothschild are putting in £2m to start off. The object – to get a TV franchise. I shall be Executive Chairman.

It's time I moved. I have lost a great deal of confidence and drive while I have been at the IBA. So easy to see ones mistakes and failings. So difficult to see at the time. On Monday I decided to tell Bridget Hayward that I felt unable to join the Really Useful Company. It would have been fun, and given me a splendid lift-off, but I think I've made a wise decision. To start off from scratch is a challenge but I shall be my own boss and I'm best when I'm that.

On Monday to Lancaster House for the farewell dinner to George Thomson given by Douglas Hurd. A jolly evening with warm words spoken by Douglas on George's achievements.

The main event of the week was the Authority Meeting with George Russell in the chair. It was good meeting; much better than I had imagined. GR has decreed that meetings will be held once a month instead of fortnightly. It will make a great difference to the internal workings of the IBA. I wish I had insisted on it earlier. I wish I had done a lot of things. I have wasted six years and lost many opportunities. I should have stood away from the IBA and looked at it from the outside instead of from inside out. Perhaps GT and I were the wrong combination. I don't know. I suppose it's too early to say. George Russell's style is very different. It's already clear that he's very much a one man band in decision taking. It's as well that I'm going. He's treading all over the ground that I expected to be mine. (I sound like a spoilt child). I believe that, if GR is going to show weakness, it will be that he is getting too close to decisions, but maybe it is the right way. He has determination and good, pragmatic logic.

The Authority agreed that ITV could sell *TV Times*. It was agreed that the remaining two channels on DBS would be complementary to BSB's three channels. All in all, a good day's work. No drinks at lunchtime but everyone seemed on a 'high'!

Anthony Smith in the current issue of *Sight & Sound* described Public Service Broadcasting: 'Public Service Broadcasting entails using a form of social power outside the justifying rituals of the marketplace'. One of the most trenchant descriptions I have read. 'PSB is considered de mode. The electronic bookstall thesis commands the high ground. Nevertheless, recognition that there is more to value in television than television itself will make its comeback as the marketplace shows itself for what it is.'

The papers last Monday were full of the details over the announcement by ITV that they were selling *TV Times*. A price ticket of £250m was struck on it with 12 possible bidders.

The row over TVS reluctance to broadcast Sky commercials rumbled on all this week. On Friday James Gatward telephoned to tell me that the Board had considered their options and decided to agree to allow Sky to purchase airtime.

Lunched on Monday with Don Moss who is being paid by James Hanson to apply for the music incremental radio station in London. He proposes putting forward the concept of 'easy listening'. We lunched at Overtons in St James's. Nothing has changed since I last went there over 15 years ago. The same Head Waiter, who recognised me I think; same menu; same air of 1930s London.

Lunched with Yorkshire Labour MPs on Tuesday, amongst them Merlyn Rees. These kind of get-togethers always prove valuable since they bring home the fact that our world of television, intrigue and power politics is relatively low on the agenda of real events.

Peter Gibbings, newly knighted, announced Anglia profits and launched a strong attack on the White Paper: 'Extraordinary that a Government keen on expanding share ownership should treat shareholders in TV companies as they are proposing to do .... now money is the touchstone, not quality'.

On Tuesday afternoon a message was handed to me that Maggie Brown on the *Independent* wanted to print a story about my going from the DG position, and GR taking over as Chief Executive as well as Chairman. George got rightly anxious about the story and we came to the conclusion that Maggie had got the wrong end of the stick, confusing a statement GR had made to the ITN Board before leaving as Chairman that he thought ITN should have a Chairman and Chief Executive position combined. In the event, no story appeared. I heaved a sigh of relief. The last thing I want is any rumours about my departure.

On Tuesday evening to The Thirty Club for a speech by Douglas Hurd. I took Bob Phillis as my guest. In the event, Douglas was delayed in the Commons and so Michael Checkland, Richard Dunn and Michael Grade were each invited to speak for five minutes. Michael Checkland delivered a rather barren discourse on BBC funding. Richard started out on a complicated analysis of 'cornerstones', ITV being the walls and BBC the cornerstone of PSB. Luckily Douglas came in, to applause and relief.

Douglas' message was simple: the White Paper was really rather green round the gills. A framework. Plenty to play for, etc. etc.

The day before, GR had had a lengthy meeting with Mrs T. It seems now almost certain that quality assessment *will* be factored into the final decision process and that networking arrangements will be part of the ITC considerations. As long as GR shares Mrs T's conviction, Douglas and the rest will stand to one side. I can see why GR appeals to Mrs T. He speaks and thinks as a businessman. His mind is constantly looking ahead, sizing up options. If anyone can combine the virtues, George can. While the critics stay silent, GR can plot and rule supreme.

Wednesday's papers were full of journalists warning of their right to challenge the legality of the ban on broadcasting interviews with named terrorist groups. The BBC and IBA are ringsiders.

Attended a presentation by BSB to the press on Thursday. A bullish statement of BSB's planning and programming. The battle between Sky and BSB is going to be, and is already, a no-holds-barred fight. Leaving the new Queen Elizabeth Conference Centre, I was exceedingly relieved that our choice of BSB appears to be a good one so far. Anthony Simonds-Gooding and his team are hard-nosed fighters and they put up a good show. With the stakes as high as they are, they will have to show true grit.

The newspapers reported Douglas Hurd's comment at a conference the day before when he laid down the law over newspaper control of the media. At last, the potential domination by Murdoch and Maxwell is sinking in.

On Friday, the papers reported the leaked findings of our monitoring on violence, presented to ITV at a PPC meeting. It could have been damaging but in the event it hasn't, I think, done any harm.

The *Death on the Rock* findings of the Inquiry have been delivered (24 copies). Members will have received their copies yesterday and no doubt are reading with interest. The IBA is totally vindicated: 'We have concluded that *Death on the Rock* did not carry any real risk for prejudice or contamination. Nor have we found there were any legal impediments to the broadcast of the programme, nor that the requirements of balance, fairness and impartiality demanded by the various statutory and contractual provisions referred to earlier in this report were infringed.' (Page 139 of Report).

This Week have invited me to take part in the programme reviewing the inquiry on Thursday. After so many weeks of uncertainty over the exact findings, the outcome is a relief. Whether Thames will now take action against the *Sunday Times* for its vicious campaign against the programme remains to be seen.

It also remains to be seen how both the Board of Thames and the IBA respond formally to the findings.

Finally, to end this week's piece, my own affairs. Meetings have taken place with my solicitors and pension advisers, and between the IBA pension advisers. I have had a meeting with GR when the terms of our parting have been discussed and I hope settled.

Change is always frightening. At the age of 58, I had always thought I would be contemplating retirement and relaxation. To leave now does not cast me in the role of a retired person looking for a job. I now feel certain in my own mind that the timing is right. Whether others think so remains to be seen.

Sunday 29th January

I need a new chapter. I don't want to 'retire'. Once someone is said to have 'retired', everyone feels a little sorry for them. No matter how hard the struggle to re-assert, everyone says nice things and behind one's back says, 'Oh dear'.

Breaking with the IBA is bound to be difficult. Will people think I've been fired? Will they think I am abandoning them? But the time has come. The last of the old guard will have gone. The IBA can find someone to take them into the new 90s. An ITC man. I don't want to be seen as a dying ember of the old IBA. If I can, I want to announce the changes before I go to America.

I need a new, stimulating challenge. I need to be creative again. I am sick of not putting something *into* the act of creation. Really Useful is small enough and eager enough to want to expand. As important, I think it will be fun and I desperately need some fun.

I think I really have a guardian angel. Last week, Consolidated was registered as a new company. I don't want to get involved in an application for a television franchise but events seemed to be taking me inexorably into this new role. Starting a new company can be fine when you are 30 but at nearly 60 it's a bit daunting.

And then, on Friday, Melvyn Bragg came to see me. He's a director of RUG. I didn't know the reason for the meeting. I thought it was to do with Border Television, of which he is a director but no, he was there as the emissary of Andrew to ask again if I would consider going into RUG as Chief Executive.

An hour afterwards I had a planned meeting with Deitch, representing the Rothschild banking interests in Consolidated. I had worked feverishly on the budget of £2.5m. It didn't add up. We simply did not have enough money to see us through the pre-contract period. I telephoned John Pringle in Miami and told him I was withdrawing. At the end of the meeting, Deitch and I shook hands and parted in friendship.

A letter from Andrew came just as I was going home:

> 'Dear John
>
> I have just been through with Biddy the position with the company and the many opportunities that we have and I genuinely can think of no one more suited to take advantage of what I believe to be a thrilling future. We have simply got to make a move fairly soon and I do beg of you to consider what we could achieve.
>
> Andrew'

That sort of letter takes some resisting!

Back to the week and its main event – Thursday 26 January and the Authority Meeting to discuss *Death on the Rock*. Members had received copies of the report the previous week and didn't take long to agree to a press statement. The main attention of the report is not on the IBA but on David Windlesham and Thames.

In the evening, Thames put out their '*This Week* special' on the *Rock*. George Thomson took part and was very good, speaking up for common sense and fairness, against the manic Andrew Neil, who appeared more and more dotty. I think he is out on a limb, having defended his troops, the *Insight* team, some of whom have been less than loyal to their leader. Michael Mates MP performed with the resolution of a tank. Not a distinguished programme and will probably open up some old scars, as did the onslaught that has poured out of the No. 10 publicity machine.

The Government was not at all happy about the outcome of the findings and the MOD hastily re-circulated its faded letters condemning the programme makers. Either the findings have had the last word, or it's the beginning of another round. Time alone will tell.

On Friday, GR spoke to the staff assembled in the Conference Room. It was a masterly and effective performance: simple, energetic and utterly convincing. I introduced him with what I think was a jolly good introduction, outlining his past achievements. He is in the middle of a fantastic honeymoon period and, for everyone's sake, long may it continue.

On Wednesday, I lunched with Luke Rittner at the Arts Council. Luke is anxious for the Arts Council to take an active part in the new broadcasting opportunities. I suggested that he should form Arts Council plc as an independent production company. This could be the way to do it, if a new funding source can be found to finance its operation. I have a number of ideas, and will speak to Luke. Perhaps RUG and the Arts Council should get together to form a partnership?

Lord Chalfont's appointment has been continuing to cause waves inside and outside Westminster. He joins the IBA in February.

Sunday 4th February

I have made up my mind to leave the IBA and join the Really Useful Company. I am both flattered and exhilarated by the prospect. The thought of coming out again into the real world of creativity makes the pulse race! The deal I have struck with RUG is a good one and should give me plenty of incentive.

I very much hope that next week, and before Friday when the Authority meets, I will be in a position to confirm my intention to leave. If the timing is right, the Members can be given the news in a private session and then an announcement can be made.

People will read all sorts of motives into my decision, but there it is. If I am going to make any money before I'm too old, I should start now.

I am also pleased to be leaving because, whilst I like GR, I don't find myself in sympathy with many of the moves he is making. He shoots from the hip and seems to change his mind almost on a daily basis. His current conviction is that a Company's future should be judged on its ratings and record in the past. Thus Granada would find favour because it has *Coronation Street* and so GR figures this will give it strength for the future. I am also afraid that GR's dislike of things political will mean that Lord Chalfont will become the guardian of IBA 'balance'.

As I write these notes, Sky television has its first night of official transmission. Estimates vary as to the number of dishes but reports estimate somewhere between 10,000 and 20,000. The size of the Astra dishes will, in time, wreck the skyline of our cities but I suppose it's inevitable.

On Wednesday, I had a meeting with John Wakeham in the Privy Council Office. Robert Hargreaves accompanied me and together we sold Wakeham on the proposition that test Parliamentary transmissions could be first started on the fourth or fifth channels on the BSB satellites. Quite an elegant solution to the dilemma facing the Commons Committee on Parliamentary Broadcasting. John Wakeham told us in confidence that Mrs T. didn't want the televising of Parliament to start with a big bang, and certainly not with the Queen's Speech. Why, I don't know. Perhaps she feels that the launch will be such a media event that nobody will pay attention to her magic words.

On Thursday an interesting meeting with Richard Dunn to brief ourselves before SCC this week. Dunn is quite seriously looking at the prospect of Thames going on the Astra satellite instead of remaining on the ground. No levy, no regulation, no licence, no hassle!

Friday 10th February

On Monday 6th, Peacock entered the fray on future allocation of television licences by repeating their concerns that to have quality in television the highest bid should not be the arbiter but the ITC should have the right to make a quality judgment.

In the evening, I went to the Broadcasting Standards Council reception. Met William Rees-Mogg, Colin Shaw, Mary Whitehouse and others bent on saving the nation's soul. It really is too ludicrous that filth and garbage can be spread across the tabloids every day and that a million pound organisation employing 20 or more staff should be set up to guard our moral values on television.

Radio Academy lunch at the Savoy on 9th February. I took Alun Chalfont, still obviously causing much speculation about his role.

In the afternoon, off to St James's Palace to see Prince Charles, who expressed his concern about the use of charity money from TV appeals. He looked rather thin and despondent.

In the evening, the opera. *Leah* at the English National Opera as guests of Grace and George Thomson. I told them about my move to RUG. George was delighted.

A red letter day today, the 10th. At 9 a.m. GR called in the Members to a private session. I sat outside with my team watching Sky television. Inside the boardroom GR told the Members I will be leaving the IBA and joining RUG. He told them of the financial package I had been offered. The private session seemed to take a long time. At 9.35am George came out and told me the Members had agreed the package and that there was a genuine warmth towards me. I went into the boardroom and the main meeting took place. Sir Donald, as we sat down, squeezed my hand under the table and said in a low whisper, 'Congratulations'.

So now the scene is set. Later in the morning I arrange the schedule of the announcement. Hopefully, if the news isn't leaked, we will issue a statement on 23rd February and I will leave on 10th April.

It is somewhat ironic, and something of a coincidence, that on the evening of 23rd February I will be chairing the Journalists Awards at the Hilton, and my very introduction to the job was the ghastly speech I made on the same occasion seven years before.

On Tuesday, Roma and I fly to California to see our daughter Fiona and her newborn son Bevan. Very odd to be a grandfather.

I told Dickie about my new job and made him promise to keep the secret. Dickie beamed on hearing what I shall be doing: 'A round peg in a round hole'. I am pleased at his reaction.

Funny to think that, after so many pages of recollections, my diary writing days may be coming to a close.

Whether in years to come what I have written will be of interest, time alone will tell.

Wednesday 22nd February

Roma and I have just stepped off Flight BA282 from Los Angeles to Heathrow so are feeling pretty jetlagged.

We had a wonderful week with Fiona, Patrick and Bevan. How instantly one can fall headlong in love with a tiny baby one has barely laid eyes upon.

Whilst there, I decided to look at some television. I was actually horrified by the tidal wave of shock-horror. The peak hours are given over to endless re-enactments of ghastly happenings in everyday life: the mother who deliberately drowns her child, the father who burns his son, the sister who knifes her sister. American viewers are riveted by this never-ending output of kill and tell.

I am glad I shall be moving out of television, for the time being at any rate. I suppose I am writing this entry tonight because tomorrow is the day when I announce my departure from the IBA. It has been a marvellously maintained secret and great credit should properly go to Sarah Thane and James Conway for keeping the news secret.

Today the interim results of RUG become public. They have slipped from last year by only about £100,000 but this has given some City analysts the chance to mock the company: 'See the shows, don't buy the shares' was a comment, I think, in *The Telegraph*. I have no idea how the media will respond to my appointment. GT has provided a really generous quote, which I hope will be used somewhere.

In a funny kind of way I am quite looking forward to tomorrow. We will see how it goes. I must learn to have a thick skin and remember most people don't read the small print anyway.

Thursday 23rd February

Arrived in early to the office. On the way, I told my driver David about the change in my job. He took it rather wearily, commenting that he had guessed as much.

At 9.45am I invited David Glencross, Kenneth Blyth and Shirley Littler into my office and broke the news to David and Kenneth. Shirley has, of course, known about my intentions for some time. Either they were both good actors or they were hearing what I had to tell them for the first time. Whatever the case, it appeared as if a bolt from the blue.

David said they were happy for me. They would miss me but readily understood. We drank coffee and they departed. The rest of the day was spent telephoning people I wanted to know before they read it in the papers.

Richard Attenborough sent me a rare bottle of champagne, with love to Roma from Sheila as well.

John Burrows from Capital sent a card with one large word: 'Brilliant!'

In the evening to the RTS Journalism Awards at the Hilton. Met a great many people who welcomed my return to the real world. David Windlesham, who was the guest speaker, said some nice things. All in all, a good evening.

On Friday to Sunday I have been at Lainston House for the Authority Weekend. The purpose was to consider the IBA submission to the Home Office as a response to the White Paper. Covered much ground and quite a few good ideas came forward, including taking BBC 2's night-time and re-allocating it to TV-am, thus releasing back to ITV the morning period. The BBC won't like it, but tough.

As I listened to the two-day discussion, I felt a strange ambivalence, part of me wanting to be in the middle of all the changes, playing a crucial role in shaping the 90s for broadcasting, part of me thankful to be out of the bureaucracy and to-ing and fro-ing and back to positives. The glad-to-be-free element won by a long margin. All the Members congratulated me. I think they meant it!

So ends part of my life – or rather the public announcement that this part will soon be over. Whether I shall continue with this diary afterwards I don't know.

I heard from Frank Willis that GR had added a postscript about me to his speech in Monte Carlo and that it had been received well. Duke Hussey called to congratulate me. It's been a long, long week and I feel horribly tired but I have nothing to complain about. The week is over. I have not suffered and, above all, I am healthy, soon possibly to become wealthy and, as a remote possibility, wise.

I am trying to keep a sense of anti-climax out of these notes but it is difficult.

Sunday 5th March

A week of transition, with more letters from well-wishers on my move: Michael Grade, Paul Fox, Alastair Burnet, David Nicholas, Richard Dunn.

I have been asked if I would mind having my farewell dinner in conjunction with Donald Maitland's leaving dinner – I think on 5th April.

The world and his wife are filing their White Paper submissions. There is no one who has come out publicly in support of auctioning to the highest bidder. The IBA, with its submission, will be pushing at an open door.

On Wednesday evening I attended the debate in the Lords on *Death on the Rock*. Lord Bonham-Carter's motion that 'whether it was Government's considered view that they profoundly disagree with the Report of Lord Windlesham and Mr Richard Rampton QC on the Thames Television programme *Death on the Rock*'.

The debate lasted some two hours, with speeches by Lords Bramall, Longford, Goodman, Warnock, Hailsham, Harris et al. All the speakers claimed their undying acceptance of David Windlesham's integrity but all those who supported the Government went on in their next breath to rubbish the report. At the end of it all, no one was any better off.

Sunday 12th March

The White Paper submissions continue to deluge the Home Office. They have received over 2,500! Mrs T should be made to read each one ten times.

I am beginning to feel very strange as I listen to IBA planning for the future. I keep saying to myself, I am glad to be leaving and then a little voice inside my head says no, I am sorry to be going, but really, I suppose, there wouldn't be much of a job in the ITC, what with Rees-Mogg delivering the tablets on sex and violence. The ITC, apart from its initial burst of activity when it appoints the licensees, could become very tedious.

We had a meeting on Monday with the Chairman of S4C. GR told them politely that they could not look to the ITC after 1992 to fund their service. We have not heard the end of this saga. Last time they had a spot of bother, an MP threatened a hunger strike.

In the evening to the 75th Anniversary Dinner at the Guildhall given by the Performing Rights Society in the presence of HRH Prince Edward. We joked about my new job. He said he was working out of a broom cupboard.

On Wednesday, a lunch with Richard Crompton-Miller of the *Daily Express*. He will probably write a stinker. I should never have agreed to be interviewed. Will I never learn?

Off in the evening to Bristol and a dinner for IBA Members given by the Board of HTV at the Society of Merchant Venturers in the Merchants Hall. George Russell in good form, telling stories about his youth when employed by ICI in Bristol.

On Thursday, the Meeting, my last but one. Members approved the White Paper submission. It should get a reasonable press.

Still saying thank you to well-wishers on my new appointment. Must say the move is very fazing. I suppose it's something to do with my age. In my late, very late, 50s it's quite a challenge to uproot and start again. I suppose it might keep me young, but right now I think I'd quite enjoy retirement. No, even as I write, I know it would send me potty.

Sunday 19th March

My time at the IBA will soon be over. Mixed feelings continue. The whole of television is in such flux, there is no time to stop and stare. Everyone in television has a great deal on their mind. Not a time for small talk. I suppose it is inevitable in this climate of uncertainty that little is done about the present. Programmes are made and are put on but I wonder how much time in boardrooms, or even in the offices of Chief Executives, is spent in considering the merit of programmes current and future.

By a twist of fate, tonight Roma and I go to the BAFTA Awards, an event which seems to run and run and run.

Earlier in the week, I attended with Roma (Tuesday 16th March) the Solus Club 60th Birthday Dinner at the Hyde Park Hotel. The Guest of Honour was HRH Duke of Gloucester who set everyone's teeth on edge by using the occasion to deliver an ill-tempered and ill-timed homily on the evil of advertising tobacco, he being the Chairman, I think, of ASH. Whilst I agreed with every word he uttered it was bad manners to turn what was intended to be a jolly occasion into a distinctly sombre one.

Next Tuesday we release our response to the White Paper. Some parts have already been leaked. It is a good response and much, if not all, the credit should go to Shirley Littler who has a magician's gift for weaving words and providing logic where emotion was before. It should get a good press.

Good news on my domestic front. Sally Munton rejoins me in my new job. This will help the change. Brompton Road to Greek Street is traumatic enough.

Monday 27th March

Beginning to clear my office and say goodbye. On Monday 20th March I went to my last ITN Board. All a bit anti-climatic. A short but nice few words from David Nicholas and that was it.

On Tuesday the unveiling of our White Paper response. The day before, I spoke on the telephone to Michael Green and Tim Bell in the hope of encouraging them to say nice things. In the event, it was unnecessary. George, Shirley, Donald and I made up the platform party. We trooped on and GR spoke for ten minutes. Strangely for George, he was nervous and unsure but the Press gave him the thumbs up. George deserves it. He has worked tirelessly to articulate a vision, and all credit to him and Shirley. Ray Snoddy asked him whether he would resign if his plan was not adopted. George said yes, he would resign. Afterwards he was worried he had overturned the balance of the press briefing. I said he had not. He ended the briefing feeling down. I told him not to worry. All the papers have been positive over the plan. The good old IBA has a new face and Timothy Renton was fast to defend and praise the new Chairman.

I shall be leaving just as the IBA returns to grace. Is it bad timing, bad luck or am I getting out at the right time? I have truly mixed feelings but the world moves on. There is plenty to do and I long for the opportunity to make things happen creatively.

Sunday 2nd April

My last week with the IBA lies ahead. Mixed feelings, some regrets but mostly a sense of looking forward.

This week mostly goodbye writing and thank you letters.

Dinner with the ROs in the Dining Room. They laid on a special Indian feast and presented me with a fine paperweight with the theatre marks engraved on the top. Very thoughtful.

On Wednesday, I entertained with DGMM colleagues Lord Chalfont. He asked that the conversation be full, frank and fearless. This it turned out to be, with Chalfont attacking our decision on *Death on the Rock* and, I think, getting as good as he gave. The *Sunday Times*, of all newspapers, appears to be adopting a less-Government stance and has run an *Insight* piece into re-assessing evidence provided to the Inquiry by the Spanish Police and evidence by one of the soldiers. All is perhaps spurred on by Richard Dunn telling a press lunch that he was considering a further programme on the subject. This time I will watch from the sidelines.

DGMM this week, my last, ended on an unexpected note. I had ordered champagne to toast DGMM at the end. All worked according to plan until I rose and, having toasted my colleagues and wished Shirley Littler good fortune, I raised the glass and swallowed the lot. The first time any alcohol has touched my lips in seven years.

Tonight, Roma and I are off to Ian Hunter's 70th Birthday concert at the Albert Hall. It promises to be a good occasion. We are having drinks with Ian and Mary beforehand.

On Thursday night I gave a cocktail party for various friends: John Mortimer and Penny, John Hawkesworth, Jeffrey Archer, Simon Jenkins et al.

Sunday 9th April

This is intended to be the final entry in my diary, marking the end of nearly seven years at the IBA.

On Monday I lunched with senior members of staff at Crawley Court. We said our mutual goodbyes and a group shot was taken afterwards. Little or no criticism has ever been levelled at the engineers. Their work has always been of the highest standard. I hope they continue to flourish in the new world of competition. They deserve to continue in some form or another. They should serve the country with a national service and not be fragmented into small lots. Whether or not the dedicated research they have previously undertaken and which earned them considerable reputation can be carried into the 1990s is doubtful. Research, like training, has few real advocates. Nowadays success is judged by immediate impact. Anything that takes time to mature is put to one side. I hope I am wrong.

On Tuesday night, a jolly dinner at the BBC with David Barlow and the BBC Controllers. An off-the-record occasion which filled me with renewed uncertainty about the BBC's future. By this I do not mean to denigrate my hosts. My uncertainty centres on doubts about the role of the BBC as construed by the Governors and Government. The fuse has been lit, to blow the old tradition asunder. There is no one within the BBC with a determination to stamp on it. Perhaps Paul Fox, but his time is short. In 1996 who will stand up for the BBC?

On Wednesday, Richard Attenborough delivered the Fleming Memorial Lecture: 'Pandora's Box. Will the 90s bring forth feast or famine.' Dickie spoke for an hour and ten minutes from autocue. His delivery was so fast it took one's breath away. Much of his ground had been travelled before by others. But this is no criticism: he made it sound fresh. His message: stand on quality and real choice. We clapped and went to Browns Hotel where the Members gave me a dinner and a camera. GR said nice things about me and I went home in a happy mood.

Thursday. My last Authority Meeting. I said little.

Friday. Goodbyes from the staff, gathered in the Conference Hall. Shirley Littler said nice things. I think she spoke from the heart. Roma received flowers, I received a briefcase that I had chosen from Aspreys. In my thank you, I spoke of early days when I went round London carrying a yellow plastic briefcase with 'Norton B. Whitney' painted on the side. I come full circle.

The office is bare. No pictures or sculpture. The drawers are cleared. I sit there quietly for a few moments before leaving. The words of Ed Murrow spring to mind: 'This instrument can teach. It can illuminate. Yes, it can even inspire. But it can do so only to the extent that humans are determined to use it to those ends. Otherwise it is merely lights and wires in a box.'

Index

10 Downing Street 6, 254–5, 256
20/20 Vision 94
60 Minutes 59

A
A-Team, The 151, 307
AAC 185, 240
ACAS 19, 66, 74
ACTT 66, 74, 245, 294
  and TV-am 269, 279, 283, 285, 288, 310, 351
Adams, Gerry 41, 326
advertising 4, 12, 16, 17, 68, 160, 191, 232
  and AIDS 194, 205, 211, 226, 246
  and BBC 81, 92, 93, 97
  and Channel 4 30, 71
  and children 185
  costs 19, 20
  and minutage 73, 201, 204, 209, 213, 240, 241, 243, 261, 262
  and radio 32, 172
  and tobacco 371
  and TV-am 48
  and White Paper 355
Advisory Liaison Committee (ALC) 209, 243
AIDS 82, 185, 191, 192, 215, 216, 331
  and advertising 194, 205, 211, 226, 246
AIRC *see* Association of Independent Radio Contractors
Aitken, Jonathan 20, 21–2, 27, 76, 286–7, 288, 355
  resignation of 289
Aitken, Timothy 21, 22, 24, 32, 33, 213, 289
  and ACTT 269, 283
  and funding 35, 36, 46, 48, 50
  and ITN 73, 74, 76, 78, 79, 81, 183
  position of 55, 129, 132
  and shareholdings 286–7, 288
ALC *see* Advisory Liaison Committee
All-Party Committee on Party Political Broadcasts 13–14
Allan, Andy 215, 241
Allen & Overy 93, 107, 113, 125, 128, 130
  and *Death on the Rock* 299, 310
  and *Scum* 97, 98
Allo, Allo 307

Amstrad 194, 229
Andrew, HRH Prince 156, 159, 174, 239, 271, 272
Anglesey, Shirley 321
Anglia TV 30, 37, 48, 194, 317
  and BSB 349, 351, 354
Anne, HRH Princess Royal 45
Archer, Jeffrey 100, 144, 255, 265, 342, 355, 372
  and scandal 189, 213, 244
Archer, Mary 243, 244
Arts Council of Great Britain 82, 314, 366
Aspel, Michael 241, 291
Asquez, Kenneth 330, 350
Association of Independent Radio Contractors (AIRC) 67, 73, 93, 162, 163, 175, 297
  and advertising 201
  and Community Radio 171, 326
  and costs 68, 77, 101, 138, 149
  and IBA 233–4, 239
  and pirate radio 61, 62
Astra Consortium 219, 220, 223–4, 253, 256, 354, 355
  and Thames TV 205, 222, 234–5, 259
Attenborough, David 226–7
Attenborough, Richard 2–3, 4, 14, 33, 53, 77, 373
  and Capital Radio 101, 226, 240–1
  and Channel 4 34, 113, 159, 210, 212, 215, 217–18, 230, 260, 265, 266–8, 303, 304, 334
  and government 316
  and Isaacs 269
  and ITN 296
  and Thatcher 252
  and Whitney 368, 369
Audley, Sir Bernard 319

B
BAFTA 119, 135, 153, 157, 212
Bailey, Sir Brian 87, 101, 102
Bailey, Peter 111
Baker, Kenneth 7, 35, 190
Baker, Mary 126, 127
Baldwin, Peter 163, 197, 210, 281, 309, 335

375

and radio 342, 357
Balhetchet, Sophie 247, 281, 289, 292
BARB *see* British Audience Research Bureau
Barlow, David 225, 291, 373
Barnett, Joel, Lord 179, 187, 198, 317
Barratt Homes 57–8, 59
Barrow, Jocelyn 323
Bass 245, 246
Bassey, Shirley 219–20, 271
BBC 6, 15, 96, 140, 223, 291, 373
  and accountability 277–8
  and advertising 92, 93, 95, 123, 131
  and Beirut 190, 192, 193
  and breakfast television 19, 20
  and costs 88
  and *Dallas* 86, 87, 89, 90, 91, 100, 110, 112, 115, 117, 118, 129, 144, 150
  and DBS 43–4, 45, 48, 49–51, 58
  and Director General 208–9, 210, 211, 212–13, 214
  and election 229, 236, 237
  and government 272
  and Hungerford massacre 250
  and Hussey 184
  and independents 275
  and IRA 116–17
  and licence fee 80–1, 97, 206, 315
  and Murdoch 294
  and *Panorama* 187, 189
  and programming 59, 75, 343–4
  as public service broadcaster 29
  and ratings 34, 145
  and satellite television 8, 9, 25, 26, 34, 35, 39, 41, 47
  and sponsorship 198
  and *Spotlight* 303, 304
  and standards 308
  and strikes 203
  and Super Channel 113, 124, 135, 136, 180, 182
  and terrorism 351
  and *Tumbledown* 309
  and violence 142, 143
  and White Paper 349
  and World Cup 170
BBC radio 4, 81, 120
BBC World Service 238
Beaverbrook Investments 283, 286, 288, 295
Berlusconi, Silvio 161
Bernstein, Alex 101, 147, 153
Bernstein, Sidney 78, 94, 108, 149, 213, 308
BET *see* British Electric Traction
BETA 192, 259–60, 262, 269, 270, 272, 288
  and ACTT 294
'Better Way' 168, 170, 171, 176, 178, 203
Bevan, Stuart 260

Bickham, Edward 262, 324
Bill, The 250, 251, 269, 270
Birt, John 210, 220, 222, 241, 278, 289, 291, 292
  and news broadcasting 227
  and Northern Ireland 318
  and *Panorama* 331
Bland, Christopher 209, 256, 328
Blyth, Kenneth 120, 169, 200, 247, 328, 369
  and DBS 60, 145, 157, 158
  and Eurosport 299
  and Northern Ireland 335
  and White Paper 344
Bond, Alan 208, 211, 213
  and BSB shares 287, 341–2, 349, 351, 354, 356, 357, 358–9
Bond, Derek 64
Bonner, Paul 210, 235
Borrie, Sir Gordon 149, 193
Bottomley, Virginia 150–1
Boulton, Roger 94
Bowe, Colette 194, 195, 202, 205, 207, 321
  and *Daily Mail* 247, 259
  and *Death on the Rock* 354
  and Home Affairs Committee 285
  and Policy Document 292, 293, 297
  and radio 241
  and terrorism 335–6
  and *This Week* 300, 301
  and TV-am 288
  and violence 253
  and White Paper 344
Bragg, Melvyn 233, 251, 252, 280, 314, 365
  and Channel 4 261, 262–3, 264
Branson, Richard 56, 57, 92, 99, 164, 192
  and ITN 335
  and satellite television 123–4
  and Super Channel 337, 342
breakfast television 19, 20–1, 27, 73, 81
  see also TV-am
Breakfast Time 19, 20, 108
BREMA *see* British Radio & Electronic Manufacturers Association
Brighton bombing 72, 73, 74, 79
Brimstone and Treacle 191, 210, 251
Brinton, Tim 67, 162, 263, 285
British Aerospace 207, 219
British Audience Research Bureau (BARB) 34
British Council 243, 272–3
British Electric Traction (BET) 126, 128, 130, 131, 274
British Film Institute 33
British Radio & Electronic Manufacturers Association (BREMA) 68, 69, 70, 39, 142, 193, 350
British Telecom (BT) 8, 78, 111, 223–4
Brittan, Leon 29–30, 60, 69–70, 100, 116, 119

Index

and community broadcasting 115
and DBS 38–9, 49, 51, 52, 56, 65, 81, 86
and Peacock Inquiry 101
and radio 24, 59, 64, 87
Britton, Sam 152, 176, 190
Broadcast 40, 164, 221, 254, 257, 295
and *Dallas* 129, 130, 131
and IBA 151–2, 155, 243, 249
Broadcasting Act (1981) 77
Broadcasting Complaints Commission 230, 264
Broadcasting Press Guild 64
Broadcasting Standards Council (BSC) 271, 302, 303, 312, 337–8, 346, 367–8
and Rees-Mogg 294, 304, 305, 323
Brompton Road 3, 19, 37, 80, 132, 133, 174, 175, 183
Brookside 12, 14, 90, 96, 248–9
Brown, Bill 95, 111, 292
Brown, George 108, 109
Browne-Wilkinson, Lord Justice 96
BSB 219, 224, 228, 261, 299–300, 303–4
and Astra 220, 223, 260
and bid 194–5, 197, 198, 199, 200
and Carlton 201
and channels 313, 314, 316, 324, 326, 327–8
and contract 237, 243
and Disney 350–1
and flotation 331, 339–40, 341–2
and investment 349
and ITN 225, 271, 273–4, 275, 281–2, 283–4, 285, 287, 292
and ITV 235
and MGM 362
and Murdoch 361
and Now Channel 279
and shareholdings 354, 356, 357, 358–9
and Sky 364
BSC *see* Broadcasting Standards Council
BT *see* British Telecom
Budd, Alan 193, 195
Burnet, Sir Alastair 45, 51, 111, 135, 162, 351
and BBC DG 209, 349
and IBA 326
and ITN 290, 350
and night programming 295, 312, 315
and Whitney 370
Burton, Humphrey 226
Burton, Richard 190
Buxton, Aubrey 30, 135, 157, 208, 265
and ITN 91, 111, 119, 155, 162–3, 181–2
and TV-am 48, 50, 73, 74, 78, 79

C

Cable Authority 203, 205, 212, 213, 281
Cable & Broadcasting Act (1984) 65, 172
Cable & Satellite Bill 46

cable television 7, 8, 9, 11, 26, 33, 124, 190
and Hunt Committee 12
and ITV 103
see also satellite television
Cable Television Association (CTA) 135, 325, 332
Cadbury, Peter 134, 155, 327
Caine, Michael 55, 70, 127, 154, 179, 191, 307
and White Paper 347
Callaghan, James 263, 331
Calvert, John 234
Camden Council 230, 244
Campaign 25–6, 231, 273
Campaign for Nuclear Disarmament (CND) 91
Capital Radio 1, 9, 101, 108, 163, 211, 226
and DevonAir 223, 232
and news broadcasting 240–1
and Oyston 333
and Whitney 2, 3, 4
Carlisle, Mark 88
Carlton 138, 178, 257, 259, 313
and Astra Consortium 201, 224, 235
and Thames 124, 125, 126, 127, 128–9, 130, 131, 312
Carlton-Green, Hugh 214
Carlton Services 61
Carrington, Peter 246
Cash, Bill 221
Casson, Sir Hugh 56
CBC Radio 123
CBS 78
censorship 51, 116, 251, 338
Central Religious Advisory Committee (CRAC) 24, 27, 44, 53, 328
Central Television 51, 57, 89, 182, 194, 312
and Astra Consortium 224, 235
and *Hardwicke House* 215
and Ladbrokes 216–17, 219
and Maxwell 119, 120, 122, 125, 136, 156–7, 159
and Super Channel 146, 148
and Zenith 259
Chalfont, Alun, Lord 362, 366, 367, 368, 372
Chalker, Linda 62
Chalmers, Pat 291
Chandler, Geoffrey 183
Channel 4 24, 96, 113–14, 145, 167, 230
and advertising 16, 17, 30, 146, 193–4, 248
anniversary 133, 134
and breakfast broadcasting 25, 285, 287, 320
and Budd 195
and budgets 71, 85, 91, 93, 104, 106, 111
and Emmy Awards 78
and funding 176, 302–3, 334
and ITV 102, 200, 266
and management 210, 215

377

and MI5 programme	90, 91, 92	Connolly, Yvonne	134, 200
and *My Britain*	152	Conservative Party	4–5, 16, 38, 72, 152, 184, 234
and news	18, 34, 35		
and opening	11, 12, 13	Consolidated	1, 2, 68, 362, 365–6
and Ponting Trial	87, 88	Constantine, King of Greece	100, 271
and privatisation	224–5	Consultation on Science	333
and programming	14, 17, 19–20, 60	Consumer Council	115
and ratings	159–60	contraception	226, 246
and Reagan	309, 311	Conway, James	297, 300, 369
and satellite	61	Cooke, Alistair	196
and snooker	59, 82, 307	Cooper, George	296, 357
and subscription	129	Coopers & Lybrand	45, 327
and terrestrial television	314	Copeland, Miles	152
and terrorism	351, 357	Coppen-Gardner, Bill	290
and warning triangle	181, 212, 213, 216, 237	copyright	67, 100, 357
		Coren, Alan	309
and White Paper	348, 349	Cork, Sir Kenneth	33, 35
Channel Five	259	*Coronation Street*	12, 120, 367
Channon, Paul	13	Cotton, Bill	26, 30, 50, 117, 261
Chappell, Frank	176, 193	and *Dallas*	99, 100
Charles, HRH Prince of Wales	33, 38, 48, 56, 122, 196, 263	and DBS	42, 43, 44, 45
		and Hussey	187
and charity	368	and *Newsnight*	278
and violence	327	and programming	59
Chat	146–7	retirement of	297
Chataway, Christopher	76, 168, 175, 224, 249	and tobacco sponsorship	153
		and World Cup	171
Checkland, Michael	107, 187, 198, 209, 262, 264	Coulson, David	235
		Coulter, Ian	290, 333
and accountability	277–8	County Bank	125, 126
and Director General	214, 215, 223, 228	Coven, Edwina	80, 197
and Eurosport	294, 296–7, 299	Cowgill, Bryan	66, 68, 74, 107, 126, 131, 150
and Fox	291		
and funding	364	and *Dallas*	86, 87, 88, 89, 90, 115
and independents	220–1	and resignation	112–13
and Obscene Publications Bill	253	Cox, Barry	227
children	29, 65, 148, 151, 185	Cox, Sir Geoffrey	63, 190
Chiltern Radio	134	CRAC *see* Central Religious Advisory Committee	
China	184, 195, 346–7		
Christmas broadcasting	203–4, 212	Crawley Court	3–4, 39, 132, 175, 257, 269, 341, 373
Churchill, Winston	143, 144, 148, 150, 160, 162		
		and changes	228
CIRCOM	315	and costs	78, 79
Clark, Peter	292	and Robson	183
Clarke, Neville	152	*Cry Freedom*	270, 296
Cleveland child abuse	317	CTA *see* Cable Television Association	
'Closed Period'	22, 23–4, 27	Cubbon, Brian	104, 105, 286, 291
Club of 21	103, 105, 109, 123, 124, 146	Cudlipp, Hugh	149
CNN	155	Cullen, Alec	70, 127, 154, 333
Coles, Ron	163, 175	Currie, Edwina	241–2
College of the Air	168, 169, 170, 174, 177, 181, 188		
		D	
Collins, Joan	138, 253, 265	*Daily Express*	370–1
Community Radio	115, 166, 213, 245, 326, 357	*Daily Mail*	247, 259, 282, 301
		and violence	250, 251, 284
and government	65, 87, 112, 123, 162, 171–2	*Daily Telegraph*	83, 96, 160, 358
		Dallas	91, 104, 107, 109, 112–13, 114–15, 119, 126, 150
and pirate radio	57, 61, 70		
and Thompson	77, 79		

Index

and Cotton 99, 100
and Cowgill 86, 87, 88, 89, 90
and Grade 117–18, 129–30
and Milne 110
and Office of Fair Trading 134
Darlow, Michael 238, 239, 244, 273, 274, 289
Davies, Geraint Talfan 291
Davies, John Howard 256, 297
Day After, The 39–40
Day, Robin 349
DBL 195, 198, 199
DBS *see* Direct Broadcasting Satellites
DBS UK 195, 198, 199
de Savary, Peter 319
de Young, Karen 147
Deakin, Michael 21, 22, 46, 55, 57, 64, 190
  and resignation 62, 63, 67
Dealey, Michael 239
Dean, Graham 241
Death on the Rock 304–5, 307, 328–30, 332, 334, 346–7, 358, 370, 372
  and Enquiry 353, 354, 355, 356, 362, 364–5, 366
decency 14, 114, 147, 262, 298, 322
Delfont, Bernard, Lord 37
Dell, Edmund 11, 14, 37, 60, 75, 96, 113, 236–7
  and advertising 193
  and Budd 195
  and IBA 108, 114, 159
  and Isaacs 21, 27, 30, 32, 35, 210, 216, 217–18
  and ITV 200
  and Peacock Committee 172–3, 176–7
  and privatisation 224–5
  and replacement 185
Dempsey & Makepeace 134, 139
Department of Education 346
Department of Employment (DofE) 333–4
Department of Trade and Industry (DTI) 47, 49, 59, 76, 89, 112
  and satellite television 124, 158
Devereux, Robert 138
DevonAir 57, 223, 226, 232
DGMM *see* Director General's Management Meeting
Diamond, Ann 235
Diamond, Aubrey 313
Diana, Princess of Wales 38, 56, 122, 183, 201, 263, 331
Dimbleby, David 210, 211, 213
Direct Broadcasting Satellites (DBS) 53, 54, 80, 103–4, 111, 157, 194–5
  and BBC 27, 43–4, 45, 47–8, 49, 50–1, 58
  and Branson 123–4
  and British Aerospace 207
  and government 7–8, 34, 56, 65, 81–2

and IBA 25–6, 30, 33, 38, 59–60, 142, 150, 160
and Tesler 69, 71–2
see also TDFI
Director General's Management Meeting (DGMM) 58, 70, 72, 79, 101, 119
  and franchises 169
  and radio 220, 236
  and satellite television 137
  and Thames takeover 126–7
  and White Paper 347
  and YTV 151
Disney Channel 350–1
Dispatches 346–7, 351
Dixons 235
Doctor Who 96, 331
Donaldson, John, Lord 96, 97
Dors, Diana 50
Douglas-Home, Charles 111
Downtown Radio 280
drama 96
DTI *see* Department of Trade and Industry
Dukes, Justin 22, 27–8, 30, 75, 96, 146, 168, 285
  and advertising 248
  and breakfast television 159
  and Budd 195–6
  and budgets 71
  departure of 338, 342
  and ITN 182, 294, 296, 302
  and promotion 207, 215, 218, 265
Dundas, Hugh 27, 66, 119, 179
  and *Dallas* 87–91, 99, 100, 104, 107, 109, 112, 115, 117, 118, 130, 131
  and takeover bid 124–5, 126, 127, 128–9
Dunn, Richard 192, 292, 318, 337, 364, 370
  and Astra Consortium 234–5, 256
  and BBC 211
  and Carlton 124, 125, 129, 131
  and *Dallas* 117, 130, 144
  and *Death on the Rock* 301, 329–30, 362
  and ITN 296
  and Super Channel 135, 248, 308
  and Thames TV 126, 205, 274, 312, 367
  and violence 251
Durex 246
Duval, Robin 250, 251, 252, 262
Dyckoff, Nigel 227
Dyke, Greg 21, 27, 32, 55, 56, 58, 183, 220
  and competition 317, 324
  and LWT 222

E
East of Eden 119
Eastenders 96, 139, 321–2
EBU *see* European Broadcasting Union
Economic League 233

379

Economist, The	54	Fleming Memorial Lectures	99, 222, 292, 373
ECS transponders	26, 113, 226	Flint, Michael	341–2
Edward, HRH Prince	211, 218, 370	Forbes, Bryan	271
Edwards, Michael	100	Ford, Anna	20, 21, 22, 27
Edwards, Owen	181, 182, 225, 256, 297	Forman, Denis	67, 77, 108, 120, 147, 186, 213
Elizabeth II, Queen of England	37, 38, 40, 45, 138, 174, 263–4, 270–1	and Granada	153, 155
		and Isaacs	292–3
and IBA	89, 140, 141	retirement of	221
Elizabeth, Queen (the Queen Mother)	92, 191	and video biographies	262
Elliot, Bill	289	Forrest, Dr John	160, 181, 183, 259–60, 285, 344
Elstein, David	146, 210, 261, 263	Foster, Christopher	28, 327
Emmy Awards	78	Fowler, Norman	192, 194, 205, 315
engineering	39, 46, 47, 62, 71, 101, 102, 343, 344	Fox, Paul	28, 85, 101, 102, 226, 234, 370
see also Crawley Court		and BBC	208–9, 263, 291, 298, 373
English, Sir David	348	and DBS	45, 46, 52, 54
Equity	4, 30, 209, 210	and Grade	266, 267
and IPA	16, 17, 19, 20, 22–3, 28, 33, 62, 64, 66, 70	and independents	206
		and ITN	111, 119, 163
Essex, Francis	65	and *The Listener*	88, 236
ethnic broadcasting	76, 134	and Super Channel	181, 188
Europe	25, 102, 124, 195, 265, 337	and TV-am	25, 183
and cable television	103–4, 105, 135	and Yorkshire Television	178, 244–5
and satellite television	7, 8, 61, 113	France	68, 69, 103, 104, 105, 161, 177, 240
see also France; Italy			
European Broadcasting Union (EBU)	15–16, 107, 112, 141, 206, 227	*see also* TDFI	
		Francis, Dick	163, 243, 272
and competition	148, 167, 231, 240	Fraser, Sir Robert	3, 13, 86, 87, 88, 94, 346
and DBS	7, 8, 68–9	Freeman, John	30, 50
and public service broadcasting	40, 61	French Cable Vision	296
European Space Agency	8	Frost, David	123, 156, 239, 265, 271–2, 355
Eurosport Channel	294, 296–7, 299	and Aitken	129, 289
Evening Standard	20	and ITN	240, 256–7
Everett, Kenny	196–7	and Thatcher	108, 109, 110
Eyre, Richard	205, 309, 336	and TV-am	19, 20, 46, 47, 218, 299
		Fulbright, J. William	196
F		Fulton, Sean	228, 232, 280, 282, 283
Face the Press	114, 147		
Falkender, Marcia	159, 265	**G**	
Falklands War	87–8, 108, 109	GAC *see* General Advisory Council	
Faulkner, Lucy, Lady	16, 123	Gale, Roger	285
Fellows, Robert	140	*Gandhi*	14, 296
Ferguson, Sarah	156, 159, 174, 271–2	Gandhi, Indira	45, 75
Ffitch, George	76, 97–8	Gatward, James	52, 101, 102, 125, 183, 315
film channels	26, 28	and Sky	363
Film Purchase Committee	115, 129	and Super Channel	246
Finance Committee	75, 197	and Thorn EMI	120, 122
Financial Times	32, 83, 118, 160, 161, 171, 180	General Advisory Council (GAC)	19–20, 23, 48, 61–2, 71, 96, 133–4, 148, 241–2
and Channel 4	268	and MAC	79
and contracts	186	and Policy Document	299
and DBS	177	and Thomson	336
and Policy Statement	298	Getty, Paul, Jnr	103, 108, 274
Findley, Richard	64	Gibbings, Peter	127, 188, 363–4
Finniston, Sir Monty	54	Gibraltar	299, 300–3, 304, 307, 328, 330, 332–3, 350
Firman, James	59		
Fleck, Tony	279, 280	*see also Death on the Rock*	
Fleet Holdings	36, 46, 47, 50, 129		

Index

Gifford, Michael 153
Gilmour, Ian 185, 186
Giscard d'Estaing, Valéry 195
Glencross, David 24, 88, 98, 139, 235, 309, 369
  and Channel 4 230
  and *Dallas* 113
  and *Death on the Rock* 299, 300, 358
  and *Dispatches* 347
  and *Hardwicke House* 215
  and independents 198, 220, 222, 244
  and ITN 229
  and ITV 232
  and MI5 91, 246
  and night programming 295
  and Northern Ireland 335
  and Obscene Publications Bill 147, 148, 252
  and Potter 191, 210
  and *Spitting Image* 116
  and Thatcher speech 91, 92
  and TV-am 56, 64–5
  and TVS 122
  and *V* 259
  and violence 150, 250, 251
  and *World in Action* 67, 69
Goldcrest 26, 194, 227
Goldstein-Jackson, Kevin 57, 87, 89, 155
Good Morning Britain 31
Goodfellow, Robin 283
Goodman, Arnold, Lord 197, 204, 239, 286, 308
Gordon, James, Lord 37
Gordon, Jimmy 43, 59, 219, 238, 246, 290
Gorst, John 14, 87, 114–15, 131, 302
Government 131–2, 141
  and broadcasting 72–3, 214–15, 217, 222, 224, 247, 314, 315–16
  and cable television 11–12, 135, 136
  and Channel 4 208, 330
  and community broadcasting 171
  and *Death on the Rock* 366
  and election 228–9, 230, 231, 232, 235
  and franchises 172
  and radio 149, 270
  and satellite television 30, 44, 46, 103–4, 113, 150, 157, 158
Grade, Michael 54, 100, 186, 187, 334–5, 364
  and BBC 78, 95, 96, 163, 209, 211, 213, 220
  and broadcasting summit 254
  and censorship 251
  and Central 194, 201
  and Channel 4 227, 230, 261, 265, 266–8, 279, 287, 302–3, 304, 322
  and *Dallas* 117–18, 129
  and Hungerford massacre 250
  and *Life of Brian* 284–5
  and Obscene Publications Bill 252
  and Reagan 309, 311
  and Rees-Mogg 307
  and tobacco sponsorship 153
  and TRIC 264
  and White Paper 349
  and Whitney 370
Graham, Jim 292
Graham, Ken 333
Grampian Television 108
Granada 48, 64, 89, 90, 233, 367
  and Barratt Homes 57–8, 59
  and BSB 317, 354
  and DBS 178
  and ITN 308
  and Ladbrokes 146, 147, 148
  as publisher contractor 314–15, 319–20
  and Rank 153–4, 158
  and satellite broadcasting 194
  and Super Channel 136
  and *World in Action* 41, 69
  and YTV 151
Granada Rental 61
Grant, Elliot 186–7, 191
Grass, Gust 161
Green, Bernard 161, 348
Green, Michael 195, 199, 216–17, 371
  and Carlton 125, 126, 127, 138
  and College of the Air 177, 181, 186, 188
  and Open College 190, 236, 325, 334
Green Papers 102, 162, 171
  and radio 203, 205, 213, 214, 216, 217, 220, 222, 224, 226, 231, 234
Greene, Graham 68
Grenfell, Morgan 158
Griffiths, Brian 206, 208, 214, 262, 273, 306, 327
Grist, Graham 235, 286, 299, 313, 316, 349
Guardian 68, 92, 148, 160, 301–2
Guinery, John 9, 250
Gulliver, James 273
Gummer, John Selwyn 39
Gunter, Barrie 85, 313
GWR Radio 226
Gyngell, Bruce 56, 57, 58, 64–5, 257, 289, 331
  and ACTT 283, 285
  and Aitken 129
  and Batman 274, 279
  and Chairmanship 310
  as Chief Executive 55, 132
  and heart attack 291, 312
  and pink 165, 238
  and standards 76, 324, 326

381

H

Hall, Peter	173, 205–6, 228, 336
Hamilton, Denis	3, 21
Hamilton, Neil	187
Happy Days	331
Hardwicke House	215
Hardy, Bert	50
Hargreaves, Robert	152, 358, 367
Harlech, David, Lord	39–40, 87
Harlech, Pamela, Lady	273
Harrison, Tony	251, 253
Harrods	40, 320–1
Haslam, Carol	257
Hastings, Max	20
Hattersley, Roy	230, 305, 344
Havers, Michael	78, 82, 93
Hawkesworth, John	1, 2, 68, 207, 372
Hayes, Brian	7, 16, 163, 246
Hayes, David	249
Haywood, Bridget	362
Healey, Denis	235
Hearn, Tony	140
Heath, Edward	51
Henderson, Brum	16
Henderson, Sir Nicholas	200
Hermon, Sir John	280
Heseltine, Michael	40, 145, 146
Highway to Heaven	115
Hill, Leslie	292, 293, 297
History of Television	89
Hobday, Gordon	89
Hoggart, Simon	176
Holdsworth, Sir Trevor	226, 303, 313
Holford, Michael	227
Holland, Geoffrey	181
Home Affairs Committee	240, 285, 293, 317, 318
Home Office	26, 29, 31, 53
see also Brittan, Leon; Hurd, Douglas	
homosexuality	14, 23, 30, 60, 82, 155
Hooper, Richard	305–6
Horn, Don	344
Horton, Brian	36
Hosking, Barbara	5, 7, 9, 10, 91, 135, 148, 348
and *Dallas*	113
and OBE	109, 110
replacement of	195, 202
and Yorkshire Television	263
House of Commons	75, 81, 114–15, 138
televising of	88, 101, 268, 283, 286, 287, 367
House of Lords	54, 80, 88, 99, 370
and White Paper	355, 356
Howard, George	7, 8, 9, 24, 29
Howard, Michael	131–2
Howard Steele Foundation	135
Howarth, Gerald	187, 216, 221
Howe, Geoffrey	299, 300, 302, 303, 307, 353
and *Death on the Rock*	347, 355
HTV	39, 87, 122–3, 155, 371
and S4C	181, 182, 225, 256, 297
Hughes, Penelope	290
Hughes Spacecraft	243
Hungerford massacre	250–1, 254, 255
Hunt Committee	7, 12
Hunter, Bob	281–2, 283–4, 292
Hunter, Ian	262
Hurd, Douglas	5, 28, 50, 119, 147, 175, 197, 217
and Astra Consortium	223–4
and BBC	179, 315
and broadcasting summit	254
and BSB	228, 313
and Channel 4	251–2
and contracts	185, 186, 187, 294
and IBA	305, 325
and independents	203, 204, 210–11, 247, 258
and Northern Ireland Directive	317–18, 335–6, 338, 341
and Policy Document	298
and radio	65–6, 123, 151, 162, 166, 171–2, 182, 213, 214, 243, 281, 282–3, 342
and satellite television	31, 46, 153, 322
and terrorism	357
and Thomson	363
and Thorn-EMI	40
and violence	142–4, 145, 225, 327
and White Paper	343, 344, 364
Hussey, Marmaduke 'Duke'	4, 192, 209, 226, 261–2, 291, 308
and accountability	277–8
and Chairman appointment	184, 187, 189
and independents	198
and Northern Ireland	318, 335
and Rees-Mogg	305, 307
and Thomson	320
and video	258
and violence	225
and Whitney	370
Hussey, Susan	140
Hyde, Wilfred	147, 343, 353

I

IBA see Independent Broadcasting Authority
ILR see Independent Local Radio

Incorporated Society of British Advertisers (ISBA)	49, 201, 237, 319
Independent	204, 295, 343, 364
and V	261, 263
and White Paper	344
Independent Broadcasting Authority (IBA)	4, 9, 102, 124, 140, 172, 179, 265

Index

and 24 hour broadcasting 164–5
and advisory groups 22–4, 308
and Astra Consortium 235
and breakfast television 19, 20–2, 27
and BSB 279
and cable television 11, 12, 105
and Channel 4 12, 14, 90, 193–4, 230, 268
and College of the Air 168
and contracts 180, 183, 185, 186, 192–3, 224, 226
and *Dallas* 86, 99, 113, 117, 130
and DBS 44, 45, 48–9, 53, 56, 57, 59, 79
and *Death on the Rock* 299–301, 329–30, 358
demise of 323–4, 325, 326, 332, 339, 341, 359, 361
and Director General position 1, 2–3, 12–13
and Granada 57–8, 153, 154
and independents 220, 222, 241, 242, 245, 249, 258
and MI5 programme 92–4
and Northern Ireland 16
and Obscene Publications Bill 252
and Policy Statement 297–9, 303
and Public Accounts Committee 105–6
and public service broadcasting 306–7
and radio 52, 57, 60, 67, 68, 77, 94–5, 209, 212, 214, 270, 273, 281, 282–3, 284
and religious broadcasting 31–2
and salaries 197, 227, 325
and satellite television 7, 8–9, 25–6, 30, 31, 41, 104, 137, 150, 157, 158, 160–1, 197–8, 199, 200
and *Scum* 54–5
and spending 123
and *Spitting Image* 118–19
and takeovers 342
and terrestrial broadcasting 61–2
and Thames Television 124–7, 128–9, 131
and TV-am 32–4, 36, 47, 56, 65, 283
and US imports 258
and violence 142, 143, 247, 250–1, 364
and White Paper 343, 344–6, 348, 369
Independent Local Radio (ILR) 38, 52, 65–6, 71, 72–3, 74, 238
and advertising 97, 171, 172
Awards 196
and diversification 156
and Green Paper 203, 213, 214, 231
and IBA 47, 112, 162, 204–5
and INR 59, 120, 149
and pirate radio 60, 67
Independent National Radio (INR) 52, 59, 76, 120, 148, 149
and community radio 77, 79

and government 147, 151, 166
and Green Paper 213
Independent Programme Producers Association (IPPA) 238, 247
Independent Radio News (IRN) 76, 240–1, 257, 328
Independent Television Contractors Association (ITCA) 25, 26, 28, 31, 93, 97, 114
and advertising 201
and competition 240
and contracts 186–7
and *Dallas* 115, 117, 118
and engineering 101, 102
and independents 203, 222, 238, 239
and satellite television 44, 45, 47, 48, 49, 50–2, 53, 58, 160
and Super Channel 135, 136, 149
Independent Television Publications (ITP) 146, 357–8
Industry Year 183
Ingham, Bernard 108, 162, 304, 326
Innes, Sheila 190, 202
INR *see* Independent National Radio
Insight 366, 372
Institute of Contemporary Arts (ICA) 5
Institute of Practitioners in Advertising (IPA) 49, 90, 116, 319
and Equity 16, 17, 19, 20, 22–3, 28, 33, 62, 64, 66, 70
International Television Festival 6–7, 8, 32, 67–8
IPA *see* Institute of Practitioners in Advertising
IPPA *see* Independent Programme Producers Association
IRA 41, 72, 116–17, 280, 301–2, 329
Iraq 351
IRN *see* Independent Radio News
Irvine, Ian 79, 289, 312, 319, 320
Isaacs, Jeremy 17, 18, 159, 168, 191, 207, 292–3
and BBC 163, 184, 209, 210, 211, 213, 278
and broadcasting summit 254
and Channel 4 11, 24, 71, 75, 96, 107, 108
and decency 14, 16, 114
and Dell 21, 27–8, 30, 217
and Grade 266–7, 268, 269, 304
and news programming 35
and Obscene Publications Bill 252
and Open College 333
and programming 25, 32, 90, 94, 134, 151, 152
replacement of 230, 245–6, 260–1, 262–3
and Royal Opera House 215–16, 225, 311
and warning triangles 237
ISBA *see* Incorporated Society of British Advertisers
Italy 142, 337, 339

383

ITC 344, 352, 359, 361–2, 364, 370
ITCA *see* Independent Television Contractors Association
ITN 75, 119, 121, 190, 192, 351
  and 24-hour programming 315, 332
  and BSB 225, 271, 273–4, 275, 279, 281, 282, 283–4, 285, 292
  and Channel 4 18, 25, 34, 35
  and competition 212, 290, 294, 350
  and DBS 178
  and diversification 155, 156, 157, 159, 165
  and election 229, 236
  and floating 236, 295
  and funding 224
  and premises 230, 244
  and satellite broadcasting 194–5
  and Super Channel 135–6, 174, 180–1, 182, 188, 207, 210, 226, 238, 307–8, 335, 338, 342
  and Thatcher 91
  and TV-am 36, 50, 63, 73, 74, 76, 78, 81, 96, 183, 256–7
  and Zeebrugge Disaster 237
ITP *see* Independent Television Publications
ITV 12, 15, 18, 88, 232, 234
  and advertising 16, 17, 46, 97, 201, 241
  and Astra Consortium 248, 253
  and cable television 103, 105
  and Channel 4 11, 17, 71, 73, 102
  and Christmas 203–4
  and *Dallas* 99
  and DBS 43, 45, 51, 60, 80
  and Emmy Awards 78
  and fee scales 281, 282
  and Hungerford massacre 250
  and independents 218, 238, 239, 247, 275–6, 279
  and ratings 34, 145
  and satellite television 7, 8, 26, 30, 42
  and standards 146–7, 308
  and subscription 129
  and Super Channel 124, 146
  and Thames takeover 126
  and White Paper 357–8
  and World Cup 170

J
Jackson, John 89, 135, 158, 195, 199, 216–17, 269
Jackson, Leslie 244
Jackson, Martin 151
James, Clive 155, 242
James, Colin, Bishop of Wakefield 23, 24, 44, 53–4
James, Howell 278
Jameson, Derek 9–10
Japan 180, 238

Jarman, Derek 139
Jay, Peter 17, 19, 20, 190
Jenkin, Patrick 286, 317
Jenkins, Hugh 13
Jenkins, Peter 343
Jenkins, Simon 184, 372
John, Brian 189
John, Elton 174, 271
Johns, Malcolm 283
Johnson, Paul 123
Johnson-Smith, Geoffrey 141
Jolliffe, Sir Anthony 228, 256
Jones, Clive 61
Joseph, Sir Keith 29
Jubilee 139, 143, 147, 148, 154–5, 162

K
Kalbermatten, Regis de 206
Kaufmann, Gerald 92, 223
Kemp, David, QC 64, 97, 99–100, 299, 347
Kennedy, Ludovick 175
King, John, Lord 178
King, Tom 137, 258, 280, 282, 317–18
Kinnock, Neil 51, 141, 231, 232, 265

L
Labour Party 38, 75, 223
Lace 68
Ladbrokes 35, 146, 147, 148, 153, 216–17, 219
Laister, Peter 39, 45
Lambourne, Pat 109
Lane, Geoffrey, Lord 141
language 148, 162, 251, 253, 256, 264
Law in Action 97
Lawson, Nigel 254
Lawson, Sarah 244
LBC 4, 76, 97–8, 163, 238, 241
Leach, Clive 349
Lee, James 26, 136–7, 194, 199, 227
Leech, Clive 151, 293
Liberal Party 152
Life of Brian, The 261, 284–5
light entertainment 145, 203
Lindsay-Hogg, Michael 68
Listener, The 88, 110–11, 118, 146, 147, 236, 282, 309
Littler, Geoffrey 109, 249
Littler, Shirley 109, 110, 131, 171, 202, 208, 247, 369
  and BETA 192
  and Channel 4 114, 230
  as Deputy DG 162, 167–8, 170
  and Home Affairs Committee 285
  and IBA 235, 361
  and ITN 296
  and ITV 232

Index

and MI5 programme 91
and Policy Document 292, 293
and retirement 249
and TV-am 288
and warning triangles 237
and White Paper 343, 344, 371, 372
and Whitney 373
Lloyd Webber, Andrew 53, 239, 265, 343, 345, 346, 356–7, 366
London Weekend Television (LWT) 7, 19, 23–4, 157, 220, 233
   and Astra Consortium 222, 224, 235, 256, 259
   and cable television 26
   and news broadcasting 227
   and shareholdings 328
   and Super Channel 136, 146
Lord, Shirley 166, 167, 175
Lords' Committee 99
Lorimer, Bob 75, 207, 268, 305
Los Angeles 106
Lucas, Christopher 262
Luce, Richard 147
Luckwell, Michael 125, 126, 295, 296, 310, 312
LWT *see* London Weekend Television
Lygo, Sir Raymond 45, 207

M

MAC *see* Multiplexed Analogue Component
McCall, David 127, 208, 227, 235, 277, 292, 294
   and independents 241, 242, 279
   and ITV 232, 289, 318
   and satellite television 160
   and Super Channel 146, 306
   and *TV Times* 357
McGarry, Ian 28
McGuinness, Martin 116
McIvor, Jill 70, 140, 168–9, 191, 195, 200, 224
McWhirter, Norris 116, 117, 118–19, 149
Maddox, Brenda 27, 118
Mail on Sunday 56, 170–1
Maitland, Sir Donald 202, 205, 211, 219, 271, 330, 356
   and Green Paper 226
   and IBA 188, 193, 194, 197
   and Policy Document 207–8, 293, 298
   retirement of 370
   and violence 253
   and White Paper 372
Mallet, Michael 231
Marcher Sound 134
Marconi 170
Margaret, HRH Princess 85
Marsh, Richard, Lord 20, 27, 32, 36, 46–7, 50, 55, 65, 127
Masham Report 281

Massiter, Cathy 91, 93, 94
Mates 246
Matthews, Paul 76, 285, 292
Maxwell, Robert 36, 74, 149, 161, 165, 182, 290, 306
   and AIDS Trust 330–1
   and satellite television 119, 120, 122, 124, 125, 136, 140, 156–7, 159, 169
   and Super Channel 332
   and Thames takeover 129
Meaney, Sir Patrick 154, 158
Media Committee 67
Media Show, The 232
Media Week 122
Mellersh, Nicholas 163–4
Mellor, David 141, 187–8, 198, 199, 210, 217, 227
   and competition 232
   and independents 211–12, 220–1, 222
Mercury Broadcasting 78
Metro Radio 289
MGM 357, 362
MI5 118, 246
MI5's Official Secrets 91, 92–4, 93–4, 94
Michael, Princess of Kent 100
Miles, Ken 201, 319
Miller, Jonathan 298
Milne, Alasdair 13, 15, 40, 46, 59, 100, 234
   and BBC 29, 81, 88, 107, 309
   and censorship 251
   and Channel 4 230
   and *Dallas* 110
   and Hussey 184
   and independents 198
   and IRA 116, 118, 123
   and *Panorama* 189, 190
   and political broadcasting 24
   and public service broadcasting 36, 61, 67–8
   and religious broadcasting 44
   resignation of 208, 228
   and RTS 6, 223
   and satellite television 8, 9, 25, 28, 50, 58
   and Thorn-EMI 41
   and violence 142
   and World Cup 170, 171
   and Young 199
Milton Committee 206, 228
miners' strike 100
Monocled Mutineer 187
Monopolies Commission 121
Montague, Michael 115
Monte Carlo 1, 90, 91, 92
Monty Python 285
Moore, Brian 324
Moore, Philip 89
Moran, Diana 19
Morgan, Brian 150

Morgan, Janet 262
Moriarty, Michael 7, 8, 30, 34–5, 41, 44, 70, 99
Morrison, Peter 225–6
Mortimer, John 123, 153, 173, 182, 273, 293, 338, 372
Moser, Claus 216
Mulholland, Clare 98, 152, 247, 332, 347
Multiplexed Analogue Component (MAC) 25, 37, 39, 82, 102
  and C-MAC 68–9, 70, 79, 104, 157, 158, 160, 163
  and DMAC 229
  and EMAC 112, 137
Murdoch, Rupert 4, 25, 56, 136, 204
  and Astra 312, 350–1, 354
  and BSB 361
  and ethics 322–3
  and Eurosport 294
  and newspapers 258, 259, 290
Murphy, Stephen 67, 97, 98
Murstill, Lord Justice 96
Museum of the Moving Image 124, 327
Music Box 151, 164, 308
My Britain 152, 153
My Country Right or Wrong 272

N
NACRO 75, 76
Naked Civil Servant, The 179
NAR (nett advertising revenue) 318, 323
National AIDS Trust 330–1
National Council for Civil Liberties (NCCL) 91
National Museum of Photography, Film and Television 226, 255
National Theatre 1, 13, 173, 205, 209, 224, 232–3, 293, 340
National Union of Journalists (NUJ) 283, 288, 338
Naughtie, James 147
NBS 194, 198, 199
Neil, Andrew 100, 156, 322, 366
Neilson 319
Nelson Mandela concert 313
Network Seven 247
News at Ten 112, 160, 192, 229, 250, 271, 295, 351
news broadcasting 96, 135, 227, 271, 295, 309, 327
  and BBC 190, 229
  and Channel 4 18, 34, 35
  see also ITN
News International 36
News of the World 9, 189, 213, 323
Newsnight 278
Newton, Sir Gordon 36
Nicholas, David 18, 60, 91, 192, 209, 273
  and ITN 121, 290, 296
  and Reagan 308, 309
  and Super Channel 157, 174, 180, 226, 350
  and TV-am 74, 81, 240
  and Whitney 370, 371
Nicholson, Mary 303
night programming 165, 245, 264, 273, 287, 343–4
  and Burnet 295, 312
  and ITN 315, 332
Nine O'clock News 96, 229
Noar, Martin 233
Norrington, John 127, 288
Norris, David 253, 332
North Sound Radio 108
Northern Ireland 16, 137, 279–80, 282, 283, 302, 303, 335–6
  see also IRA
Now Channel 273, 279, 295
nuclear defence 25, 39, 40
Nuclear Forum 102
Nuffield Foundation 54
NUJ *see* National Union of Journalists

O
Obscene Publications Act (1959) 139, 141, 143, 145, 146, 147, 149, 153
Obscene Publications Bill 206, 221, 228, 252, 253, 255
Observer, The 52, 20, 92, 118, 170, 177, 289
  and *Death on the Rock* 301, 349, 350
  and Northern Ireland 282, 283
  and radio 203, 205
O'Cathain, Detta 188
Ocean Sound 128, 196, 244
Octopus 47
Office of Fair Trading (OFT) 109, 117, 129, 130, 131–2, 149, 237
  and advertising 241, 243
  and BSB 361
  and *Dallas* 134
Official Secrets Act 90, 92
Olivier, Laurence, Lord 209, 224, 232–3
Olympic Games 48, 61
Oman 63–4, 67
One In Five 14
Open College 190, 192, 202, 216, 324–5, 333–4
  and costs 236, 311, 315
Oracle 53, 111, 170, 257
Orbital Test Satellite (OTS) 7
O'Sullivan, Kevin 107, 109, 110, 112, 113, 130, 131
Owen, David 37, 149, 271
Oyston, Owen 123, 231, 333, 337

Index

P

PAC *see* Public Accounts Committee
Packer, Kerry 55, 208, 211
Paine, Peter 111
Palmer, Derek 244, 245
Panorama 81, 187, 189, 331
Paradise Postponed 182
Paramount 245
Parker, Peter 185, 193, 196, 198, 200, 293
Parkinson, Michael 22, 100
Parliament *see* House of Commons
Party Political Broadcasts (PPBs) 13, 38, 225–6
Patten, Chris 286
pay-per-view 8
Peacock, Alan 115, 126, 139, 162, 175, 176
 and IBA 110, 119, 120, 178, 179, 194
Peacock Committee 121–2, 152, 165, 169, 170–1, 172
 and government 97, 101
 and licence fees 118, 367
Pearson 354
Peat Marwick McLintock 123, 297, 325, 334
Peat, Marwick & Mitchell 81
Philip, HRH Duke of Edinburgh 38, 41, 138
Phillis, Bob 115, 129–30, 160, 349, 354, 364
 and Carlton 201
 and Central 173, 194
 and Maxwell 120, 124
 retirement of 206
 and Zenith 257
Piccadilly Radio 219
Piece of Cake 338
Pinnell, David 169
pirate radio 47, 57, 59, 60, 61, 62, 67, 73, 78
Plouviez, Peter 28
Plowden, Bridget, Lady 108, 134, 207, 293, 304
 and IBA 347
 and Thomson 356
Plowright, David 60, 71, 151, 173, 184, 317
 and Channel 4 101, 102, 111
 and *Dallas* 89, 117
 and Granada 69, 147, 153
 and Maxwell 119, 120
 and satellite television 105, 160
 and Super Channel 113, 135, 146, 174, 182
Plymouth Sound 57
politics 4, 11–12, 13–14, 24, 37, 38
Ponting, Clive 87–8, 90
Popplewell, Margaret, Lady 188, 228, 232
Porter, David 244
Potter, Dennis 191, 210, 251
PPC 58, 115, 149, 150, 199, 332
 and Christmas broadcasting 204, 212
Pragnell, Tony 29, 94, 202
Press Association 214
press, the 258–9, 290, 344–5
 and TV-am 19–20, 50
Price, Charles 156, 174, 196, 197
Pringle, John 68, 349, 350, 352, 356–7, 362, 366
Prior, Jim 152, 317
Proctor, Harvey 221
Proetta, Carmen 301, 333, 356
Profumo Story, The 115
Protheroe, Alan 107, 220, 223
Prudential 46
Public Accounts Committee (PAC) 104, 105–6, 121, 122, 286, 287, 346
Public Service Broadcasting (PSB) 171, 174, 215, 231, 234, 290, 363
 and IBA 160, 164, 239
 and Milne 61, 67–8, 208
Public Service Broadcasts (PSBs) 82, 142, 223
Publicity Club of Great Britain 9–10
Putnam, David 188

Q

Quinn, Andrew 80, 124, 200, 220, 294
 and Granada 312, 314–15, 317, 319–20
Quinton, Anthony, Lord 179

R

radio 57, 71, 108, 111–12, 134–5, 224
 and the arts 331
 commercial 1, 2, 32, 162
 and expenditure 164
 and financing 64, 77, 85, 94–5, 101
 and Northern Ireland 280
 and rentals 75–6
 see also Community Radio; ILR; INR; pirate radio
Radio 210 244
Radio Advertising Awards 80
Radio Advertising Conference 77
Radio Authority 270, 273
Radio City 90
Radio Clyde 37, 43, 59
Radio Congress 243
Radio Consultative Committee (RCC) 61, 62, 149, 171, 172, 209
 and government 87, 239, 284, 336
Radio Jackie 67, 78, 89
Radio Joint Audience Research (RAJAR) 1, 47
Radio Liaison Group 233–4
Radio Marketing Bureau 51
Radio Orwell 37
Radio Tay 108
Radio Times 121
Radio Victory 128, 132, 134–5
Rampton, Richard, QC 334, 347, 350, 355, 370
Rank Organisation 153–4, 155, 156, 158, 274, 313
ratings 19, 34, 145, 176, 232, 361, 367
Rawlinson, Sir Peter 63–4
Rayne, Max 293
RCC *see* Radio Consultative Committee

Read, John	100	Rothschild, Evelyn	17
Readers Digest	242	Rothschild, Jacob	349, 350, 352, 362
Reagan, Ronald	161, 303, 308, 309, 311	Rothschild, Leo	17
Real Lives	116, 118, 119, 123, 152, 178, 187	Rowley, Chris	239, 244
Really Useful Company	343, 346, 356–7, 361, 362, 365, 367	*Roxy*	234
		Royal Television Society (RTS)	33, 121, 123, 150, 163–4, 172–3, 175–6, 289
Really Useful Group (RUG)	365, 366, 367, 368, 369	and Diamond Jubilee	263–4, 268–9
Red Rose	231–2	and Hurd	251–2, 255–6
Redley, Michael	285	*Royal Variety Show*	37, 138, 270–1
Redmond, Phil	90, 248	Roycroft, David	288
Reece, Gordon	258	Rudge, Alan	113, 115
Reedy, Jack	157, 185, 216	Rufus, Ian	290
Rees-Mogg, William	36, 168, 178, 234, 309, 311–12, 321–2	RUG *see* Really Useful Group	
and BSC	294, 296, 304, 305, 307, 367	Rumphorst, Werner	206
Regional Officers (ROs)	41–2, 138, 227, 279–80, 338, 372	Runcie, Robert, Archbishop of Canterbury	74
		Russell, George	45, 70, 127, 154, 159, 200, 212
reduction of	60, 63	and Channel 4	179, 185, 230, 260
and satellite television	23, 28	and IBA	352, 353, 354, 359–60, 361, 363, 364, 366, 368
Reid, Jimmy	152	and Isaacs	269
Reid, Sir John	124, 126	and ITN	296, 309, 311, 350
Reith, John, Lord	28, 50, 58, 103	and Maxwell	182
religious broadcasting	22, 23–4, 27, 31–2, 44, 54, 327, 328	and salaries	197
Renton, Timothy	238, 239, 245, 247, 254, 291	and White Paper	372
		Ryan, Michael	250
and Europe	331–2		
and ITN	295	**S**	
and Northern Ireland	318	S4C	85, 129, 155, 370
and Policy Document	298	and HTV	181, 182, 225, 256, 297
and radio	288, 289, 309, 310, 317	Saatchi, Charles	100, 260
repeats	148	Saatchi & Saatchi	235
Restrictive Trade Practices Act (1976)	132	Sainsbury, John	273, 278
Reynolds, Gillian	147, 331	Salvation Army	272
Rice, Tim	38, 239	Sandilands, Jo	221, 241
Richman, Stella	106, 297	Sapper, Alan	74, 247, 288
Riddell, Sir John	3, 32, 45, 122, 128, 140, 185, 224, 351	Sargent, Naomi	190, 202
Ridley, Paula	3, 154, 191, 356	Sat UK	195
Right to Reply	94, 139	Satellite Broadcasting Board	111
Rink, John	252, 347, 350	Satellite Broadcasting Company (SBC)	7–8, 136–7
Rippon, Angela	22		
Rippon, Geoffrey	207	Satellite Master Antenna Television (SMATV)	104
Rittner, Luke	82, 366		
Robert Fraser Lectures	107–8, 351–2	satellite television *see* DBS; SMATV; Unisat	
Robson, Tom	72, 111, 137, 140, 145, 147, 181, 183	Satellite Television Ltd	7, 16
and costs	71, 101	Satellite TV	36
and satellite broadcasting	31, 102, 158	*Saturday Night Live*	151
Roddick, Anita	311, 333	Saudi Arabia	286, 288, 290, 291, 296, 351
Rogers, Peter	11, 28, 210–11, 230, 236, 325, 344	SBC *see* Satellite Broadcasting Company	
Roland Rat	27, 31, 59	Scarman, Leslie, Lord	303
Rook, Brian	14, 91, 113, 130, 154, 197	SCC	58, 104, 145, 199, 234, 254, 294
and Carlton	125, 127	and AIDS advertising	192
death of	287, 288, 289	and contracts	173, 180
Rosenthal, Abe	166, 175	and DBS	49, 52, 105, 157, 160
Rosser, Mel	155	and night broadcasting	287, 312

Index

and Super Channel 113, 135, 141–2, 146, 151, 169
and White Paper 345
Scharf, Albert 222–3, 296
Scoble, Chris 186, 327–8, 348, 361
Scotland Yard 283
Scott, Mike 69, 101, 102
Scottish Advisory Committee 110
Scottish Nationalist Party (SNP) 228, 230
Scum 33, 48, 49, 54–5, 78, 82–3, 113
and legal proceedings 96, 97, 98–100, 102–3, 108
SDP *see* Social Democratic Party
Sebastiane 139, 143, 147, 148, 149, 154–5
SES Astra Channel 201
sex 139, 142, 216, 226
see also homosexuality
Seydoux, Jerome 161
Shackleton, Eddie 163
Shaw, Colin 2, 5, 28, 29, 149, 235
and BSC 325, 346, 367
Shaw, David 65, 97, 173, 186, 191, 235, 273, 274
and ITV 232
and Obscene Publications Bill 252
and Strategy Group 292
Shaw, Giles 75, 81, 98, 108, 135, 149, 158, 160
and radio 76, 120, 151, 164
Shea, Michael 45, 89
Sherrin, Ned 243
Shinwell, Manny 75
Sight & Sound 363
Simonds-Gooding, Anthony 260, 261, 264, 274, 287, 303, 316
and flotation 331, 339–40
and IBA 313, 324
and ITN 271, 281–2, 285
and MGM 362
and shareholders 349, 354
Simmons, Idwyl 182
Simmons, Leslie 201
Singer, Aubrey 26, 44, 50, 109
Sinn Fein 335, 338, 341
Sins 253–4
Sky 25, 103, 136, 324, 363, 367
and BSB 364
and Super Channel 273
Skyline 47, 67
SMATV *see* Satellite Master Antenna Television
Smith, Anthony 213, 215, 363
Smith, Terry 219, 290
Smith, Tony 124, 262, 265
Snoddy, Raymond 118, 164, 165, 171, 177, 180, 218, 330
and Channel 4 268
and contracts 186, 187
and White Paper 372
Soames, Mary 293, 332

Social Democratic Party (SDP) 13, 24, 38
Sondhi, Ranjit 188, 228, 320
Soundaround 192
South Africa 270
South Bank Show 280
Southgate, Colin 128
Spitting Image 51, 56, 85, 92, 113, 237, 263
and McWhirter 116, 117, 118–19
and Thatcher 114
sports broadcasting 16, 273, 294, 316
Spotlight 302, 303, 304
Spycatcher 246, 247, 270
Starstream 194
Steel, David 13, 37, 152, 200, 230, 348
Steele, Howard 39, 135
Steering Committee 319
Sterling, Jeffrey 44–5, 46, 47, 49, 306–7, 327
and IBA 286, 305, 349
Stewart, Marshall 63
Stoessel, Sue 175
Stolliday, Ivor 149
Stubbs, John 283
STV 108
Styles, Jim 324
Suchet, John 263–4
Sun, The 87, 230, 323, 356
Sunday Express 144, 153
Sunday Telegraph 179, 301, 348
Sunday Times 56, 59, 80, 112, 164–5, 179, 242, 273
and *Death on the Rock* 365
and Hussey 184
and leaks 303
and Milne 309
and Policy Document 297, 298
and *Sins* 254
and Super Channel 247–8
and Thames takeover 125–6
and *This Week* 301
and World Cup 170, 171
Super Channel 105, 141–2, 146, 206, 209, 247–8, 257
and BBC 113, 124
and IBA 151, 168–9, 198–9
and ITN 135–6, 157, 174, 180–1, 182, 188, 226, 307–8, 335
and ITV 103, 110, 111, 148–9, 205
and funding 305–6, 332, 337, 342–3

T
Taylor, Mr Justice 54
TDFI 103, 105, 156, 161, 192
and Maxwell 119, 120, 122, 125, 136, 159, 169
Tebbit, Norman 27, 53, 56–7, 89, 139, 141
and BBC 190, 192, 193
and Super Channel 210
and White Paper 350

389

technology 6, 25, 295
teletext 111, 229
Telethon 310, 311
Television & Radio Industries Club (TRIC) 88, 163, 176, 257, 264, 291, 353
    and Whitney 82, 109, 125, 169
Television South (TVS) 52, 120, 122, 125, 127, 183, 208, 363
Television South West (TSW) 57, 60, 87
Television Today 59, 149
Television Writers Guild 10
Ten O'Clock News 108
terrestrial broadcasting 61–2, 79
terrorism 91, 161, 280, 301, 335, 338, 341
Tesler, Brian 26, 45, 52, 58, 69, 160, 222, 315
    and BSB 350–1
    and CBE 169
    and DBS 71–2
    and LWT 328
    and Maxwell 119
    and Murdoch 294
    and news broadcasting 227
    and Super Channel 113, 124, 146, 182
Thames Television 7, 27, 34–5, 39, 62–3, 146
    and Astra Consortium 205, 222, 224, 234, 256, 259
    and *Dallas* 86, 87, 89, 90, 91, 100, 107, 110, 112, 115, 117, 118, 129, 130, 144
    and *Death on the Rock* 301, 302, 328, 329, 330, 334, 350, 358, 362, 364, 366
    and news broadcasting 227
    and strikes 66–7, 74, 75
    and Super Channel 135, 146, 148
    and takeover bid 124–7, 128–9
    and TDFI 192
    and unions 269, 270
    and violence 251
    and YTV 151
Thane, Sarah 268, 300, 369
Thatcher, Denis 6, 265
Thatcher, Margaret 4–5, 6, 13, 28, 62, 161, 199, 265
    and AIDS advertising 205
    and BBC 81, 95, 263
    and cable television 11
    and Congress speech 91–2
    and *Death on the Rock* 300–1, 302, 304
    and election 228–9, 232
    and Frost 108, 109, 110
    and House of Commons 283, 286
    and IRA 116
    and ITC 364
    and miners' strike 100
    and Obscenity Bill 221
    and regulations 254–5, 312
    and *Spitting Image* 114, 142
    and Super Channel 209
    and television 36–7, 63, 139
    and Westland 147
Thatcher, Mark 63
Themroc 181, 183, 216
Theobalds, Harry 169, 194, 197, 201, 240, 243, 246
This Week 365, 366
    see also *Death on the Rock*
Thomas, Howard 62–3, 108, 109, 178, 181, 192, 206–7
Thomas, Quentin 79, 88, 147, 176, 229, 262
    and broadcasting standards 271
    and BSB 235, 326, 327–8
    and Channel 4 243, 334
    and independents 242, 245, 246
    and radio 270, 288
    and V 263
    and White Paper 343
Thompson, John 38, 72, 73, 74–5, 163, 205, 264
    and community radio 77, 79
    and finance 45, 71, 94, 101
    and INR 120, 151, 166
    retirement of 70, 197, 202, 209, 210, 221, 224
Thomson, George, Lord of Monifieth 1, 2, 3, 14, 36, 99, 101–2
    and Astra Consortium 256
    and cable television 7, 8–9
    and Channel 4 11, 30, 114, 134, 159, 179, 185, 193, 207, 230, 260
    and competition 318
    and *Dallas* 90, 100, 107, 109, 110, 112, 113, 117
    and *Death on the Rock* 299, 300–1, 347, 358, 366
    and Dell 224–5
    and franchises 169
    and Grade 266, 267, 269
    and Granada 153, 154
    and independents 220
    and Maxwell 120
    and *My Britain* 152
    and news programming 34, 35
    and Northern Ireland 335
    and Policy Document 298
    and political broadcasting 24
    and public service broadcasting 290
    and radio 151, 166, 172, 205, 283
    and Rees-Mogg 305
    and religious broadcasting 32
    replacement of 334, 349–50
    retirement of 336–7, 338, 351, 353, 356, 362-3
    and salaries 197

Index

and satellite television   28, 49, 51, 52–3, 58, 111, 157
and *Scum*   55, 97, 98
and Thames TV   125, 126, 127, 128, 130, 131, 274
and Thorn-EMI   39, 41, 42
and TV-am   20, 21, 22, 32, 73, 291
and *V*   259
and violence   142, 143, 144
and White Paper   343, 344, 345, 348
and Whitney   149
and World Cup   170
and Yorkshire Television   244–5
Thorn Birds, The   81
Thorn-EMI   34–5, 61, 124, 125, 126, 128, 130
    and Gatward   120, 122
    and Thomson   38–9, 40, 41, 42
Tibet   346–7
Time magazine   6
Times, The   4, 27, 31–2, 76–7, 111, 115, 160, 229
    and Hussey   184
    and IRA   301
    and *Scum*   55
    and *V*   262, 263
    and White Paper   345, 347
tobacco sponsorship   153, 371
Tooley, John   101, 215, 216
Towler, Bob   133
Trelford, Donald   289, 354
Trethowan, Sir Ian   27, 179, 205, 256, 274
    and *Death on the Rock*   301, 302, 329, 330, 334
TRIC *see* Television & Radio Industries Club
Tucker, Geoffrey   30–1
Tugendhat, Christopher   302
Tumbledown   309, 311
Turkey   221–2
Turner, Ted   6
Tusa, John   209, 213
TV-am   13, 18, 19, 24, 25, 108, 236, 331
    and ACTT   269, 270, 272, 283, 285, 288
    and advertising   17, 20–1, 22
    aims of   64–5
    and Chairmanship   310
    and floating   132, 165–6, 173
    and funding   33–4, 35, 36, 46, 48, 50
    and ITN   96, 183, 240, 256–7
    and management   55, 56
    and news   63, 73, 74, 75, 76, 78–9
    and Princess Michael   100
    and profits   226
    relaunch of   27, 31
    and resignations   60–1, 62, 63, 67
    restructuring of   320
    and shareholdings   32–3, 129, 208, 211, 213, 286–7, 290–1, 295–6, 319, 351
and standards   324, 326
and unions   274, 279
TV Eye   144
TV Times   121, 146, 296, 357–8, 363
TVS *see* Television South
Twisk, Russell   236
Tynan, Kenneth   256, 269–70
Tyne Tees   114, 151, 195, 263, 317, 349
    and unions   269, 270, 294

U

UHF transmitters   102, 104
UK Press Gazette   118
Ulster TV   16, 41, 137, 282
Unisat   46, 105, 109, 136
    and BBC   8, 44, 45, 47, 48, 49
    costs   65, 80, 81, 86, 89, 103, 104
United Newspapers   129, 131
United States of America   2, 5–6, 26, 245, 258, 368–9
US Information Agency   193, 303
US International Communications Agency   5
Utley, Peter   96

V

V   251, 253, 255, 256, 259, 264, 271, 290
    and press   261, 263
Variety Club   53
VFH transmissions   52
Vickers, Tony   129, 265, 331
video biographies   262
Viking Group   231–2
violence   85, 133–4, 139, 142, 162, 216, 332
    and Channel 4   14, 114, 154–5
    and children   76–7, 141, 148
    and government   37, 145, 225, 327
    and IBA   150, 247, 253, 255, 364
    and press   197, 250, 251, 284
Virgin   138, 194, 306
    and BSB   349, 351, 354, 356, 357, 358
Vizard, Jane   252
'Voice of America, The'   5

W

Wakeham, John   281, 367
Walden, Brian   97, 145
Waldheim, Kurt   310, 311
Wales   122–3, 159
Walmsley, Nigel   64, 101, 112, 226, 240–1
Warnock, Mary   224
Watkins, Lord Justice   54
Weekend World   19, 97, 145, 289
Welles, Orson   33
Wembley, Mark   156
Wenham, Brian   163, 209, 211, 213, 234
    and Channel 4   223, 230, 252, 260, 265

West, Brian 73, 297
Westland affair 146
Westward Television 155
Westwood, Bill, Bishop of
  Peterborough 243, 323
What the Papers Say 89, 149, 213
Wheeler, John 293
Wheldon, Huw 156, 160, 164, 226
White Paper: 'Broadcasting in
  the 90s' 277, 293, 327,
    339, 342, 343–6, 370
  and Channel 4 330
  and IBA 262, 292, 320, 325,
    336, 347, 355, 371–2
  and ITV 337
Whitehouse, Mary 3, 16, 160,
    162, 221, 247, 251
  and BSC 367
  and Channel 4 12, 14
  and *Eastenders* 321–2
  and IBA 347
  and *Scum* 33, 48, 54, 55, 97,
    98, 99–100, 102–3, 108
  and *Sins* 253
  and *Themroc* 183
  and *V* 262
  and violence 134
  and warning triangles 212, 213, 216
Whitelaw, William 11, 52, 80,
    94, 178, 218–19, 304
  and good taste 14, 16
  and Thatcher 4–5, 30–1
  and White Paper 298, 346
Whitemore, Sir Clive 291
Whittam-Smith, Andreas 204, 343
Who Dares Wins 60
Wick, Charles 5–6, 193, 303
Willis, Ted 22
Wills, Nicholas 128
Wilson, Harold 212
Wimbledon Tennis Tournament 16
Windlesham, David, Lord 28, 179, 349, 369
  and *Death on the Rock* 334, 347, 350, 353,
    355, 358, 366, 370
Winner, Michael 153, 206, 322–3, 337–8
Wintour, Charles 36, 60–1, 63

Wogan, Terry 40, 156, 268–9
Wood, Andy 280
Wordley, Ron 39–40, 123, 215
Working Party 47, 49, 60
World Cup 170, 171
World in Action 41, 57–8,
    63–4, 69, 233, 310
Worldvision Enterprises 112, 115,
    117, 118, 119, 125
  and *Dallas* 88, 89, 90, 91, 104,
    129, 130, 131, 134
Wotton, John 126, 256, 299, 328, 342
Wyatt, Will 142
Wyatt, Woodrow 224–5, 331

Y
Yentob, Alan 265
Yorkshire Television 26, 136,
    148, 178, 218–19, 245
  and ITN 308
  and pop broadcasting 164
Young, Sir Brian 8, 9, 19, 94, 135, 202, 346
  and Channel 4 108, 304
  and retirement 1, 2
  and Thomson 356
  and Whitney 4, 12–13
Young, David, Lord 168, 190, 305, 306, 322
  and broadcasting summit 254, 255
  and BSB 313, 314
  and Open College 324–5
Young, Stuart 26, 29, 59, 81, 95–6, 107
  and BBC 97
  and *Dallas* 87, 88, 100, 110, 112, 113
  and DBS 43, 44, 45, 49, 58, 111
  death of 178, 199
  and IRA 116, 123
  and Thomson 99
  and Thorn-EMI 41
  and violence 142, 143
  and World Cup 170
YTV 151, 255

Z
Zeebrugge Disaster 234, 237
Zenith 115, 257, 259

Index

and MI5 programme 91
and Policy Document 292, 293
and retirement 249
and TV-am 288
and warning triangles 237
and White Paper 343, 344, 371, 372
and Whitney 373
Lloyd Webber, Andrew 53, 239, 265, 343, 345, 346, 356–7, 366
London Weekend Television (LWT) 7, 19, 23–4, 157, 220, 233
  and Astra Consortium 222, 224, 235, 256, 259
  and cable television 26
  and news broadcasting 227
  and shareholdings 328
  and Super Channel 136, 146
Lord, Shirley 166, 167, 175
Lords' Committee 99
Lorimer, Bob 75, 207, 268, 305
Los Angeles 106
Lucas, Christopher 262
Luce, Richard 147
Luckwell, Michael 125, 126, 295, 296, 310, 312
LWT *see* London Weekend Television
Lygo, Sir Raymond 45, 207

M

MAC *see* Multiplexed Analogue Component
McCall, David 127, 208, 227, 235, 277, 292, 294
  and independents 241, 242, 279
  and ITV 232, 289, 318
  and satellite television 160
  and Super Channel 146, 306
  and *TV Times* 357
McGarry, Ian 28
McGuinness, Martin 116
McIvor, Jill 70, 140, 168–9, 191, 195, 200, 224
McWhirter, Norris 116, 117, 118–19, 149
Maddox, Brenda 27, 118
Mail on Sunday 56, 170–1
Maitland, Sir Donald 202, 205, 211, 219, 271, 330, 356
  and Green Paper 226
  and IBA 188, 193, 194, 197
  and Policy Document 207–8, 293, 298
  retirement of 370
  and violence 253
  and White Paper 372
Mallet, Michael 231
Marcher Sound 134
Marconi 170
Margaret, HRH Princess 85
Marsh, Richard, Lord 20, 27, 32, 36, 46–7, 50, 55, 65, 127
Masham Report 281

Massiter, Cathy 91, 93, 94
Mates 246
Matthews, Paul 76, 285, 292
Maxwell, Robert 36, 74, 149, 161, 165, 182, 290, 306
  and AIDS Trust 330–1
  and satellite television 119, 120, 122, 124, 125, 136, 140, 156–7, 159, 169
  and Super Channel 332
  and Thames takeover 129
Meaney, Sir Patrick 154, 158
Media Committee 67
Media Show, The 232
Media Week 122
Mellersh, Nicholas 163–4
Mellor, David 141, 187–8, 198, 199, 210, 217, 227
  and competition 232
  and independents 211–12, 220–1, 222
Mercury Broadcasting 78
Metro Radio 289
MGM 357, 362
MI5 118, 246
MI5's Official Secrets 91, 92–4, 93–4, 94
Michael, Princess of Kent 100
Miles, Ken 201, 319
Miller, Jonathan 298
Milne, Alasdair 13, 15, 40, 46, 59, 100, 234
  and BBC 29, 81, 88, 107, 309
  and censorship 251
  and Channel 4 230
  and *Dallas* 110
  and Hussey 184
  and independents 198
  and IRA 116, 118, 123
  and *Panorama* 189, 190
  and political broadcasting 24
  and public service broadcasting 36, 61, 67–8
  and religious broadcasting 44
  resignation of 208, 228
  and RTS 6, 223
  and satellite television 8, 9, 25, 28, 50, 58
  and Thorn-EMI 41
  and violence 142
  and World Cup 170, 171
  and Young 199
Milton Committee 206, 228
miners' strike 100
Monocled Mutineer 187
Monopolies Commission 121
Montague, Michael 115
Monte Carlo 1, 90, 91, 92
Monty Python 285
Moore, Brian 324
Moore, Philip 89
Moran, Diana 19
Morgan, Brian 150

385

Morgan, Janet	262
Moriarty, Michael	7, 8, 30, 34–5, 41, 44, 70, 99
Morrison, Peter	225–6
Mortimer, John	123, 153, 173, 182, 273, 293, 338, 372
Moser, Claus	216
Mulholland, Clare	98, 152, 247, 332, 347
Multiplexed Analogue Component (MAC)	25, 37, 39, 82, 102
and C-MAC	68–9, 70, 79, 104, 157, 158, 160, 163
and DMAC	229
and EMAC	112, 137
Murdoch, Rupert	4, 25, 56, 136, 204
and Astra	312, 350–1, 354
and BSB	361
and ethics	322–3
and Eurosport	294
and newspapers	258, 259, 290
Murphy, Stephen	67, 97, 98
Murstill, Lord Justice	96
Museum of the Moving Image	124, 327
Music Box	151, 164, 308
My Britain	152, 153
My Country Right or Wrong	272

N

NACRO	75, 76
Naked Civil Servant, The	179
NAR (nett advertising revenue)	318, 323
National AIDS Trust	330–1
National Council for Civil Liberties (NCCL)	91
National Museum of Photography, Film and Television	226, 255
National Theatre	1, 13, 173, 205, 209, 224, 232–3, 293, 340
National Union of Journalists (NUJ)	283, 288, 338
Naughtie, James	147
NBS	194, 198, 199
Neil, Andrew	100, 156, 322, 366
Neilson	319
Nelson Mandela concert	313
Network Seven	247
News at Ten	112, 160, 192, 229, 250, 271, 295, 351
news broadcasting	96, 135, 227, 271, 295, 309, 327
and BBC	190, 229
and Channel 4	18, 34, 35
see also ITN	
News International	36
News of the World	9, 189, 213, 323
Newsnight	278
Newton, Sir Gordon	36
Nicholas, David	18, 60, 91, 192, 209, 273
and ITN	121, 290, 296
and Reagan	308, 309
and Super Channel	157, 174, 180, 226, 350
and TV-am	74, 81, 240
and Whitney	370, 371
Nicholson, Mary	303
night programming	165, 245, 264, 273, 287, 343–4
and Burnet	295, 312
and ITN	315, 332
Nine O'clock News	96, 229
Noar, Martin	233
Norrington, John	127, 288
Norris, David	253, 332
North Sound Radio	108
Northern Ireland	16, 137, 279–80, 282, 283, 302, 303, 335–6
see also IRA	
Now Channel	273, 279, 295
nuclear defence	25, 39, 40
Nuclear Forum	102
Nuffield Foundation	54
NUJ *see* National Union of Journalists	

O

Obscene Publications Act (1959)	139, 141, 143, 145, 146, 147, 149, 153
Obscene Publications Bill	206, 221, 228, 252, 253, 255
Observer, The	52, 20, 92, 118, 170, 177, 289
and *Death on the Rock*	301, 349, 350
and Northern Ireland	282, 283
and radio	203, 205
O'Cathain, Detta	188
Ocean Sound	128, 196, 244
Octopus	47
Office of Fair Trading (OFT)	109, 117, 129, 130, 131–2, 149, 237
and advertising	241, 243
and BSB	361
and *Dallas*	134
Official Secrets Act	90, 92
Olivier, Laurence, Lord	209, 224, 232–3
Olympic Games	48, 61
Oman	63–4, 67
One In Five	14
Open College	190, 192, 202, 216, 324–5, 333–4
and costs	236, 311, 315
Oracle	53, 111, 170, 257
Orbital Test Satellite (OTS)	7
O'Sullivan, Kevin	107, 109, 110, 112, 113, 130, 131
Owen, David	37, 149, 271
Oyston, Owen	123, 231, 333, 337

Index

P

PAC *see* Public Accounts Committee
Packer, Kerry 55, 208, 211
Paine, Peter 111
Palmer, Derek 244, 245
Panorama 81, 187, 189, 331
Paradise Postponed 182
Paramount 245
Parker, Peter 185, 193, 196, 198, 200, 293
Parkinson, Michael 22, 100
Parliament *see* House of Commons
Party Political Broadcasts (PPBs) 13, 38, 225–6
Patten, Chris 286
pay-per-view 8
Peacock, Alan 115, 126, 139, 162, 175, 176
 and IBA 110, 119, 120, 178, 179, 194
Peacock Committee 121–2, 152, 165, 169, 170–1, 172
 and government 97, 101
 and licence fees 118, 367
Pearson 354
Peat Marwick McLintock 123, 297, 325, 334
Peat, Marwick & Mitchell 81
Philip, HRH Duke of Edinburgh 38, 41, 138
Phillis, Bob 115, 129–30, 160, 349, 354, 364
 and Carlton 201
 and Central 173, 194
 and Maxwell 120, 124
 retirement of 206
 and Zenith 257
Piccadilly Radio 219
Piece of Cake 338
Pinnell, David 169
pirate radio 47, 57, 59, 60, 61, 62, 67, 73, 78
Plouviez, Peter 28
Plowden, Bridget, Lady 108, 134, 207, 293, 304
 and IBA 347
 and Thomson 356
Plowright, David 60, 71, 151, 173, 184, 317
 and Channel 4 101, 102, 111
 and *Dallas* 89, 117
 and Granada 69, 147, 153
 and Maxwell 119, 120
 and satellite television 105, 160
 and Super Channel 113, 135, 146, 174, 182
Plymouth Sound 57
politics 4, 11–12, 13–14, 24, 37, 38
Ponting, Clive 87–8, 90
Popplewell, Margaret, Lady 188, 228, 232
Porter, David 244
Potter, Dennis 191, 210, 251
PPC 58, 115, 149, 150, 199, 332
 and Christmas broadcasting 204, 212
Pragnell, Tony 29, 94, 202
Press Association 214
press, the 258–9, 290, 344–5
 and TV-am 19–20, 50
Price, Charles 156, 174, 196, 197

Pringle, John 68, 349, 350, 352, 356–7, 362, 366
Prior, Jim 152, 317
Proctor, Harvey 221
Proetta, Carmen 301, 333, 356
Profumo Story, The 115
Protheroe, Alan 107, 220, 223
Prudential 46
Public Accounts Committee (PAC) 104, 105–6, 121, 122, 286, 287, 346
Public Service Broadcasting (PSB) 171, 174, 215, 231, 234, 290, 363
 and IBA 160, 164, 239
 and Milne 61, 67–8, 208
Public Service Broadcasts (PSBs) 82, 142, 223
Publicity Club of Great Britain 9–10
Putnam, David 188

Q

Quinn, Andrew 80, 124, 200, 220, 294
 and Granada 312, 314–15, 317, 319–20
Quinton, Anthony, Lord 179

R

radio 57, 71, 108, 111–12, 134–5, 224
 and the arts 331
 commercial 1, 2, 32, 162
 and expenditure 164
 and financing 64, 77, 85, 94–5, 101
 and Northern Ireland 280
 and rentals 75–6
 see also Community Radio; ILR; INR; pirate radio
Radio 210 244
Radio Advertising Awards 80
Radio Advertising Conference 77
Radio Authority 270, 273
Radio City 90
Radio Clyde 37, 43, 59
Radio Congress 243
Radio Consultative Committee (RCC) 61, 62, 149, 171, 172, 209
 and government 87, 239, 284, 336
Radio Jackie 67, 78, 89
Radio Joint Audience Research (RAJAR) 1, 47
Radio Liaison Group 233–4
Radio Marketing Bureau 51
Radio Orwell 37
Radio Tay 108
Radio Times 121
Radio Victory 128, 132, 134–5
Rampton, Richard, QC 334, 347, 350, 355, 370
Rank Organisation 153–4, 155, 156, 158, 274, 313
ratings 19, 34, 145, 176, 232, 361, 367
Rawlinson, Sir Peter 63–4
Rayne, Max 293
RCC *see* Radio Consultative Committee

387

Read, John 100
Readers Digest 242
Reagan, Ronald 161, 303, 308, 309, 311
Real Lives 116, 118, 119, 123, 152, 178, 187
Really Useful Company 343, 346, 356–7, 361, 362, 365, 367
Really Useful Group (RUG) 365, 366, 367, 368, 369
Red Rose 231–2
Redley, Michael 285
Redmond, Phil 90, 248
Reece, Gordon 258
Reedy, Jack 157, 185, 216
Rees-Mogg, William 36, 168, 178, 234, 309, 311–12, 321–2
  and BSC 294, 296, 304, 305, 307, 367
Regional Officers (ROs) 41–2, 138, 227, 279–80, 338, 372
  reduction of 60, 63
  and satellite television 23, 28
Reid, Jimmy 152
Reid, Sir John 124, 126
Reith, John, Lord 28, 50, 58, 103
religious broadcasting 22, 23–4, 27, 31–2, 44, 54, 327, 328
Renton, Timothy 238, 239, 245, 247, 254, 291
  and Europe 331–2
  and ITN 295
  and Northern Ireland 318
  and Policy Document 298
  and radio 288, 289, 309, 310, 317
repeats 148
Restrictive Trade Practices Act (1976) 132
Reynolds, Gillian 147, 331
Rice, Tim 38, 239
Richman, Stella 106, 297
Riddell, Sir John 3, 32, 45, 122, 128, 140, 185, 224, 351
Ridley, Paula 3, 154, 191, 356
Right to Reply 94, 139
Rink, John 252, 347, 350
Rippon, Angela 22
Rippon, Geoffrey 207
Rittner, Luke 82, 366
Robert Fraser Lectures 107–8, 351–2
Robson, Tom 72, 111, 137, 140, 145, 147, 181, 183
  and costs 71, 101
  and satellite broadcasting 31, 102, 158
Roddick, Anita 311, 333
Rogers, Peter 11, 28, 210–11, 230, 236, 325, 344
Roland Rat 27, 31, 59
Rook, Brian 14, 91, 113, 130, 154, 197
  and Carlton 125, 127
  death of 287, 288, 289
Rosenthal, Abe 166, 175
Rosser, Mel 155
Rothschild, Evelyn 17
Rothschild, Jacob 349, 350, 352, 362
Rothschild, Leo 17
Rowley, Chris 239, 244
Roxy 234
Royal Television Society (RTS) 33, 121, 123, 150, 163–4, 172–3, 175–6, 289
  and Diamond Jubilee 263–4, 268–9
  and Hurd 251–2, 255–6
Royal Variety Show 37, 138, 270–1
Roycroft, David 288
Rudge, Alan 113, 115
Rufus, Ian 290
RUG *see* Really Useful Group
Rumphorst, Werner 206
Runcie, Robert, Archbishop of Canterbury 74
Russell, George 45, 70, 127, 154, 159, 200, 212
  and Channel 4 179, 185, 230, 260
  and IBA 352, 353, 354, 359–60, 361, 363, 364, 366, 368
  and Isaacs 269
  and ITN 296, 309, 311, 350
  and Maxwell 182
  and salaries 197
  and White Paper 372
Ryan, Michael 250

S
S4C 85, 129, 155, 370
  and HTV 181, 182, 225, 256, 297
Saatchi, Charles 100, 260
Saatchi & Saatchi 235
Sainsbury, John 273, 278
Salvation Army 272
Sandilands, Jo 221, 241
Sapper, Alan 74, 247, 288
Sargent, Naomi 190, 202
Sat UK 195
Satellite Broadcasting Board 111
Satellite Broadcasting Company (SBC) 7–8, 136–7
Satellite Master Antenna Television (SMATV) 104
satellite television *see* DBS; SMATV; Unisat
Satellite Television Ltd 7, 16
Satellite TV 36
Saturday Night Live 151
Saudi Arabia 286, 288, 290, 291, 296, 351
SBC *see* Satellite Broadcasting Company
Scarman, Leslie, Lord 303
SCC 58, 104, 145, 199, 234, 254, 294
  and AIDS advertising 192
  and contracts 173, 180
  and DBS 49, 52, 105, 157, 160
  and night broadcasting 287, 312

Index

and Super Channel 113, 135, 141–2, 146, 151, 169
and White Paper 345
Scharf, Albert 222–3, 296
Scoble, Chris 186, 327–8, 348, 361
Scotland Yard 283
Scott, Mike 69, 101, 102
Scottish Advisory Committee 110
Scottish Nationalist Party (SNP) 228, 230
Scum 33, 48, 49, 54–5, 78, 82–3, 113
 and legal proceedings 96, 97, 98–100, 102–3, 108
SDP *see* Social Democratic Party
Sebastiane 139, 143, 147, 148, 149, 154–5
SES Astra Channel 201
sex 139, 142, 216, 226
 see also homosexuality
Seydoux, Jerome 161
Shackleton, Eddie 163
Shaw, Colin 2, 5, 28, 29, 149, 235
 and BSC 325, 346, 367
Shaw, David 65, 97, 173, 186, 191, 235, 273, 274
 and ITV 232
 and Obscene Publications Bill 252
 and Strategy Group 292
Shaw, Giles 75, 81, 98, 108, 135, 149, 158, 160
 and radio 76, 120, 151, 164
Shea, Michael 45, 89
Sherrin, Ned 243
Shinwell, Manny 75
Sight & Sound 363
Simonds-Gooding, Anthony 260, 261, 264, 274, 287, 303, 316
 and flotation 331, 339–40
 and IBA 313, 324
 and ITN 271, 281–2, 285
 and MGM 362
 and shareholders 349, 354
Simmons, Idwyl 182
Simmons, Leslie 201
Singer, Aubrey 26, 44, 50, 109
Sinn Fein 335, 338, 341
Sins 253–4
Sky 25, 103, 136, 324, 363, 367
 and BSB 364
 and Super Channel 273
Skyline 47, 67
SMATV *see* Satellite Master Antenna Television
Smith, Anthony 213, 215, 363
Smith, Terry 219, 290
Smith, Tony 124, 262, 265
Snoddy, Raymond 118, 164, 165, 171, 177, 180, 218, 330
 and Channel 4 268
 and contracts 186, 187
 and White Paper 372
Soames, Mary 293, 332

Social Democratic Party (SDP) 13, 24, 38
Sondhi, Ranjit 188, 228, 320
Soundaround 192
South Africa 270
South Bank Show 280
Southgate, Colin 128
Spitting Image 51, 56, 85, 92, 113, 237, 263
 and McWhirter 116, 117, 118–19
 and Thatcher 114
sports broadcasting 16, 273, 294, 316
Spotlight 302, 303, 304
Spycatcher 246, 247, 270
Starstream 194
Steel, David 13, 37, 152, 200, 230, 348
Steele, Howard 39, 135
Steering Committee 319
Sterling, Jeffrey 44–5, 46, 47, 49, 306–7, 327
 and IBA 286, 305, 349
Stewart, Marshall 63
Stoessel, Sue 175
Stolliday, Ivor 149
Stubbs, John 283
STV 108
Styles, Jim 324
Suchet, John 263–4
Sun, The 87, 230, 323, 356
Sunday Express 144, 153
Sunday Telegraph 179, 301, 348
Sunday Times 56, 59, 80, 112, 164–5, 179, 242, 273
 and *Death on the Rock* 365
 and Hussey 184
 and leaks 303
 and Milne 309
 and Policy Document 297, 298
 and *Sins* 254
 and Super Channel 247–8
 and Thames takeover 125–6
 and *This Week* 301
 and World Cup 170, 171
Super Channel 105, 141–2, 146, 206, 209, 247–8, 257
 and BBC 113, 124
 and IBA 151, 168–9, 198–9
 and ITN 135–6, 157, 174, 180–1, 182, 188, 226, 307–8, 335
 and ITV 103, 110, 111, 148–9, 205
 and funding 305–6, 332, 337, 342–3

T
Taylor, Mr Justice 54
TDFI 103, 105, 156, 161, 192
 and Maxwell 119, 120, 122, 125, 136, 159, 169
Tebbit, Norman 27, 53, 56–7, 89, 139, 141
 and BBC 190, 192, 193
 and Super Channel 210
 and White Paper 350

389

technology	6, 25, 295	and Obscenity Bill	221
teletext	111, 229	and regulations	254–5, 312
Telethon	310, 311	and *Spitting Image*	114, 142
Television & Radio Industries Club (TRIC)	88, 163, 176, 257, 264, 291, 353	and Super Channel	209
		and television	36–7, 63, 139
and Whitney	82, 109, 125, 169	and Westland	147
Television South (TVS)	52, 120, 122, 125, 127, 183, 208, 363	Thatcher, Mark	63
		Themroc	181, 183, 216
Television South West (TSW)	57, 60, 87	Theobalds, Harry	169, 194, 197, 201, 240, 243, 246
Television Today	59, 149	*This Week*	365, 366
Television Writers Guild	10	see also *Death on the Rock*	
Ten O'Clock News	108	Thomas, Howard	62–3, 108, 109, 178, 181, 192, 206–7
terrestrial broadcasting	61–2, 79		
terrorism	91, 161, 280, 301, 335, 338, 341	Thomas, Quentin	79, 88, 147, 176, 229, 262
		and broadcasting standards	271
Tesler, Brian	26, 45, 52, 58, 69, 160, 222, 315	and BSB	235, 326, 327–8
		and Channel 4	243, 334
and BSB	350–1	and independents	242, 245, 246
and CBE	169	and radio	270, 288
and DBS	71–2	and V	263
and LWT	328	and White Paper	343
and Maxwell	119	Thompson, John	38, 72, 73, 74–5, 163, 205, 264
and Murdoch	294		
and news broadcasting	227	and community radio	77, 79
and Super Channel	113, 124, 146, 182	and finance	45, 71, 94, 101
Thames Television	7, 27, 34–5, 39, 62–3, 146	and INR	120, 151, 166
		retirement of	70, 197, 202, 209, 210, 221, 224
and Astra Consortium	205, 222, 224, 234, 256, 259	Thomson, George, Lord of Monifieth	1, 2, 3, 14, 36, 99, 101–2
and *Dallas*	86, 87, 89, 90, 91, 100, 107, 110, 112, 115, 117, 118, 129, 130, 144	and Astra Consortium	256
		and cable television	7, 8–9
and *Death on the Rock*	301, 302, 328, 329, 330, 334, 350, 358, 362, 364, 366	and Channel 4	11, 30, 114, 134, 159, 179, 185, 193, 207, 230, 260
		and competition	318
and news broadcasting	227	and *Dallas*	90, 100, 107, 109, 110, 112, 113, 117
and strikes	66–7, 74, 75		
and Super Channel	135, 146, 148	and *Death on the Rock*	299, 300–1, 347, 358, 366
and takeover bid	124–7, 128–9		
and TDFI	192	and Dell	224–5
and unions	269, 270	and franchises	169
and violence	251	and Grade	266, 267, 269
and YTV	151	and Granada	153, 154
Thane, Sarah	268, 300, 369	and independents	220
Thatcher, Denis	6, 265	and Maxwell	120
Thatcher, Margaret	4–5, 6, 13, 28, 62, 161, 199, 265	and *My Britain*	152
		and news programming	34, 35
and AIDS advertising	205	and Northern Ireland	335
and BBC	81, 95, 263	and Policy Document	298
and cable television	11	and political broadcasting	24
and Congress speech	91–2	and public service broadcasting	290
and *Death on the Rock*	300–1, 302, 304	and radio	151, 166, 172, 205, 283
and election	228–9, 232	and Rees-Mogg	305
and Frost	108, 109, 110	and religious broadcasting	32
and House of Commons	283, 286	replacement of	334, 349–50
and IRA	116	retirement of	336–7, 338, 351, 353, 356, 362–3
and ITC	364		
and miners' strike	100	and salaries	197

390

Index

and satellite television 28, 49, 51, 52–3, 58, 111, 157
and *Scum* 55, 97, 98
and Thames TV 125, 126, 127, 128, 130, 131, 274
and Thorn-EMI 39, 41, 42
and TV-am 20, 21, 22, 32, 73, 291
and *V* 259
and violence 142, 143, 144
and White Paper 343, 344, 345, 348
and Whitney 149
and World Cup 170
and Yorkshire Television 244–5
Thorn Birds, The 81
Thorn-EMI 34–5, 61, 124, 125, 126, 128, 130
  and Gatward 120, 122
  and Thomson 38–9, 40, 41, 42
Tibet 346–7
Time magazine 6
Times, The 4, 27, 31–2, 76–7, 111, 115, 160, 229
  and Hussey 184
  and IRA 301
  and *Scum* 55
  and *V* 262, 263
  and White Paper 345, 347
tobacco sponsorship 153, 371
Tooley, John 101, 215, 216
Towler, Bob 133
Trelford, Donald 289, 354
Trethowan, Sir Ian 27, 179, 205, 256, 274
  and *Death on the Rock* 301, 302, 329, 330, 334
TRIC *see* Television & Radio Industries Club
Tucker, Geoffrey 30–1
Tugendhat, Christopher 302
Tumbledown 309, 311
Turkey 221–2
Turner, Ted 6
Tusa, John 209, 213
TV-am 13, 18, 19, 24, 25, 108, 236, 331
  and ACTT 269, 270, 272, 283, 285, 288
  and advertising 17, 20–1, 22
  aims of 64–5
  and Chairmanship 310
  and floating 132, 165–6, 173
  and funding 33–4, 35, 36, 46, 48, 50
  and ITN 96, 183, 240, 256–7
  and management 55, 56
  and news 63, 73, 74, 75, 76, 78–9
  and Princess Michael 100
  and profits 226
  relaunch of 27, 31
  and resignations 60–1, 62, 63, 67
  restructuring of 320
  and shareholdings 32–3, 129, 208, 211, 213, 286–7, 290–1, 295–6, 319, 351
and standards 324, 326
and unions 274, 279
TV Eye 144
TV Times 121, 146, 296, 357–8, 363
TVS *see* Television South
Twisk, Russell 236
Tynan, Kenneth 256, 269–70
Tyne Tees 114, 151, 195, 263, 317, 349
and unions 269, 270, 294

U

UHF transmitters 102, 104
UK Press Gazette 118
Ulster TV 16, 41, 137, 282
Unisat 46, 105, 109, 136
  and BBC 8, 44, 45, 47, 48, 49
  costs 65, 80, 81, 86, 89, 103, 104
United Newspapers 129, 131
United States of America 2, 5–6, 26, 245, 258, 368–9
US Information Agency 193, 303
US International Communications Agency 5
Utley, Peter 96

V

V 251, 253, 255, 256, 259, 264, 271, 290
  and press 261, 263
Variety Club 53
VFH transmissions 52
Vickers, Tony 129, 265, 331
video biographies 262
Viking Group 231–2
violence 85, 133–4, 139, 142, 162, 216, 332
  and Channel 4 14, 114, 154–5
  and children 76–7, 141, 148
  and government 37, 145, 225, 327
  and IBA 150, 247, 253, 255, 364
  and press 197, 250, 251, 284
Virgin 138, 194, 306
  and BSB 349, 351, 354, 356, 357, 358
Vizard, Jane 252
'Voice of America, The' 5

W

Wakeham, John 281, 367
Walden, Brian 97, 145
Waldheim, Kurt 310, 311
Wales 122–3, 159
Walmsley, Nigel 64, 101, 112, 226, 240–1
Warnock, Mary 224
Watkins, Lord Justice 54
Weekend World 19, 97, 145, 289
Welles, Orson 33
Wembley, Mark 156
Wenham, Brian 163, 209, 211, 213, 234
  and Channel 4 223, 230, 252, 260, 265

West, Brian 73, 297
Westland affair 146
Westward Television 155
Westwood, Bill, Bishop of
 Peterborough 243, 323
What the Papers Say 89, 149, 213
Wheeler, John 293
Wheldon, Huw 156, 160, 164, 226
White Paper: 'Broadcasting in
 the 90s' 277, 293, 327,
 339, 342, 343–6, 370
 and Channel 4 330
 and IBA 262, 292, 320, 325,
 336, 347, 355, 371–2
 and ITV 337
Whitehouse, Mary 3, 16, 160,
 162, 221, 247, 251
 and BSC 367
 and Channel 4 12, 14
 and *Eastenders* 321–2
 and IBA 347
 and *Scum* 33, 48, 54, 55, 97,
 98, 99–100, 102–3, 108
 and *Sins* 253
 and *Themroc* 183
 and *V* 262
 and violence 134
 and warning triangles 212, 213, 216
Whitelaw, William 11, 52, 80,
 94, 178, 218–19, 304
 and good taste 14, 16
 and Thatcher 4–5, 30–1
 and White Paper 298, 346
Whitemore, Sir Clive 291
Whittam-Smith, Andreas 204, 343
Who Dares Wins 60
Wick, Charles 5–6, 193, 303
Willis, Ted 22
Wills, Nicholas 128
Wilson, Harold 212
Wimbledon Tennis Tournament 16
Windlesham, David, Lord 28, 179, 349, 369
 and *Death on the Rock* 334, 347, 350, 353,
 355, 358, 366, 370
Winner, Michael 153, 206, 322–3, 337–8
Wintour, Charles 36, 60–1, 63

Wogan, Terry 40, 156, 268–9
Wood, Andy 280
Wordley, Ron 39–40, 123, 215
Working Party 47, 49, 60
World Cup 170, 171
World in Action 41, 57–8,
 63–4, 69, 233, 310
Worldvision Enterprises 112, 115,
 117, 118, 119, 125
 and *Dallas* 88, 89, 90, 91, 104,
 129, 130, 131, 134
Wotton, John 126, 256, 299, 328, 342
Wyatt, Will 142
Wyatt, Woodrow 224–5, 331

Y
Yentob, Alan 265
Yorkshire Television 26, 136,
 148, 178, 218–19, 245
 and ITN 308
 and pop broadcasting 164
Young, Sir Brian 8, 9, 19, 94, 135, 202, 346
 and Channel 4 108, 304
 and retirement 1, 2
 and Thomson 356
 and Whitney 4, 12–13
Young, David, Lord 168, 190, 305, 306, 322
 and broadcasting summit 254, 255
 and BSB 313, 314
 and Open College 324–5
Young, Stuart 26, 29, 59, 81, 95–6, 107
 and BBC 97
 and *Dallas* 87, 88, 100, 110, 112, 113
 and DBS 43, 44, 45, 49, 58, 111
 death of 178, 199
 and IRA 116, 123
 and Thomson 99
 and Thorn-EMI 41
 and violence 142, 143
 and World Cup 170
YTV 151, 255

Z
Zeebrugge Disaster 234, 237
Zenith 115, 257, 259